THE LETTERS OF WILLIAM AND DOROTHY WORDSWORTH

III. *THE LATER YEARS*

PART I

1821–1828

CHRISTOPHER WORDSWORTH
from a portrait by George Robson, 1824

THE LETTERS OF WILLIAM AND DOROTHY WORDSWORTH

SECOND EDITION

III

The Later Years

PART I

1821–1828

REVISED, ARRANGED, AND
EDITED BY

ALAN G. HILL

FROM THE FIRST EDITION
EDITED BY THE LATE

ERNEST DE SELINCOURT

1978

OXFORD

AT THE CLARENDON PRESS

Oxford University Press, Walton Street, Oxford OX2 6DP

OXFORD LONDON GLASGOW
NEW YORK TORONTO MELBOURNE WELLINGTON
IBADAN NAIROBI DAR ES SALAAM LUSAKA CAPE TOWN
KUALA LUMPUR SINGAPORE JAKARTA HONG KONG TOKYO
DELHI BOMBAY CALCUTTA MADRAS KARACHI

© *Oxford University Press 1978*

British Library Calaloguing in Publication Data

Wordsworth, William
   The letters of William and Dorothy Wordsworth
   3: The later years. Part 1: 1821–1828
   1. Wordsworth, William—Correspondence
   2. Poets, English—19th century—Correspondence
   3. Wordsworth, Dorothy—Correspondence
   4. Authors, English—19th century—Correspondence
   I. Hill, Alan Geoffrey II. De Selincourt, Ernest
   821'.7   PR5881   77-30354
   ISBN 0-19-812481 3

Printed in Great Britain
at the University Press, Oxford
by Vivian Ridler
Printer to the University

PREFACE

In the course of preparing this edition I have incurred many obligations to individuals and institutions, and it is a pleasure to acknowledge here how much I owe to them: to Her Majesty the Queen, for graciously permitting me to publish the Wordsworth letters from the Royal Library at Windsor; to the present representatives of the Wordsworth family, especially Mr. William Wordsworth, Mr. Jonathan Wordsworth, and the late Mrs. Dorothy Dickson; to the Earl of Lonsdale, who allowed me to include the poet's numerous letters to the first Lord Lonsdale and his son, now deposited in the Record Office at Carlisle; and to the County Archivist for Cumbria, Mr. B. C. Jones, through whose good offices I was enabled to examine them at leisure. I am grateful to my fellow Trustees of the Dove Cottage Trust at Grasmere for allowing me to publish manuscript material in their possession: to Professor Basil Willey in particular, and to his successor as Chairman of the Trustees, Mrs. Mary Moorman, who generously handed over to me the papers of the late Helen Darbishire and Mrs. Beatrix Hogan which laid the foundations of the new edition. To the Librarians at Dove Cottage, Miss Nesta Clutterbuck and (more recently) Dr. Stephen Gill, I owe a special debt of gratitude; and to the late George Healey and Dr. Donald Eddy of the Cornell University Library, whose kindness and co-operation over the years have forwarded my work in numerous ways.

My thanks are due to the following for kindly permitting me to publish the Wordsworth letters in their possession: Lord Abinger, the Duke of Argyll, J. Robert Barth, S.J., Dr. Paul F. Betz, the Trustees of the Chevening Estate, Mrs. Spence Clepham, Mrs. Ann Coatalen, Mr. C. A. Cookson, Dr. A. B. Cottle, Miss Mary Crosthwaite, Mr. J. M. Edmonds, Mrs. Margaret Finch, Mr. P. G. Gates, Mrs. Greenwood, Mr. F. H. Harrop, Dr. Douglas Horton, Mr. Arthur A. Houghton, Jr., Mr. N. Hudleston, Mr. Leo Hughman, Mrs. Mary Hyde, Lord Inglewood, Mr. R. Jebb, Professor E. L. McAdam, Jr., Mr. J. D. McClatchy, the late Mrs. Jane Myers, Sir Roger Mynors, Messrs. Oliver and Boyd, Mr. W. Hugh Peal, Professor Willard Pope, Dr. Mark L. Reed, Mrs. M. J. Roberts, Major J. H. F. Spedding, Mr. W. A. Strutz,

v

Mr. Robert H. Taylor, Lady Thornton, Mr. W. N. Tolfree, Lord Wakefield of Kendal, Mr. R. E. Whitaker, Mr. Arnold Whitridge, Mr. T. Wilson, Mr. Jonathan Wordsworth, Mr. William Wordsworth, the late Revd. W. A. Wordsworth, and Mrs. Edmund F. Wright.

I gratefully acknowledge the courtesy of the Librarians and Trustees of the following institutions in making available to me the Wordsworth letters and related manuscripts in their collections: Amherst College Library; Arizona State University Library; Auckland Public Libraries; the Baker Library, Dartmouth College; the Bodleian Library, Oxford; the Boston Public Library; the British Museum (now the British Library); Brown University Library; the Mary Couts Burnet Library of the Texas Christian University; Bryn Mawr College Library; University of California Library, Davis; Cambridge University Library; Chicago University Library; Colby College Library, Maine; Columbia University Library; the Library of Congress; Cornell University Library; the Cumberland and Westmorland Record Offices at Carlisle and Kendal; Dr. Williams's Library; the Edward Lawrence Doheny Memorial Library (Estelle Doheny Collection), St. John's Seminary, Camarillo, California; Edinburgh University Library; Exeter University Library; the Fitzwilliam Museum, Cambridge; the Folger Library, Washington, D.C.; the John Work Garrett Library of the Johns Hopkins University; Georgetown University Library, Washington, D.C.; Haverford College (the Charles Roberts Collection); Historical Society of Pennsylvania; Houghton Library, Harvard University; Henry E. Huntington Library; University of Illinois Library; Iowa University Library; Keble College, Oxford; Kendal Public Library; the Keswick Museum; King Edward VI School, Southampton; Knox College Library (the Bookfellow Foundation Collection), Galesburg, Ill.; Lambeth Palace Library; the Lancashire Record Office, Preston; Leeds University Library (the Brotherton Collection); Lilly Library, Indiana University; Liverpool Public Libraries (Hornby, Synge, and Picton Collections); London University Library; the Archives of the Longman Group; McGill University Library; Manchester University Library; Massachusetts Historical Society; Metropolitan Toronto Central Library; Mitchell Library, Sydney; National Library of Ireland; National Library of Scotland; National Library of Wales; the New York Public Library (the Henry W. and Albert A. Berg Collection); New York University Libraries; University of Oregon Library (Burgess Collection);

Preface

University of Pennsylvania Library; Pennsylvania State University Library; the Carl and Lily Pforzheimer Foundation Inc., New York (on behalf of the Carl H. Pforzheimer Library); the Pierpont Morgan Library; Princeton University Library; the Public Record Office; the Rush Rhees Library, University of Rochester; Rice University Library, Houston; the Philip H. and A. S. W. Rosenbach Foundation, Philadelphia; the Royal College of Surgeons (Baillie Hunter Collection); the Royal Institution of Cornwall (Enys Autograph Collection); the Royal Society of Tasmania; John Rylands Library, Manchester; Sächsische Landesbibliothek, Dresden; St. Andrews University Library; St. John's College, Cambridge; the Kenneth Spencer Research Library, University of Kansas; the Miriam Lutcher Stark Library, University of Texas; Swarthmore College Library; University of Tennessee Library; Trinity College, Cambridge; Tullie House, Carlisle; University College, London (the Sharpe Collection); Victoria and Albert Museum (the Dyce Collection); Victoria University Library, Toronto; Virginia State Library, Richmond (Poe Foundation); University of Virginia Library; Wellesley College Library; Wesleyan University Library, Middletown, Conn.; Westminster City Libraries (the Broadley Collection); Wisbech Museum; Yale University Library; and the Osborn Collection, Yale.

I am also grateful to the Cornell University Press for granting me permission to reprint the Wordsworth letters originally published in *Wordsworth and Reed, The Poet's Correspondence with his American Editor: 1836–1850*, ed. L. N. Broughton, 1933; and to Messrs. Routledge and Kegan Paul for allowing me to reproduce items from *The Letters of Sara Hutchinson, 1800–1835*, ed. Kathleen Coburn, 1954.

I am indebted to the following for assistance of various kinds, and for answering my inquiries: Mrs. Elizabeth Barraclough; Mr. Alan Bell, of the National Library of Scotland; Dr. Paul Betz, of Georgetown University; Mr. E. G. W. Bill, Librarian at Lambeth Palace; Dr. James A. Butler, of La Salle College, Philadelphia; Dr. Herbert Cahoon, of the Pierpont Morgan Library; Mr. A. H. B. Coleridge (who also granted me permission to quote from Coleridge family papers); Miss A. F. Dodd, of the Ann Bryant Art Gallery, East London, South Africa; Dr. David Farmer, of the Humanities Research Center, University of Texas; Mr. R. Sharpe France, lately County Archivist for Lancashire; Miss Lorna Fraser, Librarian of Victoria College, Toronto; Dr. Philip Gaskell, Librarian of Trinity College, Cambridge;

vii

Preface

Mr. Eric Gillett; Mr. W. L. Hanchant, of Wisbech Museum; Major E. W. Hasell; Mr. H. A. F. Hohler; Mr. Derek Hudson; Dr. Felix Hull, County Archivist for Kent; Mr. D. F. James, County Librarian for Westmorland; Miss Eileen Jay, of Hawkshead; Mrs. Elizabeth Kemp; Dr. Carl Ketcham, of the University of Arizona; Dr. A. G. Lee, Librarian of St. John's College, Cambridge; Miss S. J. Macpherson, County Archivist at Kendal; Mr. J. N. S. Matthew, of Somerset House; Mr. Edward W. Milligan, Librarian of Friends House; Lord Monteagle; Mrs. Frances Pearson; Mr. Selwyn Powell; Dr. Mark L. Reed, of the University of North Carolina; Mr. Donald P. Sewell; Professor Chester L. Shaver, of Oberlin College, Ohio; Mr. R. W. Shepherd; the late T. W. Thompson; Mr. S. H. G. Twining; Dr. D. P. Waley, Keeper of Manuscripts at the British Museum; the Proprietors of the *Westmorland Gazette*; Mr. Ross Whitney, of the University of Texas; Dr. R. S. Woof, of the University of Newcastle-upon-Tyne; Dr. Marjorie G. Wynne, of Yale University Library; and Sir Robert Mackworth Young, Librarian at Windsor Castle.

Among all the institutions and individuals who have generously given their help over the years, I am particularly indebted to the Librarian and staff of the St. Andrews University Library, especially Miss Cecily Baird, for their courteous and efficient service; and to my wife Margaret, who has been my co-worker throughout this long undertaking.

My work has been liberally supported by the institutions with which I have been associated, and I would like to record here my gratitude to the Universities of Exeter and St. Andrews, and—in more recent times—to the University of Saskatchewan (St. Thomas More College) and the University of Dundee for generous financial grants towards the costs of preparing the edition.

ALAN G. HILL

June 1976

CONTENTS

List of Illustrations   xi

Abbreviations   xii

List of Letters   xv

Introduction   xxv

Text of Letters (1821–8)   1

Appendixes   701

Genealogical Table   *facing p.* 704

Index   705

Addendum   730

LIST OF ILLUSTRATIONS

Christopher Wordsworth, from a portrait by
George Robson, 1824. By permission of Trinity
College, Cambridge *Frontispiece*

Thomas Monkhouse, from a portrait by Richard
Carruthers, 1817. By permission of the Ann
Bryant Art Gallery, East London, South Africa *facing p.* 87

Brinsop Court, Herefordshire, from a drawing by
Sara Hutchinson jnr., *c.* 1855. By permission of
the Trustees of Dove Cottage *facing p.* 483

ABBREVIATIONS

PERSONAL INITIALS

W. W., D. W., M. W., R. W., C. W.: William, Dorothy, Mary, Richard, and Christopher Wordsworth.

S. H.: Sara Hutchinson. E. Q.: Edward Quillinan. S. T. C.: Samuel Taylor Coleridge. C. C.: Catherine Clarkson. I. F.: Isabella Fenwick. H. C. R.: Henry Crabb Robinson.

SOURCES

Broughton	*Some Letters of the Wordsworth Family*, edited by L. N. Broughton, Cornell University Press, 1942.
Cornell	Department of Rare Books, Cornell University Library, Ithaca, N.Y.
Curry	*New Letters of Robert Southey*, edited by Kenneth Curry, 2 vols., Columbia University Press, 1965.
DWJ	*The Journals of Dorothy Wordsworth*, edited by Ernest de Selincourt, 2 vols., 1941.
EY	*The Letters of William and Dorothy Wordsworth*, edited by the late Ernest de Selincourt, second edition, I, *The Early Years, 1787–1805*, revised by Chester L. Shaver, Oxford, 1967.
Gillett	*Maria Jane Jewsbury: Occasional Papers, selected with a Memoir*, by Eric Gillett, 1932.
Griggs	*Collected Letters of Samuel Taylor Coleridge*, edited by Earl Leslie Griggs, 6 vols., Oxford, 1956–71.
Grosart	*The Prose Works of William Wordsworth*, edited by Alexander B. Grosart, 3 vols., 1876.
Hamilton	*The Life of Sir William Rowan Hamilton*, by R. P. Graves, 3 vols., 1882–9.
Haydon	*Correspondence and Table Talk of Benjamin Robert Haydon*, edited by his Son, F. W. Haydon, 1876.
HCR	*Henry Crabb Robinson on Books and their Writers*, edited by Edith J. Morley, 3 vols., 1938.
Jordan	*De Quincey to Wordsworth, a Biography of a Relationship*, by J. E. Jordan, 1962.
K	*Letters of the Wordsworth Family*, edited by William Knight, 3 vols., 1907.
Lamb	*The Letters of Charles and Mary Lamb*, edited by E. V. Lucas, 3 vols., 1935.

LY	*The Letters of William and Dorothy Wordsworth, The Later Years*, edited by Ernest de Selincourt, 3 vols., Oxford, 1939.
Mem.	*Memoirs of William Wordsworth*, by Christopher Wordsworth, 2 vols., 1851.
MLN	*Modern Language Notes.*
MLR	*Modern Language Review.*
Moorman i, ii	*William Wordsworth, A Biography*, i, *The Early Years*, ii, *The Later Years*, by Mary Moorman, Oxford, 1957 and 1965.
Morley	*Correspondence of Henry Crabb Robinson with the Wordsworth Circle*, edited by Edith J. Morley, 2 vols., Oxford, 1927.
MP	*Modern Philology.*
MW	*The Letters of Mary Wordsworth*, edited by Mary E. Burton, Oxford, 1958.
MY	*The Letters of William and Dorothy Wordsworth*, edited by the late Ernest de Selincourt, second edition, II: *The Middle Years*: Part I, 1806–11, revised by Mary Moorman, Part II, 1812–20, revised by Mary Moorman and Alan G. Hill, Oxford, 1969–70.
NQ	*Notes and Queries.*
Pearson	*Papers, Letters and Journals of William Pearson*, edited by his widow. Printed for private circulation, 1863.
PMLA	*Publications of the Modern Language Association of America.*
Prel.	*Wordsworth's Prelude*, edited by Ernest de Selincourt: second edition, revised by Helen Darbishire, Oxford, 1959.
Prose Works	*The Prose Works of William Wordsworth*, edited by W. J. B. Owen and Jane Worthington Smyser, 3 vols., Oxford, 1974.
PW	*The Poetical Works of William Wordsworth*, edited by Ernest de Selincourt and Helen Darbishire, 5 vols., Oxford, 1940–9, and revised issues, 1952–9.
R.M. Cat.	*Catalogue of the Varied and Valuable Historical, Poetical, Theological, and Miscellaneous Library of the late venerated Poet-Laureate, William Wordsworth . . .* Preston, 1859; reprinted in *Transactions of the Wordsworth Society*, Edinburgh, [1882–7].
RMVB	*Rydal Mount Visitors Book*, Wordsworth Library, Grasmere.
Rogers	*Rogers and his Contemporaries*, edited by P. W. Clayden, 2 vols., 1889.
Sadler	*Diary, Reminiscences and Correspondence of Henry Crabb Robinson*, edited by Thomas Sadler, 3 vols., 1869.

Abbreviations

SH	*The Letters of Sara Hutchinson*, edited by Kathleen Coburn, 1954.
Southey	*Life and Correspondence of Robert Southey*, edited by C. C. Southey, 6 vols., 1849–50.
TLS	*Times Literary Supplement*.
Warter	*A Selection from the Letters of Robert Southey*, edited by John Wood Warter, 4 vols., 1856.
WL	The Wordsworth Library, Grasmere.

LIST OF LETTERS

PART I

1821

No.	Writer and Recipient	Date	Page
1	D. W. to Thomas Monkhouse	2 Jan.	1
2	W. W. to Thomas Myers	5 Jan.	2
3	W. W. to Sir George Beaumont	10 Jan.	3
4	D. W. to Catherine Clarkson	10 Jan.	7
5	W. W. to Lord Lonsdale	c. 12 Jan.	10
6	D. W. to Thomas Monkhouse	17 Jan.	13
7	W. W. to the Commissioners of Stamps	19 Jan.	14
8	D. W. to Catherine Clarkson	19 Jan.	15
9	W. W. to Lord Lonsdale	20 Jan.	19
10	C. W. Jnr. and D. W. to Thomas Monkhouse	22 Jan.	20
11	W. W. to H. C. R.	23 Jan.	22
12	W. W. to the Commissioners of Stamps	3 Feb.	23
13	W. W. to John Kenyon	5 Feb.	24
14	W. W. to Viscount Lowther	7 Feb.	25
15	W. W. to the Commissioners of Stamps	7 Feb.	26
16	W. W. to Lord Lonsdale	9 Feb.	27
17	W. W. to the Commissioners of Stamps	14 Feb.	29
18	D. W. to Catherine Clarkson	15 Feb.	30
19	D. W. to Thomas Monkhouse	15 Feb.	35
20	W. W. to Viscount Lowther	19 Feb.	37
21	W. W. to Viscount Lowther	26 Feb.	38
22	W. W. to William Myers	7 March	40
23	W. W. to Viscount Lowther	c. 10 March	41
24	W. W. to H. C. R.	c. 12 March	43
25	D. W. to Thomas Monkhouse	16 March	46
26	D. W. to Catherine Clarkson	27 March	47
27	W. W. to Viscount Lowther	28 March	54
28	W. W. to Viscount Lowther	30 March	57
29	W. W. to the Commissioners of Stamps	23 April	59

List of Letters

No.	Writer and Recipient	Date	Page
30	D. W. to Catherine Clarkson	31 May	60
31	W. W. to Viscount Lowther	June–July	66
32	W. W. to Unknown Correspondent	21 June	67
33	W. W. to John Kenyon	23 July	68
34	W. W. to Francis Legatt Chantrey	18 Aug.	69
35	W. W. to Benjamin Robert Haydon	18 Aug.	70
36	W. W. to Sir Walter Scott	23 Aug.	71
37	D. W. to Catherine Clarkson	25 Aug.	72
38	W. W. to Viscount Lowther	2 Sept.	77
39	W. W. to Walter Savage Landor	3 Sept.	78
40	W. W. to Viscount Lowther	7 Sept.	81
41	W. W. to Viscount Lowther	14 Sept.	82
42	W. W. and M. W. to John Kenyon	22 Sept.	82
43	W. W. to Lord Lonsdale	24 Sept.	84
44	W. W. to Lord Lonsdale	16 Oct.	85
45	W. W. to Francis Legatt Chantrey	October	86
46	D. W. to Catherine Clarkson	24 Oct.	87
47	D. W. to H. C. R.	24 Nov.	91
48	D. W. to H. C. R.	1 Dec.	95
49	W. W. to James Losh	4 Dec.	96
50	M. W. to John Kenyon	28 Dec.	99
51	W. W. to Robert Southey	late Dec.	101

1822

No.	Writer and Recipient	Date	Page
52	D. W. to Catherine Clarkson	16 Jan.	103
53	W. W. to Charles Lloyd	20 Feb.	106
54	W. W. to Messrs. Longman and Co.	26 Feb.	108
55	D. W. to Elizabeth Cookson	3 March	109
56	D. W. to H. C. R.	3 March	110
57	W. W. to the Commissioners of Stamps	6 March	116
58	W. W. to Robert Blakeney	11 April	117
59	W. W. to Richard Sharp	16 April	118
60	W. W. to Viscount Lowther	19 April	120
61	W. W. to Walter Savage Landor	20 April	122
62	D. W. to H. C. R.	21 April	126
63	W. W. to Lady Ann le Fleming	3 May	129
64	W. W. to the Commissioners of Stamps	7 May	131
65	W. W. to the Commissioners of Stamps	8 May	132
66	D. W. to Edward Quillinan	22 May	132
67	D. W. to Edward Quillinan	?23 May	134
68	Dora W. and W. W. to C. W.	29 May	136

List of Letters

No.	Writer and Recipient	Date	Page
69	W. W. to Allan Cunningham	12 June	137
70	D. W. to Jane Marshall	13 June	138
71	W. W. to Lord Lonsdale	18 July	142
72	W. W. to William Pearson	1 Aug.	143
73	W. W. to Unknown Correspondent	early Aug.	144
74	D. W. to Edward Quillinan	6 Aug.	145
75	W. W. to the Commissioners of Stamps	5 Sept.	151
76	W. W. to Samuel Rogers	16 Sept.	152
77	D. W. to David Laing	16 Sept.	154
78	W. W. to Richard Sharp	3 Oct.	155
79	W. W. to Richard Sharp	mid-Oct.	156
80	W. W. to Lord Lonsdale	3 Nov.	157
81	W. W. to Richard Sharp	12 Nov.	159
82	D. W. and W. W. to Mary Laing and David Laing	13–16 Nov.	160
83	D. W. to Edward Quillinan	19 Nov.	164
84	W. W. to Lord Lonsdale	29 Nov.	171
85	D. W. to Elizabeth Crump	29 Nov.	172
86	W. W. to John Keble	18 Dec.	174
87	D. W. to H. C. R.	21 Dec.	176

1823

No.	Writer and Recipient	Date	Page
88	D. W. to Samuel Rogers	3 Jan.	180
89	W. W. to Lord Lonsdale	24 Jan.	182
90	W. W. to Lord Lonsdale	25 Jan.	184
91	W. W. to William Stewart Rose	28 Jan.	185
92	W. W. to Lady le Fleming	late Jan.	185
93	M. W. to Lady Beaumont	5 Feb.	186
94	W. W. to John Keble	17 Feb.	187
95	D. W. to Samuel Rogers	17 Feb.	189
96	W. W. to John Keble	24 Feb.	190
97	W. W. to John Keble	5 March	191
98	W. W. to Allan Cunningham	6 May	192
99	D. W. to Edward Quillinan	6 May	193
100	D. W. to Edward Quillinan	7 May	195
101	W. W. to John Kenyon	16 May	198
102	D. W. to Edward Quillinan	17 June	200
103	D. W. to Edward Quillinan	4 July	201
104	D. W. to Elizabeth Crump	17 July	204
105	D. W. to Mary Laing	17 July	207
106	M. W. and D. W. to Thomas Monkhouse	20 Aug.	209
107	D. W. to Mary Laing	26 Aug.	213
108	D. W. to Elizabeth Crump	31 Aug.	216

List of Letters

No.	Writer and Recipient	Date	Page
109	W. W. to the Commissioners of Stamps	19 Sept.	220
110	D. W. to Elizabeth Crump	10 Oct.	221
111	D. W. to Mary Laing	10 Oct.	222
112	W. W. to Unknown Correspondent	21 Oct.	224
113	W. W. to Robert Southey	?Autumn	225
114	W. W. to Robert Jones	3 Nov.	226
115	W. W. to Lord Lonsdale	9 Nov.	227
116	D. W. to Catherine Clarkson	11 or 12 Nov.	229
117	D. W. to Mary Laing	25 Nov.	233
118	W. W. to Lord Lonsdale	early Dec.	235
119	W. W. to William Campbell	23 Dec.	236
120	W. W. to Henry Taylor	26 Dec.	236
121	D. W. to Mary Laing	28 Dec.	238

1824

No.	Writer and Recipient	Date	Page
122	D. W. to Edward Quillinan	7 Jan.	241
123	W. W. to Walter Savage Landor	21 Jan.	243
124	W. W. to Lord Lonsdale	23 Jan.	246
125	W. W. to James Montgomery	24 Jan.	248
126	W. W. to Allan Cunningham	1 Feb.	249
127	W. W. to Lord Lonsdale	5 Feb.	250
128	W. W. to Lord Lonsdale	17 Feb.	253
129	D. W. to Mrs. Luff	4 March	254
130	D. W. to John Kenyon	23 March	256
131	D. W. to Edward Quillinan	29 March	257
132	D. W. to John Monkhouse	16 April	258
133	D. W. to Edward Quillinan	19 April	264
134	W. W. to David Wilkie	1 May	264
135	D. W. to Edward Quillinan	3 May	265
136	M. W. to Edward Quillinan	?5 May	266
137	D. W. to Thomas Monkhouse	20 May	267
138	D. W. to Edward Quillinan	20 May	269
139	D. W. to H. C. R.	23 May	270
140	D. W. to Lady Beaumont	18 Sept.	272
141	W. W. to Sir George Beaumont	20 Sept.	275
142	D. W. to John Kenyon	4 Oct.	280
143	D. W. to [?] H. C. R.	14 Nov.	282
144	W. W. to Alaric Watts	16 Nov.	283
145	W. W. to Thomas Brydges Barrett	19 Nov.	285
146	D. W. to John Kenyon	28 Nov.	287
147	W. W. to Jane Marshall	late Nov.	289
148	W. W. to Walter Savage Landor	11 Dec.	289
149	D. W. to H. C. R.	13 Dec.	290

List of Letters

No.	Writer and Recipient	Date	Page
150	W. W. to the Commissioners of Stamps	20 Dec.	295

1825

No.	Writer and Recipient	Date	Page
151	W. W. to C. W.	4 Jan.	296
152	W. W. to Charles Lloyd Snr.	6 Jan.	299
153	W. W. to Francis Merewether	10 Jan.	300
154	W. W. to Jacob Fletcher	17 Jan.	302
155	W. W. to Lord Lonsdale	21 Jan.	304
156	W. W. to Samuel Rogers	21 Jan.	306
157	W. W. to Messrs. Bell Brothers and Co.	2 Feb.	309
158	W. W. to Viscount Lowther	12 Feb.	309
159	D. W. to Joanna Hutchinson	13 Feb.	315
160	W. W. to Samuel Rogers	19 Feb.	319
161	W. W. to Jacob Fletcher	25 Feb.	321
162	M. W. to Lady Beaumont	25 Feb.	323
163	D. W. to Catherine Clarkson	10 March	324
164	W. W. to Samuel Rogers	23 March	327
165	W. W. to John Wordsworth	late March	329
166	D. W. to John Monkhouse	3 April	330
167	W. W. to Jacob Fletcher	6 April	333
168	D. W. to H. C. R.	12 April	335
169	D. W. to Elizabeth Crump	late April	338
170	W. W. to Samuel Rogers	3 May	341
171	W. W. to Maria Jane Jewsbury	4 May	342
172	D. W. to Catherine Clarkson	4 May	344
173	W. W. to Lord Lonsdale	5 May	347
174	W. W. to Robert W. Bamford	28 May	349
175	W. W. to Sir George Beaumont	28 May	349
176	Dora W., D. W., and M. W. to S. H. and Mrs. Thomas Hutchinson	28 May	351
177	D. W. to Sir Walter Scott	30 May	356
178	W. W. to Sir Robert Inglis	11 June	358
179	D. W. and W. W. to Sir Walter Scott	13 June	366
180	W. W. to Lord Lonsdale	15 June	369
181	D. W. to H. C. R.	2 July	372
182	W. W. to Alaric Watts	5 Aug.	376
183	W. W. and Dora W. to Maria Jane Jewsbury	6 Aug.	377
184	W. W. to John Murray	6 Aug.	379
185	W. W. to Unknown Correspondent	11 Aug.	380
186	W. W. to Alaric Watts	13 Aug.	380

List of Letters

No.	Writer and Recipient	Date	Page
187	W. W. to Samuel Rogers	15 Aug.	381
188	W. W. to John Taylor	? c. 15 Aug.	382
189	W. W. to Alaric Watts	5 Sept.	383
190	W. W. to Alaric Watts	5 Sept.	383
191	W. W. to Messrs. Longman and Co.	25 Sept.	384
192	W. W. to John Brewster	26 Sept.	384
193	D. W. to William Pearson	30 Sept.	385
194	D. W. to Robert Jones	7 Oct.	386
195	Dora W. and D. W. to Edward Quillinan	17 Oct.	388
196	W. W. to Alaric Watts	18 Oct.	390
197	D. W. to Catherine Clarkson	18 Oct.	391
198	D. W. to Mary Laing	3 Nov.	394
199	D. W. to H. C. R.	8 Nov.	396
200	W. W. to Richard Heber	21 Nov.	398
201	W. W. to Allan Cunningham	23 Nov.	400
202	D. W. to H. C. R.	26 Nov.	403
203	W. W. to Lord Lonsdale	29 Nov.	407
204	W. W. to Lord Lonsdale	8 Dec.	410
205	W. W. to Charles William Pasley	9 Dec.	411
206	M. W. to Lady Beaumont	9 Dec.	411
207	W. W. to Unknown Correspondent	22 Dec.	414
208	D. W. to Jane Marshall	23 Dec.	415
209	M. W. to Alaric Watts	27 Dec.	418
210	W. W. to Lord Lonsdale	late Dec.	418
211	W. W. to Thomas Kibble Hervey	? late 1825	419

1826

212	W. W. to Robert Jones	2 Jan.	420
213	W. W. to Sir Walter Scott	2 Jan.	422
214	W. W. to [?Thomas Robinson]	17 Jan.	423
215	W. W. to Alaric Watts	19 Jan.	424
216	W. W. to Alaric Watts	23 Jan.	425
217	D. W. to H. C. R.	25 Feb.	426
218	W. W. to William Pearson	6 March	430
219	W. W. to the Commissioners of Stamps	24 March	430
220	D. W. to Mary Laing	29 March	431
221	D. W. to Catherine Clarkson	1 April	434
222	W. W. to H. C. R.	6 April	438
223	W. W. to C. W.	9 April	441
224	W. W. to H. C. R.	27 April	442
225	W. W. to Lord Lonsdale	c. 15 May	445
226	W. W. to Robert Jones	18 May	448
227	W. W. to Christopher Wilson	? 21 May	449

List of Letters

No.	Writer and Recipient	Date	Page
228	W. W. to H. C. R.	late May	450
229	W. W. to Lord Lonsdale	late May	451
230	W. W. to C. W.	9 June	453
231	W. W. to S. H.	5 or 12 June	454
232	W. W. to Alaric Watts	18 June	455
233	W. W. to Lord Lonsdale	22 June	455
234	W. W. to Lord Lonsdale	26 June	459
235	W. W. to Lord Lonsdale	28 June	460
236	W. W. to Lord Lonsdale	29 June	461
237	W. W. to Lord Lonsdale	30 June	463
238	W. W. to Lord Lonsdale	2 July	465
239	W. W. to Lord Lonsdale	5 July	468
240	W. W. to Lord Lonsdale	7 July	470
241	M. W. and W. W. to John Kenyon	25 July	472
242	W. W. to Basil Montagu	25 July	475
243	W. W. to Lupton Relfe	25 July	476
244	W. W. to H. C. R.	c. 30 July	477
245	D. W. to John Monkhouse	4 Aug.	479
246	W. W. to Maria Jane Jewsbury	early Aug.	480
247	D. W. to John Monkhouse	14 Aug.	481
248	D. W. to John Monkhouse	24 Aug.	481
249	D. W. to John Monkhouse	27 Aug.	482
250	W. W. to [? John Gregory Crump]	? 11 Sept.	484
251	W. W. to Unknown Correspondent	? Sept.	484
252	W. W. to Jane Marshall	22 Sept.	484
253	W. W. to Benjamin Dockray	17 Oct.	485
254	W. W. to Unknown Correspondent	? 17 Oct.	486
255	W. W. to Alaric Watts	22 Oct.	487
256	W. W. to Henry Taylor	23 Oct.	488
257	W. W. to Frederic Mansel Reynolds	24 Oct.	489
258	M. W. to John Kenyon	27 Oct.	490
259	W. W. to John Kenyon	c. 29 Oct.	491
260	D. W. to Thomas De Quincey	16 Nov.	492
261	W. W. to John Taylor	21 Nov.	494
262	W. W. to Messrs. Longman and Co.	22 Nov.	495
263	W. W. to Richard Sharp	22 Nov.	495
264	W. W. to John Murray	4 Dec.	496
265	W. W. to Edward Moxon	c. 7 Dec.	497
266	D. W. to H. C. R.	18 Dec.	498
267	W. W. to William Strickland Cookson	c. 22 Dec.	500

1827

268	W. W. to Mrs. Richard Wordsworth	? early 1827	501
269	W. W. to Messrs. Longman and Co.	2 Jan.	502

List of Letters

No.	Writer and Recipient	Date	Page
270	D. W. to H. C. R.	6 Jan.	503
271	W. W. to Samuel Rogers	12 Jan.	505
272	D. W. to Mary Laing	23 Jan.	506
273	W. W. to William Jackson	26 Jan.	509
274	W. W. and D. W. to H. C. R.	29 Jan.	510
275	W. W. to Frederic Mansel Reynolds	? February	512
276	W. W. and D. W. to Mary Laing	6 Feb.	513
277	W. W. to Charles William Pasley	6 Feb.	514
278	W. W. to William Sotheby	6 Feb.	515
279	D. W. to H. C. R.	18 Feb.	516
280	W. W. to Robert Southey	late Feb. or early Mar.	517
281	W. W. to Samuel Rogers	10 March	518
282	D. W. to Mary Laing	c. 10 March	519
283	W. W. to Basil Montagu	c. 20 March	522
284	W. W. to Jacob Fletcher	12 April	523
285	W. W. to Samuel Carter Hall	12 April	524
286	W. W. to Jacob Fletcher	30 April	525
287	W. W. to Samuel Carter Hall	2 May	525
288	W. W. to Messrs. Longman and Co.	10 May	526
289	W. W. to Alaric Watts	21 May	527
290	D. W. to John Wordsworth	6 June	529
291	D. W. to Mary Laing	10 June	532
292	W. W. to George Husband Baird	15 June	534
293	W. W. to William Howitt	17 June	535
293a	D. W. to C. W. jnr.	23 June	535
294	W. W. to Messrs. Taylor and Hessey	24 Aug.	537
295	M. W. to John Kenyon	28 Aug.	538
296	W. W. to Harriet Douglas	early Sept.	541
297	W. W. to Robert Southey	15 Sept.	542
298	W. W. to Samuel Rogers	20 Sept.	543
299	W. W. to William Rowan Hamilton	24 Sept.	545
300	W. W. to Thomas Norton Longman	15 Oct.	547
301	W. W. to Dora W.	26 Oct.	547
302	W. W. to Dora W.	27 Oct.	549
303	D. W. to Edward Quillinan	2 Nov.	550
304	W. W. to Thomas Crofton Croker	11 Nov.	552
305	W. W. to William Jackson	26 Nov.	552
306	W. W. to Samuel Rogers	c. 30 Nov.	554
307	W. W. to C. W. and C. W. Jnr.	c. 30 Nov.	556
308	W. W. to Lord Lonsdale	early Dec.	559
309	W. W. to Alexander Blair	11 Dec.	561
310	D. W. to John Marshall Jnr.	23 Dec.	562
311	W. W. to John Bowring	29 Dec.	564
312	W. W. to Elizabeth Palmer Peabody	late 1827	565

No.	Writer and Recipient	Date	Page
	1828		
313	D. W. to John Marshall Jnr.	8 Jan.	566
314	W. W. to Allan Cunningham	9 Jan.	568
315	W. W. to Edward Quillinan	9 Jan.	569
316	D. W. to John Marshall Jnr.	13 Jan.	570
317	D. W. to Mary Laing	21 Jan.	571
318	W. W. to Lord Lonsdale	25 Jan.	575
319	W. W. to John Taylor	30 Jan.	577
320	W. W. to Unknown Correspondent	30 Jan.	578
321	W. W. to Francis Freeling	2 Feb.	579
322	W. W. to Frederic Mansel Reynolds	c. 8 Feb.	580
323	D. W. to William Jackson	12 Feb.	580
324	W. W. to Allan Cunningham	26 Feb.	583
325	W. W. and D. W. to Harriet Douglas	29 Feb.	584
326	W. W. to William Jackson	early March	587
327	W. W. to M. W. and Dora W.	early March	589
328	W. W. to Thomas Jewsbury	c. 6 March	592
329	W. W. to Allan Cunningham	7 March	592
330	W. W. to Lord Lonsdale	7 March	593
331	W. W. to Lord Lonsdale	mid-March	595
331a	W. W. to William Jackson	late March	596
332	W. W. to James Dyer	3 April	597
333	D. W. to John Marshall Jnr.	3 April	599
334	W. W. to Barron Field	16 April	600
335	W. W. to Samuel Rogers	17 April	603
336	W. W. to Francis Merewether	5 May	604
337	D. W. to Maria Jane Jewsbury	21 May	606
338	W. W. to Allan Cunningham	late May or early June	609
339	W. W. to Julius Charles Hare	? late May or early June	609
340	D. W. to John Marshall Jnr.	2 June	610
341	D. W. to Mary Laing	3 June	611
342	W. W. to H. C. R.	16 June	613
343	W. W. to Samuel Taylor Coleridge	17 June	614
344	W. W. to Barron Field	20 June	615
345	W. W. to Frederic Mansel Reynolds	21 June	615
346	W. W. to Mrs. Elizabeth Aders	12 July	616
347	D. W. to Joseph Cottle	31 July	617
348	Dora W. and W. W. to Edward Quillinan	1 Aug.	620
349	W. W. to Samuel Rogers	2 Aug.	622
350	W. W. to Charles Aders	7 Aug.	622
351	W. W. to George Huntly Gordon	7 Aug.	623

List of Letters

No.	Writer and Recipient	Date	Page
352	W. W. to H. C. R.	7 Aug.	624
353	W. W. to Charles James Blomfield	9 Aug.	624
354	W. W. to William Jerdan	9 Aug.	625
355	D. W. to William Pearson	10 Aug.	626
356	W. W. to Sir Walter Scott	28 Aug.	627
357	D. W. to William Pearson	25 Sept.	628
358	W. W. to William Jackson	early Oct.	629
359	W. W. to George Huntly Gordon	7 Oct.	631
360	W. W. to William Jerdan	7 Oct.	632
361	D. W. to William Pearson	9 Oct.	633
362	W. W. to C. W.	mid-Oct.	633
363	W. W. to William Wood	15 Oct.	636
364	W. W. to Edward Quillinan	17 Oct.	637
365	D. W. to C. W. Jnr.	21 Oct.	638
366	W. W. to Barron Field	24 Oct.	640
367	W. W. to Alexander Dyce	29 Oct.	647
368	W. W. to George Huntly Gordon	10 Nov.	650
369	W. W. to Allan Cunningham	11 Nov.	653
370	W. W. to Edward Quillinan	11 Nov.	655
371	W. W. to C. W.	11 Nov.	657
372	W. W. to Lord Lonsdale	mid-Nov.	659
373	W. W. to George Huntly Gordon	25 Nov.	661
374	W. W. to Messrs. Longman and Co.	25 Nov.	664
375	M. W. and W. W. to Edward Quillinan	c. 25 Nov.	665
376	W. W. to C. W. Jnr.	27 Nov.	668
377	D. W. to C. W. Jnr.	27 Nov.	671
378	W. W. to H. C. R.	28 Nov.	674
379	D. W. to H. C. R.	30 Nov.	676
380	W. W. to Benjamin Dockray	2 Dec.	678
381	W. W. to Allan Cunningham	early Dec.	680
382	W. W. to William Whewell	4 Dec.	681
383	W. W. to Lord Lonsdale	6 Dec.	683
384	W. W. to Hugh James Rose	11 Dec.	684
385	W. W. to Robert Southey	mid-Dec.	686
386	W. W. to George Huntly Gordon	15 Dec.	687
387	W. W. to H. C. R.	15 Dec.	690
388	W. W. to Frederic Mansel Reynolds	19 Dec.	691
389	W. W. to Allan Cunningham	20 Dec.	694
390	W. W. to Barron Field	20 Dec.	694
391	W. W. to Lord Lonsdale	23 Dec.	696
392	D. W. to Jane Marshall	26 Dec.	697
393	W. W. to William Jackson	late Dec.	698
394	W. W. to Unknown Correspondent	1828–1829	699
395	W. W. to Sara Coleridge	before 1829	699

INTRODUCTION

LETTER-WRITING was never an easy or congenial occupation for Wordsworth. 'Southey used to say that his pen was his magic wand—with me it was and is quite otherwise,' he once confessed to Basil Montagu; '—The touch of it half benumbs me.' Those who had claims on his attention and sympathy were assured of a cordial expression of interest, but he had no time for the pleasantries that are sometimes thought part of the stock-in-trade of the successful correspondent. His unerring sense of the fitness of words to occasions made him dislike any exaggeration of expression on important matters; and while he could write with unaffected dignity and force on themes touching his vital concerns as a poet, his letters were for the most part as sober and matter-of-fact as he could make them. Too much regard had been paid to the 'casual effusions' of literary men—as the controversies about Lamb, Coleridge, and Southey would prove—and he made his own letters (he said) as dull as possible so that they would not be thought worth preserving. The measured style of writing, the product of his natural reticence and almost Roman gravity of mind, became a settled habit in later years when inflammation of the eyelids forced him to dictate many of his letters.

Business affairs apart, Wordsworth's later letters range over many subjects, but they all unmistakably reflect his judicious and comprehensive grasp of human affairs, that largeness of outlook and consistency of principle which John Stuart Mill and Gladstone both recalled as the most memorable features of his mind. Many of the letters provide 'a chain of valooable thoughts'—as Wordsworth said of *The Happy Warrior*—and are more like little essays or pamphlets. Aesthetics and literary criticism, topography, history, religion, education, politics, and the progress of society—his views on all these subjects are interconnected: indeed they spring naturally, like an organic growth, from his central preoccupations as the poet of Man, Nature, and Society. So that he never writes as a specialist, but always as 'a man speaking to men'. Dorothy's letters, in contrast, are overflowing with a superabundance of domestic and family intelligence. When read in conjunction with those of Mary Wordsworth and Sara Hutchinson, they fill out all the details of everyday events which the poet thought it unnecessary to mention. The Wordsworthian milieu seems to come across less vividly with her breakdown in health in 1835 and the loss of her regular budgets of news.

The Later Years, to which the remaining four volumes of this series are devoted, complete the picture of the poet and his circle that has been unfolding in earlier volumes, and provide a remarkably authentic record of his style of life and range of interests from 1821 until his death in 1850. By 1821, the Wordsworths had already been long settled at Rydal Mount in a pattern of life that was to remain essentially unchanged for the rest of their days. The poet's income as Distributor of Stamps for Westmorland, though modest, enabled him to live on in his native region, enjoying the communion with Nature and the traditional values of Lakeland society on which his poetic vision depended, and he resolutely refused more lucrative employment further afield. The house was enlarged and the grounds laid out according to the principles Wordsworth had applied long ago at Coleorton. Numerous visits were exchanged with family and friends, near and far. The poet assumed his place among the smaller landed gentry, and was welcomed at Hallsteads, Storrs, and Lowther Castle. The return of summer residents, the Arnolds at Fox How among many others, was eagerly awaited. The passing seasons and the changing moods of lake and mountain never ceased to delight and satisfy, and as the years slipped imperceptibly by, the poet's own days seemed to embody the 'natural piety' which he had wished for in his earlier poetry.

But the wider world was not forgotten, nor did he lose his concern for the well-being of society as a whole. He made tours of Holland (1823), the Rhineland (1828), Ireland (1829), Scotland (1831 and 1833), and Italy and Germany (1837), as well as numerous excursions nearer home. He met many of the leading churchmen and politicians of the day at Lowther; fellow writers, artists, and men of affairs made him welcome in London, and he found new friends among the Cambridge churchmen and scientists gathered round his brother Christopher at Trinity Lodge. His triumphant reception at the Oxford Commemoration in the summer of 1839 showed that he had many friends there too, who were deeply indebted to his writings. As his fame grew, so did the number and variety of influential people who flocked to visit him at Rydal Mount, and he was increasingly courted by the leaders of opinion and lionized by the younger generation. 'The callers from

day to day have been almost innumerable,' wrote Christopher
during his visit in August 1844; '. . . to me it is thoroughly
amazing how my Brother is able, from early morning, often till
late at night, to talk to, and apparently greatly to interest them
all . . .'[1] Wordsworth's election as Poet Laureate in succession to
Southey in 1843 set the official seal of approval on his achievements
as the author of *The Excursion*. But it also reflected his more
pervasive influence as the first of the great Victorian sages, one
who had outlived all his Romantic contemporaries and seemed to
carry over the certainties of a previous era into the harsher climate
of early Victorian change and uncertainty.

Wordsworth never hesitated in his life-long commitment to
poetry, and in his later years he went on producing work of value
which it is still the fashion to neglect. He continued to explore the
potentialities of the sonnet form, notably in the *Ecclesiastical
Sketches* (1822), in which all his later preoccupations as a poet are
brought into focus. His mind dwelt more and more on the loyalties
and imaginative sympathies that had developed out of the past
to become a natural and permanent part of man's inheritance and
the guarantee of his well-being, and he feared 'the march of mind'
and the gospel of Utility which seemed to be carrying all before
them. His meditative poetry, much of it inspired by what he saw and
felt on his excursions abroad, embodies his anxieties for an age
increasingly dominated by the 'calculating understanding', and
hostile to the higher visionary power of the poet. The occasional
poems (as he explained himself) offer glimpses of what might
have gone into *The Recluse*, his great philosophical poem on Man,
Nature, and Society, had it been finished. But in spite of promptings
from relatives and well-wishers the grand undertaking, by which
Coleridge had set such store, lay untouched and it is barely
mentioned in the letters. On the other hand, *The Prelude*, the
'ante-chapel' to it, was revised ready for publication after the
poet's death, and occasionally visitors were privileged to hear
parts of it read aloud. The poems were rearranged according to
their final classification, and Wordsworth continued to revise them
as new editions, and selections, were called for. He translated part
of Virgil's *Aeneid*. In his last years he joined in a scheme for popu-
larizing Chaucer. Much of the new German literature and philosophy remained a closed book to him, but he retained his abiding
love of Italian literature to the end. The letters contain much acute
and just comment on poetry and poets, and while Wordsworth

[1] C. W. to Joshua Watson, 22 Aug. 1844 (*Lambeth Palace Library MSS.*).

Introduction

never wavered in his sense of his own greatness, his judgements on his contemporaries were sometimes more generous than is often supposed.

His concerns as a poet left Wordsworth with a strong interest in public affairs, though he was sometimes profoundly pessimistic about their outcome. In many of his later letters he applies his fundamental principles to the problems of an age in many ways uncongenial to him. He followed local politics and party manœuvres at Cambridge with a practised eye; but he felt especially impelled to write on the great national issues of the day, when he felt that his views would carry weight. The appeal to expediency by those who pressed for change was abhorrent to him. The corner-stone of his Toryism was the time-honoured constitution in Church and State which seemed under threat from all the forces of intellectual and social unrest. He hotly opposed Catholic Emancipation, and wrote much about the history and prospects of Ireland; and the Reform Bill crises disturbed him more deeply still, stirring up frightening memories of the French Revolution and the Reign of Terror—though his letters to the Lowthers, now published in full for the first time, acknowledge the need for some limited measure of reform.[1] The vicissitudes of American democracy were equally disturbing for one who predicted such a great future for the English-speaking peoples, as his letters to Henry Reed, his American editor, show. Yet the movement for Italian freedom and unity won his unhesitating support.

But Wordsworth was not just a theorist or spectator of events. His convictions sprang from loyalty to the traditional leaders in his local community and to the Church as an enduring part of the English scene, and they were put to the test in the three Westmorland elections of 1818, 1820, and 1826, in opposition to Henry Brougham, the radical 'outsider', who stood for all that Wordsworth detested. His long reports to Lord Lonsdale from the hustings in 1826 prove that, for him at least, much more was at stake than the preservation of the Lowther monopoly in Westmorland politics. His zeal for Church renewal against the forces of Dissent was equally vigorous. A chapel was erected at Rydal with his support on the slopes below his house. Later, he campaigned for a new church in his native town of Cockermouth. He consistently championed the aims of the Oxford Movement, and a few letters to John Keble have now come to light; but his contacts with 'broad' churchmen and Presbyterians are equally important for an

[1] See particularly letters of 17 and 24 Feb. 1832.

understanding of his ecclesiastical thinking. The spread of a 'godless' and inhuman technology, whether in the factories of Whig magnates or in the railways that threatened the peace of the Lake District, repelled him; and the problems of industrial society, increasingly complex as the century progressed, also colour his numerous letters on the philosophy of education, the theme of his speech at the opening of the new school building at Bowness in 1836.

While Wordsworth's principles in later years were profoundly conservative, he was primarily a humanitarian with an instinct for radical solutions that were ahead of his time, and although he appeared to be fighting a rearguard action on behalf of an older order, his faith in 'the mighty stream of tendency' in history obliged him to acknowledge the reality of change and progress in human affairs. Taken together, the letters suggest that Wordsworth's complex thinking on all these problems cannot be reduced to a simple formula, and that he eludes the conventional party labels that have been attached to him.

Wordsworth saw less of the friends of earlier years as time went on, and nearly all of them predeceased him. Coleridge took part in the continental tour of 1828, but though the two poets shared many admirers among the younger generation, the ease and warmth of their earlier association could never be recaptured. Nor were friendly relations with De Quincey ever fully restored. After years of seclusion at Fox Ghyll he finally left the Lakes in 1830, and little more was heard of him until his controversial 'Lake Reminiscences' began to appear in *Tait's Magazine* in 1839. The death of Sir George Beaumont, Wordsworth's benefactor, in 1827 was the first of a long series of losses that afflicted the poet in late middle age. Scott's fatal decline set in more markedly soon after their last meeting at Abbotsford in 1831; and four years later, in one of the most moving of his later poems, the *Extemporary Effusion Upon the Death of James Hogg*, Wordsworth was mourning the passing of Coleridge and Charles Lamb as well. Robert Jones, his college friend and companion on the pedestrian tour of Switzerland, and the Wordsworths' guide through Wales in 1824, was also dead. Southey survived at Keswick for a few years more, but his melancholy end was particularly distressing to those who had known him in his prime. Soon, only Basil Montagu and Joseph Cottle were left to remind the poet of the revolutionary world of his youth and the richly productive years at Racedown and Alfoxden. But earlier times were not entirely forgotten. The later letters contain notable reminiscences of John Thirlwall and the first meeting with Coleridge. Dorothy's tragic decline often set the poet thinking of his poem on the Wye and the melancholy fulfilment of his predictions.

Yet in spite of these losses, there were other friends bringing new interests to cheer the poet in his later years: Samuel Rogers, Haydon, and John Kenyon, Henry Taylor the dramatist, Alexander Dyce the literary scholar, Edward Moxon the most generous of Wordsworth's publishers, and Barron Field, a keen critic of his textual revisions; and for a time there was a cordial correspondence with Walter Savage Landor. The long-standing acquaintance with Serjeant Talfourd, the friend and biographer of Lamb, grew into an effective alliance during Wordsworth's most sustained incursion into politics, the Copyright struggle of 1837–42, and many of the letters arising from this Parliamentary battle are now published for the first time. Wordsworth also admired scientists like Sir William Hamilton, the young Dublin astronomer, when they were men of vision as well. Nor was the younger generation forgotten. The Southey and Coleridge children became almost part of the family circle at Rydal Mount, Sara Coleridge most of all, and Hartley somehow managed to retain the Wordsworths' affection even when his drunken excesses later on might have been expected to strain their relationship beyond endurance. Edward Quillinan makes his first appearance in the correspondence in 1821. His winning ways and plight as a widower with young children more than made up in the Wordsworths' eyes for his unsettled mode of life and lack of financial security. But of all the friends of later years, two alone won their way effortlessly into the hearts of the Wordsworths and made themselves indispensable to their comfort and happiness, Henry Crabb Robinson and Isabella Fenwick. Each in their separate ways was a tower of strength in good times and bad.

The later years were a period of continuing anxiety as Wordsworth tried to provide more fully for his dependants and launch his children into the world. Many of his letters are about money matters, his attempts to get better terms from publishers, and his anger at the failure of his American investments. His financial security was at the best of times precarious. The account he gives of his Distributorship in Letter 27 to Lord Lonsdale should finally dispose of the idea, still current in some quarters, that his office was a sinecure. Much pressure had to be exerted upon the Government before he could get his territory extended, and his continued income from it depended largely on his own efforts. By prudent management (and a few timely contributions to the Annuals, which he soon regretted) he contrived to put John, his elder son, through Oxford, and saw him settled as a country parson in West Cumberland with the help of Lord Lonsdale's patronage. But Willy gave much more cause for concern. His education was interrupted by illness, no prospect of employment appeared, and after a year in Germany he had to rest content with appointment as his father's sub-distributor at Carlisle, until Wordsworth eventually obtained his Government pension from Peel, and Willy could succeed to the Distributorship. A constant need for watchfulness, even frugality, is apparent in all the poet's transactions. Yet he also showed a solicitude for others that stretched right beyond his immediate family circle to those (like his brother Richard's son) who needed his help in furthering their prospects. Perhaps it was the Wordsworths' own straitened circumstances as well as family solidarity that made them rejoice so wholeheartedly in the academic successes of their other nephews, Christopher's three sons, and the preferment which quickly followed.

These were years of tragedy and almost unbearable sorrow in the family circle. Sara Hutchinson, who had been for so long an all-but-permanent member of the household, died very suddenly in 1835, and the final breakdown in Dorothy's mental and physical condition set in soon afterwards. For the remainder of her days (she outlived the poet by nearly five years) she was a permanent invalid, her moments of lucidity rare and in themselves a painful reminder of what Wordsworth's 'exquisite' sister had once been. Dora's precarious state of health also gave much cause for anxiety— which was intensified by her growing attachment to Edward Quillinan. The story of Wordsworth's opposition to his daughter's marriage has often been told, usually to his disadvantage. But the highly charged emotional situation that built up, and his awesome agony of mind, are not susceptible of easy analysis, nor can his conflicting impulses be parcelled out for praise or blame. De Selincourt's account of the affair[1] still substantially holds good, and a vital correction to the text of Letter 327 further buttresses his contention that Wordsworth had no reason to be wary of Quillinan in the early years of their friendship. The disapproval and hostility developed much later, in 1838, when an engagement was imminent, and was based primarily on Quillinan's confessed inability to support a wife in reasonable comfort. In the end, after a long and

---

[1] 'Wordsworth and his Daughter's Marriage', in *Wordsworthian and Other Studies*, 1947.

Introduction

distressing struggle, Wordsworth survived the crisis of Dora's
marriage in 1841. It was, however, only the beginning of his
suffering. Her health continued to decline, and her death in 1847
was a blow from which he never really recovered. The picture of
Wordsworth in his last years is often painful, but never without its
moments of grandeur as well. The letters show him bending a
passionate, stubborn nature to the inevitable diminishments, the
losses and compromises of old age, but finding in the end 'the
years that bring the philosophic mind'.

'Why is it that those who can write so well in one sense, write
generally so ill in another? A very little attention would enable
even your demi-sighted friends to read without effort what now
must be rather a matter of conjecture than assurance, if ever they
read it at all.'[1] Francis Wrangham's complaint will be echoed by
many a later student of Wordsworth's handwriting. The aim of the
present edition has been to make texts accessible to the modern
reader which in their original form must often have puzzled, if not
baffled, Wordsworth's correspondents. The editorial principles of
The Early Years and *The Middle Years* have been continued in the
present volumes. The letters to Crabb Robinson and Henry Reed,
previously published in separate collections, have now been restored to their places in the chronological sequence. 'Joint' letters,
which include contributions from other members of the family,
have been printed in full in those cases where William's or
Dorothy's sections would not otherwise be completely intelligible.
Letters addressed *to* the poet have been drawn on in the commentary
together with much unpublished family correspondence and the
letters of those (like Edward Quillinan, Isabella Fenwick, and
Coleridge's daughter Sara) who were intermittently part of the
Wordsworth family circle. Other important sources for the later
years, that have not been used extensively before, include
Dorothy Wordsworth's unpublished Journals, Edward Quillinan's
fragmentary Diaries, and *The Rydal Mount Visitors Book* (which
opens in 1830 and was maintained till 1847). *The Later Years*
include well over six hundred letters of William and Dorothy
Wordsworth which have not been published before, and many more
that have appeared only in fragmentary or incorrect form.

[1] Francis Wrangham to W. W., 31 Aug. 1821 (*WL MSS.*).

xxxii

1. D. W. to THOMAS MONKHOUSE[1]

Address: To Mr Monkhouse. [?*Delivered by hand*]
MS. WL.
LY i. 1.

[2 Jan. 1821]

Have you seen Charles and Mary Lamb this Christmas? and how are they? Mrs Clarkson was reading the Morning Chronicle to us yesterday—a paper which much oftener brings vexation than[2] pleasure—and after many other things she came to a Farewell to the old Year—which at once rivetted the attention of her hearers. We recognised Charles Lamb immediately; and listened with pleasing sympathy. It appears that this Essay has been taken from the Magazine.[3]—You will perceive from Mary's letter that my Brother's eyes have been worse again. God grant that his labours at home, which no doubt he will resume as soon as he is settled there, may not make them worse again!

Have you heard from Wales? I wrote to your sister[4] about a week ago and am not without hopes of an answer from her before I leave Playford. I fear she can send no better tidings of the Farm. When your Wife writes to Miss Horrocks[5] I beg her to remember my love to her. God bless you both, my dear Friends, believe me ever yours affectionately and grateful for all your kindness.

Dorothy Wordsworth.

Have you seen Mr Johnson?[6] Mrs Hoare?[7] Mr Kenyon?[8] Do you

---

[1] M. W.'s cousin. This letter from Playford, which begins at the top of a half sheet, appears to be incomplete.   [2] than *written* and.

[3] Lamb's *New Year's Eve*, signed Elia, was first published in the *London Magazine*, iii (Jan. 1821), 5–8, and reprinted in the *Morning Chronicle* on the first day of the new year.   [4] i.e. Mary Hutchinson.

[5] Sarah Horrocks, later Mrs. St. Clare, sister-in-law of Thomas Monkhouse.

[6] The Revd. William Johnson, 'the Patriarch of National Education' (see *MY* i. 487; ii. 7), had recently been appointed rector of St. Clement's, East-cheap, with St. Martin Orgar, a living he held until his death in 1864. He continued to run the National Society's school till 1840.

[7] Hannah Hoare (1770–1856), the Wordsworths' Hampstead friend. See *MY* ii. 570. She came of a Quaker family, the Sterrys: married Samuel Hoare II (1751–1825) as his second wife in 1788, and conformed to the Church of England. She came to know C. W. soon after his marriage in 1804, when he was given the living of Oby, nr. Norwich, and stayed at Earlham with his wife's relations the Gurneys, who were also connected with the Hoares through Samuel's first marriage to Sarah Gurney (d. 1783). Thereafter the families of C. W. and W. W. were welcome guests at Mrs. Hoare's residence Heath House, Hampstead, where she entertained many of the leading men of letters, abolitionists, and penal reformers of the day. She became a second mother to C. W.'s sons when they lost their own. See Viscount Templewood, *The Unbroken Thread*, 1949, pp. 51 ff.   [8] John Kenyon. See *MY* ii. 573.

know how the Poems and the Excursion[1] sell? Two large fires have been seen from this house within the last ten days. The first it is believed was caused by some wicked Incendiary, and the second, (which only happened last night) we are afraid will be found to have had the same origin.—A sad way of mending bad times.

Mrs Clarkson desires I will give you her kind remembrances to you. She will be very happy to become acquainted with your wife. She is now in her usual state of health; but the excessive cold confines her to the house.—Now pray do write immediately; for I really long to hear from you.

I have begun to copy my journal[2] but have got poorly on. This is a very quiet place and we have no interruption of visitors—but I find it not easy to sit steadily to writing by the hour together.

2. W. W. to THOMAS MYERS[3]

MS. The late Mrs. Jane Myers.
LY iii. 1382.

Rydal Mount
Friday Evening [5 Jan. 1821]

My dear Sir,

I condole with you most sincerely on the distressing tidings which I have just heard, and pray that God will support [you] under this sudden shock.—

As the nearest Relation (by the Mother's side) of the Deceased resident in this part of the Country, and at the earnest request of his worthy Servant in which the Bearer has also joined, I have determined to go over to morrow to Pow-House,[4] where I shall await your coming if health permits; if not, which I shall much regret, I shall be glad to act upon any directions you may give; and

---

[1] i.e. the 4-vol. *Miscellaneous Poems* and the 2nd edition of *The Excursion*, both published the previous year.

[2] i.e. the *Journal of a Tour on the Continent 1820* (*DWJ* ii. 7 ff.).

[3] W. W.'s cousin (see *EY*, p. 147): elder son of W. W.'s uncle, the Revd. Thomas Myers, and his wife Anne Wordsworth (see *EY*, p. 7), and brother of John Myers the barrister (see *EY*, p. 112), who had just died. See Genealogical Table, facing p. 704.

[4] John Myers's residence near Millom. The property had been in the Postlethwaite family since the sixteenth century, but had passed to him in 1813, along with Lacra and Lowscales, on the death of his unmarried cousin John Postlethwaite, an eminent solicitor of Kendal (and nephew of the Revd. Thomas Myers). As John Myers left no male issue, the property now passed to his cousin William Myers of Deal (see L. 22 below).

I need not add how great would be my satisfaction if I could be of service on this melancholy occasion.

Julia[1] is at school, and the loss she has sustained will be communicated to the poor child to morrow, as gently as possible.

Repeating my good wishes that the Almighty may support and protect you, I remain my dear friend, truly and faithfully yours, Wm Wordsworth.[2]

3. W. W. to SIR GEORGE BEAUMONT

Address: To Sir George Beaumont Bart, Coleorton Hall, Ashby de la Zouche Leicestershire. [*In D. W.'s hand*]
Stamp: Kendal Penny Post.
MS. Pierpont Morgan Library.
K (—). *LY i. 5* (—).

10th Janry, 1821.

My dear Sir George,

Yesterday I performed a great feat—wrote no less than 7 letters, reserving yours for to-day, that I might have more leisure, and you consequently less trouble in reading. I have been a good deal tossed about since our arrival here. Mrs W. and I were first called away by the sudden death of my near kinsman, Mr Myers.[3] We went to College together, and were inseparables for many years. I saw him buried in Millom Church, by the side of his Wife.[4] The churchyard is romantically situated; Duddon Sands on one side, and a rocky Hill scattered over with antient trees on the other. Close by are the remains of the old Castle of the Huddlestones,[5] part of which are converted into farm Houses, and the whole embowered in tall trees that tower up from the sides and bottom of the circular moat. The churchyard is in like manner girt round with trees.[6]—The church is of striking architecture, and apparently of

[1] Julia Rachel Myers (1811–45), John Myers's only child, at this time a pupil at Miss Dowling's school at Ambleside. In 1841 she married the Revd. J. A. D. Meakin (1804–73) of St. John's College, Cambridge, vicar of Speenhamland, Newbury, Berks.
[2] The last paragraph has been cut away from the letter and added in pencil in an unidentified hand.
[3] John Myers. See previous letter. He was buried on 9 Jan.
[4] Rachel Phillips (d. 1816), daughter of Cyprian Bridge of Dovercourt, Essex, whom John Myers had married at Harwich in 1804.
[5] Dating from the fourteenth and fifteenth centuries. The Hudlestons of Hutton John were Lords of Millom for over 500 years, but relinquished the estates to the Lowthers in 1774.
[6] The scene today is very much as W. W. describes it here, but the interior of the church underwent considerable restoration later in the nineteenth century.

remote antiquity.—We entered with the funeral train, the day being too far advanced to allow the clergyman to see to read the service, and no light had been provided; so we sat some time, in solemn silence. At last one candle was brought, which served both for minister and clerk, casting a wan light on their faces. On my right hand were two stone figures in a recumbent Position (like those of the monument in Coleorton church[1])—Huddlestones of other years;[2] and the voice of the minister was accompanied, and almost interrupted, by the slender sobbing of a young person, an Indian by half blood, and by the father's side a niece of the deceased wife of the person whom we were interring. She hung over the coffin and continued this oriental lamentation till the service was over, everybody else, except one faithful servant, being apparently indifferent. Mrs W. I find has mentioned our return by Duddon-side, and how much we were pleased with the winter appearance of my favourite River.[3]

Since that expedition I have been called to Appleby, and detained there upon business. In returning, I was obliged to make a circuit which showed me for the [first] time several miles of the Course of that beautiful stream, the Eden, from the bridge near Temple Sowerby down to Kirkoswald. Part of this tract of country I had indeed seen before, but not from the same points of view. It is a charming region, particularly at the spot where the Eden and Emont join. The Rivers appeared exquisitely brilliant, gliding under Rocks and through green meadows, with woods and sloping cultivated grounds, and pensive russet moors interspersed, and along the circuit of the Horizon, lofty hills and mountains clothed, rather than concealed, in fleecy clouds and resplendent vapours.

My Road brought me suddenly and unexpectedly upon that ancient monument called by the Country People Long Meg and her Daughters.[4] Every body has heard of it, and so had I from very

---

[1] The monument in the S. aisle to Sir Henry Beaumont, Knight (d. 1607), and his wife Lady Elizabeth (d. 1608).

[2] The alabaster tomb of Richard Hudleston and his wife Elizabeth, daughter of Humphrey Lord Dacre and his wife Mabel Parr. The young couple died without issue *c.* 1505.

[3] At this point the letter seems to have been laid aside for about two weeks.

[4] An ancient stone circle on high ground near the village of Glassonby. See W. W.'s sonnet *The Monument commonly called Long Meg and her Daughters, near the River Eden* (*PW* iv. 47), composed about this time and included among drafts of the *Ecclesiastical Sketches* in the Cornell MS. Notebook (*Cornell Wordsworth Collection*, no. 2278): first published in 1822 in the 3rd edition of *The Guide to the Lakes* (*Prose Works*, ii. 195), included among the *Miscellaneous Sonnets* in the *Poetical Works* of 1827 and 1832, and finally transferred to the *Itinerary Poems of 1833* in 1837.

early childhood, but had never seen it before. Next to Stone
Henge, it is beyond dispute the most noble relick of the kind that
this or probably any other country contains. Long Meg is a single
block of unhewn stone, 18 feet high, at a small distance from a vast
circle of other stones, some of them of huge size, though curtailed
of their stature, by having sunk into the ground, by their own
incessant pressure upon it. Did you ever see that part of the Eden?
If not, you must contrive it. I was brought to Kirkoswald, but had
not time to visit Nunnery,[1] which I purpose to do next summer.
Indeed, we have a thought of taking the whole course of the Eden
from Carlisle upwards, which will bring us near the source of the
Lune, so that we may track that river to Lancaster, and so return
home by Flookborough and Cartmel.

It is now high time to say a word about Coleorton.[2] I often have
the image before me of your pleasant Labours, and see the landscape[3] growing under your patient hand. The large picture[4] you
were about must be finished long since. How are you satisfied with
it? I am not a little proud that our scenery employs your pencil so
sedulously after a visit to the Alps. It has lost little in my estimation by the comparison. At first I thought the coppice woods,
and alas! we have little else, very shabby substitutes for the
unshorn majesty of what I had lately seen. The rocks and crags

---

[1] The residence of Major Francis Aglionby (1780–1840), Whig M.P. for
East Cumberland, 1837–40: built in 1715 by Henry Aglionby (1684–1759),
M.P. for Carlisle, on the site of the Benedictine nunnery of Armathwaite near
the confluence of the Croglin and Eden. The estate was noted for its landscaped
walks along the banks of the Croglin.

[2] In his reply of 20 Feb., Beaumont described how he had been occupied with
re-reading the first two books of the *Excursion*: '. . . I sincerely declare to you
I enjoyed them more than ever. Your description of the glorious vision we saw
together passing Kirkstone astonishes me. I remember how much struck
you as well as myself were at the time, and I wispered to Lady Beaumont
"Mark how our comrade's rapt."—When you revived from your trance, you
told me nothing could be done with it by words—indeed I thought so—but
you have proved the contrary—such a complete blending of earth and heaven
I never saw. . . . The solid mountains entrenched almost to their tops with
burning shapes of etherial clouds of every form imagination could suggest, are
really equaled in splendor by your wonderful description, and as I read it I
really thought I saw with my bodily eye the enchanting vision again . . .'
(*WL MSS.*). See *Excursion*, ii. 834 ff. (*PW* v. 72, 417).

[3] i.e. the winter garden, which W. W. helped to plan during his residence
at Coleorton in the winter of 1806–7 (see *MY* i. 112–20). Lady Beaumont
wrote to D. W. on 19 Mar.: '. . . Pray tell your brother all the vacant scars
have been filled up with cedars, yew trees, and hollies, with other evergreens
far surpassing in beauty what were taken away . . .' And again in the following
year, on 22 Nov.: 'Had not your brother far higher claims to the admiration
of posterity, this garden almost would be a monument of his taste for the
picturesque.' (*WL MSS.*).   [4] Of Mt. Blanc.

also seem to want breadth and repose, their surfaces appearing too often crumbled and frittered. But, on the other hand, the comparison is often to our advantage. The lakes and streams not only are so much more pure and crystalline, but the surfaces of the one, and the courses of the other, present a far more attractive variety— a superiority which deserves to be set off at length, but which will strike your practised mind immediately.—It happened that Southey, who was so good as to come over to see us, mentioned to me Nichols' Book[1] with great commendation. I found also a vol. of it at Dr Satterthwaite's who says that it is both instructive, exhaustive and entertaining. When you offered so kindly to present it to me I was unwilling that you should incur the expense, but now I confess I long to possess it, with the additional value of its coming from you.—Another obligation, but this at your perfect leisure, is the little oblong picture to match with the one I possess from the pencil of a friend in Portugal. Its dimensions are marked at the foot of this sheet. A Pass on the banks of a rocky stream would please me much, or a *bit* of the Val d'enfer near Friburg, or a glade in a wood, or whatever you like.[2]—My Sister reached home last Saturday; part of her journey was very perilous on account of a blinding fog. Two Coaches that preceded her had their four horses all down together in a pit.

Ever yours,

W. W.

[1] John Nichols (1745–1826), printer and antiquarian: editor of the *Gentleman's Magazine* from 1792 till his death. His *History and Antiquities of the Town and County of Leicester* appeared in 8 vols. between 1795 and 1815, and was considered by himself as 'his most durable monument'.

[2] Beaumont replied: 'I am flattered, and shall have great pleasure in the work. I fear it may be said I sacrifice too much time to this seductive art. I was mortally struck with the love of it in early life, and those who condemn me ought first to be acquainted with the nature of my disposition and the situations in which I have been placed. I was left early to my own inclinations, and never pushed forward in public. My natural turn was for retirement. I always hated the turbulence of contention, and I always persuaded myself there would be enough who loved the bustle of the world and who would do the business far better from inclination, than I should after torturing my mind, and destroying all my comforts, and what could suit such a temper better than this silent art? . . . You who have devoted yourself to the sister art will I know be on my side. —I need not add I am not comparing myself to you.' In a later letter, of 20 Aug., he proposed sending a picture suggested by the banks of the Greta: 'I was about to send the Peel Castle, which besides being so immortally recorded I shall ever consider the best work in many respects I have ever produced. When Lady Beaumont suggested that it would be too large for your room, and that it would be better for me to paint it upon a smaller scale . . . there were two or three reasons which induced me to listen to this.' (*WL MSS.*).

4. D. W. to CATHERINE CLARKSON

Address: Mrs Clarkson, Playford Hall, Ipswich.
Endorsed: Jany. 1821.
MS. British Museum.
K (—). *LT i. 2.*

Wednesday evening [10 Jan. 1821]

My dearest Friend,

I reached Cambridge at about ½ past 6 o'clock last night; found my Brother's Servant waiting for me, and met your dear little Boy[1] in the Hall, who joyfully embraced and led me up stairs—all were glad to see me and looking blithe and healthy; but it was a great mortification to me to be told that Charles was gone to School and had only departed in the morning. Then, for the first time, I felt a pang of regret that I had not left you a day *sooner*. The first time indeed it was, for though my reasons for wishing to be a little while with the Boys[2] were very strong, my regrets were still stronger.— I was with you all the day—in your own bed-room first; then by the parlour fire; and often did I fancy you looking out of the window with melancholy eyes at the fog and rain,—which disturbed *me* much less, I have no doubt, than you. Mrs Kitchener and Elliot[3] were at the door to receive me when the coach stopped; and in about a ¼ of an hour your kind Sister[4] came in; but without her little Boy on account of the rain.—She took her dinner with us, and accompanied me to the coach at ¼ past 2. Mr and Mrs Robinson[5] called—your sister got into the Coach with me and sate till all was ready. I have had letters from Miss Horrocks and Charles Lamb,[6] with good accounts of Mrs Monkhouse. She had got into the drawing-room and all fear for the present is over. They have a Goose-pie from Mrs Anthony Harrison;[7] and Charles and Mary Lamb are to meet Talford,[8] and several other of their friends

---

[1] i.e. Willy W., who had spent his holidays with the Clarksons during his parents' absence abroad. See *MT* ii. 625.
[2] C. W.'s three sons, John, Charles, and Christopher. Charles was at this time still at Harrow, and the other two were commoners at Winchester.
[3] Mrs. Clarkson's housekeeper and her son.   [4] Mrs. Corsbie.
[5] Probably H. C. R.'s brother Thomas Robinson (1770–1860), of Bury St. Edmunds, and his wife.
[6] See *Lamb*, ii. 288.   [7] Wife of the Penrith solicitor.
[8] Thomas Noon Talfourd (1795–1854), judge and author. In 1811 he published *Poems on Various Subjects*, and in 1815 made the acquaintance of Lamb who introduced him to W. W. for whom he had a great admiration, and of whose poetry he wrote a eulogy in the *New Monthly Magazine*, which he sent to W. W. on 1 Dec. 1820. 'If it should induce any who have been hitherto strangers to these vast stores of sentiment and imagery of which it would afford a glimpse, to enter on their full contemplation, I shall greatly rejoice . . .

at the cutting of it on Friday evening. Nothing could exceed Mrs K's kindness; and she was not troublesome either with reproaches or regrets that I could not stay longer. Willy was much pleased at the sight of Elizabeth's[1] Gingerbread and returns his best thanks for it. He desires his 'love duty and compliments and everything that is good to you all'—these are his words (he is beside me) and he 'hopes you will soon be quite well'.—I think I shall certainly leave Cambridge on Tuesday morning for I see no possible reason for my Brother's desiring my longer stay—the Boys are thoroughly busy at their studies—and as Charles is not here *they* are much less likely to grieve at my departure or wish my stay. I have not, however, yet named the day of going; but I must have more talk with my Brother about Coaches, and write home to-morrow or the next day.—Willy does not like the notion of my going before *him*, therefore, at his request I shall certainly stay till Tuesday.

One o'clock—Willy and I have been to see Derwent,[2] He inquired very much after you and I am happy to tell you he looks well and as if he was doing his duty. He is in the first class; but the *arrangement* of the first class does not take place till Midsummer. He says he has not time to write for the Medal which he had ambition enough to think of doing; and my opinion is that he is wise to give it up as surely he could not have much chance against all the university, and if he fags in the more regular course I trust he may distinguish himself. Tillbrooke,[3] I believe, is not returned. Mr Townsend[4] has been very kind to Willy and given him a Book—

there is no writer who has ever lived to whom I personally owe the obligation which I owe to you, whose verse has so slid into the very current of my blood, and has so mingled with all my thoughts, hopes, and joys.' (*WL MSS.*). When the *Retrospective Review* was established in the same year, Talfourd became a leading contributor. He was called to the Bar in 1821, made a serjeant in 1833, and in 1849 a judge. He was M.P. for Reading, 1835–41 (and again in 1847), and in 1837 introduced his Copyright Bill, in which (as will emerge in later letters) W. W. took the keenest interest. Talfourd's chief works were his drama of *Ion*, successfully performed in May 1836 with Macready in the chief part (W. W. being present at the first night), and (as Lamb's literary executor) *Letters of Charles Lamb*, 1837, and *Final Memorials of Charles Lamb*, 1848.   [1] One of C.C.'s maids.

    [2] Derwent Coleridge was now an undergraduate at St. John's, where he had obtained an Exhibition. See Stephen Potter, *Minnow Among Tritons, Mrs. S. T. Coleridge's Letters to Thomas Poole 1799–1834*, 1934, p. 85.

    [3] For the Revd. Samuel Tillbrooke (1783–1835), see *MY* i. 368. He was Fellow and bursar of Peterhouse, 1810–28, and thereafter rector of Freckenham, Suffolk.

    [4] Chauncy Hare Townshend (1798–1868), minor poet, was educated at Eton and Trinity Hall, Cambridge, where he joined the circle of Derwent Coleridge and John Moultrie. In 1817 he obtained the Chancellor's English

Willy travelled with one of the Masters of the Charter House from
Bury. My dear brother is quite well and so chearful with the boys,
it is delightful to see him. I played a game at Speculation with the
Lads last night; but I found it very dull compared with our Playford pools at Commerce.

My dear Friend, I think of you continually and strangely sad
do I feel at the thought of going so far away from you, though it be
to my much-loved home and relations and to see the dear young
ones and Sara from whom I have been so long parted—yet the
thought of you is now so much with me, that I hardly seem to dwell
upon what will no doubt enliven my journey and cast out all *sorrowful* remembrances,—but as it is I cannot find in my heart to write
home till I get your letter (which I hope will be on Sunday morning). A haunting comes upon me that you may be ill again, and
that you may wish for me by your fire side; and if so, feeling that
I should be a real comfort to you and as we say in the North help
'to save your life', no consideration except a pressing duty at
home should induce me to pursue my journey northward—spite
of poverty and all other evils.

So far I wrote and was summoned by Willy to walk again. His
cousins' lessons were over at one o'clock and we sallied forth
together to Doughton's shop[1] where I was to buy something for
the Boys as a memorial in lieu of what was to have come from the
Continent. They chose a Book being busy in collecting a Library
for their own study, a nice little place. Willy pulled down a beautiful
Edition of Thomson's Seasons brought home these holidays by
Christopher a prize from Winchester School. Christ[r] is an extraordinary Boy. If God grant him health and life, he will be an honour
to his family I feel assured. We have had a nice walk together; but
I constantly regret Charles's absence, to break through the shyness
of his brothers, especially of John. He is a very thoughful, intelligent
boy, and I doubt not an excellent scholar, but his shyness is painful
to him I think; and he struck me as so exceedingly like Charles
Lloyd, when I first met him last night, that I felt uneasy at the
resemblance. Probably he would remind you of his mother. I do
not however see the particular likeness of her. When Christopher

Medal, and later, with the encouragement of Southey whom he visited at
Greta Hall, published *Poems*, 1821. He took holy orders, but was disabled by
illness from the active duties of his profession, and turned instead to collecting
and his landed interests in Norfolk. He published *Facts in Mesmerism* and
A Descriptive Tour in Scotland in 1840 and *Sermons in Sonnets*, 1851. His
friendship with W. W. suffered some ups and downs: see letters of Jan.–Feb.
1830 (in next volume).

[1] John Deighton's bookshop in Trinity Street.

asked me how long I should stay he seemed disappointed when I
mentioned Tuesday—I still think however that my Brother can have
no desire to keep me. His own engagements I am sure, make him
feel as if the Lodge were a dull place for others. My dear Friend
pray write to me if but to say how you are, I hope you have ridden
on horse-back this beautiful day. I talked of writing to you again
before my leaving Cambridge, but I think it is a pity to make you
pay for another letter; so if you do not hear you may conclude I
depart on Tuesday and may expect a letter from Rydal. I hope to
see Henry Robinson[1] to-morrow or Friday—a great pleasure.——
6 o'clock—just risen from dinner-table we have been very merry.
Christ[r] is to make tea for us. The Doctor is gone to chapel and
upon other business which will keep him till 9 o'clock, so perhaps
we may have another game at cards—but I should prefer chat
without cards unless you were here for a game at Commerce or
Whist.—I hope you have had a letter from Tom;[2] pray tell me its
contents.—Give my kindest love to Mr Clarkson and a thousand
thanks for all his goodness to me and my little nephew. God bless
you my dear Friend.—You have now just finished tea—I fancy I
see you both at the Tea table. Believe me ever your affectionate
and grateful Friend

D. Wordsworth.

I had company and the smell of Rum all the way in the Coach.
Charles had not *time* to write.

5. W. W. to LORD LONSDALE

Address: The Earl of Lonsdale, Cottesmore, Greatham, Grantham.
Stamp: Kendal Penny Post.
MS. Lonsdale MSS. Hitherto unpublished.

[*c.* 12 Jan. 1821]

My Lord,
    I am truly happy to hear of the recovery of your Lordship's health,
as is every one of my family.
    Dr Stoddart has sent me a number of his Paper containing the

---

[1] i.e. H. C. R.
[2] The Clarksons' only child. He had left Cambridge in 1818 and was now
studying at the Middle Temple. He was called to the Bar in 1825 and practised
for a time on the Northern Circuit.

resolutions of the Society.[1] It is not easy to point out in what manner an Association can act for this purpose without incurring the risk of doing more harm than good. The last Resolution seems to propose that the Society shall prosecute offenders;—now such a measure tends to take out of the hands of Government what it is the paramount duty of Government to perform. While it implies a censure of Government for remissness, it encourages the fault which could alone justify the interference. In this respect the exertions of the Association would resemble that for suppressing of vice,[2] which I always disapproved of. In the view which the Prospectus takes of the magnitude of the evil I entirely concur, and am inclined to think that a Society might be instrumental in circulating publications of a good tendency, which would in no small degree prevent the spreading of bad ones; it might also collect information and lay it before the Public, so that the extent of the mischief might become generally known. Beyond this, and perhaps occasionally rewarding the meritorious, I do not clearly see what could be done without bringing along with it more evil than good. I state these opinions to your Lordship, desirous of being corrected if you think me mistaken. As an Individual I have made a point of recommending that no one should take in a periodical publication the general conduct of which he disapproves, nor subscribe to any such. Much the largest portion of the sedition, impiety, and slander with which the country is inundated, proceeds merely from the vilest cupidity. Much good might be done, if Clergymen, Country-gentlemen, and leading Manufacturers and Tradesmen, in the several spheres would exercise their influence in introducing (especially into public Houses) loyal Newspapers. There are numberless places, thank God, yet left in the Country where a Publican would as readily take in a good Newspaper as a bad one. All Trustees of Schools ought to be especially careful as to the principles of those whom they elect as Masters. In my own neighbourhood are two School Masters, both

[1] The Constitutional Association for Opposing the Progress of Disloyal and Seditious Principles—but according to Henry Brougham 'a self-constituted body of prosecutors'. See *MT* ii. 657. On 30 May he attacked them in the House of Commons for circularizing magistrates about their duties under the law of libel.

[2] Originally founded by William Wilberforce and other Evangelicals in 1787 as the Society for Enforcing the King's Proclamation against Immorality and Profaneness (see *Life of William Wilberforce*, 1838, i. 130–8, 393–4), and reorganized in 1802 as the Society for the Suppression of Vice, it carried on an unremitting warfare against blasphemous or obscene publications, brothels, and fortune-tellers, and campaigned for rigorous Sunday observance. But while Wilberforce saw it as 'the guardian of the religion and morals of the people', Sydney Smith complained of 'a corporation of informers . . . bent on suppressing not the vices of the rich but the pleasures of the poor'.

Ultra-whigs; and Ultra-whiggism in a Master produces Radicalism in his Pupils.—But it is time to turn to another subject.

A week ago I received news of the sudden death of my Relation, Mr Myers of Millom.[1] I went over immediately. He was found dead, in the morning, lying on the floor of a House of a Relation of his, on whom his landed Estates were entailed if he should die without male issue. This he did. The County Coroner had been sent for, Mr Peter Hodgson.[2] On Sunday Evening a letter arrived from him, stating that there was no Coroner for Millom, that the County Coroner could not grant a Warrant to bury the Body without an Inquest, and suggesting that the officiating Minister might suffer the Body to be interred. The Relations of Mr Myers were not satisfied with this mode of proceeding; and we wrote a Letter to Mr Hodgson telling him so, and begging him that if he had, as County Coroner, jurisdiction in the Lordship of Millom, that he would attend without delay. This Letter produced the answer which I have the honor to enclose. On the Receipt of it I proceeded with the Gentleman in whose House Mr Myers was found dead, to beg that Mr Kirkbank[3] would act. We found him very infirm, having lost the use of one hand with the Palsy. At last we prevailed upon him to undertake the office; which with the assistance of his Son he was enabled to discharge. I have troubled your Lordship with these particulars as they shew the necessity of a Coroner being appointed for the Seignory of Millom.[4] It has been proposed, I was told by Mr Kirkbank the Younger,[5] to couple certain other offices with that of Coroner, one of which, *viz.* that of superintendent of wrecks appears to be of too mean a nature to have it probable that it would be undertaken by any person of sufficient education and respectability for an office requiring the discernment which the duty of Coroner calls for. I mention this because I am sure your Lordship would be sorry should the district suffer from any delay on this account.

I have the honor to be
my Lord
Your Lordship's
Sincerely and faithfully
Wm Wordsworth

Col: Lowther shall hear from me shortly upon the subject of officers for the Yeomanry Corps.

[1] See L. 2.   [2] Attorney, of Whitehaven.
[3] Isaac Kirkbank of Whicham, nr. Millom.
[4] An office once held by W. W.'s father.
[5] John Kirkbank of Whicham, later Coroner for the Seignory of Millom.

6. D. W. to THOMAS MONKHOUSE

Address: Thomas Monkhouse Esqre, 34 Glocester Place, Portman Square, London.
Postmark: 18 Jan. 1821. *Stamp*: Cambridge. *Endorsed*:18 Jan. 1821. D. W.
MS. WL.
LY i. 7.

Wednesday evening [17 Jan. 1821]

My dear Friend,

Soon after I parted with William yesterday morning I consented to stay a week longer at Cambridge. The Boys are not to return to Winchester till the 10th[1] and poor things! they wished me so much to stay, and talked so feelingly of their loneliness for the rest of the holidays that I could not find in my heart to leave them so soon.—I shall most probably depart next week; but though I have to them fixed next Tuesday, I do not wish to speak of it to you as a thing absolutely fixed. After my change of purpose I was very sorry that I had not sooner resolved, as you would thereby have been prevented from having the trouble of writing to me in such haste yesterday, and I should have had the hope of a longer letter tomorrow. I was very much concerned to hear that your Wife was not so well as when Miss Horrocks wrote but I hope with you that in the end all will be well. Accept my best thanks for your chearful compliance with a request of mine which no doubt appeared to you foolish and unreasonable, but you must forgive me. It is impossible not to be anxious respecting a Child subject to such severe attacks of illness, and you must remember also that all his illnesses come on with headaches. I was truly thankful to hear that he was well. I am sorry to trouble you again with another letter so soon, especially as I have no amusement to send along with it; but I have a particular reason for asking a question of you which I need not explain till I have your answer. Did William tell you what money he had when he left Cambridge? and if so, what did he say? I have some reason to suspect that he dealt disingenuously with me about it, and am anxious to have the matter cleared up; and if nothing passed between you on the subject, pray be so good as to ask him when you next see him; but without giving him cause to think you suspect any thing amiss, and above all, pray take care not to alarm him by the manner of questioning him—for if he has told one falsehood I should be very much afraid of tempting him into another.

I am truly sorry to give you so much trouble, and if you have had no talk with him, there is no need that you should write to me

[1] i.e. of February.

13

here, only be so good as not to fail to satisfy my inquiries when you write to Rydal.

I drank tea with Derwent Coleridge yesterday. Tillbrooke is [not] in College, nor have I seen Mr Robinson. My Brother is quite well—I had a letter from Mrs Hoare this morning.—She is at Bath with Mr H, who has been very nervous and poorly but is better.

This is a delightful day. I have had a long walk with Derwent Coleridge—Give my kind love to your Wife and Miss Horrocks— and believe me ever your grateful and affectᵉ Friend

D. Wordsworth.

My Brothers and the Boys send their best remembrances. God grant that the next news I have of your dear Jane may be good!

Poor William, is now, I guess, about leaving you to go to s[chool].

7. W. W. to THE COMMISSIONERS OF STAMPS

Endorsed: W. Wordsworth. Rydal Mount, Ambleside. 19 Janʸ 1821.
MS. Public Record Office. Hitherto unpublished.

[*In John Carter's hand*]

Rydal Mount, Ambleside,
19 Janʳʸ 1821—

Hon'ble Sirs,

Annexed I have the Honor to transmit a List of the Names and Residences of Persons lately appointed by me to the Collection of the Legacy Duties,[1] and I have to request that you will give directions for the Articles mentioned on the other side, to be sent to me.

I have the Honor to be
Hon'ble Sirs
Your obedient Servant
[*signed*] Wᵐ Wordsworth

Name	Residence	Occupation
Richard Bateman	Appleby	Stationer:
Joseph Sanderson	Cockermouth	Draper:
Robert Mordy	Workington	Stationer:
Joseph Millican	Maryport	Ironmonger:

[1] The towns of Cockermouth, Workington, and Maryport had just been added to W. W.'s district. See *MY* ii. 612, and *SH*, p. 202.

8. D. W. to CATHERINE CLARKSON

Address: Mrs Clarkson, Playford Hall, Ipswich.
Endorsed: 1821.
MS. British Museum.
LY i. 9.

Friday Morning [19 Jan. 1821]

My dearest Friend,

Ever since I changed my determination respecting leaving Cambridge this week, I have daily intended writing to you, but have been prevented by one cause or another. William departed on Tuesday morning. As I had good accounts of Mrs Monkhouse I thought it better that he should spend one day with his kind Friends, and I was only thankful on Monday night when we had played a merry game of cards together, to think that he had passed the whole of the holidays without a moment's sickness; but in the morning he looked very pale and complained of headache. Though I was willing to hope that the headache ought to be only such as would have been unnoticed at another time, and that the paleness of his countenance proceeded from suppressed feeling, I could not help being uneasy and therefore sent a note by him to request Mr Monkhouse to write that evening to tell me how he was on his arrival. Mr M had just time to say that he was quite well and to add a little good-humoured sneer at my 'unnecessary fears', and a word or two about his poor Wife who I am sorry to tell you had had a relapse, and though not so ill as before, I fear she will not get through her pregnancy without a miscarriage. I was not so uneasy about Willy that I could not have waited another Post, but I then thought I should have been gone on Thursday morning: the Boys however were so desirous of my longer stay, talked so feelingly of their solitude during the rest of the holidays, and complained— (especially John) so too of the missing of Willy that I could not help saying I would stay a week longer. The Father looked well pleased when he heard it and said he was lost in this huge house by himself. The fact is, that my Brother had never said a word about my longer stay from his delicacy of feeling.—Any other female but a wife resident in his house would be an encumbrance at least during his Vice-Chancellorship,[1] and he is troubled by the notion that his visitors must be dull. He says nothing of this to me; but I know that it *is* so. I never see him from breakfast till dinner except when he comes in between his different avocations. After dinner he

---

[1] C. W. was Vice-Chancellor 1820–1 and again in 1826–7.

15

goes to Chapel, then often come visitors upon Business, who go when this happens into his study. After tea he again retires to the study, where he has occupation in which no-one can assist him, generally till prayer time (ten o'clock). After that, the Boys go to bed and my Brother and I sit together till about eleven.—The Boys' time is always occupied at their Books till one or half-past from breakfast time. Their Tutor comes at 11—after his departure we walk together or they play, or talk to me, or read a little till 4, and after dinner one or other of them is generally with me till tea— after tea they generally go to their own study till 9. So you see even while the Boys are here I am much alone, but solitude is never irksome and I would willingly stay the rest of the Boys' holidays (they do not go to school till the 10th) if I thought I were of much use either to them or their Father. This I certainly am not; for as they are sometimes visiting Mr Townsend[1] and other friends of theirs, and often engaged at play by themselves in their hours of relaxation, it is not very often that they would feel the want of me— however if again they should express a very strong desire, seconded by their Father for my longer stay I could not help consenting to another week, though my wishes to see home once again, and my dear Friends there are much stronger than when I was with you. At that time indeed they never troubled me: and even now if an opportunity offered of going to Ipswich free of expense I should gladly seize it, but that is the most unlikely thing in the world; and I would not feel myself justified in going back again in the regular way, travelling so many miles and spending more money— especially when I have counter longings and wishes to be at home which would prevent a long stay—and your letter was on the whole chearing. You were going to Woodbridge and are likely now to have intercourse with other Clarksons, and to be able to ride on horseback; for the weather is delightful. Spring is coming on of itself—at least into the gardens—and in May you talk of going to London—and the summer after next I trust if God grant us life and health we may meet again in the North—and further, I feel as if there were many reasons why I should not be so long again in visiting the South.—All these thoughts have passed through my mind; and the result is, that I generally give up all idea of seeing you again at this time—unless indeed some extraordinary opportunity should offer which indeed is so far out of the circle of possibilities that I think not of it. Mr Clarkson's regrets at my departure are very flattering to me; and whenever I think of his

----

[1] Chauncy Hare Townshend. See L. 4 above.

kindness it moves me—a thousand thanks to him and to you my
dear Friend! I trust we may all live to meet again in your quiet
home at Playford, whence I hope no evil times will ever expel you.
—I have read of the arrival of letters from the West Indies, which
no doubt will bring to Mr Clarkson full accounts of what has happened and what is likely to happen.[1] I long very much to know what
you have heard, and if you do not write to me again here, I shall
hope for a letter very soon after my arrival at home.—Pray remember me to Mr and Mrs Biddle.[2] I am much obliged to him for the
kind interest he takes about me. Tillbrooke is not yet returned—
a great loss to me—nor have I seen Henry Robinson which was a
real disappointment.—I drank tea with Derwent Coleridge one
afternoon; and we had a large party of Ladies and Gentlemen to dinner on Friday. The Master was very lively and agreeable, and the
evening went off exceedingly well—No other Company.—I have
had a letter from Mrs Fisher.[3] Her Mother (Mrs Cookson) is at
Weymouth and is benefited by the air. Her disorder is an enlargement of the liver; and they hope for recovery to a certain degree;
but Mrs F says that her progress might have been quicker if her
frame would have borne rougher remedies.—I have also had a
letter from Mrs Hoare. They are at Bath and see little or no company, Mr H being still very nervous, though better since he went
to Bath.—I have heard from Sara H—she was again left alone.
William and Mary had been summoned to Po House on the sudden
death of its owner, poor John Myers,[4] who had been found dead on
the floor of his bedroom with all his cloathes on his back, at the
house of a cousin where he was going to sleep. Alas! we expected
such an end. I think it will shake his poor old Father grievously.
Myers has died without a will, which may be a great misfortune to
his Daughter. I never saw him without urging him to make a will.
I do not know whether G. Airey[5] is returned to college or not.

[1] Particularly in Haiti, after the death of King Christophe with whose cause
Clarkson had especially identified himself. See *MY* ii. 655, and L. 18 below.
[2] Arthur Biddell, neighbour of the Clarksons, a farmer and valuer, and uncle
of George Airy mentioned below.
[3] D. W.'s cousin Mary Cookson, eldest child of Canon William Cookson
(see *MY* ii. 207), had married the Revd. William Fisher (1799–1874), Student
of Christ Church, Oxford, 1815–23; and thereafter Canon of Salisbury and
rector of Poulshot, Wilts. [4] See L. 2 above.
[5] Sir George Biddell Airy, F.R.S. (1801–92), mathematician and astronomer:
Fellow of Trinity College, Cambridge, 1824; Lucasian Professor of Mathematics, 1826; Plumian Professor of Astronomy and director of the University
observatory, 1828; Astronomer Royal for 46 years from 1835. In 1812 he had
spent his holidays at Playford with his uncle Arthur Biddell and had met
Thomas Clarkson, who introduced him to his scientific and literary friends and

I mentioned the declamation to my Brother who told me the story exactly as we had heard it from George. Derwent tells me that the young men who coughed him down were very much pleased with the manner of the Master's reproof—It was 'so gentlemanly so firm, and in all respects so proper', therefore no doubt it was useful and my Brother told me that the Plaudits were almost as unreasonable afterwards on the Feast-day (I suppose when the Prizes were given). This probably proceeded from amiable feelings of compunction. This is the last day in the Senate House and I shall go to-morrow to see more of the degrees granted. My Brother keeps quite well though one engagement succeeds another the day through. Poor little Willy! I was not sorry when his holidays were over, though sorry enough to part with him. He behaved always well, so that it was impossible to say he was not a good Boy; but he was so much excited by his Cousins' company and by the notice of undergraduates, that he was restless and never once looked at a Book for pleasure; and therefore his company was not so engaging to me as at Playford, and for his own good I often wished that the holidays were shorter. Happy as he was at Cambridge there is no place he likes so well as Playford. He talks of it with much pleasure, and thankful am I that he was with us here during that fortnight. I hope before next Christmas he will have acquired some taste for Books. What do you think? He laid out 3/6 in a *'gold pin'* for his shirt, which the next day he broke. Mr Townsend found this out; and a young man with T. asked him if he would like another. You may guess Willy's answer, and the young man took him to a shop and bought him one for ten shillings!—I have now got the pin in my case. Remember me kindly to Elizabeth—I think of you more than you can possibly imagine, and of all the goings on of the day. I shall not expect to hear from you again; but should of course be glad if I do. I shall go on Wednesday at the latest if I go next week —but I should prefer Tuesday as giving me more time to get home before Sunday. If, however, you should have anything particular to say—Oh no! I cannot receive it—as the coach goes at 6 o'clock. My Brother's kind regards. Look about in all corners of this letter for scraps—In spite of your skill, I fear you will find it hard to decipher.

6 o'clock. I have just learnt from the Boys that they are going

encouraged him to go to Cambridge. In 1825 he took a reading party to Keswick for three months and saw much of W. W. and Southey. He was again in the Lakes in summer 1827 and in the autumn of 1830, when he dined at Rydal Mount. See *Autobiography of Sir George Airy*, 1896.

into [? Essex] to see Mr Walton,[1] C's[2] Godfather. This shortens the time at Cambridge so I think I shall surely go on Tuesday, but if you have any thing very particular to say to me you might write by the Coach as you did to Mrs Kitchener; should I stay another week I will write again in time for an answer from you.

I intend to go to Sedbergh to see John—God bless you ever yours

D. W.

9. W. W. to LORD LONSDALE

MS. Lonsdale MSS. Hitherto unpublished.

Rydal Mount
Jan 20th 1821

My Lord,

I am much gratified by having been made the medium of communicating to Mr Jackson[3] such important intelligence. He charges me to express to your Lordship his grateful sense of the honor you have done his Son, and hopes that his thanks will be as acceptable conveyed through me as if he had troubled your Lordship with a Letter from himself. I am sorry to add that his health does not improve.

Your Lordship, I trust, will have reason to be satisfied with the Presentation.—I have seen much of Mr Wm Jackson,[4] and with encreasing pleasure. He is a man of an upright and honorable mind, an excellent Scholar, and a man of talents. That he must be fitted for the discharge of important office, is proved by his having been pressed to undertake, a second time, that of Pro-proctor in the University of Oxford, which he now fills with a zeal and activity, from which, and from other engagements, I am sorry to hear his health suffers. It is probable that the sea air of Whit[n] may be of great service to him; he was anxious on this account to be placed by professional duty near the Sea-shore.

---

[1] The Revd. Jonathan Walton, D.D. (1774–1846), C. W.'s university friend and correspondent, and contemporary at Trinity: curate of Gosforth, Northumberland, 1800–1; rector of Birdbrook, Essex, 1801–46.

[2] i.e. Charles Wordsworth's.

[3] The Revd. Thomas Jackson, rector of Grasmere.

[4] The Revd. William Jackson, D.D. (1792–1878), son of Thomas Jackson: Fellow of Queen's College, Oxford, 1815–29; Chancellor of Carlisle, 1846–55; Archdeacon and Canon, 1856–62; Provost of Queen's, 1861–78; and rector of Lowther for 50 years, 1828–78. In 1829 he married Julia Crump, daughter of the owner of Allan Bank. He had just been appointed rector of St. James's, Whitehaven, on Lord Lonsdale's recommendation.

This morning, my Sister has had a communication from Mrs Ellwood of Penrith,[1] which the remembrance of your Lordship's past kindness to that Lady induces me to mention.

Mr Wilkin[2] has told a Friend of hers that the present House-keeper at Somerset House is very old and infirm; and this with a view that she should endeavour to procure a promise of the situation, as these things are generally disposed of before the actual vacancy. Mrs Ellwood, as I have before reported to your Lordship, is a person of excellent principles, and economic habits, well fitted, I believe, for such or similar situations: and She has been very unfortunate. Mr Wilkin can give any information upon the subject of the situation at Somerset House, if it be an affair in which it suits your Lordship to interfere; at all events I doubt not your Lordship will pardon the liberty I take in naming the matter.

The issue of the Catholic Question in the House of Lords was most happy for the Country.

I am glad to hear such good news of Sir George and Lady Beaumont.

> With most respectful regards to Lady Lonsdale,
> I have the honor to be
> my Lord
> sincerely and faithfully your Lordship's
> W. Wordsworth

10. C. W. JNR. and D. W. to THOMAS MONKHOUSE

Address: To Thomas Monkhouse Esqre, 34 Glocester Place, Portman Square, London.
Postmark: 23 Jan. 1821. *Stamp*: Cambridge. *Endorsed*: 22 Jany 1820 D. W. and C. W. Ju^r.
MS. WL.
LY i. 13.

> Trinity Lodge
> Jany 22nd, 1821.[3]

Dear Sir,

I hope you will excuse the liberty I take in troubling you with a few lines. My Brother and myself will be in London on friday

---

[1] For Mrs. Ellwood, who was still seeking employment, see *MY* ii. 406. She was Jane, daughter of Thomas Whelpdale of Skirsgill (1737–94) and his wife Jane Green (1753–1843), and was therefore a remote connection of the Monkhouses. She married Richard Ellwood (1772–1811), attorney at Penrith, in 1802, and was still living in 1843.

[2] John Wilkin. See *MY* ii. 465.   [3] 1821 *written* 1820.

the 9th of next month, and if it would be perfectly agreeable and convenient to Mrs Monkhouse and yourself, my father will be greatly obliged to you, if you will permit us to make your house our *dormitory* (N.B.—Aunt desires me make use of that word) in our way to *much-loved* Winchester and its *scientific bowers*. Hoping also that you will be kind enough to have places taken for us by the Winchester Coach, which sets off in Picadilly.

I remain

Tuus Amiculus

Christopher Wordsworth—

My Father sends his kind regards to yourself and Mrs Monkhouse.

Turn over. D W

My dear Friends,

I assure you 'Aunt' is not answerable for any part of her Nephew's letter. He dashed it off in a few seconds and looked both merry and cunning all the while.—I hope it will be convenient to you to receive them on Friday night (the 9th). That is, I hope Mrs Monkhouse will be well enough; as I do not think any thing else is likely to stand in their way. I shall not be here when your answer arrives, as I am actually going at six o'clock on Wednesday morning. I shall sleep at Leicester and at Manchester. The Boys are to spend a week in Essex, therefore their time at Cambridge will soon be over.—I have the satisfaction of seeing my dear Brother in good health and spirits; though I have but little of his company as he is busy from morning till night—I am told he makes an admirable Vice-chancellor and have no doubt that he is equally well liked as Master of Trinity.—I trust we shall hear of you soon after I reach home. Do not omit to tell me if any thing passed between William and you respecting his money. Hoping for good accounts of you, and with kind Love to Miss Horrocks I remain truly yours

D Wordsworth

It is necessary to take places for Winchester long beforehand as the Boys are flocking thither at that time.

I hope William continues well.

11. W. W. to H. C. R.

Address: To H. C. Robinson Esqre, Temple, London.
Postmark: (1) 24 Jan. 1821. (2) 26 Jan. 1821. Stamp: Kendal. Endorsed: 23^d
    Jan. 1821. Wordsworth, Southey's Vision of Judgm^t.
MS. Dr. Williams's Library.
K(—). Morley, i. 96.

Rydal Mount.
Jan. 23 1821.

My dear Friend,

We have had no tidings of the Books which were to be sent us
by the Bookseller near Charing-cross, which, if no misfortune had
happened to them might have been here, upwards of six weeks ago.
—We suffer no little inconvenience from the want of them; and
along with the Books the package contained paper, which not
having arrived, I am obliged to write to you on this shabby half
folio sheet.—Every thing has been unlucky relating to this matter
for being uneasy at not receiving the Books nearly a month since
I sent a Letter to a Friend to be franked for you, your address being
given on the inside of the cover, which had been thrown into the fire
I suppose as soon as the Letter was opened; for to my great mortification the Letter came back to me with a notice that my friend did
not know what use was to be made of it.—Be so kind as to call
upon the Bookseller, and desire him to forward the Books immediately, address'd to Mr Cookson, Kendal, no other name appearing
on the Package: which is to be sent by Pickford's Canal a conveyance which we have found both safe and expeditious. I am sorry
to give you this trouble, but the parcel is really valuable.

I have no news from this place—My Sister is still at Cambridge—
Southey came over to see me since my return, he is quite well, but
looks older than might be expected. He is about to publish a
Poem,[1] occasioned by the death of his late Majesty, which will
bring a nest of hornets about his ears; and will satisfy no party. It is
written in English Hexameter verse, and in some passages with
great spirit. But what do you think; in enumerating the glorified
spirits of the reign of George 3^d admitted along with their earthly
sovereign into the New Jerusalem, neither Dr Johnson nor Mr Pitt

---

[1] Southey's Laureate poem A Vision of Judgment (Poetical Works, 10 vols.,
1838, x. 195 ff.), with its apotheosis of George III, provoked both distaste
and ridicule, and the preface attacking the 'Satanic school' of poetry was
regarded by liberals as a direct challenge to their views. The poem is chiefly
remembered today as the subject of Byron's memorable parody with almost
the same title.

are to be found.[1]—Woe to the Laureat for this treasonable judgement! will be the cry of the Tories.

I am glad to find that Barry Cornwall's tragedy[2] has been so successful, and if you see him pray be so kind as to give him my congratulations. Say all that is kind to the Lambs, and to Talfourd, and to the Monkhouses, but with them we are in correspondence.

Mrs Wordsworth desires her kindest remembrances; we often talk of you, and your good humour, and accommodating manners.

Ever sincerely yours
W Wordsworth

12. W. W. to THE COMMISSIONERS OF STAMPS

Address: The Hon'ble Commissioners, Stamp Office, London.
Postmark: 7 Feb. 1821. *Stamp*: Kendal Penny Post. *Endorsed*: William Wordsworth Esq, Rydal Mount Ambleside. 3ᵈ Feby 1821.
MS. Public Record Office. Hitherto unpublished.

[*In John Carter's hand*]

Rydal Mount, Ambleside
3 Febry 1821—

Hon'ble Sirs,

I beg leave to state, in reply to your Letter of the 29 ult: that the Period, mentioned in my Book of Instructions of 1811, for the transmission of my Legacy Receipts is the *first* Tuesday in each month.

I further beg leave to say that a Letter on this subject, was addressed to me on the 14 March last;[3] and that in reply to my

---

[1] In Southey's poem, the King is received into Heaven and greeted by the 'lights of the Georgian age', including Wolfe, Handel, Reynolds, Hogarth, Wesley, Burke, Warren Hastings, Cowper, and Nelson (but not Pitt or Fox, as Southey pointed out delightedly in a letter).

[2] Bryan Waller Procter, or 'Barry Cornwall' (1787–1874), whom W. W. had met at Lamb's the previous November (see *MY* ii. 651), had followed up his successful poems and dramatic sketches with a far more ambitious tragedy *Mirandola*, which had just been produced at Covent Garden. The play, which owed much of its success to the acting of Charles Kemble, was financially profitable to Procter, but was never revived. In 1824 he married Anne Skepper, stepdaughter of Basil Montagu (see *MY* i. 63, 212), and thereafter his literary production, except as a writer for the annuals, declined and he devoted himself to the law.

[3] The Commissioners had written on 14 Mar. 1820: 'The regular period for your transmitting Legacy Receipts and Residuary Accounts to the Board is the

observations thereon, it was stated in your Letter of the 30 March, that it was now clearly settled in the order Book of the Office, that the *first* Tuesday in the month is the day on which I am to transmit my Legacy Receipts of Residuary Amounts, and that I must therefore continue to make my Return:—I presume, in consequence that your Letter of the 29 ult: has been inadvertently addressed to me.

I have the Honor to be,
Hon'ble Sirs,
Your obedient Servant
[*signed*] Wᵐ Wordsworth

13. W. W. to JOHN KENYON

Address: John Kenyon Esqʳᵉ, Montagu Square, London.
Stamp: Kendal Penny Post. *Endorsed*: from Wordsworth his autograph.
MS. untraced.
Transactions of the Wordsworth Society, no. 6, p. 81. K (—). LY i. 14.

Rydal Mount
5ᵗʰ Febʸ, 1821.

My dear Friend,

Many thanks for your valuable present of the Shades, which reached me two days ago by the hands of my sister.

I have tried them and they answer their purpose perfectly; Mrs W. says they have no fault but being over fine for the person they are intended for. I, on the other hand, am pleased to see Ornament engrafted upon infirmity, and promise that I will take care neither to sully nor spoil such elegant productions.

We have had a charming season since we reachᵈ Westᵈ, winter disarmed of all his terrors, and proving that it is not necessary always to run away from old England for the sake of fine weather.

Southey was so good as to come over and see us; he is well but always looks rather pale and thin in winter, which seems to add a few years to his age. He is as busy as ever, and about to publish a political Poem which will satisfy no party.[1]

---

fourth Tuesday in each month, therefore in consequence of the return which is not due until the 28 inst having been received on Friday last the 10 inst, I am directed to inform you that premature transmission causes as much irregularity in the business of the Legacy Department as those that are delayed. This being the case they desire that you will be punctual to the day fixed upon and not make your returns either before or after that period.' (*P.R.O. MSS.*). W. W.'s reply has not been traced.

[1] *A Vision of Judgment*. See L. 11 above.

George the Third is represented as entering the true Jerusalem with the deceased worthies of his reign, and neither Charles Fox, Wm Pitt, nor Dr Johnson are of the Party!!!

Cambridge is a 'pleasant place',[1] and so is Rydal Mount. Come, and make it pleasanter, or if that is not to be let us hear at least of your movements.

My sister seems to think, and yet not to think, that she ought to have answered your last letter; she stumbled out an apology to be transmitted by me.

I did not like the frame of it, and said that you will readily forgive her, if she makes up for that neglect by additional application to her journal,[2] which I am sorry to find is little advanced, talking being, as you know, a much more easy, and to one party at least a more pleasant thing than writing.

[*cetera desunt*]

14. W. W. to VISCOUNT LOWTHER

MS. Lonsdale MSS. Hitherto unpublished.

Rydal Mount
7th Febry 1821

My dear Lord Lowther,

I am sorry to have been obliged to displace Bateman,[3] recommended to you as a proper person for the Subdistributorship at Appleby. His habits I find were expensive, and his disposition such as rendered it very improbable that he could resist the temptation of public money, passing through his hands. I have substituted Mr Richardson the Tobacconist, who has property at Pooley Bridge, a regular and well disposed man.

I have no news from Westnd: The Yeomanry Corps seems much approved of,[4] though the Kendal Chronicle[5] is labouring to make it odious.

---

[1] See *Anecdote for Fathers* (1798), l. 23 (*PW* i. 242).
[2] Of their recent continental tour.
[3] Richard Bateman, stationer.
[4] The *Westmorland Gazette* for 27 Jan. carried an enthusiastic account of the muster of three new troops of Westmorland Yeomanry Cavalry at Edenhall, Kendal, and Milnthorpe. Col. Lowther was Commanding Officer.
[5] A letter signed by 'A Freeholder' in the issue for 3 Feb. attacked these increases in the military establishments. The fitting out of the three new troops would cost the taxpayer £4,000.

Poor Myers, whom you heard ranting away at my House, was found dead in his bed room.

When you can find a moment's leisure I should be glad to have a word from you upon public affairs. My Recipe runs thus, 'arm the Yeomanry and respectable Proprietors; curb the Press by vigilant prosecutions; and prepare a gradual reformation of the poor Laws.'—As to change of System, it is the cry of men wanting place, or of Revolutionists. Things may be improved, and ought to be in detail; but the system cannot be altered, as the Whigs and Lord Grey himself probably know, or would soon find out, were they in power. Mr Gee[1] is very well, he accompanied me to Lowther on my way to Appleby; we were both hospitably entertained by Dr Satt:[2] who looks very well.

Mrs W. and my sister unite with me in kind regards and believe me my dear Lord L.

ever faithfully your
Wm Wordsworth

15. W. W. to THE COMMISSIONERS OF STAMPS

Address: The Hon'ble Commissioners, Stamp Office, London.
Postmark: [? 10 Feb. 1821]. *Stamp*: Kendal Penny Post. *Endorsed*: Mr Wordsworth Ambleside 7 Feby 1821.
MS. Public Record Office. Hitherto unpublished.

[In John Carter's hand]

Rydal Mount, Ambleside,
7 Feby 1821.

Hon'ble Sirs,

I beg leave to state, that I have this day forwarded my monthly Parcel of Legacy Receipts and Residuary Accounts by the Manchester Mail.

I also beg leave to state that I have appointed Mr Edward Richardson to the Collection of the Legacy Duties, at Appleby in the Place of Mr Richard Bateman.[3]

I have the Honor to be,
Hon'ble Sirs,
Your obedient Servant
[*signed*] Wm Wordsworth

[1] George Gee, tenant of Ivy Cottage: later of Birdcomb Court, Somerset.
[2] i.e. Dr. Satterthwaite, rector of Lowther.   [3] See previous letter.

16. W. W. to LORD LONSDALE

MS. Lonsdale MSS. Hitherto unpublished.

Rydal Mount
Feb 9th [1821]

My Lord,

The reprint of the County Member's speech to his Farmers was too good a thing to be kept to myself; I wished to shew it to some Friends and neighbours, which must be my excuse for not returning it sooner. Mr C.[1] pays his Labourers not with money but potatoes, milk, flour, meal, butcher's meat, etc., all which, as our Rector was told by a man from Workington the other day, he superintends the weighing and measuring of, assisting with his own hands. Some think this extremely humane, condescending and amiable; but by the majority it is regarded as a shabby encroachment upon the profits of the small shopkeepers, and a degrading employment for a legislator.

The Kendal Chronicle has opened upon the Yeomanry Corps, and is labouring to make it unpopular on the ground of the expense.[2] Anything to carp at; but they do not like to see how much Col: Lowther is approved and admired in his management of this Corps by several of their own Party. I hope the establishment of these Corps will become universal. If a man be possessed of a horse, he will scarcely be without other property, and you have accordingly a pledge for his principles and conduct. Every one knows of what importance the Equestrian Order was in preserving tranquillity and a balance and gradation of powers in antient Rome; the like may take place among ourselves through the medium of an armed Yeomanry; and surely a preservative of this kind is loudly called for by the tendencies of things at present. Some say that Yeomanry Corps are not wanted in Cumbnd and Westnd, these districts being peaceably disposed. But have we not seen enough of the Kendal and Carlisle Rabble, without speaking of other places, to be assured

[1] John Christian Curwen of Workington Hall, Whig M.P. for Cumberland from 1820 until his death in 1828. (See *MY* i. 311; ii. 423.) For Curwen's own account of his speech on 20 Dec. 1820, in a letter to Francis Place, see Edward Hughes, *North Country Life in the Eighteenth Century*, 1965, ii. 233–4. Curwen's somewhat ambivalent behaviour in the face of the agricultural distress was due to his having interests in both land and manufactures. By 1825 he ceased to uphold protection, and came out against the Corn Laws.

[2] See L. 14. The Kendal Yeomanry mustered for the first time in full uniform, and exercised, on 19 and 20 Mar., according to the *Kendal Chronicle* for the 24th. On 31 Mar. it announced Lord Lowther's appointment as Lieut.-Col. Commandant.

that if disturbances were to become formidable, they would not be slow to play their part.[1] They probably are not strong enough to begin, but they would be ready enough to join.

If the whole Island were covered with a force of this kind, the Press properly curbed, the poor laws gradually reformed, provision made for new churches to keep pace with the population (an indispensible measure) if these things were done, and improvements carried forward as they have been, order may yet be preserved among us, and the people remain free and happy. As to the abuse of the Press, as your Lordship says[2] the Attorney Gen: being too much occupied with other duties adequately to attend to that of correcting it, could not an Assistant be appointed as has been done for the Chancellor?[3] This measure must be resorted to, in regard to other offices; the encrease of business is so great in numerous departments that the bodily strength of public functionaries is not equal to their employments. But what a clamor would be raised about extending the influence of the Crown, etc., as if (even in this view of the subject) it were not obviously politic, that as the resisting power of the People encreases, the controuling and influencing power of the Executive should be encreased accordingly.

[1] There were ugly scenes at Kendal during the Westmorland election of 1818 (see *MY* ii. 426–7); and again at Carlisle during the 1820 election, when the weavers rioted and the military were called in. Their intervention was attacked in the House of Commons on 14 Mar. 1821 by J. C. Curwen and William James of Barrock, Whig M.P. for Carlisle, and defended by Lord Lowther supported by John Beckett and Sir James Graham. The matter was referred to the Committee of Privileges.

[2] Lord Lonsdale had expressed general approval of Dr. Stoddart's proposals for curbing the Press (see L. 5) in his letter of 28 Jan.: 'Your objection to the establishment of the Society of which Dr Stoddart has apprized you, is certainly a just one, but . . . we did not think it right to put any difficulties in the way, or by stating any objections—to check a Disposition to repress an evil so formidable as that with which it proposed to contend. The spread of it is so great at this time, that it is scarcely possible for the Attorney General, with due regard to his other duties, to acquit himself of that which regards the Press in a manner either satisfying to himself or with advantage to the Interest of the Public.' (*WL MSS.*). The Attorney-General at this time was Sir Robert Gifford, 1st Baron Gifford (1779–1826): Solicitor-General and M.P. for Eye, Suffolk, 1817–19; Attorney-General, 1819–24, and thereafter Lord Chief Justice. He died of cholera just when it was generally understood that he was to succeed Eldon as Lord Chancellor.

[3] John Scott, 1st Earl of Eldon (1751–1838), Lord Chancellor, 1801–6 and 1807–27. The office of Vice-Chancellor was created by Act of Parliament in 1813 to deal with the arrears of legal business which accrued through his constant preoccupation with political affairs. It was filled by Sir Thomas Plumer (1753–1824), Solicitor-General in the Duke of Portland's administration, until 1818; and thereafter by Sir John Leach (1760–1834), later Master of the Rolls. See Horace Twiss, *The Public and Private Life of Lord Chancellor Eldon*, 3 vols., 1844, ii. 238–42, 301–3.

Young Mr Kirkbank had no objection to act as Coroner for the Lordship of Millom provided some other offices were not coupled with that.[1] He is a person perfectly competent, and upon the spot, so that if the thing be not an object to Mr Peter Hodgson, it would perhaps be more satisfactory to the neighbourhood if he would act.

Most unluckily the letter to Mr S.[2] has been mislaid. Mrs Wordsworth has been looking for it, in vain, since I began to write. We were arranging papers the other day, and I fear it may have got among them by mistake. It shall be sought for again, and taken care of.

The present juncture is interesting, and I shall be truly happy to be honoured with communications from your Lordship at your leisure. I remain

very sincerely
your Lordship's friend and servant
Wm Wordsworth[3]

17. W. W. to THE COMMISSIONERS OF STAMPS

Address: To The Hon'ble Commissioners, Stamp Office, London.
Postmark: 19 Feb. 1821. *Stamp*: Kendal Penny Post. *Endorsed*: Wm Wordsworth Rydal Mount Ambleside 14 feb 1821 rec 19.
MS. Public Record Office. Hitherto unpublished.

[*In John Carter's hand*]

Rydal Mount, Ambleside,
14 February 1821

Hon'ble Sirs,

I beg leave to state in reply to your Letter, of the 12 Inst: that Mr Edward Richardson appointed by me to the Stamp Subdistributorship of Appleby, is a Tobacconist.

:
I have the Honor to be
Hon'ble Sirs,
Your obedient Servant
[*signed*] Wm Wordsworth

[1] See L. 5.
[2] Presumably Mr. Southey.
[3] Two sentences from this letter were published by K and de Selincourt under the year 1814.

18. D. W. to CATHERINE CLARKSON

Address: To Mrs Clarkson, Playford Hall, Ipswich, Suffolk. (By Penrith).
Stamp: Kendal Penny Post.
MS. British Museum.
LY i. 15.

Feb^{ry} 15th [1821] Thursday

My dearest Friend,

A few days after writing to you from Kendal[1] I came home and found your welcome letter. Long silences often follow after the crossing of letters on the road, and this I am determined shall not happen in the present case; but besides I have been so long near you and used to you that I feel an irresistible longing to renew and keep up our intercourse. Your narration from Hayti[2] interested us all exceedingly, and I long for further accounts of your Friends[3] though with little hope of better than the last. The Newspapers have long been silent on the subject; but this is probably because no ships have arrived. The earnest expression of hatred against Boyer[4]

[1] This letter has not been traced. According to L. 8, D. W. intended to break her journey home to see John W. at Sedbergh.

[2] Ever since San Domingo—or Haiti as it was now called—was declared independent in 1804, it had been a warring ground between whites, negroes, and mulattoes; and Emancipationists in England, working for the advancement of African peoples and the freeing of the remaining slaves in the Spanish portion of the island, looked on with anxious concern. The country had become divided between two hostile camps: the predominantly mulatto republic under General Pétion in the south, centred on Port au Prince, and the Negro kingdom in the north ruled by Henry Christophe. He had originally served under Toussaint L'Ouverture and helped to drive the French from the island, and eventually had himself declared King in 1811. Threatened by Pétion and the French, Christophe turned to England for support, and Clarkson became his correspondent and adviser, and champion of his reforming activities. (For a full account see E. L. Griggs, *Thomas Clarkson, The Friend of Slaves*, 1936, pp. 122 ff.; and *Henry Christophe, Thomas Clarkson, A Correspondence*, ed. E. L. Griggs and C. H. Prator, 1952.) In 1818 Pétion was succeeded in the south by General Boyer, and after the general rebellion against Christophe two years later, and his suicide (see *MY* ii. 655), Boyer became president of a reunited Haiti.

[3] Madame Christophe and her two daughters, who were allowed to leave the country and eventually sought refuge with Clarkson at Playford Hall (see L. 46 below). Prince Joachim, Henry's young son, had been murdered by the revolutionaries, so that no pretender to the throne might survive.

[4] Jean Pierre Boyer (1776–1850), a mulatto, born in Port au Prince and educated in France. He served under General Rigaud in the south of Haiti and opposed Toussaint L'Ouverture, and on the defeat of the former he fled to France, returning with the French army in 1802, and joining in the revolution that established Haiti's independence. He was thereafter secretary to Alexandre Pétion, president of the republic in the south, and then chief of the presidential guard. When Pétion died, the army installed Boyer as president for life. He reoccupied northern Haiti after Christophe's death, and in 1822 conquered the former Spanish colony of San Domingo, thus becoming ruler of the whole island. Boyer abolished slavery and drew up a code of law, but he was

which I read as a part of Clarke's[1] letter, supposing it to be so, produced a most animating effect on my Brother and we all join in the feeling. The sentiment was yours I now discover, but I wish it had been Clarke's, for I should have taken him into my especial favour for evermore.—I found my dear Friends well and happy— our meeting was a joyful one though till afternoon there was none to share our joy. Dorothy then came and stayed till Sunday evening (I arrived on the Saturday). How I long for you to see her! She is indeed a sweet girl—I never saw a greater improvement in the time. She is grown thoughtful, steady and womanly; but is much more lively than ever she has been used to be since her first going to school. She is *as* lively as when she was ten years old; and has nothing left of her boisterousness or want of gracefulness either in manner or deportment. We are infinitely indebted to Miss Dowling,[2] to whom D. is very strongly attached. Miss D. now treats her as a Friend I can perceive by their conversation; and she told me that she had long been perfectly satisfied with D, that she had not had the smallest fault to find with her for many months. At the last holidays she brought away another elegant prize of Books. John is a thoroughly good lad and I have no doubt of his doing well though not grandly at Cambridge. My dear Friend, what shall I say at having left you? I *must* say something because I feel it— for the ease of my own mind—but I hope you will stifle regrets by a little resentment at my folly. I might just as well have stayed at Cambridge till the end of the Boys' holidays, have stayed with you till May, and brought Willy down with me, or not, as might have been hereafter judged best. The expense (which was a perfect bugbear to me when I was so far from home feeling I had spent so much) would have been a mere trifle and we should have been most happy together—you and I and your dear Husband this pleasant spring-time.

Such the time even *here*; for the sun shines as warm as in the summer, and I am able to write in the window of my own Room without a fire.—This is a digression—I was going to say that I am truly sorry I did not adopt the plan I have mentioned—the difference between three hundred miles and seventy miles being so

unpopular with the Dominicans, and lost control of the whole island in 1843 when they revolted and declared their independence. He fled to Paris and died in poverty.

[1] Unidentified—but presumably Clarkson's correspondent in the West Indies.

[2] Ann Dowling (d. 1837), now running the school at Ambleside where Dora W. was a pupil.

great. My wishes were very strong; but on the other hand came in
my longings after home; and still more than these my longings to
see John, Dorothy and Sara. Sara is gone[1] and I have not seen her,
and there being now so little occupation at home (however delightful home is) I feel as if I could have done more good elsewhere,
and I need not tell now how happily I could have spent my time. It
is now over, therefore it is folly to regret it. Rather let me be
thankful for the happiness we have had together, and for my own
especial comfort every night and morning in lying down and rising
up with the thought that whatever happened to dear little William
I was within a day's call. Before I dismiss the subject I will say one
thing. If at any time you have a particular wish to see me—as for
instance to spend two or three months of the winter with you when
you are not likely to have other inmates and then I would stay on
to see the green leaves, only tell me so—send me an invitation and
I will come. By frugality in the North I can never be so poor as not
to afford such a journey—when unconfined by active duties, or by
the sickness of Friends; it will be no effort to me to move at any
time, for you know I am one of the best travellers of my Sex. If
you should be poorly—should feel as if a Friend by the fire-side
would do you good—do not scruple to tell me so—happy again
shall I be to take my place there with you. The days have been
mild and sunny, though with a frosty air, ever since I came home,
and I have been enchanted with the beauty of the country. We
have walked daily; and had some most delicious walks by moonlight. On Tuesday we drank tea with Mr. Barber at his cottage
(formerly Mr Gell's)[2] and returned home at ½ past 11 o'clock. These
moonlight nights bring your garden and house and moat vividly to
my recollection; and often and every day many times do I think of
you. Next summer but one we trust you will be able to come North-
wards—Do not let Mr Clarkson give up the idea. We have talked
about it much together and with infinite satisfaction—and who
knows but I may return southward with you? But never forget that
at any time—even before then—if you should have strong or
particular wishes to see me I will come—God willing! Too much
of this—I am vexed with my folly and cannot help thinking of it—
nor *to you* help talking of it, as you see. But from this time forth no
more of it. We have heard from Mr Johnson that Willy was well
last Saturday. Mr J had found him with a black eye (No doubt he
had been *worsted* in fight for he did not like to talk of it) and so

[1] S. H. had gone to stay with her brother John at Stockton-on-Tees.
[2] For Samuel Barber (d. 1832) and Gell's Cottage, see *MT* i. 61.

ragged in his attire that he desired him never more to wear the old black jacket and ordered him a new suit of superfine cloth. Poor Lad! how he delights in Playford and I hope that Mr C will venture to have him again at some time or other. The Crumps[1] have left Grasmere entirely, yet their house is unsold. Mr Barber is the gayest Bachelor you ever saw—he calls at our door every day with the Morning Chronicle which for the sake of dear Playford I read with more pleasure than ever I did in my life before. We also have the Courier, therefore we stand a chance of coming to something like impartial judgement between the two. As to the Queen[2] I think both Friends and Foes seem equally tired of her. I look in vain for symptoms of something being done for the Agricultural distresses, but it seems as if all gave up the point in despair. What do you think of our Patriot Mr Curwen who at a meeting of his Farmers made them a fine speech[3] urging them, as the only means, to address Parliament—to make their own addresses not have them got up by others. As to lowering of rents that was impossible— the Landholders would sink also—They must reduce their expenses as he had done. His good Farmers went away disgusted with his fine speech and immediately resigned their Farms. He was left without Tenants and obliged to take them on again at a very *large* reduction of rent. We have had no letters from Hindwell since my return; but I find George Hutchinson[4] thinks of going either to Canada or Van Dieman's Land. There seems to be little or no distress in this country—Wages are 2/- and 2/6—and will probably be 3/- as the spring advances; and at Kendal the manufacturers are going on at a fair rate, while in Lancashire the cotton mills exhibit their dismal illuminations at night and early morning. How shall I send Mr Barton[5] 'The White Doe'? It was foolish in me not to arrange it with him. Will it not be best for me to desire Longmans to send it in one of his parcels to Woodbridge? We expect Mrs Rd Wordsworth and her little Boy[6] to stay a month with us. The poor child is very delicate and her lameness continues. William and Mary had a melancholy duty to perform at Powhouse.[7] Poor Myers, it

---

[1] For the Crumps of Allan Bank, see *EY*, p. 534.

[2] The Queen's Annuity Bill was now passing through Parliament, as addresses of sympathy continued to pour in; but two attempts to restore her name in the liturgy failed. The climax of her misfortunes came when she was refused admittance to the Coronation in Westminster Abbey on 29 July, and she died shortly afterwards.   [3] See L. 16 above.

[4] M. W.'s brother, farming at Hindwell, Radnor, with Thomas Hutchinson.

[5] Bernard Barton the Quaker poet, of Woodbridge. See *MY* ii. 269, 381.

[6] R. W.'s widow and her son 'Keswick John', as he was known in the Wordsworth circle.   [7] See L. 2 above.

appears, would have wasted his property fast away had he lived much longer. As it is there will be a very sufficient fortune for the child who no doubt will remain with Miss Dowling. Her Uncle, Thomas Myers, is to be her Guardian, and William has offered his assistance in managing the Grasmere property[1] and attending to the little girl. Notwithstanding Myers' hard conduct to his Brother (who no doubt behaved *foolishly* enough, to say the least, to him) I think he will be a judicious and faithful Guardian of his Niece. There is no motive to the contrary—and he is a sensible Man, and very clever in business. Myers's death was a great shock to the old Man.[2] He knew nothing before of his habits of drinking, nor did they come on, as we now find, till after his Wife's death.

My dear Friend, if by any accident you should ever hear of my Brother Christopher's being ill, pray let me know without delay. I am sure he will not do it himself from his constant habit of patience, and of bearing all his own sufferings himself—and when once he is ill I know well how slow he is in recovering, and should be miserable at the thought of not being near him to give every comfort in my power. He can do better alone than anybody I know; but it is a dismal thing even for him to be ill and not have one female friend near to whom he can speak. I desired Sophy[3] to write to me in case of illness; but even upon *her* I cannot depend. People are always afraid of making me uneasy. George Airey is likely to mention my Brother when he writes to Mr Biddle, and through Mr B. you might desire him when he writes to mention him and the state of his health. I find my Brother thinks very highly of George—I shall be greatly disappointed if he is not Senior Wrangler, with more than Senior Wrangler's honours.[4] My pride is a little come down before the end of my letter—I can now hardly drag the pen with my cold stiff fingers—and you, I fear, spite of your adroitness can scarcely read. I have not yet touched my journal—So much have I had to look at—so many old neighbours to see—so many letters to write. Miss Dowling and Dorothy are to drink tea with us this afternoon—What a delight do I feel in seeing that dear girl! I have very often seen her since my return. On Saturday she is to meet us at Mr Gee's to keep a Friend's Birthday.—This is a dull letter, I am sure; but I trust it will receive a speedy answer. I long to hear of your restoration to former strength—of rides on horse-

[1] John Myers's freehold (see *MY* ii. 435).
[2] i.e. his father, the Revd. Thomas Myers of Lazonby.
[3] One of the servants at Trinity Lodge.
[4] George Airy was Senior Wrangler in 1823. For his subsequent career, see L. 8 above.

back—of pleasures in the garden—and of my dear Friend Mr Clarkson's thoughts and pursuits—and how he came on with the [? Bankers][1]—and all about your poor neighbours.—Regards to the Biddles—kind love to Tom and a thousand blessings on you all—Yours ever more

D. Wordsworth.

Remember me to Elizabeth especially and to the other maids. I hope I shall see them all again some time—for I hate changes. I cannot read over what I have written.

19. D. W. to THOMAS MONKHOUSE

Address: Thomas Monkhouse Esqre, 34 Glocester Place, Portman Square.
Postmark: 19 Feb. 1821. *Stamp*: Charing Cross. *Endorsed*: 15 Feb. 1821. D. W.
MS. WL.
LY i. 20 (—).

Thursday 15th Feb^y [1821]

My dear Friend,

We begin to be anxious to hear from you especially as Mary thought you would think it necessary to acknowledge the receipt of the Bills which she sent on the 3rd. I do not mean that we are anxious on account of their safety; but are fearful that a return of your dear Wife's malady, may have been the cause of your silence and we very much wish to hear how you all are. From Mr Johnson we have heard that William was quite well though he seemed to have been worsted in fight, having got a black eye, which he did not much like to talk about, therefore Mr J concluded that he had been beaten. He was so ragged and shabby in his old black clothes that Mr Johnson desired him never to put them on again, and he ordered him a new suit of superfine cloth—I wish the Tailor may be successful in the cut. I observed that little Clarkson who called on William at Cambridge wore a round jacket without skirts and we think that a much prettier way of making little Boys' clothes; but William used to plead that it was not the fashion of the school, and most likely this plea will have served in the present instance, to induce Mr J. to order it as before. It is rather a pity that you did not happen to be the person to see William in his rags, as it would have been better to have employed your and his Father's tailor. I long to hear of John and Chris's visit to you, but if poor Jane was ill there would be no pleasure in it for any party. I left

---

[1] An obscure reference—if this is the right reading—which is unexplained.

Cambridge with great regret, turning thus away from all my kind Friends in the South, but hope that future opportunities may send me back again sometimes to see you all. If travelling were not so very expensive how pleasant it would be, at least once in two years, to have the rouzing up of a journey Southward!—As to crossing the seas it is a thing nevermore to be thought of, though I agree with you that it would be an infinite delight to revisit those noble mountains which we have seen.

Your last letter addressed to me came while I was at Kendal, and Mary supposed it was for her, and answering it as such, must have deceived you in her reply to one part of it. I am sorry to say that William did indeed tell me a falsehood, and a similar one to you. I have related the circumstance to Mr Johnson and we have requested him to give the Child such counsel and reproof as he judges best. We thought that anything coming from Mr Johnson, who once on a former occasion detected him in a falsehood, was likely to make a proper impression. During the whole of the time I was with William in the holidays I had not the slightest cause to suspect him of swerving from the truth. On the contrary his manners were particularly frank and ingenuous and his cousins tell me they have never found him guilty of lying. The case was this. Just before our parting I asked William if his uncle had given him any money and he replied 'Yes, he has given me *three* shillings' I then said to him 'I will give you half a crown'. This I did, and a shilling for the coachman. Now he must have said one shilling to you in order to conceal his having spent the additional 1/6, and three shillings to me that I might give him the more. This kind of Lying comes out of a great school where we all know that there are certain points in which it is accounted no disgrace—and probably that of money is one, so much importance being attached to the possession of it. You will speak to Willy as you think best when you see him, and I hope, as he is not habitually given to falsehood, he will not be guilty of the like again, seeing how easily it is detected, and of how little *use* it is, and how painful are the consequences—distrust and want of confidence on the part of Friends.—In addition to this I know you will in your kindness and tenderness for the dear Boy represent to him the great sin of lying.—Ever since my arrival at home the weather has been enchanting—hot sunshine, clear frost, and now heavenly moonlight nights. I can hardly tell you how much I enjoy the country and the [   ][1] of old Friends and neighbours who have [   ]fully greeted me. William's eyes [are] much

[1] *MS. torn away.*

better. He reads several [? hours in] the day; but has not yet begun [   ]. His first job will be preparing [   ] of the Lakes for the Tourists in [   ]. Do you hear anything of the Sa[le of the] Poems and Excursion. John and [Dorothy are] greatly improved. D. is a lovely [   ] most engaging in her manners [   ] yet more lively than she has [ever] been since she went to school [   ] is very satisfactory. You and you[r dear Wife will] I am sure be delighted with her. [John is] as tall as his Father and much stouter. [? His industry] is admirable and I believe his [   ] very good. God bless you my dear [Friend]. Ever your affect^e

D Wordsworth.

My Brother begs you will be so good as to call at the Booksellers Charing Cross to inquire if the Books are sent off. If not, desire they may be sent immediately and if all are not ready the package must not wait longer.

His Mother gave William 2/6 in London, [which] she told him not to spend, and he pleased me by shewing me the half-crown unbroken when he came to Playford. [? Remember me] to Mr Robinson, the Lambs and all [? our friends]. Have you seen Mrs Hoare?

[*M. W. writes*]

[   ] of Feb^ry I enclosed you 2 Bills [amounting] to £46-11-10. I hope you received it safely. M. W.

Did I request of you to pay a bill for us to Mr Prince?[1]—in my last. I have discharged that bill here thro' Miss C. Lockyer.[2] M. W.

20. W. W. to VISCOUNT LOWTHER

MS. Lonsdale MSS. Hitherto unpublished.

Rydal Mount
19th Febry 1821

My dear Lord Lowther,

Not being certain that you are a regular Reader of the K. Chronicle, I think it proper to mention, that the last number contains an Article (from the London Times) and headed 'Reply to Lord Lowther', this Reply being no other than a flat contradiction

---

[1] The bookseller.
[2] For Charlotte Lockier (d. 1825), see *MY* ii. 617.

of your statement in the House, respecting Bergami's mode of living at Paris.[1] Would you wish any notice to be taken of this Paragraph, which has manifestly been transferred from the Times, and your name put at the head of it with a view to bring you into discredit in the County, and especially among your Constituents?

Brougham's Election Bills have not been paid in this neighbourhood, at least this is the answer that Mr Newton the spiritmerchant[2] has received from the Inn-keeper when pressing them to settle their Accounts this Candlemas.

ever faithfully yours
Wm Wordsworth

21. W. W. to VISCOUNT LOWTHER

MS. Lonsdale MSS. Hitherto unpublished.

26th Febry 1821

My dear Lord Lowther,

You are quite right, I think, in recommending that no notice should be taken of the contradiction of your statement.[3] One might have opposed that anonymous contradiction, by other paragraphs from other papers, confirming and going beyond your allegation, but it was not worth while.

[1] Soon after her departure from England in the summer of 1814 the Princess of Wales, later Queen Caroline, had engaged at Milan as her courier an Italian named Bartolomeo Bergami, formerly valet to General Pino, whom she elevated to be her equerry, chamberlain, and constant companion during her three years of travel in Europe, North Africa, and the Near East, procuring him a barony in Sicily, the knighthood of Malta, and other even more extravagant titles, and taking some ten members of his family into her personal suite in various capacities. It was on the basis of this allegedly adulterous association with Bergami that Queen Caroline was brought to trial in the summer of 1820. (See *MY* ii. 643.) After the Bill of Pains and Penalties against her was dropped a committee of the House of Commons was set up on the Provision for the Queen, and it was during discussion of its report on 1 Feb. 1821 that Sir Thomas Lethbridge drew attention to Bergami's opulent style of living in Paris and advocated a reduction in her grant. His statements were corroborated by Lord Lowther on the strength of his own observations during a visit to Paris; but Brougham, who had defended the Queen at her trial, maintained that it was by his advice that Bergami had been brought to Paris in case he should be needed as a witness for the defence, and that the expense was no more than that incurred by other witnesses, on both sides. On 17 Feb. the *Kendal Chronicle* came out in support of Brougham: 'We assert from the most positive knowledge that all the statements about Baron Bergami's manner of living in Paris are false . . .'

[2] William Newton of Ambleside.

[3] Concerning Bergami. See previous letter.

Mr Wilson of Abbott Hall,[1] has heard that the Blues are *about* to pay their Bills, and to put in 60 or 70 Annuitants, and wishes to be prepared to meet them, should this be done;[2] and, for this purpose, he begs you would send him the names from Alston Moor, which you thought some time ago, might be procured there. If men are wanted, and cannot be had nearer to Appleby, would it not be easy for the Becketts to raise them among their connections at Leeds.[3] Mr Wilson mentions to me Millom—and something might be done there; but when I was in that quarter lately I was scrupulous about mentioning the subject fearing that if it were proposed to Lord Lonsdale's tenantry, and they became Freeholders upon request, they might presume upon their own consequence. I sent in one name from that district, Mr Steble[4] beneficed by Lord L— at Whichham. I shall probably have occasion to go again into Millom shortly; I will then see Mr Towers[5] of Duddon Grove, and if you think proper will push the matter in that District.

I trust the Ministers will oppose the extension of the Poor Rates to property not already subject to them. I see it has been attempted in respect to the shipping of Hull.[6] But I am sure you will be of opinion that the more you encrease the facilities of the poor being maintained at other people's expense, the more poor you will have.—The relief to the landed interest would only be temporary, and the evil would soon come back upon them aggravated, and more difficult to manage even than it now is. Nothing can be of service which does not tend to diminish the number of applicants and to regulate the allowance. Strong measures will be necessary, for which the Public ought to be gradually prepared; and such measures as the lowest orders will be disposed to resist, perhaps by force. But among many advantages to be derived from

---

[1] See *MT* ii. 417.

[2] Since the Westmorland elections of 1818 and 1820 W. W. had been playing an active part in consolidating opposition to Brougham, principally by helping to increase the number of freeholders sympathetic to the Lowther cause. See *MT* ii. 476.

[3] The family of Lord Lowther's brother-in-law, John Beckett (see *MT* ii. 515), had considerable banking interests in Leeds.

[4] The Revd. Allison Steble, b. Whitehaven and admitted Sizar at St. Catherine's College, Cambridge, in 1784: rector of Whicham, since the appointment of Dr. Satterthwaite to Lowther in 1813.

[5] Richard Towers (1770–1828), of Duddon Grove, a mansion in the Duddon Valley mid-way between Broughton and Ulpha. He was a Deputy-Lieutenant for Lancs.

[6] Through a private measure, the Hull Poor Rates Bill, which was discussed in the House of Commons on 19 Feb. It was attacked by Huskisson for extending poor rates to a new type of property. The debate was reported in the *Westmorland Gazette* for 24 Feb.

the Yeomanry Corps not the least would be their cooperation in maintaining tranquillity should the measures, which sooner or later will become necessary in remodelling the poor laws, be attended with disturbances.

Yesterday the Banns were published in church at Grasmere for a Girl 16 years of age and a drunken Shoemaker of 25, who already has a bastard child to provide for. Such marriages could never be in places like this were it not for the ruinous operation of these laws. The Girl was one of eight children all supported out of the parish Rates.

> ever my dear Lord Lowther
> faithfully yours
> Wm Wordsworth

22. W. W. to WILLIAM MYERS[1]

Endorsed: March 7th 1821.
MS. Harvard University Library.
LY i. 23.

Kendal
Wednesday [7 Mar. 1821]

My dear Cousin,

I shall be ready to attend you to the Sale. We are all glad that we shall have the pleasure of seeing you here, and hope you will come the night before, and that Mr Hutton[2] will accompany you; we can lodge you both.

I have received a Letter round by Ulverston from an Agent of Mr John[3] Manchester, addressed to the Exrs of the late John Myers of Po House and demanding of them upon the receipt thereof to forward to the address given six Pictures,[4] belonging to Mr J. Myers of Manchester and which were in the possession of the deceased. There is no description given of the Pictures alluded to.—

[1] William Myers of Deal (1774–1835), son of John Myers of Rallis (a family estate at Whicham), and nephew of the Revd. Thomas Myers. He had just inherited Po House, Lacra, and Lowscales from his cousin John, the barrister. See Genealogical Table, facing p. 704.
[2] Thomas Hutton, the Penrith solicitor.
[3] i.e. John Myers (b. 1796), a solicitor at Manchester, nephew of the new owner of Po House. See Genealogical Table.
[4] Possibly the family portraits by George Romney.

I remain with best regards to your Grandfather[1] and self
Sincerely yours
Wm Wordsworth

I dont know what to do in respect to the Piano forte; not knowing any body at Kendal who could take it in, if carried to them; and besides not thinking Kendal a good place for the Sale of Musical Instruments; there is no teacher of music in that Town.—We must determine when we meet what is to be done with it.

23. W. W. to VISCOUNT LOWTHER

MS. Lonsdale MSS. Hitherto unpublished.

[c. 10 Mar. 1821]

My dear Lord Lowther,

There is a young Man (son of Christ^r Gregg of Langdale a friendly Freeholder) who wishes to emigrate; and with that view is desirous of knowing what encouragement government gives, and what are the advantages held out to Emigrants in the different settlements of Van Diemen's Land, Algoa Bay, or Canada. Could you send me for his direction a paper of Information, or if not, would you be so kind as let me know how such could be procured?

I am just returned from Millom whither the affairs of my late Relation Mr Myers called me. I waited upon Mr Towers[2] of Duddon Grove and saw the Rev^d Mr Stables of Whicham, and begged of both to exert themselves in support of the Cause.[3] Mr Stables some time since empowered me to send his name to the Kendal Comm: and Mr Towers seems also well disposed. But they both complain of the selfishness of their neighbours and that they are not trustworthy. So that really I have little expectations from that Quarter. I think I could have effected some thing myself in that neighbourhood, but there are reasons relating to the character of the Individual with which I need not trouble you. I ought to add that both Towers and Stables promised that they would do their utmost. Mr North of Ambleside has lately added five names, of his own family and Relations.[4] I have this day received a Commission

---

[1] Unidentified, but probably his maternal grandfather. John Myers of Rallis married secondly Ann Shepherd (d. 1777), but her parentage cannot be traced.
[2] See L. 21.
[3] i.e. the Lowther cause in Westmorland.
[4] Including John North of Liverpool and Richard Ford North of Manchester.

from two of my own Relatives, Nephews of the late Mr Myers,[1] to be added, so that you see we are creeping on.

The Catholic Claims are to be referred to a Comm:[2] God grant that these people may be baffled! How Mr Canning[3] and other enemies to Reform in Parliament can without gross inconsistency be favourers of their cause I am unable to conceive. Mr Canning objects to Reform because it would be the means of sending into the House of Commons Members whose situation, opinions and sentiments differ from those of the Persons who are now elected, and who would prove less friendly to the Constitution in Church [and] state. Good Heavens! and won't this be the case to a most formidable degree if you admit Catholics, a measure to be followed up as it inevitably will, sooner or later, with the abolition of the Test and Corporation Acts, and a proportional encrease of the political Power of the Dissenters, who are to a man hostile to the Church. I know, my dear Lord Lowther, that you have great influence both personal, and belonging to your high station, and I trust that it will not sleep on this momentous occasion.

I remain
ever faithfully yours
Wm Wordsworth

Be so kind as to send the enclosed to the twopenny post.

---

[1] Two of the 'Robinson' nephews (see Genealogical Table, facing p. 704): Capt. Charles Robinson, R.N. (1788–1864), who lived in Ambleside and later in Ripon; and Lieut. Thomas Robinson, R.N. (1794–1838), for whom see also L. 214 below. Both had acquired freeholds in Crosthwaite and Lyth within the Kendal Ward.

[2] On 28 Feb. the House of Commons had resolved by a small majority to go into Committee to consider the Roman Catholic Claims, and on 2 Mar. a series of resolutions were agreed on which were embodied in the Roman Catholic Disability Removal Bill. This received its second reading on 16 Mar.

[3] Canning was at this time out of office, having retired from the Presidency of the India Board in Lord Liverpool's administration through sympathy for Queen Caroline. He rejoined the administration as Foreign Secretary in 1822.

24. W. W. to H. C. R.

Address: To H. C. Robinson Esq[re], Kings Bench Walk, Temple, London.
[*In M. W.'s hand*]
Postmark: 13 Mar. 1821. *Stamp*: Kendal Penny Post. *Endorsed*: Wordsworth, Death of Scott in a duel.
MS. Dr. Williams's Library.
K (—). *Morley, i. 98.*

[*c.* 12 Mar. 1821]

My dear Friend

The Books arrived safe
You were very good in writing me so long a Letter, and kind after your own Robinsonian way in going to inquire after our long and far banished Little one.[1] As we hear from himself never, and *of* him but seldom, we cannot but be at some times anxious, remembering the two sharp fits of illness which he had last Summer. You will be pleased to hear that the two ladies[2] are busy in transcribing their Journals; neither of them have yet reached the point where you joined us, but many a spot where we all wished you had been with us, often, I own, from our want of an Interpreter, and not unfrequently from less selfish motives.—Your determination to withdraw from your Profession in sufficient time for an Autumnal harvest of leisure, is of a piece with the rest of your consistent resolves and practices. Consistent I have said, and why not *rational* —the word would surely have been added, had not I felt that it was awkwardly loading the sentence, and so truth would have been sacrificed to a point of Taste, but for after compunction. Full surely you will do well—but take time, it would be ungrateful to quit in haste a profession that has used you so civilly. Would that I could encourage the[3] hope of passing a winter with you at Rome, about the time you mention, which is just the period I should myself select.—But the expense is greater than I dare think of facing, though five years hence the education of my eldest Son will be nearly finished; but in the mean time I cannot foresee how we shall be able to lay by any thing either for travelling, or other purposes. —Poor Scott![4] living in this solitude we have thought more about

---

[1] i.e. Willy W.　　[2] i.e. M. W. and D. W.　　[3] the *written twice*.

[4] John Scott (see *MY* ii. 237), editor of the *London Magazine*, had published a series of articles from May 1820 onwards attacking the criticisms of 'Z' in *Blackwood's Magazine*. John Gibson Lockhart (1794–1854), the chief object of his assault, was provoked into demanding satisfaction, and after fruitless negotiations a communication from Jonathan Henry Christie, a friend of Lockhart, led to a duel between Christie and Scott. They met at Chalk Farm on 16 Feb., James Traill acting as Christie's second, and P. G. Patmore (see below) as Scott's. Christie held his fire on the first occasion, but on the second

him, and suffered more anxiety and sorrow on his account, than you among the many interruptions of London can have leisure to feel. I do not recollect any other English Author's perishing in the same way. It is an Innovation the effect of others which promise no good to the Republic of Letters or to the Country. We have had ribaldry, and sedition, and slanders enough in our Literature heretofore, but no epithet which those periods deserved is so foul as that merited by the present, viz.—the *treacherous*. As to Scott he need not have lost his life, if the Coroners Inquest may be trusted but for the Intemperance and ignorance of his Second.[1]—At a proper time I should much wish enquiries to be made from myself after Mrs Scott,[2] who must know that I was acquainted with her Husband. This perhaps you could assist me in effecting; in the meanwhile could you let me know how she bears her affliction, and what circumstances she is left in.

I have read Cornwall's Tragedy,[3] and think of it pretty much as you seem to do. The feelings are cleverly touched in it; but the situations for exhibiting them, are produced not only by sacrifice of the respectability of the persons concerned, but with great, and I should have thought unnecessary violation of probability and common sense. But it does appear to me in the present late age of the world a most difficult task to construct a good tragedy free from stale and mean contrivances and animated by new and suitable Characters. So that I am inclined to judge Cornwall gently, and sincerely rejoice in his success.—As to Poetry I am sick of it—it overruns the Country in all the shapes of the plagues of Egypt— frog-poets (the Croakers) mice-poets (the Niblers), a class *rhyming* to mice that shall be nameless, and fly-poets. (Gray in his dignified way calls flies the 'Insect Youth',[4] a term wonderfully applicable upon this occasion!) But let us desist or we shall be accused of envying the rising generation. Be assured however that it is not

---

fired in self-defence, and wounded Scott in the side. He died on 27 Feb. At the inquest, a verdict of wilful murder was returned, and Christie and Traill were tried at the Old Bailey on 13 Apr. and found not guilty. Patmore absented himself from the whole proceedings. He carried considerable responsibility for the final tragedy for not stopping the duel after the first shot.

[1] Peter George Patmore (1786–1855), author and journalist, friend of Lamb and Hazlitt, father of Coventry Patmore: editor of the *New Monthly Magazine* from Theodore Hook's death in 1841 until the periodical was acquired by Harrison Ainsworth in 1853: author of the gossipy *My Friends and Acquaintances*, 3 vols., 1854. See *RMVB*, 1842.

[2] She was Caroline, daughter of the printseller Paul Colnaghi (1751–1833), founder of the famous firm in Pall Mall. She and her two children were left penniless.

[3] *Mirandola*. See L. 11 above.   [4] *Ode on the Spring*, l. 25.

fear of such accusation which leads me to praise a Youngster who writes verses in the Etonian, to some of which our Cumberland Paper has introduced me, and some I saw at Cambridge. He is an Imp as hopeful I think as any of them—by name Moutray;[1] if you should ever fall in with him tell him that he has pleased me much.— My Sister sends her[2] very kind love, and expressions of *bitter* regret, (strong terms these but natural to Ladies!) that she did not see you at Cambridge where Mary and I passed thirteen days; and, though plagued by a severe cold, what with the company (but by the bye I saw very little of him) of my dear brother, our Stately appartments with all the venerable Portraits there that awe one in to humility, old Friends, new Acquaintances, and a thousand familiar remembrances, and freshly conjured up recollections, I enjoyed myself not a little.—I should like to send you a Sonnet[3] composed at Cambridge, but it is reserved for cogent reasons—to be imparted in due time. I have been scribbling with an infamous pen, and we have no quills, which makes the further want of a penknife the less regretted.—Farewell happy shall we be to see you.

Congratulate Talfourd from me upon his new honours,[4] and add a thousand good wishes.—Muley Moloch![5]—unhappy London!

---

[1] John Moultrie (1799–1874), whom W. W. had met at Cambridge the previous December, won early renown for poems such as *My Brother's Grave* and *Godiva* contributed to the *Etonian* under the pseudonym of Gerard Montgomery in 1820–1; but he failed to live up to his early promise. At Trinity College, Cambridge, he forsook law for the Church, becoming rector of Rugby (1828) and a friend of Arnold. He published several volumes of verse and hymns: *Altars, Hearths and Graves,* 1854, included *Three Minstrels* (pp. 177 ff.), an account of his relations with W. W., S. T. C., and Tennyson. A complete edition of his Poems, with Memoir by Derwent Coleridge, appeared in 2 vols. in 1876.   [2] her *written twice.*

[3] One of the three sonnets on King's College Chapel.

[4] Talfourd was called to the Bar on 10 Feb. 1821.

[5] i.e. Thomas Samuel Mulock (1789–1869), a well-known eccentric who engaged in extensive religious controversy. He was in early life a partner in the firm of Mulock and Blood, whence the sobriquet 'Bloody Moloch'. Later this became 'Muley Moloch'—a reference to the Sultan Muli of Morocco (cf. Addison, *Spectator,* 349). Mulock's views on literary matters do not appear to have been of much importance if one may judge by Moore's opinion of a course of lectures he attended in 1820 at Geneva. (See Moore's *Memoirs,* iii. 166.) There the Wordsworths, Monkhouse, and H. C. R. met him during the Swiss tour of 1820. Mulock made himself very offensive to Monkhouse, and to H. C. R. 'began a disquisition on the character of Wordsworth's religious poetry, which he said he considered as *Atheism* and had been castigating in his lectures. . . . That rhapsodies about the beauties and wonders of nature were mystical nonsense—He aggravated this by professing the highest admiration of Lord Byron. . . . I was purposely rude and contemptuous. We saw him no more—W: used afterwards always to call him Muley Moloch.' (*HCR* i. 254; see also *DWJ* ii. 299.) This nickname was also used by Byron. See his letters to Murray, 1 Mar. 1820, and to Moore, 9 Dec. 1820. (Morley's note.)

Let Talfourd flagellate him when he becomes impertinent upon the Lake-School, i.e.

Love to the Lambs.   Wm Wordsworth

25. D. W. to THOMAS MONKHOUSE

Address: To Thomas Monkhouse Esqre, Glocester Place, Portman Square.
Postmark: 20 Mar. 1821. *Stamp*: Charing Cross. *Endorsed*: 16 Mar. 1821.
  D. W.
MS. WL.
LY i. 23.

Saturday 16th March [1821]

My dear Friend,

   Though I have nothing new to tell you I am glad to slip a few lines into a frank which my Brother is sending, thinking that the sight of a Friend's hand—writing with tidings that all is well will never be thought a dear purchase at twopence of *your* money. I had a letter from Miss Horrocks a few days ago, which gave me much pleasure. She reported favourably of your Wife's health and strength, and that was most satisfactory, though from what she says we judge that your expectations are not such as when you last wrote to Mary. I hope you will come Northward as soon as you can after the leaves are on the trees, both for the pleasure we shall have in seeing you and your Wife, and for the benefit which she will be likely to receive from country air and the joy of being amongst her old Friends. We have had only about ten days of bad weather since my return; but unfortunately I have been confined for the last three weeks with a sprained ankle, which troubled me a little at my first coming home; but I took no care of it till I found that I must give it entire rest. I have begun to walk a little in the garden; but am not suffered to go down the hill, and indeed all around us is now so chearful and beautiful that I have nothing to regret. It seems a long time since we heard of Willy—Yours was the last news of him, indeed it came about the same [time] with a letter from Mr Robinson, who had seen him in high health and spirits 'just what a schoolboy ought to be' only his hands were dreadfully chapped; but I hope the present warm weather will remove that annoyance. Pray when you see him give him my kindest love. Tell us when you write on what day his holidays are to begin. His uncle wished him to go to Cambridge if Charles' holidays should suit with his; but I rather think that Harrow School breaks up before the Charter

House. Dorothy has had one of her dreadful colds. She came to see us yesterday, but she looked extremely ill, and was very languid and weak. She is wonderfully improved, as I think you will say when you see her. She is as lively as ever yet all her turbulence is tamed down—I long for the time when she will have the privilege of being acquainted with your dear Wife.

We expect John at Easter—Would that William could be here also!

You kindly sent us two Numbers of John Bull[1] but as that light of the Nation pays weekly visits to Mr Gee's Cottage you need not trouble yourself to send it down to us again. Poor John Scott![2] You can hardly imagine how much grief and anxiety we had for him while he lay on his death bed. I think Patmore can never again have a quiet mind, as it seems his rashness, indiscretion and ignorance were the cause of Scott's death.

Mr Gee begs you will be so good as to send his Bill for Books to Rydal instead of sending it to Mr Prince.

My kind love to your Wife—I very often think of you both, and of other kind Friends in London, and shall not be unwilling to repeat my visit when time opportunity and money serve. Remember me to Mr Robinson and to C. Lamb and his sister and believe me
ever your faithful and affectionate Friend
Dorothy Wordsworth

Excuse scrawling; William waits to take the letter to Ambleside.

Wm is just returned from the Sale of Mr Myers's furniture, cattle etc. The Sale was a good one:—, a proof that this part of the North of England is in no desperate state of poverty.

26. D. W. to CATHERINE CLARKSON

Address: Mrs Clarkson, Playford Hall, Ipswich, Suffolk. By Penrith. Single sheet.
Stamp: Kendal Penny Post. *Endorsed*: Mar. 27, 1821.
MS. British Museum.
K (—). *LY* i. 25.

March 27th [1821]
In the case of the King versus Penn and Mead, the Recorder of London being dissatisfied with the Verdict, fined the Jury as

[1] A paper established towards the end of 1820 to counteract, by its scurrilous humour, the sentimental enthusiasm for Queen Caroline: its editor was Theodore Hook (1788–1841), a master of lampoon.
[2] See previous letter.

mentioned in Mr Clarkson's book,[1] but he adds that no notice was
taken of the illegality of the Act. This is not correct, for Bushel one
of the Jurors, sued out a Habeas Corpus, and the point was arranged
in Common Pleas, and decided in favour of the Juryman, see
Vaughan's Reports, Bushel's case.[2]

My dearest Friend,

The Above has been transcribed some time in preparation for a
letter to you.—April 6th. So far I wrote eight days ago and the
short transcript at the top had been made long before that. I
cannot express to you my dear Friend, how deeply I feel your
kindness in writing me such long and interesting letters, nor how
vexed I am with myself for repaying you so ill, and for being so
foolishly uneasy at not hearing from you so soon as my strong
desires led me to expect. The foolish little note I sent through the
Horrocks crossed your valuable letter on the road (that which
contained the sketch of Toussaint's[3] character). I did not suppose
that, having written, you would think yourself bound to write
again after my note, and to say the truth a scruple of delicacy prevented me from replying to that letter immediately. I thought as
I had nothing like an equivalent to send you, having been engaged
in no such interesting speculations as you had, and our goings on
being so very uniform it was unfair to put you again at once into
the situation of my debtor. But no more of this—I hope I shall be
wiser when I do not hear from you again (if that should ever
happen) so soon as I expect, only remember that the oftener you
write the better—though I would not tax you with the thought that
writing to me at this time or that is a duty—except you should be

[1] *Memoirs of the Private and Public Life of William Penn*, 2 vols., 1813, i.
64 ff. Penn and William Mead (a Quaker linen-draper) were tried at the Old
Bailey in Sept. 1670 for addressing a congregation in the open air, and acquitted;
but they were fined for not taking off their hats in court, and committed to
prison. The case was important, as it established the right of free worship.
[2] Edward Bushell was discharged by the Lord Chief Justice, Sir John
Vaughan (1603–74), in a celebrated judgement which was published by his son
in *The Reports and Arguments of Sir John Vaughan*, 1677 (2nd edn., 1706).
[3] Pierre-Dominique Toussaint L'Ouverture (1746–1803), one of the
liberators of Haiti, to whom W. W. had addressed his famous sonnet in
1802 (*PW* iii. 112). Claiming to be descended from an African chief, Toussaint
joined in the Negro uprising of 1791 and after the emancipation of the slaves
became commander-in-chief of the armies of San Domingo and gradually made
himself master of the whole country, renouncing the authority of France. In
1802 Napoleon determined to repossess the island and re-establish slavery:
Toussaint was captured and taken to France, where he died in prison near
Besançon. A year later, the French were driven from the island, and its independence was declared.

ill or in distress, and then I hope you would consider it so. You will
be puzzled by the statement at the top of the page if you have read
it. My Brother took it from Mr Raincock's[1] mouth for Mr Clarkson
to enable him to correct a mis-statement in his life of Penn. How
much more the troubles of our own particular Friends disturb one
than any detail of public distress! I read your account of the sad
prospects of Farmers with indifference comparatively as they did
seem but slightly to touch you; while I was rejoiced far more than
I can express to read the chearing reports which Mr Clarkson
brought you of Tom's well-doing. What a blessing for you after so
much anxiety to see him taking the right course! I cannot now
entertain the least doubt of his distinguishing himself in his profession, for having taken the resolution and with liking, his studies
will be persevering. It is his nature; and there can be no doubt of his
talents in the mind of any one who knows him. I can just fancy how
quietly Mr Clarkson would open out his budget of comfort when
he got back again to you after his last short absence, and how you
rejoiced together by that dear fire-side. I always fancy your sitting
in the small parlour which, perhaps because it was the first room I
entered at Playford, I shall always like better than the other. You
mention the threatening of a law-suit against Mr Corsbie[2] in your
first letter, but as in your last you do not speak of it I hope it is
over, especially as you write chearfully about your sister. I almost
wonder how she *could* remove the lilacs, yet most likely it was
wiser than to have left them to strangers, who probably would have
mercilessly cut them down and injudiciously remodelled the garden,
indeed one may be sure that no new Tenant would keep things in
the state they were in when you so fondly looked at them at the
awful time of your dear Father's death.[3] I am sorry for your sake
that your Brother William has left the house, yet no doubt he was
right as it was far too large and expensive for his needs. Do not
think that I disregard the troubles of Farmers because the chearfulness of your letters made me think little of them at that time. They
come but too closely to *us*. Poor Tom Hutchinson who is a man of
few words and still less of a complainer writes to his Brother at
Stockton that if times do not mend there will be nothing left for

---

[1] Fletcher Raincock (see *ET*, p. 70), W. W.'s schoolfellow, and brother of
the Revd. John Fleming of Rayrigg (see *ET*, p. 343): Recorder of Kendal,
1818–40, and Counsel-at law for the County Palatine of Lancaster. He resided
in Liverpool and was famed alike for his legal attainments and conversational
powers.
[2] John Corsbie, C. C.'s brother-in-law.
[3] William Buck (see *ET*, p. 296), d. 1819.

him but emigration at the end of his lease, and his wife looks to it without repining. Their Friends you may be sure cannot endure the thought—and Van Dieman's land is the spot they look to. Better, say I, live on oat-bread, milk and porridge by a fire-side like Peggy Ashburner's,[1] than go to such a banishment, and at a time of life, too, when there can be no hope of return; with a family too young to be of use for many years, and such a gem of a Woman. But I need not vex myself with this scheme—It will never be executed. It is melancholy enough to think of such a property as his sinking by little and little, without any misconduct of his own; and to see them chained down at least for four or five years to the spot. They have had, in addition to the common losses from low prices, great destruction among their cattle. Twenty three cows had slipped their calves when Mrs H wrote to us. This obliges them to change their stock. They have had the rot, too, among their sheep; but that is got under. Joanna[2] has been at Stockton with Sara and had intended to come and see us; but she says she could not be easy while Mary has the whole burthen of anxiety upon her shoulders to be away longer from her, and is returning to Wales immediately. We do not expect Sara till June. She has a visit to pay near Ripon, intends visiting Studley and Hackfall, and is to meet her Cousins Mr and Mrs Hutchinson, at Harrowgate, and return by York to Stockton. She is now perfectly well. Henry[3] has been spending the winter in that neighbourhood. He brought us last week very pleasant accounts both of Sara and Joanna. Joanna's health is renovated and she can now walk about like other people. The rheumatism had her quite an old woman when we last saw her. I cannot give you Sara's address for a longer period than three weeks; but if you write before the end of that time you must direct at John Hutchinson's esquire Stockton-on-Tees—Miss *Sarah* Hutchinson, as there are so many Miss H's at Stockton. William is quite well, and very busy, though he has not looked at the Recluse or the poem on his own life; and this disturbs us. After fifty years of age there is no time to spare, and unfinished works should not, if it be possible, be left behind. This he feels, but the will never governs *his* labours. How different from Southey, who can go as regularly as clockwork, from history to poetry, from poetry to criticism, and so on to biography, or anything else. If their minds could each spare a little to the other, how much better for both!

---

[1] The Wordsworths' one-time neighbour at Town End (see *EY*, p. 331).
[2] M. W.'s youngest sister.
[3] Henry Hutchinson, M. W.'s elder brother (see *MY* i. 231).

William is at present composing a series of Sonnets[1] on a subject which I am sure you would never divine,—the Church of England, —but you will perceive that in the hands of a poet it is one that will furnish ample store of poetic materials. In some of the sonnets he has, I think, been most successful. Mary is on the whole very well and looks so, except when certain troublesome fits of heat and head-ache come upon her, which I hope will be of no consequence, taking proper care to use purgative medicines—more important than anything else I am sure, from my own experience, where the body will bear them. The vines have not yet budded at Playford I suppose—I often image to myself the old house covered with green; and now I am glad to think of you among your spring flowers surrounded by those pretty green sloping fields. We have as yet but small appearance of spring except in the gardens. The gooseberry trees of course are in leaf but no blossoms yet on the peaches or cherries. The winter has been the pleasantest ever known; and the spring hitherto very agreeable. Sunshine has caused us many warm days; but in general the air has been rather keen, which is better liked in this country than a soft air in March, for our early springs are always blighted.—Times are certainly better in the North than anywhere else; we hear complaints of markets; the small farmers in general have con[cern] for their families, therefore to them cheapness is a benefit; and the [seal] the main dependence of both larger and smaller—Stockton [seal] I should say, the county of Durham or that part of it where Stockton lies is in no very bad way. In short we only hear dismal stories from the Newspapers and Friends at a distance. My Brother wishes very much to see Mr Clarkson's letter to Lord C.[2] and we were a little vexed when you mentioned that it was in the Suffolk paper, and that you thought we might not like to see Mr C in such bad company—a curious fancy! Mr Clarkson as a *party* man! such a thought would never enter the head of anyone who knows him as we do!

---

[1] *The Ecclesiastical Sketches* (*PW* iii. 341 ff.), begun the previous December, according to W. W.'s Advertisement, and published in 1822. D. W.'s anxiety about the progress of *The Recluse* was echoed by C. W., who wrote to W. W. on 5 Aug.: 'I was glad to hear of the Series of Sonnets "The Church of England" —Are they nearly finished—and are they to be published?—I hope they do not interfere too much with the progress of the Recluse.' (*WL MSS.*).

[2] Presumably a letter to Lord Castlereagh on agricultural distress, and published according to L. 30 in the *Suffolk Chronicle*—but unidentified. Perhaps an anonymous contribution is referred to—or D. W. may have mistaken the paper. On 5 Feb. in answer to a question in the House of Commons, Castlereagh had stated that the Government had no proposals to put forward for the relief of evils that were dependent on causes beyond the control of the legislature.

or that he could receive taint from any party. I cannot think you will have destroyed the paper, so pray send it to us immediately. William makes this request, so I am sure you will have no further scruples in gratifying us. All that you say of St Domingo is very interesting, and especially your account of Toussaint. I cannot express how grateful I am for your kindness in taking so much pains to please me by writing whatever you think will interest me. You do not in your last mention your Translation[1]—I hope it is going on and that we shall soon have it. Mr Clarkson's zeal in acquiring the French language is surprising, having so many other greater cares and more important employments, but something is always *wanted* to fill up vacant spaces and what a blessing when the mind retains zeal and vigour to seek after that something. Of course if Mr C goes into France this summer you will accompany him. I know few things I should like better than to be with you there. It is only when such pleasant schemes cross my fancy that I ever regret that we are not richer. I hope you will not take the direct route from Calais but travel through Normandy. I should like to see that country, but how many countries are there I should like to see! La Vendée, Dauphiny and not stop there. Again Switzerland and over the Alps to Rome and Naples! however I should be satisfied enough with another visit to Paris. We were there too late in the season to see it in its full splendour of out-of-door gaieties.—I think if Mr Clarkson had passed very near the Charterhouse and had had a few minutes to spare he would have called to see his favourite Willy Boy! Whenever he goes to London pray tell him to bear in mind that it would be a comfort to us to know that he had seen him, and pray ask Tom to call upon him, if he can find leisure, though but once or twice in the half-year—The best time is between one and three o'clock. Poor Fellow! he writes that he is quite well and was delighted at the sight of Mr Cowper, an Ambleside Tradesman 'The first Westmorland face he had seen for a long time'. I am afraid he does not get on so well as one would wish in the school; but his Father will judge when he comes home. We very seldom hear of Willy now! Mr M[2] you know has not so much time to 'manage him', nor for letter writing; and I doubt not he thinks we are over anxious. His wife is now quite well. She actually *had* miscarried. Henry Robinson gave us a very pleasant account of Willy. You can hardly conceive how grateful we are whenever any one sends us news of him. H. R. gives us hopes of seeing him this summer on his way to Scotland and we shall be greatly disappointed

if he changes his plans. He is one of the kindest and most friendly
creatures that ever lived, and certainly the best and most useful of
companions in travelling. I have a very great regard for him,
and remember his kindness to myself in particular with grateful
feelings. Tillbrooke has written us a pleasant letter. He says the
Vice-chancellor fills his office with great éclat, and he thinks his
year will be distinguished by several useful and important regulations.[1] Do not fail to write, if you can (but I am afraid of being
hard upon you) when you have seen George Airey. This I suppose
will be at Easter. Thank God we hear only good accounts of my
Brother's health—I have had a nice letter from his son Christopher. Have you seen Southey's *Vision of Judgment?* I like both the
metre, and most part of the Poem, very much. It is composed with
great animation, and some passages are very beautiful; but the
intermixture of familiar names pushes you down a frightful descent
at times, and I wish he had avoided the very words of Scripture.
The king has sent him a message that he had read the poem twice
over, and thanks him for the Dedication.[2] How the Queen has
passed away like a dream!—My dearest Friend never think that
your letters are dull or not worth sending—a single page from you
is always twice worth the postage—I wish I had any worthy return
for you—This is a sad dull letter; but I hope you may have the
reading of it when no other pleasure is in the way. Mary has nearly
finished her journal—I get on with mine; but not so fast, and I
think hers will be more interesting, being more brief[3]—Mine is
utterly unsatisfactory to myself as a description of Switzerland;
a land where height, depth, bulk, nay immensity—profusion—

[1] For some account of C. W.'s achievements as Vice-Chancellor, see D. A.
Winstanley, *Early Victorian Cambridge*, 1940, pp. 65 ff. Most graduates at this
period were examined only in mathematics, and came out with a perfunctory
knowledge of Classics and theology, though some of them were destined for
the Church. C. W. was convinced that the exclusive study of mathematics was
an evil, and the institution of a Classical Tripos an urgent need; and he
deplored the fact that candidates for holy orders were not examined in theology.
He put forward a scheme of reform in Apr. 1821, which was finally rejected;
but it aroused interest in the problem, and prepared the way for change. He
had clearly discussed his proposals with W. W. at Cambridge, for he repeated
them in detail in his letters of 5 and 13 Aug. 1821. 'I am disposed to agree with
you entirely in the importance of retaining the study of Mathematics unimpaired.' (*WL MSS.*)

[2] Southey's Dedication was full of exaggerated praise for the achievements
of the House of Brunswick in war and peace. 'The brightest portion of British
history will be that which records the improvements, the works, and the
achievements of the Georgian Age.'

[3] M. W.'s Journal of the recent continental tour is among the *WL MSS.*
and has never been published. It was much admired by H. C. R. (see *HCR*
i. 299).

—silence—solitude make up the grandest of our feelings, where it is utterly impossible to describe the objects except by their effects on the mind of those [*seal*] must be *felt* by the Reader, or he can have no notion of Switzerland.

My kindest love to Mr Clarkson and to Tom when you write. God bless you ever yours most affectionately   D. Wordsworth.

I open my letter to tell you that the Scarlet Fever (though in a mild form) is in the Charterhouse School. I did not like before to tell you that we had been very anxious since last Monday when we heard of it. 84 boys were then on the sick list or absent. We wrote immediately to desire if the report were true that he might be removed. Mr Johnson fetched him on Thursday. He is to remain till it be ascertained that he is clear of infection and then sent home to remain till after the May holidays.

Willy writes himself in high Spirits. He had been put up to another form—has begun with Ovid and likes it very much. We shall continue anxious as you may believe till the time of trial is over. God grant that he may have escaped infection.

Concluded on the 7th of April. William's Birthday. He is 51 years old.

27. W. W. to VISCOUNT LOWTHER

Address: The Viscount Lowther, Spring Gardens, London.
Postmark: 28 Mar. 1821. *Stamp*: Kendal Penny Post.
MS. Lonsdale MSS.
K (—). *LY i. 31* (—).

[28 Mar. 1821]

My dear Lord Lowther,

It is a pleasure to be attacked by such an intermeddling Demagogue as Hume,[1] since he has called forth so prompt and friendly

---

[1] Joseph Hume (1777–1855), radical politician, who devoted himself to questions of public expenditure. He was briefly Tory M.P. for Weymouth in 1812, and then radical M.P. for Aberdeen (1818–30), Middlesex (1830–7), Kilkenny (1837–41), and Montrose (1842–55). In a speech in the House of Commons on 22 Mar. 1821, he moved the abolition of the Offices of Receivers-General and Distributors of Stamps in the interests of economy and to reduce the baneful influence of patronage. The Distributors were sinecurists, he maintained, and received too generous a rate of poundage on their transactions—besides the interest they could earn on public money while it was passing through their hands. 'The distributors of stamps did not discharge their duties in person, but by deputy, and the consequence was, that when an idle poet (Mr Wordsworth) was appointed one of their number, he minded little in

a defender as yourself. I have sent you (as briefly as I could to be intelligible) an account of my duties and responsibilities as Stamp-Distributor. It would be well if such babbling Patriots as Hume would make their seats in Parliament sinecures and the public would be less frequently misled both as to things and Persons.

I am truly sorry for what you say as to the probable fate of the Catholic Question;[1] and feel grateful to you as an Englishman for your persevering exertions. Canning's speech[2] as given in the Morning Chronicle and Courier, is a tissue of glittering declamation and slender sophistry. He does not appear to look at the effect of this measure upon the Dissenters *at all*; and as to the inference that the Catholics will be quiet when possessed of their object, because they have been patient under long privation, first we may deny the premises—has not every concession been employed as a vantage-ground for another attack; and had it been otherwise, were it true that they had been patient, what says History as to the long-enduring quiet of Men who have an object in view. The Grandees of the Puritans, says Heylin,[3] in his life of Archbishop Laud, after the first heats were over in Queen Elizabeth's time, carried their work for *thirty* years together, like Moles under the ground, not casting up any earth before them, till they had made so strong a party in the House of Com: as was able to hold the King to their own conditions. Mr Canning finds the Catholic Peers supporters of Episcopacy in Charles 1st's time, and concluded therefore that they were friends to the Church of England because Bishops make a part of its constitution. Would it not have been more consonant to History to ascribe this care of Reformed Bishopricks to the love of an institution favorable to that worldly exaltation of Religion by which abuses were produced that wrought

what manner his deputy made his profits, provided he received his share of them.' The House set up a Select Committee to look into the matter; and from now on W. W. lived in some anxiety about the future of the office on which his financial security depended.

[1] In an undated letter to W. W. of mid-Mar. 1821, Lord Lowther had written: 'I regard the Catholic Question in the same view as yourself . . . I fear all opposition is now hopeless for we find the majority of the House is in its favor by 15 or 16. So it is mere accident whether the Question is carried or lost by a few. In another Parliament we shall have no chance, as all the young men are inoculated with liberal ideas . . .' (*WL MSS.*)

[2] On 26 Mar., during the Committee stage of the Roman Catholic Disability Removal Bill.

[3] Peter Heylyn (1600–62), Royalist, Churchman, and controversialist. His *Cyprianus Anglicus, or the History of the Life and Death of William Laud, Archbishop of Canterbury*, 1668, is a defence of Laud against the aspersions of the Puritan William Prynne, and an important source for Laud's personal character and private life. W. W. had a copy in his library.

the overthrow of Papacy in England, and to some lurking expectations that if the Sees could be preserved they might not improbably
be filled at no distant time by Catholic Prelates.

I apprehend that there will soon be an explosion in Prussia, and
the whole of North Germany;[1] so that the troubles of our time will
be perhaps renewed as formidably as ever.

Excuse this long scrawl—
Ever faithfully yours
W Wordsworth

Mrs W. will be obliged to Lord Lowther to direct the enclosed and
to allow his S^t to put it into the Post Off.

*[W. W. sent on a separate sheet the following account, in John
Carter's hand, of the duties of a Distributor of Stamps]*[2]

The duty of a Distributor of Stamps is, upon application made by
him to receive Stamps from the Head Office to supply the demands
of his District. These Stamps are forwarded by him to his Subdistributors in the quantity required by them.

At the close of every quarter, an account is sent to the Head
Office in London of the Stamps on Hand, and at the same time
Money is remitted to the amount of those sold.

The Collection of Legacy Duty which is naturally attached to
this Office is performed by supplying to Executors and Administra-
tors certain papers called Forms to be by them filled up according
to the directions contained in them and returned to the Distributor.
These papers are forwarded by him once a month to the Head
Office where (if found correct) they are stamped, then returned to
the Distributor, and from him forwarded through his Subdistributors
to the Executors, who in these papers receive a Discharge for the
Duty due under the Will.

The performance of the above two principal branches of duty
requires either the constant attendance of a Distributor himself or
that of some confidential and competent representative. The time
to be given to his duty depends upon the extent of his district or
rather the quantity of Stamps consumed in it, but as it is uncertain

---

[1] After a period of unrest and repression, the King of Prussia was preparing
to introduce a form of representative government based on provincial assem-
blies elected by the landed interest.

[2] This is the fullest account we have of W. W.'s office, the nature of which is
still occasionally misrepresented. Lord Lowther wrote in reply 'that he had
laid William's statements before the Solr. Genl., who told him that from them
he had gained more knowledge of the Nature of the Office—the responsibilities,
etc., than from any other quarter whatever' (*MW*, p. 80).

when the Stamps will be called for, he or his representative, as I have said, must be constantly on the spot.

The keeping of the accounts is a matter that requires much care and attention, and the quarterly returns must be made with the most exact Classification of the Stamps under the Heads of their several duties and the Legacy Papers demand a minute attention to Rules not a little difficult to apply without mistake.

So much for the *trouble*.—Now for the responsibility. Sureties upon undertaking the Office are required in proportion to the Profit, but even where the Profit is small they are so heavy that if there should arise a necessity to act upon them the forfiet would ruin many times over a Person of small Fortune as he must be to whom such small profit can be an object, and even where the consumption of Stamps is small it is necessary to keep on hand a large Stock, the preservation of which from Robbery, Fire or other accidents is a cause of great anxiety. For my own part so much have I felt this and the necessity of vigilance in every branch of this concern that notwithstanding I have a Clerk in whom I repose the utmost confidence, not twentyfour hours have passed during seven years in which either myself or some one of my nearest connections has not been on the spot to superintend the concern.

I was absent for some months last summer but this was by Medical advice and with the permission of the Board.

The poundage is at the rate of 4 Per Cent, from which must be deducted the Poundage to Subdistributors which varies according to circumstances.

28. W. W. to VISCOUNT LOWTHER

MS. Lonsdale MSS. Hitherto unpublished.

March 30th [1821]

My dear Lord Lowther,

The Papers so kindly sent by you have been read to Gregg,[1] and he returns his thanks for this ready mark of your attention.

[1] See L. 23. In his letter of mid-March Lord Lowther had written: 'I am told at the Secretary of State for the Colonies, that no one is sent to van Dieman's Land without he has 500 £. This is by far the best speculation, as to Climate, Land and market. But it requires this capital to undertake a farm. Under these circumstances as much Land would be given, as the person would be capable of cultivating. As to Canada if Gregg is a respectable and industrious man he might obtain a letter from the Secretary of State's office to the Governor desiring that some Land should be allotted him. But the Gov^t do not pay his passage out. The emigration to Algoa Bay [at the Cape] is stopped for the present.' (*WL MSS.*)

Since I wrote last I have seen a fuller Report of Hume's Speech.[1] He dwells much upon the balances retained in hand—what these may be in other districts I know not, but for my own part I retain seldom more than £200 of *actual cash*, at the Quarter's end, much less at the end of the year. I have latterly collected upon an average about £18,000 per ann. Of this, much more than one half never goes into Banker's hands at all; but without any profit to me is forwarded directly to the Board. On the Remainder, I might gain something that would be an object by leaving it in my Bankers hands to the end of the Quarter, were it not that the Currency in my district consists mainly of provincial notes, principally Scotch, on which the Bankers allow no interest, till they have had them six weeks. The little which I gain from Interest proceeds from the stamps sold at Kendal, principally paid for in Kendal Notes, which the Banks that issue them are obliged to receive as Cash.

If a reference to my annual Quarterly Returns at the Stamp office should appear to make my Balance larger than I have now declared, it is owing to my not having always repeated in the Margin of the account explanatory observations, which have been given by Letter to the Board. Enough of this.

I have read with the utmost attention the Debates on the Catholic Question. The opinion I share with you remains unaltered. We have heard much of candour and forbearance etc., but these qualities appear to be all on one side; viz on that of the advocates of existing laws;—among the Innovators there is a haughtiness, an air of insolent superiority in light and knowledge which no strength of argument could justify; much less the sophisms and assumptions which they advance. I am aware that if the Catholics are to get into Parliament, ambition and worldly interest will have their sway over them as over other men, and it need not be dreaded, therefore, that they will all be upon every occasion, upon one side. But still the Esprit du Corps cannot but be stronger with them than other bodies, for obvious reasons; and looking at the Constitution of the House, how nicely-balanced Parties have often been, and what small majorities have repeatedly decided most momentous questions, I cannot but tremble at the prospect of introducing men who *may* turn, and (if they act consistently with the spirit of their Religion and even with its open profession) *must* turn their mutual fidelity against our Protestant Establishment; till in co-operation with other Dissenters and Infidels, they have accomplished its overthrow.

[1] See previous letter.

I repeat my thanks for your exertions in behalf of the enactments
of our Forefathers, and remain

> my dear Lord Lowther
> your faithful friend and Servant
> Wm Wordsworth

29. W. W. to THE COMMISSIONERS OF STAMPS

Address: The Hon'ble Commissioners, Stamp Office, London.
Postmark: 26 Apr. 1821. *Stamp*: Kendal Penny Post. *Endorsed*: William
  Wordsworth Esqᵣ Rydal Mount Ambleside 23 April 1821.
MS. Public Record Office. Hitherto unpublished.

[*In John Carter's hand*]

> Rydal Mount, Ambleside
> 23 April, 1821—

Hon'ble Sirs,
   In reply to your Letter of the 11 Inst, I beg to forward the Copy
of a Letter from Messrs: Sherwen and Son,[1] and also the Copy of
a Letter received from Mrs: White,[2] which will explain the cause
of the delay.—
   I deem it right to add, in justice to Mr: White, that having been
appointed by me at the commencement of my Distributorship, I
have not had occasion, in any one Instance, to complain of inattention
or irregularity, during the eight years which he has held the Office.

> I have the Honor to be,
> Hon'ble Sirs,
> Your ob: Servant
> [*signed*] Wᵐ Wordsworth

Copy   Whitehaven
                                                          14 April 1821

Sir,
   The Residuary Amount of the Revᵈ Wᵐ Thompson[3] as Executor
of his Sister Eliz: Fisher, deceased, was delivered into Mr: White,
the Stamp Distributor in this Town and the Duty thereon, amounting to £3.13.4 paid to him on the 3ʳᵈ Day of April Inst:
   The Letter addressed to the Revᵈ Mr: Thompson dated '4ᵗʰ Ap:
1821' containing a palpable misstatement and Falsehood, was

---

[1] Richard Sherwen and Son, Whitehaven attorneys.
[2] Wife of William White, W. W.'s Sub-distributor at Whitehaven.
[3] Unidentified.

written and sent off to Mr: Thompson by our Clerk, unknown to us, and we should be sorry indeed if Mr: White should incur any blame, in consequence of the negligence and inattention of those in our employment.

We are Sir,
Your ob^t Servants
[*signed*] Richard Sherwen and Son

To Wm Wordsworth Esq.—

Whitehaven 21 Apr: 1821—

Sir

The enclosed was put into the Post Office on the 14 Inst: in a Letter from Mr: White to Mr: Wordsworth but by not being addressed (an oversight I cannot account for) had gone to the General Post Office, I suppose, and was returned here last night.— Mr: White being from home I delayed opening it until his return, but receiving your Letter this Evening, stating your uneasiness in not having an Answer, I take the liberty of stating the Reason.

I am Sir,
Your ob: Servant
[*signed*] B. White.

[*John Carter adds*]

Mr: Wordsworth's Day of transmission is on the *first* Tuesday in the month, that of his Subs: on the Tuesday preceding, so that the Rec^t: in Question could not have been sent in Mr: Wordsworth's Par¹ of the 3rd Inst.

30. D. W. to CATHERINE CLARKSON

Address: Mrs. Clarkson, Playford Hall, Ipswich, Suffolk. (Single sheet. By Penrith).
Stamp: Kendal Penny Post. *Endorsed*: May 1821.
MS. British Museum.
K (—). *LY i. 33.*

[31 May 1821]

My dearest Friend

On the receipt of your last letter I felt an impulse to write immediately and pictured to myself your pleasant looks by the

---

¹ i.e. Parcel.

well-known fire-side of my bedroom, when Elizabeth should give you a letter (no doubt she knows whence they come as well as Susan used to do) from Miss Wordsworth—to interpose a little variety during your watchings by the poor stranger's[1] bed-side. Such were my first thoughts; but recollecting that Sara Hutchinson would soon be at Rydal Mount and that I had no novelties to communicate I awaited her arrival. She had not been two hours in the house before she said she must write to you. I then put your letter into her hands; and thinking she would have much more interesting matter than I had, and that two letters were useless I trusted to her—but you know the way of putting off, and though I believe she will soon write, my conscience can be no longer at rest. Poor Mr Clarkson! I think I felt more for his condition than yours or that of the unfortunate young man when he was brought back to the house in a helpless state. His (Mr C's) sufferings must have been dreadful however he might wish to conceal them from you. To estimate them in some small degree I need only look back to the feeling manner in which he sometimes spoke of poor little William's illness and his own anxiety. I cannot express my thankfulness on reading how you supported yourself under the first alarm; and in the whole of the circumstances of this melancholy accident how much cause is there for thankfulness! That you were so near to the Surgeon's house was indeed a blessing, and though it is certainly not ordinarily considered as such, to be confined to the anxieties and cares of nursing for six weeks, I am sure *you* are a hundred times thankful that if such an accident *was* to happen to this young man so far from home they fell to your lot. For me much as I rejoice to find that your strength is equal to great trials I cannot help a little grieving that they should so often come to you out of their natural course. It is but nine months since you watched over our dear William. Your letter is concluded on the 11th of May—It is now the 31st —therefore I trust that as your Patient's state was so hopeful and his condition of mind so happy you will have him in your pleasant dining-room in the course of a fortnight after you receive this.

Sunday afternoon June 3rd.—It is a few days since I began this letter. The country was then pining under the blight of frosty nights, snow-showers and north east winds, which had prevailed more or less for the last three weeks, having checked the ash-trees in their budding, arrested those of the oak in their first stage of bursting into yellow leaf, and destroyed most of the blossoms of

[1] i.e. Benjamin Laroche, the French refugee. See L. 37 below.

the fruit trees. The air changed on Friday: and the difference in the hue of the woods is astonishing; but they will never have their proper share of leaves; and as rain is not come with the warmth, the fields are not yet cheared. We have all been at Church and though M and S were a little oppressed by the heat, they do not seem to be tired. As for me the hotter the better if the air be dry—especially along the foot path under the crags where one can rest at pleasure upon sloping turf. How you will be charmed with that walk upon which we enter from our own terrace! Not as a path *for you* to *church*—the distance would be too much—but as a retired walk, of which every step is pleasant and which may be made as long or short as you like. You will judge that we are all strong and well, indeed I never saw Sara look better in my life, or appear to suffer less from walking, and this is very lucky for her, as she is now deprived of the use of her pony.—I told you she was going to Harrowgate. There she spent more than a fortnight, much to her satisfaction, and to the benefit of her health. She rode daily on her pony with Mrs Hutchinson,[1] whom she accompanied to H, and when they were about to send these ponies home and follow themselves in a day or two, Sara, ten minutes after she had seen them led past the window to water, was informed that both were struck dead by lightning, but the boy uninjured who was on the back of Mrs H's. This was such a providential escape that the loss was at first little thought of. Mrs H's pony was actually dead, but S's revived, and hopes were given of its recovery, and that she might even ride it this summer. The expense and trouble you may guess were great, and she was obliged to leave it at H—, but last week it was removed to Stockton, where it must remain in her cousin's fields for a summer's run. This is really a serious misfortune, as of late Sara has never continued long in perfect health without her exercise.—Mary has not quite got rid of those burstings-out of heat but nearly so, and she is much better than when I last wrote to you, though she is very thin—and you will be sorry to hear that my fatness has now entirely disappeared. I was never leaner in my life except at the beginning of our travels last summer before I got to wandering among the Alps, and I am sure I do not eat one fifth of what I then did; but these things are of little consequence as I can walk with as little fatigue as when I was twenty. Not long ago my Brother and I spent a whole day on the mountains, went by a circuitous road to the top of Fairfield, walking certainly not *less* than 14 miles; and I was not the *least tired*. My brother is still

[1] S. H.'s cousin. See L. 26 above.

hard at work with his sonnets.[1] I hope he will have done before
Mr Tillbrooke, Henry Robinson, or the Monkhouses arrive—all of
whom we expect to see; but exactly when I do not know. John
is expected with one of his schoolfellows for a few days at Whitsuntide—His great holidays will be in July. My Brother is well
satisfied with his progress at school, and with his Master's[2] mode
of proceeding. This often makes in me a lingering wish that
William were at Sedbergh also, London being at such a frightful
distance in case of sudden illness, and the expense of coming
down rendering it impossible (except in the case of friends
chancing to come just at the time of his holidays, who could find
room in their carriage) that he should meet his Family at home
oftener than once a year. Poor Fellow! he is now on his road
from Preston to London. He left us on Wednesday, stayed Thursday
at Kendal, and on Friday proceeded to Preston, whence he was to
depart to-day with two of his schoolfellows. He had a slight indisposition the second week after his arrival at home; but has since
been perfectly well, and full of life and spirits. The parting was
painful enough as you may judge. He had striven with his feelings
all day, and when forced to yield to his anguish was piteous; but
even when sitting on top of the Coach as he went down Ambleside
Street, I could see that he was ready to be a little comforted by the
kind notice of a Gentleman sitting beside him; and Mrs Cookson
tells us that after the first evening (when he appeared a little low-
spirited) he was in joyous spirits while he remained at Kendal.
Dorothy will be home in a fortnight. She was to have left school
entirely this Midsummer; but Miss Dowling has kindly invited her
to stay with her another half-year, and Dorothy is delighted with
the privilege. She is deeply attached to Miss Dowling; who is
now perfectly satisfied with her in all respects, and treats her with
the tenderness of an affectionate relative. We spent yesterday very
pleasantly. After Breakfast all went to Mr Barber's cottage at
Grasmere, and Dorothy and Miss D and one of her sisters joined
us there in the afternoon and we came home together in their Cart.
I thought much of you when I was sitting under the shade of one
of the old Pollard oaks before his house, which I daresay you
remember. The cottage is much enlarged since you saw it, and
Mr Barber has purchased some adjoining fields, which will be a
public benefit, as the trees will be preserved. Sad work has been
made at Grasmere by larch plantations; but even yet, I thought

[1] The *Ecclesiastical Sketches*.
[2] i.e. the Revd. Henry Wilkinson of Sedbergh. See *MY* ii. 565.

last night it was the sweetest of all our Vales. You must not give over thinking and talking of coming to see us next summer—Do not let Mr Clarkson lose sight of the scheme after having looked at it with pleasure as he did when I was with you. Yet how can I hope it if times do not mend? My Brother desires me especially to return his sincere thanks for the letter contained in the Suffolk Chronicle.[1] He was exceedingly pleased with it, and thinks the Arguments unanswerable. Yet things go on as they were, and I fear are likely to do so, till hundreds more are reduced from the comfortable state of middle life to begging or to seek their fortunes elsewhere—and no place for settlement except Van Dieman's land seems now to offer much temptation. The accounts brought to Liverpool from the Cape are as bad as can be, and it is, at best, a chearless thing to go to the cold climate of Canada. George Hutchinson I suppose will go thither—Van Dieman's land requires too much money; and emigrate he must—there is nothing else for him. It will be a great weight removed from his Friends at Hindwell when he is gone. Joanna writes that Mrs Hutchinson is but in very delicate health. She had a miscarriage during Joanna's absence.— I have not yet finished my journal,[2] though at times I have worked very hard from ten o'clock in the morning till dinner time, at four; and when it is done, I fear it will prove very tedious reading even to *Friends*, who have not themselves visited the places where we were. Had not my Brother so very much wished me to do my best, I am sure I should never have had the resolution to go further than just re-copy what I did by snatches, and very irregularly, at the time; but to please him I have amplified and arranged; and a long affair will come out of it, which I cannot think any person can possibly have the patience to read through; but which, through sympathy and a desire to revive dormant recollections, may in patches be interesting to a few others. For my own sake, however, the time is not thrown away; and when we are dead and gone, any memorial of us will be satisfactory to the children, especially Dorothy. Her mother's journal[3] is already transcribed, and not being so lengthy as mine, it cannot but be interesting, and very amusing. She has read it to Mrs Gee and Miss Lockier[4] and they were delighted. Her course was much wiser than mine. She wrote regularly and straightforward, and has done little more than re-copy, whereas all that I did would have been almost worthless, dealt with in that way. There is some excuse for me in my illness

[1] See L. 26 above. [2] Of her continental tour. [3] Of the same tour.
[4] One of the Lockier sisters (see *MY* ii. 612), probably Charlotte.

which threw me back. I have not read a single word of Mary's, being determined to finish my own first, and then make comparisons for correction, and insertion of what I may have omitted. What a weary way I have been leading you with this dull subject! Let me now ask what news from St Domingo! and what is to become of the gentleman who went from Ipswich. You do not mention your translation[1] in your last letter. If you go on with it and publish it you must let us have a copy through Longman who sends parcels to Southey, and if Mr Clarkson writes again on Agriculture or any other subject do not fail to remember us.—Pray write as soon as you can; as we shall be anxious to hear of the recovery of your patient. How happy for you and Mr Clarkson that he is so interesting a companion! I expect to hear that you can chatter French as fast as English, and that with the Frenchman's help you will furnish Mr Clarkson with as much pleasant matter for good-humoured jesting as you and I used to do when he sate beside us.—Give my love to Tom. I am delighted with your account of him.—Remember me to Elizabeth—I cannot tell you how often I think of you all— and even while looking round in this beautiful garden of our own surrounded by mountains, and now full of blossoming shrubs, I picture to myself the beauties of Playford in its own green hollow— the old walls covered with vine leaves—the garden full of flowers.— Tell Mrs Thistleton[2] that Sara H enquired much after her and we both send our regards to her. When you write tell me all you are doing and think of doing. Everything interests me coming from you. This is a full letter—a poor [*seal*] return for yours—but it is better to have nothing new to tell, than to have to talk of misfortunes or sorrows—and thank God in our own Family we have kept clear of these so long that we ought to be grateful. If you see Mr Tillbrooke tell him I would have written but so many letters were sent from Mr Gee etc that I thought mine would not be worth postage, and tell him that we hope he will stay with us much longer than he talks of. God bless you my dearest Friend ever yours

D. Wordsworth

When I began this letter in the cold Sara desired me to say she would write to you when it was warm weather. Remember me to Mr and Mrs Biddle and do not forget my kind regards to your Friends at Woodbridge. I am glad the girls are recovered—Poor things. They are sweet good creatures.

My very best love to Mr Clarkson—

---

[1] See below, L. 37.   [2] One of C. C.'s Playford friends.

31. W. W. to VISCOUNT LOWTHER

MS. *Lonsdale MSS. Hitherto unpublished.*

[June–July 1821]

My dear Lord Lowther,

Mr Sykes,[1] Solicitor of the Stamp Off. has just called on me, in his way to the Stamp Off. of Edinburgh. He is an old School-fellow of mine, but his object in calling was to beg that I would furnish him with any considerations arising from my duties and responsibilities as a Stamp-Distributor, which he might urge when examined by the Committee, in support of the present system, and in opposition to that which Hume is contending for.[2] Hume's plan goes to the annihilation of the off: of Stamp Dis. and to offer the Collection of the duties to the lowest Bidder, in other words to have the duties collected by persons dispersed over the Country like the present Sub Dis^rs and collecting for two per cent or under. With this view Hume has already been putting persons upon making such proposals, and no doubt his invitations will be readily met.

Mr Sykes says that he should have had no fears but that such a plan would have been rejected by the House and the Government had they not already given up the Receiver General; at present he is full of apprehension of the worst consequences. It is impossible that the present administration should be so imbecile as to give way to this extent to a vulgar Demagogue like Hume, were not his plans supported by influences that do not appear. Is there any considerable portion of the Landowners who support these schemes with a view to reducing the taxes, and so lessen the burthens upon their Estates?—I suspect this to be the case. It is a short-sighted Policy. Why not attack the poor Laws? Which would prove an effectual Relief, instead of stripping government of that influence which it stands so much in need of. The tendency of the present reforms is to throw the Collection of the Revenue into the hands of persons of the lowest situation in life—men without education or stake in the Country or influence in it for any good purpose.

As to Mr Sykes' application to myself I can do little more than furnish him with the substance of what you were so kind as to lay

---

[1] Godfrey Sykes (1772–1828), barrister-at-law and Solicitor to the Board of Stamps and Taxes since 1814: b. Sheffield, educated at Hawkshead School and Sidney Sussex College, Cambridge, of which he became a Fellow in 1796.
[2] See L. 27.

before the Sol^r Genl.[1] Persons of Parliamentary influence must write and speak boldly, if they are persuaded that these schemes are injurious.

This morning's interview has forced me to look round upon my own situation in this Country. If the intended changes take place, my plans must alter accordingly—As far as concerns my own expenditure, I can reduce it as low as may be necessary, but the education of my younger son, now ten years of age, must unavoidably be attended with difficulty; or I ought rather to say will prove impossible upon the plan commenced, except in case of accomplishing, what I am well aware is most difficult; viz, getting him upon the *foundation* of the Charterhouse (where he has been already two years) through the interest of some powerful Friends. I should not mention this now, but on account of his age which allows no time to be lost. He will be twelve next May, and after that period, I believe, he cannot be admitted on the foundation. I do not presume to ask your assistance, or that of Lord Lonsdale, in this matter; but I feel that it is no abuse of your kindness to state that this is one of the ways in which I might be served.

I remain my dear Lord Lowther
ever faithfully yours
W. Wordsworth

32. W. W. to UNKNOWN CORRESPONDENT

MS. Cornell. Hitherto unpublished.

Rydal Mount
June 21st 1821

Sir,

My handwriting has inflicted so much punishment upon my Friends, that it is not without some hesitation that I comply with your request. Such as it is, you have it now before you.—

I am Sir
your ob^nt Servant
Wm Wordsworth

[1] Sir John Singleton Copley, later 1st Lord Lyndhurst (1772–1863), Solicitor-General since 1819: Attorney-General, 1824–6, and three times Lord Chancellor, 1827–30, 1834–5, and 1841–6.

33. W. W. to JOHN KENYON

Address: To John Kenyon, Esqre, at the Granby Hotel, Harrowgate.
Postmark: Kendal Penny Post.
MS. untraced.
Transactions of the Wordsworth Society, no. 6, p. 78. K(—). LT i. 39.

[*In D. W.'s hand*]

Rydal Mount, July 23rd, 1821.

My dear Sir,

My eyes have lately become so irritable that I am again forced to employ an amanuensis.

I learned with much concern from Monkhouse and Tillbrooke that you had been unwell for some time, and am truly grieved not to find in your last an assurance that your health is restored.

I hear from Miss Hutchinson such striking accounts of the benefit which invalids derive from Harrowgate waters, and of their general salutary effect (in which she speaks from experience, having been there lately with a sick Friend), that I more than hope you will have reason also to speak highly in their praise for their effect upon yourself.

We are disappointed at not seeing you before you go into Scotland, myself more particularly so, because I have held out expectations to an Irish Gentleman[1] who has lately taken lodgings in this neighbourhood that I might accompany him on a Tour through a considerable part of his country, including the two extremities, Killarney and the Giant's Causeway, which he says might easily be accomplished in five weeks by our shipping at Whitehaven for Dublin. If this plan should be adopted, I fear I must purchase the pleasure at the cost of not seeing you unless you could be tempted to prolong your stay in the neighbourhood till towards the end of September. If I *do* go (which certainly I should not have thought of this summer, were it not for the disordered state of my eyes), I shall make all possible speed back for the sake of seeing you and your Brother,[2] to whom I have a strong wish to be made known. Happy should I be, could what I have thrown out tempt you to make Ireland your object instead of Scotland. I have myself made three tours in Scotland, but cannot point out anything worthy of notice that is not generally known. Of particular sights and spots those which pleased me most were (to begin with the

---

[1] Edward Quillinan. See L. 37 below.
[2] John and Edward Kenyon came to Ambleside a month later. See L. 42 below.

northernmost) the course of the river Bewley up to the Sawmills, about twenty miles beyond Inverness,—the fall of Foyers upon Loch Ness, (a truly noble thing, if one is fortunate as to the quantity of water), and Glen Coe. These lie beyond the limit of your route— and within your route I was not much struck with anything but what every body knows.

I cannot hasten my departure for Ireland so [as] to suit your arrangement on account of the expected confinement of the Gentleman's wife whom I am to accompany.

I am glad you have seen Bolton Priory. You probably know that Gordale, Malham Cove, and Wethercote Cove, which lie north of Bolton, are interesting objects, though dependent—two of them— upon water, and we have had such a drought as was never before known.

Mrs Wordsworth, Miss Hutchinson, and my Sister, who writes for me, join me in kindest remembrance and sincere wishes for the recovery of your health. We are all well, and shall be most happy to see you.

Ever sincerely yours,
[*signed*] Wm Wordsworth

If you have not an Introduction to Sir Walter Scott, and should wish for one, pray let me know and I will write to him.

34. W. W. to FRANCIS LEGATT CHANTREY

Address:—Chantry Esq., Pimlico, London.
Franked: Penrith Aug[t] nineteen 1821 J. Beckett.[1] *Postmark*: (1) 19 Aug. 1821. (2) 21 Aug. 1821. *Stamp*: Penrith.
MS. Harvard University Library. Hitherto unpublished.

August 18th [1821]
Lowther Castle
Westmorland.

My dear Sir,

I am pleased to hear that Sir George and Lady Beaumont were satisfied with the Bust.[2]

In addition to the Casts which I mentioned, another will be

---

[1] John, later Sir John, Beckett, Lord Lonsdale's son-in-law.

[2] For Chantrey's bust of W. W., see *MT* ii. 615. On 20 Aug. Sir George wrote to W. W.: 'I greatly admire your bust, it is admired by all, and especially by judges—of art or countenance; it does high honor to Chauntry.' (*WL MSS.*)

wanted for Mr Kenyon, a friend of mine. It may remain with you
till further directions.—

> ever faithfully yours
> Wᵐ Wordsworth

35. W. W. to BENJAMIN ROBERT HAYDON

Address: B. R. Haydon Esq., Lisson Grove North, London
MS. untraced.
LY i. 41.

> Lowther Castle Westⁿᵈ
> August 18ᵗʰ [1821]

My dear Sir,

Having an opportunity of procuring a Frank, I write this short
note to express a hope that you are well, happy, and flourishing.

A female Friend of mine has seen your resurrection of Lazarus,[1]
and was highly delighted with it.

For many reasons with which I need not trouble you, I could
not subscribe to Scott:[2] I was much shocked at his melancholy end,
which I am afraid will not have produced the Reformation of those
who occasioned it. Shall we see you again at Rydal Mount;[3] I hope
so—it would give us great pleasure.

I left all well at Home, a week ago. I return to morrow.

> Believe me my dear Sir,
> with high respect
> your sincere friend
> Wm Wordsworth

[1] 'The Raising of Lazarus', begun in the summer of 1820, and not finally
completed until the end of 1822, is now in the Tate Gallery. See *Diary of
Benjamin Robert Haydon* (ed. Pope), ii. 299, 391. Mary Russell Mitford
describes a visit to Haydon's studio at the inception of the work: 'He is now
painting another great picture, the "Resurrection of Lazarus", different from
any of the many paintings on this subject. All the other pictures represent
Lazarus as rising from a horizontal position. Mr Haydon, following the custom
of Jerusalem, where all the tombs were excavations in the rock, and the bodies
placed upright, represents him as walking from the hollow in which he had
been enclosed, and throwing off the grave-clothes at the command of Christ,
"Lazarus, come forth!" Nothing can be finer than the sketch, which I have
seen. It contains about twenty figures, and will occupy, I suppose, nearly two
years.' (A. G. L'Estrange, *The Life of Mary Russell Mitford*, 3 vols., 1870,
ii. 101.)

[2] John Scott. See L. 24 above.

[3] Haydon had called at Rydal Mount on his return from Scotland the
previous December, while W. W. was staying at Coleorton on the way home
from his continental tour.

36. W. W. to SIR WALTER SCOTT[1]

Address: Sir Walter Scott Bart.
Endorsed: 1821 Aug. 23rd Wordsworth to Walter Scott. Letter of introduction.
MS. Dr. Williams's Library.
K. Morley, i. 103.

[*In M. W.'s hand*]

Rydal Mount.
Aug: 23. 1821.

Dear Sir Walter

    The Bearer, Mr Robinson, being on a Tour in Scotland is desirous of the honour of an introduction to you; which though aware of the multiplicity of your engagements, and sensible of the value of your time, I have not scrupled to give. Mr R. is a highly esteemed Friend of myself and of those who are dearest to me; he accompanied us during our Tour among the Alps, last summer, and I can say from experience that he will prove no unworthy Spectator of any thing which you may be kind enough to recommend to his notice in that Country which you have so nobly illustrated. Mr R. has been much upon the Continent, and is extensively read in German literature, speaking the language with the ease of a native.—

    In the last Letter I had from you, you spoke of the pleasure you should have in revisiting our Arcadia. I assure you that you would be most welcome. When I think how small is the space between your Residence upon the Tweed and mine, in the Valley of Ambleside, I wonder that we see so little of each other. In all cases however believe me with sincere regard and high admiration

faithfully yours
[*signed*] Wm Wordsworth

    Mrs W— and my Sister unite with me in remembrances to yourself and Mrs Scott.

---

[1] This letter arrived too late to be delivered, according to H. C. R.'s letter to his brother written on 7 Oct. from Rydal Mount, where he stayed for a few days on his way home. (*Dr. Williams's Library MSS.*)

37. D. W. to CATHERINE CLARKSON

MS. British Museum.
LY i. 41.

Rydal Mount
25th August [1821]

My dearest Friend,

Why did you mortify me in the first sentence of your letter by telling me that you had before you three sides of a sheet of paper which had been nearly filled a long time before? Your letters never become flat or uninteresting however long they lie on hand, and you ought instead of taking a new sheet to have filled up the old one and crossed as much as you liked, for *you* have a right to cross your letters which I must say some of the young ones, so fond of that practice, have not, but whatever you were to do with yours they would not be rendered illegible. Poor Mr Clarkson! I am sorry indeed to hear that his good habit of falling asleep as soon as his head is laid upon the pillow has been broken by his late cares and disappointments; yet I hope that when his present labours[1] are concluded it may return, being a part of his natural constitution, which has been little changed since I knew him. There seemed when I was at Playford little or no difference except that he might not have been able to walk from Poolley to Penrith and back without fatigue, and that he was somewhat less active in his motions. Whatever grief he may yet have to endure for the sake of the poor Africans, and whatever labour though without apparent results, he will still have the satisfaction that good must come out of it in the end, though probably none of us will live to see the day when the atrocities now practiced shall be wholly prevented. What a blessing for La Roche[2] that he was under your roof at the time of his confinement and suffering, and that you can still keep him till he is fit to travel with comfort. I often think that in future years he will look back to this period as the happiest of his life. As for you you must

---

[1] Clarkson was at this time writing *The Cries of Africa, to the Inhabitants of Europe; or, A Survey of that bloody Commerce called the slave-trade,* [1821].

[2] Benjamin Laroche (1797–1852), radical journalist, and opponent of the Bourbon regime in France, was sentenced to six years' imprisonment for his work *Lettres de M. Grégoire, ancien évêque de Blois ... à M. le duc de Richelieu ... et à M. Guizot ...* Paris, 1820. He fled to England and took refuge at Playford Hall, remaining there till 1827, teaching French and propagating the cause of Abolition. On his return to France, he achieved fame as a translator of English writers, including Canning (1827), Byron (1836), Fenimore Cooper (1835–7), and Shakespeare (1843). He returned to active journalism during the revolution of 1848, and published the first part of *Histoire de l'abolition de l'esclavage dans les colonies françaises.*

have a wonderful strength somewhere or you could never have
gone through the labour of writing, explaining construing etc.—
and it gives me so much pleasure to perceive this that I can hardly
regret that you were forced to this trial of yourself; though if you
had not been straitened for time it would have been only an agreeable employment, and that does at first seem to be what one *should*
regret. I hope we shall see the fruit of your joint labours.[1] Through
Longman a parcel can at any time be sent to us, as he has frequent
communications with Southey. I am sure I need not tell you how
much we all rejoice in the hopeful prospects which Tom's good
conduct and steady industry set before you. There cannot now be
any doubt of his well doing if it please God to preserve his health—
and then in a few years your private worldly cares will be over.—
Public cares Mr Clarkson will have as long as he lives—but I try
to see the day when the casting up of the year's accounts and the
price of grain shall be a matter of little consequence, and you can
come and go among your friends wherever your kind hearts would
lead you. Then my dear Friend, if we are alive, and our hitherto
allotted share of quiet good fortune does not desert us, I trust we
may see something more of each other—and even as it is I sometimes venture to hope that you will come next year—though Sara
Hutchinson (probably wiser than I from past experience) checks
me with saying—'nay, nay, it will be put off again till another
year!' With respect to myself whenever I think of taking a journey
(and when I think of going Southward Playford is one of my first
objects) the expense seems to be now the main impediment.
Formerly there were more cares to bind me to home, yet on the
other hand when more of life was before us, there seemed to be more
time to spare. One could then *afford* to be separated for half a year
from best friends, and the thought how few years or half years
must we inevitably have to spend together did not interpose in the
same spirit of nice calculation. However, costly as was our last
year's rambling, and heavy as are the expenses of schools and
colleges, I trust it will be far from as long a time between my seeing
you again at your own home as it was in the former case, nine
years between the happy weeks I spent with you at Bury and Playford—It is fit I should endeavour to tell you something of our
goings-on at Rydal; but as nothing very important has happened,

---

[1] From Ls. 26 and 30, it would appear that C. C. had begun to translate
Clarkson's pamphlet *The Cries of Africa* into French. She was now joined in the
task by Laroche, and the completed version was published in London in 1821
(Paris, 1822).

and for another strange reason, as it is so long since I wrote to you I seem to have little to say. Had letters passed between us once a month I should have had a hundred things to write about, now forgotten or not worth the telling. The most important matter is the state of my poor Brother's eyes. During the winter he daily read several hours, and could use them freely without the slightest inconvenience, except by candle-light, and we flattered ourselves that the weakness was overcome; but in the spring he worked hard and incessantly and under great mental excitement, and the consequence was, that often, having the first threatenings of slight inflammation for a few days he was obliged to lay aside all employment, and if he had not been exceedingly careful in all respects he might probably have been as bad as ever again; but happily the inflammation never became violent, and it is now almost entirely gone; though still he cannot read more than a quarter of an hour without heat and prickings in the eye, and if he were to exercise his mind in composition all would be to be begun again. Undoubtedly the malady proceeds from the stomach, and it is attended with heat and flushings in the face. I still hope as he is now going on perfectly well, that before winter he may be able to take to his studies. He has now two works unfinished (the Recluse and the Sonnets[1]) and you may believe that it often disturbs him that he is forced to spend so much of his time in idleness. It is, however, a great consolation to us that he enjoys air, exercise, company and all the pleasures this delightful country spreads before us, and these are the best means of cure—and as I said I hope he will be cured before winter. The inflammation is solely in the eye-lids. We have had Mrs Richard Wordsworth for five weeks and her son, a nice little Boy— very like Willy, a pretty genteel looking child—but when he speaks the revolution is astonishing! he has the very worst and most barbarous of all the dialects of Cumberland. He goes to school at Hunsanby near Lazonby. His mother lives there beside her Father; but about a year hence she will probably remove to Sedbergh with him. She is very lame—walks with two sticks or crutches, and I fear will never be much better. She is a very worthy, sensible and discreet woman, of an excellent temper; and exceedingly well-behaved. I believe she is attached to us all and would in all things respecting her son be governed by my Brother's advice. You will be surprised perhaps to hear that your dear little friend William is at home. Various circumstances combined to induce us to incur the expense and risk of this long journey so soon after the former; but

[1] i.e. the *Ecclesiastical Sketches*.

in future we shall only look for the indulgence once a year. He is in high health—looks strong and his spirits are inexhaustible—too soon will arrive the dismal day of departure. Yesterday we were all over at Grasmere and dined on the Island with Mrs Robinson,[1] one of her Daughters[2] and a fine young man her Son[3] who have been staying with us. It really seemed they had hardly ever in all their lives spent so happy a day. Mr *Kenyon* and his Brother were of the party—the Brother as pleasant as he is himself. They have lodgings at Ambleside and will stay a little while, then go to Lymington—thence to London, thence to Rome. They live in all places, are at home every where and are most entertaining companions. You recollect I had a letter from Mr K when at Playford. The Monkhouses are not coming—a great disappointment. Mrs M is again in a situation which makes quiet necessary, and unfortunately she has taken a journey to Hindwell and not being able to consent (except in case of absolute necessity) to stay there till her confinement, there will be great anxiety in the management of her journey. What a misfortune that she should be so delicate! Poor Mrs Robinson has had great sorrow in the lamentable end of her Brother John,[4] and the dissensions between the two Brothers. She entered into all the particulars of the dispute; and as I know I probably contributed to strengthen your dislike of Tom Myers I must say that I see that many points of his conduct towards his Brother when explained were not unjustifiable. Others proceeded from irritation, certainly only to be excused from the weakness of human nature; but I really believe if he had not himself been illused by Mr Robinson, and disappointed by the folly and misconduct of his Brother, he would have behaved in all respects kindly and honourably to him. He is a man of haughty spirit, but has not a hard heart. Mrs Robinson loved both her Brothers and their dissensions were a clinging sorrow to her. Her eldest daughter[5] has been with her Uncle more than a year and he cannot part with her. Last year they had a frightful visitation—the Daughter[6] and Niece

[1] D. W.'s cousin Mary, daughter of the Revd. Thomas Myers and widow of Admiral Hugh Robinson (see *EY*, p. 11). She lived at York.
[2] Presumably, from D. W.'s remarks later on, one of the younger daughters is meant, either Elizabeth (1792–1832), Hannah (1793–1834), or Julia (1796–1826). All died unmarried. See Genealogical Table, facing p. 704.
[3] One of the younger sons: either John (b. 1798), a naval chaplain; Jeremiah (1799–1836), an army officer in India; or Henry (1800–58), who became a solicitor at York. See Genealogical Table.
[4] i.e. John Myers, the barrister.
[5] Mary Ann (1789–1868). In 1832 she married the Revd. W. H. Dixon (1783–1854), vicar of Bishopthorpe and Canon Residentiary of York.
[6] Mary Catherine Ann Myers. She died unmarried.

in bed in the same room lay panic-struck during a storm of thunder, lightning and hail. They lay till the window frames were driven in and the lightning danced along the Bell wires—[?] quitted their rooms and found all the house in the same state and the next morning a heap of hail stones as large as a marble and four feet deep was found lodged in one of the sitting-rooms. What is wonderful neither man nor beast was hurt though all fruit, corn and young Buds were destroyed, and the lightning more than once entered the house following the bell-wires. This only daughter of his was stung by a Viper and her life despaired of two years ago. These are awful visitations, and with the death of his Brother I think must have softened him. He seems very tenderly disposed towards Julia Myers[1] and I doubt not will do his duty as her Guardian and protector. Mrs Robinson is delighted with Miss Dowling's school and Julia is to remain there. She and Dorothy spent their holidays here very happily and as happily are now enjoying the quiet and regularity of school. Dorothy is a sweet girl and I trust will be a constant comfort when she comes home, which will be next Christmas. She improves in music; she likes it; but will never be a fine player, it is however enough for us if she can amuse herself and her Friends. I think she will draw well with practice. She has a great wish to sketch from Nature and begins very prettily. John has gone back to school—His industry is unexampled.—I have had very nice letters from my Nephews at Cambridge. My Brother C is quite well and determined (God willing!) to bring the Boys into the North next summer. We have had a few weeks of rainy weather, now succeeded by summer heat—most delightful. Hills and vales are as green as Emeralds—the country is much more woody than it used to be, as I am sure you will say when you come. We were in Windermere the day before yesterday—with the Robinsons, and splendid as was the Lake, we all preferred the green vale of Grasmere and its tiny lake. Tillbrooke only stayed 5 days with us—He was in good spirits in spite of family distresses, and intends to take his house[2] into his own hands the year after next. *So* long the Gees will remain beside us, and we have now other pleasant neighbours very near; but they will not long abide, a Mr Quillinan[3]

[1] Thomas Myers's niece. See L. 2 above.
[2] i.e. Ivy Cottage.
[3] Edward Quillinan (1791–1851), W. W.'s future son-in-law. Son of an Irish wine merchant of Oporto, and educated a Roman Catholic, he saw active service with the dragoons during the Peninsular War, and later published several volumes of verse and engaged in controversy with John Wilson and Lockhart. In 1817 he had married Jemima (1794–1822), second daughter of

married to a daughter of Sir Egerton Brydges. They are very
amiable. He is a clever man and a scholar—an officer on half-pay.
They keep a gig and horses and are very glad to make them useful
to us. We sit much out of doors as heretofore, read to William in
the shade—chat a little—saunter a little—and so on—and Sara
plants and tends her flowers. She is copying Mary's journal a second
time which you will be glad to see. It is much shorter than mine,
and therefore I think you will (and everybody else) find it more
entertaining.—Mine is written now, but not yet fit to be read by
others I write so carelessly; but when the *Season* is over and we are
quietly by ourselves again I shall rewrite it in a *plain hand*. This
you will hardly perhaps believe with the present specimen before
your eyes, yet you must remember that I *can* do this when I am
fairly resolved upon it. How often do I think of you and your
garden and your motes[1] and the old hall and the covering of vines.
Well should I like to pluck a Bunch of Grapes this Autumn! Give
my kindest love to Mr Clarkson—to Tom when you write and
as I am sure our names are familiar to Monsr La Roche, pray
present my regards and best wishes to him. My love to your Sister
and a kiss to her sweet Boy—and God Bless you dearest Friend—
I cannot read over this dull letter—so excuse blunders and write as
soon as ever you can to your

faithful and affectionate
D Wordsworth.

38. W. W. to VISCOUNT LOWTHER

MS. Lonsdale MSS. Hitherto unpublished.

Rydal Mount
Sep^{br} 2nd 1821

My dear Lord Lowther,

I shall have great pleasure in transferring the business to Faraday
and Grime,[2] if upon further enquiry I find them reported as proper
persons. After having been so deceived in the case of Bateman, you
will agree with me that I must not be hasty. From carelessness,

Sir Egerton Brydges of Denton Court, Kent (see *MY* ii. 169), and he was now
retired on half pay and living at Spring Cottage, Loughrigg (later The Stepping
Stones), with his wife and daughters, Jemima and Rotha. For his MS. account
of his first meeting with W. W. in May of this year, see Appendix I.
[1] i.e. the *moats* around Playford Hall.
[2] Of the Market Place, Kirkby Stephen.

timidity, and other causes, people are perpetually recommended by their neighbours, to situations for which they are quite unfit; but this case I hope will prove an exception.

I saw Mr Southey at Keswick yesterday. He has written to Mr Senhouse[1] to know when it will suit him to go to Lowther Castle and will let me know his answer. I shall meet them there, and hope you will not be gone.

Ever sincerely yours
my dear Lord L.—
W. W.

39. W. W. to WALTER SAVAGE LANDOR[2]

MS. Victoria and Albert Museum.
K (—). *LT i.* 47.

[*In M. W.'s hand*]

Rydal Mount, near Ambleside,
September 3ᵈ, 1821.

My dear Sir,

After waiting several months in the hope that an irritation in my eyes which has disabled me both from reading and writing would abate, I am at last obliged to address you by means of the pen of Mrs Wordsworth, which however I should not have had courage to do, had not an opportunity occurred of forwarding my letter by a private hand, that of my esteemed Friend Mr Kenyon who is not unknown to you. I felt myself much honoured by the present of your

---

[1] Humphrey Senhouse (1773–1842) of Netherhall, nr. Maryport: High Sheriff of Cumberland, 1826. See also *MT* ii. 338. The family dated back at least to the sixteenth century, but its fortunes had risen considerably in the eighteenth with the development of Maryport by Humphrey Senhouse's grandfather. See Southey, v. 91–3.

[2] Walter Savage Landor (1775–1864), author of the *Imaginary Conversations*, had removed himself from Trinity College, Oxford, and adopted republican principles, living off an allowance from his father until the latter's death in 1805 made him independent. In 1798 he published *Gebir* (2nd edn. and Latin version, 1803); in 1812 *Count Julian: A Tragedy*. Since 1815 he had been living in Italy, first at Pisa, and now Florence. He had met Southey in Bristol in 1808, and at Como in 1817, and through him received copies of W. W.'s *Excursion*, *White Doe of Rylstone*, and *Poems* of 1815, and Landor's evident admiration led W. W. to send him his next volumes. This opened the way for a regular correspondence, though the two poets did not meet until 1832. Landor's letters to W. W. (among the *WL MSS.*) are reprinted in full by R. H. Super, 'Landor's Letters to Wordsworth and Coleridge', *MP* lv (1957), 73–83.

book of Latin Poems,[1] and it arrived at a time when I had the use of my eyes for reading; and with great pleasure did I employ them in the perusal of the dissertation annexed to your Poems, which I read several times—but the Poems themselves I have not been able to look into, for I was seized with a fit of composition at that time, and deferred the pleasure to which your Poems invited me, till I could give them an undivided attention; but alas the complaint in my eyes, to which I have been occasionally subject for several years past, suddenly returned and I have since suffered from it as already mentioned. I have also to thank you for a letter[2] containing several miscellaneous observations in which I had the satisfaction of concurring.

We live here somewhat singularly circumstanced—in solitude during nearly nine months of the year, and for the rest in a round of engagements. I have nobody near me who reads Latin, so that I can only speak of your Essay from recollection. You will not perhaps be surprized when I state that I differ from you in opinion as to the propriety of the Latin language being employed by Moderns for works of taste and imagination. Miserable would have been the lot of Dante, Ariosto, and Petrarch, if they had preferred the Latin to their Mother tongue (there is, by-the-by, a Latin translation of Dante[3] which you do not seem to know), and what could Milton, who was surely no mean master of the Latin tongue, have made of his Paradise Lost, had that vehicle been employed instead of the language of the Thames and Severn! Should we even admit that all modern dialects are comparatively changeable, and therefore limited in their efficacy, may not the sentiment which Milton so pleasingly expresses when he says he is content to be read in his Native Isle only, be extended to durability, and is it not more desirable to be read with affection and pride, and familiarly for five hundred years, by all orders of minds, and all ranks of people, in your native tongue, than only by a few scattered Scholars for the space of three thousand? My own special infirmity moreover gives me an especial right to urge this argument—had your Idylliums been in English I should long ere this have been as well acquainted with them as with your Gebir, and with your other

[1] *Idyllia heroica decem*, Pisa, 1820, to which is appended an essay *De Cultu atque Usu Latini Sermonis*.

[2] Landor's letter of thanks, 23 Sept. 1820, had commented on W. W.'s views on planting in his *Topographical Description of the Country of the Lakes*, and described his own feelings on selling off his family estates. 'Your poem on Repentance has harmonised all this . . .'

[3] *Della Commedia di Dante Alighieri. Transportata in verso latino eroico da Carlo d'Aquino* . . . 3 vols., [Rome], 1728.

Poems—and now I know not how long they may remain to me
a sealed book.

I met with a hundred things in your Dissertation that fell in with
my own sentiments and judgments; but there are many opinions
which I should like to talk over with you. The ordonnance of your
Essay might, I think, be improved, and several of the separate
remarks, upon Virgil in particular, though perfectly just, would
perhaps have been better placed in notes or an appendix; they are
details that obstruct the view of the whole. Vincent Bourne[1]
surely is not so great a favourite with you as he ought to be,
though I acknowledge there is ground for your objection upon the
score of ultra *concinnity* (a queer word for a female pen, Mrs W.
has boggled at it) yet this applies only to a certain portion of his
longs and shorts. Are you not also penurious in your praise of
Gray? The fragment at the commencement of his fourth book,[2] in
which he laments the death of West,[3] in cadence and sentiment,
touches me in a manner for which I am grateful. The first book also
of the same Poem appears to me as well executed as anything of
that kind is likely to be. Is there not a speech of Solon to which the
concluding couplet of Gray's sonnet bears a more pointed resemblance than to any of the passages you have quoted? He was told,
not to grieve for the loss of his son, as tears would be of no avail;
'and for that very reason,' replied he, 'do I weep.'[4] It is high time I
should thank you for the honourable mention you have made of
me.[5] It could not but be grateful to me to be praised by a Poet
who has written verses of which I would rather have been the
Author than of any produced in our time. What I now write to you,
I have frequently said to many. Were I able to recur to your book
I should trespass further upon your time, which, however, might
prove little to your advantage. I saw Mr Southey yesterday at his

[1] Vincent Bourne (1695–1747), Fellow of Trinity College, Cambridge
(1720), and master at Westminster School, published *Poemata, latine partim
reddita, partim scripta*, 1734. Lamb had praised his poetry in a letter to W. W.
of 1815 (see *Lamb*, ii. 154; and iii. 319).

[2] Of Gray's fragmentary Latin poem *De Principiis Cogitandi*.

[3] Richard West (1716–42), schoolfellow of Gray and Horace Walpole at
Eton, and a poet of promise, died of consumption at an early age.

[4] Landor had discussed (*Idyllia heroica*, p. 186) the source of the last lines of
Gray's sonnet *On the Death of Richard West*: 'I fruitless mourn to him, that
cannot hear,/ And weep the more because I weep in vain.' In his reply of
22 Feb. 1822, Landor agreed that Solon's speech was doubtless the source, but
that the actual debt was more probably to verse than to prose, and that Gray
was copying the Italian 'Mi piango più perchè mi piango indarno'.

[5] In his essay (p. 215), Landor had addressed W. W. as 'vir, civis, philo-
sophe, poeta, praestantissime! qui saeculum nostrum ut nullo priore minus
gloriosum sit effeceris'.

own house—he has not had his usual portion of relaxation this summer, and looked, I thought, a little pale in consequence—his little Boy[1] is a stout and healthy Child and his other Children have in general good health, tho' at present a little relaxed by the few days of extreme heat. With best wishes for your health and happiness,

I remain, my dear sir, sincerely yours,
[*signed*] Wm Wordsworth

40. W. W. to VISCOUNT LOWTHER

MS. Lonsdale MSS. Hitherto unpublished.

Rydal Mount
Septbr 7th 1821

My dear Lord Lowther,

I am truly obliged by your most friendly and ready notice of my communication respecting the Charter House.[2] I have been informed that there was no admission upon the Foundation after the age of 12 but my Son says, that Boys are admitted between the ages of 10—and 14; if so, I shall have a better chance of profiting by the exertions you are disposed to make in my Son's favor, and by Lord Lonsdale's influence. Though having had this matter at heart for a long time I had resolved never to apply to my friends of the Lowther name; being a person who has never regarded one substantial Favor, and important service, as a ground for applying for another; but you will not wonder, that I am under apprehension as to the proposed changes, and there was not time to lose, on account of my Son's age.

I have written to the Head Master of the School Dr Russel,[3] for information as to which of the Governors have the next and succeeding presentations, and other particulars.

Ever yours thankfully
my dear Lord Lowther
your obliged friend and Servnt
Wm Wordsworth

[1] Cuthbert, b. Feb. 1819.
[2] See L. 31 above.
[3] The Revd. John Russell. See *MY* ii. 513.

41. W. W. to VISCOUNT LOWTHER

MS. Lonsdale MSS. Hitherto unpublished.

Rydal Mount
14 Sept[r] 1821

My dear Lord Lowther,

Dr Russel informs me that a Boy is admissible to the Charter-house Foundation, till the age of 14;[1] my Son was eleven last May. The next presentation is with the King; I begged Dr Russel to inform me respecting the succeeding ones, but he has neglected to do it.

James Brougham[2] talking lately with Calvert[3] upon the subject of Ministers stripping themselves of Patronage, said, that they, viz, the Opposition, had a right to goad the Ministers to do foolish things, and then laugh at them!

Ever my dear Lord Lowther
faithfully yours
W. Wordsworth

42. W. W. and M. W. to JOHN KENYON

Address: John Kenyon Esq[re], Leamington.
MS. untraced.
Transactions of the Wordsworth Society, no. 6, p. 83. K. LT i. 50.

[*In M. W.'s hand*]

Rydal Mount, Sept. 22[d], 1821.

My dear Sir,

My eyes are better than when you were here, but an amanuensis is still expedient, and Mrs W. therefore writes for me to the whistling of as melancholy a wind as ever blew, coming as it does after a long series of broken weather, which has been injurious to the harvest, and when we were calculating upon a change for the better. The season with us has been much less unfavourable, I fear, than in many other parts,—though our exercise has never been altogether prevented, and we have had some beautiful days. Two schemes of 'particular pleasure' have been frustrated thus far, a 2[d] trip to Borrowdale—including the summit of Scawfell—and,

---

[1] See previous letter. This rule had disqualified John W. from admission to the Charterhouse in 1819 (see *MT* ii. 519).
[2] See *MT* ii. 420.
[3] i.e. William Calvert of Greta Bank, brother of Raisley. See *ET*, p. 97.

for my daughter and her school-companions, an excursion to Furness Abbey. Anxiously have they looked in vain for steadily bright weather—thinking, poor things, little about the spoiling of the crops by the damp days, rains, and winds.

Since your departure we have seen no Persons of note except Dr Holland,[1] the Albanian Traveller, and otherwise less agreeably distinguished. We have two additional neighbours (not to speak of the new-born Rotha, for that name the infant is to bear in honour of the stream upon whose banks she was born) under Mr Quillinan's roof, in the persons of Colonel Holmes[2] and his lady, sister to Mrs Q. The Col is a good-natured old soldier, who has risen without purchase to his present rank, and stood the brunt of war in the Peninsula and in America. At Ambleside there was a *gay* ball; for such it appeared to many contributors to its splendour but not so to the paradoxical lady of Calgarth:[3] *she* thought nothing of it, because there was no gentleman there, *as she said,* 'above five feet 8 inches,'—though there were present two handsome officers, one a Waterloo Medalist, and both of good stature. This Lady's ideal of a partner, and such she hoped to meet—is a '*tall* slender person with black hair and a bald front'—what a pity that you, or your Brother, could not have been put into a stretching Machine, and conveyed to Ambleside by steam, through the air, or under the Earth. Fashion and fancy, I can assure you, run high in this neighbourhood as to these matters.

At Keswick resides a Miss Stanger, her Father[4] a Cheapside Trader who has built a house near the Vicarage: this Lady, celebrated for beauty, enviable for fortune, would not allow that a Ball could be mustered at Keswick by all the Collegians there—'send for

[1] Sir Henry Holland, Bart. (1788–1873), physician, related through his mother to the Wedgwood family, and a cousin of Mrs. Gaskell the novelist. In 1815 he published *Travels in the Ionian Isles, Albania, Thessaly, Macedonia, etc., during 1812 and 1813* (2nd edn., 1819). His 'less agreeable distinction' was that he had been medical attendant to the Princess of Wales, later Queen Caroline, and in 1820 testified before the Parliamentary Committee that, so far as he had seen, her conduct with Bergami had been free from impropriety. In his later years he was a well-known figure in London society. His second wife was the elder daughter of Sydney Smith, and author of the *Memoir* of her father.

[2] Col. George Holmes, C.B. (d. 1833), of the dragoons, who had married Elizabeth (d. 1853), eldest daughter of Sir Egerton Brydges, in 1817. His epitaph in Doncaster Parish Church was composed by E. Q. See his *Poems . . . with a Memoir by William Johnston,* 1853, p. 215.

[3] i.e. Mrs. Watson, widow of the Bishop of Llandaff, who lived at Calgarth Hall (see *MY* ii. 332).

[4] James Stanger (1796–1866) of St. Anne's Hill, Wandsworth, and Lairthwaite, Keswick, an estate adjoining Crosthwaite Church: philanthropist and Evangelical churchman.

a parcel of officers from Carlisle,' said she, 'and then something may be done.' What a slight upon the gown, and from a Blue-stocking Lady too, who is an Eléve of Mrs Grant[1] of the Mountains! 'Come, come,' said she to a young Oxonian, 'let us walk out this evening that I may catch a cold, and have an excuse for not going to the thing!' [*S. H. adds: Not true*, she said the Ball. S. H.]

Dear Mr Kenyon,

Writing in my own name, I thank you, while William is taking a turn, after dictating the above flourish, for your agreeable and acceptable present which was duly received. The Chart shall be forwarded to the address, as soon as we can procure any that we know to be excellent. I shall anxiously expect your *next commission*, which I hope will be to look out for a house—by-the-bye Mr. Gee has taken one at Keswick so it will be well to know what Mr Tillbrook means to do with the Ivy Cot, which will be vacant next Whitsuntide. But I must not consume more space, as W. is not done. Very sincerely yours,

Willy leaves us to-morrow.

M. W.

[*W. W. adds*]

I was going to say something about your tour, but Mrs W. tells me that what I meant to speak of was mentioned when you were here, so nothing remains but good wishes in which all my family join, both to yourself and to your brother, who stands in particular need of them if he meditates Marriage.

Very affectionately yours,
Wm Wordsworth

43. W. W. to LORD LONSDALE

MS. Lonsdale MSS. Hitherto unpublished.

Monday morning 24th [Sept. 1821]
My Lord,

Mr Senhouse[2] of Netherall is now at Mr Southey's, and Saturday next is the day they promise themselves the pleasure of being at

[1] Mrs. Anne Grant of Laggan (1755–1838), author of the popular *Letters from the Mountains*, 3 vols., 1806. Her beliefs were markedly Evangelical. See J. P. Grant, *Memoir and Correspondence of Mrs Grant of Laggan*, 3 vols., 1844. [2] See L. 38 above.

Lowther, should it suit your Lordship to receive them. I shall be happy to meet them there, if the state of my eyes will allow me; but lately they have been so much distressed by Candlelight, that I am afraid of going into Company; but Lady Lonsdale is very indulgent and will allow me to retire if I cannot bear the light for any length of time.

We have here an unquestioned report that Mr Curwen is about to marry a Daughter of Willan the Horsedealer;[1] he is Uncle to our neighbour of Blue notoriety, Mrs Edmunds,[2] who, perhaps upon the strength of this alliance, appeared with her Daughter, as I am told, at a Ball in Ambleside, dressed in a fantastic style of expense, which amused and astonished the gayest of the Party.

I hope Lady Frederic[3] is still at Lowther, and in good health.

ever my Lord
most sincerely yours
Wm Wordsworth

44. W. W. to LORD LONSDALE

MS. Lonsdale MSS. Hitherto unpublished.

Rydal Mount
Oct^{br} 16th 1821

My Lord,

Sincerely do I thank you and Lady Lonsdale for your prompt exertions in my behalf.[4] I am sensible also of Lord Camden's[5]

[1] For Jacob Willan and his daughter, see *SH*, p. 223. He was a freeholder of Underbarrow, nr. Kendal, and owned a livery stable in London.

[2] For Edmunds, the Ambleside Attorney, see *MY* ii. 515.

[3] Lady Mary Lowther (d. 1863), Lord Lonsdale's second daughter, had married Maj.-Gen. Lord Frederick Cavendish Bentinck (1781–1828), youngest son of the 3rd Duke of Portland, the previous autumn. See *MY* ii. 643. He was M.P. for Weobley, 1812–24, and thereafter for Queenborough, Kent.

[4] i.e. to get Willy W. placed on the Foundation at the Charterhouse. Lady Lonsdale's brother was John Fane, 10th Earl of Westmorland (1759–1841), a distinguished Carthusian and powerful member of the Cabinet by virtue of his office of Lord Privy Seal, which he held almost continuously from 1798 until the end of Lord Liverpool's administration in 1827.

[5] John Jeffreys Pratt, 2nd Earl and 1st Marquess of Camden (1759–1840), governor of the Charterhouse since 1811, and one of the tellers of the exchequer, a post he held for the extraordinary period of sixty years, voluntarily giving up the growing emoluments of the office and receiving a vote of thanks from Parliament. He was Lord Lieutenant of Ireland in the troubled period leading up to Wolfe Tone's rebellion, Secretary of State for War under Pitt, and thereafter Lord President of the Council, but otherwise his political career was undistinguished. In 1834 he became Chancellor of Cambridge University.

favorable dispositions and obliging expressions. The Result has not caused me much disappointment; nor can I lament that I did not make my wishes earlier known to my Friends of the House of Lowther, as I could not have felt justified in applying for their assistance, had it not been for the course now pursuing in respect to the public office with which, through your Lordship's patronage, I am connected.

Mrs Wordsworth returns her respectful acknowledgements for the present of game.

The Report concerning Mr Curwen's marriage seems dying away.

What enchanting weather we now have!

Ever my Lord
most faithfully your obliged Friend and Servant
Wm Wordsworth

45. W. W. to FRANCIS LEGATT CHANTREY

Address: Francis Chantry Esqre. [*Delivered by hand*]
Endorsed: October 1821 Wordsworth to Chauntrey.
MS. Dr. Williams's Library.
K. Morley, i. 104.

Rydal Mount Octr. 1821

My dear Sir

If I recollect right I ordered 7 Casts—one of them was intended for the Bearer of this, my Friend Mr Robinson—he wishes to have another, and possibly more, with which I beg he may be furnished and for which himself will pay, and give directions whither they are to be sent. If I am not mistaken the price which the person making these casts charges is 4 Guineas—allow me to ask whether in case 15 or 20 were required he could not supply them at a lower rate for the accommodation of my Friends—

Since my last I have heard from Sir George Beaumont[1] who expresses himself in the highest terms of the Bust—and adds a world of most agreeable things concerning its Author, both as an Artist and a Man—which it would give me pleasure to repeat but I spare your blushes—

[1] See L. 34 above.

THOMAS MONKHOUSE
from a portrait by Richard Carruthers, 1817

I have requested Mr Carruthers[1] who painted a Portrait of me some years ago, to call for a sight of the Bust—He is an amiable young Man whom a favorable opening induced to sacrifice the Pencil to the Pen—not the pen of Authorship—he is too wise for that—but the pen of the Counting House which he is successfully driving at Lisbon—I remain, with sincere regards from Mrs W. and my Sister to yourself and Mrs Chantry,

most faithfully
Yours—
Wm Wordsworth

46. D. W. to CATHERINE CLARKSON

Address: Mrs Clarkson, Playford Hall, Ipswich, Suffolk.
Postmark: [?28] Oct. 1821. *Stamp*: Kendal Penny Post.
MS. British Museum.
K (—). *LY i. 52.*

Rydal Mount Wednesday Oct 24th [1821]

My dearest Friend,

Shamefully indeed have I delayed from day to day to thank you for your great kindness in sending me the old letter with the interesting account of poor La Roche's[2] sorrow for the death of his Mother. It was indeed an affecting sight for you to see him struggle with mental agony, when you had cause to think his body could so ill bear it—I trust you have had happy tidings from him since he left you, and hope you may meet again in England before his departure from this country. How Sorrow and Friendship must have endeared the soil to him!—Your last letter was indeed a treasure; such a long one! and every bit of it interesting! but that is nothing new—Your letters are always so. What a splendid figure does 'Playford Hall the seat of Thomas Clarkson Esqre' make in every London, in every provincial newspaper! If you could see the lively picture I shaped to myself of the sable Queen[3] sitting with

---

[1] Richard Carruthers (1792–1876) gave up art for a career in business, and retired *c.* 1840 with a small fortune to Crosby-on-Eden, nr. Carlisle. His portrait of W. W. (see *MY* ii. 402; *SH*, pp. 111, 115) was commissioned in 1817 by Thomas Monkhouse, who also sat to the artist himself. See Frances Blanchard, *Portraits of Wordsworth*, 1959, pp. 53–8.   [2] See L. 37 above.

[3] Madame Christophe and her daughters had now escaped from Haiti to England. Their arrival at Playford Hall was reported in the *Courier* for 15 Oct. For Thomas Clarkson's own account of his difficulties in accommodating them, see his letter to Zachary Macaulay, quoted by Griggs in *Thomas Clarkson, The Friend of Slaves*, pp. 144–6.

her sable daughters beside you on the sofa in my dear little Parlour at Playford you would thank the newspapers for being so communicative respecting your visitors! I placed them in the *little* parlour because it is always first in my thoughts when I turn them thither; but Sara says 'No, they will sit in the great room.' I was forced to accede and now my Fancy espies them through the window of the court upon the larger Sofa—them and you—and your dear Husband talking French to them with his old loving-kindness. I hope they are good and grateful—and know the value of such a Friend.—If so they have won their way into your heart, and you will have comfort and pleasure while they are with you. All this I want to know, and how you spend your time—what they think of England, and rural life;—the splendours of Royalty and presentations and Balls left so far behind. You will also tell us what you gather of Christophe's character and private conduct, and whether there was a great change in him in that respect after he had the full and free exercise of regal power. A paragraph in the newspaper stating that Madame Christophe was to swear to her property (under £9,000) gave us great satisfaction. If she has no *more* property (but I hope she has more) this will at least support her and her Daughters; and it will save Mr Clarkson from a trouble and anxiety which we much feared would fall upon him. How busy you have been kept ever since I left you! and what a number of things you have furnished me to think about. When we sate so quietly by the fire-side (no visitor for a week together, but by chance Mr Biddel or Mr Walford[1]) we little thought that Playford Hall would soon be graced by the presence of a Queen! Does it not seem strange to you after all your thoughts and cares for this poor Family during their splendours and after their downfall you should see them seated in humble quiet, and happy comfort beside you! At the end of my letter I *must* copy a parody (which I hope will make you laugh) that William and Sara threw off last Sunday afternoon. They had been talking of Mr Clarkson's perseverance in the *African* cause—*especially* of his kindness to every human being and of this last act of kindness to the distressed Negro Widow and her Family. Withal tender thoughts of merriment came with the image of the sable princess by your fire-side. The first stanza of Ben Johnson's poem slipped from W's lips in a parody—and together they finished it with much loving fun—Oh! how they laughed. I heard them into my Room upstairs, and wondered what they were about—and when it was finished I claimed the privilege

[1] A Playford neighbour.

of sending it to you. Sara and I are alone. William and Mary left us this morning to spend a week at Keswick, and I am glad of this as he has had three weeks of labour in poetry, and I should fear that his eyes may suffer without a little pause. They are very much amended, and I do not think he has been at all the worse for his labour. He cannot bear the full light of a candle; nor can he read at all by candle-light. Sara will write I think, very soon, because she often reproaches herself for her idleness; but she is not a person who makes promises either to me or to anyone else, therefore I cannot answer for her. It seems not probable that she will go southward this winter, as Mrs Monkhouse is to have one of her sisters with her previous to and during her confinement and they will not have room for her—At least so we think, though the last time Mr M wrote he said they hoped to see her. They have left Wales—Mrs Hutchinson writes in better spirits. She is now so used to losses and disasters that she has learned to bear them chearfully. Mr Lewis[1] has refused to lower their Rent and to permit them to leave the Farm, so they must make the best of it. Though he has refused to lower their Rent, there seems reason to hope that he will not persist. Henry Robinson left us far too quickly. We very much enjoyed his company,[2] and had many a pleasant retracing of his travels. He read Mary's journal of that part of the journey, after he came,[3] with comments; and was greatly delighted with its minuteness and faithfullness; and liveliness of observation.—Of mine he read all that I had recopied—and though he had not been our companion in that part of the Tour, he was much interested. I am hard at work with it, and if you can summon half the patience I have had and must yet have, when we meet you shall travel along with us—but you will be frightened when you see so many pages— all written about the outside of things hastily viewed! Nothing could surely be more tiresome if it were not for personal regards. Dorothy will be at home in two short months. She is a sweet creature—no beauty now but interesting to look upon, though her health is by no means *established*. She looks puffy and heavy, and is indeed far from being right in all respects, though she makes no

---

[1] Sir Thomas Frankland Lewis, 1st Bart. (1780–1855), of Harpton Court, Radnor: M.P. for Beaumaris (1812–26), Ennis (1826–8), Radnorshire (1828–35), and Radnor borough (from 1847): successively Secretary of the Treasury, Vice-President of the Board of Trade, Treasurer of the Navy, and Commissioner of the Poor Law. He was made a Baronet in 1846.

[2] H. C. R. had spent September in Scotland. On the way back he called at Greta Hall, and spent four days (5–8 Oct.) at Ambleside and Rydal Mount. See *HCR* i. 270–3.

[3] See *MY* ii. 615.

complaints. Willy writes that he is quite well. How I wish you may see him! We are anxious and uneasy, he is so very idle at his Books—No improvement last year. Sara Coleridge's translation[1] is out but not yet come to us. A wonderful work of perseverance. My kindest love to Mr C and the same to Tom when you write. I hope he will come to see the Queen of Hayti at Playford. God Bless you my dearest Friend. Pray write and tell us all particulars. Yours ever D. W.

Ben Johnson's poem begins 'Queen and Huntress chaste and fair', you *must* know it.

> Queen and Negress chaste and fair!
> Christophe now is laid to sleep
> Seated in a British Chair
> State in humbler manner keep
> Shine for Clarkson's pure delight
> Negro Princess, Ebon-Bright!
>
> Let not *'Wilby's' holy shade
> Interpose at Envy's call
> Hayti's shining Queen was made
> To illumine Playford Hall
> Bless it then with constant light
> Negress excellently bright!

3rd Stanza.

> Lay thy diadem apart
> Pomp has been a sad deceiver
> Through thy champion's faithful heart
> Joy be poured, and thou the Giver
> Thou that makest a day of night
> Sable Princess, Ebon-Bright!

*Mrs Wilberforce calls her Husband by that pretty diminutive 'Wilby'—you must have heard her.

---

[1] *An account of the Abipones, an equestrian people of Paraguay. From the Latin of M[artin] D[obrizhoffer]*, 3 vols., 1822. See *Minnow Among Tritons*, pp. 88–9. 'God love her—', wrote Charles Lamb to Bernard Barton, 'to think that she should have had to toil thro' five octavos of that cursed . . . Abbey-pony History, and then to abridge them to 3, and all for £113. At her years, to be doing stupid Jesuits' Latin into English, when she should be reading or writing Romances.' (*Lamb*, ii. 370.) S.T.C. later declared that Sara's translation was 'unsurpassed for pure mother English by anything I have read for a long time' (*Table Talk*, 4 Aug. 1832).

You say that Mr C willingly thinks of coming to see us—and next Summer! Keep him to it I pray you my dear Friend. I shall long for a letter from you so you *must* find time to write.

47. D. W. to H. C. R.

Address: To H. C. Robinson Esqre, 3 King's Bench Walk, Temple.
MS. Dr. Williams's Library.
K (—). *Morley, i. 105.*

Friday Night
24th November [1821]

My dear Friend,
The three or four days after you left us were most provokingly sunny and delightful—I cannot say that we have had much vexation of the like kind since that time;—for the rain has day by day fallen in torrents with a chance twenty-four hours of fine weather between; and we consoled ourselves as well as we could for our mortification in having lost you before the fine weather came, in thinking that it would make your journey pleasant on the outside of the coach; and also in remembering how chearful and merry we were in spite of wind and rain during the short time you were with us. I write now, because I can send a letter post free,—and because I have to ask your advice for a young Man, the son of our Friend Mrs Cookson of Kendal, who is in the last year of his Clerkship with a Solicitor at Kendal, and is looking forward to his removal to London.[1] Will you be so good as to point out what seems to you most likely to be serviceable in the regulation of his views? And perhaps you may know some respectable Solicitor who may be inclined to take him into his office. Mr Strickland Cookson is a remarkably steady and sensible young Man, very attentive to business, and has I doubt not given great satisfaction to his present Master,—and you already know from us that he is come of good Parents. He has no particular wish to settle in the country, after his Clerkship, rather the contrary, though we think that he would have a better chance than most young men in his native Town. If there should be an opening for him in London he would prefer settling there.

I mention these circumstances that you may be the better able to judge what kind of practice for the time he has yet to serve may

---

[1] Strickland Cookson, later W. W.'s solicitor, was articled the following year to Richard Addison (see *MY* i. 366), formerly partner to R. W., as D. W. anticipates later on in this letter.

be most likely to profit him; and perhaps in thinking the matter over you may hit upon some judicious Friend or acquaintance in the Law who may be glad to take such a young Man into his service.—

I should have continued to wait yet a week or two longer in hopes of a letter from you, but for the present opportunity—You know you had several matters to write about.—Do not forget the pulpit at Brussels, and if you have any notes respecting Milan Cathedral, I should be grateful if you would send them. We have been going on in much the same way as when you were with us, only my poor Sisters motions are sadly cramped by the lameness in her Toe. So far from being in a condition to climb St Gothard at present, She is obliged to be indebted to the Ass or Mr Quillinan's gig if she would go much more than a mile from home. We hope, however, that as the enlargement of the joint seems to have yielded in some degree to twice blistering and bleeding, she may, by perseverance in that course, advised by a medical Man, again have the free use of both her feet. She has little or no pain except from using the foot too much. My Brother's eyes are no worse—I think rather better. He has written some beautiful poems[1] since you left us, which as Miss Hutchinson has transcribed them for Mr Monkhouse you will have an opportunity of seeing—I am sure they will delight both you and him. The Sonnets[2] have been at rest.

Poor Mrs Quillinan has been removed to Lancaster;[3] and you will be sorry to hear that her mind is not more settled than when Mrs W. was attending upon her, though she is less turbulent. Her eldest little Girl is with Mrs Gee; and her Husband at present gone to visit her. My Brother accompanied Mr Q. on a Tour[4] to the Caves, Studley Park, Knaresborough and York, and this was of

[1] *Memorials of a Tour on the Continent, 1820* (*PW* iii. 164 ff.), published in 1822. See L. 55 below.

[2] i.e. the *Ecclesiastical Sketches*.

[3] Mrs. Quillinan was undergoing mental treatment at Lancaster after the birth of Rotha the previous spring, and E. Q., in a distraught state, had left Rydal for Lancashire. His unpublished Diaries (*WL MSS.*) record his restlessness: [Liverpool, 23 Nov.] 'What am I doing here? Without object, without motive except the vain hope of beguiling this dreadful anxiety by movements and change of place. I have left my romantic cottage in the mountains, and my children, and kind and valuable friends, for the smoke and dirt and noisy cheerless bustle of this over grown Mart, where I am alone in the midst of thousands.' But by 20 Dec. he was back in Rydal: his wife made a good recovery in the new year (see *SH*, p. 229), and by the following March the family was reunited and had moved into the Ivy Cottage.

[4] E. Q.'s incomplete MS. Diary records that they left Rydal on 3 Nov., and visited Kirkby Lonsdale, Sedbergh (where they saw John W. and Henry Wilkinson), Leyburn, Middleham Castle, Jervaulx Abbey, Masham, Ripon, Studley, and Fountains Abbey—where the entries break off on 6 Nov.

great service to the forlorn husband, who is sadly unsettled at home. My Brother very much enjoyed his Tour; and this reminds me that both we at home, and they, had a whole week of fine weather. Shame on my treacherous and ungrateful memory!—I have not had a single line from my dear and good Friend Mrs Clarkson since Playford Hall had the honour of becoming a royal Residence;[1] and we have been anxious to hear how the parties were satisfied with each other on nearer acquaintance.—Mrs C. talked of going to London before Christmas; and perhaps she is there now, for as the papers tell us the Queen and Princesses have left Playford. Pray if you have any tidings of her tell us.—

It gave us great concern to hear of the death of John Lamb;[2] Though his Brother and Sister did not see very much of him the loss will be deeply felt; pray tell us particularly how they are; and give our kind love to them. I fear Charles's pen will be stopped for a time. What delightful papers he has lately written for that otherwise abominable magazine![3] The Old King's Benchers is exquisite—indeed the only one I do not quite like is the Grace before Meat.

I hope you see the Monkhouses often, though he is become a home-stayer. I cannot express how it would grieve me if any thing should prevent their intended journey next summer. It seemed quite unnatural not to have him amongst us during some part of the last.

I wish you may have seen Willy when you write; but I am well aware of the trouble of making calls for a man of business in London.—You must excuse this worthless scrawl. It is near eleven o'clock—I have yet another letter to write, and the packet is to go

[1] See previous letter.

[2] 'Nov. 18th . . . I stepped into the Lambs' cottage at Dalston. Mary pale and thin, just recovered from one of her attacks. They have lost their brother John and feel their loss. They seemed softened by affliction and to wish for society.' (*HCR* i. 276.) John Lamb (1763–1821), who died on 26 Oct., had drifted apart from his younger brother and sister long before this, after the tragic death of their mother. He entered the South-Sea House as a clerk in the early 1780s, prospered, and *c.* 1805 became Accountant, taking up residence in Threadneedle St. In 1815 he acquired the portrait of Milton (see *MY* ii. 239 and *Lamb*, ii. 154, 159) which he bequeathed to Charles Lamb, and which is now in the New York Public Library. While for Talfourd he was 'John Lamb the jovial and burly', H. C. R. found him 'grossly rude and vulgar'; but a fuller portrait of him as 'James Elia' had recently appeared in Lamb's essay 'My Relations' (*London Magazine*, iii (June 1821), 611–14), and he was to be recalled among childhood memories in 'Dream Children' (v (Jan. 1822), 21–3).

[3] The *Essays of Elia* were continuing to appear in the *London Magazine* throughout 1821 and 1822. The essays mentioned here were published in iv (Sept. and Nov. 1821), 279–84, 469–72.

early in the morning.—My Brother and Sister and Miss Hutchinson send their best wishes and remembrances.

Believe me,

dear Friend and Fellow traveller,

Yours faithfully

Dorothy Wordsworth.

Have you been able to forward my letters to Rome and Paris[1] through your Friend? If not, I hope you have already paid the postage—but should you still have them pray do so even yet; for as they contain no News they will answer their purpose.—Better late than never.—

I have been reading to my Brother what I had written concerning Strickland Cookson, and he desires me to add that Mr Wilson[2] of Kendal whom he serves at present, has respectable connexions in London, among whom is Mr Addison of Staple Inn, Successor to, and formerly Partner with our late Brother; but it is thought here that it would be more advantageous to the young Man to be placed in an office where he might meet with more extensive practice.

Among the poems is one to the Memory of poor Goddard,[3] which probably would never have been written but for your suggestion.—How often do I think of that night when you first introduced that interesting youth to us!—At this moment I see in my mind's eye the lighted salon—you in your great Coat, and the two[4] slender tall figures following you!

My Brother says that you will probably like to have yourself a copy of the Stanzas above-mentioned; and also you promised to seek an opportunity, (if ever it should be composed,) to send this tribute to poor Goddard's memory, to his Mother in America. [*W. W. adds*: By no means read the poem to any Verse-writer—or *Magazine Scribbler*] Have you seen the Edinburgh Magazine[5] with

---

[1] i.e. to Lady Beaumont and the Baudouins.

[2] There were several solicitors of this name in Kendal: W. W. is probably referring to Isaac Wilson, whose talents he came to admire during the 1818 election, and who eventually rose to be Mayor of Kendal in 1832; or to the younger Mr. Wilson of Messrs. James Wilson and Son. For both, see *MY* ii. 418.

[3] *Elegiac Stanzas* (*PW* iii. 193), in memory of Frederick Warren Goddard (or Frederick *William*, as H. C. R. miscalled him). See *MY* ii. 642 and *HCR* i. 243, 247, 250.

[4] i.e. Goddard and his young friend Trotter. Alexander Trotter (1804–65) came of an old Midlothian family: entered St. John's College, Cambridge, 1822; and met H. C. R. again later in life as a fellow member of the Athenaeum. See *HCR* ii. 615.

[5] i.e. *Blackwood's*, in which there appeared in Oct. 1821 (x. 243–62) five letters entitled *A Selection from Mr Coleridge's Literary Correspondence with Friends, and Men of Letters*. They are somewhat desultory, as Morley notes, but there is no doubt about the authorship. See Griggs, v. 166.

the articles signed S. T. Coleridge? My Brother has not; for he will not suffer it to come into his house, as you know—but we females *have*—we found the Matter too dull to be read by us; mostly unintelligible, and think it cannot be Coleridges.

48. D. W. to H. C. R.

Address: To H. C. Robinson Esqre, 3 King's Bench Walk, Temple.
Postmark: 3 Dec. 1821. *Endorsed*: Novr 1821, Miss Wordsworth. Sent A^r.
1st March.
MS. Dr. Williams's Library.
K (—). *Morley, i. 109.*

[1 Dec. 1821]

A thousand thanks for your interesting letter, this moment arrived—Luckily the enclosed, was detained or I should not have been able to have told you how much pleasure your's has given us—yet we have been greatly shocked with the sad news of Mary Lamb's recent attack. It must have been *before* the death of her Brother;[1] and the awakening to that sorrow how very dismal. Your account of Charles is just what we expected—And are those articles *really* Coleridge's?[2] It was much more pleasant to me to accuse the Blackwoodites of having libelled him than to believe that he had really been a contributor to the Magazine—besides, there seems to me to be a perplexity—(and even a *poverty* often,) in the *style*, which do not belong to Coleridge—His matter is, God knows, often obscure enough, to unlearned Readers like me.

My Brother very often talks of you—and of our Tours *with* you— He has laid no Irish scheme, but most likely you will hear of one.

Your account of William gives great delight to all—yet we are lingering after tidings of the beginning of pains-taking at his Books.

God bless you!—Believe me your affectionate Friend

D Wordsworth.

No doubt the Letters were sent, as you do not name them— I am very glad you met with so good an opportunity for the needles etc[3]—and again I thank you for all kindnesses—

Saturday morning

This letter is a libel on Bramah's pens![4]

[1] i.e. John Lamb. See previous letter. [2] See previous letter.
[3] Presents for Annette Vallon and the Baudouins. See Morley, i. 105.
[4] In 1809 Bramah patented a machine for cutting a quill into separate nibs. This familiarized the public with the appearance and use of a nib slipped into a holder. (Morley's note.)

49. W. W. to JAMES LOSH[1]

MS. WL.
Mem. (—). Grosart (—). K (—). LY i. 56.
[In M. W.'s hand]

Rydal Mount, Decr 4th 1821.

My dear Losh,

Your letter enclosing the Prescription ought to have been much earlier acknowledged, and would have been so, had I not been sure you would ascribe my silence to its true cause, viz procrastination, and not to indifference to your kind attention. There was another feeling which both urged and indisposed me to write to you,—I mean the allusion which in so friendly a manner you make to a supposed change in my Political opinions. To the Scribblers in Pamphlets and Periodical publications who have heaped so much obloquy upon myself and my friends Coleridge and Southey, I have not condescended to reply, nor ever shall; but to you, my candid and enlightened Friend, I will say a few words on

---

[1] For W. W.'s early association with James Losh, see *EY*, pp. 185, 213, 219, 222–3, 225–7. Since the turn of the century Losh had been settled in Jesmond, a prominent figure in the political and cultural life of Newcastle, intimate with Grey and Brougham, and a staunch supporter of Parliamentary and educational reform—but debarred by his Unitarian beliefs from public office until the close of his life (he became Recorder of Newcastle in 1833). Though diverging in politics, W. W. and Losh had maintained their friendship, and his MS. Diaries (at Tullie House, Carlisle: published in part, ed. Edward Hughes, for the Surtees Society as *The Diary and Correspondence of James Losh 1811–1833*, 2 vols., 1962–3) record several meetings between the two in their later years; and they dined together at Woodside shortly before Losh's death. The genesis of the present letter lies in Losh's visit of 12 Sept.: 'I called upon my old friend W. Wordsworth, the poet. He looks thin and old but is, I believe, in good health and seems to be contented with his situation. We both (from the wish I have no doubt to avoid unpleasant discussion) avoided the subjects either of general or local politics.' (*Diary*, i. 138.) But in an otherwise conciliatory letter on 7 Oct. Losh did refer specifically to a 'change' that had come over W. W.'s views: 'They tell me you have changed your opinions upon many subjects respecting which we used to think alike; but I am persuaded we shall neither of us change those great principles which ought to guide us in our conduct, and lead us to do all the good we can to others. And I am much mistaken if we should not find many things to talk about without disturbing ourselves with political or party disputes.' (*Mem.* ii. 22–3.) W. W.'s reply is a full and careful defence of his political philosophy, which he regarded as important enough to keep by him; for the only surviving MS. is a draft, or more likely a copy, of the letter actually sent. But his argument did not convince Losh who recorded on 7 Dec.: 'I received a long letter from my old friend William Wordsworth (the Poet) containing a laboured but (in my opinion) very unsuccessful apology for his political *apostacy*. Towards me, however, he expresses himself in the most friendly terms and I mean to reply to him in a mild but decided manner.' (*Diary*, i. 144.) Losh's reply, if sent, has not survived.

this Subject, which, if we have the good fortune to meet again, as I hope we may, will probably be further dwelt upon.

I should think that I had lived to little purpose if my notions on the subject of Government had undergone no modification—my youth must, in that case, have been without enthusiasm, and my manhood endued with small capability of profiting by reflexion. If I were addressing those who have dealt so liberally with the words Renegado, Apostate etc, I should retort the charge upon them, and say, *you* have been deluded by Places and Persons, while I have stuck to Principles—I abandoned France, and her Rulers, when they abandoned the struggle for Liberty, gave themselves up to Tyranny, and endeavoured to enslave the world. I disapproved of the war against France at its commencement, thinking, which was perhaps an error, that it might have been avoided—but after Buonaparte had violated the Independence of Switzerland, my heart turned against him, and the Nation that could submit to be the Instrument of such an outrage. Here it was that I parted, in feeling, from the Whigs, and to a certain degree united with their Adversaries, who were free from the delusion (such I must ever regard it) of Mr Fox and his Party, that a safe and honourable Peace was practicable with the French Nation, and that an ambitious Conqueror like B[uonaparte] could be softened down into a commercial Rival. In a determination, therefore, to aim at the overthrow of that inordinate Ambition by War, I sided with the Ministry, not from general approbation of their Conduct, but as men who thought right on this essential point. How deeply this question interested me will be plain to any one who will take the trouble of reading my political Sonnets, and the Tract occasioned by the Convention of Cintra, in which are sufficient evidences of my dissatisfaction with the mode of conducting the war, and a prophetic display of the course which it would take if carried on upon the principles of Justice, and with due respect for the feelings of the oppressed nations. This is enough for foreign politics, as influencing my attachments. There are three great domestic questions, viz. the liberty of the press, Parliamentary reform, and Roman Catholic concession, which, if I briefly advert to, no more need be said at present.

A free discussion of public measures thro' the Press I deem the *only* safeguard of liberty; without it I have neither confidence in Kings, Parliaments, Judges, or Divines—they have all in their turn betrayed their country. But the Press, so potent for good, is scarcely less so for evil; and unfortunately they who are misled and abused by its means are the Persons whom it can least benefit—it is the fatal characteristic of their disease to reject all remedies coming from the quarter that has caused or aggravated the malady. I am *therefore* for vigorous restrictions—but there is scarcely any abuse that I would not endure, rather than sacrifice, or even endanger this freedom.

When I was young, giving myself credit for qualities which I did not possess, and measuring mankind by that standard, I thought it derogatory to human nature to set up Property in preference to Person, as a title for legislative power. That notion has vanished. I now perceive many advantages in our present complex system of Representation, which formerly eluded my observation; this has tempered my ardour for Reform; but if any plan could be contrived for throwing the Representation fairly into the hands of the Property of the Country, and not leaving it so much in the hands of the large Proprietors as it now is, it should have my best support—tho', even in that event, there would be a sacrifice of Personal rights, independent of property, that are now frequently exercised for the benefit of the community.

Be not startled when I say that I am averse to further concessions to the Catholics. My reasons are, that such concessions will not produce harmony among the Catholics themselves—that they, among them who are most clamorous for the measure, care little about it but as a step, first, to the overthrow of the Protestant Est^nt in Ireland, as introductory to a Separation of the two Countries—their ultimate aim. That I cannot consent to take the character of a Religion from the declaration of powerful Professors of it disclaiming Doctrines imputed to that religion; that, taking its character from what it actually teaches to the great mass, I believe the Catholic religion to be unchanged in its doctrines and unsoftened in its spirit,—how can it be otherwise unless the doctrine of infallibility be given up? That such concessions would set all other Dissenters in motion—an issue which has never fairly been met by the Friends to concession; and deeming the Church Establishment not only a fundamental part of our Constitution, but one of the greatest Upholders and Propagators of civilization in our own Country, and, lastly, the most effectual and main Support of religious toleration, I cannot but look with jealousy upon Measures which must reduce her relative Influence, unless they be accompanied with arrangements more adequate than any yet adopted for the preservation and increase of that influence, to keep pace with the other Powers in the Community.

I do not apologize for this long letter, the substance of which
you may report to any one worthy of a reply who, in your hearing,
may animadvert upon my Political conduct. I ought to have added,
perhaps, a word on *local politics*, but I have not space; but what I
should have said may in a great measure be deduced from the
above.

[*unsigned*]

50. M. W. to JOHN KENYON

Address: John Kenyon Esqre, Fladong's Hotel,[1] London.
Postmark: 31 Dec. 1821. *Stamp*: Kendal Penny Post.
MS. untraced.
Transactions of the Wordsworth Society, no. 6, p. 85. K (—). LY i. 59.

Rydal Mount, Dec. 28th [1821]

My dear Sir,

  I have been waiting for your address for some time to tell you
that Fleming's House at the bottom of the hill is vacated, and that
I have a promise of the refusal and therefore, want your directions
about it—under existing circumstances I suspect that I am not to
have the pleasure of taking it for you—but I must hear this from
yourself before I give up my claim.

  Tillbrook some time ago mentioned your *wise intentions* to us,
which we had before half suspected—indeed Sarah bids me tell you
that she was always sure 'you were *in love*,' and that it was you,
and not your Brother (as you cunningly hinted), that was to
become a married Man.[2] May your happiness go *beyond* your
anticipations is the sincere wish of all your friends under Nab
Scar, who by the bye want no packages from Twining's to remind
them of you, and your Br, and of the days of *particular pleasure* that
you passed among them—that *season* has been long gone by, and
Rydal Mount is now as *notorious* for its industry as at that time it
was for its idleness.

  The *Poet* has been busily engaged upon subjects connected with
our Continental journey,[3] and if you have leisure and inclination to

---

  [1] In Oxford St.
  [2] Kenyon's second marriage, the following year, was to Caroline (d. 1835),
sister of John Curteis (d. 1849), a wealthy bachelor of Devonshire Place, who
left Kenyon the bulk of his property. See also Mrs. Andrew Crosse, 'John
Kenyon and his Friends', *Temple Bar*, lxxxviii (1890), 477–96.
  [3] *Memorials of a Tour on the Continent, 1820*. The plan, which M. W. goes

call upon Mr Monkhouse 34 Gloster Place you have permission to ask for a perusal of certain Poems in his possession—he was charged not to give copies, and for obvious reasons you would not wish for an exception in your case. You will also see another *late production*[1] in Gloster Place, which will be shown, I doubt not, with no little pride. Miss W. is going on with her journal, which will be ready to *go to press* interspersed with her brother's poems, I hope before you return. I do not say this *seriously*, but we sometimes jestingly talk of raising a fund by such means for a second and a further trip into Italy!

Lady Beaumont writes from Rome that she has rec[d] the letter which was entrusted to your care but not by your hands: they will remain in Rome 2 months longer, and will be glad if you will call upon them.

In addition to our home employments we have lately been much occupied by our sick neighbours. Old Mr Jackson[2] is dead—Mrs Quillinan had had a melancholy confinement since the birth of her second little girl (who is called Rotha after the brook upon whose banks she was born)—the Mother is doing well however at present, under medical care at Lancaster, where the family mean to spend the winter months, and return in the spring. Mr Q. and the children are yet here, but depart next week.

Poor Barber has had a hair-breadth's escape from the grave, and is still confined to his bed—his disease, an inflammation on the chest, this is subdued—but he now suffers dreadfully from spasms to which he has for many years been subject.

Now pray do not go on without writing to us—if we could be sure of this, we should be spared much trouble in examining the list of marriages, which we have regularly done for many weeks past. With affect[e] regards to y[r] Br and yourself from all under this roof,

Ever yrs
M. Wordsworth.

We had a most elegant Ball at Miss Dowling's last Wed[y] evening, on the occasion of Miss Wordsworth and Miss

---

on to mention, of interspersing D. W.'s Journal of the same tour with W. W.'s poems (on the analogy of her Journal of the Scottish Tour of 1803), and publishing them together, was soon dropped. See L. 52 below.

[1] Thomas Monkhouse's recently born daughter Mary (1821–1900), for whom W. W. wrote a sonnet in 1824 (see *PW* iii. 46). She married the Revd. Henry Dew (1819–1901), a pupil of Arnold at Rugby, and rector of Whitney, Hereford, 1843–1901.

[2] Rector of Grasmere since 1806.

Harden[1] leaving school. 48 persons (not children) present—all the Beauty and Fashion of the neighbourhood—the Ball was led off by Miss W. the younger and Mr Harden, who were followed by *Mr W.* and Miss H.—the Company (and Dancing) lingered till after 4 o'clock! ! !

W. wrote to you at Leamington.

[*There follows an itinerary of the continental tour of 1820*]

51. W. W. to ROBERT SOUTHEY

MS. Mr. Roger W. Barrett.[2]
Chester L. Shaver, '*Wordsworth on Byron: an Unpublished Letter to Southey*', *MLN lxxv (June 1960)*, 488–90.

[late Dec. 1821]

Dear S—

The only part of the charge[3] you are any way called upon to notice is that of slander, as this is given with his name, we think

---

[1] For John Harden and his family, see *MY* ii. 109 and Daphne Foskett, *John Harden of Brathay Hall, 1772–1847*, Kendal, 1974. His daughter Jane Sophia (1807–76), married in 1840 the Revd. Frederick Barker (1808–82), perpetual curate of Edgehill, Liverpool, 1835–54, and thereafter Bishop of Sydney and Metropolitan of Australia.

[2] But now (1974) no longer in his possession.

[3] For the progress of Southey's quarrel with Byron and the 'Satanic school', see *The Works of Lord Byron: Letters and Journals*, ed. R. E. Prothero, 6 vols., 1901, vi. 377 ff. Byron had been smarting under the rumour (which he supposed Southey had inspired on his return from Switzerland in 1817) that he and Shelley were 'in a league of Incest'; and now, further incensed by Southey's *A Vision of Judgment* and its preface (see L. 11 above), Byron assailed him not just as a political turncoat, but as a slanderer as well. 'I am not ignorant of Mr Southey's calumnies', he wrote in an appendix to *The Two Foscari*, published on 21 Dec., '. . . which he scattered abroad on his return from Switzerland against me and others.' Southey saw that some immediate rebuttal was necessary, at least to the charge that reflected on his personal honour, and after consulting W. W., he published a reply, dated 5 Jan. 1822, in the *Courier* for the 7th (reprinted by Prothero). After an outright denial that he had spread the slander attributed to him, Southey returned to his previous charges against the 'Satanic school': 'Lord Byron . . . has not ventured to bring the matter of these animadversions into view. He conceals the fact that they are directed against authors of blasphemous and lascivious books; against men who, not content with indulging their own vices, labour to make others the slaves of sensuality like themselves; against public panders, who, mingling impiety with lewdness, seek at once to destroy the cement of social order, and to carry profanation and pollution into private families, and into the hearts of individuals.' He ended with a word of advice to Byron, which in the event was only too well heeded: 'When he attacks me again let it be in rhyme. For one who has so little command of himself, it will be a great advantage that his temper should be obliged to *keep tune*.' Byron's triumphant parody *The Vision of Judgment* followed within a few months.

it ought to be met. As to the rest—one would never think of it but
for the opportunity it gives of chastising the offender. Ever yours
most faithfully,

W W—

Turn over—

The Girls[1] may be amused—

> Critics, right honorable Bard! decree
> Laurels to some, a nightshade wreath to thee,
> Whose Muse a sure though late revenge hath ta'en
> Of harmless Abel's death by murdering Cain.[2]

On Cain a Mystery dedicated to Sir Walter Scott

> A German Haggis—from Receipt
> Of him who cook'd 'The death of Abel'
> And sent 'warm-reeking rich' and sweet
> From Venice to Sir Walter's table.[3]

After reading a luscious scene of the above—

> The Wonder explained
> What! Adam's eldest Son in this sweet strain!
> Yes—did you never hear of Sugar-Cain?

On a Nursery piece of the same, by a Scottish Bard—

> Dont wake little Enoch,
> Or he'll give you a wee knock!
> For the pretty sweet Lad
> As he lies in his Cradle
> Is more like to his Dad
> Than a Spoon to a Ladle.[4]

---

[1] i.e. Southey's daughter Edith and his niece Sara Coleridge.

[2] Byron's drama *Cain* had appeared on 19 Dec. As Shaver notes, this quatrain and the next were first published by Knight in his *Poetical Works of William Wordsworth*, 8 vols., 1896, but the letter itself he had apparently not seen. De Selincourt, likewise, prints only the first two epigrams (*PW* iv. 378).

[3] Byron says in his preface to *Cain*: 'Gesner's *Death of Abel* I have never read since I was eight years of age, at Aberdeen.' Salomon Gessner (1730–88), published *Der Tod Abels* in 1758. It was translated into English soon afterwards, and contributed much to the contemporary cult of sentimentality. Cf. *Prelude* (1805), Bk. vii., ll. 558–9, where W. W.'s 'comely Bachelor' parson has felt its influence. De Selincourt identified the phrase 'warm-reeking rich' as a quotation from Burns's *To a Haggis*.

[4] See *Cain*, Act III, sc. i.

52. D. W. to CATHERINE CLARKSON

Address: Mrs Clarkson, Playford Hall, Ipswich, Suffolk. (Single).
Postmark: 16 Jan. 1822. *Stamp*: Kendal Penny Post. *Endorsed*: 1822.
MS. British Museum.
K (—). *LY i. 61.*

16th Jan. [1822]

My dearest Friend,

On the faith of the old proverb I am willing to believe that if any evil had befallen you we should have heard of it; yet I cannot be easy under your long silence.—I did indeed anxiously expect a letter for a long time, till at last at the opening of the leather bag I have said, or thought—'there will be no letter from Mrs Clarkson!' and am now completely settled in my mind that I shall hear no more from you till you are roused by a letter from me.—Sometimes (but I instantly rejected that thought) I have fancied that our joke on poor fallen royalty[1] had in connection with us been displeasing to you—that you had felt in reading the foolish rhymes, as if we had played too lightly with sacred feelings, and *therefore* (wanting sympathy with us) had felt no inclination to write.—Yet still I am sorry that I ever committed them to paper; thinking that, at all events, while those innocent Beings were at your side, who had suffered so much from the Death of Christophe (and perhaps still more from his ungovernable passions) you were little likely to cast off serious thoughts and feelings at once and transport yourself to our fire-side partaking of its half-hour's mirth. I am afraid you have not seen Henry Robinson since he was at Rydal, as, when he wrote to us some weeks after the time was passed at which you talked of going to London, and you had not been there, nor had he heard you were expected. I wish you may tell us that, instead of a journey to London, you are meditating a journey to the North next summer. You said in your last that your Husband seemed to look with favour on the scheme; and the recollection of that gives me some hope that it will be executed—even in spite of the low price of corn, and all other grievances. I had just left you this time last year. My dear Friend I marked the anniversary of the day of our meeting—have thought of you every day since, more than usual, and especially upon those two when we always look back, and forward—Christmas day and New Year's day. I suppose your little scholars were assembled again in the decorated kitchen to their plum pudding and Beef—Poor things! what a cold day it was last

[1] i.e. the parody of Ben Jonson's 'Queen and Huntress chaste and fair' in L. 46 above.

year! and how they enjoyed your good fire! This year we have had no frosts of the same kind as that short but severe one which bound up the moats round Playford Hall. There has been with us one week of delightful sunshine and frost—and now we have weather as mild as the best in spring-time. But what a stormy season for the four months preceding! Yet this country never suffers from floods—and as to winds, we, at Rydal Mount are so sheltered that we only hear their music among the trees—or their driving through the valley below us, or over the mountains above our heads. This is indeed a great blessing. We have not so much as had a slate blown off while some of our neighbours have been so terrified as not to be able to lie in their beds. William and I have walked daily through all the stormy Season—but poor Mary has a stiffness in one of her toes, which though in itself a trifle, prevents her from walking with her accustomed freedom. In other respects she is quite well. William has written some beautiful poems in remembrance of our late Tour. If you should go to London Mr Monkhouse will show them to you, he having a copy. I think of their kind he never wrote anything that was more delightful. He began (as in connection with my 'Recollections of a Tour in Scotland'[1]) with saying 'I will write some Poems for your journal', and I thankfully received two or three of them as a tribute to the journal, which I was making from notes, memoranda taken in our last summer's journey on the Continent; but his work has grown to such importance (and has continued growing) that I have long ceased to consider it in connection with my own narrative of events unimportant, and lengthy descriptions, which can only interest friends, or a few persons, who enjoying mountain scenery especially, may wish for minute details of what they can never hope to view with their own eyes—or perhaps a few others who have themselves visited the countries which *we* visited.—The poems are as good as a descriptive tour—without describing. I was going to say more about them; but I will leave you to judge for yourself. The Ecclesiastical Sonnets, meanwhile, are at rest. Dorothy has left school; and you may be sure we are happy to have her at home. She is not yet in *confirmed* good health, though not so subject to take cold as formerly, and, as she has no apparent weakness we trust that fresh air and regular exercise (she cannot now bear long walks) will in the course of a few months restore her to that state in which it is so pleasant to see young people—equable looks and fearless activity. John leaves us next Monday. He is wonderfully improved

[1] *DWJ* i. 195 ff. Cf. *EY*, pp. 605–6, 652–4.

in appearance during the last half-year, has cast off a portion of his rusticity, and his limbs are knitting together—they do not look so large and clumsy as last year. When I returned last year I thought him a perfect Langdale Rustic in appearance.—But these things are trifling. He has a manly generous mind—gentle dispositions and a serious love of study. Indeed he is a thoroughly excellent Youth. And will, I am confident, in time, be more than a respectable scholar. It is greatly to be lamented that he was not earlier sent from home. As to dear little William—*he* has been sent away soon enough; but he has not profited by the advantage. His attainments were worse than nothing in Latin the last holidays, and his Uncle gives no better report at present; therefore his Father intends in three months to take him from the Charter House. You will perceive that without reasonable grounds for believing that his improvement was in some degree proportionate to the expense, it would be very unwise in my Brother to let him remain there. It is not yet decided to what school he is to go. Probably it will be Sedbergh, yet the objections to that, and any *Northern School* are very great; while on the other hand, if he were sent to a school in the South, it would be making a second experiment, when there is no time to be lost—and the distance from home was always an object of the utmost importance. Have you seen George Airey this Christmas? I hear from all the Cambridge men that he, decidedly, is to be the Senior Wrangler[1] of his year.—I wish you may have had both your Son and your Brothers to enliven your Christmas. How is your Sister? and how goes on the little Boy? and how the Farm?—and are you at Playford making greater gains or rather smaller losses than last year? They are doing no better in Wales—I trust Tom is flourishing though not rapidly—for that is not to be expected—pray tell us how the business advances. If he keeps his health I have no doubts about him for what he likes he will do and do well. Remember me kindly to Mr and Mrs Biddle—and to Elizabeth, and give my very best love to Mr Clarkson. All join in wishing you both many happy years believe me ever, my dearest Friend your

affectionate Dorothy Wordsworth.

Willy does not yet know he is to leave the Charter House and perhaps may not be told immediately.

I hope you have good tidings from your Friend La Roche.[2]— How is the family at Woodbridge?

---

[1] See L. 18 above.   [2] See L. 37 above.

53. W. W. to CHARLES LLOYD[1]

MS. Cornell. Hitherto unpublished.

Feb 20th 1822

I begin this letter without the usual expressions of regard, because till I have explained myself, they might be understood not altogether as I could wish. You need not doubt that every one in this family, myself included, sympathized with you in the loss of your excellent parent,[2] of whom probably too much could not be said, and we all thank you for the memorial which you have sent. The little volume you last sent to me, I have not read. The subject would at no period have interested me, and coming as it did in the wane of the trash that had just been scribbled by others, upon the character of Pope, I could not, from respect to your intellect, and from general disgust bring myself to the perusal.[3] I am sorry you should have imagined that anything connected with myself as a literary person, could have given me offence. This is not an age, which will allow an author's feelings to be in that state without disgrace to his philosophy. I come now to the point—

From a wish to see certain writings of C. Lamb in the *London Mag.* a few numbers were procured: in one of them I found an abusive article, no doubt by Hazlitt,[4] in which inferences were

---

¹ Charles Lloyd, who was still living in Kensington, had recently sent W. W. his *Poetical Essays on the Character of Pope as a Poet and Moralist; and on the Language and Objects most fit for Poetry*, 1821, and he wrote on 16 Feb. from a place called Woodfield to inquire why he had received no acknowledgement. 'I have feared that you were not quite pleased with my last little volume, as you have neither noticed its receipt, nor have we heard from any branch of your family since it was sent. Of its merit as a performance it is not for me to speak, but this I can truly say, that nothing in it was written with the slightest intention of displeasing you, indeed I am incapable of harbouring such a feeling towards you.' (*WL MSS.*) W. W.'s reply is quoted by Lloyd in the copy of their correspondence which he sent to Talfourd on 6 Mar. for his perusal and advice. See also Vera Watson, 'Thomas Noon Talfourd and His Friends', *TLS* 20 and 27 Apr. 1956.
² Mrs. Mary Lloyd had died on 9 Dec. 1821. Lloyd's letter of 16 Feb. was written on a copy of the tribute he had composed to her memory.
³ W. L. Bowles's hostile *Life* of Pope, prefixed to his edition of 1806, stirred up a bitter controversy to which Campbell (in his *Specimens of the British Poets*, 1819), Hazlitt, and Byron all contributed. Lloyd's own *Poetical Essays* added to this prolonged debate on the rival claims of 'nature' and 'art' in poetry: had W. W. opened the book, he would have found himself criticized (p. 56) for confining the true subject-matter of poetry to the 'peasants'.
⁴ In 'Table Talk, No. XII—On Consistency of Opinion', *London Magazine*, iv (Nov. 1821), 485–92, in the course of attacking the apparent inconsistencies between W. W.'s early poetical creed and his recent stance in Westmorland politics, Hazlitt had illustrated W. W.'s 'impertinence' and 'ostentatious

drawn to my prejudice from a trivial story, which, as I know from several quarters, you repeated at Keswick (observe not from Southey), but treating it then as neighbourly gossip I did not notice it. The same story must have passed from you to Hazlitt, a person who you knew was malignantly disposed towards Southey, Coleridge, and myself. The particulars upon which you *grounded* this misrepresentation came to your knowledge as a guest invited to my table, and therefore could not have been repeated in any miscellaneous society with a view to lower my character, without a breach of the rules of gentlemanly intercourse; but persuaded as I was that you had talked in this strain to the individual in question, I was disinclined to write untill I should be called upon to explain in sincerity my notion of this mode of dealing with one's friends. I will conclude the subject with a word. Such silly tales throw no light whatever upon the character they are brought forward to illustrate[1]—what light they may throw upon that of those who report, or listen to them, I should be loth to trouble myself to ascertain.

Be so good as to remember me affect[ly] to your father, to M[rs] Ll.

servility' with the following anecdote about Lloyd, W. W., and Lord Lowther, which he must have heard from Lloyd's own lips: 'A gentleman went to live, some years ago, in a remote part of the country, and as he did not wish to affect singularity he used to have two candles on his table of an evening. A romantic acquaintance of his in the neighbourhood, smit with the love of simplicity and equality, used to come in, and without ceremony snuff one of them out, saying, it was a shame to indulge in such extravagance, while many a poor cottager had not even a rush-light to see to do their evening's work by. This might be about the year 1802, and was passed over as among the ordinary occurrences of the day. In 1816 (oh! fearful lapse of time, pregnant with strange mutability), the same enthusiastic lover of economy, and hater of luxury, asked his thoughtless friend to dine with him in company with a certain lord, and to lend him his man-servant to wait at table; and just before they were sitting down to dinner, he heard him say to the servant in a sonorous whisper—"and be sure you don't forget to have six candles on the table!" ' (*Works*, ed. Howe, xvii. 26–7.) W. W.'s version of what happened is reflected in M. W.'s indignant letter to Thomas Monkhouse, in which she attempted to set the record straight. W. W. had once snuffed out a candle at Brathay, 'after he had walked to see the reptile [i.e. Lloyd] thro' the darkness, and the glare hurt his eyes . . . The cant about the poor who only have a rush light, etc., is utterly false, as any one who knows Wm will know.' As for the dinner party, the servant was present to watch over and restrain Lloyd as his insanity increased, not to wait at table. Lord Lowther had brought his own servant for that purpose. (*MW*, p. 84.)

[1] In his letter to Talfourd, Lloyd justified the publishing of such trifles about celebrities on the ground that 'people in trifles are less on their guard than in matters of greater importance, and that consequently the real character by means of them is often best detected . . . This is one instance of that want of *truth* of character, which in all that relates to *self* is perpetually conspicuous in W.'

and to your children, in whose welfare I shall always feel much interested, and I may now say that I remain my dear Lloyd with sincere truth and regard

affectionately yours
W. Wordsworth.[1]

54. W. W. to MESSRS. LONGMAN AND CO.

Address: To Messrs Longman and Co, Paternoster Row, London. [*In M. W'.s hand*]
Postmark: 1 Mar. 1822. *Stamp*: Kendal Penny Post. *Endorsed*: W Wordsworth Feb. 26/22.
MS. Mr. Robert H. Taylor. Hitherto unpublished.

Rydal Mount Feb^ry 26th 1822

Dear Sirs,

Being apprehensive of some mistake I think it best to have the Revise and the Proof[2] sent back to myself—I therefore beg that you would be so kind as to forward them as speedily as possible to Mr Becket,[3] Downing Street to whom I have written requesting him to frank them for me, through whom, also they will be returned immediately.

If it should happen that they are struck off before this letter reaches you, then let them be published.

Pray send two copies to Dr Wordsworth Trinity Lodge Cambridge—

I am, dear Sirs
Yours sincerely
Wm Wordsworth

[1] Talfourd's efforts at mediation met with little success, but—as W. W.'s closing words suggest—there was no permanent breach with Lloyd, and they seem to have met again in 1827 when W. W. was staying with Charles Lloyd senior on his way through Birmingham.
[2] *The Memorials of a Tour on the Continent, 1820* were now going through the press, followed closely by the *Ecclesiastical Sketches* (see *SH*, p. 231).
[3] John Beckett.

55. D. W. to ELIZABETH COOKSON[1]

MS. WL. Hitherto unpublished.

Sunday [3 Mar. 1822]

My dear Friend,

I have long expected an answer from Mr Robinson to my inquiries respecting a Situation for Strickland.[2] It is at last arrived; but I am afraid that it brings little or no information that will be new either to you or him. Such as it is, however, I will transcribe it for you—premising that (speaking of Strickland's future views when his Clerkship in London should be ended,) I had inaccurately used the words 'if an *opening* should offer in London,' in allusion to S's wish to settle there rather than in the country provided he could be taken into partnership—or otherwise could find means for advancing himself there. M^r R says, 'The uniform practice is, for Clerks in the Country to spend the last year of their time with the Agent of their Principal. If not an inconvenient tax on their Parents, it is adviseable for the young Men to be a year with a conveyancer, if he is ultimately to practise in the country, and for that a fee of a hundred Guineas is required. This my Nephew has done. But when with the Agent, no Salary is given, and no fee paid. You suggest there being an opening for young C. in London. The expression raises a smile. An army might be raised of the London Attornies and their Clerks; and were the first Ranks killed off there would be enow to fill their places. There is no other hope of your Friend's obtaining an eligible situation here than what may arise out of very particular connexions, or his displaying extraordinary qualifications.' (This I was well aware of and only mentioned S's future views thinking the knowledge of them might possibly serve M^r R as a Guide in his advice). 'A large sum is frequently given for an advantageous partnership with a Senior practitioner, when the Junior is willing and competent to undertake the labour of the profession. But the ordinary situation of an Atty's Clerk in London is that of hard work and small pay. At present Mr C. can only make himself Master of country practice. In Town he may learn the practice of the Courts; and even if he intend to practice in the Country a residence for a year or two is adviseable, were it only for the sake of reputation.' (This of course we all know, and I told M^r R that S's time in the North was nearly expired). M^r R then goes on 'As to Mr Addison's practice I dare say it would be quite enough for purposes of instruction; but the

---

[1] i.e. Mrs. Cookson of Kendal.   [2] See above, L. 47.

object is, if possible to find a situation that would be likely to lead to permanent employment.' This is all — — If, after having read the above you or Strickland think that by putting any further questions to Mr R. I can be in any way serviceable I shall be most glad to do it.

We have not yet heard from Mr Gee—The Quillinans talk of coming to the Ivy Cottage in the course of a fortnight. We have every reason to expect pleasant neighbours in them; but it is very grievous to us to part with our old and tried Friends, especially as they might as well have stayed at Rydal a year longer.—My Brother's eyes are better, though very weak—Sara is better—and all else are well. My Br, S. Coleridge[1] and I were at Dungeon Gill yesterday; so you may judge *I* am pretty stout. My Sister's Toe is less troublesome. She has walked to Mr Barber's without injury— We were much concerned to hear of your distressing attack in the head. I trust you have had no return of it, as Mr Gee gave a good account of you, in a note we had from Kendal. — — My Brother's two publications[2] will very soon be out. The printing is nearly finished—Excuse this hasty scrawl—

Ever, my dear Friend
Your affectionate
D Wordsworth

56. D. W. to H. C. R.

Address: To H. C. Robinson Esqre, No. 3. King's Bench Walk, Temple, London. *Single*.
Postmark: 8 [?Mar.]. *Stamp*: Kendal Penny Post. *Endorsed*: 3d March 1822, Miss Wordsworth.
MS. Dr. Williams's Library.
K (—). *Morley, i. 112.*

3rd March 1822.

My dear Friend,

It is fit that I should begin with my reason for writing to you on the very day of the receipt of your letter,[3] that you may not be afflicted with the thought that you had no sooner cast a burthen off your shoulders than another was ready to be cast *upon* them. It is

---

[1] Sara Coleridge.
[2] i.e. *Ecclesiastical Sketches* and *Memorials of a Tour on the Continent, 1820*, both published by Longman in 1822.
[3] Of 25 Feb. Parts of it, discussing the *Memorials* which H. C. R. had seen in MS. at Thomas Monkhouse's, are printed in Morley, i. 110.

very unfair in managing a correspondence for one party, in the
first motions of gratitude for pleasure received to write off immediately, but indeed it is a species of selfishness of which I confess
I have been too often guilty; however in the present case; having
nothing very interesting to communicate, much as it has delighted
us to receive yours, I would have spared you had I not wished that,
if you have opportunity you would tell Mrs Montagu[1] that I never
recommended Miss Fletcher[2] as a Governess. She has very good
dispositions and I believe a good temper. She was thought by many
(but of this we are no judges) to be able to give instruction in
Music, and I have reason to think she has a sufficient knowledge of
French; but she was very deaf when resident in this country; and
though I am told this infirmity did not hinder her from detecting
false notes and perceiving gradations of sound in music, I am afraid
she would be utterly unfit to give accurate instructions in other
matters—not to speak of the ill effects that might be produced on
the manners and habits of Children by being under the government
of a deaf person. I was quite shocked to hear of 'exertions made
by me'—The Fact is that poor Miss Fletcher wrote to Mrs W.
and me requesting us to recommend her. This letter *I* replied to[3]
telling her that neither Mrs W. nor I were judges of her qualifications in many points, and that we could not know in what degree
her unfortunate deafness might disable her from giving instructions;
adding that those Ladies who had employed her would be the
judges of this.

I suspect that Miss F has copied those parts of my letter in
which I spoke of our favourable opinion—omitting all that was said
of our incompetence to judge, and of our apprehensions concerning
her deafness. Otherwise Miss Benson[4] could not have supposed
that I would recommend her as a Governess. Miss Fletcher is a
good kind-hearted creature, and I wish it were in my power to
serve her; but should never think, whatever were my means, of
attempting to do it in that way. Do excuse this long story, which,
if you were not the kindest creature in the world, I should not have
oppressed you with (and this is what you get by your kindness.)
I know that you will perceive what a painful thing it would be to
me to be supposed to have recommended a person to an office,
which I am convinced she would not, through natural infirmity, be

[1] The third Mrs. Basil Montagu, formerly Mrs. Skepper (see *MY* i. 63,
212).
[2] See *MY* ii. 120.   [3] D. W.'s letter to Miss Fletcher is untraced.
[4] Unidentified. Presumably a friend of Mrs. Montagu and perhaps a relation
of the Benson of *HCR* i. 357–8.

able to discharge.—And now for that other burthen of debtorship which you might fancy I was laying upon you—I can only say, that sooner or later—whenever your letters come they are joyfully received and highly prized—the oftener the better—but however seldom and however slowly we are never inclined to think ourselves neglected or ill used.—My Brother will, I hope, write to Charles Lamb in the course of a few days—He has long talked of doing it: but you know how the mastery of his own thoughts, (when engaged in composition, as he has lately been), often prevents him from fulfilling his best intentions; and since the weakness of his eyes has returned, he has been obliged to fill up all spaces of leisure by going into the open air for refreshment and relief of his eyes. We are thankful that the inflammation (chiefly in the lids) is now much abated. It concerns us very much to hear so indifferent an account of Lamb and his Sister. The Death of their Brother,[1] I have no doubt, has affected them much more than the death of any Brother, with whom there had in near neighbourhood been so little personal or family communication, would affect any other minds—We deeply lamented their loss—wished to write to them as soon as we heard of it, but it not being the particular duty of any one of us—and a painful task—we shoved it off—for which we are truly sorry and very much blame ourselves. They are too good and too confiding to take it unkindly; and that thought makes me feel it the more.

Sergeant Rough[2] was an intimate Friend of my Brother Chris[r] at College. I used to hear him much spoken of, but never saw him— Poor Man! his lot in this world has been a hard one—A thoughtless wife and an undermining Friend—what sorer evils can beset a Man! Your affecting comment on her Death reminded me of a Sonnet of my Brother's on the subject of ruined Abbies,[3] which I will not quote as you will so soon have an opportunity of reading the Sonnet among the Ecclesiastical Sketches. The thought in that part to which I allude is taken from George Dyer's[4] History of Cambridge.

[1] John Lamb. See L. 47 above.

[2] For William (later Sir William) Rough, see *MY* ii. 182. In 1816 he had been appointed a judge in the united colony of Demerara and Essequibo, but in Oct. 1821 he was suspended by the Governor for usurping the privileges and functions of the executive. His appeal to the Privy Council was finally upheld in 1825. Rough married a natural daughter of John Wilkes, and she had recently died of yellow fever at Demerara along with one of her children. The 'undermining friend' is apparently Basil Montagu, to whom H. C. R. had attributed all of Rough's misfortunes.   [3] *Old Abbeys* (*PW* iii. 401).

[4] For George Dyer, Lamb's Unitarian friend, see *EY*, p. 511 and, for a

With respect to the Tour poems, I am afraid you will think his notes not sufficiently copious—Prefaces he has none—except to the poem on Goddard's death. Your suggestion of the Bridge at Lucern set his mind to work; and if a happy mood comes on he is determined, even yet, though the work is printed, to add a poem on that subject[1]—You can have no idea with what earnest pleasure he seized the idea—yet before he began to write at all, when he was pondering over his recollections, and asking me for hints and thoughts, I mentioned that very subject and he then thought he could make nothing of it.—You certainly have the gift of setting him on fire—When I named (before your letter was read to him) your scheme for next Autumn,[2] his countenance flushed with pleasure, and he exclaimed 'I'll go with him!'—and then I ventured to utter a thought which had risen before and been suppressed in the moment of its rising—'how *I* should like to go.'—Presently however, the conversation took a sober turn—My *'unlawful desires'* were completely checked—and he concluded that *for him* the journey would be impossible—and then, said he, 'if you or Mary or both were not with me I should not half enjoy it;—and THAT (*so soon again*) is impossible'.—We have had a letter from Mr Monkhouse today. He talks of taking a house in the neighbourhood of London; but as they had once an idea of coming into Lancashire, which circumstances in Mr Horrocks's[3] family have prevented, we can see no reason why they should not, instead, take lodgings for the spring and early part of the summer in this neighbourhood; and Miss Hutchinson has written to them to that effect—It will be a pity if the circumstance of having already taken a house should prevent our having the pleasure of having them as neighbours. The Quilli[n]ans have taken Mr Tillbrooke's house; and will be settled there in about a fortnight. They are at present at Lancaster —You will be glad to hear that Mrs Q. is quite recovered. We are

sketch of his life, *HCR* i. 4–5. His best-known works were *Memoirs of the Life and Writings of Robert Robinson*, 1796, pronounced by W. W. to be the best biography in the language, and the *History of the University and Colleges of Cambridge*, 2 vols., 1814, to which (I. vii–viii) W. W. was indebted in the concluding lines of the sonnet.

[1] See *Desultory Stanzas*, ll. 55 ff. (*PW* iii. 200). '. . . I should rejoice', H. C. R. had written, 'to find among the unseen poems some memorial of those patriotic and pious bridges at Lucerne suggesting to so *generative* a mind as your brother's a whole cycle of religious and civic sentiments . . .'

[2] In the unpublished part of his letter H. C. R. had described his plans for a tour of the Tyrol and Austria in the autumn. 'I shall almost excite unlawful desires by the enumeration of places so inviting . . .' (*Dr. Williams's Library MSS.*)

[3] Samuel Horrocks, the Preston manufacturer and M.P. See *MY* ii. 592.

exceedingly sorry that the Gees are gone entirely from Rydal—
No neighbours could have been kinder or better suited to us, in age
and all other respects.—Poor Mrs Gee was called away a fortnight
ago to attend the sick-bed of one of her Sisters, and the next week
Mr Gee followed her to be present at the sister's funeral.—They
had before taken a house at Keswick; but they are so loth to leave
the neighbourhood and us, that they are determined to be at
Ambleside instead of Keswick, and to get rid of their house there.

We have had a long and interesting letter from Mrs Clarkson
with an account of the manners, characters, habits etc, of the sable
Queen and her Daughters. Notwithstanding bad times Mrs C
writes in chearful spirits, and talks of coming into the North this
summer; and we really hope it will not end in *talk*, as Mr Clarkson
joins with her; and if he once determines, a trifle will not stop him.
—Pray read a paper in the London Magazine by H. Coleridge on
the Uses of the Heathen Mythology in Poetry[1]—It has pleased us
very much. The style is wonderful for so young a man—so little of
effort—and no affectation.—Poor Coleridge! have you seen his
advertisement for pupils?[2] How beautifully Charles Lamb speaks of
Gray's Inn Gardens, and his meeting with the Old Actor there.[3]

Miss Hutchinson has just reminded me that you are now on the
circuit;—Perhaps I might have something to add before your
return, but, as a letter is safe and off my mind when put into the
post office, and it will keep very well and be ready to welcome you
when you return to your solitary Chambers I will e'en send it off.
At that time you may have more leisure than at any other, to read
(perhaps I ought to say *decypher*) my scrawling.—I hope the poems
will then be published; but, if not, you must not indulge the hope
of finding the Bridge of Lucern among them. I do not think that

[1] *London Magazine*, v (Feb. 1822), 113–20, signed Thersites: repr. in
Essays and Marginalia, ed. Derwent Coleridge, 2 vols., 1851, i. 18–39. It
included appreciative comment on W. W.'s use of Classical mythology. Since
leaving Oxford, Hartley had been settled with the Montagus in London, but
despite the success of his series of papers in the *London Magazine* he was
unsettled and restless, and S. T. C. contrived soon after this to have him taken
on as Mr. Dawes's assistant at Ambleside, and he left London at the close of
1822. See *Letters of Hartley Coleridge*, ed. Grace Evelyn Griggs and Earl
Leslie Griggs, 1936, pp. 56, 71–4.

[2] The following paragraph appeared in the *Courier* for 25 Feb. among items
of domestic news: 'Mr COLERIDGE proposes to devote a determinate portion of
each week to a small and select number of gentlemen not younger than 19 or
20, for the purpose of assisting them in the formation of their minds and the
regulation of their studies. The plan, which is divided between direct instruction and conversation, the place, and other particulars may be learnt by
personal application to Mr COLERIDGE at Highgate.'

[3] In 'On Some of the Old Actors', *London Magazine*, v (Feb. 1822), 174–9.

work can be accomplished in time, much as my Brother would wish it; but you may depend upon it that something will come of your suggestion. My Sister says, 'mind you thank Mr Robinson a hundred times for his kindness to Willy.—Poor little Fellow! he will certainly I think be removed from the Charter-house, but my Brother is undecided in the choice of another school. We have every reason to be dissatisfied with his late progress—rather I should say we are satisfied he has made no progress at all in learning—All join in kind remembrances.—Remember, when you happen to have half an hour's leisure we shall always be glad to hear from you.—You must think nothing of what I have said of my Brother's longings to roam with you among the Tyrolese. It will be quite impossible I am sure. God bless you.

Believe me your grateful and affectionate Friend
D Wordsworth.

The Transcript of my Journal is nearly finished—There is so much of it that I am sure it will be dull reading to those who have never been in th[ose¹ coun]tries—and even to such *I* think *much* of it at [? least] must be tedious. My Brother is interested when I read it to him—So are the young ones; but they have not been much tried—My Sister too, never complains of over much—but that is because the subject is so interesting to her.—When we meet, you shall read as much or as little of my journal as you like. I long to try it on you and Mr Monkhouse. Mary seems to have succeeded so well in the brief way that I can hardly hope my lengthiness will interest in like degree. I shall not read hers till my transcript is finished.

When you next write pray sign your name at full length. This I particularly request for the settling of a dispute among us—Thanks for the description of the Brussels pulpit. It revived my recollections.—I hope you have found Friends well at Bury.

I have transcribed what you say for Mrs Cookson² and thank you for it.

¹ *Seal.*   ² See previous letter.

57. W. W. to THE COMMISSIONERS OF STAMPS

Address: To The Hon'ble Commissioners, Stamp Office, London.
Postmark: 9 Mar. 1822. *Stamp*: Kendal Penny Post. *Endorsed*: Mr Words-
worth Rydal Mount Ambleside 6 March 1822.
MS. Public Record Office. Hitherto unpublished.

[*In John Carter's hand*]

Rydal Mount, Ambleside
6 Mar: 1822—

Hon'ble Sirs,

I beg to lay before you the Copy of a Letter received from Emal[1]
Theobalds, one of the Executors of Alice Theobalds, late of Kearstick,[2] and to state that since the Receipt of the same, I have written
to his Brother, calling upon him to execute the Trust without delay, of
which he has taken no notice. I have in consequence ventured at the
earnest solicitation of this poor Man, to lay the case before the Board.

I have the Honor to be
Hon'ble Sirs,
Your obedient Servant

Copy—

[*signed*] Wm Wordsworth

Honour'd Sir,

With a degree of solicitude I humbly beg your endeavours to
write to Edmund Theobalds of Cow Brow near Kirkby Lonsdale or
to write to the proper Office, requesting them to do so—The
purport is:

Alice Theobalds late of Kearstick near K^y Lonsdale died in June
1819 and a few days after her interment her will was proved by
Edward Theobald one of the Executors who collected all the monies
etc: but will not give any Account whatever:—by this means I am
deprived of my Legacy and also one of the Executors, and feeling
desirous to finish the Business but cannot on account of my
Brother's proving the Will and collecting the money, all without
my knowledge. Mr. Sharp[3] Vicar of Kirkby wished me to write you,
desiring as above, and I humbly hope your Candour will excuse the
liberty I have presumed, and oblige, Sir

with sentiments of respect
Your obedient Servant
Eman[1] Theobalds.

Wm Wordsworth Esq.

[1] i.e. Emanuel.
[2] i.e. Keartswick, a hamlet one mile north of Kirkby Lonsdale.
[3] The Revd. Joseph Sharpe (1755–1831), Fellow of Trinity College,
Cambridge, 1781: vicar of Kirkby Lonsdale, 1791–1831.

58. W. W. to ROBERT BLAKENEY[1]

MS. Cornell. Hitherto unpublished.

April 11th. [1822] Rydal Mount.
[*In M. W.'s hand*]

My dear Sir,

You will no doubt have heard that Mr White[2] declines to continue *Sub*: upon the new arrangement, which the Treasury retrench-
ments, and other considerable fallings off in my Office have forced
me to adopt. The collateral advantages to Mr White were of no
importance as he does not keep a Shop. I am very sorry to part
with him, but I must now look out for Some one to whom these
may be an object—so that it may be worth the Parties while to
distribute Stamps in Whitehaven at 15/- per cent—which if the
Sale does not diminish much, will leave a profit on the *poundage* of
nearly £30 a year. Do you know of any Person whom you could
recommend that would accept the Stamps upon these terms? If I
may judge from applications in other Towns where the profits are
not one fourth of the reduced profit at Whitehaven, there will be
no difficulty in meeting with such a Person.

We are looking for you on the 15th and perhaps you may be
able to make enquiries that may lead to something decisive before
you come.

Mrs W. and my Sisters unite with me in kind regards to yourself
and Mrs Blakeney

and believe me very faithfully Yours
[*signed*] W[m] Wordsworth

[1] Secretary and Treasurer of the Whitehaven Harbour Trust and owner of
Fox Ghyll (see *MY* ii. 98, 120, 135), which he had let to De Quincey towards
the end of 1820 (Jordan, pp. 292 ff.).
[2] W. W.'s Sub-distributor at Whitehaven, who held a post at the Customs
House. Blakeney recommended Mrs. Frances Hodgson in his place.

59. W. W. to RICHARD SHARP[1]

Address: Richd Sharp Esqre, Mansion House Sq^r, London.
Postmark: 19 Apr. 1822. *Stamp*: Kendal Penny Post.
MS. University Library, Davis, California.
K (—). *LY i. 64.*

[*In M. W.'s hand*]

Rydal Mount, April 16th [1822]

My dear Sir,

I took the liberty of sending you the Memorials, for every thing of this sort *is* a liberty (inasmuch as, to use Gibbon's phrase, it levies a tax of civility upon the receiving Party), as a small acknowledgement of the great advantage I and my Fellow-Travellers had derived from your directions; which, as you might observe by the order in which the Poems are placed, and the limits of our Tour, we almost literally followed. The Ecclesiastical Sketches were offered to your notice merely as a contemporary Publication. It gratifies me that you think well of these Poems; but, I own, I am a little disappointed that considering these obligations to you, and your familiar acquaintance with all the spots noticed in the Memorials, they should have afforded you less pleasure than a single Piece,[2] which, from the very nature of it, as allegorical, and even imperfectly so, would horrify a German Critic; and, whatever may be thought of the Germans as Poets, there is no doubt of their being the best Critics in Europe. But I think I have hit upon the secret. You, like myself, are, as Smollet says in his translation of the French phrase, 'd'un certain age', no longer a chicken; and your heart beat in recollection of your late glorious performance, which has ranked you as a demigod among Tourists—

> Mounting from glorious deed to deed,
> As thou from clime to clime didst lead.[3]

You recollect, Gray, in one of his letters (a book by the bye I value more, as I owe it to your kindness), affirms that description, (he means of natural scenery and the operations of Nature) though an admirable ornament, ought *never* to make the subject of poetry.

---

[1] 'Conversation' Sharp (see *EY*, p. 468, *MY* i. 39), man of business, critic, and traveller, was at this time out of Parliament, having resigned his Irish constituency of Portarlington to his friend David Ricardo in 1819. He returned, as M.P. for Ilchester, in 1826.

[2] W. W. had included *To Enterprise* (*PW* ii. 280) with the *Memorials*. It eventually found its place among the *Poems of the Imagination*.

[3] *To Enterprise*, ll. 45–6.

How many exclusive dogmas have been laid down, which genius from age to age has triumphantly refuted! and grossly should I be deceived if, speaking freely to you as an old Friend, these local poems do not contain many proofs that Gray was as much in the wrong in this interdict, as any critical Brother who may have framed his canons without a spark of inspiration or poetry to guide him. I particularly recommend to your second perusal the Eclipse,[1] to be valued I think as a specimen of description in which beauty majesty and novelty, nature and art, earth and heaven are brought together with a degree of lyrical spirit and movement which professed Odes have, in our language at least, rarely attained. I am sure you cannot have overlooked this piece. But, fearing that it may have failed to interest you as much as I could wish, I have thus adverted to it, being sure that your taste leads you to rate a perfect idyllicism or exquisite epigram higher than a moderate epic—perfection you will agree with me, in humble kinds, is preferable to moderate execution in the highest.

The Ecc. Sketches labour under one obvious disadvantage, that they can only present themselves as a whole to the reader, who is pretty well acquainted with the history of this country; and, as separate pieces, several of them suffer as poetry from the matter of fact, there being unavoidably in all history, except as it is a mere suggestion, something that enslaves the Fancy. But there are in those Poems several continuous strains, not in the least degree liable to this objection. I will only mention two: the sonnets on the dissolution of the Monasteries,[2] and almost the whole of the last part, from the picture of England after the Revolution, scattered over with Protestant churches, till the conclusion. Pray read again from 'Open your Gates, ye everlasting Piles'[3] to the end, and then turn to *your Enterprise.*

Has the Continent driven the North out of your estimation? I hope not, and that we may see you here again, when it would be a great treat to us all to have the particulars of your exploits from your own mouth. What time had you for Venice? I think you must have been obliged to quit the Venetian School with regret. How did you travel etc etc? I have a 100 questions to ask. Pray when is Rogers expected home?[4] I wish to know for a literary reason. Would you be so kind as to give me this information, or to request, if he

---

[1] *The Eclipse of the Sun, 1820 (PW* iii. 184).
[2] *PW* iii. 371–4.   [3] *PW* iii. 404.
[4] Samuel Rogers had been in Italy since the previous autumn. He returned home in May.

should arrive unexpectedly, that he would apprize me of his return.
I remain with best regards from all this Family, who are all well,
very faithfully yours

[*signed*] Wm Wordsworth

I have in the press a little book on the Lakes,[1] containing some
illustrative remarks on Swiss scenery. If I have fallen into any
errors, I know no one better able to correct them than yourself,
and should the book (which I must mention is chiefly a *re*publication) meet your eye, pray point out to me the mistakes. The part
relating to Switzerland[2] is new. One favour leads often to the
asking of another. May I beg of you a sketch for a tour in North
Wales? It is thirty years since I was in that country, and new ways
must have been opened up since that time.

60. W. W. to VISCOUNT LOWTHER

Address: The Lord Viscount Lowther, Spring Gardens, London.
Postmark: 20 Apr. 1822. *Stamp*: Kendal Penny Post.
MS. Lonsdale MSS.
K (—). *LY* i. 66(—).

Rydal Mount
19th April 1822

My dear Lord Lowther,

It is a long time since any communication passed between us;
nothing has occurred in this neighbourhood which was likely to
interest you. The 'hardness of the times'—a phrase with which you
must be pretty well tired—urges me to mention to you a case in
which I am not a little interested, and Mrs W. still more so, as the
Party is her Brother. To come at once to the point; in the wide
circle of your acquaintance, does any one want a land agent, of
mature experience in agriculture, and who can be recommended
as a thoroughly conscientious and honourable man, of excellent
temper, and mild manners. Mr Thomas Hutchinson the person in
question was brought up to farming, under his uncle Mr Hutchinson
of Sockburn, in Durham—a person of much note as being a principal

---

[1] *A Description of the Scenery of the Lakes in the North of England . . . With
Additions, and Illustrative Remarks upon the Scenery of the Alps*, Longman, 1822.
This was the third but the first *separate* edition of this work. (See *Cornell
Wordsworth Collection*, no. 65.)
[2] For the major changes and additions to what eventually came to be called
A Guide Through the District of the Lakes, see *Prose Works*, ii. 133.

teacher in the improvements in breeding cattle, for which Durham and the adjoining part of Yorkshire have become so famous. About 1808, knowing that Wales was backward in Agriculture, he took a Farm, under Mr Frankland Lewes[1] in Radnorshire, and since that period has been a leading agriculturist in that quarter, to its great improvement; but I am sorry to say that he has suffered from the change of times, to the degree that a private fortune of not less than £14,000 has been reduced so as to determine him to retire from farming, if he could find a situation such as I have named. During the first years of his lease, which was 14 years, he sunk large sums in improvements; and when he looked for his return, the 'times changed'; and notwithstanding his judgement, his prudence, and his care, he must have gone to ruin, if it had not been for his private resources. Mr Lewes, who I remember said in Parliament,[2] in speaking against the Corn bill, that *he* was prepared to reduce his rents, has constantly refused to do so in this case; or to relinquish the lease till now, when it is nearly expired. He had a fat tenant, and has kept him by force, till he is becoming lean as a church-mouse. Mr Lewes conditionally remitted the landlord the amount of income tax, when the Property tax was abolished.

I must add, that I have known Mr Hutchinson from his childhood, and therefore can speak confidently to his moral merits, his daily habits, and the soundness of his principles as a good subject; and am certain that he is not reduced to this situation by any fault of his own. He is 47 years of age,[3] prudently did not marry early in life. His eldest child[4] is about 8 years of age; he has still enough left for his own needs, but he is naturally anxious for the sake of his children.

You will excuse this long story; but, if you should have an opportunity of serving this excellent man in the way in which he wishes to be, he would prove an invaluable servant.

I called on Mr Barton[5] yesterday to take my Oath[6] but he was too ill to see me—he is going fast, I fear.

Pray, how are they going on in France? Courtenay,[7] the Barrister,

[1] Thomas Frankland Lewis. See L. 46 above.
[2] W. W. seems to be referring to the debate on Agricultural Distress on 30 May 1820, but his recollection of Frankland Lewis's remarks on the Corn Bill of 1815 does not quite tally with the *Hansard* report.
[3] Thomas Hutchinson was in fact 48.   [4] Thomas (1815–1903).
[5] The Revd. William Barton (1748–1823), rector of Windermere for 43 years. See also *MY* ii. 468.
[6] As a magistrate. See *MY* ii. 521, 532, 539. Up to this date W. W. was apparently still willing to qualify, though he finally dropped the idea.
[7] Philip Courtenay, K.C. (1782–1842), barrister, and (later) W. W.'s

took a bed with us a few nights ago, while rambling through these hills, between the Lancaster and Appleby Assizes. He talked with pleasure of having seen you in Paris; and of the information you had given him about the state of affairs.[1] Brougham, he seemed to think, was mortified at not being the Manchester Cause at Lancaster.[2]

We are all rejoiced to have such good accounts of Lord Lonsdale's eyes. Believe me, dear Lord Lowther

ever faithfully your
obliged friend and Servant
Wm Wordsworth

61. W. W. to WALTER SAVAGE LANDOR

Address: W. S. Landor Esqre, Florence, Italy.
Postmark: [   ] 1822.
MS. Victoria and Albert Museum.
K (—). *LY i. 68.*

[*In M. W.'s hand*]

Rydal Mount Ap. 20th [1822]

My dear Sir,
Could I have assured you that my eyes were decisively better I should have written instantly on the receipt of your last most

'fac-totum in money matters', entered the Inner Temple from Trinity College, Cambridge, and was called to the Bar in 1808. He was M.P. for Bridgwater, 1837–41, and Treasurer of the Inner Temple, 1841.

[1] There was widespread disaffection among the French provincial garrisons at this time, and interest was focused in February on the insurrection at Saumur of the Napoleonic General Jean-Baptiste Berton, who was arrested in June and executed later in the year. This, and the threat of war between Russia and Turkey in the Near East, had depressed the French funds, in which, as will emerge later (see L. 78 below) W. W. had invested.

[2] A legal action arising out of the 'Manchester Massacre' of 16 Aug. 1819 (see *MY* ii. 553), which opened on 4 Apr. It was nominally an action brought against four of the cavalrymen by one of the victims, Thomas Redford, to recover damages for injury; but it was really aimed at procuring a full investigation of the whole affair. On 9 Apr. a verdict was given for the defendants, on the grounds of the illegality of the meeting at St. Peter's Fields and the imminent danger it presented to life and property. 'The most incredulous must now be convinced', remarked the *Courier* on 12 Apr., 'that the Manchester Yeomanry had been basely calumniated by a seditious Press.' But the *Kendal Chronicle* of the following day condemned the verdict: 'Thus may the subjects of this realm be cut, maimed, or injured; thus may our laws and liberties be violated with impunity by Yeomanry Cavalry . . .' Henry Brougham might have been expected to have taken part in this controversy, but he had been ill and absent from Parliament. But he did appear briefly at Lancaster on 1 Apr. to defend a publisher prosecuted at the instigation of the Constitutional Association for seditious libel.

friendly letter,[1] but in fact they were rather worse at that time, and I thought you would infer from my silence that there was no improvement. I am truly sensible of the interest you take of this infirmity of mine, which makes me so dependent on others, abridges my enjoyments by cutting me off from the power of reading, and causes me to lose a great deal of time: and the worst of it is, that from the long standing of the complaint, I cannot encourage a hope of getting rid of it. The first attack was 18 years ago[2] when I had an inflammation in my eyelids, which by frequent returns has weakened them so much that they enflame upon slight occasions, and are scarcely ever both well at the same time: this affects the eyes by sympathy, and latterly the eyes themselves have been much annoyed by heat, and suffusions, proceeding from a weakness in the stomach, mainly caused by feelings stronger than my frame can bear and ill regulated application.

I am happy to hear of any intended Publication[3] of yours and shall be proud to receive any public testimony of your esteem. Mr Southey left me a few hours before I received your last, he had been so kind as to come over for two or three days; he was very well, and making regular progress in many works—his history of the Peninsular War,[4] a Book on the Church in England,[5] two Poems,[6] with regular communications in the Quar[ly] Review[7] into the bargain. Have you heard of the attacks of Byron upon him and his answer?[8] his L[dsp] has lost as much by this affair as S. has

---

[1] Dated Florence, 22 Feb.

[2] i.e. on New Year's Day, 1805. W. W.'s first attack of trachoma occurred after a walk over the Kirkstone Pass to visit the Hutchinsons at Park House. See the I. F. note to '*A little onward lend thy guiding hand*' (*PW* iv. 422), and *EY*, pp. 527–8.

[3] The *Imaginary Conversations*, which Landor had been planning for some time. (See R. H. Super, *Walter Savage Landor*, 1957, pp. 158–9.) 'I have inscribed them to you, in few lines', he had written to W. W. But the proposed dedication has not survived.

[4] 3 vols., 1823, –27, –32. See Warter, iii. 259. It was entirely superseded by Sir William Napier's volumes, the first of which appeared in 1828. Unlike Southey, Napier had access to the Duke of Wellington's papers and showed a surer grasp of military policy.

[5] *The Book of the Church*, 2 vols., 1824. It led to a controversy with Charles Butler, who published *The Book of the Roman Catholic Church* the following year. Southey answered him in *Vindiciae Ecclesiae Anglicanae*, 1826.

[6] *A Tale of Paraguay*, 1825 (*Works*, vii. 11 ff.), in Spenserian stanzas, founded on an incident in Dobrizhoffer's Latin *History*, had been occupying Southey since about 1814 (the date of the dedication to Edith Southey): *Oliver Newman, a New England Tale*, 'an Anglo-American Iliad of King Philip's War', was begun about the same time, but published unfinished by Herbert Hill in 1845. See Southey, v. 195.

[7] Recent contributions had included the 'Life of Cromwell', xxv (1821), 279–347.   [8] See above, L. 51.

gained, whose letter was circulated in almost every newspaper in England. S. means to send you a parcel of books, and I have requested him to include in it two things which I have lately published, the one, Ecclesiastical Sketches, a sort of Poem in the sonnet stanza, or measure, and the other, Memories of a Tour on the Continent in the year 1820—the tour brought me to Como a place that, with the scenery of its Lake, had existed in my most lively recollection for upwards of 30 years. What an addition would it have been to my pleasure if I had found you there! Time did not allow me to get further into Italy than Milan, where I was much pleased with the Cathedral especially, as you will collect if you ever see these Poems, from one of them entitled 'The eclipse of the Sun'.

I am surprized, and rather sorry, when I hear you say you read little, because you are removed from the pressure of the trash which hourly issuing from the Press in England, tends to make the very name of writing and books disgusting. I am so situated as to see little of it, but one cannot stop one's ears, and I sometimes envy you that distance which separates you altogether from this intrusion. It is reported here that Byron, Shelley, Moore, Leigh Hunt (I do not know if you have heard of all these names) are to lay their heads together in some Town of Italy, for the purpose of conducting a Journal[1] to be directed against everything in religion, in morals and probably in government and literature, which our Forefathers have been accustomed to reverence,—the notion seems very extravagant but perhaps the more likely to be realized on that account.

Mr Kenyon left us in Sept[r] with the intention of proceeding directly to Italy, but omitted to forward my letter when he changed his purpose and took a wife instead—he talks of starting for the continent, with his Lady, but only for the summer, so I am afraid you will not see him. We have as a near neighbour another amiable Person, an old Acquaintance of yours, Mr Quillinan, who knew you

---

[1] In 1821 Byron and Shelley proposed that Leigh Hunt should join them in establishing a quarterly liberal magazine. Soon after Hunt's arrival in Italy in June 1822 Shelley was drowned (8 July), and Moore declined an invitation to assist; but Hunt and Byron went ahead with the undertaking, in spite of their increasingly strained relationship, and the first number of *The Liberal, Verse and Prose from the South*, London, 1822, printed by and for John Hunt, appeared in the October. It opened with *The Vision of Judgment*, which had been written for almost a year, and held back by Murray the publisher; and Hazlitt contributed five papers, including 'My First Acquaintance with Poets' in the third number. As a friend of Southey, Landor himself did not escape criticism, but the whole project collapsed the following year, after only four numbers had appeared. See Leigh Hunt, *Autobiography*, chs. xix–xx, and William H. Marshall, *Byron, Shelley, Hunt, and 'The Liberal'*, Philadelphia, 1960.

at Bath. He was lately of the Third Dragoon Guards, but has retired on ½ pay. He married a daughter of Sir Egerton Brydges, and they live, with two nice children, at the foot of our hill. He begs to be kindly remembered to you.

In respect to Latin Poetry, I ought to tell you that I am no judge, except upon general principles. I never practised Latin verse, not having been educated at one of the Public Schools. My acquaintance with Virgil, Horace, Lucretius, and Catullus is intimate; but as I never read them with a critical view to composition great faults in language might be committed which would escape my notice; any opinion of mine, therefore, on points of classical nicety would be of no value, should I be so inconsiderate as to offer it. A few days ago, being something better in my sight, I read your Sponsalia;[1] it is full of spirit and animation, and is probably of that style of versification which suits the subject; yet, if you thought proper, you could produce, I think, a richer harmony; and I met some serious inaccuracies in the punctuation which, from the state of my eyes encreasing the difficulty of catching the sense, took something from the pleasure of the perusal. The first book whic[h I read] unless it be one in large type, shall be these Poems. I must express a wish, however, that you would gratify us by writing in English—there are noble and stirring things in all that you have written in your native tongue, and that is enough for me. In your Simoneida,[2] which I saw some years ago at Mr Southey's, I was pleased to find rather an out-of-the-way image, in which the present hour is compared to the shade on the dial. It is a singular coincidence, that in the year 1793, when I first became an author, I illustrated the sentiment precisely in the same manner.[3] In the same work you commend the fine conclusion of Russel's sonnet upon Philoctetes,[4] and depreciate that form of composition. I do not wonder at this; I used to think it egregiously absurd, though the greatest poets since the revival of literature have written in it. Many years ago my sister happened to read to me the sonnets of Milton, which I could at that time repeat; but somehow

---

[1] *Sponsalia Polyxenae*, the third of the *Idyllia heroica*: later translated by Landor and published in his *Hellenics*, 1847, as *The Esposals of Polyxena*.
[2] i.e. *Simonidea*, English and Latin poems, Bath, [1806].
[3] *Evening Walk*, ll. 37–42 (*PW* i. 6).
[4] Thomas Russell (1762–88); his *Sonnets and Miscellaneous Poems* were published in 1789. In Southey's *Vision of Judgment* he is coupled with Chatterton; and Landor said of the Philoctetes sonnet that it 'would authorize him to join the shades of Sophocles and Euripides'. W. W. introduced the last four lines of his tenth sonnet into his own sonnet *Iona* (*Upon Landing*) in the *Itinerary Poems of 1833* (*PW* iv. 43).

or other I was singularly struck with the style of harmony, and the gravity, and republican austerity of those compositions. In the course of the same afternoon I produced 3 sonnets, and soon after many others; and since that time, and from want of resolution to take up anything of length, I have filled up many a moment in writing Sonnets, which, if I had never fallen into the practice, might easily have been better employed. The Excursion is proud of your approbation. *The Recluse* has had a long sleep, save in my thoughts; my MSS. are so ill-penned and blurred that they are useless to all but myself; and at present I cannot face them. But if my stomach can be preserved in tolerable order, I hope you will hear of me again in the character chosen for the title of that Poem.

I am glad that you are a Father and wish for a peep at your boys, with yourself to complete the trio.[1] Southey's Son[2] continues to thrive and promises well, and his family is flourishing.

I expect your book with impatience and shall at all times be glad to hear from you. I remain faithfully yours,

[*signed*] Wm Wordsworth

62. D. W. to H. C. R.

Endorsed: 21 April 1822, Miss Wordsworth.
MS. Dr. Williams's Library.
K. Morley, i. 117.

Rydal Mount, Ap. 21ᵗ [1822]

My dear Friend

If you have not seen Mr Monkhouse before this reaches you, no doubt you will seek *him* out, or *he* you, ere another day passes over your heads, therefore I need not tell you any Rydal news.—We were truly sorry as you may believe to part with him so soon—and for *his* sake as well as our own; for he is leaving this Country just at the time when, he (being an ardent and very successful angler) would find the most pleasure here.

I wish very much for that reason, that his stay had been *now*, rather than in the Autumn—besides—a Bird in the hand is worth two in the Bush.—We know not what may happen to prevent his fulfilling his present scheme of returning hither. However, having

---

[1] 'I never wished for children,' Landor had written, 'having disciplined myself in early life to wish for nothing—but my two children and I are the three noisiest children in Florence . . .' Arnold Savage Landor was just four at this time, Julia Elizabeth two.   [2] Cuthbert.

taken a house exactly to his Wife's mind and his own, is a good
security that nothing but necessity will turn him aside. Mrs Monkhouse will be our neighbour at the foot of the hill, so that she will
not find her situation lonely.—

No doubt you are as busy as possible yet I have been unreasonable enough—not to *expect* to hear from you; but often to think to
myself, 'Perhaps there may be a letter from Mr Robinson today.'—
If you had been a formal person (but I am glad you are not; and as
poor Coleridge used to say) I 'like you the better there*fore*'—you
certainly would have written after having looked over the
Memorials,—(finding yourself one of the *Dedicatees*)[1] to express
your sense of the high honour.—Seriously, however, I should like
to know how you like the whole volume,—*which* poems you like
best—and what you do *not* like—if any—and my Brother wishes,
too, to know if the Desultory Stanzas have given you pleasure, as
they were inspired by your letter.[2]

It is generally supposed that Longman has an interest[3] in the
'Literary Gazette'—Do you know whether he actually has, or has
not? If he has, he has used my Brother very ill by suffering his
'Ecclesiastical Sketches' and 'Memorials' to be reviewed by a
person who could give such a *senseless* criticism[4]—Besides, a sacrifice is made of W. Wordsworth to obtain for the Literary Gazette
the Reputation of impartiality. This is clearly the object of the
criticism, as is plain from the last paragraph of the review of the
Memorials; wherein the Writer declares that, that Journal proves
its impartiality, by censuring without reserve those whom he is
pleased to call the heads of their several schools when they write
such stuff as Mr W. has now given to the public—It would not
have been worth while to have said so much about so despicable

[1] W. W. dedicated the *Memorials* to his 'Fellow-travellers'. See *PW* iii.
164, and *MY* ii. 615.
[2] See L. 56 above.
[3] In 1820 Longmans had become part-proprietors and publishers of the
Literary Gazette, then under the editorship of William Jerdan (see *MY* ii. 547).
[4] The *Ecclesiastical Sketches* were reviewed on 30 Mar. 1822; the *Memorials*
on 6 Apr. Along with the severe criticism that runs through each article is a
more personal note of animosity against the poet himself. 'The disease of
mind which manifests itself in eruptions of poetry, is certainly an extraordinary
phenomenon, and as likely to puzzle the acumen of the critic as the symptoms
of the plague are calculated to perplex the skill of the physician. With Mr
Wordsworth it is evidently chronic . . . It is astonishing to see a man of genius
so far delude himself as to fancy he can render any thing popular, no matter how
untractable the subject, how prosaic the verse, and how absurd the plan.' The
conclusion of the first article is that 'The chaff is out of all proportion to the
grains'. The summary judgement on the *Memorials*, 'these teemings of egotisti-
cal complacency', is even harsher: 'there is hardly one . . . worth reading at all'.

a criticism, if it were not on account of my Brother's connection
with Longman[1]—We should not otherwise have given it a thought,
after the trifling vexation, that such an opinion of the poems
should even have *preceded* their publication, robbing us of the little
profit which might have arisen from a first flush of sale—the only
profit which could be expected from these little volumes.—

We had a letter from my Brother Christopher a few days ago.
He is in excellent health and good spirits; but so busy that he has
hardly time to think of his own affairs, and cannot yet say whether
it will be in his power to come into the North this summer. We
expect the Clarksons in a few weeks.—

My Brother is anxious to know what your plans are for the
autumn—not that there is the smallest chance of his benefiting by
them; but being so fond of travelling himself he sympathizes with
you in all your hopes and schemes in that line.—His eyes are better,
yet almost useless in reading—I think he will satisfy himself this
summer with a little Tour not far from home.—We had an interesting letter from Charles Lamb[2] not long ago. Pray mention him and
his Sister when you write; but I fear you do not see them often as
they are so much in the Country.—How is poor Barry Cornwall?—
I mean Mr Proctor. When I asked the question I had forgotten that
it was not his true name. We were very sorry to hear of his illness.

The Montagus, I doubt not, are very kind to him.—Do excuse
this stupid letter with all its blunders—Miss Hutchinson, a determined French Scholar, is puzzling over her lesson beside me and
every two minutes she asks me the meaning of a word—She gets on
admirably, without having studied a word of the Grammar—and
will very soon be a fluent Translator, stimulated by the hope, at
some time or other, of travelling on the Continent, and being able
at least to make her wants known on French ground She begs her
kind Regards to you—My sister, were she here, would send her
Love.—Adieu—

Believe me affectionately
Yours D Wordsworth.

[1] Longman hastened to reassure W. W. on 26 Apr. that he had no responsibility for the *Literary Gazette*: '. . . we have felt exceedingly chagrined at the
notices of your last two books. We have no more connexion with the writers in
that paper than yourself. When we purchased a share in it about three years
ago, there was a stipulation in the Articles of Agreement, to render the work
free from bookselling influence . . .' (W. J. B. Owen, 'Letters of Longman and
Co. to Wordsworth, 1814–36', *The Library*, 5th series, ix (Mar. 1954),
25–34.)

[2] Describing the personal losses he had suffered recently. 'Every departure
destroys a class of sympathies.' See *Lamb*, ii. 318.

63. W. W. to LADY ANN LE FLEMING[1]

MS. Fleming MSS., Record Office, Kendal.
Historical MSS. Commission, Twelfth Report, Appendix, Part VII, pp. 363–
4(—). LY i. 71(—).

[In M. W.'s hand]

Rydal Mount May 3ᵈ [1822]

Madam,

Knowing your Ladyship to be indisposed, I am sorry to trouble you with this letter, but as *your Tenant* I should not feel myself justified on the present occasion were I to omit stating to your Ladyship the nature of the repairs necessary at Rydal Mount, which have been from time to time delayed, and, as we are now informed, are not to be done at all.

The back apartments of the house ever since we entered upon it, have not been habitable in winter on account of the damp, and in wet seasons not even in Summer. Lord Suffolk's Agent some years ago, from the state of the timber gave an opinion that a new roof was necessary, and estimated the expence at £10. Since that time temporary repairs have been made, which were to have been completed at the first convenient season. Those repairs never made the house watertight; and to give your Ladyship an idea of its present state, I need only say, that, during the last heavy rains, an empty trunk standing in the best of the three rooms, was half filled with water.

Last summer, the late Mr Jackson[2] and the workmen examined with me the Premises, and it was our joint opinion that when the rooms were unroofed, if the walls were raised, it would be an advantage to the house very far beyond the additional expense, and one which we had little doubt would be approved by your Ladyship. Ld. Suffolk's agent was consulted; and as I understood, the plan was not, in the end, opposed by your Ladyship. On my part I was to pay interest upon the sum laid out, and on this supposition my family prepared for the workmen. To my surprize it was *afterwards* required that I should relinquish the barn, or part of the barn, and other out buildings or the work in the Dwelling was not to be

---

[1] Ann Frederica (1784–1861), only daughter and heiress of Sir Michael le Fleming, 4th Bart., and his wife Lady Diana, only daughter and heiress of Thomas Howard, 14th Earl of Suffolk and Berkshire, had married her cousin Sir Daniel le Fleming, 5th Bart. He had died the previous year, but she continued to reside at Rydal Hall.

[2] The Revd. Thomas Jackson, who died the previous December, had acted as Lady le Fleming's agent. His son Thomas, of Waterhead, succeeded him.

done. This, not only on account of the comfort and convenience to myself and family, but from respect to your Ladyship's property, I could not consent to; the character of the place would be entirely changed and vulgarized, were these premises turned into a common farmer's yard. This we have proved by experience, for upon our first coming to R. M., as a temporary accommodation, the farmer had the use of some of the buildings, and the annoyance of cattle hanging about the gates causing filth and intercepting the way upon the public road to the house may easily be conceived. To palliate this (and various other inconveniences) Mr J. proposed that the yard should be divided by a wall, and a gate broken out below, but this, without removing the evil from us, would only have thrown it nearer to the gates of the Hall, and probably have occasioned the felling of trees, and exposed the fold yard to the road. Besides, a part of the barn we could not possibly do without, and an apprehension of that very evil—fire (which has already taken place in our neighbour's premises) from the ingress and egress of a large family, many of them children, over whom I should have no control, was of itself sufficient to prevent my acceding to such an arrangement.

I have nothing to add to this long, but necessary statement, except to remind your Ladyship, that the rooms under consideration only in one part allow a person to stand upright, and that it remains to be considered whether it may not be better to raise the walls according to the plan proposed, or merely to make them water-tight, which can only be done by means of a new roof. For notwithstanding what I have heard, I cannot conceive that it is your Ladyship's intention that it should remain in its present state, especially after the long inconvenience we have suffered.

I have the honour to be Madam,

Your Ladyship's obedient St.

[*signed*] W. Wordsworth

64. W. W. to THE COMMISSIONERS OF STAMPS

Address: To the Hon'ble Commissioners, Stamp Office, London.
Postmark: 11 May 1822. *Stamp*: Kendal Penny Post. *Endorsed*: Mr Words-
worth Rydale Mount Ambleside 7 May 1822. Ansd 13 May 1822.
MS. Public Record Office. Hitherto unpublished.

[*In John Carter's hand*]

Rydal Mount, Ambleside,
7 May 1822—

Hon'ble Sirs,

I beg to be informed how the Executor under the Will of the
late Mr: Backhouse,[1] must account for the duty on the Annuities to
Mrs: Backhouse and Miss Backhouse, which are bequeathed under
the following peculiar circumstances.—

I have the Honor to be
Hon'ble Sirs
Your obedient Servant
[*signed*] Wm Wordsworth

Testator directs his Executor to deduct from Miss B's Income £50
per Annum, to be paid to Mrs: B towards Housekeeping so long
as they live together:—In case they do not live together, *then* to
deduct from Miss B's Income £25 pr. Ann: and pay the same to
Mrs: B:

The Parties yet live together: The Executor considers £25 pr:
Ann: as a sufficient compensation for Miss B's Board and that the
additional £25 was left in order to induce the Parties to live
together.—

---

[1] According to a memorandum added to this letter, an annuity of £50 out
of income was bequeathed by the Will to the Testator's sister Cicely. The
executors were to pay this amount as her share and contribution towards
housekeeping expenses to Elizabeth Backhouse (the wife) as long as they lived
together. An annuity of £25 to the wife was to take the place of this arrangement if the two separated.

65. W. W. to THE COMMISSIONERS OF STAMPS

Address: To The Hon'ble Commissioners, Stamp Office, London.
Postmark: 11 May 1822. *Stamp*: Kendal Penny post. *Endorsed*: Wm Words-
worth Esq Rydal Mount Ambleside, Westmorland.
MS. Public Record Office. Hitherto unpublished.

[*In John Carter's hand*]

Rydal Mount, Ambleside,
8 May 1822—

Hon'ble Sirs,

I beg leave to state that the undermentioned Persons are appointed by me to the collection of Legacy Duties.

I have the Honor to be
Honble Sirs
Your obedient Servant
[*signed*] Wm Wordsworth

P.S. My parcel of Legacy Rects. was forwarded this day.

Messrs: Faraday and Grime—Drapers, Kirkby Stephen.
Mrs: Hodgson, Widow, Whitehaven.

66. D. W. to EDWARD QUILLINAN

Address: Edward Quillinan Esqre, No. 17 Fludyer St., Westminster, London.
Stamp: Kendal Penny Post.
MS. WL.
LY i. 73.

[22 May 1822]

My dear Friend,

I sit by your dear Wife's bed-side.[1] She *was* to dictate for me;
but I must put it into my own words—'Tell him, she says, I am
doing as well as can possibly be expected.'—I stop again—and
ask her a question 'Have you no message to send?' 'Oh yes, about
the Children. Say they are both uncommonly well.' That is the
truth and they give their Mother as little disturbance, and as much
comfort as possible—Sunday night was a good one—Monday
morning no worse; but in the afternoon there was an accession of
fever—and we had a *bad* night. Last night was very good—Today

[1] For the details of Mrs. Quillinan's accident, see L. 70 below. She died
on Saturday, 25 May. E. Q. had gone away on business the previous Saturday
and left her in D. W.'s care, and this letter was written the following Wednesday, while she was still making progress towards recovery.

she has been perfectly composed—and now (at 7 o'clock) is cool and without fever. So far very good—I feel little or no doubt of her now going on with the most perfect regularity. But having told you how we stand at present I must revert to the past—Monday night was indeed a very bad one—not that I was alarmed, but the fever ran so high that I thought it right to send for Mr Carr;[1] which we did at 12 o'clock. He stayed with us till past 3—the fever, then was almost gone—she took her draught and in the morning was very composed and had no fever or very little—and at about 2 being quite cool, we gave her the Bark—but, the heat returning, we only gave it once. This morning at 6 she took it again, has continued to do so every three hours—and is at this moment a great deal cooler than I am—in short has no fever whatsoever—has taken by Mr C.'s orders $\frac{1}{2}$ a glass of port wine, and it really now seems that we have nothing to do but strengthen her—to enable her to bear the pain which is yet for her to endure.—The sores give her less pain—and are going on perfectly as they ought to do.

I think you will be quite satisfied, if not already so, when I add to this good account of Mrs Q. that she has been without her two head nurses today from nine o'clock in the morning till 6 tonight. A trifling accident befel my Brother on his way to Haweswater— God be praised it was but a trifling one, though it might have been very bad.—He had got from the Back of his pony to go into a Cottage when within two miles of Bampton, where they intended to halt for the night. In mounting again, fumbling between his portmanteau and umbrella the horse was frightened and threw him against a stone wall and the Back of his head was cut. Of these particulars I knew nothing this morning—only that he had had a fall—and being at the house of Dr Satterthwaite, wanted female attendance, therefore Mr Monkhouse[2] wrote to desire my sister to set off immediately. The messenger arrived at a little after 11 o'clock she being just parted from Mrs Q. and me—The letter said nothing of the nature of the wound—nothing but that it was in the head—that the Dr had dressed it and that my dear Brother was very composed. My sister durst not send down to me for fear of our poor sick Friend's alarm—D[3] and she set off—and this

---

[1] Thomas Carr (1795–1856), the Ambleside surgeon. He married Ann Dowling.

[2] In the spring Thomas Monkhouse and his family had rented a house 'at the foot of the hill' in Rydal. He had been called away towards the end of April (see L. 62 above), but had since returned. W. W. had evidently gone with him and Mr. Gee on a fishing expedition when the accident occurred.

[3] Dora W.

morning Miss Horrocks sent for me—attempted to break the force
of the tidings by preparations—more frightful than the letter itself
—and from the letter I could gather no hope but what was chased
away by a frightful fear. All day I lay on a bed at Mrs Monkhouse's
and till 4 o'clock past when the happy news arrived—two letters—
one from D one from her mother. Nothing in this world ever made
me so happy as D's letter. Before she finished she talked of being
at *home* at Lowther and delighted with Dr Satterthwaite's kindness
and hospitality! She said her Father was in good spirits had no
fever and even *wished* to come home in the chaise; but quiet was
necessary. I shall urge them to stay till he is quite well.—I will not
attempt to describe my own wretched state—all this day.—My only
comfort that I could rest upon was the thought that D was gone with
her Mother. Mrs Monkhouse and Mr Carr explained away my
long absence (which grieved your wife) by saying that I was unwell
with the heat, my Sister's by saying that she had been called away
from home by the sickness of a Friend. My first business, as it was
my first duty, when sufficiently composed after the inrush of thankfulness and joy—was to come and see your wife—who received me
joyfully, but was anxious for an explanation. I gave it chearfully.
She saw I was happy in my own feelings and is now as chearful as
I am; and was never thrown into agitation—Rotha has just been
giving her Mother the evening kiss before undressing. God bless
you, my dear Friend! and bring you back safe again to the Ivy
Cottage. We shall be anxious to hear from you. I will write daily—
and I trust you will find a great change for the better at your return.

Yours truly   Dorothy Wordsworth.

You will not wonder at my penmanship,—nor even if my letter
is not perfectly coherent. The past is like a horrible dream to me.

67. D. W. to EDWARD QUILLINAN

Address: Edward Quillinan Esq., 17 Fludyer St^r, Westminster, London.
Postmark: 27 May 1822. *Stamp*: Kendal Penny Post.
MS. WL.
LY i. 75.

Wednesday Evening. [?Thursday, 23 May 1822]

My Dear Mr Quillinan,
    I think you will look long for a letter before next Monday,
therefore I write to tell you merely that we have gone on very well

to-day. It is 7 o'clock—and no return of fever—and the port wine and bark have been taken as before with broth and a *little* animal food.

After I closed my letter of yesterday the fever came on, but not very strong, and she had some pain in the bowels—which with constant affliction of the back and arm it was hard enough to bear— but before I went to bed she had taken her draught (between 3 and 4 o'clock) and was quiet and settled. Yet her sleeps were but by snatches. It is now near 8 and no fever, indeed I think I may say that *to-day* she seems as if she were *gaining ground*, which before I could never absolutely be satisfied that she was, for many hours together.

I am writing in her room—and (asking her what I must say) she answers—'I think you may say I am a good deal better', and this neither in a weak or a disturbed voice.

Mr Carr spoke well of the arm to-day, and seemed to think the sores were going on well.

I sent Wilson Morris[1] to Lowther to-day—and he has returned with the most satisfactory accounts of my dear Brother. He has no fever—has nothing to complain of but being fed on slops, and the only difficulty in managing him is to keep him from talking.

Mr Gee will return to-morrow—Mr Monkhouse on Thursday[2]— so that we shall have the speediest tidings possible.

My poor sister and Dora had a dismal journey in their way over Kirkstone, but their suspense was in some degree relieved at Pooley Bridge, where they were told there was no danger, but this you may be sure could not satisfy *them*. *My* suspense was of longer duration. Never in my whole life did I pass so wretched a day. The short lived hope—a perplexing shadow of good, was chased away instantly by the most dreadful of all fears, and thus I struggled from before 8 till 5 or after.

To-day I have been very anxious but I kept it from your Wife —anxious I could not help being in the fear of fever, but now I am quite satisfied. Excuse this, I must write to the Boys, God bless you. Your dear wife says you must not make yourself uneasy about her that she now feels herself doing well—longs to hear from you— and sends her best love.

Do not expect to hear from us again till Tuesday—I will write again on Sunday and not before—unless something unlooked for occurs.

[*unsigned*]

[1] A Rydal neighbour mentioned in L. 83 below.
[2] i.e. Thursday, 30th. He was still at Lowther on the 29th (see next letter).

Address: The Rev^d. Dr. Wordsworth, Trinity Lodge, Cambridge.
Postmark: 30 May 1822. *Stamp*: Penrith.
MS. WL. Hitherto unpublished.

Lowther Rectory
May 29th. 1822.

My dear Uncle,

Dr Satterthwaite has just received your letter containing the most delightful news we have heard for a very long time,[1] and he requested me to answer it as he was going out with my Father and Mother to walk towards Askam Church; from this you may conclude he is quite well. Indeed we ourselves have had, since the first two or three days, so little anxiety about him, that we forgot you who were at so great a distance, could not know how things were going on, and must have been kept in great suspense and anxiety. But I trust you have considered no news as good news, which it most certainly has been. The only thing now to be attended to, is to keep him perfectly quiet, so we could not be in a better place than we are, and we shall be grateful all our lives to the D^r for his great kindness and hospitality to us during the time we have been under his roof.

I suppose we shall go home about the end of this week or the beginning of next, the Clarksons are there now[2] which makes us— [*W. W. writes*] Here Dorothy was interrupted last night, and this morning she is gone with her mother and Mr Monkhouse to Haweswater; so I shall add a few words. I am truly sorry, my dear Brother, that Mary did not write to you but we had taken for granted that Dr S's Letter had been so expressed, as that you would conclude I was doing well if you did not hear to the contrary, and as D has said above, not being anxious ourselves, we were not considerate enough for others. In fact I have suffered no pain, and little inconvenience, but it is necessary from the depth of the cut in my head that I should continue to be very cautious. I was bled the day after the accident and had lost much blood from the wound previously. Nothing can exceed the kindness of Dr S. to whom we feel greatly indebted.—I am truly happy to hear of your coming

---

[1] The news of C. W.'s proposed visit in the summer. W. W. and Dora W. were still at Dr. Satterthwaite's following the accident described in L. 66.

[2] Thomas Clarkson had written to W. W. on 16 May (*WL MSS.*) that they were leaving London in a day or two and expected to arrive at Rydal in eight or nine days. They actually arrived on the 27th, and stayed a fortnight. W. W. did not return home till their second week.

along with Boys; Mrs W. says every thing you mention shall be supplied, and particulars given when we return. Lord Lonsdale, perhaps you would hear, has had also an ugly fall from his horse; providentially no wound in the head—and he is doing well, though with the Collar Bone and two ribs broken.—The weather is most beautiful, and this place truly charming.—The D^r will add a few words.¹

ever my dear B^r, most faithfully yours
W Wordsworth

69. W. W. to ALLAN CUNNINGHAM²

Address: To Mr Cunningham at Mr Chantry's, Pimlico. By favour of Mr Gee.
Postmark: 21 June 1822. *Stamp*: Chancery Ln.
MS. Mr. W. Hugh Peal.
K (—). *LY i.* 77(—).

[*In M. W.'s hand*]

Rydal Mount
June 12th 1822

Dear Sir,

Mr Gee being upon the point of returning to London, I wish him to be the Bearer of my thanks for the Present of your Book³ rec^d thro' his hands; and your obliging Letter, which I forwarded to Mr Southey as the best means of communicating Mr Chantry's wishes respecting the transfer of the Bust.⁴ Before I rec^d Mr S's answer I had the misfortune to fall from my Horse, and was so much hurt in my Head that I could not return home for more than a fortnight—during which time, and previously, my House was in great confusion and trouble, from other causes, so that whether any

¹ Dr. Satterthwaite added a note, expressing his pleasure at W. W.'s recovery, and at the prospect of C. W. coming north with his boys in the summer: 'If they remember me at all, it must be as a Patron of fishing, and you may tell them, I have both a Lake and a river here and all the other necessary etc^s for giving them as good Trout fishing as I believe the Island affords, and a more cordial welcome they can have under no roof in Christendom.'
² Allan Cunningham (1784–1842) trained as a stonemason, left Scotland for London in 1810, and became Chantrey's secretary and superintendent of works from 1814 to 1841. In 1829 and 1830 he edited an Annual entitled *The Anniversary*; from 1829 to 1833 wrote his *Lives of the Most Eminent British Painters, Sculptors, and Architects*; and in 1834 published an edition of Burns. He was also a minor poet, and published songs and ballads, and a collection of *The Songs of Scotland* (1825), as well as tales and romances. His *Life of Sir David Wilkie* was published posthumously.
³ *Sir Marmaduke Maxwell, a Dramatic Poem*; *The Mermaid of Galloway*; *The Legend of Richard Faulder*; *and Twenty Scottish Songs*, 1822.
⁴ W. W. was continuing to present his friends with casts of his bust by Chantrey.

answer has been sent to me from Mr Southey I am unable to say—but I think it probable that he has written to Mr Chantry expressing his pleasure and satisfaction at this mark of attention.

Mrs W. begs you to be so kind as to mention to Mr C. that the more she is familiar with the Bust the more she likes it, which is the case with all my Family. As to my own opinion it can be of little value as to the likeness, but as a work of fine Art I may be excused if I say that it seems to me fully entitled to that praise which is universally given to Mr Chantry's Labours.

The state of my eyes for a long time has only allowed me to read books of large Print, and from this, and the unfortunate causes above alluded to, which have occupied the time of those of my family who read for me,—I have not yet been able to make myself acquainted with more than a few of the first scenes of your drama, one of your Ballads, and the Songs. I am therefore prevented from accompanying my thanks with those notices which to an intelligent Author give such an acknowledgement its principal value. The Songs appear to me full as good as those of Burns, with the exception of a *very* few of his best,—and The Mermaid is wild, tender, and full of Spirit. The little I have seen of the Play I liked, especially the Speeches of the Spirits, and that of Macgee, page 7th. I hope, in a little time, to be acquainted with the rest of the volume.

Mr Gee will tell you how we have been harrassed and troubled, by the Affliction of our neighbour Mr Quillinan, in which he himself has fully participated.

I remain dr sir very sincerely yours
[*signed*] Wm Wordsworth

70. D. W. to JANE MARSHALL

Address: [Mrs] Marshall, Post Office, Leamington, Warwickshire. [*readdressed to*] [   ] Hotel, 16 Bond St., London.
Stamp: Kendal Penny Post. *Endorsed*: Alarming accident to Mr W. Mrs Quillinan's death—1822.
MS. WL.
K (—). *LY i.* 77.

13th June, 1822.

My dear Friend,

Your kind letter reached me yesterday; but I was then so hurried that it was impossible to find a quarter of an hour for writing, and I am now too late to catch you before your departure from London.

Truly glad was I to find that Cordelia[1] and John[2] had so much benefited by the Leamington waters; and that you were all enjoying yourselves so much in London; a pleasant preparation for the quiet of the country, which, by contrast, will appear the more delightful. As you do not mention that the original disorder was the hooping-cough, I conclude it was not; and that you will have no fears of bringing infection to Hallsteads when you have stayed your time at Leamington.

I hope that ere this you have heard of my Brother's perfect recovery—yet bad news flying generally with more speed than good, though the bad reached you soon enough, the good may have lingered on the road. The accident *might* have been terrible indeed! Had the horse been one inch nearer the wall his Death would have been inevitable—the sharp stone which gave a grazing side-cut to the skull would have penetrated into the head. Indeed we can never be sufficiently thankful to Providence for the many favourable circumstances attending this accident. It happened, not at Haweswater; but about 2 miles on this side of Bampton. My Brother had kind and judicious Friends at hand. He was removed to Dr. Satterthwaite's and very soon after he reached that quiet comfortable house Dr Harrison[3] arrived. At first, he could not exactly ascertain the degree of injury, nor was it known when a messenger was despatched to Rydal. He arrived at 12 o'clock at night, when my Sister was undressing to go to bed to her Daughter, after having left me with poor Mrs Quillinan then in a very feverish state, as she always was from the ev^{ng} till a certain time in the morning. They set off over Kirkstone immediately, not daring to inform me of the letter, for fear of injury to our suffering Friend. The next morning (and you may judge of my Terror and distress when I tell you that the intelligence, though with due caution respecting Mrs Q., was communicated to me in the most alarming way possible) I was informed what had happened. My wretchedness and anxiety were extreme till 4 o'clock when I heard from my Sister that all was likely to go on well—only that absolute quiet would be needful for a long time. He was in the very place that if we had had

[1] Mrs. Marshall's third daughter, Cordelia (1803–53). In 1841 she married William Whewell, C. W.'s successor as Master of Trinity.
[2] Her second son, John Marshall II (1797–1836), of Headingley and Keswick: partner in the family flax business, and M.P. for Leeds from 1832. He married Mary (1803–74), eldest daughter of J. D. B. Dykes of Dovenby (see *MY* ii. 466).
[3] Thomas Harrison of Kendal. See *MY* ii. 427.

the whole world to chuse from, we should have selected—both for quietness and kindness—therefore I returned to my sick Friend with chearful composure.

I have spoken of Mrs Quillinan as if you knew all the dismal particulars of her case; but perhaps you have not heard a word of them and know no more than that she was the Wife of Mr Q., a Lieutenant in the 3rd Dragoon Guards, that they lodged a while at Penrith, afterwards came to live here, and that she was afflicted with mental derangement after the Birth of her last child. She recovered from this affliction and was settled entirely to her satisfaction and her Husband's in Mr Tillbrook's house, the Ivy Cottage, but what a change have 5 weeks brought about! Her clothes accidentally took fire—she was grievously burnt—put to bed, and never rose after but to have her bed made. The Burn spread over a great part of her Body, but the abdomen was spared—in consequence of her having on a flannel petticoat and that being the case, as the Burns (except under one arm) were not very deep, and the *fire* (as we express it) was soon got out, every one hoped for her speedy recovery: but, when the wounds ought to have begun to heal—they grew worse—and at the end of a fortnight, from languor of constitution she expired. It was my lot to attend her death-bed. Her Husband had been obliged to go to London on especial Business the Saturday preceding her Death. (I was to stay with her during his absence, and how little did he, or any of us, foresee what was to happen!) (She died on the morning of the following Saturday.) My Sister, as you will have gathered, was at Lowther; Miss Hutchinson was at Harrowgate—thus I was quite alone, and thankful I am that it *was* so; for the dear Creature wanted no other help except that of the Servant who attended upon her. My Sister, in the beginning had been called upon to perform a trying part, the assisting to dress the wounds; her absence was not missed, and it was well she was spared the last awful scene.

You will be glad to hear that I, though as you may suppose, much harassed and exhausted when all was over, soon recovered myself; and it was a great satisfaction to me to find how well able I had been to go through the trial, and I pray that I may never in sickness and sorrow for[get the] example of patience and sweetness of disposit[ion the s]ufferer exhibited throughout the [? whole illness].[1] Not a word of complaint even. [Mr. Quillin]an has left the Cottage. [   ] He departed y[ester]day evening. [My sis]ter is gone with him as far as Matlock, on his way to the neighbour-

[1] *MS. torn.*

hood of Canterbury.[1] She and my Brother and Dorothy did not come home till the day after the Funeral. Since that time we have had every kind of arrangement to make in the melancholy house. Mr Q. and two of his Wife's Brothers[2] did not arrive till 6 days after Mrs Q.'s death.

They attended the funeral three days after their arrival. Mr Gee was my kind support and helper, in all preparatory arrangements, and he and I had the melancholy satisfaction of following the body to the Grave. It was a most fortunate circumstance that Mr Gee happened to be at Ambleside at the time. He remained in Mr Q.'s house till the arrival of the afflicted Husband and Brothers; and the Children were at Rydal Mount.

Mrs Quillinan is buried in the same corner of the church-yard where lie our little Catharine and Thomas. I went to order the grave, and chuse the spot on the morning of Mr Quillinan's return.

It happened very unfortunately for Mr and Mrs Clarkson that they came only two days after Mrs Q.'s death to pay a visit promised for years—and no one of the Family but myself was at home during the first half of a fortnight allotted to us. They left us last Tuesday for Scotland.

My Brother and Sister called at Hallsteads in their way to Lowther. Unluckily none of your sisters were there; and they only saw Julia;[3] but they could not have made any stay had they been more fortunate in finding others of the Family at home. Do excuse this sad scrawl—I have other letters to write and am hurried to get done in post-time.

My Brother and Sister thank you heartily for your kind anxiety concerning them. My Sister is *pretty* well—not quite strong.

Remember us to all and believe me

Yours aff[ectionately,]
D. Wordsworth.

[1] E. Q. left his children with his brother-in-law at Lee Priory, and embarked the following month on an extended tour of the Continent.
[2] Capt. Thomas Brydges (1789–1834), of the Grenadier Guards, who assumed the additional surname of Barrett on inheriting the Lee Priory estate from his maternal uncle; and John William Egerton Brydges, 2nd Bart. (1791–1848), of the dragoons. Both died unmarried.
[3] Julia Anne (1809–41), Mrs. Marshall's sixth daughter. In 1833 she married the Revd. Henry Venn Elliott (1792–1865), Fellow of Trinity College, Cambridge (1816), and perpetual curate of St. Mary's, Brighton, from 1827.

71. W. W. to LORD LONSDALE

MS. Lonsdale MSS. Hitherto unpublished.

Rydal Mount
July 18th 1822

My Lord,

Mr Monkhouse who is now in London, begs that if I were writing to your Lordship, I would request leave for two or three days shooting on some of the Moors for himself and Mr Horrocks jun[1] of Preston, from the 12th of August. Though aware of the embarassments which these numerous applications some times occasion, I do not scruple to make this request, more especially as it furnishes me with an opportunity of congratulating your Lordship, directly, as I have previously done through others, upon the happy issue of the operation upon your eyes, and likewise upon the recovery from the effects of the severe accident which befel you in the Park. In these heart-felt congratulations all my family unite, with wishes and prayers for the blessing of heaven upon you and yours.

From various causes this last spring and the present summer have been melancholy to my Family. Our heaviest trouble was caused by my younger Son who nearly three weeks ago returned from School suffering under dropsy,[2] without our having heard a word of anything ailing him. Mr Harrison[3] was called from Kendal; he had I believe little hope of his recovery; but I am happy to say that within these last three days a most favorable change has taken place; so that we are full of hope. The anxiety I have suffered on his account has made me feel that my head is not so strong as before my late accident.

We hear nothing of Sir George and Lady Beaumont.

Sir Richard le Fleming[4] is our present Rector; he has done duty in the Church and is said to read agreeably.

Mr Dawes the clergyman of Ambleside a few days ago was

---

[1] Thomas Monkhouse's brother-in-law. He owned property in Kirkby Lonsdale and was a freeholder of Westmorland.

[2] Willy did not return to the Charterhouse after his recovery, but remained at home and attended Mr. Dawes's school in Ambleside, where he was taught for a time by Hartley Coleridge.   [3] See previous letter.

[4] The Revd. Sir Richard le Fleming, 6th Bart. (1791–1857), of Trinity Hall, Cambridge, succeeded his brother Sir Daniel in 1821. He had also just succeeded William Jackson as rector of Grasmere, a living he held (along with that of Windermere) until his death. He was, according to S. H., 'tho' a Reverend, . . . even more of a Graceless than his Brother Sir Daniel' (*SH*, p. 230); and the Clarksons, during their visit to Rydal, were much put out by W. W.'s praise for him (see Morley, i. 120).

struck with apolexy; his recovery was despaired of; but there are
expressed hopes of his getting better.

    With respectful remembrances to Lady Lonsdale, in which Mrs
Wordsworth and my Sister unite

I have the honor to be

my Lord

ever faithfully your Lordship's friend and Serv^(nt)

Wm Wordsworth

72. W. W. to WILLIAM PEARSON[1]

MS. untraced.
Pearson. K. LY i. 81.

1^(st) August, [1822]

Dear Sir,

    The weather having been so bad, you will scarcely have set out
on your Tour, therefore I hope these few notes will be in time to
be of service to you.[2]

    We were pleased with the vale of Nith.—The ruins of Lin-
cluden Abbey or Priory are near Dumfries, on the road up the
vale; but little of them remains. Drumlanrig, the mansion of the
late Duke of Queensbury, which is a long way up the Vale, we did
not see—turning off to Lead Hills, a village inhabited by miners;
thence nothing interesting to Lanark,—at Lanark, falls of the
Clyde and Mr Owen's[3] establishment. Beautiful country to Hamilton, where in the Duke's palace, a fine collection of pictures.
Thence to Bothwel Castle, Glasgow,—Dumbarton,—Loch Lomond,
—Luss, fine view of the islands of Loch Lomond from the top of
Inch ta Vannoch, Tarbet, Arroqher,—Glen Crow, Inverary,—
Kilchurn Castle on Loch Awe, very striking; Dalmally. Thence we
went to Loch Etive,—to Portnacroish on Loch Linnhe, interesting

---

  [1] William Pearson (1780–1856), born at Crosthwaite, nr. Kendal. After
seventeen years in a Manchester bank he returned in 1820 to take up farming in
his native village, and interested himself in natural history and local antiquities.
He was an early admirer of W. W. and wrote him a long letter in criticism of
Peter Bell and *The Waggoner*, 'the most lively and humourous of all your poems',
on 30 July 1819: '. . . You may not dislike to hear the real opinions of some of
your less learned admirers' (*WL MSS.*).
  [2] The itinerary given below mainly follows the route pursued by W. W.,
D. W., and S. T. C. during the Scottish Tour of 1803. See *DWJ* i. 195 ff., and
Coleridge Notebooks, i. 1426 ff.
  [3] Robert Owen (1771–1858), whose famous experiments in education and
community living were carried on in the mill town of New Lanark. For D. W.'s
visit there on her second tour, later this year, see *DWJ* ii. 381–9.

143

all the way up to Ballachulish; from hence we went up Glen Coe and back to B——. Glen Coe very sublime. By Fort William, Fort Augustus to the Fall of Foyers, very fine; and so on to Inverness, from whence, fifteen miles north to some beautiful Saw Mills upon the river Bewley, the scenery of which is very romantic.

Homeward, by the main coach-road to Blair Athole,—a little before reaching it you cross the stream of Bruar below the waterfalls, interesting on Burns's account,[1]—Killicrankie and Fascally on the way to Dunkeld, very striking; Dunkeld also interesting. The narrow glen,[2] a pleasing solitude. I have omitted Killin at the head of Loch Tay and the Trossachs, as they lie in the country between the two main roads; but the Trossachs are very fine, and Killin a striking situation. Stirling and Edinburgh; and I have nothing more to say, unless I mention Perth, which lies low, in a beautiful valley.

The letter you sent to the Gazette[3] was just the thing, and I hope would produce some effect. Wishing you fine weather and a pleasant journey,

I remain, dear sir,
With very sincere regard
yours,
Wm Wordsworth

73. W. W. to UNKNOWN CORRESPONDENT[4]

MS. Cornell. Hitherto unpublished.

[*In M. W.'s hand*]

[early Aug. 1822]

My dear Sir,

I have delayed thus long thanking you for your very acceptable letter in the hope (which thank heaven has been realized) of

---

[1] See *The Humble Petition of Bruar Water to the Noble Duke of Athole* among the poems of 1787.

[2] i.e. Glenalmond, or 'Glen Almain' as W. W. calls it in the *Memorials of a Tour in Scotland, 1803*. See *PW* iii. 75.

[3] In the *Kendal Chronicle* for 6 and 13 July 1822, W. W.'s *Description of the Scenery of the Lakes* had been ridiculed as part of 'the literary quackery of the day', and the poet was the butt of some very uncomplimentary verses. His literary character was defended in the *Westmorland Gazette* for the 13th with a long quotation from a favourable review of the *Ecclesiastical Sketches* in the *Monthly Repository* for June 1822: 'His poetry has made its way—an unobtrusive, gentle proselytizer—like the great stream of knowledge and improvement . . .'

[4] Perhaps the Revd. John Russell, of the Charterhouse, or a medical practitioner there.

accompanying my acknowledgements with the tidings that my Son was recovering. A plan nearly the same as you recommended had been entered upon, previous to the receipt of your letter—and has been successful—and his Surgeon considers him now as advancing towards perfect recovery. An old enemy, tho' in this case it may perhaps be stated a *friend*—the nettle rash, has come back upon him and torments him much.

I have directed Mr Longman, my Publisher, to send you a Copy of my principal Poetical Works, hoping that you will accept it, as the return most suitable to my feelings which I could make, for your attention to the Case of my Son. And believe me to be

very sincerely your obliged
Friend and S^t
[*signed*] Wm Wordsworth

74. D. W. to EDWARD QUILLINAN

Address: Edward Quillinan Esqre, Lea Priory, near Wingham, Kent.
Postmark: 12 Aug. 1822. *Stamp*: Kendal Penny Post.
MS. WL.
LT i. 82.

Rydal Mount. August 6th, 1822

Turn to the next Page; below black line—for I begin with accounts,[1] to get rid of perplexities before I tell you of our goings-on. Observe I only give you a rough Draft reserving particulars till your return to England, when I shall be able to say exactly what sum will be wanting to make up deficiencies after Dr Wordsworth's Debt[2] to you—and ours for Wine and sundry articles are discharged.
Received from Mr Q. in cash
including 21 £ from Mr Horrocks—   £   s
the sum of—   70– 13– 6
Paid for Mr Q—   61– odd– —therefore   I
have in cash—about 9 £—, having paid all the smaller Bills—and all the larger (except those connected with the mourning, and Mr Carr's Bill, which for reasons to be explained below I have not

---

[1] When E. Q. left Rydal after his wife's death D. W. undertook, with S. H., the management of the accounts etc. arising from his tenancy of Ivy Cottage, and the business connected with its sub-letting.

[2] C. W. and his sons were now on holiday in Ivy Cottage. Charles Words-worth later recalled as a highlight of their holiday the visit of Canning to Rydal Mount with John Bolton of Storrs (*Annals of My Early Life*, 1891, p. 13). See also Warter, iii. 323–5.

paid). The Bills for Funeral expenses, now on hand, amount to upwards of 70 £—(some of the smaller are not yet come in—for instance those from Grasmere—and the final covering for the Grave is not yet put over it.)—Say 100 £—will cover all claims against you—except the amount of Mr Carr's Bill. Towards this I have about 9 £.

To this add—the Wine from your Father—and the Stores remaining in your house—Some of which Dr W has taken, *we* some—and a part of the Liquor in the Cellar will be left for Mr Elliot,[1] *or you.* At Dr W's departure this will all be settled, and you shall have an account of [the] Rydal Mount debt to you on that score. We shall add to it the price of the Portugal Wine, and you can then remit the Remainder. I have informed the Trades-people that all will be paid in September, when I hope the Wine will have safely arrived and my Brother will thankfully pay his share. He is very glad of the privilege of keeping the extra hogshead of which Mr Southey will no doubt be very glad of a share.

As to Mr Carr's Bill, I was going to discharge it according to your directions—with 15 £. The amount of the Bill is—18 £-2-7 from which you deducted 5 £ which he notes down that he has received—and you and I agreed that 15 £ would be a sufficient remuneration, having as you supposed overpaid him 5 £—. But on looking over Mr Carr's Bill I found that you were under a mistake. The first article is 'attending Mrs Quillinan in labour'—with a Blank.

Now I recollect perfectly that you consulted my Brother (and he also recollects it) respecting the Sum to be given to Mr Carr on that score. You determined together on 5 £—and I recollect (as does Mrs Wordsworth) that you told us you *had* given Mr Carr that Sum for his attendance on Mrs Q's labour. This being the case you remain Mr Carr's Debtor for the whole of his present Bill 18 £-. *2s-7d-* which we think you cannot pay with less than 20 £—*Say 20 guineas.* I think—as the Bill is very reasonable considering the length of time which each dressing occupied—(half a crown for each journey and the same for each dressing)—that 20 guineas would not be more than you would wish to give on reconsidering the matter, and on perceiving your mistake respecting the 5 £, but till I have your approbation I shall not venture to pay Mr Carr.—My dear Friend I know that you will be little inclined

---

[1] The next tenant, who took over from C. W. in September. The Elliots were apparently a West Country family. Mrs. Elliot was formerly a Miss Maltby of Norwich.

to weigh the expences of the last sad Duties to your poor Wife; but as they are certainly somewhat greater than were necessary for respectful ceremony I cannot dismiss the subject of the demands against you without stating that if I had had the sole management of them they would not, in some few particulars have been so heavy—but as all was done for the best I can blame no one—nor will you I am sure—but will be thankful in the remembrance that whatever was done or ordered was all in affectionate regard for the Deceased.

I think I have nothing further to add concerning money, except that I should like Mr Carr's Bill to be paid as soon as we can receive your answer—and that we must not be later than the end of September with the others. The Wine is not yet arrived at Whitehaven. Mr William Jackson[1] has engaged to do all that is necessary when it *does* arrive. Your Cook will be hired by the Elliots for the half year—and Hannah goes to Liverpool with a Relative of Mrs Harrison's,[2] so that business is settled. I have received a letter (for you) from the Lancaster housemaid's Mother —complaining of injury in her Daughter's sudden dismissal—and demanding her wages. I shall write to Mrs Donovan[3] to beg her to pay what is proper.

My dear Friend,

Truly glad shall I be when we have no more to say to each other respecting money, the most tiresome subject to me in the world, and it has so dried up my brain that I hardly know how to take to any thing better. First let me give you the best news I have that dear little William's danger has been passed for three weeks, and that he is now in health strength, spirits—and *shape* nearly as well as we could desire. You may conceive what an anxious time we had after his arrival at home—with death on his countenance— a dry fever on his emaciated Body—that was swoln to a great size. Mr Carr treated him most skilfully and through the Blessing of God I trust that the remedies used have struck at the root of the Disease. He gains flesh daily; but still looks very pallid in the face; and the utmost care and attention to the state of his Bowels etc will be necessary for some time so that he cannot be sent to school again—at least not for many months. His dear Mother's health

[1] Rector at Whitehaven.
[2] It is not clear which of the several Mrs. Harrisons of D. W.'s acquaintance is referred to here.
[3] An old Lancaster friend of E. Q.'s, referred to in his MS. Diaries.

has not suffered so much as one might have expected from her constant anxiety and attendance on him; yet I cannot say that she is well. As to my Brother—though *his* anxiety has been greater than upon any other occasion during the four and twenty years that I have lived with him—his health is not to be complained of, and he is now in excellent spirits though the inflammation never wholly leaves his eyes, and the slightest exposure to over-heat or cold increases it, so that he is obliged to be constantly on the watch. Dora is neither well nor ill—that is—she complains of nothing; but looks wretchedly and, when not excited by pleasure, is apt to be dull in spirits—and sluggish in motion. Poor thing! Many a time have I seen her turn away to hide her gushing tears at the mention of your Dear Wife's name—or when circumstances have brought her to her recollection at some particular time and place; but she can talk of her not only with composure but pleasure. This brings me back to the time of your departure; and you have scarcely heard of or from us since then. When the Clarksons had stayed their fortnight D and I went into Borrowdale, where we had fine weather—went to Buttermere, Wastdale—and all over the Vale of Keswick, so that in spite of herself, D was cheared, returned with amended health and looks—and full of hope—for her Brothers were to come home in three days.—You know what followed. For three weeks we had little hope of William's life: and before he was decidedly convalescent two Aunts[1] came from Wales. The one is returned thither—the other remains and will be our Visitor in Winter—a chearful old Lady, 73 years of age, who plays at Whist with Willy. In addition to this company we have had a succession of others. Col. Lowther[2] was here last week. The Monkhouses (with whom our old Aunt is now staying) are to have their christening tomorrow—and will depart to attend Preston Guild,[3] leaving the old Lady with us. Mrs Ellwood is here, and Miss Joanna Hutchinson,—so that you see my Brother's number of Ladies has increased and is not likely soon to be much diminished. The Horrocks's are gone. Dr Wordsworth and his Boys are delighted with the Ivy Cottage. The quiet spot often makes him think of you and yours (though unknown to him) and of what a loss you have had. I think he will stay till the 2nd week of September. Dora is now at Coniston with her Aunt Joanna. They will return tomorrow. We hope D's

---

[1] M. W.'s aunt, Elizabeth Monkhouse of Penrith (see *EY*, p. 141), and Mary Hutchinson of Hindwell, with whom she was now living.

[2] For Col. H. C. Lowther, M.P., see *MY* ii. 407.

[3] A two-week festival and trade exhibition held by the Merchants' Guild of Preston since the Middle Ages. See *Liverpool Advertiser* for 3 Sept. 1822.

health may have been bettered by the change; and if not she must go from home—to Stockton, or elsewhere, as Mr Carr thinks that change of that kind is the best thing for her. My Brother sometimes talks of a short excursion—but whether to Scotland—or whither—he is undecided; and he will not stir (except with our Brother in this neighbourhood) till after *he*, Dr W., is gone—and in the mean time we expect Mr Jones (*Robert Jones*[1] the companion of his pedestrian Tour in Switzerland two and thirty years ago) to spend three weeks under our Roof. Thus, you see, the summer—past and to come—is wholly filled up—and I trust I have sufficiently explained to you why you have not heard from us sooner or oftener. When we have been at rest from anxiety our time has been wholly filled up—indeed I can scarcely recollect a period in my life in which I have had so little leisure.

We have received your letter with the extract from the Magazine.[2] You cannot doubt that it gave us pleasure; for never was there a panegyric more true to Nature. It has been written by someone well acquainted with Jemima Quillinan, and the truth and delicacy of discrimination would make one entirely overlook any faults in expression—yet in considering and reconsidering the words, one would have wished that what is so well done had been still better. One would have liked to have seen it more concisely and correctly expressed. I hope you have ere this made up your mind respecting the Marble Tablet.[3] The stone on the Grave would have been done before this time; but we were obliged to wait for our new Rector's consent. Sir Richard le Fleming[4] has had the living for some weeks, and is settled in the Parsonage House. He has given us 3 excellent sermons and two very bad ones—we fear the good are exhausted. My Brother called on him very soon but he has not returned the call. We have heard nothing amiss in his conduct hitherto; but reports of the past are so very bad that we cannot but expect some outbreak, in which case I think Mr Barber will represent to the Bishop. William Jackson's health is much improved—we expect him next week—and I think Miss Hutchinson and Willy, who have each got a nice pony of their own, will

[1] See *EY*, p. 32; *MY* ii. 613.
[2] Probably the verses referred to in *MW*, p. 89.
[3] The tablet to Mrs. Quillinan's memory by Chantrey on the south wall of Grasmere Church, for which W. W. was meditating some memorial verses (see D. W.'s postscript and *MW*, pp. 88, 92, 95–6). It seems clear that the Epitaph (*PW* iv. 378) was mainly the work of E. Q. with revisions by W. W., and that the *Mem.* is probably wrong in stating (i. 444) that the first six lines were by W. W.
[4] See L. 71 above.

accompany him back to Whitehaven. Miss H. has finished her labours at the Ivy Cottage, after many a battling with—and grumbling against—Mr [Halhead's][1] stupidity. After all Mr Tillbrooke is not coming this summer. Southey has been with us lately.[2] He now looks well, after having had a seven weeks' cold which alarmed us somewhat; for we never before had seen him so much disordered. Poor Derwent Coleridge has been at Death's door—6 weeks confined to his Bed in the Typhus fever—carried from Cambridge to Highgate, where, under the same roof with his Father and Brother, he was taken care of. His poor Mother and Sister remained at Keswick—suffering greatly in mind as you may suppose. Miss Coleridge looks very ill. The same Fever has caused the Death of five young Men belonging to St John's College. John Wordsworth is not to go to College *this* year. He will return to Sedbergh after the holidays. There is to be a Regatta at Low Wood next Thursday and John is to be one of a company of ten (mountaineers) who are to row against a company of Cantabs now lodging at Ambleside, who have challenged the mountaineers. If *strength* will gain the Victory I think it will be on our side. What sort of weather have you had on the Continent? From the time of your departure till within the last month *we* have had the finest weather ever remembered; but now we have only a fine day now and then—and whole days and nights of gushing showers—with a few minutes' pause between.

The Harp strings are arrived in a beautiful case. It was a great disappointment that the [?profile][3] could not be sent at the same time. Mrs Wordsworth begs you will thank Capt[n] Barrett[4] for his note, which brought us happy tidings concerning your sweet Darlings. We trust that they continue to go on well—or we should have heard again from him. We long for a letter from you, and shall rejoice in your safe return to England. Tell us all you can about your Travels—about your Friends in Geneva[5]—and above all tell us, if you write again before your return to Lea Priory, what you have heard concerning the children—and when you have seen them yourself you cannot tell us too much of their ways and their doings.

[1] John Halhead, the Kendal upholsterer.
[2] According to his letter to W. W. of 26 July (*MS. Mrs. Ann Coatalen*), Southey's visit was to take place on the 28th and 29th.
[3] A profile of the late Mrs. Quillinan. See also *MW*, pp. 89, 92.
[4] For Capt. Brydges Barrett, see L. 70 above.
[5] Sir Egerton Brydges had been living abroad, principally at Geneva, since 1818. E. Q. arrived there some time after 15 Aug., when his MS. Diary for 1822 breaks off: 'I long to be at Geneva, and to have the meeting over, but I cannot stir today.'

Do excuse this poor scrawl—I have not said half of what I felt I *had* to say—and I am sure you will want to know a hundred things which I have omitted—but you must be thankful and contented that we are all well—we shall never forget you. May God bless you—my dear Friend

Ever yours

Dorothy Wordsworth.

My Brother has not composed a single verse since you left us. At this you will not wonder. His feelings will I am sure lead him to pour out his first renewed song to the memory of her who is departed; but *when* that will be I cannot say—and will not.

75. W. W. to THE COMMISSIONERS OF STAMPS

Address: To The Hon'ble Commissioners, Stamp Office, London.
Postmark: 9 Sept. 1822. *Stamp*: Kendal Penny Post. *Endorsed*: W Wordsworth Esq Ambleside 5 Sept^r/22 Mr. Campbell to Report to the Board on the subject of this Letter. Ansd 10 Sept. 1822.
MS. Public Record Office. Hitherto unpublished.

[*In John Carter's hand*]

Rydal Mount, Ambleside

5 Septr: 1822.—

I beg leave to state in reply to your Letter of the 3rd Inst: that this is the *third* Letter which I have received upon the subject of the transmission of my Parcels of Legacy Receipts, calling upon me to explain the cause of my not transmitting these Parcels on the *fourth* Tuesday in each Month. The letters are dated 14th Mar: 1820 29th Jany 1821 and 3rd Sepr 1822.—

In reply to the Letter of the 14 Mar: it was stated that my transmissions had been made on the *first* Tuesday, in conformity to the Instruction of 1811 which the Board in its printed Circular of 15 Decr 1819 *insists* upon being punctually complied with. The Board by Letter dated 30 Mar: confirms this Period of transmission by stating that '*it is now clearly settled* in the Order Book of the Office that the *first* Tuesday in the Month is the day on which Mr. Wordsworth must transmit his Legacy Receipts and Residuary Accounts'.

In my reply to the Board's second Letter, viz that dated 29 Jany 1821 I again referred to my book of instructions of 1811 and quoted the above Paragraph, in confirmation from the Letter of

30th March; and as no further notice was taken by the Board I concluded that my reply was satisfactory, and accordingly have continued to transmit my Legacy Parcels on the *first* Tuesday in each Month.—It is therefore with much regret that I find the application again renewed, which subjects me, without grounds, to a charge of neglect of Duty.

I have the Honor to be
Hon'ble Sirs,
Your obedient Servant,
[*signed*] Wm Wordsworth

76. W. W. to SAMUEL ROGERS

Address: Saml Rogers Esq., St. James's Place, London.
Franked: Penrith Sepr sixteen 1822 Cecil Jenkinson.¹ *Postmark*: (1) 16 Sept. 1822. (2) 18 Sept. 1822. *Stamp*: Penrith. *Endorsed*: not to be published. S.R.
MS. Sharpe Collection, University College, London.
Rogers K (—). *LY i.* 88.

Lowther Castle [16 Sept. 1822]

My dear Rogers,

It gave me great pleasure to hear from our common Friend, Sharp, that you had returned from the Continent in such excellent health, which I hope you will continue to enjoy in spite of our fogs, rains, east winds, coal fires, and other clogs upon light spirits and free breathing.—I have long wished to write to you on a little affair of my own, or rather of my Sister's; and the facility of pro-curing a frank in this house has left my procrastinating habit with-out excuse. Some time ago you expressed (as perhaps you will remember) a wish that my Sister would publish her Recollections of her Scotch Tour,² and you interested yourself so far in the scheme, as kindly to offer to assist in disposing of it to a Publisher for her advantage. We know that your skill and experience in these matters are great; and she is now disposed to profit by them provided you continue to think as favorably of the measure as heretofore. The

---

¹ The Hon. Charles Cecil Cope Jenkinson, later 3rd Earl of Liverpool (1785–1851): M.P. for Sandwich (1807), Bridgnorth (1812), and East Grinstead (1818): Under-Secretary for the Home Department, 1807, and for War and the Colonies, 1809. He succeeded to the title on the death of his half-brother, the former Prime Minister, in 1828.

² Of 1803. See *DWJ* i. 195 ff. These (and later) negotiations finally fell through, and the Journal was not published in full until J. C. Shairp's edition of 1874. See also L. 88 below.

fact is, she was so much gratified by her tour in Switzerland, that she has a strong wish to add to her knowledge of that country and to extend her ramble to some part of Italy. As her own little fortune is not sufficient to justify a step of this kind, she has no hope of revisiting those Countries, unless an adequate sum could be procured through the means of this Mss. You are now fairly in possession of her motives; if you still think that the publication would do her no discredit, and are of opinion that a respectable sum of money might be had for it, which she has no chance of effecting except through your exertion, she would be much obliged, as I also should be, if you would undertake to manage the Bargain, and the Mss shall be sent you as soon as it is revised. She has further to beg that you would be so kind as to look it over and strike out what you think might be better omitted.—

I detected you in a small collection of Poems entitled, Italy,[1] which we all read with much pleasure. Venice, and The Brides of Venice, that was the title I think, pleased as much as any; some parts of the Venice are particularly fine. I had no faul[t] to find but rather too strong a leaning [to][2] the pithy and concise, and to some peculiarities of versification which occur perhaps too often.

Where are the Beaumonts? and when do they come to England— We hear nothing of them.

Lord and Lady Lonsdale are well, Lady Frederic[3] is here, so is Lady Caroline,[4] both well. Before I close this I will mention to Lady F. that I am writing to you. My own family were well when I left them two days ago. Please remember me kindly to your Sister, and believe me, my dear Rogers, faithfully yours,

Wm Wordsworth

PS. Lady F. says, if Holland House were but where Brougham Hall is, we should see more of Mr Rogers. She adds that we have really some sunshine in this country and now and then a gentle day like those of Italy.—Adieu—

[1] The First Part of *Italy*, [anon.], 1822.
[2] *MS. torn.*
[3] i.e. Lady Frederick Bentinck.
[4] Lady Caroline, Lord Lonsdale's fourth daughter. In 1815 she had married William John Frederick Vane, 3rd Duke of Cleveland (1792–1864).

77. D. W. to DAVID LAING[1]

Address: To D. Laing, Esq[re], 49 South Bridge St, Edinburgh.
Postmark: 17 Sept. 1822.
MS. Edinburgh University Library.
Geoffrey Bullough, 'The Wordsworth–Laing Letters', *MLR* xlvi (1951),
1–15(—).

Black Bull[2]
Monday Night. [16 Sept. 1822]

Dear Sir,

After parting with you, (having rested a while) we proceeded to Holy Rood House—thence to Arthur's Seat, where we highly enjoyed the splendid prospect in sunshine—differing from what we saw from the same place yesterday. We returned by the Canon gate and High street to M[rs] Wilson's[3] where we spent a pleasant evening—and now at our return, find your note with your acceptable present for my Brother, which will be of great use to us in our future progress.

Miss Hutchinson joins with me in thanking you for your great kindness to us. We are sorry it has not been in our power to see you again; but I shall hope to have that pleasure at Rydal Mount if you again visit the Lakes.

I am, Sir,
Yours respectfully
D Wordsworth.

[1] David Laing (1793–1878), antiquary and bibliographer, became a partner in his father's (William Laing) bookshop in Edinburgh in 1821, Librarian of the Signet Library from 1837, and Secretary and adviser to the Bannatyne, Wodrow, and Abbotsford Clubs. His chief works were an edition of Dunbar (1834) and the *Collected Works of John Knox*, 6 vols., 1846–64. He had visited the Lakes in the summer of 1822, with an introduction from Southey to W. W., and D. W. was now returning the visit to Laing and his sister Mary (d. 1871). See Gilbert Goudie, *David Laing, LL.D.: A Memoir . . .*, [privately printed], 1913.

[2] The coach terminus in Catherine St., Edinburgh. D. W. had set off from Rydal Mount on her second tour of Scotland on 13 Sept. in the company of Joanna Hutchinson. For full details see her Journal in *DWJ* ii. 339 ff.

[3] Mrs. Margaret Wilson (d. 1824), mother of Professor John Wilson (see *MY* i. 260, ii. 594). She lived in Queen St.

154

78. W. W. to RICHARD SHARP

Address: Richd Sharp Esqre, Park Lane, London.
Stamp: Kendal Penny Post.
MS. University Library, Davis, California.
K (—). *LY i. 89.*

[In M. W.'s hand]

Octr 3^d 1822

My dear Sir

I hope you will not think I press too much upon your friendly disposition when I beg that if it should be necessary you would take some little trouble on my acc^t in a money transaction. We have lodged nearly £2,000 of our little fortune in the french funds, but having no reliance on the good faith of that Gov^t I am anxious, in case its stability should receive a shock, to sell out with expedition which residing at such a distance from Town as I do, would be impossible unless some Friend would interest himself on my acc^t— A young Gent of the name of Cookson[1] of Kendal who I believe was here when we had the pleasure of seeing you, is going in about 10 days to London to complete his clerkship with Mr Addison Solic^r of Staple Inn—to him I have entrusted the Certificate I hold from the French Gov^t, and expressed my wishes that he might make inquiries as to what further documents or powers if any may be required to enable him to act for me—and now my d^r Sir I have reached the point where I solicit your interference. If you should receive, extensively connected as you are, any intimations that it would be expedient to sell out, may I entreat that you would address a note to him at Mr A's Staple Inn, and he will instantly wait upon you for instructions. He is himself inexperienced and out of consideration for his responsibility as well as my own interests, I have ventured to request this assistance, which I shall consider a great favour.

I have had a kind letter from Rogers in answer to mine about my Sister's publication; he profers every assistance, but is strongly against my proposal to sell the Copyright at once.[2] If you happen to

---

[1] Strickland Cookson. See L. 47 above.

[2] See above, L. 76. Rogers had written in September: 'I never knew a single instance of the sale of a Copyright by a young writer or a writer before unknown, where reasons of repentance did not follow . . . and wherever there is *real merit* in a work, and you know my opinion of your Sister's, I think when it *can be done* it is best to enter the Lottery oneself and not sell the ticket for little or nothing to the bookseller . . . The bookseller I should go to myself in such a case would be Murray. He will consult Gifford, who will certainly be charmed with a talent such as hers . . .' (*WL MSS.*).

see him shortly, say that my Sister is at present in Scotland and that as soon as she returns we shall write to him.

During these last three weeks we have had a glorious season, such a one as scarcely occurs in seven years—would that you and Rogers had been here to enjoy it—even he could not have regretted Italy—and I am sure you would not.

We hope that your Sister was benefitted by her Tour, with best regards from Mrs W.

I remain my d^r Sir
faithfully yours
[*signed*] Wm Wordsworth

79. W. W. to RICHARD SHARP

Address: Richd Sharp Esqre, 9 Mansion Ho: Place, London. By favor of Mr Cookson.
MS. University Library, Davis, California.
K (—). LY i. 91.

[*In M. W.'s hand*]

[mid-Oct. 1822]

My dear Sir,

Many thanks for your kindness in meeting my wishes so promptly.[1] Your view of the case appears quite just, but is it not probable that, if the present French Ministers can keep their ground, the Death of the King[2] would prove less injurious to the credit of the Govern^t; as I understand that their system is approved of by the Heir to the Throne, and his Friends? There is yet another reason for confidence,—the desire which the Continental Powers have to raise the credit of their funds, from the conviction that Public Credit enabled England principally to make such mighty exertions during the late War. Nevertheless, I know how difficult it is for unprincipled men to resist a temptation of present advantage for a remote benefit; and I regard the French as destitute of public principle.

I should be most happy to submit the whole of my little Venture to your discretion; and with this view, I have requested Mr Cookson to deposit the Certificate in your hands, to sell out or leave in as you judge best, and I should be thankful for instructions how

[1] See previous letter.
[2] Louis XVIII (1755–1824), now a permanent invalid, lingered on for nearly two more years, but the government had already passed into the hands of his ultra-royalist ministers led by his brother the Comte d'Artois, later Charles X (1757–1836), King from 1824 till 1830.

to vest you with the necessary Powers, as something more, I apprehend, must be wanting.

You talked of going to the Continent in the Spring. In this case Mr Davis[1] would perhaps be so kind as to represent you for my benefit.

This morning the wind is blowing a perfect Hurricane, tearing the leaves off the trees in myriads, so that the splendour of the Autumn is destroyed. My Sister has not returned from Scotland, being detained at Edinburgh[2] by the indisposition of her Companion Miss Joanna Hutchinson.

We are glad to learn that your Sister derived benefit from her journey in spite of the unfavourable weather. We are gratified by her remembrances, and those of Miss Kinnaird.[3]

How singular is the fate of Fonthill![4] The Papers give a sentimental and silly account of the Place, but one cannot help longing to see it, with all its wonders.

With best regards from Mrs W, I remain,

faithfully, your oblg[d] friend,

[*signed*] W[m] Wordsworth.

80. W. W. to LORD LONSDALE

MS. Lonsdale MSS. Hitherto unpublished.

Rydal Mount
Nov[b] 3rd [1822].

My Lord,

I thank your Lordship for a present of Game which reached us yesterday.

[1] Business partner of Richard Sharp.
[2] On the way back from the Highlands. See *DWJ* ii. 396.
[3] Maria Kinnaird (1810–91), Richard Sharp's ward and adopted child, was born in the West Indies. In 1835 she married Thomas Drummond (1797–1840), engineer and administrator, who was Head of the Boundary Commission in connection with the great Reform Bill, and Under-Secretary at Dublin Castle, 1835–40. She outlived him for many years and became a prominent figure in London society.
[4] In Wiltshire, the home of William Beckford (1760–1844), author of *Vathek*. Beckford spent a gigantic fortune inherited from his father (the Lord Mayor of London, and friend of Wilkes) on James Wyatt's Gothic extravaganza of Fonthill (1795), and crowded it with valuable collections of books, pictures, and engravings. In 1822 he found himself in straitened circumstances, and sold the whole estate to a wealthy merchant named Farquhar (who had made a fortune in India out of an improved method of manufacturing gunpowder), and went to live in Bath. For a full account of Fonthill and its new owner, see *Courier* for 9 and 10 Oct.

I left Lowther with the hope that I might have the pleasure of again seeing your Lordship and Family before you returned to the South, and purposing to wait upon you at Whitehaven. But alas the illness which we thought was quite removed has returned upon my poor little Boy, the seat of it only changed from the abdomen to the chest. His Surgeon has hopes of him, in which I but imperfectly sympathize. We are indeed all much distressed; if he recovers, I shall be happy to pay my respects to Lady Lonsdale, and your Lordship at Whitehaven.

I hope that the University of Cambridge upon the present vacancy[1] will shew that it is not fairly represented by *two* Advocates for further concession to the Catholics—but I have heard no news upon the subject.

The enclosed was received this morning from Mr Gee; I have read it with much concern. I cannot but forward it to your Lordship, as to express the matter in other words would be unjust to the Writer. To write thus on his personal affairs must have cost much to a man of Mr Gee's spirit.[2]

> I remain
> with high respect
> my Lord
> your Lordship's
> faithfully and sincerely
> Wm Wordsworth

[1] John Henry Smyth (1780–1822), of Heath Hall, nr. Wakefield, M.P. for Cambridge University since 1812, had died on 22 Oct. As many as eight names were canvassed for the vacancy, but by the beginning of November they had been narrowed down to four: Lord Hervey, later 2nd Marquess of Bristol; Robert (later Sir Robert) Grant, Governor of Bombay; James Scarlett, later 1st Baron Abinger, the Whig lawyer (see below, L. 236); and the favourite, Charles Manners-Sutton, Speaker of the House of Commons (see *MY* ii. 309). When he later withdrew, W. J. Bankes (see L. 212 below) took his place as the candidate uncompromisingly opposed to the Roman Catholic claims, and—at the election in the Senate House on 26 Nov.—he secured a large majority. The other representative was Lord Palmerston (1784–1865), the famous statesman, who sat for Cambridge University from 1811 till 1831, and was Secretary at War till 1828.

[2] The reference here (and in L. 84 below) is unclear. Perhaps Gee was seeking Lord Lonsdale's good offices for some purpose connected with his sporting activities. Two years previously, Lord Thanet (see *MY* ii. 412) had brought a suit against Gee to try the right claimed by Lord Lonsdale to shoot over the wastes of the manor of Kirkby Lonsdale: Lord Lonsdale had dropped the claim, and Gee had come rather badly out of the affair (see *Lonsdale MSS.*).

81. W. W. to RICHARD SHARP

Address: Richard Sharp Esqre, Mansion House Square, London.
Postmark: 13 Nov. *Stamp*: Kendal Penny Post.
MS. University Library, Davis, California.
K (—). *LY i. 92.*

[*In M. W.'s hand*]

Rydal Mount Novr 12th [1822]

My dear Sir,

I am much concerned to hear of your indisposition, which I sincerely hope is by this time abated.

Our house has, for these last ten days, been filled with anxiety on account of the illness of my younger Son; he has had a relapse, and we have been much alarmed, but we hope he is something better, though his fever is still very high.

Dorothy is at Stockton upon Tees.[1] She will be consulted by letter upon your obliging offer, of which I know she will be duly sensible.

My Sister returned from Scotland a few days since, having been detained three weeks at Edinburgh by the illness of her Companion, Miss Joanna Hutchinson. She would have written to Mr Rogers immediately had she not been prevented by her Nephew's severe sickness. She went from Edinburgh to Stirling by water, thence to Glasgow, chiefly by the Track-boat, thence to Dumbarton and to Rob Roy's Caves, and Tarbet by the Steam Boat. To Inveraray by land, and returned to Glasgow by steam; coming home by Lanark, etc. She has made notes of her tour, which are very amusing, particularly as a contrast to the loneliness of her former mode of travelling.

I was not aware how much I was asking when I requested you to undertake my little concern in the French Funds, or I should not have ventured to make the proposal. I knew indeed that everybody must be averse to incur such a responsibility, but was encouraged to hope that your confidence that, whatever the result proved, I should not complain, but should be content, would do away much of your dislike in my particular case. On carefully referring to your letter I feel myself not justified in expressing the wish that you should act for me.[2]—At present I have only to say that I should be

---

[1] She had gone on a visit to John Hutchinson with S. H.
[2] See above, L. 78. Sharp had written on 8 Nov.: 'All funded property, and most especially *foreign*, varies so much, and so often, in value, that it defies any man's sagacity to form even a reasonable conjecture. For this reason I have uniformly, for many years, even when requested by my partners, and my female relations, intreated to be excused from the painful responsibility of

willing to stand a few of the depressions of the French Funds, even
if considerable, provided I could feel assured that the French
Government would honestly abide by its engagements. I am not
anxious for profit, by selling in and out; or desirous to have the
command of my money: all I look for, for some years to come, is
the regular payment of good interest which I now have. Were I
to take the money out, I should not know what to do with it. After
stating this, as the principal point I look to, and the only one to me
of great importance, I may add that I should be perfectly contented
to have my Cork-boat tyed to your Seventy-four. If *you* thought
it advisable to sell out, so should I, therefore, should *you* see reason
to change, I have only to beg that you will be so kind as to let me
know.

I have not heard from Mr Cookson,[1] and therefore do not know
whether the document he took is in your hands or his; but I expect
to hear from him in a day or two, and no doubt he will [tell][2] me.

With much regret that I should have troubled you thus far,
and grateful for your kind attention to my letter, I remain, with
Mrs Wordsworth's and my Sister's best Regards

my dear Sir

very faithfully your obliged Friend

[*signed*] Wm Wordsworth

82. D. W. and W. W. to MARY LAING and DAVID LAING

Address: Messrs W. and D. Laing, Booksellers, South Bridge Street, Edin-
burgh. *For Miss Laing*.
Postmark: 18 Nov. 1822. *Stamp*: Kendal Penny Post.
MS. Edinburgh University Library.
The Wordsworth–Laing Letters(—).

[13–16 Nov. 1822]

My dear Miss Laing,

Our House has been a house of distress and anxiety ever since
Miss Hutchinson and I arrived (on the Thursday after we parted

buying or selling without their own orders. . . . There is no man for whom I
would sooner undertake this anxious trust than for yourself, but I always
decline the requests of this nature, and I am sure you will on reflection approve
my doing so . . . I shrink even from advising: yet on the whole, I will on this
occasion own that my judgment inclines to recommend it to you to dispose of
your French funds, should the present prices continue: yet I have and must of
course have doubts.' (*WL MSS.*)

[1] Strickland Cookson.   [2] *Word dropped out.*

from you).[1] We found my Brother's younger Son very poorly—
with a difficulty of breathing—a cough on the slightest exertion
and other symptoms, very alarming, as he had but recently recovered from an attack of dropsy. The disorder continued to encrease till the Sunday, when the application of leeches to his Chest
considerably relieved him; but our anxiety hardly abated, his pulse
continuing very quick, and respiration difficult. Thank God! we
now consider him recovering; and trust that with extreme care as
to diet and exercise, he has a fair chance of [?now][2] very slowly
regaining his strength, which the very remedies used would alone
have been sufficient completely to upset. His poor Mother has been
employed in watching him night and day, and his Father's anxiety
has been extreme. I was truly thankful (things being in this state)
that we had not lingered two days longer at Edinburgh which I
assure you we had the strongest inclination to do—myself especially
—having to pack up, to walk to Frederick Street, and a hundred
little matters to arrange.

Though not painfully fatigued with our trip to the Lions Head[3]
etc etc—I would gladly have taken an evening's rest by the fireside,
had another ramble with you the next day and made leisurely
preparations for our departure. It was the fear of a change in the
weather that decided us. Thus far I wrote three days ago, was
interrupted and have not till now (Saturday the 16th) been at
liberty to return to my writing desk. I was going to say that it was
most fortunate we had the resolution to leave Edinburgh on the
Tuesday morning; for we had three delightful days for our journey
—golden sunshine on the soft hills of Tweed and Teviot; and a
bright moon to light us through the Vale of the Esk. We slept at
Carlisle, spent the next day at Penrith—and the day after (Thursday) travelled in our favorite vehicle, a Cart along the Banks of the
finest of our English Lakes (Ullswater) to Patterdale. Thence,
over Kirkstone Mountain, to Ambleside and Rydal. A storm of
wind and rain came on when we were at the top of Kirkstone—
and till the Friday following the rain was unceasing—Friday and
Saturday fine—Sunday as wet as ever—and such has been the
weather ever since until today, which is very fine. The only variety
we have had, has been a storm of Thunder light[e]ning and hail—
except one showery day with sunny gleams. I wonder what sort of
weather you have had in Scotland. My Friend, Miss Joanna

---

[1] D. W. and Joanna Hutchinson had revisited David Laing (see L. 77
above) and his sister Mary in Edinburgh on their way home.
[2] *Written* not.   [3] Presumably the Lion's *Haunch*, at Arthur's Seat.

Hutchinson, left us yesterday—and today the sun shines again upon us, and the barometer rises. I am grieved that she is gone; for after so much bad weather we surely shall have better; and she departs with her former prejudices strengthened, having scarcely ever paid a visit to Rydal or Grasmere in fair weather. As for Scotland—she is half inclined to believe that you have never two thoroughly rainy days together—at least on the Eastern side of the Island. You and your good Mother will be happy to hear that she not only was not the worse for her journey from Edinburgh, but the better; and has, in spite of wet and damp, been pretty well during her stay at Rydal. She will never forget the pleasure she enjoyed in Scotland—notwithstanding all she suffered. I tell her she is more than half a Scotch woman in her heart. The hospitality and kindness of Friends—the simplicity and decency of manners in the peasantry—the wholesome air—the green hills—and chearful streams are the daily theme of her praise. Within the last hour before I parted with her she charged me to give her best Love to you and your Mother, with a thousand thanks to you both, and to your Father and Brothers for the great kindness you and they shewed to us during our stay at Edinburgh. In expressing her feelings I express my own; and you must receive, and deal out, my acknowledgements with hers.

Mr David Laing will be glad to hear that my Brother's eyes are stronger than when he was at Rydal; and that my Brother and Mrs Wordsworth are both pretty well, notwithstanding their late anxiety. I am truly happy to inform you that, since I began this letter my Nephew has made even rapid advances towards recovery; and I hope that, if the weather continues fine, he will soon be able to resume his exercise on horseback, which is of more use to him than any thing else. Poor Boy! he has had great pleasure in hearing of what we saw and did in Edinburgh, and in listening to the Journals of our Travels. My Friend, Joanna, has not forgotten the Isle of Skye any more than myself—nor the pleasure we are to have in coasting the Western shores of Scotland in a Steam Boat to meet you at Glasgow—but we are afraid you will be getting married—and then Joanna says 'farewell to travelling!' She intends to send you a little counsel on the affair of Matrimony . . . Seriously speaking, however, there are few things we should like better than a journey with you to Skye and Staffa,—and we have often since parting from you talked of it as not altogether merely a pleasant dream. This little Bit I must leave for my Brother—cut it off and give it to Mr D. Laing.

13–16 November 1822

[*D. W. continues for W. W.*]

Dear Sir,

I hold the pen for my Brother, whose eyes do not suffer him to write by candle light. 'I have to thank you for a letter received some time ago, mentioning that you bear in mind my wish to be possessed of the 1st Edition of Milton's Minor poems, and I am much obliged by a Mark of your remembrance, thro' my sister, the Pleasure Tours of Scotland[1] by which I hope to profit when I revisit Scotland. I have looked it over and it seems well done. I have got into the house the Bride of Lammermoor;[2] but my anxiety on account of my Son's illness has prevented me from reading it. I cannot conclude without expressing my gratitude for the many attentions received from you and each Member of your Family which my Sisters received from you during their stay at Edinburgh. I remain dear Sir very sincerely yours

[*signed*] Wm Wordsworth

We shall hope to see you again in this country—and remember your Sister has not seen our Lakes.'

[*D. W. continues*]

I have been latterly writing almost in the dark—and my scrawl not being familiar to you I fear you will be a little puzzled. A Candle is just arrived—and, casting my eyes back upon the last page I am really ashamed of it—but were I to suppress this letter, intending to write another, many Posts might be lost, and I am sure you have had good right to expect to hear from me ere this. You must therefore excuse whatever trouble the reading may give you. Before I conclude I must say a word in favour of our Lakes, in which I hope your Brother will join me; and that he will contrive to bring you to see them. I need not say what pleasure I should have in conducting you to many of the pretty spots in our neighbourhood, whose names are no doubt familiar to you—and to others which are less known. Thanks for the Jelly and the Recipe. Miss Joanna will send your Mother the prescription for her eyes when she sees her Friend. Again my kind regards to all your Family—Believe me your obliged and sincere Friend

D Wordsworth

[1] *An Account of the Principal Pleasure Tours of Scotland*, Edinburgh, 1819 (2nd edn., 1821).
[2] Published with *A Legend of Montrose* in June 1819.

Concluded Novr 16th.

I have forgotten your number both in Town and at Laureston: therefore will direct to the Firm—W. and D. Laing.

The Mr Wilkinson to whom Mr Laing was sending Books I find from my Brother is not Mr Wilkinson of Sedbergh as I supposed; but a Roman Catholic Priest[1]—a great collecter of Books.

[written at top of letter]

Recipe from Miss Hutchinson for Mrs Laing

Two Teaspoonfuls of Rochelle Salts and half a Teaspoonful of the Super Carbonate of Potass to be taken in a large Tumbler of water, as warm as it can be drunk. To be taken before Breakfast. Better before rising in the morning.

83. D. W. to EDWARD QUILLINAN

Address: Edward Quillinan Esqre, Lee Priory near Wingham Kent. (Single Sheet).
Postmark: 20 Nov. 1822. *Stamp*: Kendal Penny Post.
MS. WL.
LY i. 93.

Finished 19th Nov^r [1822]

My dear Friend

Your delightfully interesting letter to my Sister is just arrived —not to spur me on—for I was at my writing-table ready (after having finished one letter) to begin to write to *you*. I should not have waited three weeks at home without congratulating you on being reunited in one house with your dear Children had all been going on chearfully with us, but I was unwilling to make you a sharer in our anxieties, and therefore waited till I could tell you (which now, thank God! is in my power) that the whole Family, was (if not in strong health) in hopeful spirits. Miss J. H. and I, on our return from Scotland (It will be 3 weeks ago on Thursday) found William looking so much better than at our departure that we were quite delighted. His countenance had cast off its wrinkles: he was again the Boy William. We had met him and his Father and Mother on the hill going by moonlight to drink tea with the Elliots[2]

---

[1] The Revd. Thomas Wilkinson of Kendal. The Roman Catholic chapel there was rebuilt in 1793.
[2] The new tenants of Ivy Cottage.

(for the first time). They turned back with us; but after ten minutes' chat, went to pay their visit, leaving William, Aunt J—and me to the fire-side. We were very merry—and, through the evening, discovered nothing amiss in him but a little quickness of breathing, which we had attributed to hurrying up the hill—with the excitement occasioned by the pleasure of seeing us. When my Br and Sr returned they told us, however that they were uneasy about him. The next day there was plainly cause for this—the day after he was worse;—and on the third day—breathing bad—and pulse very quick, with other alarming symptoms. The usual reducing remedies were resorted to; and the disease has yielded to them. He is now (though weak and looking very ill—wrinkled and hollow-cheeked —with his nose in proportion higher than his dear Father's)—in good spirits, eats with appetite, sleeps well—and is without pain, or difficulty in respiration. For the last three days he has ridden round and round the garden with great benefit and if the weather be fine I doubt not he will gather strength fast; but for long—many a day and many a month he must be guarded and watched as an invalid. The strictest rules are prescribed as to diet, *gentle* exercise —and cessation from application to Books—except of amusement. This you will say no hardship for him! I am happy however to tell you that he finds great amusement in being read to; and seems to take pleasure in reading to himself—only his weakness will not permit him to do this long together, he having yet no facility in catching up sentences: but while another is reading he listens steadily, and long together, and his natural quickness enables him to gather ideas without any injurious effort of the mind. He is charmed with Parry's voyage to the N. Pole,[1] which I now overhear his Mother reading to him. They are in the dining-room— *I* at my bed-room window. I am sure you have not forgotten that window—out of which I peeped many a time last winter to give you a nod, and to hear your pleasant voice, while I was muffled up in my Cloak copying that enormous journal which I can never expect any one (except a few idle folks such as our Cousins the Robinsons[2] who have nothing else to do) ever to read through. Well, here I sit again—muffled in my furs and cloak; but though snow is on the hills, summer flowers are lingering in the garden— the mount is as green as in spring-time—indeed so are the Fields—

[1] Sir William Edward Parry (1790–1855), rear-admiral and Arctic explorer. In 1821 he published his *Journal of a Voyage for the Discovery of a North-West Passage . . . performed in the years 1819–20, in H.M. Ships Griper and Hecla.*
[2] i.e. Admiral Robinson's widow and her numerous children.

and the sun now shines sweetly upon the green grass and brown
leafy oaks. The air, though changeable is often very mild; but
alas! it is from the rain that so much greenness comes—Only four
fine days since our return—the rest not gushing showers—but all-
day and all-night rains. Last year a little before this time you were
about returning from your Yorkshire Tour with my Brother.[1] We
were talking of this only yester night—and I went on musing to
myself on other events sad and sorrowful—and on the return of
innocent hopes and pleasures when the Ivy Cot was again echoing
with the little prattler's voice—and of the changes that too harshly
followed:—But we talked with chearfulness of you and your little-
ones; and today your account of them almost brings them back
again to us—so lively is your description—the same sweet, loveable,
spirited interesting creatures—yet with the change that five months
have made at their changeful age. Jemima is certainly established
the very best child in the world—I thought her so before she went
away; and now she is proved. Rotha's hair will be a fine auburn—
depend upon it—whether you shave her head or not—so pray let it
keep its natural covering, during the winter, at least. Dora's heart
will flutter with pleasure when she reads your description of her
own Darling! but only think of the feeble, delicate pretty (I *will*
call her pretty in spite of Dora's jealousy) Mary Monkhouse,[2]
having so far got the start of your little roundabout as to show eight
teeth in her wee mouth! My Sister is much pleased with what you
say of the Nurse, and thinks it was the best good fortune that you
met her at Matlock. We are truly glad that Eliza pleases you so
well; and you may be sure that we (my Sister and I) are not inclined to think the worse of her for spending some of her time,
which she might employ at her needle, in reading my Brother's
poems. Do you think she is partly swayed by the pride and pleasure
she has in thinking of this country, and of having *herself* known the
poet?—or would she have taken delight in them if she had found
the Book by chance and had known nothing of Westmorland or the
Author?—You may rest assured that if any one, or two, or all of us
—should go to London we shall not come away again without
going to Lee Priory if you or your Children be there—and even
though not—*I* should be tempted thither, though but to look at
the place and empty rooms. I hope at some time that we shall see
Captain Barret again. Perhaps he may have a wish to revisit Rydal
and Grasmere, even if you and your little Girls should not take up

---

[1] See L. 47 above.
[2] Thomas and Jane Monkhouse's daughter (b. 1821).

your abode at the Ivy Cottage—or we may meet in London—or at Lee Priory. Miss Hutchinson and Dora will probably not return from Stockton much before Xmas as we are desirous that William should be completely recovered before D comes home. Many a time did we express our thankfulness that they (and D especially) had been spared from sharing our sorrow and anxiety. It would certainly have had a bad effect upon her health, which her Aunt says is now quite restored. She rides out daily, is very happy, and in excellent spirits—busy with music and drawing—and (to my great satisfaction) has cast away Dictionaries and Grammars. She is much beloved (and admired too) by all her Friends—Her Aunt says that her looks are wonderfully improved. She is like *herself* again (which you hardly ever saw her)—Nothing remaining of that dullness and heaviness—that inactive appearance which she had had for so many months before she left home. Her cough has been quite well for some time.

As to Miss Hutton,[1] if she has not written to you or sent you messages it has only been that she has had nothing to say but that she affectionately remembered you and Jemima and Rotha. If she had had a scold, or a grumble for you—depend on it she would have given it. I know not whether she may not, after all, go to London from Stockton instead of coming back hither, as she seems determined to spend the earliest of the Spring (or rather the end of winter) in London. In that case my Brother would fetch his daughter home. I hope you will very soon find her out after her arrival of which you will have timely notice. Her first visit will be to the Monkhouses. We are sorry you did not see them when in town. Poor Mr M. has lately heard of the Death of one of his two Brothers,[2] in the West Indies—where he has been toiling for more than twenty years without profit. Mr M had lent him considerable sums of money which will all be lost to him; but this seems to give him small concern. The death of his Brother has affected him very much.

I hope you will be able to see the M.'s the next time you go to Town.

We have not heard from the Gees for many weeks—I wrote to Mrs Gee a few days ago to inform them that Mr Dixon[3] has given up Old Brathay[4]—not that we think it likely they would now have

---

[1] The name by which S. H. was called by E. Q.'s little daughters.
[2] Joseph Monkhouse (1785–1822), 'honest Joe', the sailor brother. See *SH*, pp. 95, 99, 246.
[3] See *Letters of Hartley Coleridge*, p. 84.
[4] The house formerly occupied by Charles Lloyd and his family.

any thing to do with it—but as they used to wish for that house in preference to any other we thought it right to tell them. Poor Mr Blakeney[1] is dead, so it is probable that Fox gill will be to be sold; for Mrs Blakeney is not likely to come to it herself. Mr de Q. is here shut up as usual—the house always blinded—or left with but one eye to peep out of—*he* probably in bed—We hear nothing of him. Your Friend Wilson Morris[2] has offered himself to Mr Elliot —as a servant—told the same story of Mr Wordsworth's *promises* —and was rejected by Mr E. He is still *studying* with John Carter, and gallanting the Ladies. John Fleming[3] is no doubt again in his glory; for both his houses are empty—he himself flourishing—for he looks well and always smiles graciously upon *me* at least. Meanwhile Mr Monkhouse profits from the interest of his rent. Mr Barber is vexed with himself that he cannot support the solitude of his Cottage the year through. Labours out of doors are at an end— He is not confined or employed, as last year, by sickness—yet he has not the resolution to go away. He talks of Edinburgh—and that would be the best [thing] for him; for he says that if he goes to London he shall never come back again. This is all very strange for [he] says alw[ays] that he has had enough of London. The [?Campbells][4] have been in L. above a month. Mrs and Miss Mac-Clochan[5] (They have never taught me to spell their name) are at Allan Bank—the Quakers still at Tail End[6]—Mr Harden has had a fit of Lumbago and is bleached by it; but he will soon be on horseback again, and among his workmen, and then as young as ever.

Hartley Coleridge is with Mr Dawes.[7] He has not been long

---

[1] Robert Blakeney, the owner of Fox Ghyll (see L. 58 above). He had been having difficulty with his tenant De Quincey for some time. 'I regret the necessity of letting Fox Ghyll,' he had written to W. W. on 25 Apr., 'I do not understand Mr De Quincey—he has promised by two different Letters to pay his rent—but the Bill is not yet come to hand . . .' (*WL MSS.*).

[2] The Rydal neighbour mentioned in L. 67 above.

[3] Farmer, and owner of the cottage occupied by the Monkhouses the previous summer.

[4] *MS. torn.* Col. and Mrs. Campbell, tenants of Allan Bank, moved to the Isle of Mull the following spring.   [5] Unidentified.

[6] i.e. Dale End, on the western side of Grasmere lake, at the opposite end from Allan Bank.

[7] Hartley Coleridge's move north, at the earnest entreaty of his father (see Griggs, v. 228–33, 243–5), had not been accomplished without a good deal of opposition from the Southey and Wordsworth households, who feared the deterioration in his personal life that only too quickly came about. Southey had expressed his anxiety to W. W. as early as 11 Apr.: 'My sincere hope is that H. may not accept Mr Dawes' invitation. The scheme of sending him to be under his mother's eye is preposterous . . . As to his living under my roof, for to this the question comes—I certainly will not suffer any such disturbance of my peace or comfort as such an arrangement will inevitably bring with it.' And

enough to have proved his skill and patience as a Teacher; but Mr D. says he is very steady. He is the oddest looking creature you ever saw—not taller than Mr de Quincey—with a beard as black as a raven. He is exactly like a Portugueze Jew. Mrs Coleridge and Sara are at Derby—going to Mr Clarkson's in Suffolk—and thence to London. Sara quite well. You will be glad to hear that her horsemanship is going to turn to some profit. The Southeys all well. You do not forget your neighbours, and now I think I have told you enough of them.

Oh no—poor Curran, the coach-man at the hall—our proud letter-carrier—is dead and buried. He died of a fit of apoplexy— a fate which my Brother had long foretold. The Church[1] *is* to be built—in the orchard adjoining our Field. We hear nothing of Tillbrooke, except that he and my Brother are both much interested in the Election[2]—both of course against *your* side. [The] Miss Dowlings are well—and your little favorite Julia[3] improving in all respects.

As to our Scotch Tour I can only say that it was delightful— though not extensive. I liked it the better for being over known ground. Afterwards we returned to Edinburgh—found quiet benefit for Miss J H in the warm sea, and vapour baths, and in spite of rheumatism, she had great pleasure in 3 weeks residence at Edinburgh. We were at Lanark. I thought of you—and yours in passing through Hamilton, especially when I saw the Barracks. You will wonder I have not said a word of Bills and Business—all will be settled I hope in the course of a week—and I will then send you a statement of D^r and C^r and all particulars. The principal Bills are discharged. Mr Carr very much obliged to you—and begged me to say so.—And now my dear Friend I must turn for a moment to the most interesting part of your very interesting letter. You desire to have no criticism—and I assure you I am not disposed to criticize. The verses[4] are very affecting—and I think they will set

later, when events had borne out the foolishness of the move: 'What to advise about Hartley I know not. The event has shown that you and I judged rightly when we thought it no hopeful experiment to bring him from London. *There* he was at least out of sight, when he chose to wallow in disgrace;—and he was in the way of employment. And he could not, as he does here, throw himself into these miserable situations in full reliance that he will be sought for, and extricated . . .' (*WL MSS.*).

[1] Rydal Chapel, opened late in 1824. See below, L. 153.
[2] Of a new Member for Cambridge University (see above, L. 80). W. W. was particularly anxious that the successful candidate should be opposed to the Roman Catholic claims, which E. Q. as a Catholic himself, naturally supported.
[3] Julia Myers. See L. 2 above.
[4] In memory of Mrs. Quillinan. See L. 74 above.

my Brother's mind to flow in numbers, as they have already wrought on his feelings. He has mused upon your lines—but he must be left to himself—at present his nervous anxiety concerning William is not sufficiently settled down. He cannot go to any thing but vagrant reading by day light. He walks much it is true—yet seldom alone except to the Doctor's. My poor Sister has been her son's constant attendant—night and day—but now her rest is not broken. She is thinner, as you may suppose—and looks ill; but her health has not, I think, materially suffered. My Brother's eyes are better—and he looks pretty well. I am perfectly well—Truly thankful I reached home when I did; for my poor Brother would have been lost without a companion during his heavy anxiety. Joanna Hutchinson, I am sorry to tell you, has left us.

This is a sad, sad scrawl; If I were as witty as you I should contrive with some nicely turned apology to beg you to excuse my brevity—As it is, I must say my weary lengthiness.

I began to write yesterday—in sunshine and fair weather—the rain came on again at night with renewed freshness—goes on now at 12 o'clock briskly—and so I suspect will continue to do— perhaps for days to come. Poor William is confined to the parlour and our wooden house—but he desires me (very merrily) to tell you that he too has got the littlest of little houses. He is doing very well. Kiss the Darlings for each of us—give my kiss with the name 'Dortee Wordsworth'. The wine and all other things you shall hear of when I write again.

Yours ever
aff^{cly} D. W.

My Sister returns a hundred thanks for yr letter. She will write when quite at ease and more at leisure.

I have broken open my letter for a message from my Brother. His state of mind has hindered him from doing what he hopes now soon to be able to do—he says it is much in his thoughts.

My Brother begs his kindest regards.

Mr Kenyon desired to be informed when Old Brathay was vacant—if ever. You perhaps know where he is and could contrive to write or send him word,—but first learn if the Gees think of it.

This surely will prove the most troublesome letter you ever received—You must have a sharp eye to discover all the scraps.

84. W. W. to LORD LONSDALE

MS. Lonsdale MSS. Hitherto unpublished.

Rydal Mount
29th Nov[br] 1822

My Lord,

Mr Gee expresses himself as deeply sensible of your Lordship's kind consideration. He has probably written to you, ere this, to state his own views.

Lord Lowther honored me with a call the other day. I should have gone over to meet him at Keswick on Tuesday, but his Letter announcing his intention of being there did not reach me till Wednesday.

Mr White[1] of the Custom House Whitehaven has been over here, on poor Mr Blakeney's affairs, and has mentioned to me a regulation which will probably take place in the Custom House at Whitehaven which will materially affect the interests of that Body; and will also bear upon the Stamp Office, so as very much to reduce the profits of the Distribution which I hold. Mr White states that from the correspondence of the Commissioners he is persuaded, that Ireland (as is the case with Scotland) will be subject only to coasting duties; in which case the sale of Stamps at the Custom House Whitehaven will be diminished from upwards of 2,000 per Ann (which is the average for the last four years) to £200.

Your Lordship is probably aware of the reduction of the rate of poundage from 4 per Cent to three, after the first ten thousand pounds returned; and likewise of the new regulation requiring monthly remittances, so that the little profit which has heretofore been derived from interest on the money in hand may be said to be at an end; I am sorry to add that the sale of stamps is diminished considerably through the whole of my district, and in some parts is reduced one half. If the apprehended change in the Custom House takes place, that alone will entirely take off the advantages derived from the addition, through your Lordship's kindness, of the three Towns to my district.[2] I could not forbear mentioning the above particulars, because I know and gratefully feel how desirous your Lordship has been at all times to serve me; and I have thought it prudent to mention them thus early, not as presuming to ground any proposition or immediate request upon them, but that you might know how I stand and am likely to stand, so that if an opportunity

---

[1] Formerly W. W.'s Sub-distributor.
[2] Maryport, Cockermouth, and Workington, added in 1820. See L. 7 above.

should occur, my interest might not suffer from your Lordship being ignorant of the situation.

I was much concerned to hear of Col. Lowther's servere accident; Lord Lowther told me he was doing well. My little Boy is recovering.

Ever most faithfully your Lordship's
W. Wordsworth

85. D. W. to ELIZABETH CRUMP[1]

Address: Miss Eliz[th] Crumpe, at J. G. Crumpe's Esq[re], Liverpool.
MS. WL.
LY i. 100(—).

Rydal Mount, Nov. 29th, 1822.

My dear Elizabeth,

I am glad of an opportunity of sending you a line by E. Wilkinson[2] who will depart this evening for Liverpool and will return in a fortnight when I hope she will bring good tidings of all your family, and of Mrs King,[3] who I suppose is now with you.

You were very kind in thinking of us at the time of your affliction. Mrs Harden[4] delivered your message and I should have written, but shrinking from the pain of it myself, I said—'What consolation can be given at this time? They will ere long find the best consolation in thinking of their departed sister as removed from an uncertain life to that happiness which her meek spirit seemed almost to be fitted for while she was in this world.' I trust your dear Mother has regained her chearfulness and that she enjoys the same good health as formerly. Mrs King's account of Louisa gave us great pleasure. Little did I once think that she would ever again have been able to join in the pleasures and employments of other young people, but it now seems she is as stout as the best of you.

We have heard that *you* are coming to Mrs Harden's this winter,

---

[1] Elizabeth Crump (d. 1835), younger daughter of the Liverpool attorney who built Allan Bank (see *EY*, p. 534). In 1826 she married William Wardell of Chester and Liverpool, a banker. She was a close friend of Dora W. and the younger Coleridges at this time; after her marriage she mainly corresponded with Sara Coleridge. She had two brothers, George and John (mentioned below), and several sisters, including Sophia, Louisa (mentioned below), and Julia, who later married the Revd. William Jackson.

[2] A servant.   [3] See *EY*, p. 636.

[4] John Harden's second wife, formerly Janet Allan (1776–1837), of Edinburgh, whom he had married in 1803.

and shall be sincerely glad if it be true. We will again, God willing, go again to the sheep-fold[1] together—and who knows but you may even reach the top of Fairfield? I was there twice last summer. I addressed a letter to Mrs King at Liverpool. From her you will have heard of William's[2] last illness. He is (I am thankful in being able to say so) much better now, than when I wrote to her, and we trust that with constant watchfulness, he may in course of time overcome the present internal weakness which has caused his last two—and indeed several other serious illnesses. His spirits are excellent and he submits chearfully to all privations, having at the same time some pleasures which he is privileged to enjoy only as being an invalid. He has a nice little poney and rides whenever the weather will permit.

Miss Hutchinson is still at Stockton with Dora. We hope to have them àt home before Xmas, when John will come for the holidays from Sedbergh. Dora's health seems now to be quite re-established. Miss Joanna is at Kendal, and I am sorry to say she has again been poorly, since she left us. I had a delightful little Tour with her in Scotland, and a three weeks' residence in Edinburgh, where though she suffered great pain from rheumatism, she enjoyed much pleasure, and at our return to Rydal she was, I hoped, nearly well.

My Brother had a letter lately from your Brother John. He bids me say that he heartily wishes him success, and would have been very glad to have given him an order, but he happens now to have an unusual stock of wine, having imported through Mr Quillinan, whose father is an Oporto merchant, two hogsheads of port. You know that at best our consumption of wine is but trifling, but my Brother will not forget that John Crumpe can supply him when he wants white wine again. The stock of port will last us for years and years to come. Hartley Coleridge is with Mr Dawes. Mrs C. and Sara are at Derby, on their way to London.

I send you a specimen of my Brother's handwriting. You will be glad to hear that he is well in health and his eyes not very bad. My Sister is quite well, notwithstanding her late anxiety—it has however made her *look* ill and thin. My Brother and Sister join with me in kindest remembrances to your Father, Mother, Miss Crumpe and all the Family and to Mrs King. Believe me, my dear Elizabeth, your affectionate Friend,

Dorothy Wordsworth.

[1] i.e. Michael's sheepfold in Greenhead Ghyll.
[2] i.e. Willy's.

29 November 1822

[*Enclosed is a copy in W. W.'s hand of the first five stanzas of* The Eclipse of the Sun, 1820, *as in PW iii. 184, except that for ll. 7–12 read*:

> *We* sailed beneath Italian skies
> Through scenes as fair as Paradise
> While in the face of things was wrought
> A silent and unlook'd for change
> Which, even for us, did check the range
> Of joy and spritely thought.]

86. W. W. to JOHN KEBLE[1]

Address: To The Revd John Keble, Oriel College, Oxford. *To be forwarded.*
MS. Keble College, Oxford.[2] *Hitherto unpublished.*

Rydal Mount
Decr 18th. [1822]

My dear Sir

Prompted by a respect for your character, and encouraged by marks of attention which I have received from you on different occasions, I take leave to address you on a subject which concerns me nearly—viz the education of a Son. Two years ago he was admitted at St John's College Cambridge and it was my intention that he should go thither next October—but after having read with his present Master Euclid and made some little progress in Algebra, he is convinced in his own mind that his future progress in Mathe-

---

[1] John Keble (1792–1866), poet and Tractarian divine: Fellow of Oriel College, Oxford (1811), and tutor (1818–23), Professor of Poetry (1831–41), and vicar of Hursley, Hants (1836–66). In 1827 he published anonymously *The Christian Year*, which achieved phenomenal success, and his famous Assize Sermon of July 1833 initiated the Oxford Movement. He contributed to the *Tracts for the Times* and *The Library of the Fathers*, edited Hooker's *Works* (1836), and published a *Life* of Bishop Wilson and edited his *Works* for *The Library of Anglo-Catholic Theology*. In 1841 Keble dedicated his poetry lectures to W. W., who had first met him as early as May 1815, when W. W. had escorted Hartley Coleridge to Oxford. Keble wrote enthusiastically to J. T. Coleridge (see *MY* ii. 235) on 18 May 1815: '... have you seen Wordsworth? and is he not a delightful man? I met him one evening at Wm Coleridge's, and really I do not know when I have been better pleased. It is certainly one of the prime, as well as, I fear, one of the rarest, enjoyments of life, to find such a writer coming up to your conceptions of him. In one respect he was even better than I expected; there was no affectation of poetical or metaphysical talk in him; rather he seemed to avoid it. We took him into Magd. Chapel and shewed him the picture by candle-light, with which he was evidently affected. Cornish and I have been speculating on a sonnet ever since.' (*Bodleian Library MSS.*)
[2] The MSS. of this and later letters to Keble have now (1974) been mislaid.

174

matics will bear no proportion to the time which he must give to the Study, if he perseveres in the course followed at Cambridge—in short, he is strongly persuaded that the system at Oxford would suit him much better.—

My Son is as industrious as a Parent could wish—and is indeed passionately fond of Classics, in which he must have made great progress had he been more fortunate in his Teachers—especially in the earlier part of his life—but on this I need not dwell—as you will be assured that I should not have mentioned a subject of this kind to you, had I the smallest reason to believe, that, either from want of attainments, or any other cause, he were likely to do discredit to any Coll: that should receive him.

If it were practicable, I could wish him to enter upon keeping his terms in some leading Coll: in Oxford, before the expiration of the approaching year—but I fear the regulations of that University will not allow it, as I understand none are received who cannot be admitted within the Walls. He will be 20 years of age next June—he has no time to spare, therefore he must be contented to go to Cambridge unless there be found room for him within the time before mentioned in some respectable Coll. at Oxford—those I should prefer, are your own, Christ Church—Brazen Nose and Exeter.

I have ventured to trouble you with this, with a hope that you will endeavour to ascertain if my wishes can be carried into effect—You are probably out of Coll: and I should have deferred writing till after the Christmas holidays, but for the pressure of the occasion.

I need not add that as speedy an answer as the case, and your own convenience will allow, will greatly oblige, dear Sir,

Yours faithfully and respectfully—

Wm Wordsworth

87. D. W. to H. C. R.

Address: To H. C. Robinson Esqre, No. 3 King's Bench Walk, Temple, London.
Postmark: 26 Dec. 1822. *Endorsed*: 1822, Dec. 21st Miss Wordsworth including a Sonnet.
MS. Dr. Williams's Library.
K (—). *Morley, i. 120.*

December 21st 1822.

My dear Friend,

Disappointment often follows hope long deferred. Not so in our case when your promised letter arrived, which did and *does* interest us much more than you could possibly imagine, when you kindly took so much trouble for us. It has had many readings; and is not yet laid up among our records; but will for some time be kept out for reference and re-perusal. You do not say you intend us a second part;—but that hint at the last, that you could fill another letter with what you saw, and observed of the people[1]—(no doubt including many adventures characteristic both of you and of them) set our greedy desires at work yet we are not unreasonable enough to ask the favour; but if you could find leisure, and could make of it a pleasant task, it would render this your delightful sketch of Cities Towns—ruins and scenery quite complete.— I have had many a transient wish that we could have been with you. —and exclaimed to my Brother—'Nay had *I* been there—(at Grenoble)—no weather should have deterred him—We *would* have seen the Grande Chartreuse'—but *he* interposed to check my boasting, with the irrevocable decree that no Female is to tread on that sacred ground. Seriously, however, my Br is very sorry that you should have missed the Chartreuse. I do not think that any one spot which he visited during his youthful Travels with Robert Jones[2] made so great an impression on his mind: and, in my young days, he used to talk so much of it to me; that it was a great disappointment when I found that the Chartreuse was not to come into our Tour—We were all mortified that you turned away from the Pyranees,—yet the reason was quite sufficient—(being alone)— Not that perhaps you would have been safer with a companion— but you would have thought less of danger—and most likely none would have reached you; though in the unsettled state of the

---

[1] H. C. R. had spent the previous summer in France, where he had run into the Lambs and acted as Mary Lamb's escort to Paris. See Sadler, ii. 235–8; *HCR* i. 284–5.

[2] In Aug. 1790. See *EY*, p. 32. For the impact of the Grande Chartreuse on W. W.'s mind, see *Descriptive Sketches* (1793), ll. 53 ff. (*PW* i. 46); *Prel.*, pp. 196 ff., and Moorman, i. 135–7.

country, with the recent provocation you mention, you probably made a wiser choice than you might have done under the temptation of pleasant company. As to Italy I do not so much lament that you did not go thither; for perhaps the scheme we have so often talked of may at some time be accomplished—and then we shall once again be fellow-travellers.—We have had an anxious time as you well know, having heard of poor William's illness; He recovered from the first attack (at Midsummer) sooner than we expected; and we had much enjoyment in the company of my Brother and his three Boys for seven weeks notwithstanding almost incessant rain.— They were no sooner gone than the weather changed, and Miss Hutchinson and Dora went on a visit to Stockton upon Tees— whence they only returned the day before yesterday, Dora's health much improved, and both in good spirits. I set off to Edinburgh with Miss Joanna Hutchinson on the day of Miss H's and D's departure—intending to return home in a fortnight but we stayed seven weeks!—I had for years promised Joanna to go with her to Edinburgh—that was her object; but we planned a little Tour—up the Forth to Stirling, then by Track-boat to Glasgow—from Dunbarton to Rob Roy's Caves by steam—stopped at Tarbet— thence in a cart to Inverary—back again to Glasgow down Loch Fyne and up the Clyde—thence on the Coach to Lanark—and from Lanark to Moffat in a cart. There stopped two days, my companion being an Invalid;—and she fancied the waters might cure her— but a bathing-place which nobody frequents is never in order— A Bath that *was* to have been warm proved worse than cold—and we were glad to leave Moffat—crossing a wild country—again in a cart—to the Banks of the River Esk—in our way home. There we intended staying two days at a Friend's house; but were detained *four* by Joanna's having an attack of lumbago, which determined us to return to Edinburgh for the sake of warm Baths. We were three weeks in lodgings at E.—The Baths proved very beneficial and we very much enjoyed the time—though we saw little or no company— The Laings[1]—your Friends—were very kind to us—and theirs was the only house which we visited. Miss Laing is a clever good-natured, frank Scotch Lassie—and as stout a walker as myself—and was as glad to take with me a long wild walk as I to accompany her. Poor Joanna could not do much in this way; but she was delighted with Edinburgh—had much of that sort of pleasure which one has in first seeing a foreign country—and in our Travels—whether on the outside of a coach—or the deck of a steam-boat—or in whatever

---

[1] See L. 77 above.

way we got forward she was always chearful—never complaining of bad fare—bad Inns—or anything else. We had only six wet days —and of these only one was very bad—during all the 7 weeks! How different your lot last year! The rain set-in, the day after our return home, and for five weeks it was almost incessant—At first that was not of much consequence to the inmates of our house—for poor William then began to be ill a second time—the symptoms were very alarming, but now thank God! he is recovered—rides on horseback daily, and seems to receive daily benefit from the fine weather we have lately had. The Family is gathered together for the Christmas holidays—John arrived last night; and we had a happy meeting, far happier than we could have expected six weeks ago! for the best we could then look to, for William, was a long and tedious illness. I now hope that his constitution may in course of time over come that internal weakness which has caused the late serious attacks. He is kept to a strict regimen and there is no reason to fear that rules will be broken after such awful warnings. He cannot be put to school again for a long time[1]—nor will the physicians allow of any thing like study—This is a great misfortune at his age.—My Brother's mind, since our summer company left us has been so much taken up with anxiety that till within the last 3 weeks he has done nothing. Our first job was to prepare, with additions—a second Edition of his little Book on the Lakes.[2] He is now giving his mind to Poetry again, but I do not think he will ever, in his life-time—*publish* any more poems—for they hang on hand— —never selling—the Sketches and the Memorials[3] have not, I daresay *half* sold—I will transcribe a Sonnet which he felt himself called upon to write in justification of the Russians whom he felt he had injured; by not having given them *their* share in the overthrow of Buonaparte in conjunction with the elements. Refer to the Political Sonnets for that which is to precede the following.[4]

> By self-devoted Moscow—by the blaze
> Of that dread sacrifice—by Russian blood
> Lavished in fight with desperate hardihood—
> The impassive elements no claim shall raise
> To rob our human nature of her praise.

[1] Willy did not return to the Charterhouse.

[2] Strictly speaking the fourth edition, but the second *separate* edition. See *Cornell Wordsworth Collection*, no. 73.

[3] i.e. the *Ecclesiastical Sketches* and *Memorials of a Tour on the Continent, 1820.*

[4] See *PW* iii. 140–2. The sonnet as first published in 1827 differed in several respects from the version given here.

Enough was done and suffered to insure
Final deliverance, absolute and pure;
Enough for faith, tracking the beaten ways
Of Providence. But now did the most High
Exalt his still small voice, his wrath unshroud,
And lay his justice bare to mortal eye;
He who, of yore, by miracles spake aloud
As openly that purpose here avow'd,
Which only madness ventures to defy.

When you see Mr Monkhouse you will read the Sonnet to him, as it is always a treat for him to have a few verses from Rydal Mount. The Guerilla sonnets[1] must have been selected by the Newspaper Editor on account of the circumstances of the times. We had not seen—or heard of—them. The French have stayed their hands it is to be hoped for the present,—but whether they meddle or not —I think it is very likely that some thing more may come out of my Brother in connexion with Spain.—and certainly *will*, if they do after all send their Armies across the Pyranees.[2]—We shall be delighted to see Elia's Essays collected in a Book by themselves— I hope they will soon appear.[3] Thank you for your good account of Miss Lamb Pray give my kind Love to her and her Brother. They will be glad to hear that Miss Hutchinson talks of going to London in the Spring. She often speaks of the pleasure she shall have in seeing *them*—and I assure you, she does not forget *you* in numbering her London Friends.

We have been much concerned at the recent accounts of Mrs Monkhouse's state of health.—I hope you see them as often as ever you can—There is no one so likely to chear our good Friend as yourself—when his spirits are sinking under anxiety, which I fear they must often do, during his Wife's confinement to the Sofa.

[1] See *PW* iii. 138–9. The details about this republication of the sonnets cannot be established as H. C. R.'s letter has not survived.
[2] In 1820 there had been a revolt in Spain against the harsh rule of Ferdinand VII (1784–1833), who had abolished the Cortes and restored absolutism. A liberal regime followed, and for three years he was a prisoner of a section of his subjects who proclaimed once more the Constitution of 1812. Ferdinand appealed for help to the monarchies of the Holy Alliance; and late in 1822 at the Congress of Verona France proposed to invade Spain. This attempt to revive traditional Bourbon pretensions in the peninsula was opposed by Great Britain. But on 7 Apr. 1823 Louis XVIII sent his nephew, the Duc d'Angoulême, into Spain at the head of an army. Ferdinand was delivered out of the hands of the liberals, and a new reactionary regime was set up.
[3] *Elia. Essays which have appeared under that signature in the London Magazine* appeared in 1823.

This is a sad dull letter in return for y[ours[1]]—and I am ashamed of blots—scrawling with a bad pen etc, etc, etc—ashamed indeed after your legible pen[man]ship—and to write so to YOU! who repaired my loss in the Vale of Leuk with such a nice silver pen—which I still daily use! It is almost like ingratitude. We all join in wishing you as happy a coming year as the last with your usual good health and spirits—God bless you. Believe me ever your faithful and affectionate Friend

Dorothy Wordsworth

Mrs Coleridge and her Daughter are at Playford—Remember me to Tom Clarkson. Your good Report of him gives us the sincerest pleasure.

As you are so much interested in the Ecclesiastical Sonnets[2] William will send you hereafter—a poem which he has just written upon the foundation of a Church which Lady Fleming is about to erect at Rydal.[3]—It is about 80 lines,—I like it much.

My Brother who is now beside me, desires sincere remembrances. He tells me to say he sympathises with you entirely in what you say respecting the interference of France with Spain.

88. D. W. to SAMUEL ROGERS

Address: To Samuel Rogers Esq[re] St James's Place, London.
Postmark: 7 Jan. 1823. *Stamp*: Kendal Penny Post. *Endorsed*: not to be published S R.
MS. Sharpe Collection, University College, London.
Rogers. K (—). *LY i. 102.*

Rydal Mount Jan[ry] 3rd, 1823.

My dear Sir,

As you have no doubt heard, by a message sent from my Brother through Mr Sharpe, I happened to be in Scotland when your letter arrived, where (having intended to be absent from home only a fortnight) I was detained seven weeks by the illness of my fellow-traveller. Having not had it in my power to thank you immediately for your great kindness to me, and your ready attention to my Brother's request,[4] I was unwilling, after my return, to write for

---

[1] *MS. torn.*

[2] 'I read the glorious sonnets of Wordsworth—the *Ecclesiastical Sketches*, which are lessons of wisdom and stimulants to inquiry . . . one of his greatest publications.' (*HCR* i. 282.)

[3] *To the Lady Fleming on seeing the Foundation preparing for the Erection of Rydal Chapel, Westmoreland.* See *PW* iv. 165, 439 (for the I.F. note). The poem was clearly only in its first version at this stage, as the final text is 100 lines long. See Ls. 90 and 92 below. [4] See L. 76 above.

that purpose merely, many circumstances occurring to prevent me from coming to a decision upon the matter in which you are inclined to take so friendly an interest. The most important of these was a protracted and dangerous sickness of my Nephew William, which began the day after my arrival at home, and engrossed the care and attention of the whole house. He is now recovered; but his looks continue to shew that his frame is far from being restored to its natural strength.

I cannot but be flattered by your thinking so well of my Journal as to recommend (indirectly at least) that I should not part with all power over it till its fortune has been tried: you will not be surprized, however, that I am not so hopeful, and that I am apprehensive that, after having encountered the unpleasantness of coming before the public I might not be assisted in attaining my object. I have then to ask whether a middle course be not possible, that is, whether your favorable opinion, confirmed perhaps by some other good judges, might not induce a Bookseller to give a certain sum for the right to publish a given number of copies. In fact, I find it next to impossible to make up my mind to sacrifice my privacy for a certainty *less* than two hundred pounds, a sum which would effectually aid me in accomplishing the ramble I so much, and I hope not unwisely, wish for. If a bargain could be made on terms of this sort, your expectation of further profits (which expectation I would willingly share) need not be parted with; and I should have the further gratification of acting according to your advice.

I have nothing further to say, for it is superfluous to trouble you with my scruples, and the fears which I have that a work of such slight pretensions will be wholly overlooked in this writing and publishing (especially *tour*-writing and *tour*-publishing) age—and when factions and parties literary and political are so busy in endeavouring to stifle all attempts to interest, however pure from any taint of the world, and however humble in their claims.

My Brother begs me to say that it gratified him to hear you were pleased with his late publications. In the 'Memorials' he himself likes best the Stanzas upon Ensiedlen,[1] the three Cottage Girls, and, above all, the Eclipse upon the Lake of Lugano; and, in the 'Sketches' the succession of those on the Reformation, and those towards the conclusion of the third part. Mr Sharpe liked best the poem on Enterprise, which surprized my Brother a good deal.

---

[1] i.e. Einsiedeln. The reference is to the poem *Composed in One of the Catholic Cantons* (*PW* iii. 173).

We hope to see you in summer; you will be truly welcome, and we should be heartily glad to see your Sister as your companion, to whom we all beg to [be m]ost[1] kindly remembered.

If you knew how much it has cost me to settle the affair of this proposed publication in my mind, as far as I have now done, I am sure you would deem me sufficiently excused for having so long delayed answering your most obliging letter. I have still to add that if there be a prospect that any Bookseller will undertake the publication, I will immediately prepare a corrected copy to be sent to you; and I shall trust to your kindness for taking the trouble to look over it, and to mark whatever passages you may think too trivial for publication, or in any other respect much amiss.

My Brother and Sister join with me in every good wish to you for the coming year—and many more. Believe me, dear Sir,

yours gratefully, and with sincere esteem,

Dorothy Wordsworth

89. W. W. to LORD LONSDALE

MS. Lonsdale MSS. Hitherto unpublished.

24th Jan[ry] 1823

My Lord,

I should have been sorry if your Lordship had been at the trouble of answering my former Letter,[2] which was merely a statement of facts. In one instance things have not turned out quite so ill as I had then reason to fear. In some parts of my District the consumption of Stamps had fallen off one half; but the whole amount having just made up my annual Account, I find to be only £3,000 less than the year preceding, while there is an encrease of £300 in the Coach duty. Your Lordship will excuse my being so minute; but I wish to be accurate. My last year's return is £17,000, and a few pounds.

If the apprehended Reduction at the Custom House Whitehaven takes place, I cannot but think that the addition of Ulverston, small as it is, to this district would on general grounds be desirable. As far as I am myself concerned, I could on no account wish it, unless the Lancaster Distributor had an Equivalent from the late Mr Myers's District,[3] which might easily be done were the Treasury so disposed; but it is certainly not worth while to encounter any thing unpleasant for so small an advantage. Let me at all events,

[1] *MS. torn.*   [2] L. 84 above.   [3] i.e. Millom.

thank your Lordship for so readily meeting my wishes. I have written to Lord Lowther by this Post.[1]

I take the liberty of enclosing a short Poem which I have just addressed to Lady le Fleming upon the occasion of erecting a Chapel at Rydal.[2] I hope it will afford some pleasure to your Lordship and to Lady Lonsdale. I have been honoured lately by a Tirade of abuse in the Edinburgh Review.[3] This is as it should be. Attachment to the institutions and Religion of our Country is enough to make a man odious with the Whigs, as they call themselves, who are indeed running a desperate course.

Lord Holland[4] is much galled by Mr Southey's peninsular War.[5]

The King as probably your Lordship knows has expressed in strong terms his approbation of the Work.[6]

My Son is at present well; but preserved so, I believe, only by care as to his diet, exercise and exposure. I dare not send him to School; and am restricted by his Medical Adviser from putting him upon over much application at home.

I hope that the Col. feels no bad effects from his Accident, and that the family are all well.

The frost is very severe; we have excellent skaiting upon the Lake.

Ever with highest respect
I remain gratefully
your Lordship's friend
and Serv^{nt}
Wm Wordsworth

[1] In a letter of 20 Jan. Lord Lonsdale had not held out much hope for an extension of W. W.'s Distributorship, and he enclosed a letter from Lord Lowther two days earlier which argued that the addition of the Lonsdale North district 'would make but a trifling addition to Mr W's income'. But he wrote again on 31 Jan. more hopefully: 'Lord Lowther I am sure will do all in his Power to effect the change you have suggested—and the Difficulty seems to be diminished, as there is very great Dissatisfaction express'd by our Friends at Lancaster, as the appointment of Distributor is given to a Hornby, on the recommendation of Lord Stanley.' And a few days later he sent on to W. W. a letter from the Stamp Board of 4 Feb. formally agreeing to the arrangement contemplated by W. W. (*WL MSS.*).   [2] See L. 87 above and next letter.

[3] This abusive article by Francis Jeffrey on the *Memorials of a Tour on the Continent*, *Edinburgh Review*, xxxvii (Nov. 1822), 449–56, began: 'The Lake School of Poetry, we think, is now pretty nearly extinct', and went on to speak of 'a sort of emphatic inanity', in W. W.'s latest compositions, 'a singular barrenness and feebleness of thought, disguised under a sententious and assuming manner and a style beyond example verbose and obscure'.

[4] The famous Whig statesman. See *MY* ii. 304.

[5] The first volume of Southey's *History of the Peninsular War* had just appeared. See L. 61 above.

[6] In a letter from Sir William Knighton, the King's private secretary, to Southey. See Warter, iii. 369–70.

90. W. W. to LORD LONSDALE

Address: The Earl of Lonsdale.
MS. Lonsdale MSS. Hitherto unpublished.

Rydal Mount 25th Jan^ry 1823

My Lord,

On reviewing the lines which I ventured to send yesterday,[1] they seemed to me in some respect not sufficiently appropriate; I felt also that there was an abruptness in the mode of introducing the 4th stanza and that there was a disproportion between the middle and the other parts of the Poem. These several objections seem in a great measure obviated by the Introduction of a new stanza, as on the opposite page. It follows the third, ending,

'To interrupt the deep repose.'

Ever most faithfully
Your Lordship's,
W Wordsworth

A corrected copy is enclosed, of the whole.

[In M. W.'s hand]

To interrupt the deep repose.

Well may the Villagers rejoice!
Nor storms, henceforth, nor weary ways
Shall be a hinderance to the Voice
That would unite in prayer and praise:
More duly shall wild-wandering Youth
Receive the curb of sacred truth;
The Aged shall be free to hear
The Promise, caught with steadfast ear;
And *All* shall welcome the new ray
Imparted to their Sabbath-day.[2]

Lives there a man etc.,

[1] See previous letter and L. 87 above. W. W. had now expanded the original draft of *To the Lady Fleming* with a new stanza, making a poem of ninety lines in the second MS., dated 24 Jan. 1823. One more stanza, the fifth in the final version, had yet to be added.
[2] The final version of this stanza, as in *PW* iv. 166, varies slightly from the text printed here.

91. W. W. to WILLIAM STEWART ROSE[1]

MS. Cornell. Hitherto unpublished.

Rydal Mount
28th Jan^{ry} [1823]

Dear Sir,

I have to thank you for the obliging present of your Translation of the 1st 12 Cantos of Ariosto.—I have looked it nearly through, but without having time to compare it with the Original; if when I am able to do so any remarks should occur worthy of being communicated, I will not fail to attend to your request. In the mean time accept my acknowlegements for a work which promises to make the English Reader acquainted in a faithful and agreeable manner with a charming Writer.

I remain your obliged Ser^{vnt}
Wm Wordsworth

92. W. W. to LADY LE FLEMING

MS. WL transcript. Hitherto unpublished.

[late Jan. 1823]

Mr Wordsworth is far from desiring to entangle Lady le Fleming in a troublesome correspondence but he cannot refrain from expressing his sympathy with those feelings which have induced Lady le Fleming to decline meeting his wishes to honor the Verses by prefixing to them her name[2]—he will therefore not only abstain from introducing her Ladyship's name but will also alter the line in which Rydal is mentioned and take care that nothing shall be left in the poem which must obviously localize it—

Thus far Mr W. happily concurs[3] with Lady le Fleming but tho aware that the Structure arose out of a view to private accomodation Mr W. cannot think that the founding of any building which

---

[1] William Stewart Rose (1775–1843), author and translator, second son of George Rose, the politician: M.P. for Christchurch, 1796–1800; thereafter Clerk in the House of Lords until 1824. After travelling on the Continent, 1814–18, he began to translate from the Italian, and the first part of his metrical version of Ariosto's *Orlando Furioso* appeared in 1823. It was completed in 1831.

[2] In an undated letter of this time, she had written: 'Lady le F. returns her thanks to Mr Wordsworth for the obliging wish expressed of placing her name with the Verses upon Rydall Chapel, but this she must *decidedly decline* as it would be most inconsistent for a Person whose general mode of life is so quiet and retired thus to intrude herself upon the Public . . .' (*WL MSS.*).

[3] agrees *crossed out*.

forms a constituant part of the Church Establishment of England can under any circumstances take place without interesting a respectable portion of the community. Mᴿ W. may be permitted to observe that Lady le F's view of the present case proceeds from that humility which leads the sincere Christian to think little of his own works—the same feeling which induced Lady le F. to wish that her name should be withheld. The Chapel which forms the subject of this poem cannot but be an object of general concernment both as an elegant Edifice ornamenting a most beautiful situation in a country resorted to by travellers from all parts of the world and as an instance of individual munificence unhappily too rare in this age.

The purpose of the verses being to support however humbly and feebly the cause of religion and piety especially as connected with the ordinances and institutions of the Church of England Mᴿ W. is desirous that they should be published at this time when the Church is assaulted openly and unceasingly by enemies in all orders of society from the highest to the lowest. In a few days Mᴿ W. will enclose a revised copy and if after what has been said and notwithstanding that this foundation has already at great length been noticed in newspapers and will be so again when it is consecrated Lady le Fleming should object to the verses being published[1] Mᴿ W. will suppress them altogether out of respect to the private feeling of *One* to whom this neighbourhood of Rydal is upon this as it has been upon many other occasions so deeply indebted.

[*unsigned*]

93. M. W. to LADY BEAUMONT

MS. untraced.
K (—). *LY i. 104*(—).

February 5ᵗʰ, 1823

My dear Lady Beaumont,

I have delayed sending you the poem,[2] and also to reply to your last kind letter, in the hope of being able to speak decisively about the intended visit to Coleorton. . . .

---

[1] Lady le Fleming finally agreed to the publication of the verses the following Easter: 'The whole strain of the poetry is of so pious a nature that there can be no doubt of its strongly interesting all persons of a serious turn of mind' (*WL MSS.*). The poem was published in the *Poetical Works* of 1827.

[2] *To the Lady Fleming on seeing the Foundation preparing for the Erection of Rydal Chapel, Westmoreland.*

Mrs C. and Sara have been some time at Highgate.[1] She wrote soon after their arrival there, and gave a cheerful account of C.[2] She spoke of going into Devonshire about the middle of March. We seldom see Hartley, but as we hear little of him, and that little in his favour, we hope he is spending his time to some good purpose; but as to the discipline of Mr Dawes' school, that cannot much restrain him, as I believe there are not more than four boys. . . .

I hope the verses will afford you pleasure. Her ladyship wrote a very proper reply when they were sent to her; but how far they may have power to act as a 'peace-offering' we much doubt, but heartily wish they may.[3] The severe weather has put a stop to all progress with the work. If you or Sir George could send us any hints, or sketch for a chapel that would look well in this situation, it is possible that we could have it made useful—through her[4] agents. We are very anxious that nothing should be done to disfigure the village. They might, good taste directing them, add much to its beauty. The site chosen is the orchard opposite the door leading to the lower waterfall. . . .

[cetera desunt]

94. W. W. to JOHN KEBLE

Address: To the Rev[d] John Keble, Oriel College, Oxford.
MS. Keble College, Oxford. Hitherto unpublished.

[17 Feb. 1823]

My dear Sir

I do not write on purpose to thank you for the ready kindness with which you met my wishes in respect to my Son being settled

[1] On their way south they had stayed at Coleorton, and Lady Beaumont had been much struck with Sara. She wrote to D. W. on 8 Dec. 1822: 'I never saw at her age such a delicate little sylph, so thoughtful, yet active in her notions, she would represent our ideas of Psyche or Ariel, Juliet would be too material, but she looks so delicate I should tremble at her becoming a wife or mother . . .' (*WL MSS.*)
[2] S. T. C. was at this time at work on his *Logic*. See Griggs, v. 263–5. He seems to have resented W. W.'s and Southey's opposition to Hartley's removal to Ambleside, and took the occasion of a recent dinner at the Aderses', when he was the 'star' of the evening, to speak somewhat slightingly of their achievements. See *HCR* i. 288.
[3] The strained relations between the Wordsworths and Lady le Fleming may be explained by L. 63.
[4] i.e. Lady le Fleming's.

at Oxford,[1] but to beg that any communication you may have to make to me, from this time until about the middle of next Month, may be addressed to Sir Geo: Beaumont's Bart Coleorton Hall Ashby de la Zouche—to which place I set off tomorrow.

You would understand by my silence that your recommendation was sufficient to make me quite satisfied with the addition of the two Colleges you mentioned, to those I had named. If your exertions to place my Son at Oxford during the course of this year, prove unsuccessful—I should like to know the earliest period at which he could be admitted,—yet it is scarcely worth while to ask the question—as his age will not allow delay.

Do you happen to know Mr Augustus Hare[2] of New College? He was here last Summer and I think it likely he would interest himself in the matter, if his cooperation would be of any service.

Hartley Coleridge is at present with his old Schoolmaster near Ambleside, and going on, as far as I know, very steadily—tho' his Manners have lost nothing of their oddity.

I have not had the pleasure of seeing either Mr Southey or Mr W Jackson since I heard from you—but Mr J. will be here on Tuesday when my Sister will not fail to deliver your message to him.

Deeply sensible of your kindness, I remain dear Sir, with best regards from Mrs W,

very sincerely yours
Wm Wordsworth

¹ See above, L. 86. Keble had written on 6 Jan.: 'I shall be greatly disappointed if we cannot get your son at Oxford, and it will be a real kindness to point out any little service that I can render to him, or any one connected with you, there or any where else. For I feel deeply your debtor for the real advantage (as I trust it will prove to be) as well as for the great pleasure which I find in reading your publications.' (*WL MSS.*)
² Augustus William Hare (1792–1834), Fellow and tutor of New College, Oxford, from 1818, and rector (from 1829) of Alton-Barnes, Hants, where his *Sermons to a Country Congregation*, 1836, were originally given: co-author, with his brother Julius Charles (see L. 123 below), of *Guesses at Truth*, 1827 (enlarged edn., 1848). He had first visited W. W. in the Lakes in 1819.

95. D. W. to SAMUEL ROGERS

Endorsed: not to be published S R.
MS. Sharpe Collection, University College, London.
Rogers. K (—). *LY i. 104.*

17th February 1823

My dear Sir,

I cannot deny myself the pleasure of thanking you for your last very kind letter, as Miss Hutchinson is going directly to London, and through her you will receive this. At present I shall do no more than assure you that I am fully sensible of the value of your friendly attention to the matter on which I have troubled you,[1] as I hope that my Brother and Sister will soon have the pleasure of meeting you in London, and he will explain to you all my scruples and apprehensions. They will leave home tomorrow with Miss Hutchinson and (parting with her at Derby) will turn aside to Coleorton, where they purpose spending about three weeks with our kind friends Sir George and Lady Beaumont; and will then, if nothing intervene to frustrate their present scheme, proceed to London. Their visit will be a short one; but I hope they will have time to see all their Friends.

My Brother is glad that you came upon the stone to the memory of Aloys Reding[2] in such an interesting way—he and Mrs W, without any previous notice, met with it at the moment of sunset, as described at the close of those stanzas. I was rambling in another part of the wood and unluckily missed it. I was delighted with your and your Sister's reception at that pleasant house in the vale of Schuytz, which I well remember. Mr Monkhouse and I (going on foot to Brennen from Schuytz) were struck with the appearance of the house, and inquired to whom it belonged—were told, to a Family of the name of Reding; but could not make out whether it had been the residence and Birth-place of Aloys Reding or not.

The passage in Oldham is a curious discovery.[3]

[1] See L. 88 above. Rogers had subsequently written to D. W. in mid-January inviting her to send her MS. Journal for submission to John Murray. 'Of the Longmans, I confess, I have no good opinion. . . . I believe them to be narrow, unenterprizing and penny-wise.' (*WL MSS.*)

[2] Captain-General of the Swiss forces opposed to Buonaparte, whom Rogers in his letter recalled visiting in 1802. 'There was a noble simplicity in his manner, and a courtesy, a cordiality in the reception they all gave us that sent us away enchanted.' See *PW* iii. 172.

[3] 'I have lately met with a remarkable instance of your Brother's sagacity,' Rogers had written. 'He had always maintained that Gray's line "And leave us leisure to be good" was not his own—It is in Oldham. "I have not yet the leisure to be good." ' (*WL MSS.*) The reference is to John Oldham's *Satyr against Value*, stanza v. See Gray's *Hymn to Adversity*, l. 20.

You say nothing of coming northward this summer. I hope my Brother and Sister may tempt you to think about it. I am left at home with my Niece and her Brother William, now quite well.

Pray make my very kind remembrances to Miss Rogers. You must not leave her behind when you come again to the Lakes.

So, my dear Sir, excuse this hasty scrawl, we are in the bustle of preparation for the long journey—a great event in this house!

Believe me to be
with great respect,
Yours very sincerely
Dorothy Wordsworth

96. W. W. to JOHN KEBLE

Address: To The Revd John Keble, Oriel College, Oxford.
MS. Keble College, Oxford. Hitherto unpublished.

Febry 24 [1823]
Coleorton Ashby de la Zouch

My dear Sir

Had it not been for the mention you make of Mr Hare's[1] kindness I need not to have troubled you with this, but should directly have opened a communication with Mr Forshall.[2] If my Son could only be admitted at New Col: as a Gen^t Com: that is entirely out of the question, both as to my judgement and as to my *means*—but, as your expression 'I *fear* he must be admitted'—allows of the *possibility* of its being otherwise—may I entreat, with my best thanks to Mr Hare, you would take the trouble of ascertaining that point—My Son is of a very retired disposition and would be much benefitted by the countenance of a Gentleman like Mr H. who, to the attentions which as a Tutor, from a general sense of duty he would pay him, would unite that personal interest which I have good reason to believe Mr H. would feel for a Son of Mine.[3] If, as is too probable he will be precluded from this great benefit, then may I beg, as there may be no time to lose, that you would signify

[1] Augustus Hare. See L. 94 above.
[2] The Revd. Josiah Forshall, F.R.S. (1795–1863), Biblical scholar: Fellow of Exeter College, Oxford, 1819–26, and tutor from 1822; Keeper of MSS. at the British Museum, 1827, and Secretary, 1828–51: chaplain of the Foundling Hospital, 1826–59.
[3] The choice at this stage lay between Exeter and New College, and John W. was eventually accepted by the latter, but only after further uncertainty. See next letter.

to Mr Forshall my wish that he would write to me here, letting me know the *latest* period at which my Son may be matriculated without loss of time, and also when he must enter into residence—or any other necessary information, for I am quite ignorant of the ways at Oxford—a previous journey is not required at Cambridge for the purpose of matriculation.

Many thanks for the interest you have taken in this matter, and for your wish to see me at Oxford—I remain here with M^rs W till the 15th of March—and if it be not necessary for my Son to go to O. previous to that time, we hope to meet him there, when we shall have the pleasure of mak[ing] our acknowledgements to you in person.

With kind regards from Mrs W., and in the mean time I remain my d^r Sir

Very sincerely your obliged
Wm Wordsworth

97. W. W. to JOHN KEBLE

Address: To The Revd John Keble, Oriel College, Oxford.
MS. Keble College, Oxford. Hitherto unpublished.

Coleorton Hall
Ashby de la Zouch
Mar 5th. [1823]

[*In M. W.'s hand*]

My dear Sir

Not hearing from you in answer to my last[1] respecting New College, I have been obliged this day to write to Mr Forshall—begging to know from him the latest day on which my Son can be matriculated at Oxford during the present term—it is proper to mention to you that 2 posts since M^r F's letter to H. Coleridge reached me. I am very sorry that I troubled you upon the Subject of New Coll at all—as I have since learnt, that that Society consists of Winchester Men only, so that a Person having not been educated at that School would be uncomfortably Situated—therefore if the advantage of Mr Hare's tuition had been within my reach, I must have declined them on this account.[2] I mean to be at Oxford

[1] See previous letter.
[2] Augustus Hare wrote on 14 Mar. to assure W. W. that not all members of the College were Wykehamists, and to keep open the possibility of John W. being entered there: 'I regret much that your Son is not to be entrusted to us; not for the trust's sake, for one would not court responsibility, but because from our very limited numbers, I should perhaps be able to pay him more attention

about the 20th inst[1]—when I shall hope for the pleasure of thanking you in Person for your kindness in this rather troublesome affair— and believe me Dr Sir

very faithfully your obliged S^t
[*signed*] W Wordsworth

98. W. W. to ALLAN CUNNINGHAM

MS. Mr. W. Hugh Peal.
K (—). *LY i. 105*(—)

Lee Priory near Wingham, Kent,
May 6th 1823.

Dear Sir,

On my return to Gloucester Place[2] the morning I received your directions for Mr Cannings,[3] I found your obliging present of your

than he is likely to meet with elsewhere, however zealous the tutor under whom he has been placed. Our independent members for some time past have been heirs to little or no fortune . . . The present Warden talks of taking as many as six or eight. They will then be numerous enough, if they wish it, to form a little society themselves; but I should hope, for the sake of both parties, that they will continue, as at present, to mix with the undergraduates on the foundation. The latter it is true are all from Winchester; but an athletic, sensible, gentlemanly and open-hearted lad is free of all schools . . .' (*WL MSS.*).

[1] W. W. and M. W. left Coleorton on 19 or 20 Mar. for Birmingham where they met John W. and went on to Oxford for his matriculation. On the 22nd or soon after, they all moved on to Thomas Monkhouse's London residence in Gloucester Place, where they rejoined S. H., and remained for over two weeks, caught up in a busy round of social engagements. On 1 Apr. they dined with Rogers to meet Cary (the translator of Dante), Hallam, Sharp, and Moore (*Memoirs*, iv. 47–8). On 2 Apr. there was a visit to Sir George Beaumont's to examine his newly acquired Michelangelo, and meetings with Moore and the Lambs (*HCR* i. 291–2). On the 4th W. W. gave a dinner at Thomas Monkhouse's for Coleridge, Rogers, Moore, the Lambs, and H. C. R.—'half the Poetry of England constellated and clustered in Gloster Place', according to Lamb; though the conversation was dominated by Coleridge who 'was in his finest vein of talk' (*Lamb*, ii. 376–7; *HCR* i. 292–3 and his later account in *Athenaeum*, 25 June 1853). The next evening W. W. saw Coleridge again at a musical party at the Aderses', with the Gillmans and Flaxman the sculptor (*HCR* i. 293). On the 6th W. W. was again with Rogers. There were also meetings with William Godwin (see Moorman, ii. 293), and Haydon (*Diary*, ed. Pope, ii. 470–1: for W. W.'s temporary estrangement from Haydon after this, and the artist's wild attack on W. W. in his correspondence, see Stanley Jones, 'B. R. Haydon on Some Contemporaries', *RES* xxvi (1975), 183–9). About 9 Apr. the Wordsworths moved down to Lee Priory in Kent, and remained there for five weeks before setting off on their continental tour.

[2] The residence of Thomas Monkhouse.

[3] Canning's private residence in London was at Gloucester Lodge, Old Brompton. Canning had returned to Lord Liverpool's administration as Foreign Secretary the previous autumn after Castlereagh's death, exchanging his constituency of Liverpool for that of Harwich.

Book,[1] and the Medallion of Sir Walter S—,[2] with both of which I was much pleased; both for their several sakes, and as marks of your attention. They are forwarded to Westmorland; and in a day or two I quit this place[3] for a trip, I hope of not more than three weeks, chiefly in Holland. If I return through London it will not be to stop 24 hours there, so that I shall be unable to call, and inquire after Mr and Mrs Chantrey: for whose recovery I assure you I feel not a little anxious. Pray present my best regards and wishes to them both in which Mrs W. sincerely joins.—

Mr Quillinan who is here begs me to repeat the assurance of his sense of Mr Chantrey's kindness in offering to sketch the monument[4] himself, and he further entreats (having the performance of this mark of respect to his deceased wife much in his mind) that you would be so good as to communicate with him as soon as Mr C's state of health and engagements allow him to fulfill his obliging intentions.—Excuse this hasty scrawl; and believe me my dear Sir

very faithfully your obliged Serᵛⁿᵗ

Wᵐ Wordsworth

Mr Quillinan's address
is Lee Priory, Wingham, Kent.

99. D. W. to EDWARD QUILLINAN

Address: Edward Quillinan Esqʳᵉ, Lee Priory, near Wingham, Kent (Single Sheet).
Stamp: Kendal Penny Post. *Endorsed*: Rydal Mount, May 6 1823. Miss Wordsworth. Accounts etc.
MS. WL.
LΥ i. 106 (—).

Tuesday May 6ᵗʰ 1823.

[After two pages of Accounts]

After this will be another account on the score of the Bed, which (how soon will the anniversary[5] return!) was spoiled. I had thought,

[1] Probably *Traditional Tales of the English and Scottish Peasantry*, 2 vols., 1822.
[2] An engraving by Edward Lacey of the medal executed by Thomas Stothard, R.A. (1755–1834), from Chantrey's marble bust of Scott; with surrounding ornaments engraved by Mitan from the designs of Henry Corbould (1787–1844).
[3] W. W. and M. W. actually left on the 16th, held back by bad weather and W. W.'s old trouble of inflammation of the eyes. See L. 101 below.
[4] The proposed monument in Grasmere Church to Mrs. Quillinan's memory, for which the verses had already been composed (see L. 74 above). It was placed in the church in Feb. 1824 (see *MW*, pp. 105–6).
[5] Of Mrs. Quillinan's death on 22 May 1822.

as I now find no need to step in between Mr Gee and you for the sake of justice, I might have safely left him to take care of himself; but his prepossessions that in between Friends—at such a time!—such things could not be considered—that it was a mere nothing—that he should take no notice of it etc etc—completely duped me (do not suppose that I imagine that at such a time he could *intend* that I should be his dupe). So however it was. I told him that it was *just*, you should know—and that his loss should be repaired. I now find him resolved to repair it according to *the letter*. A new Ticking is to be provided for bed and Mattress with other Costs. Luckily I went to Kendal the day after the arrival of the Bed etc. with Mr Gee's orders to Mr Halhead, and I have so modified the order that I hope the expence will not be frightful—and our good Friend Mrs Cookson will dispose of the damaged articles to the best advantage. When this matter is settled I will send you the final account. In the meanwhile you remain my Debtor—9£-16s-3d. I have all the Bills and vouchers, and will, if you please, send them by Mr Gee; but unless you wish to see them, perhaps they might as well remain with me. They will be perfectly safe till we meet.

—You will think I am a strange Blunderer to say to my Br and Sr that the Balance would be *against* you after the Wine was paid for. The truth is, I have no passion for accounts—hastily glanced my eye on John Carter's Statement and *read* 10£ for 100£. Truly glad was I when I found the truth—as, when I made my calculation when you were abroad I reckoned 100£ to be more than enough, though it is true I did not calculate upon the 42£ to Mr Tilbrooke for Rent. Before I have done with this subject, I must say once again that had the last business been wholly in my hands, the expence would have been much less; but my spirits were so much exhausted that I willingly submitted to Mr Gee and Mrs C.[1] who might better understand such arrangements. There is however one satisfaction that a pleasing remembrance of you and that blessed creature now at rest in Grasmere Church-yard has been the more often renewed in the neighbourhood—and that whatever was done on that last day is looked upon here as a mark of love and respect from you to her memory.

My dear Friend,

Dismissing money matters, let me now tell you that much and often and long together has my heart been with you at Lee Priory and truly have I sympathized with my Brother and Sister in the

---

[1] Mrs. Cookson.

happiness they have enjoyed under that hospitable roof. We are and have been most comfortable at home, but you may be sure had duty permitted such a wish I should many a time have wished to be at Lee Priory and should now wish to be setting out on the Holland Ramble. My dear Niece sends a thousand Loves to you and your sweet Jemima and Rotha. She never lets half a day go by without talking of you all. God be thanked we are all quite well. I have had a most severe cold during which D. was a tender nurse and faithful housekeeper. I have not quite regained my strength but have cast off the malady completely. I have just returned from a ride in a cart with Miss Dowling. My walks since my recovery have not been beyond the garden and I assure you I am disposed to take great care of myself. According to Mary's last letter, they will leave you to-morrow. Perhaps you will go with them to Dover and perhaps may write to tell us they are gone. I pray you in love and charity to write to us—you cannot think what pleasure a letter from you would give us. Do excuse my scrawling—though my Disorder has been nothing worse than a bad cold—or Influenza—I am strangely weakened, and the writing of a letter tires me more than any thing. Pray make my affectionate regards to Captn Barret and believe me your ever faithful and affectionate Friend

D. Wordsworth.

Poor Mr Gee is with us. He looks dreadfully—sadly harrassed he had the Rheumatism in his head. He complains of his [?Fates]— but *I* think (and every one else) that they have been very good. He will stay with us till he is recovered.

100. D. W. to EDWARD QUILLINAN

Address: Edward Quillinan Esqre, Lee Priory, near Wingham, Kent.
Postmark: 10 May 1823. *Stamp*: Kendal Penny Post. *Endorsed*: Rydal Mount
  May 7, 1823. Miss W.
MS. WL.
LY i. 107 (—).

May 7th Wednesday. [1823]

My dear Friend,
    On retracing in my mind the hurried letter which I sent off yester-day it has occurred to me that I left some matters worse than unex-plained. I hope however that you will have found the main point—the accounts—sufficiently clear: whence you will have gathered

that you remain my Debtor—9 £–16ˢ–3ᵈ. To this I should have added another half year's Taxes (one I paid myself and it is charged in the account). The other half year was paid last week by John Carter when I was confined to my Room by the Influenza, and (not wishing to teize me at that time) he did not send me information of it; but this morning, on talking with him about money affairs in general, he informed me that he had done so. In the course of a few days, Mr Elliott will pay his rent, and one half year's taxes for the house.—I shall pay John Carter 42 £ for Mr Tillbrooke on your account. The overplus will be placed in my favour—and as soon as I have paid Halhead for the Bed, Mattress, etc. the accounts shall be finally closed; and I will send you a correct Statement. Tell me if you wish the Bells to remain in my possession—or if they are to be sent to London by Mr Gee.

As to the bed, I am sure I said just enough to puzzle you—and leave you altogether uninformed. So, for my own satisfaction, I will, once for all, detail the matter from the beginning.

On mentioning to Mr Gee the injury that had been done—he replied as I have told you, 'It was not worth speaking of etc etc'—but the result was (after I had named the damage to you) that I was to get it repaired. Mrs W. and I on examining the Bed thought a new Breadth or a little more would repair it. We however judged it best to wait *Mrs* Gee's arrival, as they would have no immediate need of it. Mr Gee comes down—He tells me nothing less than a new Tick will do—This I could not oppose—'Anything less would look patched'.

—And accordingly he despatches bed, mattress, etc to Kendal with a letter to Mr Halhead. Mr H was confounded with the order for the '*best* ticking', best feathers etc etc. No reference to the actual quality of the old Ticking! ! Luckily I arrived at Kendal the same day—and so modified the order that Justice, complete justice, as between trader and trader, has been done to Mr Gee. And by disposing of the damaged articles at an auction at Kendal, I hope considerably to lighten the expence to you.

I hope to sell poor little Mima's Crib to Mrs Robinson.[1] The Bed is finished by Halhead, and with the Mattress, packed up to be sent into Somersetshire. The cost I do not yet know, as I desired Mr Halhead to send the Bill to me—not immediately for there was no hurry. The truth is that I do not wish Mr Gee to know any thing about the cost.

[1] Daughter-in-law of Mrs. Robinson, the admiral's widow. See L. 108 below.

7 *May 1823*

My dear Friend,

It grieves me to have to write thus of Mr Gee—so kind a man—and now actually under our Roof—but you understand him—and know with me that, in such little matters as these he casts off the Gentleman in feeling. Indeed I am obliged to call to mind his patience, his tenderness last year, and the deep havoc made in his feelings—otherwise I should be utterly indignant. It is now over and settled, and I will no more recur to it, and you will, I am sure, gladly burn this letter as soon as read.

I *hope* my Brother and Sister have left you this day and are now actually sailing with a mild breeze towards Ostend. The air here is charming—I *hope* so, (i.e. that they have left you) for it has occurred to me that if my last should reach you when they are still at Lee Priory, my account of the bad cold which I have had may have half frightened my Brother, though I spoke of it only as a thing gone by. I am very sorry I mentioned it at all—yet surely they must be gone. I was yesterday pleasantly jolted with Miss Dowling in a cart round by Skelwyth Bridge and Skelwyth Fold—came home quite in glee—strong and hearty—to-day I have been visiting our neighbours the Elliotts and Robinsons. My first walk down the hill—and I almost feel as if I could mount Nab Scar, but you need not fear me. I have no temptation to take long walks, having no long-walking companions—and all is so delightful immediately around us. William has never had a moment's illness since his Father and Mother left us. D.[1] is quite well at present. Miss E. Crump here—a very pleasant companion for both of us. I hope that my dear Brother and Sister will return to us with renewed health and spirits. He stood in great need of a change, and so long as they are enjoying themselves, and he laying in stores of spirits etc for the winter—we are quite contented and happy; feeling no impatience for their return. I speak at least for myself. I would have them leave nothing undone that their means can accomplish, which may be pleasant and beneficial. Do write to us—and tell Miss Hutton[2] to write often and long letters—I shall write to her as soon as I hear again from Mary. My kind love to the Monkhouses. I should like to be among you now and then. How happy Miss Hutton and Mima will be picking up pretty shells together. God bless you all. Believe me, ever your affec^te

Dorothy Wordsworth.

[1] Dora W.
[2] i.e. S. H., who did not accompany W. W. and M. W. on their tour of Holland, but remained behind at Lee Priory, spent several weeks at Boulogne, and then moved to London and Ramsgate in the autumn, where she continued to see much of the Monkhouses and the Lee Priory circle.

101. W. W. to JOHN KENYON

Address: John Kenyon Esqre 59 Pulteney Street, Bath.
Postmark: 17 May 1823.
MS. untraced.
Transactions of the Wordsworth Society, no. 6, p. 91. K (—). *LT* i. 108.

[*In M. W.'s hand*]

Lee Priory, May 16th [1823]

My dear Friend,

Your very welcome letter followed me to this place; the account it gave of your happiness and comfort was such as we wished to hear—may the like blessings be long, very long, continued to you —changing their character only according to the mildest influences of time! You gave me liberty to reply to your letter as might suit what you knew of my procrastinating disposition—I caught at this, but be assured you would have heard from me immediately if I could have held out any hopes, either to myself or you, that we should be able to accept of your kind invitation to visit you and Mrs K. (with whom we should be most happy to become acquainted) at Bath. We came hither 5 weeks ago, meaning after a fortnight's stay to cross the Channel for a little Tour in Flanders and Holland —but we had calculated, as the saying is, without our Host—the Spring was tardy and froward—when a day or two of fine weather came, they were followed by blustering, and even tempestuous, winds—these abated, and out came my own vernal enemy, the Inflammation in my eyes, which dashed our resolutions, and here I am, still obliged to employ Mrs W. as my amanuensis.

This day however being considerably better we shall go to Dover with a view to embark for Ostend to-morrow; unless detained by similar obstacles. From Ostend we mean to go to Ghent, to Antwerp, Breda, Utrecht, Amsterdam—to Rotterdam by Harlem, the Hague and Leyden—thence to Antwerp by another route, and perhaps shall return by Mechlin, Brussels, Lille and Ypres to Calais—or direct to Ostend as we came. We hope to be landed in England within a month.[1] We shall hurry thro' London homewards, where we are naturally anxious already to be, having left Rydal Mount so far back as February.

---

[1] The tour in Belgium and Holland, which followed the route outlined here by W. W., began on 16 May and ended on 11 June. M. W.'s unpublished MS. Journal (among the *WL MSS.*) concludes, 'Adventures we have had few— William's eyes being so much disordered and so easily aggravated made him shun society and crippled us in many respects, but I trust we have stored up thoughts and Images that will not die.' See also *Mem.* ii. 116–20.

Now for a word about yourself, my d^r Friend. You had long been followed, somewhat blindly, by our good wishes; we had heard nothing of you, except thro' Mr Quillinan and from Mr Monkhouse. If there was any fault in your not writing sooner, you made amends by entering so kindly into the particulars of what you had done and proposed to do; where you are living, and how you were as to estate, body and mind. It is among my hopes that, either in Westmoreland or West of England, I may at no very distant time be a witness of your happiness; and notwithstanding all my faults and waywardnesses, have an opportunity of recommending myself to the good graces of your Help-mate.

I have time for little more; as, in an hour and a half, we must leave our good friends here—this elegant Conventual Mansion,[1] with its pictures and its books, and bid a farewell to its groves and nightingales, which this morning have been singing divinely—by the bye it has been so cold that they are silent during the season of darkness. These delights we must surrender and take our way on foot three miles along the pleasant banks of Stour to fall in with the Dover coach. At this moment the S.W. wind is blustering abominably, and whirling the leaves and blossoms about in a way that reminds me of the tricks it is playing with the surf on the naked coast of Ostend—but courage! we depart with many good wishes, to which yours shall be added as no act of presumption on our part. God bless you and yours! and grant us a happy meeting if not in this world, in a better! to which my wife says Amen.

Ever aff^ly yours,

[*signed*] Wm Wordsworth

If you should be in London about a month hence let us know by a letter to the Post Off. Dover, as we should be sorry to pass thro' without a glimpse of you.

John is at New Coll. Oxford. Should you pass enquire after him —he would be overjoyed to see you.

---

[1] W. W. is speaking in fun of James Wyatt's Gothic mansion built for Thomas Barrett in 1783 (and now demolished): acknowledged by Horace Walpole as 'a child of Strawberry, prettier than the parent'. It was here in 1813 that Sir Egerton Brydges set up the private printing press famed for its reprints of earlier English literature.

102. D. W. to EDWARD QUILLINAN

Address: Edward Quillinan Esqre, Lee Priory, near Wingham, Kent. [*Re-addressed to*] To the care of Messrs Cane and Co, Army Agents, Dublin, to be left till his arrival.
Postmark: 20 June 1823. *Endorsed*: Rydal Mount. June 19 1823, Miss Words-worth.
MS. WL.
LY i. 110 (—).

June 17th [1823]

My dear Friend,

John has brought his letter[1] for me to fill up—and I have but three minutes. The Maid of Paraguay[2] and her Mother wait for me to go out. They arrived on Saturday morning and are to leave us to-morrow. The young creature has returned to her native mountains unspoiled by the admiration that has been showered upon her[3]—indeed I think her much improved. She is a sweet Girl to look upon and is truly amiable. Doro is to stay another fortnight at Harrowgate, that is she will set off homewards on Tuesday (I believe it is the first day of July). Mr Barber is to meet her if he is well enough but he is beginning a course of the Blue Pill—and is therefore, he says, doubtful. For my part, I think he ails little more than usual, only the old Bachelor is unhinged by the late addition to his family and his housekeeper's consequent disability to wait upon him. I am not without hopes that her Father and Mother may, after all, meet Doro at H.[4] I forwarded yesterday a letter to them through Mr Johnson hoping it might catch them in London, or be forwarded to them at Cambridge, which letter was from her pro-tectress Mrs Hutchinson,[5] and decided me to let her stay the full six weeks prescribed by the Doctor. We have now delightful

---

[1] This note follows a letter from John W. about some translations from Greek which he had done for E. Q.

[2] i.e. Sara Coleridge, who had translated Dobrizhoffer's *History of the Abipones* to help defray her brother Derwent's college expenses. (See L. 46 above.) This work was the source on which Southey drew for his poem *A Tale of Paraguay* (published 1825).

[3] Sara Coleridge had spent the early part of this year in London, on a visit to her father at the Gillmans'; and in Devon where she stayed with other members of her family. In May she visited Thomas Poole at Nether Stowey with her mother.

[4] Harrogate. According to H. C. R., W. W. and M. W. returned to London on 17 June, stayed a night with Talfourd, and on the 19th saw Macready, the actor, who visited Rydal Mount later in the summer (*Reminiscences*, ed. Sir Frederick Pollock, 2 vols., 1875, i. 284–5). Thereafter they moved on to Cambridge (*HCR* i. 296), and then joined Dora W. for some three weeks at Harrogate, finally returning home to Rydal Mount on Tuesday 15 July.

[5] Mr. and Mrs. Hutchinson of Harrogate were M. W.'s cousins.

weather—to me *most* delightful, for the sun shines the day through, and the air is clear and bracing. I am now quite well in all respects —that is I seem to have regained my strength, which fell away sadly under the Influenza. I was at Kendal on Sunday and spent 3 hours with the Cooksons. Poor Elizabeth grows weaker—her breathing worse and the pain in the side more fixed. She wastes very slowly, but even her Mother has now no hope. Her countenance is angelic and she looks affectingly beautiful. Her good Mother bears up wonderfully, I thought her as well as I have seen her for years: but Mr Cookson is sadly changed. He feels deeply—so does she, but she has so many duties to keep her up—and above all the necessity of chearfulness in the Daughter's presence, who poor thing, is very patient, and I believe prepared for the worst, though she talks of recovery now that the weather favours her, and of coming to Rydal Mount. I am very glad you have written to Doro. Some trifles in the accounts are not yet settled. Ever your affectionate Friend

Dorothy Wordsworth.

—Delighted with all I hear of your Darlings. God bless you and them. Remember [me] most kindly to Egerton Brydges as well as Captain Barrett, whom I seem to know, from all I have heard of him, as well as if I too had been at Lee Priory: I hope tomorrow will bring us a letter from my sister.

103. D. W. to EDWARD QUILLINAN

Address: Edward Quillinan Esqre, Post Office, Limerick, Ireland. [*Readdressed to*] care of Major Birch, Royal Artillery, Ballincolly.[1]
Postmark: (1) 8 July 1823. (2) 9 July 1823. *Stamp*: (1) Kendal Penny Post. (2) Cork. *Endorsed*: Miss Wordsworth, Rydal Mount, July 4. 1823.
MS. WL.
LY i. 111.

Friday 4th July 1823

My dear Friend,

On Wednesday I forwarded a letter to you from Captn Barret into which I contrived to insert a few words telling you that I would *not* write in case our Travellers returned not as was expected, on Thursday, but thinking you will hardly grudge the cost if this letter should reach you, and that if it be too late the loss will be

---

[1] E. Q. had now embarked on a tour to SW. Ireland and Killarney. Major and Mrs. R. H. Birch, whose names crop up from time to time in E. Q.'s MS. Diaries, were close friends with whom he later stayed in London.

4 July 1823

nothing. I take the pen just to tell you that they are at Harrowgate, and will remain there 'at least a fortnight'—that was my Brother's expression, but Mary says she thinks nothing will tempt him to stay longer, and that if he receives benefit it will be an encouragement to him to go again at a cheaper season. I, however, think it will be much cheaper to get cured at once, and have urged them to stay longer if good comes of the fortnight's trial. On Thursday morning I went down to the Coach, and in spite of my heroical wishes for their stay at Harrowgate I was disappointed at not seeing Father, Mother, and Daughter on the top of it—at first grievously disappointed; but I soon got the better of that: and an hour after had the pleasure of receiving a joint letter from Wm and M.[1] with a delightful account of Doro's good looks, her strength and spirits—of every thing but the pimples on her face which still keep their station. The doctor advised a fortnight's longer stay at H. for her, and this no doubt had much influence on their decision. Immediately they sought out lodgings and were comfortably settled on Monday morning at 2£– 16s– per week (fire and attendance included) next door to the Robinsons and little Julia,[2] who were to remain at H. till to-day, and who I hope will persuade my Brother to take Doro and her Mother to see York when the business at the Spa is over. My Sister was in a great puzzle about you, having heard that the Holmes's[3] had not yet arrived at York, and she thought, as you would be obliged to go to Newcastle, you would hardly come back again to see us at Rydal. It was indeed very kind in you so to do—but Oh! that I could have kept you longer! I was very sad and melancholy all the morning after you left me, wandering about the garden while the young ones were at Church. Poor Mr Barber! I have seen him twice at his own house, but he comes not near us, nursing his ailments, and being one ferment of suspicion and rage after another. I went on Monday evening with Mr Todd[4] —we drank tea with him; and Todd was quite astonished with the feverish violence of his language. He seemed positively to *hate* our meek neighbour at the foot of the hill, because he had talked with you a quarter of an hour—he! who knew nothing of you! he who had

[1] This letter is untraced.
[2] Julia Myers, who was staying with her aunt Mrs. Robinson, the admiral's widow, and her family.   [3] E. Q.'s sister-in-law and her husband.
[4] Perhaps Capt. George Todd, a Dragoons officer, of Hampstead, who in 1827 married Mary Jane, daughter of Sir Egerton Brydges by his second marriage. The reference appears to be to a temporary visitor to Rydal, rather than a resident. The nature of the disagreement which D. W. goes on to unfold (and in which Elizabeth Crump and Hartley Coleridge seem to have been involved as well) is only partially explained in the next letter.

no claims on you! I delivered your message before a word of this broke out: and told him that you not only had expected to see him on Sunday, but that we had been on the look-out for him at Rydal on Saturday afternoon. The next day I went again with Mr and Mrs Dowling,[1] who were so charmed with the place that he was happy and pleasant in spite of himself. In neither of these interviews having an opportunity of speaking to him alone, I left a note, very kindly expressed, explaining how I had been the innocent cause of his suspicions against myself after the mysterious words—old Wife—overheard by him in the passage. He has made no reply to the note, and I have heard nothing of him since. But more than enough of such nonsense! When I see him again, if he renews the subject, I shall make no reply, still less shall I be inclined to shew resentment—indeed how could I? for I do not feel it, and am only sorry for his unhappy lot.

We have had delightful weather since you left us, and I hope you have been as much favoured on your solitary journey. It would be a great kindness if you would write to me before you leave Ireland. Remember that your letter would be a double treat to me, as it would arrive before our Friends return.

Do not, I pray you, wait for a frank. Miss E. Crump will leave us on Monday morning—she begs to be most kindly remembered to you. So does Hartley Coleridge. He has been writing a pretty sonnet: and many a Run has he had up and down the Terrace while he was composing it—a Run such as he used to take at 'six years old'.

Well! if you do not settle at the Ivy Cottage, I hope sometime to see you and your dear little Ones at Lee Priory. God bless you all and grant you a happy meeting! Yours ever affectionately

D. Wordsworth.

My kind regards to Capt[n] Barrett and Egerton Brydges. John and William are out on their ponies with the three young Hardens—Miss H. and her Brothers[2]—a gallant cavalcade.

[1] Vincent George and Elizabeth Dowling of Kentish Town, parents of the Misses Dowling. Dowling had been one of the principal managers of *The Observer*, a Tory paper founded in 1791, and in 1816 was employed as a Home Office agent to report the speeches of the Radical orators at the famous Spa Fields meeting (see A. Aspinall, *Politics and the Press, c. 1780–1850*, 1949, pp. 83–5, 406–7). He achieved local notoriety later this year when he was charged at Carlisle on 13 Oct. with stealing a report of the proceedings at a dinner given for Brougham at Glasgow intended for the editor of *The Times*. Dowling brought a countercharge of conspiracy and malicious prosecution, but both cases were dismissed.

[2] i.e. Jane Harden (see L. 50 above), Allan (1803–75), later of Edinburgh, and Joseph (1805–72), later curate of Hawkshead and incumbent of Coniston.

104. D. W. to ELIZABETH CRUMP

Address: Miss E. Crump, St Anne's Street, Liverpool.
Stamp: Kendal Penny Post. *Endorsed*: July 1823.
MS. WL.
LY i. 113 (—).

Thursday afternoon [17 July 1823]

My dear Elizabeth,

I doubt not you have thought me slow in writing, as you left us in so much anxiety respecting Hartley, but as there was nothing in the termination of that affair but just what you might fancy, I waited to tell you either that our Friends meant to prolong their stay at Harrowgate or were actually come home, and now I have the Happiness of seeing them all gathered together again at Rydal Mount and have only to lament that you were not here to receive them. They arrived at $\frac{1}{4}$ before two o'clock on Tuesday morning, I had sate up till 12 and was just dropping asleep when I was rouzed by a pattering of gravel against the window and starting out of bed saw two female figures and a postchaise on the Front. You may be sure we were presently all in a bustle, but this did not last long, for the Travellers were in their beds before an hour was over. I could not at first judge of their looks for all were heated with their journey from H. (since 6 o'clock in the morning) but had the pleasure of seeing D. lively-looking and much improved when she had been refreshed with sleep. She is active and strong, her pimples however are as fresh as ever. My Brother having been overtired was very poorly all day, heated in the eyes with a dreadful headache, but yesterday he was quite well, and *looked* well also. He set off to Ulverston directly after dinner and is not yet returned. My Sister I am sorry to say is thinner than when she left home, and I do not think her looking quite so well, but thank God! she *is* well and I hope that D.[1] will help her to lay a little flesh upon her slender body.

Hartley and John arrived 5 minutes too late, they followed me up the hill after I had parted from you and after a moment's deliberation turned their steeds towards Ambleside in hopes of overtaking you. The coach had just driven away. H. seemed much hurt when I said how you lamented his going at that time, therefore I did not give him your letter the same evening, and all I said further on the subject was simply this—the first moment we were alone together —that I had one thing to require of him, that he would never again

---

[1] Mary Dawson, the cook.

leave home while he remained here without informing us. Poor fellow, he looked down ashamed, and made his ready promise like any repentant little Boy. Mr Barber was in the garden with his two friends. I received him much more coldly than even I wished to do, and he was evidently confounded. The next evening I received a long letter from him. He had not discovered mine till five minutes before he wrote (mine was left when I was there with the Dowlings): next morning I began to answer his, but finding it would never be done if I were to go on writing I resolved to walk over with my unfinished letter in my pocket. I told him I was come to end this foolish affair and said as to myself and Dora I thought no more of it, but you and Hartley were not to be given up by me. He disbelieved your word and then by implication charged you with the crime of lying. He was warm at first, but with firmness and a full comment and explanation on my part he was softened even to tears, and sent an apology by me to Hartley and requested me to say to you that he was very sorry for his misconception of what was said and done, and hoped the next time he should meet you you would give him your hand on his offering his. Having fought your Battles so well I must now on my part exact from you perfect forgiveness of our old Bachelor friend and full indulgence to his humours, besides oblivion of the whole affair. This I *will* say, that no other of Mr Barber's female friends except Mrs W. (and perhaps Miss Hutchinson) would ever have been on speaking terms with him again. This being the case you see how much it behoves *you* to send your free pardon. I mean on my account. He called yesterday and was delighted to see Mrs W. and he and I were as friendly as usual. Miss Laing[1] did not arrive till Thursday evening and left us on Monday morning. She is truly a delightful creature and I was very sorry you were not here to enjoy her company. On Friday she rode round Coniston water with John, Saturday morning was very wet and we went no further than the garden. On Sunday too late for church I walked to Mr Barber's—did not see him, and on Monday having packed a few necessaries for John and Hartley in the carpet bag, slung it on the side saddle and we (all on foot but Miss L.) set forward to Ambleside, John and Hartley intending to go with her to Edinburgh. Hartley was delighted with the scheme—so was John, but a letter telling us that his Father and Mother would be at home the same night checked their progress. John could not bear the idea of absenting himself on the very day, nor indeed could I have consented, therefore Hartley

[1] Mary Laing, of Edinburgh.

with a dolorous heart parted from Miss L. and John at Miss Dowling's door, they proceeding over Kirkstone, he with me back to Rydal. John intended walking by Miss L.'s side to Penrith: but half way down Ulswater she would not consent that he should go a step further, leapt from her pony and hurried forward on foot by the side of the man who carried her luggage. She parted from us in no bad spirits, for we had given her hopes that J. and H. might follow her in a few days: but I am now going to write and tell her that the Father cannot part with John at present, and they must look to some future opportunity. Hartley only stayed to get a luncheon after we had parted from Miss L. and proceeded to Keswick, thinking to finish his visit there before John would be ready to start for Edinburgh. I am quite sorry for his disappointment, he behaved so well and gave up the journey with so good a grace when the letter arrived, though it was plain he would have gone on without John, had I encouraged him. My Brother and Sister are delighted at finding themselves at home and seem to have nothing to complain of but the wet weather of our North of England. They declare that during their whole absence of 21 weeks, they have not seen so much rain as has already fallen since their return. Poor Mrs J. Harden has been very ill in the Erisypelas. I have not seen her, having never felt myself strong enough to undertake such a walk. She is now downstairs and happy, as Mrs Elliott tells me, in being surrounded with a host of her Friends. God bless you dear Elizabeth. Give my kind love to Father, Mother, Sisters and Brothers and to Mr Jackson. We must see him on his return and pray tell him so. I leave the little scrap below for Dora.[1] Yours ever affectionately

D. Wordsworth.

I had a sad missing of you after you were gone.

[1] The rest of the sheet was in fact taken up by Hartley Coleridge: '. . . Just this moment come from Keswick—can't let the letter go off without shewing that the dear *little scissors* have not quite cut off all remembrance of you . . . John and I gallop'd a felon's race to catch you—but all in vain. Mind, I don't mean to make this do instead of a letter, which I mean to plague you with soon, with a leaden weight of stanzas appended thereto. Sara is very well . . . she plays over the 'infinity of Waltzes' you copied out for her, and hopes you won't forget to write to her. Edith is much better, but still weak and pale. And now, dear little Bessy, don't think worse of me for my naughtiness than you can help, and all shall be made whole in good time. Expect Prometheus [his tragedy] in a month or so. I hope you'll admire it, for I don't believe many people will. . . .'

105. D. W. to MARY LAING

Address: To David Laing Esqre, South Bridge Street, Edinburgh. *For Miss Laing*.
Postmark: 19 July 1823. *Stamp*: Kendal Penny Post.
MS. Edinburgh University Library.
The Wordsworth–Laing Letters (—).

Thursday, July 17th—[1823]

My dear Miss Laing,

I so little expected John's return on Monday that when I heard his foot along the passage I could not guess *who* was coming; and hardly recognised the *voice* when he called 'Aunt!' You ought not to have parted from him so soon; I assure you he would much more gladly have gone with you on to Penrith; and I was very sorry to see him with half his errand unperformed. I was not, however, uneasy concerning you: as you are so good a Traveller; but after having taken so much pains to come and see us I should have wished your journey to have been made as pleasant as possible under the circumstances; and to have known that you were safely mounted on the Coach and on your way to Edinburgh. You did me another wrong. You paid the Man who carried your luggage over Kirkstone, who, you know, was to have been paid by me with the 2/- which I owed you and a trifle added to it. Well! I must remember my debt when we next meet; and shall know better how to deal with you in future.

My Brother and Sister would have been greatly disappointed had they not found their Son John at home, therefore you may be sure I was glad that he had not set forward before the arrival of the letter, and had at first some hope that the Father would have consented to John's going at the end of this week; but hints and petitions were alike vain: he cannot consent to part with him now; for various reasons, which I need not detail; but John (and I hope Hartley Coleridge) will certainly take the first opportunity of accepting your proffered hospitality, for which they are very grateful—and my Brother says, 'Next summer it will be all very well—but now, after so long an absence, I wish to have John a little settled with me at home'. As to Doro, whenever she can be indulged with such a journey—(and that will probably be the first time that either her Brother or I have the power to take a journey merely for pleasure)—she will be indeed delighted to see *you* and Edinburgh. She regrets very much that she did not see you here. So do her Father and Mother; and I blame myself for not having pressed you more to stay a few days longer; which I certainly

207

should have done, had you not been so eager to be at home, and had I not hoped that John and Mr H. Coleridge would speedily follow you. On Monday night I sate up till 12 o'clock; and was just dropping asleep at ¼ before two, when I was rouzed by a pattering of gravel against the window, and starting up from my bed I saw two female figures on the Front, and a post chaise. Instantly the whole house was rouzed; and before an hour was over, the three Travellers were quietly laid down in their Beds.

You will be glad to hear that all are well and in good spirits; Doro, however, has not parted with the crop of pimples on her face; nor are my Brother's eyes wholly free from inflammation. He and Mrs Wordsworth have been much pleased with their Tour; and are now delighted to find themselves at home again. They seem to have nothing to complain of but our moist climate. Tuesday was a day of streaming rain, which I am encouraged to hope was confined to our Mountains and did not touch you on your way to Edinburgh—encouraged because my Brother and Sister declare that during the whole of their 21 weeks' absence they had never seen so much rain as in the *two* days after their return to Westmorland. This is a beautiful morning; and I am again, like you, full of hope that in spite of the prophecy of the followers of St Swythin we shall have some settled weather; for the Barometer rises. My Brother left us again yesterday; but to return today. He is gone to Ulverston by Hawkshead, and will come home up Coniston Water, as John and you did. You may be sure that it was business;[1] and of an urgent nature [that] carried him away so soon.

M^rs W[ordswor]th[2] and I have done little more than talk and [sau]nter in the garden; and poor Doro seems hardly to know what to do with herself she is so glad to find herself on her own ground once again, and with limbs that do not ache—and no uneasiness in head or stomach. William talks much of you—and in the same language which when you were present we called flattery. His spirits are never-failing. I wish they would be quieter; for he has certainly the look of a person whose strength is not equal to the demands upon it; and since the return of his Parents I think he looks worse. They were disappointed in his appearance, having, during their absence, received such encouraging accounts of the state of his health. John was exceedingly shocked when in talking with me he discovered that he had been at home when your Brother was here;[3] he thought you would consider him so very neglectful

---

[1] Connected with the extension of W. W.'s Distributorship.
[2] *MS. torn.*   [3] i.e. the previous summer.

in having apparently forgotten him. The fact was, that he being in the habit of so frequently seeing strangers at Rydal Mount, did not recall your Brother to mind when you were here; but when I mentioned the Poet Dunbar[1] to him, every circumstance connected with that day when Mr David Laing dined with us flashed upon his mind; and he remembered him perfectly; and now begs to be kindly remembered to him. My Brother begs me to say that it is so long since he read Dunbar's Works that it is impossible for him to give any critical opinion of them at present; and he has no opportunity here of referring to the works themselves; but this he affirms, that Dunbar was a man of very powerful genius; and his poetry left a strong impression upon his mind. He regrets very much that the works of that Writer are not now within his reach, as it would have given him great pleasure to be in any degree useful to your Brother. Pray remember me most kindly to your good Mother—and to both your Brothers.[2] I heartily wish your Father a prosperous journey and safe return. I am anxious to hear how you found all Friends; and how you feel yourself on being settled again at home. Pray take the earliest leisure you have for writing, and let me have a letter full of all particulars concerning yourself and family. Believe me

Yours affectionately
D Wordsworth

Mr H. Coleridge went to Keswick, as you advised, and is this moment returned.

106. M. W. and D. W. to THOMAS MONKHOUSE

Address: To Thomas Monkhouse Esqre.
MS. WL.
LY i. 116 (—).

Wed Aug 20th [1823]

My dear Cousin,

Immediately upon the rec^t of your letter Dorothy and I walked over to make the enquiries you desire of Robin Clark the farmer at

---

[1] William Dunbar (*c.* 1460–*c.* 1530), whose poems David Laing later edited.

[2] Mary Laing in fact had four brothers: David, William and Gilbert who were both ministers, and James who became a public official and journalist in Ceylon.

Fox Ghyll[1]—as being the only means of coming accurately at the information required—and the following is the result.

The whole property including Coppice and Intack comprises 38 Acres. Intack 8 Acres worth 5/- per A. p^r Ann: wood 7 acres value £10 per acre every 15 years—now ready. These 7 A. together with the Standard trees scattered over the Land, he values at this time at £150. Reduced Rent £30 per Ann.

The House Stable etc Garden Orchard and Shrubbery ¾ of an A. this he values £400 (too low I think). A comfortable farm House and Barn. The house, Garden etc stands on freehold ground and there are 9 acres besides, free—the rest is under the Rydal property paying 2 years value on the death of Ld and Tenant etc etc (Mrs B[2] compromised for £20 upon the death of Mr B.—£30 was first demanded). Land tax 2/11 per year—Tithe a trifle, 2^d for every 20 Stooks. There are annuities that reduces the value of the Property as Mr White told D[3] (Mrs B Executing) about £200.

This coming from an interested person may be reckoned a low estimate. Upon my putting the question to him of what *he* thought it might be sold for he said—'if it was his concern he would be loth to refuse £12,00—but it might fetch 1300'—Mr de Q. pays about £50 for House and furniture. The furniture is not to be sold till May when the purchaser may have it at a valuation, or be sold by auction—the wood of course sold with the land.—As to what the House might be let for unfurnished, or indeed furnished, it is impossible to say—these things here depend so much on the need of the tenant as you may guess. *Unfurnished* I should say it was worth from 20 to 25 pound a year—the tenant says from £15 to 28.—From the above you may form your own opinion—when we read your letter we all said 'then he won't get it at that rate'—nor do I think it desirable that you should be purchaser unless you furnish with a view to your being *occasionally* your own Tenant and letting your pleasure make up to you for the loss of interest. In turning it to account by any other way, the possession I think will be a plague to you. This I hope you will consider to do. Till:[4] talks of being his own tenant after Mr Q's lease is expired.

We are expecting Strickland Cookson here every hour to stay a few days, his mother having spoken of his being or going to, set out upon a 'tour to the lakes'—if he has had any commission from

[1] After the death of Robert Blakeney, his widow wished to dispose of the Fox Ghyll property. Robin Clark was tenant of the farm land, and De Quincey of the house. Thomas Monkhouse was interested, but did not in the end buy it.
[2] Mrs. Blakeney.   [3] i.e. D. W.
[4] Tillbrooke, owner of Ivy Cottage, at present leased to Edward Quillinan.

you (as I suppose he must have had from your having mentioned him in your last, in connection with this business), perhaps he will contrive to be here upon the day of Sale. At any rate I am sure he would with pleasure attend at your request. Just before your letter arrived W^m had said to me that *he* should attend.—I must not omit to tell you that the wood immediately *behind* the House (not that which clothes the Ghyll and belongs to the Estate) belonging to T. Fleming[1] is felled, and at present, except under the evening light, the beauty of the place is sadly injured by the loss—this will soon be restored again, and if it becomes yours you will have the pleasure of seeing it improve for the next 15 years.

We are very glad of the improving account of the Invalids, and of the gaieties expected at Lee. Why does not Sarah write herself to us—Tell her that John hopes she may be detained so long as not to pass thro' Oxford before the 12th of October, when with God's blessing he hopes to be there—he is better but still unable to read as long at a time as his inclination and his duties require. Much against his own will he began last night with a course of the blue pill etc.—(I did not mean to make a rhyme)—this I trust will set him to right again, which I believe he never has been since his Christmas cold. I am sorry that Sarah should have found us so inattentive to her commissions or requests as that she should have recommended it to you, as the only way to be answered, to write *an especial* letter. I had always fancied that, some of us at least, were unusually ready to serve our friends, but she must have found it otherwise!—I hold in my hand 9 pounds for your three shares of the Langdale farm[2]—supposing Mr Gee to have rec^d his share from the tenant of the small house, but of this I am not quite sure. Therefore as we hope to see you so soon I will not remit your's.

Dear John's[3] is an affecting letter—heaven grant that his hopes may be realized—well does he deserve the blessing of eyesight who so patiently bears his sufferings. My Aunt's[4] complaint I do not understand, for Joanna speaks of her appetite being good, and at the same time says her complaint is in the throat which I should suppose a good appetite would ill agree with, but this she does not allude to. I had no idea from the former accounts that she was able to go out. I am very glad that her spirits do not sink.—The improvement in the times will cheer them all—flour with us has risen above 3/- a Stone

---

[1] Thomas Fleming (1763–1840), owner of Spring Cottage.
[2] Ivy How. See *MY* ii. 509–10, 583.
[3] John Monkhouse (see *MY* i. 39, 390) had an affection of the eyesight which led a few years later to total blindness.
[4] For Miss Elizabeth Monkhouse, see L. 74 above.

14 lb.—this I suppose is nearly the highest it ought to be, before the ports are opened—the average must be kept under if possible.

Kind love to all, not forgetting our good friends at Lee. Miss W. has something to add. Dora still in her *situation*.

ever yours
M Wordsworth

[*D. W. writes*]

My dear Friend,

I am sure I had no wish to humble you when I gave you my feelings and opinion of the passage in Mr Irving's 'Oration'.[1] Still less, I am sure, did I feel myself superior to you in entertaining a different opinion of the Composition. As to the propriety or impropriety of bringing living Characters (as Authors especially) into notice in a place of public worship I think there is not probably much difference between your opinion and mine. Since I wrote to you I have seen passages from Irving which give me a much higher idea of his powers than the little I had seen before. I allude chiefly to what he says of the withdrawing of the visible interposition of the Divinity, and the calling upon us to seek for it within;—in our own minds and hearts. But his description of the joys of Heaven (which appeared in the same newspaper) is to me *worse* than a Methodist Rant—as Mary called the other. However in reading a favourable character of one poet we were perhaps as you say prejudiced by our disgust by having seen Southey so abused and coupled with the Blasphemer Lord Byron. *Yours* was the amiable feeling I will allow; and I heartily hope with you that my Brother's writings may be served by the Orator, who undoubtedly must be a man of no common talents.

Your most affect^e D Wordsworth

Your dear Brother John's letter affected me very much. We had heard from Joanna the opinion of the surgeons in Wales, and were

[1] Edward Irving (1792–1834), the famous preacher, was at first a school-master at Haddington and Kirkcaldy (where he got to know Carlyle), until in 1819 he went to Glasgow as assistant to Thomas Chalmers. In 1822 he was invited to the Hatton Garden Chapel, London, where his magnetic personality and eloquence commanded an instant following, and he soon numbered Canning, Hazlitt, and Coleridge among his many admirers. In Oct. 1823 he published his *Orations*, which included 'An Argument for Judgment to Come', a protest against the *Vision of Judgment* of both Southey and Byron, whom he thought equally profane. On the other hand, he praised W. W. from the pulpit. (For their meeting in Apr. 1824, see L. 133 below.) Later Irving moved to a new church in Regent Square, but with the appearance of the 'Tongues' among his followers, he was deposed for unorthodoxy (1832), and founded the 'Catholic Apostolic Church'. A year later he was deprived of his ministry in the Church of Scotland for heresy.

much distressed; but comfort comes from the sufferer himself, who shows an example of Christian resignation and true philosophy which we may all wish to imitate. May God grant him a perfect recovery, but it cannot be a speedy one.

[*M. W. adds*]

Mr Jackson says that the price demanded from Mr Blakeney for enfranchisement of the estate was about £40, but it is not certain that Lady F.[1] would now enfranchise.

107. D. W. to MARY LAING

Address: To David Laing Esqre, South Bridge Street, Edinburgh. *For Miss Laing*.
Postmark: 29 Aug. 1823. *Stamp*: Kendal Penny Post.
MS. Edinburgh University Library.
The Wordsworth–Laing Letters (—).

Rydal Mount, August 26th [1823]

My dear Miss Laing,

I had long and impatiently expected your letter, yet so confidently had I trusted to your good fortune that I never once suspected the true and distressing cause of your silence. Tuesday was indeed with us a day of downright rain; but as it did not begin early in the morning I flattered myself that you would have the start of it, which probably would have been the case had you travelled in the same coach that we did last year. It left Penrith at 5 o'clock in the morning, reached Carlisle at seven, and immediately after breakfast, we departed on the 'Sir Walter Scott'—the Mail no doubt gaining upon us all the way; but we preceded it in our arrival at Edinburgh. *That* coach would have set you down in South Street; for I well remember that a number of passengers left us opposite the College and crowds of porters came round. But it is all over now; and except for the future there is no use now in turning to past mischances. I cannot express how much I and all the Family, whether personally known to you or not, have been concerned at your illness. As it happened so unfortunately it is well that John and Mr C.[2] did not accompany you, for without your society they would have missed one half of the pleasure of being at Edinburgh; and they look forward to the excursion at some future time when the thought that prudence ought to have detained them elsewhere will not intrude,

---

[1] Lady le Fleming.   [2] i.e. Hartley Coleridge.

to interrupt their enjoyments. The bad weather, too, was another consolation—and to this I may add yet another reason for being reconciled to the disappointment, but perhaps had not the rainy season come on, change of air might have prevented the existence of *that*. Very soon after our Friends' return, poor John became subject to headaches, could not read above an hour at a time, and was altogether uncomfortable. A very bad cold then came on attended with fever and slight delirium. It was thought there was a determination of blood to the head; but the internal bursting of an abscess, above the nose, proved that we were in some degree mistaken. He now rides, and walks about as usual; but is yet far from well; and unless he casts off the disorder still hanging upon him, I fear he will be very unfit for his studies at Oxford. He has a great aversion to medicine; but is undergoing (under our Apothecary) a course of the blue Pill, which at present encreases his uncomfortable feelings; we hope however for final good effects. Willy is as lively as ever—has been successful in fishing of late, and when the weather is fine, rows himself about (or takes the Ladies along with him) in the Boat upon Rydal Water, which Lady Fleming has kindly permitted him to do. Doro is quite well— no traces left of the eruption on her face except the old marks. Your advice respecting her is very good; indeed it corresponds in many points with her physician's prescriptions and general advice. She is grateful to you for thinking so much about her, and wishes exceedingly for the pleasure of knowing you. She and her Father and Mother regretted much that you were gone when they arrived. You will be surprized to hear of Doro's present engagement. She has actually, for a whole month, been sole Teacher in Miss Dowling's School, under Miss D., whose two Sisters, having gone to Paris in the holidays for pleasure and improvement, are not yet returned, nor expected till next week. No doubt Doro will then be very glad to resign her office, though she never utters a wish to that effect, and suffers neither in health nor spirits; and she performs her many duties surprizingly for so young a person, wholly un-practised in that way. The Children are all very fond of her; and Miss Dowling says that she should be quite 'set up' if she could procure such a Teacher, one with so much zeal and activity. I should have written to you some days ago; but Mrs Coleridge's answer respecting the veil did not arrive till the day before yester-day; and now I seize the first hour of leisure. She and all the Family at Keswick were much concerned to hear of your illness, and Mrs C. returns you her best thanks for your kindness in remembering her commission at a time when you were so little able to execute it. She desires me to say that as the summer is now nearly over she thinks her Daughter may get through with her old veil therefore she will not now trouble you.

My dear Miss Laing I pray you not to *fash* yourself about my caps. If you can make the muslin one and purchase the new one, as we settled it—without fatigue to yourself or much trouble, I shall be very glad, and shall value them the more for your sake; but as I can do very well without them take no thought about the matter, unless leisure and opportunity throw themselves in your way. Should you have the parcel to send, (and it is not worth while except you hear of somebody coming this way) it might be directed to be left with Mʳ Garnet, Stamp Office, Penrith, for Miss Wordsworth of Rydal Mount—or, at Kendal to the care of Mʳˢ Cookson. By the Bye I must not forget to tell you that the Cap which you manufactured for me at Rydal has been much admired. I reckon it the choicest cap I have.

How is the weather with you? We had some very fine days last week; and much *spoiled*, and some *un*spoiled hay was got in; but on Sunday we had a fresh fall of rain. Yesterday was very fine; and today again the mountain, misty, almost invisible, rain puts a stop to all the business of the Hay-field. Unless the Sun will favour us more steadily there will hardly be time to get in the crops. The corn is turning yellowish in some places. We heard from Miss Joanna Hutchinson lately, who is pretty well. She desires kind regards to you, your good Mother and all the family. I was glad to hear of your Father's safe return. I cannot but be sorry you did not go with him. You need not have been prevented from visiting us by the way (provided he came from London by land) and perhaps you might have been spared your illness; but you are young, and may look for another opportunity of going abroad with your Father or one of your Brothers. How I should enjoy a trip to Paris with you, who are so alive and watchful, and so little annoyed by trifling inconveniences! I have never seen Willy destroy many flies since you were here; and doubt not that the remembrance of you will check him in future when so disposed. We have seen fewer friends from a distance this summer than I ever remember; and there has been very little company at the Lakes. The bad weather, no doubt, has kept some at home and perhaps others have sought a dryer climate. The elder Miss Hutchinson[1] writes from Ramsgate and Boulogne, that they have seen nothing like *rainy weather*. Now

[1] i.e. S. H.

and then a shower to refresh the earth; but mostly unclouded sunshine (which truly I envy her) though accompanied with sharp winds, and often a nipping air. I hope you will write again very soon, as I am anxious to hear of your perfect recovery. Make my best regards to all your Family and believe me, my dear Miss Laing

Yours affectionately

D Wordsworth

My Brother has been a good deal interested with the specimens of ancient poetry,[1] sent to eke out your parcel. He preserves them carefully. We have not seen the Professor Wilson.—Do excuse this scrawl of a letter

108. D. W. to ELIZABETH CRUMP

Address: Miss Eliz[th] Crumpe, Queen Anne Street Liverpool.
Stamp: Kendal Penny Post. *Endorsed*: August 31st 1823.
MS. WL.
LY i. 117 (—).

Sunday afternoon, August 31st [1823]

My dear Elizabeth,

I have no fears that you may have thought me either forgetful or ungrateful in being so long silent: but am sure you have been sorry for it, and have often wished for news from Rydal. The truth is that I have been loth to put you to the expense of postage, so many opportunities occurring of sending letters to Liverpool, but when such have occurred (which has really been not seldom) I have not had leisure to write: and as now I foresee no fresh ones I am determined to wait no longer for chances of which I may not be able to avail myself. My Brother and Sister are fully sensible of your Father and Mother's kindness and that of yourself and all your Family in wishing to see Dora this winter, but they cannot consent to her leaving home again so soon, and her Father says her first visit must be to see her nearest relatives whom she has never yet visited. Liverpool is in the road into Wales, and whenever she goes thither (but no time is at present fixed) no doubt she will halt at Liverpool, a great pleasure for herself. She is now no inmate of Rydal Mount and has actually been absent a month and a day, on

---

[1] *Select Remains of the Ancient Popular Poetry of Scotland*, 1822.

duty at Miss Dowling's, as her assistant in the school. I think she will be released next week as Miss M.[1] or Miss Eliza Dowling is daily expected. She however expresses no impatience and is both well and happy in the regular discharge of her duties.

Only think of your young Friend instructing the whole school (thirty 8 or 9) in penmanship—the younger classes reading and French—walking as Governante of the tribe, superintending drawing and music lessons—and having the charge of 5 or 6 little ones in her Bed-room? It is very fortunate for Miss D. that she happened to be at liberty, otherwise I know not how she would have got through, having been disappointed in the hope of engaging either one or two Teachers.

You will have gathered that D. has entirely regained her strength from what I have said of her exertions, and will be glad also to hear that she has now very few spots on her face. Surely I have written to you since my Brother and Sister returned, and I have now nothing to say of them except that his eyes, though delicate, are on the whole much improved, and that my Sister is much stronger and healthier than when she left home, though thinner and perhaps at first sight you might think her not looking well. Miss Hutchinson returned from Boulogne three weeks ago without having seen anything beyond that place and Calais. Had I [? gone] off with Mr Quillinan matters would have been different: but it is perhaps better as it is, though certainly had my Brother and Sister been a few weeks settled at home, I should have been likely to yield to so strong a temptation as his pleasant company to the shores of Kent. Miss H. is now at Hendon, the Monkhouses still at Ramsgate—Mrs M.'s health much improved; and Miss Anna Eliza Horrocks[2] who has been dangerously ill recovering. Mr M. is expected at the Penrith Races and Hunt. I hope Dora will be at the Balls with her Father and Mother but it is yet uncertain. Poor John has been very unwell. He had an abscess above the nose which was attended with fever and slight delirium for some days; the abscess burst internally, he was much weakened, and is still very far from well: but I hope a part of his uncomfortable feelings are attributable to the Blue Pill which he is taking as an alternative. I have had a letter from Miss Laing. She had a dismal journey to Edinburgh in streaming rain and could not ride in the inside of the coach from sickness. The next day a fever came on which confined her to her room for three weeks. She was recovering when she wrote and in her usual good

[1] Mary Dowling (1791–1830).
[2] Daughter of Samuel Horrocks, and sister of Mrs. Monkhouse.

spirits. Your friend Hartley does wonders.[1] He has been regularly at his post ever since school began and parents and children are satisfied. I can answer for William that he has improved very much since he went to school, and he is strong active and lively. We have had rainy weather with few and short intermissions for the last seven weeks. This day is fine and so was yesterday, but with showers. The hay is spread abroad in many parts and much of it uncut. Mrs Robinson[2] is out of her month and the Baby really worth much talk much expectation and all the needle work bestowed upon it: but poor thing (entre nous) I wish the parents were not themselves quite so much of Babies. Thomas[3] and Jeremiah Robinson[4] (his[5] brothers) are with them, both pleasant young men, especially Tom (Dora's protector on her walks at Harrowgate). They are all coming to tea this afternoon. Daniel Green[6] is with us to dinner and Strickland Cookson. Mrs Elliott is overflowing with friends, all very pleasant people. Sir Francis and Lady Drake[7] at Spring Cottage, (she is Mrs Elliott's cousin a sweet creature, beautiful at 50 years of age and by candle light and well-dressed, you might take her for 6 and twenty. At Mr Fleming's little cottage are two nephews of Mr E and in their own house Mr E.'s sister (Mrs Anne E.) a clever intelligent lively old lady and her Nieces. Mr Tillbrooke has been with us for a few days, he talks of coming to the cottage himself after Q.s leave. Mr Monkhouse is in treaty for Mr Blakeney's cottage which is on sale. The opium eater must have left off his opium: he is returned quite well,[8] and looks younger

[1] Hartley Coleridge's own view of his achievements at the Ambleside school was somewhat more sceptical, as his letter to Elizabeth Crump of 28 Nov. makes clear: 'As to what you say of my future fame as a schoolmaster, I set it down under the head of golden visions. The utmost I hope for, is to lay good foundations.—I have not, and cannot gain, the art of commanding any but mere children. Neither do I profess the sort of learning or talent that tells in Great Schools and Universities. But still, I believe, all will be well—better at least than I deserve, and as well as I hope for.' (*WL MSS.*)

[2] Daughter-in-law of Mrs. Robinson, the admiral's widow. She was Charlotte Kearsley of Manchester and married their eldest son Captain Charles Robinson (see L. 23 above), who fought against the Dutch and Spanish in the East Indies, before retiring to Ambleside and joining the Wordsworth circle. They had ten children. See Genealogical Table, facing p. 704.

[3] For Lieut. Thomas Robinson, see L. 23 above and L. 214 below.

[4] See L. 37 above.   [5] i.e. Captain Robinson's.

[6] The Revd. Daniel Green (1798–1829), fourth son of John and Molly Green of Mosshead, Grasmere: perpetual curate of Langdale, 1828–9. He had just graduated at St. Catherine's Hall, Cambridge.

[7] Sir Thomas Fuller Eliott Drake, Bart. (1785–1870), of Nutwell Court, Exeter, and Buckland Abbey: a descendant of Sir Francis Drake, he served throughout the Peninsular War, and married Eleanor, only daughter of James Halford of Laleham, Middlesex.

[8] De Quincey had spent a good deal of time in London recently. Since the

than he did seven [years] ago. He drank tea with us lately. William Jackson was [there] on his way to John Wakefield's.[1]—he too much improved. I fell in for two rides in his gig. Had I not reason to say it would make him more welcome? Anne Harrison[2] is recovering, she crawls about like a shadow but every week grows stronger. Our new maids give great satisfaction in essentials only we cannot brush off poor Mary's awkwardness. She makes up, however, (at all times but when we have company) by her zeal in serving every member of the Family, and by increasing industry. Anne is much admired not for her beauty but for her sensible countenance and respectable appearance. We had a large party last Sunday, all the Elliotts, Mr Barber, etc., etc., and fortunately Mary had had a tooth drawn, therefore Anne waited. Dear Elizabeth, what a gossiping letter this is. I know you want to know all that concerns us and I flit from one thing to another. Edith Southey spent a week with us. She is very delicate and has had two sore throats. Sara quite well. She talks of riding over with Mary Calvert[3] when D.[4] comes home. D. dines with us to-day. She sends her very best love to you and says the first thing she does when she comes home again shall be to write to you. She longs to hear how the Doctor and you are going on[5] You must not expect her letter in less than three weeks, for I find she intends staying a while after Miss M. Dowling's return to have the benefit of the fresh import of Parisian steps. Will and Dora are playing on the Front with Strickland Cookson. Poor E. Cookson is just in the same state, talks of coming to Rydal when she is strong enough. We were all at Grasmere Church to-day, the Vale beautiful, and nothing so pretty from the other side as the Wyke. I have not been at Mr Barber's for many weeks, and he has been making grand improvements: I must go the first Sunday. And now dear Elizabeth, it is time to ask after you and all yours, to whom give my very best love. The

---

publication of his *Confessions* in the *London Magazine* for Sept. and Oct. 1821, he had continued his contributions—most recently the *Letters to a Young Man whose Education has been Neglected* in the issues for Jan.–Mar., May, and July 1823.

[1] Probably the *younger* John Wakefield (1794–1866), the Kendal banker (see *MY* ii. 428), who continued his father's opposition to the Lowther cause, and was five times Mayor of Kendal between 1837 and 1860. In 1839 the Wakefield Bank merged with the Kendal Bank of W. D. Crewdson and Co., and John Wakefield became senior partner in 1850. See George Chandler, *Four Centuries of Banking*, 2 vols., 1964–8, ii. 86–7, 99–101.

[2] Perhaps a daughter of the Mrs. Harrison of L. 74 above.

[3] William Calvert's daughter, educated with Dora W. at Miss Dowling's school (see *MY* ii. 496).

[4] Dora W.   [5] See below, L. 110.

Hardens well, we saw them the day before Jane's departure, whom
you will soon see at Liverpool. John has been so thrown back by his
illness that I fear he will only have time for one day with you when
he goes to Oxford. I have written in great haste between dinner and
time to dress for the afternoon company. It is 6 o'clock—I am in my
dressing gown and have not time to read over, so excuse all
blunders. God bless you. ever yours.

D. W.

My Brother's and Sister's best regards to Father and Mother
and all of you.

109. W. W. to THE COMMISSIONERS OF STAMPS

Address: To the Hon'ble the Commissioners, Stamp Office, London
Stamp: Kendal Penny Post. *Endorsed*: Wm Wordsworth Esq Rydal Mount
  Ambleside 19th Septr 1823.
MS. Public Record Office. Hitherto unpublished.

[*In John Carter's hand*]

Rydal Mount, Ambleside,
19 Septr: 1823.—

Honble Sirs,
  My Subdistributor of Stamps at Ulverston[1] having referred to
the Books of the late John Soulby in pursuance of the Board's letter
of the 26th Ult: to Henry Hesketh Esq[2] respecting the duty on a
Legacy of fifty Pounds to [   ] Brockbank[3] under the will of Geo:
Redhead,[4] states to me that a Duty of £2 was paid thereon to Mr:
Soulby on the 9th March 1813 and that the same was remitted
by him to Mr: Hesketh on the 11th of the same month—

I have the Honor to be
Honble Sirs,
Your obedient Servant
[*signed*] Wm Wordsworth

The Hon'ble the Commissioners.—

---

[1] Stephen Tyson, bookseller: successor as Sub-distributor to John Soulby,
printer and bookseller.
[2] Apparently an official of the Stamp Office.
[3] Christian name illegible: perhaps the reference is to Thomas Brockbank,
an Ulverston grocer.
[4] Unidentified—but perhaps a partner in the Ulverston grocery firm of
Redhead and Seatle.

110. D. W. to ELIZABETH CRUMP

Address: Miss Elizabeth Crumpe, Queen Anne S^t. Liverpool.
Stamp: Kendal Penny Post. *Endorsed*: Oct. 10th 1823.
MS. WL.
LY i. 121.

Rydal Mount October 10th [1823]

My dear Friend,

Poor John left yesterday and I am very sorry he could not take the Liverpool road which he himself regretted much. He lost so much time by his illness in the summer, and slow recovery, that he has none to spare for pleasure, yet if it had not been for a swelled face which came on at the end of last week, and continued for several days, I think he would have stolen one day to have spent with you at Liverpool. He desires me to give his kind remembrances to all of you with many thanks for your kind wish to see him. Perhaps we may have him in the north again at Christmas but that will not be the season for halting on the road, or for seeing Liverpool to advantage, therefore I think it is hardly likely he will travel by that way except in Summer. Your Father must have reached home after his journey into Scotland, and we have neither seen nor heard anything of him. We were in hopes that he would have been induced to look at Allan Bank on his return, and that we should have seen him. Your letter came from Kendal without a postmark. I suppose it was left by some one at the bottom of the hill, to whom your Father had entrusted it. Why have we not seen your brother John? or having put off his journey so long does he not intend coming at all? I wish he had arrived when John was at home, but whenever he comes it will give us great pleasure to see him. My dear Elizabeth, it gives me much pain to find you are in such bad spirits, and truly shall I rejoice when your mind is completely made up and settled. In whatever way the present suspense is decided there will be much matter for consolation; for at best it is a dreary thing to give up country and friends for so many years.[1] We are very glad that Dora is again at liberty. She is quite well, and her face comparatively little flushed. Poor Miss Eliza Dowling is still very weak and it will be long before she can take her place in the school. Miss D. has engaged two Teachers but only one has arrived, the other daily expected. Mr William Jackson was well when my Brother parted from him at W.haven last Saturday—We

---

[1] Elizabeth Crump had become engaged, against her own inclinations, to a doctor who was bound for India, and for rather more than a year her future was uncertain until the engagement was broken off.

expect him shortly. You were very kind in wishing for Dora at your Musical Festival. We expect Mr Monkhouse next week on his way to Penrith. I fear Dora and her Mother will not be able to go to the Balls, as my Brother's eyes are in a very weak state. Your letter was most acceptable and I return you a thousand thanks for it. Believe me ever your affectionate friend

D. Wordsworth.

I assure you I shall not forget my promise when your fate is decided.[1]

111. D. W. to MARY LAING

Address: To Miss Laing, Messrs W. and D. Laing's, South Bridge Street, Edinburgh.
MS. Edinburgh University Library.
The Wordsworth–Laing Letters (—).

Rydal Mount, October 10th. [1823]

My dear Miss Laing,

A neighbour of ours is going to Edinburgh next week, and as I know you are always pleased at hearing of us I shall trouble her with a letter, to be put into the post office at E., and, unless you write to me before Mrs Harden leaves your neighbourhood, I hope you will send me a letter by her, with a full account of yourself—and all the members of your family with whom I am acquainted. I trust you had no relapse after you last wrote and that you are now perfectly well, and enjoying your usual good spirits. Poor John left us yesterday for Oxford.[2] He was in no very good plight for travelling, having never regained his former strength since the severe illness he had after you left us. Perhaps had he gone with you it might not have happened; yet if it *had* how much worse for him! and what a distress for your poor Mother—who had to nurse *you* at the same time! I have often thought of this, and that perhaps on the whole (independent of my Brother's probable disapprobation) it was much better that we all turned back from Ambleside.

---

[1] Dora W. adds a note at the bottom of this letter: '. . . Oh that you were by me. How well I remember the delightful evenings we passed together by our bed-room fireside after my Aunt was gone to her own room—but I fear those happy hours will never come over again—*never* if that horrid Dr. carries you far away which I confess I am selfish enough to hope and trust he will not do. The time is now fast approaching for your lot to be fixed. How anxious am I to know your fate. . . .'

[2] To commence his studies with **Augustus Hare** at New College.

Doro is at length again at liberty. She has only been a week at home, having been detained after Miss Mary and Miss Eliza Dowling's return from Paris by the non-arrival of Teachers, and a more distressing cause, the illness of Miss Eliza, who is still in a state of extreme weakness, and unable to attend to the school; but her place is now supplied by a very competent Teacher. Doro is no worse for her labour and confinement—and has great satisfaction in having been useful to her excellent Friend Miss Dowling.

We are going on pretty much in the same way as when I last wrote. Willy has had the pleasure of drowning five kittens, and catching a few score of fish. I do not know that he has practised the taking away of life in any other line since the Lecture you gave him, and I have the pleasure to tell you that he has been perfectly well. His Master, Mr Coleridge,[1] has stuck to his post wonderfully, and though his school is not characterised by strict discipline, I think the Parents are satisfied. The Boys, of course, make no complaint on that score. You will be sorry to hear that my Brother's eyes have been troublesome of late but in other respects he is pretty well. I have quite regained my strength, and could now attack Arthur's Seat and the Braid Hills as lustily as when you and I trudged together. My Sister is quite well.

I had a letter not long ago from Miss Joanna Hutchinson, who desired particularly to be remembered to you and your Mother. Her health is in its better way at present. Miss Hutchinson[2] intends very soon to join her in Wales, having spent her summer at Ramsgate, Boulogne, and in London and the neighbourhood.

The Seasons, I think, will go their round as they began. In Spring, we hoped for a fine summer, in summer for a fine autumn—and now the autumn is almost over, and we have had only one week of steady fine weather; and now, it is worse than ever. I hope the rain which is here at this moment falling in torrents will not attend poor John on his journey [? for he is][3] not fit to be exposed to wetting; and as he detests the inside of a Coach we are apprehensive that he may go all the way to Oxford on the outside. Some Friends of our Neighbour, Mrs Elliott, are just returned from a Month's [? tour][4] in Scotland, and it appears they have not had nearly so much rain as we have had.—Perhaps you have seen my Brother's Description of the Country of the Lakes; but I feel assured that you will value the Copy which I send, as coming directly from Rydal Mount, and will keep it for my sake. If you have got a Cap for me, Mrs Harden will be so kind as to bring it, and I shall request her to

---

[1] i.e. Hartley Coleridge.   [2] i.e. S. H.   [3] *MS. damaged.*   [4] *Seal.*

send you her address, along with the parcel, and to state to you *when* she is likely to leave Edinburgh, that you may send your pacquet to her in proper time. Pray remember me most kindly to your Father, Mother and Brothers and believe me, dear Miss Laing,

ever affectionately yours
D Wordsworth

My Brother begs his best Respects to your Brother David, and hopes that business or pleasure will again conduct him into our neighbourhood.

This time last year we were at Edinburgh. How much finer the season! On second thoughts I shall enclose this letter by Mrs Harden. If you have not procured the Cap pray do not give yourself much trouble about it.

112. W. W. to UNKNOWN CORRESPONDENT

MS. Mr. W. A. Strutz. Hitherto unpublished.

Rydal Mount
Oct^br 21st—1823

Dear Sir,

Upon returning home, after an absence prolonged greatly by unforeseen circumstances, I find your Letter among so many others that my Reply, which I am sorry will reach you so late, must be very brief.

You are yet very young, and I can therefore without any regret say that I know of no infallible test for ascertaining whether you are capable of becoming a poet or not: '*Try*, and *merit*', and in these two words lies the substance of what can with reason be said upon the Subject.—Nevertheless as my own experience may not be useless to you, I will add that at your age I had full as much of the poetic Spirit in me as I have ever had since—but with regard to Art and the power of expression I had made all advances, nor was it untill my 28th year, though I wrote much, that I could compose verses which were not in point of workmanship very deficient and faulty.—

With many good wishes, I am dear Sir
Sincerely yours
Wm Wordsworth

P.S.

Long ago I found myself compelled to lay down a Rule not to undertake the perusal of Mss Verses from any Quarters, and therefore you will not think it unkind if I should decline inviting you to send a Specimen of your own.—

113. W. W. to ROBERT SOUTHEY

MS. untraced.
K. LT i. 167.

[? Autumn 1823]

My dear Southey,

Colonel Campbell, our neighbour at Grasmere, has sent for your book;[1] he served during the whole of the Peninsular war, and you shall hear what he says of it in due course. We are out of the way of all literary communication, so I can report nothing. I have read the whole with great pleasure; the work will do you everlasting honour. I have said the whole, forgetting, in that contemplation, my feelings upon one part, where you have tickled with a feather when you should have branded with a red-hot iron. You will guess I mean the Convention of Cintra.[2] My detestation—I may say abhorrence—of that event is not at all diminished by your account of it. Bonaparte had committed a capital blunder in supposing that when he had intimidated the Sovereigns of Europe he had conquered the several nations. Yet it was natural for a wiser than he to have fallen into this mistake; for the old despotisms had deprived the body of the people of all practical knowledge in the management, and, of necessity, of all interest, in the course of affairs.

The French themselves were astonished at the apathy and ignorance of the people whom they had supposed they had utterly subdued when they had taken their fortresses, scattered their armies, entered their capital cities, and struck their cabinets with dismay. There was no hope for the deliverance of Europe till the nations had suffered enough to be driven to a passionate recollection of all that was honourable in their past history and to make appeal

---

[1] The first volume of Southey's *History of the Peninsular War*.

[2] For full discussion of W. W.'s tract and the circumstances in which it was written, see *Prose Works*, i. 193 ff., and *MT* i. 291 ff. Southey's treatment of the Convention of Cintra was somewhat perfunctory. He stressed the military advantages of the settlement: 'But some political errors were committed in framing it; and the British Generals did not assume that moral tone which the occasion justified, and which the soundest policy required' (i. 577).

to the principles of universal and everlasting justice. These sentiments the authors of that Convention most unfeelingly violated; and as to the principles, they seemed to be as little aware even of the existence of such powers, for powers emphatically may they be called, as the tyrant himself. As far, therefore, as these men could, they put an extinguisher upon the star which was then rising.

It is in vain to say that after the first burst of indignation was over the Portuguese themselves were reconciled to the event, and rejoiced in their deliverance. We may infer from that the horror which they must have felt in the presence of their oppressors; and we may see in it to what a state of helplessness their bad government had reduced them. Our duty was to have treated them with respect, as the representatives of suffering humanity, beyond what they were likely to look for themselves, and as deserving greatly, in common with their Spanish brethren, for having been the first to rise against the tremendous oppression and to show how, and how only, it could be put an end to.

W. Wordsworth.

114. W. W. to ROBERT JONES

Address: Revᵈ R. Jones, Plas yn lan, Ruthin, N.W.
Franked: Penrith November four 1823 Fred. Bentinck.[1]
MS. WL. Hitherto unpublished.

Lowther Castle
3ᵈ Novᵇʳ. 1823.

My dear Jones,

Many thanks for your kind Letter which we had long looked for. —I think you express yourself rather too strongly when you say that I *promised* a visit to you in Wales, last summer. I did indeed express a *strong wish* which I yet feel to do so, but I think I could scarcely have said that I relied upon your being able to fulfill my wish last summer—I went into Leicestershire in Febʳʸ with Mrs W. but we did not return to Rydal Mount till July, having been in Flanders and a tour in Holland, besides a residence of five weeks in Kent. You may be sure if I can I shall profit by your kind invitation, but I dare not engage for next summer: If I am at liberty I will take care to let you know.

I am truly concerned to hear that you have been unwell—though

---

[1] For Lord Frederick Bentinck, see L. 43 above.

your account speaks of a Recovery. Exercise and spare diet are the things for a habit like yours. Remember this, and the strength of your constitution will carry you probably a healthy man to old age.

My Son is at New College, pray if you return to Oxfordshire[1] let him know, and most likely he may find leisure to pop in upon you for a day or two. Do not omit calling upon him when you pass through Oxford.

I am at present on a visit to Lord Lonsdale. D[r] Satterthwaite begs his best regards, adding that he has a beautiful parsonage like your own, where you would have a most hearty welcome.

Mrs Monkhouse[2] did mention her having been so fortunate as to fall in with you at Preston.

I often fear that you were not so comfortable with us,[3] on account of the bustle we were in, as we all wished you to be. Happy shall I be to see you again—and believe me my dear friend with best regards to your Brothers and those about you who may remember me very faithfully yours

W[m] Wordsworth

115. W. W. to LORD LONSDALE

Address: The Earl of Lonsdale, Lowther Castle, Penrith.
Postmark: 11 Nov. 1823. *Stamp*: Kendal.
MS. Lonsdale MSS. Hitherto unpublished.

Nov[r] 9th [1823].

My Lord,

With much pleasure I return thanks for a present of beautiful Game of which Dr Satterthwaite had taken charge as far as Kendal —it would have made a charming Picture in the hands of a Dutch Artist; and arrived very opportunely for the more humble purpose of entertaining several Friends who dined with us today.

Our journey home[4] was full of adventures. We were much indebted to the Gig, which, however, we should not have been able to get through some of the Gates without the assistance of your Lordship's Serv[nt]. The distance is much greater than I thought; and

---

[1] Robert Jones was rector of Souldern, Oxon., from 1806 until his death in 1835, but he had a licence of non-residence for long intervals, the benefice house being unfit for occupation, and he spent much of his time at the family home in Denbighshire.
[2] i.e. *Miss* Elizabeth Monkhouse.
[3] During his visit of Aug. 1822. See above, L. 74.
[4] From Lowther Castle.

we did not reach home till near ten o'clock, having halted an hour only on the road.

I mentioned Mr Myers's[1] illness—it was brought on in a singular way. He had suffered his grey hair to be cut off, for the gratification of one of his Grandsons.[2] They imprudently cleared away the greatest part of it, and the consequence was most alarming; violent pains in the back of the head, and the eyes, attended with giddiness. We used to joke with Mr O'Callaghan[3] about the state of his locks, I hope he will take care not to give the hair-cutter carte-blanche. My Sister, who had been visiting Mr Myers, happened to regret that more pains had not been taken to cure one of Mr Parkin's[4] Sons of Stammering. 'Yes', replied the Quondam School-master, now ninety years of age, 'much may be done for relief in these cases; you are a Reader, and will recollect that Demosthenes got the better of this disadvantage by declaiming on the seashore with a pebble in his mouth. This, said he, was in the time of Cicero!'

Be so kind, my Lord, as to say to Lady Lonsdale, that we saw nobody of whom we could enquire about the nine Lakes visible from some of the mountains at the head of Haweswater.

I have just finished a Translation into English Rhyme of the first Aeneid.[5] Would your Lordship allow me to send it to you at Cottesmore? I should be much gratified if you would take the trouble of comparing some passages of it with the original. I have endeavoured to be much more literal than Dryden,[6] or Pitt,[7] who keeps much closer to the original than his Predecessor.

---

[1] W. W.'s uncle, the Revd. Thomas Myers, rector of Lazonby, now entering his ninetieth year.

[2] i.e. the sons of Mrs. Robinson, the admiral's widow.

[3] The Hon. George O'Callaghan (1787–1856), youngest brother of Cornelius, 1st Viscount Lismore (1775–1857), of Shanbally Castle, Co. Tipperary: younger brother of General Sir Robert O'Callaghan (1777–1840), Commander-in-Chief at Edinburgh Castle.

[4] Probably Hugh Parkin of Skirsgill House, on the Eamont at Dacre. He had two sons, James (b. 1798) and Charles (b. 1800) who entered Brasenose College, Oxford, in 1815 and 1818 respectively. Thomas Myers perhaps had had some hand in tutoring them.

[5] See *PW* iv. 286 ff., 468–70. It is now clear that W. W. began his translation in the autumn of 1823, and that the chronological reconstruction by de Selincourt must be amended accordingly.

[6] Dryden's Virgil was first published in 1697. For W. W.'s opinion of it, see J. P. Collier, *An Old Man's Diary* . . ., 4 vols., 1871–2, i. 90: 'He admired Dryden more as a writer of paraphrases than as a translator: he read the passage he wished to render, until he took in the full and entire meaning of the author, then threw aside the original, and expressed the thought in his own happy and truly English phraseology.

[7] Christopher Pitt (1699–1748) published his complete translation of the *Aeneid* in 2 vols. in 1740.

With kindest wishes to everyone about you, in which Mrs
Wordsworth and my Sister unite, I have the honor to be my Lord
Ever your Lordship's
faithfully obliged Ser^{vnt}
Wm Wordsworth

Mrs Wordsworth takes the liberty of sending the enclosed with
a request that you would be so kind as to frank it at your convenience. It was sent here by mistake.

116. D. W. to CATHERINE CLARKSON

Address: Mrs Clarkson, Playford Hall, Ipswich, Suffolk.
Postmark: 17 Nov. 1823. *Stamp*: Kendal Penny Post.
MS. British Museum.
K (—). *LT i. 122.*

Wednesday, 11th or 12th Nov^r. [1823]

My dear Friend,
I thought your husband's visit to us and our Friends at Hindwell
together with the request for the Recipe for the cure of the Rheumatism would have insured us a letter and this has furnished me
with an excuse for delay, though had I had ten minutes at command
I should certainly have written when the Ipswich Ladies[1] departed
whom, by the bye I took the liberty of troubling with a m[?essage][2]
respecting the medicine—and this too I flattered myself [would be]
an additional spur to your writing. Twenty years a[go I should]
have been uneasy and concluded you were ill; but [   ] myself
that it is merely the press of every day employments [which] give
you little leisure and that having once put off, you go on fro[m day
to day.] So it is with me in most cases. I think I told you that we
thought Mr Clarkson looking ten years younger than when he was
here with you,[3] and at Hindwell they were quite charmed with his
chearfulness and good looks. We were very glad that he made so
long a stay there, which would greatly tend to restore whatever
strength he may have lost by his exertions—then completed.—
What does Mr C think of the insurrections at Demerara?[4] I fear

---

[1] Probably Mrs. Lloyd and her daughters, mentioned further on. They were
friends of the Clarksons, and perhaps related to the Lloyds of Birmingham.
[2] *MS. damaged.*   [3] In late May and early June 1822.
[4] The emancipation cause had been gaining momentum this year: Wilberforce had issued his 'Appeal on Behalf of the Slaves' and founded the Anti-
Slavery Society, and on 15 May Sir Thomas Fowell Buxton (1786–1845),
M.P. for Weymouth, had brought forward a motion in the House of Commons

there will be many a bitter struggle before the Negroes will be free—and able to manage themselves in a state of freedom. My Brother strenuously advised Mr C, when he was here, to undertake a History of Africa, as the finishing of his literary labours, and the most appropriate one for him who has so nobly spent his life in the service of the poor natives of that country. He seemed to be impressed with what my Brother said, and I hope has already begun to turn his thoughts to the subject, and mode of treating it.

Southey will probably be at Playford ere long. He set forward on his long intended journey with his Daughter on Monday sen'night; but what is the plan of their route I know not—or whether they intend to go into Suffolk at the beginning or end of their stay in London.[1] No doubt you have heard from Sara H. of her late movements and present plans—She is at this time at Hendon, and will, I suppose, very soon, go into Wales, unless poor Mrs Luff's[2] present illness should detain her in London. I fear this last residence in the mountains has injured her constitution more than the former; for she appears to have been but weak and delicate ever since her arrival,—I hear she is now seriously ill.—My Brother and Sister and Dora had much pleasure at the Penrith Races. Many persons told me that no one looked so happy in the Ball-room as they; and they had the choice week of [? October] for the out-door amusements. I was left a[t home with] Willy; but a gig was sent to take me over Kirksto[ne on Th]ursday to meet my good and dear Friend Mrs Rawson[3] and [? her Husband]. Willy accompanied me, and *he* had the pleasures of the Races [on one] day and on the Saturday we all together (with Mr [?]) returned home. He only stayed over Monday, and on Wednesday my Br and I again crossed Kirkstone. We rode to the top, and thence walked to Hallsteads (13 miles) with great pleasure and no fatigue. I saw Mrs Rawson again and her Husband who had come to fetch her home. The pair seem not to have been touched at all by the lapse of seven years.[4]

in favour of gradual Abolition which was carried unanimously, subject only to Canning's amendment safeguarding the rights of the planters. The government recommended immediate reforms; but these were rejected by the planters, and tension rose. On 19 Aug. the united colony of Demerara and Essequibo was declared under martial law, and two days later there was a Negro insurrection. By the time reports reached the English papers in October, the rebellion had been crushed and a thousand Negroes executed as a reprisal.

[1] Southey spent about eight weeks in the West Country and London, and made up his temporary difference with Lamb (see Southey, v. 149–53).

[2] For Mrs. Luff, see *EY*, p. 334 and *MY* i. 11.

[3] D. W.'s cousin, formerly Elizabeth Threlkeld (see *EY*, p. 2).

[4] i.e. since D. W. stayed with them at Halifax in the autumn and winter of 1816. See *MY* ii. 352–4.

Mrs R is 78 and as chearful and gay as if only 16—and notwithstanding her lameness, on every fine day while at Hallsteads she
walked out alone—a mile or a mile and a half at a stretch—besides
numerous little trips in the garden. When Mrs R was gone I went
to Penrith to stay with Mrs Rd Wordsworth. She is a good creature,
and I have a great affection for her—which grows every time I am
with her. My nephew is a mild and amiable child—still delicate in
health; but I think he will be reared, having already gone through
so much, and becoming stronger as he does.—From Penrith last
Wednesday, I went to Lowther in a gig, breakfasted with Dr
Satterthwaite, and there William joined me from the Castle, where
he had been staying, and we proceeded together up Hawes-water,
in another Gig lent us by Lord Lonsdale. The first time I saw
Hawes-water was from your house;[1] and many thoughts did our
beautiful journey revive of you and yours, and the happy day we
spent in going to Mardale with Mr C. and you. We took the gig as
far as we could, and then proceeded over the Fell, on foot, to the
head of Long Sleddale, a very interesting valley, crossed at the first
houses to Kentmere (Bernard Gilpin's Birthplace)[2] thence over
another fell to Troutbeck, crossed that vale also, and home by Low
Wood. I never spent a more rememberable day, seldom a pleasanter; though the latter part of our journey was performed in the
dark (which, however, was of little consequence, as it was over
familiar ground). It would be a charming journey for any one,
either on horseback, or on foot, on a long summer's day, but certainly except under favour of bright calm weather such as we had, is
unfit for a *winter's* day. I was neither stiff nor tired the next day.
It is indeed a fact that I can take mountain walks with much less
fatigue than in my youth. I cannot say the same of the vallies—at
least on damp warm days. Shall you be in London in the Spring?
I guess you will as you had not your journey [   ] last May.
When and where shall we meet again? [? Let it] be before another
year elapses. We talk of a jour[ney   ] but plans are not laid
therefore all is uncertain [   ] once again stirred
from home I shall [? certainly not] return without first having had
a sight of you. [   ]

[1] Eusemere, in Nov. 1799. See *EY*, pp. 271–2.
[2] Bernard Gilpin (1517–83), known for his zealous independence as a
preacher and his devotion to the poor as the 'Apostle of the North'. After a
successful career at Oxford, where he gradually conformed to the views of the
Reformers, he became vicar of Norton, Durham, and (following his exile in
the early years of Mary's reign) Archdeacon of Durham, and rector of Houghton-
le-Spring, where he founded the Grammar School. C. W. reprinted Carleton's
Life in the third volume of his *Ecclesiastical Biography*.

William's eyes much better than they have been [   ] Doro
caught a cold at the races; but that was [? likely to] have happened
to anyone, so much excited as *she* was; and it is now quite gone.
She has lately been much less subject to colds than formerly, and
this last attack does not shake my persuasion that her constitution
is strengthened in that point as well as several others—Willy
continues perfectly well and his school-master[1] keeps at his post—
taking much pains at lesson-time; but as you may suppose he is no
disciplinarian and the Boys make strange fun. Mr Calvert[2] has
sent his two sons from Keswick for a short while. Poor Sara
Coleridge has a weakness in her eyes—very distressing for one of
her habits. I think I have nothing new for you in the way of common
occurrences. The bad season has kept people at home—and prevented them from staying when passing among the Lakes;—at
least we have had fewer visitors of that kind than I ever remember.
Mrs Lloyd and her Daughters were particularly unfortunate in the
weather. There was many a day, while they were at Spring Cottage,
when all females, except ourselves, would have thought it impossible to go out of doors for pleasure. This of course entirely
prevented short walks, therefore they were only in the precincts of
Rydal Mount, I believe, twice or three times. They made use of the
few chance fine days, and wisely, in going to places at a greater
distance. Soon after the Ladies arrived they wrote to request
permission to see the views—etc from our grounds and Mary and
I called immediately. They seem to be very good people, but never
in my life did I see such a set of chatterers as the young ones. Each
seems to think herself bound to be agreeable and all talk at once—
and so loud! They are much liked by Mrs Fleming with whom they
lodged. *We* saw very little of them owing to the unfortunate
weather, which we really often lamented for their sakes, thinking
it very hard to have come so far to be shut up in a cottage and see
nothing. Pray do not fail to send the Recipe for Rheumatism—
Many of our friends are anxious to have it. Mr Quillinan gives up
his lease of Ivy Cottage to the Elliots, having now no thoughts of
living there himself. This we think is well both for himself and
children. We have just had a pleasant letter from Henry Robinson

[1] Hartley Coleridge.
[2] William Calvert of Greta Bank (see *EY*, p. 97). He had *three* sons, but the
eldest, Dr. John Calvert (1803–42), was now away at Oxford. The younger two
were the Revd. Raisley Calvert (1804–38), later of Barton, Derbyshire, and
William Calvert (1810–41), later a surgeon in Bombay.

after his long Tour[1]—and what delightful accounts from all quarters of your Son! He will certainly if he have health and strength be heard of among the Lawyers—and we shall be seeing his name in the newspapers with the best of them. No news lately from Wales. Poor Mrs M[2] is I fear not likely to get through another summer. Tillbrooke writes in good spirits; but longing after the Ivy Cot. for himself at the end of Mr Q's lease. God Bless you dearest Friend. I shall anxiously expect a letter, and may it bring good tidings of you and your husband—and all who are near and dear to you.

Yours ever more D. Wordsworth

All send best love— Our church is near finished on the outside and is very pretty and you can have no idea how beautiful in connexion with the village, especially seen from the other side of the Lake.

I have a stupefying cold which prevents my looking over this letter to correct blunders, and must be my excuse for dullness.

117. D. W. to MARY LAING

Address: To Miss Laing, South Bridge Street, Edinburgh.
MS. Edinburgh University Library.
The Wordsworth–Laing Letters (—).

Nov[r] 25th 1823

My dear Miss Laing,

I am not doing as you desired, taking a long sheet of paper and a long evening to write to you, having at present no opportunity so to do. I yesterday heard of a Friend going to Edinburgh, whom I am going to trouble with a package to M[r] Wallace the Dentist, in which I shall enclose this (as better than nothing) though I have but ten minutes before the package must be closed and sent off. I know not how long my Friend will stay at Edinburgh but he is to bring back my package from M[r] Wallace (alas! I have lost one of my teeth which M[r] W. is to replace) and if you send a letter to M[r] Wallace he will enclose it; a letter just to say how you all are— for I am not so unreasonable as to expect a long one in return for this—only I assure you I shall write ere long with leisure and quiet before me, and endeavour to satisfy your wishes. I am really anxious to hear of the re-establishment of your health; and must

[1] During October H. C. R. had made an extended tour of Germany, Switzerland, and the Tyrol.
[2] Miss Elizabeth Monkhouse, who survived four more years.

intreat that you will abide strictly by your physician's orders. There is not much fear of your transgressing in the visiting line; but as to walking, I do fear for you: however this I believe, that if you stop short of fatigue you cannot be far wrong, and strength will grow with well-regulated practice.

Since I wrote to you my Niece has been very gay, having been first introduced at a *public* Ball—at the Penrith Races. She very much enjoyed herself. So did her Father and Mother enjoy *them*selves[1]— and were no worse for it; but poor Doro came home with a bad cold, from which, however, she is now recovered, and is in very good health. My Brother's eyes are much better, without taking snuff; but I think he will be induced to try it, when the inflammation returns, as full surely it will.

Many thanks for all the trouble you have had with my Caps. You have set me up for the winter—and I assure you the caps are pronounced very becoming, and not unsuitable to my years.

You have sent no Bill of costs; but pray when you write by Mr Wallace's parcel tell me what I am indebted to you. A [?][2] of mine will be going to Edinburgh by whom I will write the promised letter in which I shall enclose the money. So pray do not forget.

Willy returns a hundred thousand thanks for the Seal. 'Poor Miss Laing! how good it was of her to send it me! But she should not have robbed herself of it!' So says William, while at the same time he is most proud in seeing it hanging upon his steel watch-chain.

A letter yesterday from [Miss][3] Joanna Hutchinson. Thanks for yours and her kind love to you. She is quite well at present.

[1] See *SH*, p. 267. D. W. does not describe her own activities here, but she wrote about them to Joanna Hutchinson, who relayed them to Mary Laing on 5 Dec.: 'I had a very entertaining letter the other day from Miss Wordsworth, giving me an account of a visit she had been paying in Penrith amongst her old school fellows, and she had joined in one or two of their gay Tea parties, and gave me a very nice description of all the pretty young ladies she had seen, their dress, etc. From Penrith she and her Brother went to Lowther . . .' (*Laing MSS., Edinburgh University Library*).

[2] *MS. torn.*

[3] *Tear.* In her letter to Mary Laing, Joanna described her life at Hindwell and nearby Qwerndovenant: 'I am writing this letter from a very retired place, where I am surrounded by rocks, woods and wild streams, and some of the most beautiful Picturesque Cottages you can imagine. Qwerndovenant is the name it bears, *Welch enough* you will say. It is a small Estate my brother purchased soon after he came into Radnorshire, and he has kept it in his own hands to improve it, and I have lately fitted up two appartments in the old Farm house and furnished them according to my fancy, and I have much pleasure in coming and spending a few days in this sweet retirement—for tho' perhaps you might say Hindwell was retired enough for any thing yet we are a large family there, and I find a little quiet leisure very desireable . . .'

Do excuse this sad scrawl. Best remembrances to all under your
Roof—and believe me,

Your affect^e Friend

D Wordsworth

If I could just now afford it, I should have a great mind to desire
Mr Wallace to make me a new set of Teeth, having no comfort in
the London ones—and if I live I must some time have another Set;
I do not however *know* that he can do it without my presence—but
if I should be long in going to Edinburgh I may again send the old
ones by a Friend.

118. W. W. to LORD LONSDALE

Address: The Earl of Lonsdale.
MS. Lonsdale MSS.
K (—). *The Middle Years* (1937) (—).[1]

[early Dec. 1823]

My Lord,
  Many thanks for your obliging letter. I shall be much gratified if
you happen to like my Translation,[2] and thankful for any remarks
with which you may honor me. I have made so much progress with
the 2nd book, that I defer sending the former till that is finished: It
takes in many places a high tone of passion, which I would gladly
succeed in rendering. When I read Virgil in the original I am
moved, but not so much by the translations; and I cannot but think
this owing to a defect in the diction; which I have endeavoured to
supply, with what success you will ere long be enabled to judge.
  Mr North[3] pleased me the other day with the account he gave of
the manner in which he had followed to Pooley Bridge and there
apprehended a worthless Fellow who had robbed his Cornstack.
Mr N. will I hope prove a useful magistrate.

Ever my Lord
most faithfully your obliged
Friend and serva^{nt}
Wm Wordsworth

May I request a cover for the Enclosed—

John Wordsworth Esq.,
New College
Oxford.

---

[1] Printed by de Selincourt under the year 1819.
[2] Of the first book of Virgil's *Aeneid*. See L. 115 above.
[3] Ford North of Ambleside. See *MY* ii. 549.

119. W. W. to WILLIAM CAMPBELL[1]

Address: To Wm Campbell Esq: Somerset Place London
Postmark: 27 Dec. 1823. *Stamp*: Kendal Penny Post. *Endorsed*: From W^m
   Wordsworth Esq Rydal Mount 23^d Decr 1823.
MS. Public Record Office. Hitherto unpublished.

[In John Carter's hand]

Rydal Mount,
23 Decr: 1823.

Sir,

I beg leave to state that having in pursuance of your Letter of
the 13th Inst: applied to my Subdistributor at Ulverston, for the
particulars therein called for, he informs me in reply that the
additional duty on the Legacy Receipts under the Will of late Rev^d.
Wm Wilson[2] has not been paid.

I am Sir,
Your obedient Servant
Wm Campbell Esq: *[signed]* Wm Wordsworth

120. W. W. to HENRY TAYLOR[3]

Address: To Henry Taylor Esqre, 11 Chapel Street, Grosvenor Square.
Postmark: 31 Dec. 1823. *Endorsed*: Wordsworth 26 Decr 23.
MS. Bodleian Library.
K (—). *LY i. 129.*

[In M. W.'s hand]

Rydal Mount, Dec^br 26th [1823]

Dear Sir,

You perhaps are not aware that the infirmity in my eyes makes
me afraid of touching a pen, and, tho' they are always much better

---

[1] Comptroller of Legacy Duties in the Stamp Office.

[2] Perhaps the Revd. William Wilson, rector of West Shefford, Berks., who
died on 13 Feb. 1818. He was a native of Sandbach, Cheshire.

[3] Henry Taylor (1800–86) of the Colonial Office, where he was the colleague
of Villiers, Stephen, and Spedding, all of whom figure in W. W.'s later correspondence. He was concerned with the slavery question at a crucial moment,
and devised schemes for the gradual amelioration and emancipation of the
Negroes. In autumn 1823 he met Southey during a visit to the Lakes, and
became his intimate friend, and in the same year began to contribute to the
London Magazine, of which he was offered the editorship. He was the author
of three dramas, *Isaac Comnenus* (1827), *Philip van Artevelde* (1834), and
Edwin the Fair (1842). In 1839 he married Theodosia, daughter of Thomas
Spring Rice, later Lord Monteagle (who came to the Colonial Office in 1834),
and became intimate with her cousin Aubrey de Vere. W. W.'s friend Isabella
Fenwick was his step-cousin. He was knighted in 1852. On 29 Nov. 1823,
Taylor had written to W. W. that he was contributing to the *London Magazine*
a paper on 'Recent Poetical Plagiarisms', and asking him what he had noted in
Byron as borrowed from him (*WL MSS.*). Taylor enclosed examples of Gray's
debts to Catullus, Lucan, Seneca, Le Moyne, and Pope's *Rape of the Lock*.

in winter than in the Summer Season, I am obliged mostly to employ an Amanuensis, as I do at present. I should not, however, have failed to answer your obliging letter immediately, if I could have been of any service to you in the point to which you directed my attention I have not, nor ever had, a single poem of Lord Byron's by me, except the Lara, given me by Mr Rogers, and therefore could not quote any thing illustrative of his poetical obligations to me: as far as I am acquainted with his works, they are most apparent in the 3rd canto of Childe Harold; not so much in particular expressions, tho' there is no want of these, as in the tone (*assumed* rather than natural) of enthusiastic admiration of Nature, and a sensibility to her influences. Of my writings you need not read more than the blank verse poem on the river Wye to be convinced of this. Mrs W. tells me that in reading one of Lord B.'s poems of which the story was offensive she was much disgusted with the plagiarisms from Mr Coleridge—at least she *thinks* it was in that poem, but as she read the Siege of Corinth in the same volume, it might possibly be in that. If I am not mistaken there was some acknowledgment to Mr C. which takes very much from the reprehensibility of literary trespasses of this kind. Nothing lowered my opinion of Byron's poetical integrity so much as to see 'pride of place' carefully noted as a quotation from Macbeth, in a work where contemporaries, from whom he had drawn by wholesale, were not adverted to. It is mainly on this account that he deserves the severe chastisement which you, or some one else, will undoubtedly one day give him: and may have done already, as I see by advertisement the Subject has been treated in the London Mag.

I remember one impudent instance of his thefts. In Raymond's translation of Coxe's travels in Switzerland,[1] with notes of the translator, is a note with these words, speaking of the fall of Schaffhausen: 'Lewy, descendant avec moi sur cet échaffaud, tomba à genoux en s'écriant: *Voilà un enfer d'eau!*' This expression is taken by Byron and beaten out unmercifully into two stanzas, which a critic in the Quarterly Review is foolish enough to praise. They are found in the 4th Can: of Childe Harold.[2] Whether the obligation is acknowledged or not I do not know, having seen nothing of it, but in quotation.

Thank you for your parallels; I wished for them on Mr Rogers'

[1] See *EY*, p. 235 and Moorman, i. 198–9.
[2] In *Childe Harold* (iv. 69) Byron describes the falls of Terni, not those of Schaffhausen, as 'the hell of waters': it is possible, moreover, that in this he was influenced not by Ramond, but by Addison's *Remarks on several parts of Italy*— see *Poems of Byron*, ed. E. H. Coleridge, ii. 383. (De Selincourt's note.)

account, who is making a collection of similar things relating to
Gray. There are few of yours, I think, which one could swear to as
conscious obligations—the subject has three branches—accidental
coincidences without any communication of the subsequent Author;
unconscious imitations; and deliberate conscious obligations. The
cases are numerous in which it is impossible to distinguish these by
any thing inherent in the resembling passage, but external aid may
be called in with advantage where we happen to know the circumstances of an Author's life, and the direction of his Studies. Do not
suffer my present remissness to prevent you favouring me with a
letter if there is the least chance of my being of Service to you.
I shall reply immediately if I have any thing to say worthy your
attention. With best wishes from myself and family, I remain,
dear sir,

very sincerely yours,
[*signed*] Wm Wordsworth.

[*W. W. writes*]

When you write to your Father,[1] be so good as to make my
respectful remembrances to him.

121. D. W. to MARY LAING

MS. Edinburgh University Library.
The Wordsworth–Laing Letters (—).

December 28th [1823]

My dear Miss Laing,

As you will see by the date, the enclosed[2] was written some time
ago: my Friend did not go to Edinburgh; the letter was not worth
postage, and I kept my package for another opportunity. Before
entering on other matters I must talk of business. If you write in
a few days after the receipt of this, and send your letter to M^r
Wallace (taking care to fold it in small compass so as to fit the
little Box in which I send this along with my teeth,—wanting

---

[1] George Taylor (1772–1851), of Witton-le-Wear, was brought up in
Durham and Sunderland. He wrote occasionally for the *Quarterly Review* on
literature and political economy, and was secretary to the commission of
inquiry into the poor laws, 1832–4. He wrote the memoir of Robert Surtees,
prefixed to vol. iv of his *History of Durham*, 1840. He was 'a most remarkable
person for strength of character, as well as for intellectual powers,' according
to Southey, 'the sort of person with whom Cato might shake hands, for he has
the better parts of an antique Roman about him'. (*Correspondence of Robert
Southey with Caroline Bowles*, 1881, p. 93.)   [2] i.e. L. 117.

repair) Mr W. will forward it to Carlisle, as I shall direct, whence Miss Dowling, who is spending a part of the holidays there, will bring it to me. The Box is conveyed to Edinburgh by Col. Campbell's servant. You may remember to have seen the Colonel's house (formerly Mr Crump's) at Grasmere. He, with his Family, is going to pass the winter at E.—(No. 8 Abercrombie Place.) You must not fail to let me know, in your next, what I am indebted to you for the Caps etc., as Mrs Campbell has kindly promised to discharge that debt for me, and also to pay Mr Wallace what I shall owe him after the necessary repairs are made.

Your kind and pleasant letter ought to have had a speedier answer; and I think if I had not written the worthless one which I now enclose, you would have heard from me ere this; but having written that little letter, I was loth wholly to waste it, and looking forward to an opportunity (earlier than the present, which failed me) I determined to wait for it.

The best news I now have for you is that my Brother's eyes have continued to be in their very best way since the enclosed was written, though he has been constantly busy, which usually of late years has brought on the inflammation. Your Friend Willy continues stout and well, and improves as much in scholarship as can be expected (while under this indulgent roof) of one so lively and volatile as he is. There is now good ground to hope that he may be trusted from home in course of time, to some place where more will be exacted from him, and where he may be under stricter discipline than it is in Mr Coleridge's power to exercise. At present, however, we think that what is going on is very well, and his constitution is evidently strengthening. John is at home for the holidays—much improved—and his health re-established—but again we have lost the company of his Sister. She left us on Saturday the 19th, accompanied to London by Miss Jane Dowling.[1] She will remain in Gloster Place till after New-year's-day, and then will go to Hendon (near Hampstead) to remain there till March or April when she will return to her Friends in Gloster place and will then have an opportunity of seeing London at leisure, and at the pleasantest season of the year. Her going was very sudden—a most pressing invitation came:[2] at the same time a Companion was ready, and the opportunity could not be resisted, though we (and especially her Father to whom she is very useful) were loth to part with her; and she herself unwilling to leave home again so soon after her long

[1] Jane Martha Dowling (1795–1851).
[2] Probably from the Misses Lockier.

absences at Harrowgate, and at Miss Dowling's; however, when it *was to be* she got up her spirits, and anticipated much pleasure—yet what she *most* thought of was the meeting her Aunt Sarah (Miss Hutchinson) and her Friend Miss Southey, who happens now to be staying in Gloster Place, and is to accompany Doro to Hendon. So much for my Niece's travels, which, by the bye, will be crowned by a visit to Oxford and Cambridge. I must now speak of my own—which indeed may probably end in a journey by way of Liverpool to the neighbourhood of Ashby de la Zouche in Leicestershire—a month's stay there, and a direct return to Rydal by way of Liverpool. My Brother talks of setting off in the middle of February to spend a month with our Friends Sir George and Lady Beaumont; and I am to accompany him. Perhaps we may go to Cambridge, and if to Cambridge probably to London for two or three weeks—but all this is uncertain. No plans are laid beyond the visit to Coleorton (Sir George Beaumont's residence.) My Sister will remain at home with her Son William. You will be surprized to hear that Miss Dowling[1] is to be married in the Spring. I know not whether you saw Mr Carr when you were here—or heard us speak of him. He is our Surgeon and Apothecary: very clever in his profession, and an amiable and very worthy Man. He will besides have a handsome independent fortune in the course of a few years. Her Sisters[2] will then be at the head of the school; but she will not withdraw her superintendence. They are admirably qualified to conduct the Establishment, and I trust it will in no degree suffer in reputation from the change. Miss Eliza Dowling is with us for the Christmas holidays. I am sure you will be glad to hear that she is now in perfect health, and even stronger than before her late tedious and dangerous illness.

We heard not long ago from Miss E. Crump. She wrote in good spirits. I shall of course see her at Liverpool. I hope, my dear Miss Laing, that you will be able to give a good account of yourself. It gave me most sincere concern to hear of your illness, but, as you were recovered when you wrote, I trust that, using the precautions recommended, you have now wholly regained your strength. I am quite well; but have been comparatively a prisoner since writing the enclosed, having had a very troublesome cough. I wish you could see this place in *winter*; for (in comparison with others—) it is far more beautiful at that season then even in Summer. Whenever the sun shines in a morning we have it glittering upon the Lake—and

[1] i.e. Ann Dowling, the eldest of the sisters. See L. 66 above.
[2] i.e. Elizabeth, Mary, and Jane Dowling.

are at all times sheltered from Storms. I have enjoyed the situation this winter perhaps the more, from not having been allowed to trudge along the roads. My walks have therefore been confined to the Garden and Terrace. My Brother begs particular regards to Mʳ David Laing. I hope your Father, Mother, and all the Family are well. Remember me to all—not forgetting James.[1]

Good tidings from Wales of Miss Joanna Hutchinson's health. Forgive this scrawl and believe me, dear Miss Laing, affectionately your Friend,

D Wordsworth

If you cannot write with the little Box—pray do not fail a letter by post very soon.

122. D. W. to EDWARD QUILLINAN

Address: Edward Quillinan Esqʳᵉ, Lee Priory, Wingham, Kent. [*Readdressed to*] 14 Fludyer Street, Westminster, London.
Postmark: (1) 10 Feb. 1824. (2) 12 Feb. 1824. *Stamp*: (1) Kendal Penny Post. (2) Canterbury. *Endorsed*: 1824. Miss Wordsworth. Rydal Janʳʸ 7.
MS. WL.
LY i. 131 (—).

Rydal Mount 7ᵗʰ Janʳʸ 1824

My dear Friend,

On the other side of the paper you will find our present *final* accounts—not very neatly drawn out, it must be confessed: but I hope sufficiently plain for your satisfaction. The Bills etc are all safe, and when you come to Rydal you shall have them to keep, or burn. You will say this is a shabby way of setting about writing a letter after so long a silence, a few lines scrawled at the fag end of pounds shillings and pence; but in truth I am much hurried, and should not have written at all at this time but for the sake of casting Business off my mind. My Brother and I are going to Coleorton next week, and as I shall set off on Monday I am now in the last bustle of preparation. He will join me at Kendal on Tuesday Evening, and on Wednesday we take the coach for Preston, where we shall halt one day at Mr Horrock's[2]—another day at Liverpool with the Crumps,[3] and hope to be with Sir George and Lady Beaumont on Saturday. Our further movements are all uncertain.

---

[1] For Mary's brother James Laing, see L. 105 above.
[2] At Lark Hill, outside Preston.
[3] At their house in Queen Anne St.

My Brother *has* talked of our going to Cambridge after three weeks or a month spent at Coleorton, and if so I think (though he does not talk of *that*) we should take a peep at London rather than come home direct from Cambridge. Miss Hutchinson writes in good spirits. She wants us to turn aside into Wales, and it is not impossible that we may, but there are so many reasons both for and against that plan (i.e. Wales) at this particular time that I do not like to think of it—or any other till our visit to Coleorton draws near its close, when my Brother will have made up his mind either for some deviation or for our return straight home. Mrs **W**. will certainly visit Wales this summer. And I—if not now—in the course of another year. She tells us you talk of going thither also.

My Brother's eyes have been much better this winter, though he has worked very hard. It has not been Doro's fault that the transcript of the 'Nightingale'[1] was not finished before she left home, and no doubt she has explained to you how it happened. We have had charming weather on the whole this winter—a greater number of bright days than I recollect ever noticing at this season, except with hard frost. The frost has been very slight,—no skaiting—and snow in the vallies but once. Every winter has confirmed our opinion that Rydal Mount, as a residence, surpasses all other places at that time—and I feel the truth of this now more than ever, and am very sorry that our going away does not happen six weeks or two months later. Pray give our kind remembrances to Captain Barrett, and when you give love and kisses from Mrs Wordsworth to your dear little Girls, add the same from me, and try if Jemima remembers me. Poor Doro, how glad she will be to see Jemima when you take her to London in the Spring, as D. tells me you have promised.

This letter does not deserve an answer, but I will venture to say that if you would write to me at Sir G. Beaumont's, Coleorton Hall, near Ashby de la Zouche it would give me great pleasure.

My Brother and Sister send kind remembrances. Believe me ever your faithful and affec^te Friend,

D. Wordsworth.

If we *should* go to London I take it for certain that you will either be there or come to meet us, and I need not say how glad I should be to see you there, or anywhere.

Pray do not let the quest of a frank shorten your letter, or the not being able to procure one prevent your writing—and remember, we shall be at Coleorton this day week—Saturday.

---

[1] E. Q.'s poem, mentioned in L. 135 below. See also *SH*, pp. 276–7.

7 *January 1824*

[Accounts follow on last two pages of the sheet]

I was going to write to you this morning to enclose a Bill for the above amount (16 £–18ˢ–5ᵈ) intending to pay for the putting up the monument[1] (which I am sorry to say is not yet arrived) from the overplus of Mr Elliott's Rent, but a letter just received from Miss Hutchinson informs us that henceforward you have nothing to do with the Rent, but have given it up to Mr Tillbrooke. I shall therefore not send the Bill; but when those expences are defrayed will then remit you the final Balance. Here I will just observe that I think (and my Sister agrees with me) that you ought not to have parted with your right till after next May-day, the Rents already received not having defrayed all Charges. I said something to this effect when I wrote to Mr Tillbrooke some time ago; but it is done and therefore the matter must rest as it is. No doubt *his* steward leans to him and, of course, I as *yours* lean to you.

123. W. W. to WALTER SAVAGE LANDOR

Address: W. S. Landor Esqʳᵉ, Florence, Italy.
Postmark: 29 Jan. 1824.
MS. Victoria and Albert Museum.
K (—). *LY i. 133.*

[In M. W.'s hand]

Rydal Mount, Janʳʸ 21, 1824

My dear Sir,

I am both tired and ashamed of waiting any longer: many months have I looked for your dialogues[2] and they never appear; the expectation of the book prevented my answering your former letter in which were mentioned some unpleasant topics relating to your own feelings;—as you do not advert to these in your second letter, recᵈ about a fortnight ago,[3] I trust the storm is blown over. I am

---

[1] The memorial to Mrs. Quillinan.

[2] For the delay in the publication of the *Imaginary Conversations*, which Landor had entrusted to Julius Hare, see Super, *Walter Savage Landor*, pp. 158 ff. The first volume finally appeared in Mar. 1824.

[3] i.e. Landor's letter of 24 Nov. 1823. His earlier letter of 8 Sept. 1822 had referred to an acrimonious dispute he was having with the English diplomatic colony in Florence: 'Since I wrote last to you, an occurrence has taken place, which has altered the tendency of my Dialogues, increased their number, and planted rue where there were roses. Delicacy towards you will not permitt me to inscribe them with your name. Resentment has lighted up a fire which has cracked the column on which my glory was to have been erected. I have received first insult, and afterwards injustice and contempt from people in power.'

truly sensible of your kindness, as testified by the agreeable, and allow me to say valuable present of Books from your hand, but you will be mortified to hear as I was bitterly vexed, that some of them have been entirely spoilt by the salt water; and scarcely one has escaped injury. The two Volumes of de Re rustica[1] in particular which I did not possess and had often wished to consult, are sorely damaged—the binding detached from the book, the leaves stained, and I fear rotted:—the venerable Bible is in the same state—indeed all to pieces. These are such unpleasant facts that I doubt whether I ought not to have suppressed them.

You promise me a beautiful Copy of Dante, but I ought to mention that I possess the Parma folio of 1795,—much the *grandest* book on my shelves,—presented to me by our common friend, Mr Kenyon (who, by the bye, is happily married since I last wrote to you and has taken up his residence at Bath.)

When at Mr Southey's last summer, my eyes being then in a very bad state, he read me part of that dialogue of yours, in which he is introduced as a speaker with Porson. It had appeared (something I must say to my regret) in a Magazine,[2] and I should have had the pleasure to hear the whole, but we were interrupted. I made out part of the remainder myself. You have condescended to minute criticism upon the Laodamia.[3] I concur with you in the first stanza, and had several times attempted to alter it upon your grounds. I cannot, however, accede to your objection to the 'second birth', merely because the expression has been degraded by Conventiclers. I certainly meant nothing more by it than the *eadem cura*, and the *largior œther*, etc., of Virgil's 6th Æneid. All religions owe their origin or acceptation to the wish of the human heart to supply in another state of existence the deficiencies of this, and to carry still nearer to perfection whatever we admire in our present condition; so that there must be many modes of expression, arising out of this coincidence, or rather identity of feeling, common to all Mythologies; and under this observation I should shelter the phrase from your censure; but I may be wrong in the particular case, though certainly not in the general principle. This leads to a remark in your last, 'that you are disgusted with all books that treat of

[1] See *R.M. Cat.*, no. 361.
[2] 'Southey and Porson', which included some discussion of W. W.'s poetry, appeared in the *London Magazine* for July 1823, by arrangement with Hare, to give the reading public a preview of what the forthcoming volume would contain. '... in a Conversation', Landor wrote, '... I could say more than a dedication would have permitted; and I have added weight to what is said by attributing it to Southey, the vanquisher (as he should be) of Porson.'
[3] *PW* ii. 267.

religion.'[1] I am afraid it is a bad sign in me, that I have little relish for any other—even in poetry it is the imaginative only, viz., that which is conversant [with], or turns upon infinity, that powerfully affects me,—perhaps I ought to explain: I mean to say that, unless in those passages where things are lost in each other, and limits vanish, and aspirations are raised, I read with something too much like indifference—but all great poets are in this view powerful Religionists, and therefore among many literary pleasures lost, I have not yet to lament over that of verse as departed. As to politics, what do you say to Buonaparte on the one side, and the Holy Alliance on the other, to the prostrate Tories, and to the contumelious and vacillating Whigs, who dislike or despise the Church, and seem to care for the State only so far as they are striving,—without hope, I honestly believe,—to get the management of it? As to the low-bred and headstrong Radicals, they are not worth a thought. Now my politics used always to impel me more or less to look out for co-operation, with a view to embody them in action—of this interest I feel myself utterly deprived, and the subject, as matter of reflection, languishes accordingly. Cool heads, no doubt, there are in the country, but moderation naturally keeps out of sight; and, wanting associates, I am less of an Englishman than I once was, or could wish to be. Show me that you excuse this egotism, if you can excuse it, by turning into the same path, when I have the pleasure again to hear from you.

It would probably be wasting paper to mention Southey, as no doubt you hear from him. I saw Mrs S. and 4 of his Children the other day; 2 of the girls most beautiful Creatures. The eldest Daughter is with her Father in town. S. preserves excellent health, and, except that his hair is gryzzled, a juvenile appearance, with more of youthful spirits than most men. He appears to be accumulating books in a way that, with my weak eyes, appalls me. A large box of them has just strayed into my house through a blunder in the conveyance.

Pray be so good as to let me know what you think of Dante—it has become lately—owing a good deal, I believe, to the example of Schlegel[2]—the fashion to extol him above measure. I have not read him for many years; his style I used to think admirable for

---

[1] 'I am disgusted at all things treating of religion', Landor had written in his second letter, describing the books he was sending W. W., 'but Savonarola and Molinos are two such rich weeds that they are well worth climing the dung-hill for.'

[2] August Wilhelm von Schlegel (1767–1845), the great German critic and scholar, whom W. W. met at Bonn during his continental tour of 1828.

conciseness and vigour, without abruptness; but I own that his fictions often struck me as offensively grotesque and fantastic, and I felt the Poem tedious from various causes.

I have a strong desire to become acquainted with the Mr Hare[1] whom you mention.—To the honour of Cambridge he is in the highest repute there, for his sound and extensive learning. I am happy to say that the Master of Trinity Coll. (my brother) was the occasion of his being restored to the Muses from the Temple. To Mr H's Br, Augustus, I am under great obligation for having *volunteered* the Tuition of my elder Son, who is at New Coll. Oxford, and who, though he is not a youth of quick parts, promises, from his assiduity and passionate love of Classical literature, to become an excellent Scholar. By the bye he seems very proud of your Idylls and the accompanying Elegy,[2] as an honour to modern times. Farewell—be so kind as write soon, and believe me, ever sincerely and aff^ly. yours,

[*signed*] Wm Wordsworth

124. W. W. to LORD LONSDALE

MS. Lonsdale MSS.
K (—). *LY i. 161* (—).

Rydal Mount
23rd Jan^ry 1824

My Lord,

I am quite ashamed of being so long in fulfilling my engagement. But the promises of Poets are like the Perjuries of Lovers, things at which Jove laughs. At last, however, I have sent off the two first books of my Translations,[3] to be forwarded by Mr Beckett. I hope

---

[1] The Revd. Julius Charles Hare (1795–1855), broad-churchman, disciple of Coleridge, and one of the profoundest Germanists of his generation, had been elected a Fellow of Trinity College, Cambridge, in 1818, but left for the Temple a year later to study law. In 1822 he returned to a Classical lectureship at Trinity, and was ordained in 1826. He translated (with Thirlwall) Niebuhr's *History of Rome* (2 vols., 1828–32), and joined his brother Augustus (see L. 94) in *Guesses at Truth*. In 1832 he took the family living of Hurstmonceaux, Sussex, where John Sterling was his curate, and Bunsen a resident; and in 1844 he married the sister of his former pupil F. D. Maurice. He published numerous sermons and his *Charges* as Archdeacon of Lewes. At this time Landor knew him through his brothers Francis and Augustus, whom he had met in Italy: W. W. seems to have met Julius Hare for the first time later this year while staying in Cambridge.
[2] See L. 39 above.   [3] Of Virgil's *Aeneid*.

they will be read by your Lordship with some pleasure, as having caused me a good deal of pains. Translation is just as to labour what the person who makes the attempt is inclined to. If he wishes to preserve as much of the original as possible, and *that* with as little addition of his own as may be, there is no species of composition that costs more pains. A literal Translation of an antient Poet in verse, and particularly in rhyme, is *impossible*; something must be left out and something added; I have done my best to avoid the one and the other fault. I ought to say a prefatory word about the versification, which will not be found much to the taste of those whose ear is exclusively accommodated to the regularity of Pope's Homer. I have run the couplets freely into each other, much more even than Dryden has done. This variety seems to me to be called for, if any thing of the movement of the Vergilian versification be transferable to our rhyme[d] Poetry; and independent of this consideration, long narratives in couplets with the sense closed at the end of each, are to me very wearisome. I should be grateful for any communication of your Lordship's feelings on these parts of my labour, or any other.

I have had a piece of good luck in the Stamp Off: the other day; particularly acceptable after the loss of the Custom House Stamps at Whitehaven. Mr Thompson[1] Lord Egremont's[2] Agent at Cockermouth paid into my office upwards of £4,000 duty upon the personal Estate of his late Uncle Mr Allan Pearson of Bridekirk; this large sum would have been paid directly to the office in London, without passing through my hands, if it had not been for strenuous exertions on my part. Mr Thompson seems heartily sick of his Whig Gentry connections about Cockermouth.

I have deferred to the conclusion my congratulations upon your Lordship's escape with no severe injury, bad as it was, from your late accident. These misadventures are nearer to my feelings than it would become me to express.

Since I last wrote to your Lordship, we received a second present of game from Lowther, for which though late, accept our best thanks; ever most sincerely and faithfully your Lordship's

W Wordsworth

[1] Henry Teshmaker Thompson (d. 1855) of Bridekirk, nr. Cockermouth: a relative of Andrew Green (see *MY* ii. 590), whose son succeeded to his property.
[2] George O'Brien Wyndham, 3rd Earl of Egremont (1751–1837), of Cockermouth Castle, and Petworth House, Sussex.

125. W. W. to JAMES MONTGOMERY[1]

Address: To James Montgomery Esq, Sheffield.
Stamp: Kendal Penny Post.
MS. Yale University Library.
K (—). *LY i. 136* (—).[2]

Rydal Mount
Jan^{ry} 24th 1824

Dear Sir,

I am truly sorry that the benevolent society[3] with which you are connected should have been at the trouble of addressing themselves to me, to write something in behalf of the poor Chimney-boys. I feel much for their unhappy situation, and should be glad to see the custom of employing such helpless creatures in this way abolished.—But at no period of my life have I been able to write verses that do not spring up from an inward impulse of some sort or other; so that they neither seem proposed nor imposed. Therefore I have no hope of meeting either the wishes of the Society or my own on this humane occasion.—If you are in communication with them may I beg you to mention my regret, accompanied with my earnest desires that their endeavour may prove successful.

I am dear Sir
with great respect
very sincerely yours
Wm Wordsworth

I should have written sooner, but it was possible that I might have fallen into a track that would have led to something.

---

[1] James Montgomery (1771–1854), Scottish poet and philanthropist, author of *The Ocean* (1805), *Wanderer of Switzerland* (1806), *World before the Flood* (1812), *Pelican Island* (1826), and other volumes, a frequent contributor to the *Eclectic Review*, and editor of the *Sheffield Iris*, 1795–1825. In 1824 he was engaged in editing *The Chimney Sweepers' Friend and Climbing Boys' Album*, with the object of rousing public opinion to insist on legislation to render illegal the practice of sending boys up chimneys. Montgomery applied to many poets of the day to contribute to his volume. Barton and Bowles, among others, complied: Lamb sent 'The Chimney Sweeper' from Blake's *Songs of Innocence* (see *Lamb*, ii. 425–7).

[2] Part of this letter is also quoted by John Holland and James Everett, *Memoirs of the Life and Writings of James Montgomery*, 7 vols., 1854–6.

[3] The Society for Ameliorating the Condition of Infant Chimney-Sweepers. Sydney Smith had put in a humane plea for its objectives in the *Edinburgh Review* for 1819.

126. W. W. to ALLAN CUNNINGHAM

Address: A. Cunningham Esqre, F. Chantrey's Esq, Pimlico.
Postmark: 4 Feb. 1824. *Stamp*: Lombard St.
MS. Mr. W. Hugh Peal. Hitherto unpublished.

[*In M. W.'s hand*]

> Rydal Mount
> Feb^ry 1st [1824]

My dear Sir,

Some time ago, in answer to my requesting two Casts of my Bust to be prepared for two friends, you told me that they should be sent in a short time. As one of the parties at least, has not received that intended for him, I trouble you with this, lest the circumstance, in your press of more important engagements, may have escaped your memory, and beg to repeat that I will be obliged to you as soon as convenient to forward one cast to Edward Coleridge[1] Esq Eton, and another to A. Hare Esqr New Coll Oxford—for this last mentioned, as well as for the Carriage of it, which I must request you to be so obliging as pay for me, I shall desire my daughter (who is in the neighbourhood of London, and will be in Town in Spring) to call upon you and discharge the debt. With many thanks for various attentions, believe me dear Sir very sincerely yours

> W Wordsworth[2]

My kind regards to Mr and Mrs Chantry who I trust are better than when I last heard from you.

Mr Quillinan some time ago mentioned that a Monument[3] would shortly be sent to Grasmere from your Warehouse. I take this occasion to say that it has not arrived.

---

[1] The Revd. Edward Coleridge (1800–83), S. T. C.'s nephew, youngest son of Col. James Coleridge of Ottery St. Mary: Fellow of Exeter College, Oxford, 1823–6; master at Eton, 1824–50, and Fellow (1857); rector of Mapledurham, Oxon., from 1862. He had been a welcome guest at Rydal Mount in Aug. 1822, and wrote to W. W. on 30 Jan. 1823; 'I must tell you all with a frankness, which you will perchance all laugh at, that I think you as good and entertaining sort of people, as it ever was my lot to fall in with. . . .' (*WL MSS.*)

[2] Not apparently signed by W. W.

[3] The memorial tablet to Mrs. Quillinan. See L. 74 above.

127. W. W. to LORD LONSDALE

MS. *Lonsdale MSS.*
Mem. (—). *K* (—). *The Middle Years* (1937) (—).[1]

Febry 5th [1824]

My Lord,

I am truly obliged by your friendly and frank communication. May I beg that you would add to the favor, by marking with a pencil, some of the passages that are faulty in your view of the case. We seem pretty much of opinion upon the subject of rhyme. Pentameters, where the sense has a close, of some sort, at every two lines, may be rendered in regularly closed couplets; but Hexameters (especially the Virgilian, that run the lines into each other for a great length) cannot. I have long been persuaded that Milton formed his blank verse upon the model of the Georgics and the Aeneid, and I am so much struck with this resemblance, that I should have attempted Virgil in blank verse; had I not been persuaded, that no antient Author can be with advantage so rendered. Their religion, their warfare, their course of action and feeling, are too remote from modern interest to allow it. We require every possible help and attraction of sound in our language to smooth the way for the admission of things so remote from our present concerns. My own notion of translation is, that it cannot be too literal, provided three faults be avoided, *baldness,* in which I include all that takes from dignity; and *strangeness* or *uncouthness* including harshness; and lastly, attempts to convey meanings which as they cannot be given but by languid circumlocutions cannot be said to be given at all. I will trouble you with an instance in which I fear this fault exists. Virgil, describing Aeneas's voyage, Third Book, Verse 451,[2] says

> Hinc sinus Herculei, si vera est fama, Tarenti
> Cernitur.

I render it thus,

> Hence we behold the bay that bears the name
> Of proud Tarentum, proud to share the fame
> Of Hercules, though by a dubious claim.[3]

I was unable to get the meaning with tolerable harmony into fewer words, which are more than to a modern reader perhaps it is worth.

---

[1] Printed by de Selincourt under the year 1819.
[2] Actually l. 551.
[3] See *PW* iv. 354 for the final version of these lines.

5 February 1824

I feel much at a loss without the assistance of the marks which I have requested, to take an exact measure of your Lordship's feeling with regard to the Diction. To save you the trouble of reference I will transcribe two passages from Dryden, first, from the celebrated appearance of Hector's Ghost to Aeneas. Aeneas thus addresses him.

> O Light of Trojans and support of Troy
> Thy Father's Champion, and the Country's joy,
> O long expected by thy friends, from whence
> Art thou returned so late for our defence
> Do we behold thee wearied as we are
> With length of labours, and with toils of war,
> After so many funerals of thy own
> Art thou restored to thy declining Town?[1]

This I think not an unfavorable specimen of Dryden's way of treating the solemnly pathetic passages. Yet surely here is *nothing* of the *cadence* of the original, and little of its spirit. The second verse is not in the original, and ought not to have been in Dryden, for it anticipates the beautiful Hemistich; Sat patriae Priamoque datum; bye the bye there is the same sort of anticipation in a spirited and harmonious Couplet preceding,

> Such as he was when by *Pelides slain*
> Thessalian Courses dragg'd him o'er the plain.[2]

This introduction of Pelides here is not in Virgil, because it would have prevented the effect of 'redit exuvias indutus Achillei.'

There is a striking solemnity in the answer of Pantheus to Aeneas.

> Venit summa dies et ineluctabile Tempus
> Dardanneae, fuimus Troes, fuit Ilium et Ingens
> Gloria Teucrorum etc.[3]

Dryden thus gave it

> Then Pantheus with a groan,
> Troy is no more, and Ilium was a Town,
> The fatal day, the appointed hour is come
> When wrathful Jove's irrevocable doom
> Transfers the Trojan state to Grecian hands,
> The fire consumes the Town the foe commands.[4]

---

[1] Dryden's *Aeneid*, ii. 367–74.   [2] Ibid. ii. 354–5.
[3] *Aen*. ii. 324–6.   [4] Dryden's *Aeneid*, ii. 435–40.

251

My own Translation runs thus, and I quote it because it occurred to my mind immediately on reading your Lordship's observations.—

> Tis come the final hour
> The inevitable close of Dardan power
> Hath come; we *have been* Trojans, Ilium *was*
> And the great name of Troy; now all things pass
> To Argos. So wills angry Jupiter
> Amid a burning Town the Grecians domineer.[1]

I cannot say that we *have been*, and Ilium *was* are as sonorous words as 'fuimus' and 'fuit'—but these latter must have been as familiar to the Romans as the former to ourselves. I should much like to know if your Lordship disapproves of my Translation here.

I have one word to say upon ornament. It was my wish and labour that my Translation should have far more of the *genuine* ornaments of Virgil than my predecessors. Dryden has been very careless of these, and profuse of his own, which seem to me very rarely to harmonize with those of Virgil. As for example, Describing Hector's appearance in the passage above alluded to,

> A *bloody shroud* he seemed, and *bathed* in tears.
> I wept to see the visionary man,[2]

again

> And all the wounds he for his country bore
> Now streamed afresh, and with *new purple ran*.[3]

I feel it however to be too probable, that my Translation is deficient in ornament, because I must unavoidably have lost many of Virgil's, and have never without reluctance attempted a compensation of my own. Had I taken the liberties of my Predecessors, Dryden especially, I could have translated nine books with the labour that three have cost me. The third Book being of a humbler Character than either of the former, I have treated with some less scrupulous apprehension, and have interwoven a little of my own; and with permission I will send it erelong for the benefit of your Lordship's observations, which really will be of great service to me if I proceed. Had I begun the work 15 years ago I should have finished it with pleasure—at present, I fear, it will take more time than I either can or ought to spare. I do not think of going beyond the 4th Book.

As to the MS, be so kind as to forward it at your leisure, to me at

---

[1] See *PW* iv. 321.
[2] Dryden's *Aeneid*, ii. 353, 365.   [3] Ibid. ii. 363–4.

Sir George Beaumont's, Coleorton Hall, near Ashby; whither I
am going in about ten days. May I trouble your Lordship with our
respectful compliments to Lady Lonsdale

and believe me
Your Lordship's faithful
and obliged friend and Ser^{nt}
Wm Wordsworth

128. W. W. to LORD LONSDALE

MS. Lonsdale MSS.
K (—). *The Middle Years* (*1937*) (—).[1]

Coleorton Hall
near Ashby de la Zouche
17th Febry [1824]

My Lord,
  Your Lordship's very obliging Letter reached me this morning,
having been forwarded from Rydal Mount. I am sorry to have
given you so much trouble, but I attach so much importance to
your Lordship's judgment, that I was anxious for a clear understanding which could scarcely be effected without a few *particulars*.
May I hope to be favored with these if I have the pleasure of seeing
you in the course of next summer. Five minutes will do more than
hours of Letter-writing.
  I began my translation by accident; I continued it with a hope to
produce a work which should be to a certain degree *affecting*, which
Dryden's is not to me in the least. Dr Johnson has justly remarked that Dryden had little talent for the Pathetic, and the
tenderness of Virgil seems to me to escape him. Virgil's style is an
inimitable mixture of the elaborately ornate, and the majestically
plain and touching. The former quality is much more difficult to
reach than the latter, in which whoever fails must fail through
want of ability, and not through the imperfections of our language.
  In my last I troubled you with a quotation from my own translation in which I feared a failure; 'fuimus Troes,' etc., 'we have
been Trojans' etc.: It struck me afterwards that I might have
found still stronger instances. At the close of the 1st Book Dido
is described as asking several questions of Aeneas,

Nunc, quales Diomedis equi, nunc quantus Achilles—[2]

---

[1] Printed by de Selincourt under the year 1819.
[2] *Aen.* i. 752.

which Dryden translates, (very meanly I think) thus 'The Steeds of Diomede varied the discourse', etc.: My own Translation is probably as faulty upon another principle,

> Of Hector asked—of Priam o'er and o'er—
> What arms the Son of bright Aurora wore,
> *What Horses those of Diomed; how great*
> *Achilles—but o queen the whole relate.*[1]

These two lines will be deemed, I apprehend, harsh and bald. So true is Horace's remark 'in vitium ducit culpae fuga' etc.

With many thanks and I hope to be excused for being so troublesome, I remain,

my Lord
your faithful and obliged Serv[nt]
Wm Wordsworth

Sir George and Lady B. are quite well and beg best Compl[ts] and wishes. I received the MSS through Mr Beckett. Mrs Wordsworth is much obliged by your Lordship's kind offer to frank her Letters—I now take the liberty of enclosing one to my Son for that purpose.

129. D. W. to MRS. LUFF

Address: Mrs Luff, 13 Bruton St, Berkeley Square.[2]
MS. British Museum.
LY i. 136.

Thursday 4th March [1824]

My dear Friend.

You have no doubt heard from Mr Monkhouse of our wish to go to London, and I may now say it is our *intention* so to do, provided my Brother continues well in health; but the state of his eyes has long been so uncertain that he always feels obliged to put in an 'if' to every scheme of this kind. We shall leave this place[3] on Wednesday the 17th and unless you hear from us to the contrary you may conclude that we bend our course to Oxford, where we shall arrive on Thursday. Perhaps my Brother may remain there a few days, in which case I shall certainly precede him to London—probably on the Saturday. I shall however

---

[1] See *PW* iv. 310 for the final version of these lines.
[2] The residence of Sir Robert Farquhar (see L. 131 below), with whom Mrs. Luff was staying.   [3] Coleorton.

write again to Mr Monkhouse from Oxford or Birmingham. I have had a letter to-day from Mrs Clarkson who is anxious to hear from you. She says she hopes to be in London in May, and to carry you back to Playford. Now I suppose you will not defer your visit so long; but will wish to go thither when (or *before*) we go to Cambridge. Now I, (when so near as Cambridge) shall feel a very strong desire to join you there—indeed it would be unkind to Mrs Clarkson, and inconsistent with our long friendship if I did not—and to this I have only one objection, that I do not like the thought of parting with William to send him home alone after he has taken me with him so long a Round; that objection, however, I shall set aside, and if all be well I shall most likely go from Cambridge to Playford, and you and I can travel Northward together, staying as far into the month of May as suits our good Friends at P. I shall not write to Mrs Clarkson till I have seen you, and when you write, pray, with my kind Love tell her I am indulging the hope of seeing her at P. She desires, if there be any chance, that I will inform her, in order that she may not be visiting any of her relations at the time. As we hope to meet so soon I need not say more. God grant that we may find you in tolerable health and good spirits!
Believe me ever your affect^e Friend   D. Wordsworth.

We shall probably stay a fortnight or three weeks in London. Say the latter which would make it the middle of April before we go to Cambridge, and alas that would leave little time for Playford—but I hope Mrs C may not go till the *end* of May— You might tell her, however, when we are likely to be at liberty, and she must tell me whether I shall be too late for her or not— but there is no need to write to me about it *here*. *All* will be plain when we talk together in London. Our stay in Cambridge will not I think be *more* than a fortnight—perhaps not so much.

Friday morning.
It occurs to me that as you are good at procuring franks you might send this letter to Mrs Clarkson,[1] which would save you the trouble of reporting. With this view, I say for her information, that I have sent word to Mary W. how to dispose of the Books, and that when I write to her from London my Br will reply to Mr Clarkson's kind communication respecting the Slave-

---

[1] This letter was in fact sent on to Mrs. Clarkson, and is now preserved among the Clarkson Papers.

trade. We congratulate him on the picture[1] and shall go to see it with the greatest pleasure. I am much hurried this morning and ought to write a long letter to Joanna H., but having only time for a note, I will enclose it to you hoping you may be able to procure a Frank for it in the course of a few days, and to write, with it, to Sara.

130. D. W. to JOHN KENYON

Address: John Kenyon Esq—Bath.
Postmark: 23 Mar. 1824. *Endorsed*: Miss Wordsworth.
MS. Cornell. Hitherto unpublished.

67 G[loster][2] Place, Portman Square
23ᵈ—March [1824]

My dear Sir,

My Brother has desired me to write to you to say that he is in London and intends to remain here (at Nᵒ 67. Gloster Place Portman Square, with our good Friends Mʳ and Mʳˢ Monkhouse) about three weeks, and that he should think it a most fortunate chance if any thing should bring you and Mʳˢ Kenyon to London during that time—or if not both, *you* alone. My Niece tells us that you were here for a few days about Christmas, and the like might happen now, and if you did not know of our being here we might miss the great pleasure of seeing you.

My Brother and I left Rydal five weeks ago, spent a month with Sir George and Lady Beaumont, and came hither on Friday, having visited John at New College. We have pleasant accounts from home. My Sister is quite well, excepting a slight touch of rheumatism at times—and William is very hardy, and, we hope getting on with his Books under our new School-master, Hartley Coleridge.

My Brother, who is now *sparing* his eyes by keeping them shut upon the sofa, says 'tell Mʳ Kenyon I was disappointed on our return from Holland[3] at not finding a letter from him at Dover'. He hopes, and so do I, that we shall have the pleasure of hearing from you in a few days with good tidings of yourself, Mʳˢ Kenyon and your good Brother—Where is he? and what is he doing?

Though my Brother's eyes are not certainly strong, or securely

[1] The portrait of Thomas Clarkson by A. E. Chalon, R.A. (1780–1860), exhibited this year.
[2] *MS. torn.*
[3] i.e. the previous June.

well even at any time, you will I am sure, be glad to hear that they are much more useable than formerly. His Daughter is with us in Gloster Place. Poor Mrs Monkhouse is again condemned to the Sofa, and I am sorry to say that her Husband is far from well, and looks wretchedly. I hope much worse that he actually is.—

My Brother begs you will present his Respects to Mrs Kenyon, and I hope you will add mine to her.

Wishing much that we may have the good fortune to see you, I remain

dear Sir,
Yours faithfully
D. Wordsworth

131. D. W. to EDWARD QUILLINAN

Address: Edward Quillinan Esqre, Lee Priory, Wingham, Kent.
Postmark: 29 Mar. 1824. *Endorsed*: 1824. Miss Wordsworth, Gloster Place.
  March 29.
MS. WL.
LY i. 138.

Gloster Place, Monday, 29th March [1824]

My dear Friend,

Captain Barret called yesterday and sate an hour with us. You will be concerned to hear that Doro has had one of her bad colds. We imprudently suffered her to walk to Charles Lamb's with Miss Horrocks and ourselves, to dinner on Friday, came home in a hackney coach—her voice gone the next morning— and very feverish. The cold has yielded to the usual remedies— she says she is now quite well, but the East wind continuing we do not venture to let her leave her own Room to-day, but I hope, when you arrive, she will be free to come amongst us as usual. Poor Mr Monkhouse looked wretchedly when we arrived—the next day better and for two or three more days; but he was very unwell yesterday. To-day a little better—yet, as long as these East winds continue, I think his going out will be hazardous. Country air, and spring breezes, I hope, will set him to rights, and till he can get into the country—whatever the weather may be, I have no hope of his regaining either strength or good looks. My Brother has a cold, too, but it is only in his head—and does not affect his health or spirits.

Pray come to Town as soon as you can. It grieves me to think

I shall not see your dear little Girls, but I must submit, and hope that our meeting with *you* will be a happy one.

Do excuse this hurried scrawl—I have many letters to write—We are going with Sir G. and Lady B. to see Wilkie[1] and his pictures at one o'clock, and at ½ past 5 to dinner at Sir Robert Farquahar's.[2]

God bless you—no more till we meet

Yours ever   D. Wordsworth.

Doro's Love, her Father's and the Monkhouses' kind regards —Mr Coleridge and other Worthies are to dine here on Saturday.[3] We hope you will be here to join the party.

My Brother just arrives. He begs you will come before *Thursday*. Captain Barret dines with us on Thursday and he hopes, as does Mr Monkhouse, that *you* will also. My B[r] is engaged for Friday to dine with Dr Holland[4]—and on Wednesday we go to Hendon[5]— shall return on Thursday morning. Doro will remain in Gloster Place—we shall not venture to take her to Hendon.

132. D. W. to JOHN MONKHOUSE

Address: John Monkhouse Esq[re].
MS. WL.
LY i. 139 (—).

Friday 16 Ap[r]. 1824

My dear Friend

As your Brother[6] has a frank and asks me to write to you I cannot refuse, though I am no where in so bad a mood for letter

---

[1] For David (later Sir David) Wilkie, see below, L. 134.

[2] Sir Robert Farquhar, Bart. (see *MY* ii. 456), had recently resigned the Governorship of Mauritius, where he did good work in grappling with the evils of the slave trade, to return to a political career at home as M.P., first for Newton, Lancs. (1825), and then for Hythe (1826).

[3] See Griggs, v. 347, 353–4. It was on this occasion that W. W. seems to have given S. T. C. his translation of the first three books of the *Aeneid* for comment. Coleridge's verdict did not offer him much encouragement to proceed with the work: 'Since Milton, I know of no poet with so many *felicities* and unforgettable lines and stanzas as you. And to read, therefore, page after page without a single *brilliant* note, depresses me, and I grow peevish with you for having wasted your time on a work *so* much below you, that you cannot *stoop* and *take*. Finally, my conviction is, that you undertake an *impossibility . . .*' But W. W. had already indicated to Lord Lonsdale (L. 127) that he had no plans to translate the whole poem. See also *Letters of Hartley Coleridge*, p. 87.

[4] For Henry (later Sir Henry) Holland, see above, L. 42.

[5] Probably to visit the Misses Lockier.   [6] Thomas Monkhouse.

writing as in London, where, having so much to tell, it seems as
if I had nothing, being unable to utter my thoughts—yet this
is a day to set doggedly to any indoors work—Good Friday—
and so cold, wet and windy that no one will go out of doors but
to church—that can stay at home. I am the only one of the house,
that has left the fire side—with cloak and umbrella paddled to the
new Church in York Street, where I heard a very good sermon
suited to the day from Mr Dibdin[1]—yet came home in bad
humour with the churlishness of London people,—in London
churches at least—for I had hard work to get a place to sit down
in though many pews were not half filled, and some were actually
empty. I am thankful at being enabled to tell you that your good
Brother is very much better than when we came to London three
weeks ago—though since that time he has been very ill—twice
unable to dine with us when there was company that he much
wished to see. I trust, that a disorder which has long hung upon
him was then passing the crisis; for his looks have gone on improving; and he is now in good spirits, though his wife is confined
to the Sofa—and one day perhaps very poorly and unable to leave
her bed-room—the next however pretty well and quite chearful;
yet one can never have any confidence that this state of comfort
will last through the twenty four hours; and this is so depressing a
thing to the spirits that I wonder to see him so chearful as he is.
They have had thoughts of letting the house and going to Ramsgate,
Sea air having been advised for Mrs. M., I have no dependence on
such removal being of any service, therefore am not sorry that a
suitable Tenant has not yet offered.—With respect to the mode
of Dora's travelling into Wales I cannot say anything decisive.
If your Brother should go he would take charge of her—and if not,
the Miss Lockiers *would* as far as Bristol, where Sara[2] says she
would meet her. In the meantime, if Mrs M. should be at Ramsgate,
after having made short visits to Mrs Anstie,[3] Mrs Johnson,[4]
and Mrs Parry,[5] she will go to Hendon; there to remain till her
departure for Wales.—You have heard the doleful history of our
colds—Dora's confined her a whole week and hindered her from

---

[1] The Revd. Thomas Frognall Dibdin (1776–1847), bibliographer, had
studied for the Bar under Basil Montagu, but was ordained in 1805, and had
just been appointed rector of St. Mary's, Bryanston Square.
[2] i.e. S. H., who had recently spent some six weeks with John Monkhouse at
the Stow, and had now returned to Hindwell.
[3] A London friend. See *MY* ii. 613.
[4] Wife of the Revd. William Johnson, the schoolmaster.
[5] Probably the wife of Hugh Parry of the Stamp Office (see *MY* ii. 356,
where W. W. refers to him as *Henry* Parry by mistake).

going to a play and the Opera—besides two dinner visits. She has been quite well, except during that week and has had much enjoyment. As to my Brother, his cold still hangs upon him and still gives him fits of dolefulness when we are alone, though it does not now much affect either his spirits or his looks when in company—As to mine, it did but last three days and I have made as good use of my privilege of health and strength as I could possibly have expected to do—though often thwarted by showery, and pinched by cold, weather. We have seen the first of all sights, the Diorama—Dora's second visit and we floated 5 or 6 times between Sarnen and Canterbury—Dora declared against the Swiss giantess so our kind and active fellow traveller[1] accompanied me thither and to the Swiss Models calling for me at St James's Place, where I breakfasted with my 'admirer' as D calls him, Mr Rogers, and his Sister. The giantess has no un-comely face, and a chearful Swiss countenance which brightened up in discourse with my companion. The Models are but poor things yet I was glad that I had gone to see them, and found much pleasure in tracing our route and pointing out where in-teresting objects—Crosses and Buildings remembered by us, ought to have been placed.

Last Tuesday was a fine bright day and my Brother and Dora, and Mr Robinson and I went to Piccadilly to the Mexican Curiosi-ties—the modern very amusing and the live Mexican not the least interesting object—Mr R. talked Spanish with him. The *Antient* Curiosities for which you pay another shilling are but a collection of ugly monstrous things—thence to the Panorama of Pompeii, where we were all much delighted—looked at Somerset House and paid our Toll on Waterloo Bridge, for the sake of the prospect—arrived at home not tired. Dora is very strong, and since her cold left her has had no return of it. I find she has been subject to colds all the winter; but never till we brought her to London has had a violent one. On Wednesday we walked through the Regents Park to Hampstead—sate an hour with Mrs Parry and saw her two beautiful children. She is just recovered from the feverish cold which everybody has had.—Thence to Mrs Hoare's where we sate another hour—and reached Hendon at half past two—none of us the worse for the walk. All the Miss Lockiers quite well and Miss Charlotte astonishing—She trips about—and runs errands almost like a Scholar of the school—I was delighted to see her so changed a creature. Next morning she and Miss

[1] H. C. R. See *HCR* i. 303.

Lockier took us to Mrs Hoare's (where we breakfasted) on their way to London—and Mrs Hoare brought us home in her carriage. We then went to the British Museum with Sir George and Lady Beaumont and after that to dinner at Mr George Philips[1]—Mr Chauntry was the most interesting person there—Mrs Philips, Dora, and I were the only ladies. Poor Chauntry is in bad spirits. He is in great apprehension of losing his Wife to whom he is tenderly attached. She has been ill more than a year. Their lot is remarkable in one respect, that neither of them has a relative male or female, nearer than distant cousins—so that the sole care of her in her sickness seems to fall on him. Tomorrow our nephews are to dine here; and Mr Monkhouse has invited Captain Barrett. I think, after all, we shall not go to Lee, Mr Quillinan and Dora got my Brother persuaded to go—and he fixed next Thursday or Friday *'in case he should be well'*. His heart now fails him—he does not like the journey; and I think I shall have to write to Quillinan to retract. I am sorry any half promise was made—and now that the house does not lett, your Brother and Sister would be glad to have us here a week longer. Your kind Brother likes company, and now that he is better, seems much to enjoy our being here. Captain Barrett is to dine with us to-day, and I shall wait till Wm has seen him before I take his final decision. If we do not go to Lee we shall be at Cambridge on the 30th. If we *do*, probably a day or two later, as on our return we shall spend one day with Mr Johnson at Clapton House—and provided we stay in London shall in like manner halt one day there on our way to Cambridge. All this is more for Sara H. than for you. I am afraid she will not be with you when you receive this letter, but pray send it to her and excuse whatever may be dull to yourself—

Saturday   Another rainy cold morning! William is gone to breakfast with Mr Courtenay the lawyer—and we *were* to have met Mr Robinson at Mr André's. Sara knows the place—Mr A. has some old pictures—and thence gone to the Exhibition—Dora cannot go—the streets are so wet—nor even I, unless the rain ceases—Your Brother is just gone, per Stage, into the City. He looks well this morning but is soon jaded—and often comes home the worse for having left the house. Mrs M. is confined to her room by a cold—but we hope she will be able to come down into

[1] George Richard Philips (1789–1883) of Weston, Warwick, and Sedgley, Lancs., M.P. for Steyning (1820–32), Kidderminster (1835–7), and Poole (1837–52): succeeded his father as 2nd Baronet in 1847.

the drawing room in the evening. We have often seen the Lambs—
and are to meet them at Miss Kelly's[1] on Wednesday—Charles,
though not in his best spirits has always been very agreeable.
At Sir George Beaumont's he was charming—Both Sir George
and Lady B. were delighted with him. On Monday Wm and I
are to meet Mr Irving[2]—and a few others at Sir G's—and Dora
is going with Miss Horrocks and your Br to hear Matthews[3]
tell how they manage in America. We have at present no other
engagements—Bye the Bye of Mr Irving—we have heard him
twice—and were very much interested. His person is very fine,
in my opinion—and his action often graceful—though often far
otherwise—his voice fine—reading excellent, and, while he keeps
his feelings under, nothing can be finer than his manner of preaching—but it is grievous to see him wasting his powers—as he
does in the latter part (especially) of his discourses—the more
grievous as it is plain he must sink under such exertions while yet
a young man. When I say *wasting* his powers, you will understand
that I mean that with less effort—the effect on his hearers would be
more beneficial. He wholly wants taste and judgment—but one
essential I give him full credit for—*sincerity*—without which no
preaching that would address the feelings can be efficacious.

   I have been interrupted by dear Mrs Luff's arrival through the
rain—(of course in a carriage) with Walter Farquahar[4]—to see
my Brother, who is breakfasting out—Mrs Luff has put off her
journey to Playford in hopes of her pension—and now to our
utter astonishment—she tells us that the Farquahars are probably to set off to Paris tonight or tomorrow. Thus suddenly
are things done in London. Mrs Luff will, I doubt not, go with
them though she talks of it hesitatingly—and she will be in
London again by the time we finally leave it—the 29th of this
month. Your sweet little warbling-voiced niece[5] has been playing
in the room beside us a full hour. She is a child by herself—
Such an one as was never born before and never will be again.

   [1] Fanny Kelly, the actress, thought by Lamb to be very little if at all inferior
as a *comédienne* to Mrs. Jordan in her best days. See *MY* ii. 613.
   [2] Edward Irving. See L. 106 above and next letter.
   [3] Charles Mathews (1776–1835), the actor, had visited the United States in
1822–3, and in his *Trip to America* produced at the Lyceum in Mar. 1824, he
imitated various types of Americans, black and white. His performance caused
much irritation when it was put on ten years later in New York.
   [4] Sir Walter Minto Farquhar (1809–66), 2nd Bart., entered Christ Church,
Oxford, in 1827 and was subsequently called to the Bar. He was M.P. for
Hertford, 1857–66.
   [5] i.e. the infant Mary Monkhouse.

There seems to be no seed of evil in her; but I trust when she is old enough to be touched by it externally she will have the spirit of self-defence—like the little Birds or young lambs—which now her ways and notions far more resemble than those of other children. She is constantly happy—and everything that is new and everything that is old affords her amusement. It is a great pleasure to see her with her Father. This morning he happened to be standing with his legs out-stretched like the Colossus of Rhodes—the little creature whose eye is very quick, chanced to see him and she ran under the pointed arch—and was quite de-lighted with her trick.

Mary Wordsworth seems to accede to the plan laid down by Sara of going into Wales before the end of June. This I am very glad of, and you and our Friends at Hindwell may depend on my being at home—not later than the first week in June but more probably the last in May. Mrs. Luff is very anxious to be in the North, and will go to Playford as soon as possible after her return from Paris—(if she goes thither). The affair of her Pension will not be decided till after the holidays. Nothing on my part shall prevent Mary W's being at liberty to leave home as soon as she *can*, in the month of June—*can* or is desirous of doing it. Had we not come to Town from Oxford it would have given me very great pleasure to visit you all this year, but having much enjoyed our stay here, in spite of a few drawbacks, I do not regret that it was not so arranged—and shall hope to see you at Hindwell and Stowe at another not very distant opportunity.

It seems little likely that they will leave Hindwell before the end of another year.

Many thanks to dear Sara for transcribing Mrs Donaldson's[1] affecting letter! No doubt, poor woman she will end her days among her Children in America. I enclose for Sara a letter which she sent to us, and which ought to have been returned before. This sad penmanship will, I fear distress your eyes—and I have no right to trouble you with so much of it. Lucky will it be for me if Sara or Joanna be by your side to decipher for you——

Dora's kind love—

adieu, my dear Friend

Believe me yours affectionately

Dorothy Wordsworth

Excuse all blunders. I have not time or patience to read over, and correct.

[1] A Hindwell acquaintance.

133. D. W. to EDWARD QUILLINAN

MS. WL.
LY i. 145.

My dear Friend,   Monday morn^g [19 Apr. 1824]

It is fixed that we set off[1] next Friday, but whether by Steam[2] or by one of the Charing Cross coaches is not decided, only I declare against the Tallyho for the reason which recommends it to you, its speed.

Captn Barret and Mr Irving[3] and my two nephews are breakfasting with us. Mr Robinson just arrived to walk about with me, and see sights—so do not wonder that my pen wants to be done, and as we shall meet so soon there is no need to say much.

Your watch key is found. I will drop you a line when our mode of travelling is fixed.

Do's love to the Toots—and mine
                                        Ever yours truly
                                        D. Wordsworth.

134. W. W. to DAVID WILKIE[4]

Address: David Wilkie Esq, Kensington.
MS. Cornell. Hitherto unpublished.

                                        Bread Street[5]
                                        May 1st [1824]

My dear Sir,

The Rev^d Mr Birkett[6] the Bearer of this, is fond of Painting, and of course anxious for a sight of any work of yours; I have not

---

[1] For Lee Priory, where the Wordsworths stayed for a week.

[2] i.e. by steamboat to Ramsgate.

[3] For W. W.'s meeting with Edward Irving and their 'interesting hour's conversation' on this occasion, see *HCR* i. 304.

[4] Sir David Wilkie, R.A. (1785–1841), the celebrated artist (see *MY* i. 79, 95, 182), moved from Edinburgh to London in 1805 to study at the Royal Academy, and a year later was commissioned to paint 'The Blind Fiddler' for Sir George Beaumont. He stayed at Coleorton in 1809: visited Paris with Haydon in 1814; and in 1817 stayed at Abbotsford and painted the Scott family. In 1830 he was appointed Painter in Ordinary to the King and was knighted in 1836. He visited Rydal Mount in 1834 and 1839 (*RMVB*).

[5] On their return to London from Lee Priory, the Wordsworths called at the Revd. William Johnson's rectory in Bread St., off Cheapside, before moving on the next day to Clapton to stay with Joshua Watson. See next letter.

[6] The Revd. William Birkett (1794–1875) of Lancaster, who married Mary Horrocks—sister of Mrs. Jane Monkhouse—later this year, and was appointed vicar of South Tawton, Devon (see *SH*, p. 291). He was rector of Haseley, Oxon., from 1846.

scrupled therefore to offer him this Note; as I am sure you will have pleasure in showing him any Study you may have by you, which would much oblige your sincere

Friend and admirer
Wm Wordsworth

This afternoon I leave London, having returned yesterday from the neighbourhood of Canterbury.

135. D. W. to EDWARD QUILLINAN

Address: Edward Quillinan Esqre, Lee Priory, Wingham, Kent.
MS. WL.
LY i. 145.

Monday Morn^g. Clapton.[1] [3 May 1824]

My dear Friend,

We had amusing company and a very pleasant ride in spite of dust. The rough Fellow who got up in his patched coat covered with dust proved a worthy Pilot who plies the river and who had a large share of human kindness, and gave my Brother no little information in *his way*. Found dinner ready at Bread Street.[2] Mrs Johnson could not receive us that night, so we were to sleep at a Coffee house in St Paul's Churchyard.

Next morning very busy till our departure for Clapton from the Flower-pot at four—and here we shall remain till to-morrow morning—hoping to dine with the Master of Trinity and his Nephew John.

I will not say a word of Lee and the nightingales—I was too sorry to leave them—and poor Doro could think of little but what she had left behind, for some miles of the journey. I very much rejoice with her in the happy opportunity we have had of seeing your dear little Girls. I can never forget them as they are now—and whatever notion you may entertain of my likings I assure you Rotha is an especial favorite with me.

All well in Bread Street. They cannot leave London till Wednesday. We shall see them to-day, as we are going to the Exhibition.

---

[1] The purpose of W. W.'s visit to Clapton was probably to dine with C. W. and the latter's old friend the Revd. Henry Handley Norris (1771–1850), a prominent high-churchman, and rector of near-by Hackney from 1809. Mr. Johnson may well have been of the party as well (see L. 132 above). Norris and his family visited W. W. in the company of Joshua Watson in summer 1835 (*RMVB*).
[2] i.e. at Mr. Johnson's rectory.

I got a letter forwarded by you from Lee and heard a rumour of some verses[1] which never alas! reached my hands—I was busy with a long letter from Rydal, and Doro (after reading them) gave the verses to Mrs Monkhouse. Doro has repeated a part of them to me; but cannot remember them all—I hope to pursue the same poem in Bread Street to-day.

You will look for news of us—therefore I write—and because I can procure a Frank. I would not have the conscience to send such a scrawl to be *paid* for. Breakfast ready—off to London! and not a moment to spare.

A thousand loves from Doro and self to the little ones. Remembrances to all kind Friends—not forgetting Mrs Lucas.[2] God bless you

Yours ever truly
D Wordsworth.

Doro read your verses to her Father, who just now tells me 'They are very pretty verses' if he may be allowed to say so of any so panegyrical of himself. God bless you—a week at Lee Priory is far too little.

Bread Street. Monday morn^g 12 o'clock. Your letter just received by hand from Mrs Monkhouse. Many thanks! and for the pretty verses! we are going to the Exhibition at St House,[3] and back to Clapton to dinner.

136. M. W. to EDWARD QUILLINAN

MS. untraced.
K.

Trinity Lodge, May 5 [? 1824][4]

My dear Friend,

. . . *Then*, on Saturday the 10th, God willing, we purpose to commence an attack upon your hospitality. W. will take the first Cambridge coach, and Dora and I shall follow with Dr Wordsworth, and hope to reach Bryanston Street in the course of the day. Indeed, the Dr is engaged to dine in town. Therefore we shall not be long after W.; but do not disarrange your plans in expectation of us, as you know we are no great *dinerites*, and would rather fall in at your

---

[1] For E. Q.'s poem *The Nightingale*, see L. 122 above.
[2] Nanny to Rotha and Jemima Quillinan.   [3] Stafford House.
[4] This text, which appears to be a fragment rather than a complete letter, is misdated by *K* and seems to belong to this year.

tea hour than at any other. In hope of seeing you so soon, and having a host of letters to write, I will say no more: only that we trust we are not to be disappointed in our expectation of seeing the dear Rotha. Love to sweet Mima, and believe me,

Ever affectionately yours,
M. Wordsworth.

137. D. W. to THOMAS MONKHOUSE

Address: Thomas Monkhouse Esqre.
Endorsed: D. W. Senr. to T. M. Cambridge 20 May 1824.
MS. WL.
LY i. 148.

Trin. Lodge
Thursday May 20th [1824]

My dear Friend

At six o'clock yester evening I little thought I should have to tell you of Doro's travelling northward with her Father, instead of southward with her uncle. Such is, however, the case. At seven o'clock this morning, her Cousin John and I saw them seated on the back part of the Stamford coach (i.e. from Stamford) whence they are to proceed by Leeds, and they expect to reach home on Saturday morning.

You, I am sure, will be much disappointed—and so will many other kind Friends; and on many accounts, I assure you this arrangement does not please me—but I will neither trouble you nor myself with the details of my arguments in opposition to it. Had not her Father's promise that she should accompany her Mother into Wales (he either going with them or joining them there to return with them) in some degree reconciled me as far as our kind Friends at Hindwell and Stowe are concerned—I should have really at this moment been very unhappy. Doro will write to you herself a day or two after her arrival at home— and she will tell you how she sickened at the thought of her Father's going without her—how he yielded—and also how desirous he was to take her with him. The point he most dwelt upon was, that her absence from home and from her Mother and himself would be too long—more than could be afforded—'nine or ten months being a long portion of human life after 53 years of age', but I am insensibly getting into details that I wished to avoid.

I very much regret that the present plan had not been settled before we left London. In that case notwithstanding Mrs Luff's wish to have a companion on her journey—and notwithstanding my wish to see Mrs Clarkson (all things being convenient for it) —I should have made no engagement with Mrs Luff and instead of going to Playford (which I intend to do, tomorrow) should have gone as far as Leicester with my Brother and Doro—thence to Birmingham, and from Birmingham to Hereford—and thence to the Stowe and Hindwell. This would have been for myself a very pleasing scheme, and would, in some degree, have made amends to them for the putting-off of Doro's visit.

My Brother C. left us this morning at ½ past nine; so I have now no companion in this large and quiet house but my Nephew John who is now hard at his studies.[1] At 12 he attends his Tutor, and after that time we shall walk out together and conclude with a last visit to King's College Chapel—I assure you we both feel very queer, now that we are quite deserted—yet that would disturb me little were it not for the breaking of engagements, which I do not see sufficient reason *for* breaking. My Br C. will be at Mr J Watson's[2] most part of his absence from Cambridge. He thinks of returning about Monday sen'night but is uncertain. John would gladly join a party if he could hear of one with a Tutor, to the Lakes—but his Father seems to think the Idle Mount is too pleasant a spot for *mathematical* studies, to prosper in. I have at least half a dozen letters to write that *must* be written —the greater part of them on account of this change of purpose— which falls rather hard on me—having had no hand in the business. Had the resolution been formed one day earlier, Doro should have had the telling of her own Tale. So far not a word of you or your concerns! We much rejoiced over your good accounts from Ramsgate—God grant that your hopes of a perfect restoration of your dear Wife's health and strength may be realised before the end of the summer! Give my very kind love to her and Miss Horrocks —and tell little Good Good that Dorothy sends her many kisses— and that 'Do' is 'gone'.

I shall not write to Sara Hutchinson till I reach Playford, when I hope to have something pleasant to communicate concerning our Friends there, to set against her disappointment.

Adieu, my dear Friend,

Believe me ever, yours faithfully and affectionately

D Wordsworth.

---

[1] John Wordsworth was now an undergraduate at Trinity.
[2] For Joshua Watson, see *MY* ii. 605.

A letter from Mary W received yesterday says (quoting from Sara) 'I hope William will not let the French have his money at reduced interest'—and the quotation goes on to this effect that 'she (Sara) wishes to have hers sold out—' No doubt she has written to you on the subject since we left you.

Do let me hear from you when you can find leisure. I hope the change in weather may have set you right again—yet though this is a very hot day in the sunshine—we have a sharp East wind, and *that* wind, I know—wet or fair—never agrees with you—It would give me great pleasure to hear that your Sports at Lee, and the Lee Ale have agreed as well with you as the last time.

138. D. W. to EDWARD QUILLINAN

Address: Edward Quillinan Esqre, Lee Priory.
MS. WL.
LY i. 147 (—).

Trinity Lodge, Thursday 20th May. [1824]

My dear Friend,

I have just written to Mr Monkhouse to tell him that Doro is now travelling northward with her Father, instead of southward with her Uncle. She was home-sick—the Father sick to have her at home, and so they settled it—and this morning at 7 o'clock I saw her seated on the top of the Stamford Coach by his side. Instead of going into Wales as before intended, at Midsummer, she is to accompany her Mother in the autumn, and my Brother will either go with them, or join them there to return with them. I hope Egerton Brydges will find his way to the Lodge either this morning or at Chapel time in the evening. My Brother and Doro saw him since his return from London, but I happened not to be out with them. This house which seemed so chearful until to-day is now (deserted as we are) quite melancholy in its still-ness; though the sun shines brightly, and the sight of it chears me a bit for the Travellers' sake. The Master set off for London at ½ past 9.—I shall be at Cambridge again on my return from Playford with Mrs Luff, but probably only for one night.

I am sorry I was so careless as to bring away Miss H.'s letter, which I now enclose.

Poor Rotha! how anxious you must have been when she was so ill! I hope to hear from you while at Playford with good accounts of both your dear little Girls—and a pleasant history of your sports at Lee with Mr M., visits to Ramsgate etc etc. Excuse this poor scrawl. I have many letters to write, and would much prefer musing in the Garden—or lying on a sofa with a Book from which my thoughts would wander far away—halting oftentimes at Lee— a place which will always be dear to my memory. God bless you and your bonny Lasses (I assure you Rotha was right bonny in my eyes long before they cast on her their last look). Do not fail to remember me to Mrs Lucas—Yours ever truly

D Wordsworth.

Direct [to] Playford Hall n^r. Ipswich.

139. D. W. to H. C. R.

Address: To H. C. Robinson Esqre, 3. King's Bench Walk, Temple.
Postmark: 26 May 1824. *Stamp*: Lombard St. *Endorsed*: 23^d May 1824, Miss Wordsworth.
MS. Dr. Williams's Library.
K (—). *Morley, i. 126.*

Playford Hall, near Ipswich.
Tuesday Morn^g. 23rd May [1824]

My dear Friend,

In my way from Cambridge last Friday, as soon as I had secured my luggage etc I set off towards your Brother's house; stopped at Mrs Kitchener's to enquire after her, and just as I was setting out again your Brother and Sister were coming up the Square. Instead of proceeding to Southgate I turned in again with them, and Mrs R.[1] stayed till the Coach took me up.

—I was much pleased to see a chearful countenance when she met me, and though I marked the traces of age coming on—and of past suffering, on the whole she looked much better than I had expected. In fact she told me she had rallied wonderfully since her late distress.—I shall stop in Southgate on my return— Mrs Luff, who will be my companion to Rydal—going forward to the Inn—where she will take care of Luggage, etc. My time will be very short, as the Coach only remains half an hour at Bury—We shall travel with our Family cares—the whole of Mrs Luff's living Stock, three singing Birds of gay plumage brought from the Mauritius.

---

[1] Mrs. Thomas Robinson, H. C. R.'s sister-in-law, who was now suffering from cancer.

Thank you for your letter, which I received at Cambridge with the parcel and two Books for my Brother's use. He has taken them into the North, as, he told me, you were not in immediate want of them.

Your advice respecting my Continental Journal[1] is, I am sure very good, provided it were worth while to make a Book of it,—provided I *could* do so—and provided it were my wish: but it is not—'Far better', I say, 'make another Tour and write the journal on a different plan!' In recopying it, I should—as you advise omit considerable portions of the description—These would chiefly be, what I may call duplicate descriptions—the same ground travelled over again either actually or by retrospect.[2] Such occur several times. I should also omit or compress much of what is detailed respecting dress etc etc—and would insert all the poems.[3]

But, observe, my object is not to make a Book but to leave to my Niece a neatly penned Memorial of those few interesting months of our lives.

I have heard of your being at the Exhibition. I hope you liked Leslie's[4] picture of Sancho and the Duchess—We were charmed with it—What did you think of Mr Clarkson?[5] and of the Master of Trinity?[6]

You will be surprized to hear that Dora is gone home with her Father. They left Cambridge on Thursday morning, and,

[1] H. C. R. had been reading D. W.'s Journals during the London visit. See *HCR* i. 305: 'That of her first Scotch tour preferable to the Swiss journal, from its brevity and the insertion of Wordsworth's delightful poems. The last a hurried composition not much better than my journals.'

[2] *Written* retroscept.

[3] i.e. W. W.'s *Memorials* of the 1820 tour.

[4] Charles Robert Leslie, R.A. (1794–1859), who specialized in painting scenes from Shakespeare, Cervantes, Sterne, and Goldsmith. He came to London from Philadelphia in 1811, studied under Benjamin West and Washington Allston, and through him got to know Coleridge. 'Sancho Panza in the Apartment of the Duchess', one of the most successful of his humorous pictures, is now in the National Gallery. In 1845 he published his *Memoirs of John Constable, R.A.*

[5] For Chalon's portrait of Thomas Clarkson, see L. 129 above.

[6] Robson's portrait of C. W. (see *Frontispiece*), which he commissioned and presented to his College. George Fennel Robson (1788–1833), born in Durham of a Cumberland family, moved to London in 1804, and began to exhibit at the R.A. from 1807 onwards, specializing in romantic landscapes. It is not known why C. W. chose him, or how he came to know him—but possibly they had met in the Lakes. The portrait was not well received by his family. As Charles Wordsworth put it to his brother Christopher on 24 June: 'Father's picture . . . is disliked by every body—as being too amazingly glum—and as for your friend Robson he is reckoned nothing more than a mere dauber.' (*MS. Jonathan Wordsworth*.)

I hope, reached Rydal on Saturday to breakfast. I expect a letter tomorrow.—My Brother was well and in good spirits at Cambridge, and we all enjoyed our visit there very much. The weather was delightful the first week.—Then came the Flood—a new scene for us—and very amusing—on the Sunday when the sun shone out again. The Cam, seen from the Castle Hill resembled one of the lake-like Reaches of the Rhine. The damage was, I fear very great to the Farmers; but though the University Grounds were completely overflowed up to Trinity Library, in the course of four days most of the damage was repaired. I think we shall remain here about a fortnight longer—We intend to stay two nights at Cambridge—two in Leicestershire—two in Yorkshire—and after that one day's journey, a night spent at Kendal, and a three hours' ride before breakfast will take us to Rydal Mount. Mrs Luff is a bad traveller—and short journeys and long rests suit her.—Adieu, my dear Friend,

Truly yours
D Wordsworth

I have had good reports from Mr Monkhouse of our friends at Ramsgate—I hope you and he contrive to meet when he is in Town—Dora is to go into Wales with her Mother in the Autumn. My Brother will either accompany them, or join them there.

140. D. W. to LADY BEAUMONT

Address: To Lady Beaumont, Coleorton Hall, Ashby de la Zouche, Leicestershire.
Stamp: Kendal Penny Post.
MS. Pierpont Morgan Library.
K (—). *LY* i. 150 (—).

Rydal Mount, 18th Sept., Saturday [1824]

My dear Lady Beaumont,

I think you will like to hear of the Travellers, besides I have tidings for Sir George respecting his Friend Major Machell.[1] Not long ago, in walking to Ambleside, I met a very striking company,

---

[1] Col. Christopher Machell, of Beverley, Yorks. (1747–1827), a descendant of the Machells of Crackenthorpe Hall, Westmorland, lost his arm in the battle of New York. His only daughter Matilda, mentioned further on, married Edward William Smith, of Routh. It is impossible to identify the other young man, as Col. Machell had three sons surviving at this time.

a young and beautiful Lady on horseback, attended by two *young* men on foot (both with unusually large black whiskers, and one of them smoking a Segar) and an old gentleman, who under his single arm carried a port-folio: his coat-sleeve hung on the other side. They stopped to admire the prospect of Nab Scar and the Bridge, therefore we had time to look at them, and on their slow approach we had been prepared for a gaze.—In the first place, the Tobacco, scenting the sunny air, and the whiskered youths in their fur caps, reminded one of Switzerland or Germany, and I exclaimed to my Companion 'These must be foreigners, or people who have spent much of their time abroad.' The old man's appearance was very gentlemanly, and I really admired him more than his beautiful Daughter; and had I known who he was I certainly should have addressed him for Sir George's sake. The next day Miss Dowling mentioned to me that a *great Beauty* had been some days at Ambleside with her Father, Major Machell, her Husband, and Brother. I was then assured that the Gentleman without an arm must be Sir George's Friend, and begged to be informed if the Party had not left Ambleside, intending to call and tell him how much he had been inquired after at Coleorton, and very sorry I was to hear that he was gone. Sir George will be glad to be informed that Major M. looked so stout and well, that when the thought first crossed me that it must be him I had seen, I dismissed it saying 'No, *he* must be a much older man; besides I was told he was very infirm.' But, laying all circumstances together, I was persuaded it would be no other. He appears *old* (I should have said about 60) but not aged—and walks with a firm step.

Now for our own Travellers.[1] They have thridded North Wales, and hardly left a celebrated spot unseen. Mr Jones, my brother's first pedestrian companion on his Tour in Switzerland, joined them with his car and servant, and travelled with them every where. They were to part at the Devil's Bridge last Tuesday, and on Wednesday expected to reach Mr Hutchinson's house at Hindwell. They had had fine weather, and no drawback from their pleasure except my Brother's poor eyes, which at some times were much inflamed; he, however, kept up his spirits, enjoyed every thing, and the whole journey seems to have gone off very well. My letters have been from Dora, who gives a most lively account of what she has

[1] i.e. W. W., M. W., and Dora W., who had left on their Welsh tour about 25 Aug., travelling to Liverpool and from there by steamboat to Bangor and on to Caernarvon, where they spent a day with the Crumps and William Jackson, before commencing their tour with Robert Jones. D. W. had stayed behind at Rydal Mount to look after Willy.

seen, especially of the ladies[1] at Llangothlin (I cannot spell these Welsh names), with whom they spent an evening; and were well pleased with *them* and their entertainment. Dora says of Conway Castle, 'Having left the vale of Clwyd, we soon came in sight of Conway, which I think the King of castles. All that I have heard of it, all that I have seen—even Sir George's picture—nothing gives one a sufficient idea of its grandeur. Here we spent more than three hours, but it would take more than three days to become acquainted with it. The longer I stayed the longer I wished to stay. They are erecting a Bridge[2] across the River, on the same plan as at Bangor Ferry, which I think will be an improvement to the appearance of the Castle when the newness is worn off.'

So much for the distant travellers; but we, at home, have had our travels. Mrs Luff,[3] William, and I spent three days in Borrowdale very agreeably—not wholly in Borrowdale, for William and I went over the Stye to Wasdale, with a party of our Friends. Bright sunshine after torrents of Rain set off the charms of Borrowdale and the sublimities of Scawfell to the best advantage, and all were delighted.

You will be glad to hear that William who is my first charge and care during his parents' absence, is much improved in strength and good looks since they left us. John is at Whitehaven with Mr William Jackson.—Sara Coleridge rode over to us in Borrowdale. I cannot discover any ailment in examining her eyes, nor is there any inflammation on the Lids; but, poor girl, she says the uneasiness is often very great, and she cannot endure a strong light. She is extremely thin; I could not but think of a lily Flower to be snapped by the first blast, when I looked at her delicate form, her fair and pallid cheeks. She is busy with proof sheets,—a labour that she likes,—yet I should be glad if it were over, and she could be employed and amused at the same time without exercising her mind by thought and study. Southey is much better, and I think he looks pretty well. He had been on Helvellyn the week before last, a proof of recovered strength! Mrs C. and the rest of the family

[1] Lady Eleanor Butler (1745–1829), sister of the Earl of Ormonde, and the Hon. Miss Ponsonby, cousin of the Earl of Bessborough, retired from society in 1779 and for fifty years lived together, as 'sentimental anchorites' in the vale of Llangollen. Their devotion to each other, and their eccentricities of dress and manner, brought them great notoriety, and they were much visited. (De Selincourt's note.) See *To the Lady E. B. and the Hon. Miss P.* (*PW* iii. 42, 432).

[2] Thomas Telford's suspension bridge at Conway was completed in 1826.

[3] Mrs. Luff had returned to Westmorland with D. W. at the end of May, and was now negotiating to purchase Fox Ghyll. See L. 143 below.

well, except Mrs Lovel.[1] Southey seemed to be very sorry to give up the expectation of seeing Sir George in the North. I told him, however, that there was perhaps a little chance of his coming, recollecting your message to Lord Lonsdale.

I hope I shall ere long hear of you indirectly from Wales, or directly from yourself, if you have not written to Hindwell. Should you have written thither, pray do not give yourself the trouble of writing to me also.—With best wishes and affectionate regards to Sir George, Believe me, dear Lady Beaumont, your faithful and affectionate Friend,

D. Wordsworth

141. W. W. to SIR GEORGE BEAUMONT

Address: Sir Geo. Beaumont Bart, or Lady Beaumont, Coleorton Hall, Ashby de la Zouch, Single Sheet.
Stamp: Radnor.
MS. WL.
Mem. (—). *K* (—). *LY i. 151* (—).

[*In M. W.'s hand*]

Hindwell, Radnor, Sept[br] 20th [1824]

My dear Sir George,

After a three weeks' ramble in North Wales, Mrs Wordsworth, Dora, and myself are set down quietly here for three weeks more. The weather has been delightful, and everything to our wishes. On a beautiful day we took the steam-packet at Liverpool, passed the mouth of the Dee, coasted the extremity of the vale of Clwyd, sailed close under Great Orme's Head, had a noble prospect of Penmaenmawr, and having almost touched upon Puffin's Island, we reached Bangor Ferry a little after six in the afternoon. We admired the stupendous preparations for the bridge over the Menai,[2] and breakfasted next morning at Carnarvon. We employed several hours in exploring the interior of the noble castle, and looking at it from different points of view in the neighbourhood. At half-past four we departed for Llanberris, having fine views, as we looked back, of C. Castle, the sea, and Anglesey. A little before

---

[1] Robert Lovell's widow (see *EY*, p. 441): Southey's sister-in-law, and a permanent member of his household.
[2] Thomas Telford's suspension bridge, now nearing completion.

sunset we came in sight of Llanberris Lake, Snowdon, and all the craggy hills and mountains surrounding it; the foreground a beautiful contrast to this grandeur and desolation—a green sloping hollow, furnishing a shelter for one of the most beautiful collections of lowly Welsh cottages, with thatched roofs, overgrown with plants, anywhere to be met with: the hamlet is called Cwm-y-Glo. And here we took boat, while the solemn lights of evening were receding towards the tops of the mountains. As we advanced, Dolbardin Castle came in view, and Snowdon opened upon our admiration. It was almost dark when we reached the quiet and comfortable inn at Llanberris. Here we passed the morning of the Sabbath in a quiet strole round the upper lake—Dora *not* being strong enough on that hot day to accompany us, attempted to sketch the Church and some of the Cottages—often wishing, as we all perpetually did, that you would pop upon us.

In the afternoon there being no carriage-road, we undertook to walk by the Pass of Llanberris, eight miles, to Capel Cerig; this proved fatiguing, but it was the only oppressive exertion we made during the course of our tour. We arrived at Capel Cerig in time for a glance at the Snowdonian range, from the garden of the inn in connection with the lake (or rather pool), reflecting the crimson clouds of evening. The outline of Snowdon is perhaps seen nowhere to more advantage than from this place. Next morning, five miles down a beautiful valley to the banks of the Conway, which stream we followed to Llanrwst; but the day was so hot that we could only make use of the morning and evening. Here we were joined, according to previous arrangement, by Bishop Hobart,[1] of New York, who remained with us till two o'clock next day, and left us to complete his hasty tour through North and South Wales. In the afternoon arrived my old college friend and youthful companion among the Alps, the Rev. R. Jones, and in his car we all proceeded to the falls of the Conway, thence up that river to a newly-erected inn on the Irish road, where we lodged; having passed through bold and rocky scenery along the banks of a stream which is a feeder of the Dee. Next morning we turned from the Irish road three or four miles to visit the 'Valley of

[1] John Henry Hobart (1775–1830), rector of Trinity Church, Bishop of New York since 1816, and one of the chief architects of the Church in America, which had suffered greatly during the revolution and the first years of independence. He paid a protracted visit to Europe in 1823–5, and spent a day with W. W. on 23 Aug. this year. In a letter of 1 Sept. 1825, he recalled his two meetings with W. W.: 'The day when you honored me with your attentions at the Lakes and that which I subsequently passed with you in Wales, I shall always look back to, with pride and with the highest pleasure . . .' (*WL MSS.*)

Meditation' (Glyn Mavyn), where Mr Jones has, at present, a curacy, with a comfortable parsonage. We slept at Corwen, and went down the Dee to Llangollen, which you and dear Lady B. know well. Called upon the celebrated Recluses,[1] who hoped that you and Lady B. had not forgotten them; they certainly had not forgotten you, and they begged us to say that they retained a lively remembrance of you both. We drank tea and passed a couple of hours with them in the evening, having visited the aqueduct over the Dee[2] and Chirk Castle in the afternoon. Lady E. has not been well, and has suffered much in her eyes, but she is surprisingly lively for her years. Miss P. is apparently in unimpaired health. Next day I sent them the following sonnet from Ruthin, which was conceived, and in a great measure composed, in their grounds—

> A stream, to mingle with your favourite Dee,
> Along the *Vale of Meditation* flows;
> So named by those fierce Britons, pleased to see
> In Nature's face the expression of repose;[3]

The allusion to the Vale of Meditation in the above, would recal to the Ladies' minds, as it was meant to do, their own good-natured jokes of the preceeding evening, upon my friend Mr Jones, who is very rubicund in Complexion and weighs about 17 stone, and would, as they said, make 3 good hermits for the Vale of which he is Curate. We passed 3 days with Mr J's friends in the vale of Clwyd, looking about us, and on the Tuesday set off again, accompanied by our friend, to complete our tour. We dined at Conway, walked to Benarth, the view from which is a good deal choked up with wood. A small part of the castle has been demolished, for the sake of the new road to communicate with the suspension bridge, which they are about to make to the small island opposite the castle, to be connected by a long embankment with the opposite shore. The bridge will, I think, prove rather ornamental when time has taken off the newness of its supporting masonry; but the mound deplorably impairs the majesty of the water at high-tide; in fact it destroys its lakelike appearance. Our drive to Aber in the evening was charming;

[1] See previous letter.
[2] Thomas Telford's aqueduct at Pont-y-Cysylltau, over 1,000 feet long and supported on 19 piers, carries the Ellesmere Canal over the vale of Llangollen 121 feet above the River Dee. It was opened in 1805.
[3] The rest of the sonnet follows, as in *PW* iii. 42.

sun setting in glory. We had also a delightful walk next morning up the vale of Aber, terminated by a lofty waterfall; not much in itself, but most striking as a closing accompaniment to the secluded valley. Here, in the early morning, I saw an odd sight —fifteen milkmaids together, laden with their brimming pails. How chearful and happy they appeared! and not a little inclined to joke after the manner of the pastoral persons in Theocritus. That day brought us to Capel Cerig again, after a charming drive up the banks of the Ogwen, having previously had beautiful views of Bangor, the sea, and its shipping. From Capel Cerig down the justly celebrated vale of Nant Gwynant to Beddgelert. In this vale are two small lakes, the higher of which is the only Welsh lake which has any pretensions to compare with our own; and it has one great advantage over them, that it remains wholly free from intrusive objects. We saw it early in the morning; and with the greenness of the meadows at its head, the steep rocks on one of its shores, and the bold mountains at *both* extremities, a feature almost peculiar to itself, it appeared to us truly enchanting.

The village of Beddgelert is much altered for the worse; new and formal houses have supplanted the old rugged and tufted cottages; and a smart hotel has taken the place of the lowly public-house in which I took refreshment almost[1] thirty years ago, previous to a midnight ascent to the summit of Snowdon. At B. we were agreeably surprised by the appearance of Mr Hare, of New Col: Oxford. We slept at Tan-y-bwlch, having employed the afternoon in exploring the beauties of the vale of Festiniog. Next day to Barmouth, whence, the following morning, we took boat and rowed up its sublime estuary, which may compare with the finest of Scotland, having the advantage of a superior climate. From Dolgelly we went to Tal-y-llyn, a solitary and very interesting lake under Cader Idris. Next day, being Sunday, we heard service performed in Welsh, and in the afternoon went part of the way down a beautiful valley to Machynlleth, next morning to Aberystwith, and up the Rheidol to the Devil's Bridge, where we passed the following day in exploring those two rivers, and Hafod in the neighbourhood.

I had seen these things long ago, but either my memory or my powers of observation had not done them justice. It rained heavily in the night, and we saw the waterfalls in perfection. While Dora was attempting to make a sketch from the chasm in

---

[1] In fact, thirty-three years before. See *Prelude* (1805), xiii. 1 ff.

the rain, I composed by her side the following address to the torrent:

> How art thou named? In search of what strange land,
> From what huge height descending? Can such force
> Of water issue from a British source,[1]

If the remembrance of 34 years may be trusted, this chasm bears a strong likeness to that of Viamala in the Grisons, thro' which the Rhine has forced its Way. Next day, viz., last Wednesday, we reached this place, and found all our friends well, except our good and valuable friend, Mr Monkhouse,[2] who is here, and in a very alarming state of health. His physicians have ordered him to pass the winter in Devonshire, fearing a consumption; but he is certainly not suffering under a regular hectic pulmonary decline: his pulse is good, so is his appetite, and he has no fever, but is deplorably emaciated. He is a near relation of Mrs Wordsworth, and one, as you know, of my best friends. I hope to see Mr Price,[3] at Foxley, in a few days. Mrs Wordsworth's brother is about to change his present residence for a farm[4] close by Foxley.

Now, my dear Sir George, what chance is there of your being in Wales during any part of the autumn? I would strain a point to meet you anywhere, were it only for a couple of days. Write immediately, or should you be absent without Lady B. she will have the goodness to tell me of your movements. I saw the Lowthers just before I set off, all well. You probably have heard from my sister. It is time to make an end of this long letter, which might have been somewhat less dry if I had not wished to make you master of our whole route. Except ascending one of the high mountains, Snowdon or Cader Idris, we omitted nothing, and saw as much as the shortened days would allow. With love to Lady B. and yourself, dear Sir George, from us all, I remain, ever most faithfully yours

[*signed*] Wm Wordsworth

[1] The rest of the sonnet follows, as in *PW* iii. 43, except that in ll. 10–11 read

> High O'er the yawning fissure, piny woods
> And Sun bright Lawns, and everlasting snows

and in l. 13 read 'sway' for 'power'.

[2] Thomas Monkhouse.

[3] Uvedale Price. See *MT* i. 3, 505. He was made a baronet in 1828.

[4] Brinsop Court, to which Tom Hutchinson was about to move from Hindwell. See *SH*, p. 287.

142. D. W. to JOHN KENYON

Address: John Kenyon Esqre, Bognor, Sussex.
Postmark: 9 Oct. 1824. *Stamp*: Kendal Penny Post. *Endorsed*: Miss Words-
   worth 10th Oct.
MS. untraced.
Transactions of the Wordsworth Society, no. 6, p. 93. K (—). *LY i. 156.*

Rydal Mount,
October 4th [1824]

My dear Sir,
   About three weeks ago, on returning from a walk, a letter in
which I instantly recognised your handwriting, was given to me.
I knew it must have been left by a Friend[1] of yours, and was
heartily grieved that I should have been absent, and the more
so, as the servant told me he had neither visited the Terrace nor
the Mount. Such was my first feeling and then I opened and
read your letter. I am truly glad that both you and Mrs Kenyon
are in good health, and seemingly in good spirits; and was
reconciled to your having been compelled to visit the sea and the
grey-green Fields of Bognor, instead of our brighter vallies,
as you would have found neither my Brother, nor Sister, nor Niece
at home; and I hope that you will have free choice next summer,
and that choice will lead you hither. I am sure you will be glad
to hear of us, and this reconciles me to sending a poor scrawl
without a Frank; besides I ought to have written to you from
London after the very kind letter which I there received; but you
know how Country folks are bustled about in London, and will
therefore excuse that failure in duty.
   I need not say how glad we should have been to accept your
friendly invitation, had it been in our power to visit you at Bath,
and to take a ramble on the Quantock Hills, on which, through
God's mercy, we can yet walk with as light a foot as in the days
of our youth. But it is time to begin with what has been done.
My Brother and Dora left me at Cambridge in May; they re-

   [1] John Kenyon had written on 15 Aug. to introduce two friends, Mr. and
Mrs. Guillemard, who were making a tour of the Lakes. 'Mrs G. is . . .
passionately fond of such scenery as you have about you, and renowned, as I
hear, for knowledge in Botany—not however "one that would peep and
Botanize etc"—at least I hope not. Mr G. once intended himself for "Physician"
and has always been "Philosopher"—but early in life he went to the United
States as Commissioner for settling the debts between the two Countries, and
is also well acquainted with Europe . . .' (*WL MSS.*) The reference is to John
Lewis Guillemard, F.R.S. (1765–1844).

turned directly to Rydal Mount, and I followed them in June, after paying a short visit to Mrs Clarkson near Ipswich. Since that time we have had scarcely anything but fine summer weather, such as *you* ought to have when you first introduce Mrs Kenyon to these Lakes and mountains; and though as I say I am not sorry that you did not come in the autumn months I wish you could have been here in the summer. It will be six weeks to-morrow since Mrs Wordsworth and my Brother left us. Three of those weeks they spent in North Wales, thridding that romantic country through every quarter. My Brother, to whom it was familiar ground when a very young man, has been pleased beyond expectation and remembrance, and his Wife and Daughter (to *them* all was new) have been delighted. They have, however, had a sad draw-back from the agreeable thoughts and feelings which they carried along with them to *South* Wales. There, on the banks of the Wye, they met our friend, Mr Thomas Monkhouse, who by the advice of Physicians had come thither, to his Brother,[1] for the sake of quiet, dry and pure air, and chearful society, with strict injunctions to withdraw his mind from business. That injunction was totally unnecessary, for he is, alas! unfit for all business. My Brother and Sister were heart struck at the first sight of him. He looks like a person far gone in consumption, but as the London Physicians, attributing the disorder entirely to a derangement of the digestive organs, speak confidently of a cure, I am willing to hope, though the Surgeon at Kington[2] holds out little or no hope of his recovery. You know what a good creature Thomas Monkhouse is, and how much he is valued by all his Relatives and Friends, and will, I am sure, rejoice with us if we have the happiness to see him restored to health. Removal to a warmer climate for the winter has been recommended, but I know not what will be done.

You will be glad to hear that my nephew William is, though not a thriving plant, what, but for his looks, we should call healthy at present—not fit for a public school, therefore he attends Hartley Coleridge, who has now fourteen Scholars—a flourishing concern for an Ambleside schoolmaster!—and he is steady and regular.

I have just had a letter from Mrs Coleridge, by which I learn that your Friends, Mr and Mrs Guillemard, are at Keswick. I shall desire her to say to them that I hope, if they return by this road, they will turn aside to look at Rydal Mount, though there is no chance of their finding my Brother and Sister at home. I think we shall hardly see them before the middle of November,

[1] John Monkhouse.　　　[2] A small town near Hindwell.

as they think of paying a short visit to Sir George and Lady Beaumont at Coleorton, on leaving Wales, and most likely it will be the third week of this month before they leave Wales. You do not mention your Brother. I hope you hear good tidings of him. May I beg to be most kindly remembered to him when you write? With best wishes to yourself and Mrs Kenyon, believe me, dear Sir

Yours truly
D. Wordsworth

John has been three weeks at Whitehaven with Mr Wm Jackson. I expect him home this week, to leave us soon for Oxford. My Brother's address is Thomas Hutchinson's Esqre, Hindwell, near Radnor. All pretty well at Keswick.

143. D. W. to [?] H. C. R.

MS. Cornell. Hitherto unpublished.

Sunday—November 14th
[1824]

My dear Friend

Mrs Luff is very grateful for your kindness, and she thinks you so admirable an agent that she has begged me to trouble you again, rather than write directly to Mrs Blakeney.[1] I will however write the business part of my letter, so that, if you please, you may cut it off and send or give it to that Lady, which may a little diminish your trouble.

Mrs Luff is willing to adhere literally to her offer. She meant to include the timber on the premises, and also an oak Tree that is just on the outside of the fence, which Mr Carter spoke about to Mr White. It is of the utmost consequence to Mrs Luff to get immediate possession of the place: she consents unwillingly to wait till April; but would relinquish the purchase altogether if it cannot be completed at that time. It can scarcely be necessary to add that the House, Fixtures, Barn, trees and every thing within the Field are to be included in the purchase.

Miss Joanna Hutchinson is here, and Mr Henry H. also—on his way to winter quarters near Stockton. Mrs Luff is going to Graystock for a few weeks—perhaps a couple of months, and she is very anxious to have the Fox Ghyll affair decided before her departure. Whatever the answer may be, *I* hope it will be speedy;

---

[1] Owner of Fox Ghyll, which Mrs. Luff was still trying to purchase.

indeed I am sure she will give it up altogether, if it cannot be *at once* decided, by a direct declaration on the part of the De Quinceys, whether they mean to go out in April or not.

Mrs L. is sitting beside me. She desires me to say that if ever she *be* Mistress of Fox Ghyll, she hopes to have the pleasure of seeing you there before Summer is over, and that we must all spend a Merry day together.

Mrs Luff is particularly anxious for an immediate answer as she intends leaving Rydal next week. She supposes that possession may be had of the Land *before* April—and, as she means to plant, She would wish to enter upon it as soon as possible.

Since writing the above Mrs Luff has seen Mrs de Quincey, who says that her Husband, before his Departure, fully intended quitting Fox Ghyll at May-day; and, further; she has no doubt of his willingness to quit before that time. It will be proper (in case Mrs Blakeney accedes to Mrs Luff's condition) that Mr White should write immediately to Mr de Quincey.

Mrs Luff requests an immediate answer.

[cetera desunt]

144. W. W. to ALARIC WATTS[1]

MS. untraced.
Alaric Alfred Watts, Alaric Watts, A Narrative of His Life, 2 vols., 1884, i. 199.
K. LY i. 158.

Rydal Mount, Ambleside,
November 16, 1824.

Dear Sir,

On my return home, after a prolonged absence, I found upon my table your little volume and accompanying letter, for both of which I return you sinceré thanks. The letter written by my sister upon their arrival does not leave it less incumbent on me

[1] Alaric Watts (1797–1864), editor of the *Leeds Intelligencer* since 1822. In 1825 he moved to Manchester, where he edited the *Courier*; in 1824 he edited, and from 1826 to 1838 was sole proprietor of the *Literary Souvenir*, one of the first of the popular annuals. In 1850 he published *Lyrics of the Heart*; in 1853 he provided a memoir and commentary for Turner's *Liber Fluviorum*; and in 1856 he initiated the series *Men of the Time*. On 23 July 1824 he had written to W. W., sending his *Poetical Sketches*, and acknowledging the delight W. W.'s poems had given him: 'They have been to me a source of pure and unfailing pleasure for many years . . . I was (until the regeneration of my taste had been effected by the perusal of *your* compositions) in a state of intellectual blindness; and I cannot but feel inexpressibly grateful to him from whose simply beautiful and dignified muse I have derived so many new and exquisite perceptions . . .' (*WL MSS.*)

to notice these marks of your attention.[1] Of the poems I had accidentally a hasty glance before; I have now perused them at leisure, and notwithstanding the modest manner in which you speak of their merits, I must be allowed to say that I think the volume one of no common promise, and that some of the pieces are valuable, independent of such consideration. My sister tells me she named the *Ten Years Ago*. It is one of this kind; and I agree with her in rating it more highly than any other of the collection. Let me point out the thirteenth stanza of the first poem as— with the exception of the last line but one—exactly to my taste, both in sentiment and language. Should I name other poems that particularly pleased me, I might select the *Sketch from Real Life*, and the lyrical pieces, the *Serenade* and *Dost Thou love the Lyre?* The fifth stanza of the latter would be better omitted, slightly altering the commencement of the preceding one. In lyric poetry the subject and simile should be as much as possible lost in each other.

It cannot but be gratifying to me to learn from your letter that my productions have proved so interesting, and, as you are induced to say, beneficial, to a writer whose pieces bear such undeniable marks of sensibility as appear in yours. I hope there may not be so much in my writings to mislead a young poet as is by many roundly asserted; but I am not the less disposed strenuously to recommend to your habitual perusal the great poets of our own country, who have stood the test of ages. Shakespeare I need not name, nor Milton; but Chaucer and Spenser are apt to be overlooked. It is almost painful to think how far these surpass all others.

I have to thank you, as I presume, for a *Leeds Intelligencer*, containing a critique on my poetical character,[2] which, but for your attention, I probably should not have seen. Some will say, 'Did you ever know a poet who would agree with his critic when he was finding fault, especially if on the whole he was inclined to praise?' I will ask, Did you ever know a critic who suspected

---

[1] D. W.'s letter is untraced.

[2] 'On the Writings of Wordsworth', reprinted in the *Leeds Intelligencer*, 26 Aug. 1824, from the first number of the *South African Journal*. The author was Thomas Pringle (1789–1834), Scottish poet and journalist, and one of the editors, who lived at the Cape, 1820–6, and subsequently returned to England to work for the Anti-Slavery Society. In his article, Pringle praised W. W. for concentrating on 'the slow and solemn operations of the primary affections'; but he found several poems quite unacceptable. 'Some of his subjects are whimsically unimportant, and no where except in his self-willed imagination, invested with relations of worth or pathos; and his manner of treating them sometimes so capricious and unwarranted by matter of fact, as to prove entirely ludicrous and even reprehensible . . .'

it to be possible that he himself might be in the wrong?—in other words, who did not regard his own impressions as the test of excellence? The author of these candid strictures accounts with some pains for the disgust or indifference with which the world received a large portion of my verse, yet without thinking the worse of this portion himself; but wherever the string of his own sympathies is not touched the blame is mine. *Goody Blake and Harry Gill* is apparently no favourite with the person who has transferred the article into the Leeds paper; yet Mr Crabbe[1] in my hearing said that 'Everybody must be delighted with that poem.' The *Idiot Boy* was a special favourite with the late Mr Fox[2] and with the present Mr Canning. The South American[3] critic quarrels with the *Celandine*, and no doubt would with the *Daffodils*, etc.; yet on this last the other day I heard of a most ardent panegyric from a high authority. But these matters are to be decided by principles; and I only mention the above facts to show that there are reasons upon the surface of things for a critic to suspect his own judgment.

You will excuse the length of this letter, and the more readily if you attribute it to the respect I entertain for your sensibility and genius.

Believe me, very truly,
Your very obedient servant,
Wm Wordsworth

145. W. W. to THOMAS BRYDGES BARRETT

Address: I. B. B. Barrett Esqre, Lee Priory, near Wingham, Kent. To be opened by Edwd Quillinan Esq. in case of Capt. B's absence.
Endorsed: From Mr Wordsworth dated Rydal Mount, Novr 19th 1824; received at Lee, on Nov 24th 1824. This letter is in Mr Wordsworth's own hand.
MS. Historical Society of Pennsylvania.
LY i. 160.

[*In M. W.'s hand*]

To Capt. Barrett Rydal Mount Novr. 19th [1824]
My dear Sir

The other day, upon returning home after a long absence, I found additional proofs of your regard in two valuable volumes

---

[1] George Crabbe (1754–1832), the poet, had been rector of Trowbridge, Wilts., since 1814. W. W. almost certainly met him during one of his more recent visits to London, for Crabbe regularly visited Samuel Rogers and the Hoares in Hampstead whenever he came up to London.
[2] For Fox's comments on the *Lyrical Ballads*, see *Mem.* i. 171–2.
[3] i.e. South *African*.

from the labours of your learned Father[1]—with much pride and pleasure I placed them by the side of those which I have previously received from your hands: and now return you my sincere thanks for those interesting memorials of your esteem. How much do I regret that the state of my eye-sight is so great an obstacle to my profiting, as speedily as I otherwise might do, from the information, much the greater part of which is new to me, contained in the Polyanthea and Cimelia.[2]

I sympathized with your regrets on the loss of your beautiful Trees by tempestuous weather, and I am sure you would share mine could you behold the havoc which a late storm has made in the grounds and woods of Rydal. I cannot conceive any danger to surpass what would have been encountered by a Person in the midst of these woods during the hurricane. In one quarter you might imagine that giants had been hurling the Oaks and Pines at each other after tearing them up by the roots—or rather that they had been endeavouring to do so, for most of the prostrate trees adhere to the ground with large masses of earth attached to them; in one instance, a space, of 7 yds by 3, had been torn up by a single tree from the surface of the ground—some were snapped off by the middle,—and one I noticed whose trunk was split nearly to its root—$\frac{1}{2}$ left standing—but the whole riven into fibres. Sixty trees have been overthrown, and out of 15 hundred the greater part shew vestiges of this tornado, which raged with its utmost fury in the Cove of Rydal.

You will have heard from Q. of poor Mr Monkhouse's melancholy state—we have heard of him since his arrival in Devonshire,[3] but without any assurances of any improvement—so that his friends are preparing themselves for the worst. He will be a great loss, for he was an example of a Man upright in all his dealings and a most affectionate friend.

Be kind enough to pass the other $\frac{1}{2}$ sheet to Quillinan—reading it yourself, if you think proper.

My Wife, Sister and Daughter join me in sincere regards and believe me my d[r] Sir to be your obd[t] and sincere Friend

[*signed*] Wm Wordsworth

[*There follows in M. W.'s hand* To Rotha Quillinan, *as in PW iii.*

[1] Sir Egerton Brydges.

[2] *Polyanthea librorum vetustiorum* . . ., Geneva, 1822, and *Cimelia* (a supplement to *Res literariae*), Geneva, 1823; only seventy-five copies of both were printed.

[3] Thomas Monkhouse, now in an advanced stage of tuberculosis, had moved with his family to Torquay. S. H. had gone with them.

47, except that in ll. 11–12 read . . . whose Name is thine to bear/
Hanging around thee; *and* Mary Monkhouse, *as in PW iii. 46,
except that in ll. 5–6 read* . . . a trace/ . . . ne'er bedews her cheek,
l. 8 That one who has been gazing on her face, *and in l. 11* Might
see, in no unholy mood of faith.]

146. D. W. to JOHN KENYON

Address: John Kenyon Esqre, Bath. 7 Upper Church Street. [*Delivered by hand*]
Endorsed: Miss Wordsworth, W's sister.
MS. untraced.
Transactions of the Wordsworth Society, no. 6, p. 96. K (—). *LY i. 162.*

Rydal Mount, 28th Nov. [1824]

My dear Sir,

    An offer, just received from a Friend to execute commissions
for us at Bath, tempts me to send a few lines to you, knowing
that you will be glad to hear we are gathered together again at
Rydal Mount, the usual Family, except Miss Hutchinson (whose
duties to poor Mr Monkhouse will I fear long detain her in the
South) and John (whom we expect in about a fortnight from
Oxford). The Travellers returned delighted with North Wales,
all in good health and with improved looks. My Brother's eyes
have mostly during the summer been in their better way, and
are still so—very useable for a short while at a time by day-
light: but hardly at all by candle-light, and this, I fear, is the
best that we may be allowed ever to expect from them. I told
you of Mr Monkhouse's deplorable state of health in a letter
addressed to you at Bognor, and have written thus far as if I
were assured you had received it, but perhaps you might have left
the place, as it was some weeks after the receipt of yours that I
wrote: however, you have probably heard by other means of the
Tour in N. Wales, and the long visit in S. Wales and Herefordshire, therefore I will not tell the tale over again; but must repeat
that I very much regretted that I had not the opportunity of shewing
Rydal Mount to your Friends,[1] and, in any other way, of doing
my best to make some amends for the absence of my Brother and
Sister.

    Our friends at Keswick are pretty well. Southey has got rid
of his summer cold, Sara Coleridge's eyes are no worse—Miss

---

[1] Mr. and Mrs. Guillemard. See L. 142 above.

Southey is expected at home early in the Spring. After a long stay in Devonshire she is now in London. Derwent keeps his situation as third master of Plymouth school,[1] and we (hearing nothing amiss) conclude he is going on well. As to poor Hartley he sticks to his school-hours, is liked by his scholars, and is still 'Hartley' among them; even (out of school) the bigger address him 'Hartley!' This will give you a notion of the nature of the discipline exercised by him.

Miss Hutchinson is at Torquay with Mr and Mrs Monkhouse. The Invalid is not, in appearance, worse than at his going thither, about 5 weeks ago, but Miss H. thinks him no better.

My Brother and Sister, Dora, and William, join with me in kindest remembrances to you, and to your Brother, when you write to him. We often talk of you both. I wish he may be in England next summer, that you may bring Mrs Kenyon to the Lakes, and that he may make a third in the party.

It would give us great pleasure to hear how you are going on; I do not ask you to write; but at some half-hour of leisure, the Rydal folks coming into your head, you may be seized with the inclination to say a few words to us. Pray present our united regards to Mrs Kenyon, and believe me, dear Sir,

> Yours faithfully,
> Dorothy Wordsworth.

Do you hear frequently of or from Mr Poole?[2] and how is he? Do you know whether Coleridge has lately been at Harrowgate,[3] or not? A rumour of his having been there has reached these parts, but we think there must be a mistake in the name, and that it has been some watering-place in the South.

[1] Derwent Coleridge had graduated at Cambridge the previous summer. In 1825 he was appointed master of Helston Grammar School, Cornwall, where he remained till 1841. He was ordained in 1827.

[2] After his first marriage in 1808, John Kenyon had settled at Woodlands, between Alfoxden and Nether Stowey, and his friendship with Thomas Poole dated from that time.

[3] S. T. C. had been at Ramsgate in October and November of this year, not Harrogate.

147. W. W. to JANE MARSHALL

MS. University of Iowa Library. Hitherto unpublished.

[late Nov. 1824]

. . . Pray if you see your Sisters,[1] tell them that the beauties of North Wales much exceeded my expectations as regulated by the impaired remembrance of thirty three years. I was indeed highly gratified as were Mrs W and my Daughter to whom the objects were new. I should . . .

[   ] of the stuff with which it is *every* morning encrusted.[2] He is dieted . . .

[*cetera desunt*]

148. W. W. to WALTER SAVAGE LANDOR

Address: Walter Savage Landor Esqre, Florence, Italy.
MS. Victoria and Albert Museum.
K (—). *LY i. 165.*

[Keswick December 11, 1824.][3]

My dear Sir,

I have begged this space from S., which I hope you will forgive, as I might not otherwise for some time [have] had courage to thank you for your admirable Dialogues.[4] They reached me last May, at a time when I was able to read them, which I did with very great pleasure; I was in London then, and have been a Wanderer most of the time since. But this did not keep me silent; I was deterred, such is the general state of my eyes, by a consciousness that I could not write what I wished. I concur with you in so much, and differ with you in so much also, that, though I could have easily disposed of my assent, easily and most pleasantly, I could not face the task of giving my reasons for my dissent! For instance, it would have required almost a pamphlet to set forth the grounds upon which I disagreed with what you have put into the mouth of *Franklin*[5] on *Irish* affairs, the object to my mind of constant anxiety. What would I not

---

[1] See *EY*, p. 5.   [2] Presumably a reference to Willy's ailments.
[3] This letter is written at the end of one by Southey, with this heading.
[4] The first two volumes of *Imaginary Conversations*.
[5] In the dialogue *Washington and Franklin*. Among several suggested remedies for the Irish problem, Franklin is made to advocate the abolition of the Protestant establishment.

give for a few hours' talk with you upon Republics, Kings, and Priests and Priestcraft.[1] This last I *abhor*; but why spend our time declaiming against it? Better endeavour to improve priests, whom one cannot, and ought not therefore to endeavour to do without. We have far more to dread from those who would endeavour to expel not only organised Religion, but all religion from society, than from those who are slavishly disposed to uphold it; at least I cannot help feeling so—Your Dialogues are worthy of you, and great acquisitions to literature. The classical ones I like best, and most of all that between Tully and his Brother. That which pleases me the least is the one between yourself and the Abbé de Lille.[2] The observations are invariably just, I own, but they are fitter for illustrative notes than the body of a Dialogue, which ought always to have some little spice of dramatic effect. I long for the third vol: a feeling which after my silence I should not venture to express, were you not aware of the infirmity which has been the cause of it. I sent a message of thanks from Cambridge through Julius Hare, whom I saw at Cambridge in May last.

Ever affectionately and gratefully yours,
W Wordsworth

149. D. W. to H. C. R.

Address: To Henry C. Robinson, Esqre, 3. King's Bench Walk, Temple.

Postmark: 20 Dec. 1824. *Stamp*: Tottenham C. R. *Endorsed*: Decr 1824, D. Wordsworth Sonnets on Miss Quillinan etc etc etc.

MS. Dr. Williams's Library.

K (—). *Morley, i. 128, 130.*

Rydal Mount 13th December. [1824]

My dear Friend

I should have written to welcome your return to England, having about that time an opportunity of making a letter-carrier of one of our visitors to the Lakes, but I shrunk from being the first to communicate to you the sad tidings of poor Thomas Monkhouse's hopeless state, and merely sent a message through Miss Lamb begging for news of you and an account of your continental Travels.[3] We have heard from Mrs Clarkson of your being well

---

[1] In a brief letter to W. W. of 20 Sept. Landor had written, 'The other great evil, priestcraft, sticks to the hand like pitch and sulphur.'

[2] The abbé Jacques Delille (1738–1813), conversationalist, poet, and translator of Virgil and Milton. For W. W.'s debt to him in *Descriptive Sketches*, see *PW* i. 325.

[3] H. C. R. had spent the previous September and early October in Normandy.

and in good spirits. That is all—not a word of where you have been
or what doing—Pray write to us—do not suppose I require a
journal; but, spoiled by former kindnesses in this way, I really
have been disappointed at not receiving one before this time—write
however; and if the journal comes hereafter it will be thankfully
received.—My Brother and Sister, with their Daughter, arrived at
home a month ago after an absence of eleven and a half weeks.
Their Tour in North Wales was delightful—much surpassing
remembrance and expectation—To my Brother the ground had
been familiar in the days of his youth; but all was new to the Females. They spent five weeks among their Friends in Herefordshire
and Radnorshire, and bore away one great consolation in parting
from Thomas Monkhouse, as they all feared, for the last time—
that he had been cheated out of many a melancholy thought by their
presence. My Brother's society was an especial comfort to him.
Two days before *our* Travellers left Wales, the sick man had set
off for Torquay with his Wife and Child, and Miss Hutchinson.
She, our only correspondent, writes to us but seldom, having
nothing to say. What ever change there ma[y] be it is not percep-
tible—or hardly so—but as he is no better he must be worse; and
I suspect, that in looking back to the time of their arrival at
Torquay, Miss Hutchinson perceives that he is weaker. The little
Girl never has a bodily ailment; and is in temper just as you have
always seen her—'Good good'. Her Mother is in excellent health;
and (considering that she must be haunted by apprehensions)
keeps up her spirits wonderfully. I expect, however that she
deceives herself, dreading to look at the worst—and is, besides,
buoyed up by favorable opinions given by a physician whom they
have lately consulted,—and in fact those who have thought the
worst of the case, would not be likely to say the whole truth to
her. Poor Miss Hutchinson has a melancholy office; and I fear she
is not in good plight to bear up under it. The mild and damp air of
Torquay relaxes her frame, and she is plagued with constant
toothache.—

Miss Horrocks[1] who is very good in sending us whatever tidings
she receives from Torquay, inquires after you and your travels.
She is pretty well, though much harassed in mind—two of her
Sisters just married to Clergymen,[2] not over wealthy, a third

---

[1] Sarah Horrocks.
[2] i.e. Mary, married to the Revd. William Birkett (see L. 134 above); and
Susannah, who married the Revd. Thomas Raven (1793–1868), perpetual
curate of Holy Trinity, Preston, 1824–49.

waiting till her intended Husband has got a living[1]—or pupils!! and the fourth Sister[2] has been for some weeks extremely ill— requiring constant attendance night and day.—My Brother and Dora were at Keswick for four days last week. Southey has got rid of a cold which hung upon him all the summer and autumn, and is in his usual good spirits,—happy in his various employments—Sara Coleridge (whose eyes are still weakly though not worse) is busy correcting the press—She has translated a Book from the French[3] either written by the Chevalier Bayard or by some other person concerning him and his times—I know not which.—Cuthbert Southey is a fine clever Boy, and I hope it will please God to preserve him for the comfort and delight of his poor Father, whose loss seemed irreparable when Herbert (then his only Son) died.[4] Mrs Southey and the rest of the Family are well. Miss Southey is again in London and not expected at home till February or March—

Now for ourselves—We are all quite well—the Travellers were much improved both in looks and health by their journey, especially my Brother, whose eyes have been less troublesome than usual since his return—Notwithstanding bad weather we have had our daily walks. My Brother has not yet looked at the Recluse; he seems to feel the task so weighty that he shrinks from beginning with it— yet knows that he has now no time to loiter if another great work is to be accomplished by him—I say another—for I consider the Excursion as one work though the Title-page tells that it is but a *part* of one that has another Title. He has written some very pretty small poems—I will transcribe two of them,[5] which have been composed by him with true feeling, and he has great satisfaction in having done them—especially that on Mary Monkhouse for her dear Father's sake, who prizes it very much—

John is just arrived from Oxford and your old friend William is very well in health, though not fit to be trusted off to school at a distance. My Sister sends her very best love to you, and heartily joins with me in the wish that your travels next summer may lead you into Westmorland. It is too soon to begin to tattle of these

[1] i.e. Alice, who married the Revd. James Streynsham Master (1799–1878) of Balliol College, Oxford: rector of Chorley, Lancs. from 1846, and Hon. Canon of Manchester, 1854.
[2] Probably Ann Eliza, rather than the eldest of the sisters Eliza, who had married Charles Whitaker (1790–1843), of Symonstone Hall, Lancaster, in 1812.
[3] *The right joyous and pleasant History of the feats, gests, and prowesses of the Chevalier Bayard the good Knight without fear and without reproach. By the Loyal Servant.* 2 vols., 1825.   [4] In 1816. See *MY* ii. 305.
[5] They were enclosed in the second half of the letter.

things—and I hardly think my Brother will stir away from Rydal next summer—yet he sometimes hints at going into Ireland and says when he *does* go he will take me along with him.—but we have all been such wanderers during the last twelve months that the pleasantest thought at present is that of being gathered together at home, and all quietly enjoying ourselves. There is no country that suffers so little as this in bad weather—none that has so much of beauty (and *more* than beauty) in the winter season—and at Rydal Mount especially we are favoured, having the sun right before our windows both at his rising and setting.—My Brother, who is famous for providing opportunities for his Friends to do him a service, desires me to ask you to be so good as to inquire what is the present price of shares in the Rock Insurance. He has a little money to dispose of, and you know he was fortunate in his purchase from that office. Can you recommend any other mode of laying out money?[1]

I am further to ask you if it be possible, through your man or through anyone whom you know of, to have a Daily Paper sent to my Brother the day after publication. We have lost our good neighbours from the Ivy Cot (Mr and Mrs Elliott) and with them their newspaper, and now we only see our own provincial papers, and in these long winter evenings, my Brother feels a want of the little break-in, which our Friends paper used to make among us.— You will have heard of us from Mr and Mrs Field[2]—at least they assured me that they should see you ere long, and I sent messages by them. Perhaps they forgot all but my remembrances, for I begged them to urge you to *write*—My Brother is very sorry he did not see Mr Field, being much interested about him. I was much pleased with his Wife. I hope you often see Charles and Mary Lamb, and that they are well. Mrs Field brought a very good account of her. What a loss the Lambs, not less than you, must feel this winter of the chearful resting place and never-failing cordial welcome by Thomas Monkhouse's fireside!——We all join in Kindest remembrances.

Believe me ever your faithful and affectionate Friend,

Dorothy Wordsworth.

I know you are not tolerant of bad penmanship. What, then, will you say to this letter? I have no excuse for giving you so much

---

[1] In his (unpublished) reply of 10 Feb. 1825, H. C. R. advised an investment in North American securities. (*Dr. Williams's Library MSS.*)
[2] For Barron Field of the Inner Temple, see L. 334 below.

trouble except the bad habit of scrawling whenever I write to my best Friends.—

Because this comes to you by a private hand, do not suppose that your letter will be the less welcome if to be paid for—and I pray you wait not for a Frank.

[*There follows*[1] Mary Monkhouse *as in PW iii. 46, except that in ll. 5–6 read* . . . a trace/Of fretful temper sullies not her cheek.]

My Brother desires me to beg you (this I know is unnecessary) not to give copies of these Sonnets to any one; but they having been composed only for the love of private Friends; and for the sake of expressing his own peculiar feelings with regard to the two Infants, he is particularly desirous that they should not be spread abroad either by copies—or by being read to any persons but such as may have an interest in the parents or Children.—You have heard of the melancholy Fate of Mrs Quillinan, Rotha's Mother. She died at the age of 28—at Ivy Cottage.

[*There follows* To Rotha Quillinan *as in PW iii. 47, except that in ll. 11–12 read* . . . whose Name is thine to bear,/Hanging around thee.]

Pray give our united love and best wishes to Charles Lamb and his Sister.—I should now write a few lines to her, but have nothing to say but what you may tell them from my letter, only be so good as to ask Charles if my Brother's Translation of Virgil is in his possession. Tell him, too, that if he would send us a letter either from his India House Desk or from Colebrook Cottage, we should all be well pleased,—and if addressed to my Brother I can insure him an answer from himself.

[2][Postscr]ipt after postscript! Did you ever read the letter of orders for a Scarlet Cardinal? If you did I am sure this will remind you of it. First a *morning* Paper is desired, (to be forwarded the same evening). If that cannot be, an Evening paper next day— if not, a *morning* paper sent *next* day . . . and last of all—if none of the above can be had, an *evening* three-days-a-week paper—

I fear you will not succeed, knowing that there is great difficulty in obtaining second-hand newspapers—

---

[1] The rest of this letter was printed by Morley as a separate item—but it seems to be part of a single letter, though possibly added a day or two later.
[2] *MS. torn.*

150. W. W. to THE COMMISSIONERS OF STAMPS

Address: To The Hon'ble the Commissioners, Stamp Office, London.
Postmark: 24 Dec. 1824. *Stamp*: Kendal Penny Post. *Endorsed*: From W^m
Wordsworth Esq Rydal Mount 20th Decr 1824.
MS. Public Record Office. Hitherto unpublished.

[*In John Carter's hand*]

Rydal Mount, Ambleside,
20th Decr 1824.—

Hon'ble Sirs,

I beg leave to state in reply to your letter of the 16th Inst: that as the several Receipts therein mentioned were not returned to me by the Parties to whom they had been given for corrections, they could not possibly be forwarded by me, in the monthly Parcel of Receipts; but, that the Account (sent in pursuance of the Board's directions) which accompanied the Parcel, contained the said Receipts, amongst others, *regularly reported* as not having been returned to me.

The instructions of the Board do certainly enjoin an 'endeavour' on the part of the Distributors to obtain a return of Receipts of this description within the prescribed time, which Instructions were in the first Instance pressed upon the Subdistributors as a general Rule, and their attention has subsequently been directed thereto in special cases:—nevertheless a punctual return of those Papers can in very few cases be obtained, even through the exertions of the Subdistributors, and I am not aware that I possess, either in my own person, or by my Agents, any power to *compell* Parties to deliver in their Accounts.—

I have the Honor to be
Hon'ble Sirs,
Your obedient Servant
[*signed*] W Wordsworth

151. W. W. to C. W.

Address: To The Revd Dr Wordsworth, Trinity Lodge, Cambridge.
Stamp: Kendal Penny Post. *Endorsed*: My brother. Jany 4.
MS. WL.
LT i. 168.

[In D. W.'s hand]

January 4th 1825

My dear Brother,

During the former part of this letter I shall hold the pen for William at his request. Southey would inform you that he had delivered the Icon[1] to me at his own house. In his judgment[2] you had made out the case. My Wife, your Relation Mr Robinson,[3] and Mr Carr, our Apothecary all of whom have read your Book are of the same opinion. I have had considerable portions of it read, and find it improve upon me in effect. You ask for remarks—I have only one—that when you argue from the inherent baseness of Gauden's[4] mind that he was incapable of entertaining the noble sentiments of the Icon, and therefore of personating the King, sufficient allowance is not made, I think, for his dramatic talent, as I may call it, as exhibited in the hypocrisy of his episcopal Charge and his other works; yet, I own, it would be little less than marvellous that Gauden had kept the Icon so clear from stains of vicious

[1] In 1824 C. W. published *Who wrote ΕΙΚΩΝ ΒΑΣΙΛΙΚΗ? considered and answered, in two letters, addressed to . . . the Archibishop of Canterbury*, in which he argued for the authorship of Charles I. In 1825 he published *A Documentary Supplement*, and in 1828 *King Charles the First the author of Icon Basilike, further proved in a letter to his Grace the Archbishop of Canterbury, in reply to the objections of Dr. Lingard, Mr. Todd, Mr. Broughton, the Edinburgh Review, and Mr. Hallam*.

[2] On 11 Dec. 1824 Southey had written to C. W.: 'I am not a little pleased to think that our conversation on the Rydal road should have led you to undertake and execute a task, which in my view of the subject, is of considerable importance to English feeling, as well as English history. You have completely destroyed Gauden's credibility as a witness, and completely removed the difficulty arising from Clarendon's silence, which I am quite satisfied is rightly explained. Whenever that age shall be regarded without any feelings of party, it will be admitted that you have thoroughly sifted the question, and finally decided it.' (*MS. Jonathan Wordsworth.*)

[3] Capt. Charles Robinson, now living in Ambleside.

[4] John Gauden (1605–62), Bishop of Exeter at the Restoration, and Bishop of Worcester in 1662. In the early years of the Civil War his sympathies were with the Parliament: he became vicar of Chippenham in 1640, and Dean of Bocking, 1642, and in 1643 he was for a short time a member of the Westminster Assembly, though he was soon 'shuffled out' for episcopalianism. He contrived, however, to retain his benefices throughout the Commonwealth: welcomed the Restoration, and claimed authorship of the *Icon* to promote his claims to high office in the Church.

moral sentiment and bad taste. In that, I think, would lie the wonder, and not in the production of any *strains* of piety and purity that may be found there.

Mary, Dora and I reached home on the 13th Novr. after an absence of eleven weeks and ½, three of which were spent in a delightful ramble through North, and a part of South, Wales— five in a residence in Radnorshire and Herefordshire with Mr Hutchinson and Mr Monkhouse—and three at Sir George Beaumont's. Our abode in South Wales, notwithstanding the pleasure we had in seeing such excellent Friends was made very melancholy by the state of Mr Thomas Monkhouse's health, who, you will be grieved to hear, is dying of a pulmonary Consumption —dying very, very slowly. He is now in Devonshire with his Wife and Child and Miss Hutchinson. Their situation is sad, for he is not allowed by his physicians to speak above a whisper, from which you may judge in what condition they suppose his lungs to be. I cannot help saying on this occasion that Mr M. has proved to us in all our various connexions a faithful and invaluable Friend, so that our loss will in every respect be severe.

Jones met us at Llanroost, and was our companion during 13 days. We parted at the famous Devil's Bridge. If I find I have room I will send you a Sonnet, which I poured out in the chasm there, during a heavy storm, while Dora was at my side endeavouring to sketch the body of the place, leaving, poor Girl! the soul of it to her Father. Jones was the best of companions, being master of the language, very extensively known in the Country, a most affec- tionate Man, and, I verily believe, the best-tempered Creature imaginable; to me, who am apt to be irritable in travelling, an inestimable qualification. We did not ascend Snowdon nor any high mountain, but in other respects did justice to the country, by travelling very leisurely. It much exceeded in interest the expecta- tions which the imperfect observations of one or two and twenty, and the faded recollections of two or three and thirty years allowed me to entertain. We were indeed all much delighted, and often wished for Dorothy and you. Jones spoke of you with that interest which is natural to him—and of your Sons. We went round by Worcester to see Sir George and Lady Beaumont, then in atten- dance upon Mrs Fermor,[1] Lady B's Sister, a most highly gifted and excellent person, who is since dead. We were anxious about her

---

[1] She was Frances, eldest daughter of John Willes of Astrop, Northants (see *EY*, p. 409), and married Henry Fermor of Fritwell, Oxon, in 1784. See the *Elegiac Stanzas* in her memory and the I. F. note, *PW* iv. 269, 457.

during the whole of our stay at Coleorton, though accounts were more favorable. She died about three weeks ago. As a mark of regard—or rather, if I may be allowed to say so, as a testimony of her sense of the value of my writings, she has left me a Legacy of £100—'a small token' as she terms it; but in fact not so, as her means were inconsiderable. Sir George (writing soon after the melancholy event) says that Lady B and himself are a good deal worn down. By this time I hope they are recovering.

We were much concerned to hear of our Nephew John's[1] deranged health. He did not seem to be strong when we were at Cambridge. I think you have taken the best plan possible for restoring him. Remember us all kindly to him and his Brothers. I have not forgotten the prize exercise which Charles sent me, which did him great credit. What have you to say of them all? They are often talked of, and still more in the thoughts of, this family.—William's health is tolerable but we dare not send him from home. John is here for the Christmas vacation, and perhaps to remain till Easter, but this will depend on his Friend Mr William Jackson being at liberty to give him a little of his time.

My eyes are on the whole better, though very subject to derangement—The Females are well. I, that is here meaning Dorothy Wordsworth, have to thank my Nephew John for a very pleasant letter from Cromer,—now I deliver up the pen to W.——

Dearest Brother,

I am truly glad that the Speaker's[2] connection is broken off for his sake; but as far as you are concerned in the politics connected with the affair, I see nothing to rejoice in; first because the matter has been so public, (Dr Satterthwaite for instance spoke of it as the common talk among the younger Members of the Lowther Family, and all their town acquaintance) and next, because one cannot rely upon good conduct being preserved where it originates so obviously in a selfish motive. I should have been much better pleased to hear that the Speaker had declined the Representation altogether, and

---

[1] C. W.'s son John, now an undergraduate at Trinity.

[2] Charles Manners-Sutton, 1st Viscount Canterbury (1780–1845), Speaker of the House of Commons, 1817–35: son of C. W.'s patron who was responsible for his appointment as Master of Trinity (see *MT* ii. 309, 614). In Nov. 1822 he had withdrawn as a candidate for Cambridge University on account of the inconvenience he might cause in the workings of the House (see above, L. 80); but Lord Lowther, as Chairman of his election committee, had expressed the hope that he would stand at the next general election, and he seems to have been pressing his claims again at this time. Manners-Sutton was not elected for Cambridge until the general election of Dec. 1832, when he was returned with Henry Goulburn as colleague.

I cannot see how you can escape censure for supporting him after what has passed; and if he does come forward, still less do I see how you can avoid supporting him; it would be cruel to decline it, both on his own account and his Father's. The dilemma I cannot get out of and it causes me much uneasiness. Do let me hear from you again, if you can say any thing satisfactory.—I had such bad accounts of Dr Satterthwaite's health that I went over to see him; and found him much better than I expected—ever most affectionately yours

W W.

Sonnet, composed in the *Chasm of the Devil's Bridge*, after a Flood [*as in PW iii. 43 but ll. 10–11*

> High o'er the yawning fissure, piny woods,
> And sun-bright lawns, and everlasting snows,

and in l. 13 Sway *for* power.]

152. W. W. to CHARLES LLOYD SNR.[1]

MS. untraced.
E. V. Lucas, Charles Lamb and the Lloyds, 1898, pp. 274–5.

Rydal Mount,
January 6, 1825.

My dear Sir,—You will be surprised with the matter which this letter will turn upon—viz., something like money business, and I feel that I ought not to approach you, without previously resting my apology on your known friendly disposition. To come to the point at once, I have been led to consider Birmingham as the point from which the railway companies now forming receive their principal impulse, and I feel disposed to risk a sum—not more than 500*l.*—in purchasing Shares in some promising Company or Companies. I do not wish to involve you in the responsibility of *advising* an Investment of this kind, but I hope I do not presume too much when I request that you would have the kindness to point out to me what Companies are thought the most eligible, adding directions as to the mode of proceeding in case I determine upon purchasing.

We heard from Dr. Wordsworth about 3 weeks ago; as he does

---

[1] The Quaker banker of Bingley House, Birmingham (see *EY*, p. 217): father of Charles and Priscilla Lloyd. W. W. and D. W. used to stay with him when passing through Birmingham on their way south.

not mention Owen,[1] we infer that his health is improved. He speaks of his Son John being much benefited by Horse exercise. I hope you receive good tidings from France.[2] We are all very well here, and with our united best regards to you and your numerous Family, believe me to be, dear Sir, very sincerely yours,

Wm Wordsworth

153. W. W. to FRANCIS MEREWETHER[3]

Address: Rev^d. Francis Merewether, Coleorton Rectory, near Ashby de la Zouche, Leicestershire.
Stamp: Kendal Penny Post.
MS. Cornell. Broughton, p. 61.

Rydal Mount
Jan^ry 10th 1825

Dear Sir,

You were very kind in bearing my request in mind; and I should have written sooner to thank you had there been any thing for me to suggest. I infer that nothing important has occurred or probably I should have heard from you again. It would give me much pleasure to learn that this troublesome business[4] is at rest.—

Many thanks for your long Extract from Mr Walters[5] Letter. As he seems, not without good reason, afraid of the length of his Abstract, it might perhaps be better to confine himself to his own first plan, that of giving the assailant side *only*. But he will be the best judge of this. I have nothing further to observe upon his little work, which I cannot but think will prove serviceable, and ought to be continued hearafter if occasion should call for it; and this from the temper of our age, is too probable.

---

[1] The Revd. Owen Lloyd (1803–41), son of Charles Lloyd jnr., born at Brathay, educated at Shrewsbury, was at this time an undergraduate at Trinity College, Cambridge. He was perpetual curate of Langdale, 1929–41.

[2] i.e. from Charles Lloyd jnr., now living in France.

[3] The Revd. Francis Merewether (1784–1864), rector of Coleorton, 1815–64, and vicar of Whitwick—where John W. was later his curate—from 1819: a high-churchman of traditional views, and author of several pamphlets on Church questions. [4] The reference here is obscure.

[5] Probably the Revd. Henry Walter (1785–1859), divine and antiquary: Fellow of St. John's College, Cambridge, 1806–24; Professor of Natural Philosophy and Mathematics at Haileybury, 1806–30; and rector of Hazelbury-Bryan, Dorset, from 1821. He published a *History of England* in 1840, and edited Tyndale for the Parker Society. The 'Letter' referred to here is probably *A Letter to the Rt. Revd. Herbert Lord Bishop of Peterborough, . . . on the independence of the authorized version of the Bible*, 1823: *A second letter . . .* appeared in 1828.

10 *January 1825*

Lady Fleming's Chapel of Rydal[1] though not yet consecrated was opened on Christmas day. The weather was tremendously stormy, and 60 or 70 persons at least had through means of this new Edifice an opportunity of attending public worship, which without it they could not have had. This sight must have been highly gratifying to the munificent Foundress. The cost of the Structure has much exceeded what was needful; but when time has softened down the exterior a little it will prove a great ornament to the Village. The Clergyman promises to be a sort of 'rara avis', in this Country, where there is a sad want of zeal among Members. His name is Fleming[2] and he is a distant Relative of her Ladyship's F[amily.]

I heard from Dr Wordsworth lately upon the delicate matter[3] which I believe we alluded to when I was at Coleorton. The connection is broken off; but how much is it to be lamented that such a thing should ever have been!

I hope that Lady B. and Sir George are recovering from the effects of their late loss. Mrs Fermor was an inestimable Person, and the thought of her departure from this world, blessed as no doubt it is for herself, will often cast a shade of sadness over my mind, when I think of the apartments and the groves of Coleorton. Perhaps you may have heard that she has left me in her Will a token of Remembrance; solemn Testimonies of regard from so pious and exalted a mind, prized as they must be, are attended with this danger that they may tempt the object of them to think more favorably of himself than he ought to do. The caution of St Paul ought never to be out of a man's thoughts, when he receives any striking evidence of the good opinion of his Friends.—

We are all pretty well at present except that I have a slight cold which would not be worth naming, but that it is the *third* I have had since the sharpness of autumn set in. Every one sends the best wishes of the season to you and Mrs Merewether.

---

[1] Built by Lady le Fleming at a cost of £1,500, and now opened. Dora W. described the event in her letter to Elizabeth Crump of 27 Dec. 1824: 'I never was out in such a storm nor does my Father ever remember experiencing so violent a one. My Lady walked thro' it all—how thoroughly she must have been imprest with the utility of her work . . . Fletcher Fleming is a Treasure in these parts where, as my Father says, we are so ill-parson'd, he is very earnest, has a remarkably distinct articulation and good voice—*his* fault is reading *too* slowly . . .' (*WL MSS.*)

[2] The Revd. Fletcher Fleming (1795–1876), son of W. W.'s school friend John Fleming of Rayrigg, and nephew of Fletcher Raincock (see L. 26): educated at Hawkshead and Sedbergh, and St. John's College, Cambridge: perpetual curate of Rydal and Loughrigg, 1825–57, and rector of Grasmere from 1857. He lived at Rydal Lodge, Ambleside, and latterly at Rayrigg.

[3] The candidature of the Speaker for Cambridge University. See L. 151 above.

What do you think of the 'Eikon'?[1] We reckon it convincing; ever most sincerely yours

W W—

If you write to Mr Walter pray tell him I shall bear his obliging message in mind about his parsonage, and this with thanks—I ought to have thanked you again for your Pamphlet[2] which I have read at leisure. It is extremely well done.

154. W. W. to JACOB FLETCHER[3]

Address: To J. Fletcher Esqre, Allerton, near Liverpool.
Stamp: Kendal Penny Post.
MS. Cornell.
K (—). *LY i. 171.*

[*In M. W.'s hand*]

Rydal Mount Jan^ry 17th 1825

Sir

I should have acknowledged the receipt of your obliging communication by return of Post, had it found me at home.[4] It would have been gratifying to me to have made your Acquaintance when we were thrown together on that gloomy evening, and in those not very comfortable Quarters.

The interesting Observations you have sent me I have not yet had time read more than once—so that I do not feel competent to make any remarks worthy the attention of so accurate an Observer as you are, and so reflecting a mind as you possess. One or two notices, however, I will hazard. I object to nothing which you say upon the Scenery of N.W.[5] considered per se. Your analysis of it is, as far as it goes, undeniably just—but it seems next to impossible to discriminate between the claims of two countries to admiration with the impartiality of a *Judge*; in one's mind one may be just to both, but something of the *advocate* will creep into the language— as an office of this kind is generally undertaken with a view to rectify some injustice. This was the case with myself in respect to a comparison which I have drawn between our Mountains etc and

---

[1] i.e. C. W.'s book, just published. See L. 151 above.
[2] *Thoughts on the present State of Popular Opinion in Matters of Religion in England* . . ., 1824.
[3] Jacob Fletcher (1790–1863), a Liverpool merchant, of Grove House, Allerton: educated at Brasenose College, Oxford: friend of John Bolton of Storrs.
[4] W. W. had been away for a few days at Cockermouth, presumably on Stamp Office business.　　　　　[5] North Wales.

the Alps; the general impression is, I am afraid, that I give the preference to my native region, which was far from the truth. But I wished to shew advantages which we possessed that were generally overlooked, and *dwelt* upon these, slightly adverting only to the points in which the Alps have the superiority. The result then is, that I may *appear* to have dealt unfairly with that marvellous portion of the Earth that is presented to view in the Swiss and Italian vallies.—In like manner you have the *appearance* of being unjust to Scotland. I am indeed not acquainted with any tract in Scotland of equal compass so worthy of admiration as Snowdon, and its included and circumjacent vallies—and this is the district which has suggested the principal part, if not the whole of your observations; but there are tracts in N.W. that are as tame and uninteresting, and almost as desolate as the worst in Scotland, tho' certainly not so extensive. I cannot but think that if the Landscape interests of the Highlands were as condensed as those of N.W., or of *this* Country, they would bear a comparison more favourable than you are inclined to allow them. We employed three weeks in exploring N.W.—far too short a time:—a complete circuit ought to be made of Snowdon and the like of Cader Idris—centres to a pair of magnificent circles. We went from Dolgelly to Barmouth by land, and returned by water—but it was with the utmost regret that I left the shore on our right, as we returned, wholly unexplored. We saw something more of the Tal-y-lyn side of the Mountain, but owing to the state of the weather far less than we wished. I am so much pleased with your communication that I am desirous to know what use you mean to make of it. If I do not visit Scotland during the ensuing Summer I shall in all probability re-examine N.W. not with any view to writing a Tour thro' the Country but of giving an analysis of Snowdon, Cader Idris and their several dependencies, with a sketch of the characters of the principal rivers. But you appear to be so well qualified for this employment, that I should be happy to hear that you meant to undertake it—my wish being to teach the *Touring World*, which is become very numerous, to look thro' the clear eye of the Understanding as well as thro' the hazy one of vague Sensibility. But let me have the conclusion at your earliest convenience, and tell me precisely what you mean by objects being picturesque—and yet unfit for the pencil. Many objects are fit for the pencil which are not picturesque—but I have been in the habit of applying the word to such objects only as are so.

I remain d^r Sir your obd^t S^t

[*signed*] Wm Wordsworth

155. W. W. to LORD LONSDALE

Address: The Earl of Lonsdale, Cottesmore, Grantham.
Stamp: Penrith.
MS. Lonsdale MSS. Hitherto unpublished.

Lowther Rectory
Jan^ry 21st [1825]¹
My Lord,

You will be surprized with the date of this. Messrs Harrison² and Nicholson³ having a spare place in their Chaise, I was glad to avail myself of it to go over and see Dr S.⁴ of whose health I had heard unfavorable accounts. It gives me great pleasure to say, that I found my excellent Friend very much better than I had been led to expect, and upon the whole I should say that his health is improved since I last saw him.

I was much gratified by your Lordship's attention to my Report of what was passing in Grasmere.⁵ You have learned, no doubt, from Mr Nicholson the result of the meeting, and the turn the affair is likely to take. The *meeting* broke up without anything being done except passing a Resolution that a debt which had been incurred under the authority of a previous Vestry meeting for defraying the expenses of running a fence between Grasmere liberties and those of Wytheburn should be paid by a Rate upon the Township. Before this was settled (which might have been disposed of in a moment except for the presence of Captn Robertson Walker⁶ who has a small Estate in Grasmere in right of his Wife, Sister of the late Mr Walker of Gilgaren near Whitehaven) so much time was consumed and the Parties put into such ill-humor, that nothing further could be agreed upon. Mr Harrison stated your Lordship's wishes to concur in anything which in the opinion of the Proprietors might tend to their common benefit, and the meeting was dissolved. We retired into different Rooms for Refreshment, and during this time a Paper was circulated by Mr Johnson⁷ of Kendal,

---

¹ *Written* 1824—but the year is clearly 1825 from other references in the *Lonsdale MSS.*

² Anthony Harrison, the Penrith attorney, acting for Lord Lonsdale.

³ William Nicholson, agent at Lowther. See *MT* ii. 585.

⁴ Dr. Satterthwaite.

⁵ This letter, which is untraced, must have contained an account of the move to enclose the wastes and commons of Grasmere and Loughrigg. In his reply of 10 Dec. 1824 Lord Lonsdale wrote, '. . . as far as I am able, I shall have great Pleasure in doing what I can to allay the present Irritation and alarm' (*WL MSS.*).

⁶ Capt. James Robertson, R.N., High Sheriff of Cumberland, 1841, married Miss Walker of Gilgarran, nr. Whitehaven, and assumed the additional surname of Walker by Royal Licence.

⁷ James Johnson, the Kendal attorney. See *MT* ii. 418.

containing a proposal for converting the Common into a stinted pasture, without division of enclosure; certain parts to be sold for to pay the expenses. This measure met with the countenance of so many who were utterly averse to *dividing* and *enclosing*, that in all probability with your Lordship's approbation, it will take effect. The expense is estimated at about £1,200, application to Parliament and Commissioner included. The Meeting however unsatisfactory as *such*, furnished fresh evidence that the alledged abuses had been greatly exaggerated, and that these abuses were *not* the principal motives with the few who first agitated the Question. In some cases it had not been convenient or deemed advisable to make use of the Common and in others the Parties expected to profit by that portion of the Common which must be sold for to pay the expenses. The proposed plan will certainly lead to a more equitable enjoyment of rights, and I hope will in the end prove to the benefit of the Proprietors. Those who have had more than their share will of course be discontented. For my own part, as deeply interested in the well-being of the neighbourhood, I must say that I wish the Townships of Loughrigg and Grasmere had been kept separate in this affair; as I do not think that the abuses were sufficient to call for a change in the case of *Grasmere*, and I am afraid of such a change in a Township which could affirm a little time ago and probably may not be able to say the same since, that the only Resident Pauper in a population of 56 Dwellings was an old woman who received a shilling or two per week.

Mr Nicholson has promised that a draught of the Bill[1] shall be sent over for my Inspection which I flatter myself your Lordship will approve of.

Sir George and Lady Beaumont have suffered a severe loss by the death of Lady B's Sister, Mrs Fermor.[2] Sir George writes me that they are both worn down a good deal by the event. Mrs Fermor I knew well, she was worthy of the affection they bore her.

We have no better accounts from Mr Monkhouse.

I am sorry I was not at Rydale when your Lordship did me the honor of calling.[3] I should have liked much to show you the view

---

[1] To promote the enclosure.
[2] See L. 153 above.
[3] 'I call'd at your House as I went to Storrs, but at that time they had no Tidings of you. We called likewise on your neighbour, who has just entered, into what she call'd her Winter Quarters, from which she opines she will not emerge till the Spring. For my own Part, I had rather be divorc'd to the Treadmill, than become the Inhabitant of this mansion with such a Hostess.' (*WL MSS.*)

from the garden and Terrace of Rydal Mount, which are universally admired.

Pray present my best respects to Lady Lonsdale, and believe me my Lord

Ever faithfully
your Lordship's
obliged Friend and Serv^{nt}
Wm Wordsworth

May I beg the favour of a Frank for the enclosed—

156. W. W. to SAMUEL ROGERS

MS. Sharpe Collection, University College, London.
Rogers. K (—). LT i. 173.
[In M. W.'s hand]

Rydal Mount, Jan^{ry} 21st, 1825.

My dear Rogers,

I take the liberty of enclosing a letter which I have just rec^d from Messrs Longman,[1] which be so kind as to peruse: it was in reply to one of mine, wishing to know whether they could not make it answer for them to publish my Poems on terms somewhat more advantageous to me than hitherto; what those terms were you learn from the letter, and I need scarcely add that after the first expense of printing and advertising was paid out of an Ed: the *ann^l* expence of advertizing consumed in a great measure the residue of Profit to be divided between Author and Publisher. So that, as I frankly told them, it was not worth my while to undergo the

---

[1] For some time W. W. had not been entirely happy with Longman as his publisher; and now, in contemplating a new edition of his poems, he was hoping to find another who would offer him better terms. On 18 Jan. Longman had replied: 'We regret with you that your works have not been more productive to you; and it would give us great pleasure could we propose terms more favorable to you, but, seeing what the demand has been, we can only propose, as before, to take the expenses upon ourselves, and divide the profits . . . If you can find terms with another respectable house which you may consider more to your interest, we cannot feel that you have acted unhandsomely towards us, and only regret the dissolution of a publishing connexion with a gentleman for whom we have felt the highest regard.' (W. J. B. Owen, 'Letters of Longman and Co. to Wordsworth, 1814–36', *Library*, 5th series, ix (Mar. 1954), 25–34.) W. W. accordingly approached Murray, through Samuel Rogers (see L. 164 below); then Hurst and Robinson through Alaric Watts (see L. 182 below); and in 1826 he made a fresh approach to Murray. But nothing eventually came of these overtures, and he reverted to Longman, on somewhat better terms than before. See L. 264 below.

trouble of carrying my works thro' the Press unless an arrangement more favourable could be made.

The question then is, whether there be in the Trade more liberality, more enterprize, or more skill in managing the Sale of Works charactered and circumstanced as mine are, than have fallen to the lot of Messrs Longman and Co. Of this you are infinitely a better judge than myself; I therefore apply to you for advice and assistance before I make a new engagement with any one. Observing by the bye to you, that I have no *positive* ground for complaint against my present Publishers.

Would you be so kind as to try for me wherever you think it most likely to effect a favourable bargain. I am aware that I am proposing a very disagreeable office, but it is not more than I would readily do for you, if I had the same advantage of experience, influence, and judgement over you in these matters that you have over me. The letter shews that if Messrs L. and I part, it is amicably. I must add that they have an interest in the Ecc. Sketches and the Memorials of a Tour etc which must be given up before I could incorporate them, according to my wish, into a new Edition, which I think would contain besides, 4 or 500 lines of verses which have not yet seen the light. I have no objection to any Publisher whom you might approve.

Where were you last summer? Mrs W, my daughter, and I spent three weeks in a delightful ramble thro' North Wales, and saw something of S.W. particularly the course of the Wye above Hereford nearly to its source.

I saw Southey the other day, he was well, and busy as usual; and as his late letter[1] shews, not quite so charitably disposed to Don Juan deceased as you evidently are, if I may judge by a tribute to his memory bearing your name, which I accidentally met with in a newspaper—but *you* were the Don's particular Friend, an equal indulgence, therefore, could not be expected from the Laureate, who, I will not say was his particular enemy, but who had certainly no friendship for him. Medwin[2] makes a despicable Figure as the

---

[1] Published in the *Courier* for 13 Dec. 1824, and repr. in Southey's *Essays Moral and Political*, 2 vols., 1832, ii. 196 ff.

[2] In 1824 Thomas Medwin (1788–1869) had published his controversial *Journal of the Conversations of Lord Byron*, based on his association with the poet in Italy in 1821–2. In his letter, Southey treated Medwin as an authentic witness, answered Byron's allegations against him quoted by Medwin, and defended his original stand against the 'Satanic school'. 'It was because Lord Byron had brought a stigma upon English literature, that I accused him; because he had perverted great talents to the worst purposes; because he had set up for pander-general to the youth of Great Britain as long as his writings

Salesman of so much trash. I do not believe there is a man living, from a Shoeblack at the corner of your street up to the Archbishop of Canterbury or the Lord Chancellor, of whose conversation so much worthless matter could be reported, with so little deserving to be remembered—as the result of an equal number of miscellaneous opportunities. Is this the fault of Lord B. or his Boswell? The truth is, I fear, that it may be pretty equally divided between them.

My Amanuensis Mrs W says that it is not handsome in me to speak thus of your friend—no more it is, if he were your friend *mortuus* in every sense of the word, but his spirit walks abroad, to do some good I hope, but a plaguy deal of mischief.

I was much shocked when I heard of his death[1]—news which reached me in the cloisters of that College to which he belonged.

Where and how is Sharp, and what does he report of Italy? Last autumn I saw Uvedale Price,[2] our common friend (so I presume to call him, tho' really only having a slight acquaintance with him), striding up the steep sides of his wood-crowned hills, with his hacker, *i.e.* his silvan Hanger, slung from his shoulder, like Robin Hood's bow. He is 77 years of age and truly a wonder both for body and mind—especially do I feel him to be so when I recollect the deranged state of his digestive organs 12 years ago. I dined with him about that time at your table and elsewhere.

Poor Mr Monkhouse, you will be sorry to hear, is wintering in Devonshire, driven thither by a disease of the lungs, which leaves his Friends little hope of his recovery. He is one of my most valued friends, and should he sink under this complaint, one of the strongest of my inducements, and the most important of my facilities for visiting London, and prolonging my stay there, will be removed.

Remember us all most kindly to your Sister, and believe me with all our united regards my dear Rogers most faithfully yours,

[*signed*] Wᵐ Wordsworth

Pray send me Longman's letter back at your convenience.

should endure; because he had committed a high crime and misdemeanour against society, by sending forth a work, in which mockery was mingled with horrors, filth with impiety, profligacy with sedition and slander. For these offences I came forward to arraign him. . . .'

[1] At Missolonghi, on 19 Apr. 1824.
[2] See L. 141 above.

157. W. W. to MESSRS. BELL BROTHERS AND CO.[1]

MS. Cornell.
Broughton, p. 63.

[*In M. W.'s hand*]

Rydal Mount
Feb 2d 1825

Gent,

I have to acknowledge the receipt of your letter of the 24th of Janry stating that you had paid into the Bank of Messrs Masterman and Co,[2] on my account £161–12–10 being part of the Life Annuities due to me—and have now to desire you to pay any balance you have since received, or may hereafter receive *immediately* to Mr Courtenay;[3] he having made purchases for me, I wish to put funds into his hands. And in future also, please to pay what may become due to me, not into Masterman's but to Mr C. directly.

I am Gentlemen
respectfully yours
[*signed*] Wm Wordsworth

158. W. W. to VISCOUNT LOWTHER

MS. WL.
LY i. 175.

[*In M. W.'s hand*]

Rydal Mount Febry 12th 1825

My dear Lord Lowther

Your obliging letter was very acceptable—from what you mention respecting the new Lord Thanet,[4] and from what I have heard from Lord Lonsdale on the same subject, I infer there is little probability of Westd being disturbed—yet one cannot but be anxious, and I shall be truly glad to be informed when you have any thing positive to communicate.

Your account of the angry temper which prevails in the House adds much to the concern which I felt in reading the debates upon

---

[1] Stockbrokers.
[2] The Lombard St. bankers: W. W.'s local bank, John Wakefield and Son of Kendal, drew on them.
[3] Philip Courtenay, W. W.'s man of business.
[4] The 9th Earl of Thanet (see *MY* ii. 412), who actively supported Brougham in the Westmorland elections of 1818 and 1820, died on 24 Jan. 1825. He was succeeded by his brother, the Hon. Charles Tufton (1770–1832).

the King's speech; and sorry am I to say, not so much on account of what fell from Opposition, as from the conduct of Ministers. I do not judge of motives on either side, being too far from the spot for accurate observation—but who can see without emotion things carried on as if the maintenance of Protestant Ascendancy in Ireland were to be abandoned? While Opposition is affirming that the Catholic Association[1] is eminently beneficial, Mr Canning *as* positively asserts that it is a pest—but why? only because it must impede, instead of advancing the views of the Catholics; and he bewails its constitution, and grieves for its misconduct accordingly.[2] This would be all very well for discontented Persons out of power, or for those who care little for Catholic or Protestant principles either in Church or State—in Religion or politics—But that a leading Minister should utter these regrets and *confine himself* to the uttering them, does grieve me who am heartily glad that the Romanists have thus prematurely shewn themselves, so as to open the eyes, one would think, of the most simple. Glad should I have been to have heard from Mr Canning a word of regret upon the bearing of the Catholic Association upon the Protestant interest— and still more to have heard him acknowledge that late events had proved he had thought too favourably of them—that he was becoming suspicious, and that if their future conduct were not more wise and temperate, which he scarcely dared to hope for, he must give them up, and side with their opponents. Let us ask what reasons can be adduced for putting down the Catholic Association but such as are drawn from circumstances and characteristics which belonging to them as Papists, make them dangerous to the tranquillity, if not to the existence of the State. There are, we all know, numerous Societies in this Kingdom that raise large sums of money, by voluntary contribution, which are in most cases applied to avowed ends—we do not dread these—nor do we legislate against

---

[1] The Catholic Association was founded by Daniel O'Connell (1775–1847) in 1823 to take up the practical problems and grievances of the Irish peasantry. In the following year he started the system of 'Catholic rent' whereby those who paid a shilling a year to the Association became members. On 10 Feb. 1825 a Bill was introduced to suppress the Association.

[2] In reply to the King's Speech opening the Session on 3 Feb., Brougham, speaking for the Opposition, had contrasted the liberal policy adopted towards the new South American states with the oppression in Ireland: he drew attention to a recent conciliatory proclamation of the King of Hanover to the effect that all professors of the Christian faith in that Kingdom should enjoy equal civil and political rights; and he defended the Catholic Association as expressing the feelings and wishes of the Irish people. In answer to Brougham, Canning supported the principle of emancipation, but saw the Catholic Association as the greatest impediment to the further progress of the movement.

them. Wherein is the Catholic Association formidable? from its Numbers—from the contribution, which is professedly voluntary, being in fact compulsory thro' the power of the Priests, and from that disposition in all men to deem false pretence justifiable for favourite ends—a disposition to which Papacy gives a religious sanction. It is in vain to say that such principles are disavowed by great Leaders on formal occasions: we know they are, and ever have been, acted upon in the Romish Church. But many believe, along with Mr C., that concession would conciliate; and that these principles not being called for as helps to get rid of injustice, would die away in general content. Impossible if there were no other obstacle than envy of the protestant Ch: establishment. 'What would satisfy you?' said not long ago a gentleman to a very clever R.C. Lady, whose husband by the bye is an Agent of the present Duke of Norfolk. 'That Church' replied she, pointing to a large parish Church in Sheffield where the conversation took place— This, at the bottom of their hearts, is the feeling of them all; and can we wonder at a worldly ambition which comes recommended to the Members of this Church, by a belief instilled into them from infancy, that there is no safety out of the pale of their Faith. Intolerance under this impression becomes a duty, nor ought we to blame, however we may dread them, if they feel and act upon it as such. But we are told that these tenets are abandoned—by Persons who forget, no doubt, that infallibility (and consequent immutability) is a fundamental principle of the Romish Faith.

Mr Brougham exults in the late application of his liberal notions to Hanover, but in Hanover the Protestants are more than ten to one, and the Govt. is military; and, like the other German States, has the whole Germanic league to back it, in case of a tendency to commotion. Hanover indeed possesses a Legislative Assembly, but its powers are so ill defined that it could not attempt to do any thing important without bringing on immediately its own dissolution from the military force. It has, on the other hand, a Censorship of the Press—and, if Mr B. should say that this is very indulgent, let him be told that it can afford to be so, thro' the tranquillizing virtue of the standing Army of Hanover, and of all Germany if required.—Why does nobody think it worth while to put down this Cant? which, though harmless in the House of Commons perhaps, does a world of mischief in the country.

I return to Conciliation. The Mover of the Address of thanks in the House of Lords is a Concessionist[1]—and Lord

---

[1] John William Ward, 4th Viscount Dudley and Ward, later 1st Earl of

Liverpool[1] is obviously giving way under Canning's superior influence. Now my dear Lord Lowther, I do not undertake to calculate what change the introducing Catholics into the two Houses of Parliament,—followed up, as such Measure must necessarily be, by the repeal of the Corporation and Test Acts,—would produce[2]— I do not enquire how the Measure might affect the composition and proceedings of the two Houses; I will even grant for a moment, notwithstanding we have often seen how the scale when nicely balanced can be turned by a small party steadily united, that the acquisition of organized political Power would be less than an equivalent for the irregular influence the Catholics derive from being regarded by so many as a Body unfairly dealt with.—Still remembering that every concession hitherto has only served them as a 'vantage ground for making new demands, let us recur to the Protestant Church establishment, which, should the existing restrictions be removed, would become a more conspicuous object for discontent to point at. At first we might possibly hear less of an ambitious and factious Bar; but the hopes of the Priesthood would be quickened, and when it had succeeded in inflaming the popular Mind to a convenient degree, *in* would step the Lawyers to raise themselves to power and consequence at any cost. A maxim of the Roman Catholics is, never to give up any claims.—I do not say I would be as unbending as they—but I would copy to a certain degree their firmness, and would defend the exclusive laws, not so much for their own sakes, but as an outwork; and not give them up and have to fight the enemy under the gates of the City.

There is neither honour, nor hope in any course that does not aim at the maintenance of Protestant ascendancy. We hear much of the hardship of such an Establishment as the Protestant Church in Ireland, where the Catholics so far outnumber the Protestants, and are encreasing upon them so fast—but, in legislative measures, are mere numbers to be considered? Has the property or the knowledge in Ireland increased relatively to that of the Protestants in

Dudley (1781–1833), of Castle Dudley, Staffs., a follower of Pitt and subsequently a close associate of Canning: he was Foreign Secretary, 1827–8, under Canning, but resigned from Wellington's administration with Huskisson and Palmerston.
[1] In his speech in the House of Lords, Lord Liverpool confined his remarks about Ireland almost entirely to an attack on the Catholic Association and its activities.
[2] Following a motion by Sir Francis Burdett on 28 Feb., the Roman Catholic Relief Bill was introduced in the Commons on 23 Mar., and O'Connell subsequently appeared in person before committees of both Houses. The Bill was passed by the Commons on 10 May, but rejected by the Lords a week later.

the same proportion? Certainly No. Let us enquire the cause of the increase of the Catholic population, and we shall find that it arises principally from a want of Protestant Ministers; felt much more in consequence of uniting and consolidating Parishes, in order to furnish an adequate support for a Person filling the respectable situation of a Protestant Minister. This want has made an opening for the lowest orders of the Catholic Priests, who find even poverty, inasmuch as it is favourable to ignorance, favourable to their views —for no man is so poor but, if superstitious, he will spare something to his Priest. If we are to believe one Party the calamitous state of Ireland is caused by the oppressions of the English Govern[t]— these have been had enough in former times, and much may be amiss at present. But the true causes of the miseries of Ireland are, Papacy and the State and Management of landed Property; of the former I have said, I fear, more than enough—of the latter, what good can be expected while the soil is occupied by tens of thousands of petty Farmers of 5 or 10 pounds a year—immense tracts altogether without a Resident Gentry—the Protestant Clergyman, where there happens to be one, being the only Person with pretentions to such a character. Look at any tract of Country without a Resident Nobility or Gentry—take, for instance, the District now ceded to Prussia, from Mentz[1] towards France in the direction of Metz, and including France as far as Metz itself—and you will find similar poverty and wretchedness.—Lamentable is it to acknowledge, that the Irish people are so grossly ignorant, and from that cause subject to such delusions and passions, that they would destroy each other, were it not for the control exercised over them by the power of England. This power it is, which protracts their existence in a state, which otherwise the course of human nature would provide a remedy for, by reducing their numbers thro' mutual destruction. Hence, for our Govt., an awful responsibility.—We must have in our Rulers no *luxuries* of sentiment, none of those persuasions which flatter the feelings at the expence of the understanding—no self-applauding spirit of unreflecting liberality —we must look sternly at the case, and we shall find that it is vigour, and not indulgence, that must save us.—Person and Property must be placed in security in Ireland.—English Capital, Manners, Arts, and aspirations would then make their way among the grovelling Peasantry—they would have Property, without which they can have no attachment to tranquillity: the Absentees could have no plea for remaining out of the Country—they would begin to unite

[1] ?Mainz.

and consolidate their farms—and the increase of vicious population would be stopped; part of it in course of time might be got rid of, by extensive schemes of colonization: the Protestants would recover ground—the people of the two Countries would be intermixed to their mutual benefit;—knowledge, industry, riches would increase, and with these, dispositions to loyalty and good order.

The sincere Liberals suppose *that* to be dead which only sleeps —those weapons to be thrown away that are only concealed—in short *that* to be true which they wish for. A careful perusal of Ecclesiastical History would put an end to these dreams—The system of the Romish Church is so exquisitely contrived for the subjugation of the many to the few, that it never can cease to be formidable; the celibacy of the Clergy alone, armed with indulgences, and made Master of the Conscience by auricular confession, discriminates the Romanists from all other Bodies of Christians, in a way that must call forth jealousy on the part of all those, whom the good sense of their Ancestors has delivered from a Church so constituted, and from such a thraldom.

Such is the result of my reading, and of my personal experience— which is not so confined as might appear—for I have passed much time abroad—and live at a short distance from the Strong-holds of the Papists in England, and I give it to you as my deliberate opinion, that all analogies drawn from foreign Countries are illusory: those Countries are not free, in the sense in which we are, and I am convinced, that in a Country which is free, I mean in spirit as well as form, Power and Office cannot be indiscriminately distributed among Protestants and Catholics, and both placed upon the same footing of religious Establishments. One must be uppermost —happily for us, Protestantism is paramount—and while it is treason by our laws to attempt the subversion of the Protestant succession, we have the satisfaction of knowing that in defending a Government, resting upon this basis, we are working for the welfare, and supporting the dignity of human nature.

I ought to apologise for troubling you at such length—on so hacknied a subject, the more so as I may not have started one thought that is not familiar to you—but it is becoming every day more momentous—and be assured the liberal policy of being so ready to acknowledge the independence of the revolted South Americans will not easily be forgiven by Spain, or any Continental Gov^t.—this Measure will both furnish an impulse and an excuse for the Catholic States interfering to foment the disturbances of Ireland. Symptoms of dissatisfaction among the Holy Alliance are obvious—the Catholics will be emboldened from a reliance upon foreign countenance and assistance, and if the proceedings, which I have been arguing against, be continued, we shall have either to re-conquer Ireland by force of arms or submit to a dismemberment. Where then would be the liberties of Great Britain, with a Standing Army, which would be necessary to guard us from France in our front stretching, as sooner or later she will do, her Coast from Bayonne to the mouths of the Rhine, with hostile or suspected Ireland at our backs? If the Irish Catholics will not be incorporated with us under a Protestant Ascendancy, they must, if Providence gives us the means, be *compelled* to it; our own safety requires it.

[*The conclusion of the letter has been cut away*]

159. D. W. to JOANNA HUTCHINSON

MS. WL. Hitherto unpublished.

Kendal, Sunday 13th Feb^{ry}. [1825]

My dear Joanna,

I have talked of writing to you ever since I came to Kendal, but Elizabeth[1] did the same, and poor Girl! till yesterday and today has never been well enough to write; and I was unwilling to prevent her doing so as soon as she should be able, which would have been the case had I *alone* availed myself of the privilege of the Frank. It was a fortnight yesterday since I came to Kendal, intending to stay but a week, however my kind Friends have been so unwilling to part with me that, having no particular object to call me home, I could not refuse. My Stay has been very comfortable—bad weather has kept away callers—and I have insisted on not visiting —glad to seize upon a plea which no one could gainsay—the fear of catching cold. In fact, all towns are cold-taking places for me. I have never been without one since I came, and a *trail* in the streets with a Stand in the Shops has been sure to make it worse; I have, however, when the weather has not been desperately bad, always had a walk with Sarah, on the Canal Bank, as far as Natland Beck— or up the Castle Hill. M^{rs} and even Mr Cookson had written very favorably of Elizabeth, so I was grievously disappointed at her appearance when I first saw her. She did not look nearly as well as

[1] Daughter of the Kendal Cooksons, with whom D. W. was staying, 9–15 Feb. Several others of their large family are mentioned in the course of this letter.

at Natland. Mrs C., however, said as there was a reason for it, we might expect her to return to her old state in a day or two. The reason passed away and still she was no better—when she attempted to read, the Book was soon laid aside—and work she never took up —side bad—chest weak—sharp weather affecting her breath. In short I was quite heartless. Thank God! She has been wonderfully better the two last days—has read—worked talked and written without fatigue. Her letter to you is not finished but I doubt not *will be* before night. She flushed a little in the cheeks, and folded it up, saying she would take it again after dinner. The flushing is passed away, and she is now looking very sweet and chearful upon her little Bed, to which she moves every morning, and at night sleeps with her Mother in the large one. The little bed is placed with its foot to the fire-side, its head to the lower end of *side* of the great bed—So that there is no space to walk between—but between the little bed and the wall is a little waste room—convenient enough to Elizabeth, only, to pop to it, you have to climb over her bed. I think you can now fancy how the dear creature lies. She has just finished her letter and seems a little fatigued; but talks of getting up and having her cloaths put on, for the first time since I came. Before that, she had often been down stairs, and every day sate in her chair. Mr Cookson is the only one come in for afternoon meeting. I have stayed with Eliz. all day. On Thursday, if weather be tolerable, Edwin is to go with me to Rydal—Sharpe our driver— they are to stay all night. He is a proud child at the thought of his journey. He says to me two or three times every day—'I am going with you to Rydal!' and talks of the Waterfalls and all that he is to see. Edwin and Mary are sweet-tempered children, and to me very interesting and pleasant companions. All the Family here and abroad are quite well. Thomas is happy—Strickland prospering—and John as a traveller seems to give great satisfaction. Sarah is wonderfully improved by being at home—and is so very quiet, industrious, and tractable that she gives no trouble to Eliz.^th with teaching her. Poor Edwin! Elizabeth tells me he said to his Mother this morining—'I *must* have a pair of new Garters!' 'Well you *shall* have a pair soon.' 'Nay I must have them *now* before I go to Rydal, for it would be such a thing if I had to ask Miss Wordsworth for a pair of scissors to cut loose my Garters—and I *must*, if I have not a *pair* of new ones!' Things are much better managed in one important point than formerly. The room is kept very quiet—the young children are not suffered to come in without leave. In short it is to Elizabeth's, not the *Family's* room. She tells me she is indebted to you for this blessed change. Richard and James are most attentive, coming to sit with her whenever they have a little spare time. Visitors, as I said, have been very few—and they are not admitted up stairs immediately. The Harrisons[1] are at school (Miss Lambert's[2]) and only come on Saturdays. Mrs Cookson does not come home, and I suspect she is gone to see Mrs Johnson,[3] who is now on the List of M^rs C's unhappy Friends, on whom the charge falls of being sole comforter. A fortnight ago, poor Mrs J. on discovering that Mr J. had paid attentions not very delicate to her cook left the house with her 3 children. By Mrs C's advice she returned on Wednesday. Johnson is penitent and forgiven; but his affairs are in a sad state. It is apparent he cannot long hold out. Books and Plate have been parted with. Poor Miss Braithwaite[4] has, I fear, paid her last visit to Elizabeth. She drank tea with us last Sunday but one—I liked her much—and especially for her honest friendship, and her regard for you. We laughed and talked of your partnership. She now lies speechless.

Talking of plans, brings me to the Bobbin Mill, which I do suppose is seriously thought of, though Thomas H's promised letter is not arrived. John Cookson seems to see no reason why it should not answer—and Mr C. says that the article produced will certainly be easily disposed of. I have nothing to say but that I hope you, dear Joanna, will not nail yourself to the spot; and that if constant residence of one of the principals is necessary it may be given up. I am pretty easy as to the expense and risque, for your Brother, I am sure, would embark in no scheme without seeing his way before him.

All are well at Rydal. I have had a good escape from dirt and workmen, the passage wall having been pulled down to make a place for Greatcoats etc., much needed since the dining-room closet was done away. Mr Southey is expected next week[5]—and a Gentleman from Cockermouth to meet him, who brings a Servant. So we shall be a house-full. Mrs Luff writes that we must send her a chaise next Thursday to meet her at Patterdale, therefore we

---

[1] Probably the children of the Revd. John Harrison, the Unitarian minister (see *MY* ii. 128, 420), since the Cooksons were members of his congregation.

[2] Probably Miss Ann Lambert of Kirkland.

[3] Probably the wife of James Johnson, the Kendal attorney. See L. 155 above.

[4] Probably sister of Isaac Braithwaite, drysalter and dyer, one of the leading Kendal Quakers, who in 1808 married Anna, fourth daughter of Charles Lloyd of Birmingham, C. W.'s father-in-law. His house in Highgate was frequently visited by the Wordsworths.

[5] In fact he did not arrive till early March. See L. 162 below.

must be obliged to take her a lodging at Mrs Fleming's for the week—and perhaps she will wish to return to it, when there is any work for her at Fox Ghyll; but *when* that will be I know not; for Mr de Quincey is still in London and till he returns, his Wife will not dare to touch a Book, or do any thing towards removal. They promise fair; but cannot be *forced* to quit before October. Poor Mrs Luff was in such haste to have possession that she set labourers into the Garden 3 months since—now was not this foolish? taking possession and thus having all the risk and all the trouble of ousting the de Quinceys, which Mrs Blakeney may now be easy enough about, whereas if no steps had been taken by Mrs Luff, she and her agents would have left no stone unturned to get the house free. We cannot turn Mrs L. from building her kitchen—or any scheme. There is, however, this comfort that she will never be like Miss Barker.[1]

John Monkhouse had done a good Office in persuading the removal from Torquay—at least I hope so—the Invalid[2] was so much better at Exeter. I hope in a day or two we shall hear of their arrival at Clifton. It is a blessed removal for poor Sara—who must have spent a wretched time at Torquay. It will be comfortable to have the Gees within Reach, while they remain at Clifton; and I trust that your dear Cousin will have strength to go to the Stowe, where his heart is fixed, as soon as the Spring is sufficiently advanced. John Wordsworth will be going to Whitehaven before the end of this month, to stay till Easter. I am thankful he is not at Oxford having just heard of the Typhus fever being in the University. Mrs Jackson (the organist's widow) is gone up to attend upon her Son, at Queen's College. The Tutor had written to his Brother in London, who went off immediately and then wrote for his Mother. I wish much to hear how the Tutor is approved at Hindwell. If he is likely to do his duty, what a comfort and relief to dear Mrs Hutchinson! I wish she were stronger and am fearful of the bustle and fatigue of her removal; but very glad to find that Miss Sandford[3] is still at Hindwell, hoping she will not go away before matters are a little settled.

Dear Joanna, I have said nothing of your wish expressed in former letters to see me this Spring. It is not a time to tell of plans when our good and dear Friend Thomas Monkhouse is in so precarious a state—rather I ought to say—in such a state that one can only look to his getting through as peaceably as possible—to

---

[1] Mary Barker, late of Keswick, now living in Boulogne.
[2] Thomas Monkhouse.   [3] Presumably the governess.

the *end* of all *his* cares and of all ours! for him. This being the melancholy truth, it is not the time one would chuse for a visit of pleasure. In fact how could one think of pleasure in connexion with the nearest Friends of a dying man so justly beloved! Therefore I accede not unwillingly to my Brother's suggestions that it would be better for me to go into Herefordshire when the Family have been settled a while in their new home[1]—and also that it would be a pity for me to go from home again so soon after our several long absences. All this, however, would be nothing could I be of any particular use.—Enough on this subject, only remember that I should shrink neither from pain nor fatigue could I lend a helping hand or alleviate distress.

7 o'clock Sunday night. Tea over, and Elizabeth risen and dressed. She is fatigued; and breathes rather louder—but not much.— She now settles herself and looks comfortable, and I hope will be the better for sitting up a little while. Her Mother thinks her coming round to the state in which she was a fortnight ago.— I wish this letter may find you not very busy—or you will be provoked with the difficulty of making it out—and will have good cause to wish there was not so much of it. I am very glad to hear of your being so well. Give my kindest Love to Thomas, Mary, your Aunt, and my valued Friend John Monkhouse, and believe me, dear Joanna, ever your affectionate and faithful Friend

D Wordsworth

160. W. W. to SAMUEL ROGERS

Address: Sam[l] Rogers Esq[re], St. James Place, London.
Postmark: 22 Feb. 1825. *Stamp*: Kendal Penny Post. *Endorsed*: not to be published S. R.
MS. Sharpe Collection, University College, London.
Rogers. K (—). *LY i. 181.*

[*In M. W.'s hand*]

Rydal Mount Feb[ry] 19th [1825]

My dear Rogers,

I wrote at least six weeks ago[2] enclosing a letter I had rec[d] from Longman, etc, and being unwilling to put you to the expence of

---

[1] Brinsop Court, home of the Danseys from the fifteenth century until *c.* 1820 when it was sold to David Ricardo of Gatcombe Park (see L. 249 below), whose son leased it to the Hutchinsons.

[2] See L. 156 above.

double postage upon my own business, I enclosed it to Lord Lowther for the 2^d post-off:. Not having had your answer, I am afraid his S^t 1 has not attended properly to it.

The letter was to beg your assistance in the republication of my poems with some Bookseller either more liberal, more adventurous, or more skilful in pushing off unfashionable books than Messrs Longman. I have been accustomed to publish with them—they facing all risks and halfing the profits. This is a wretched way for books of some established credit, but of slow, tho' regular Sale. For the expence of advertizing eats away (as conducted by Longman) all the profit which would otherwise accrue after the cost of printing, etc has been discharged. L. declines publishing on other terms, but says that an Ed: both of the Poems and the Excur: is called for, and if not by them, ought immediately to be published by *some* one. I have no [other]² fault to find with Messrs L. and Co than is implied above—if we part, it is on good terms, as his letter expressed, and I should not wish for a change without the hope of a better bargain.

Now you may think that I ought to undertake this disagreeable business myself, and so I should think, if I had not so kind a Friend who has 50 times the talent for this sort of work which I possess, and who besides could say 100 handsome things, which, egotist as I am described to be, and as *in verse* I am *willing* to be thought— I could not say of myself.

I have additional short pieces to the amount of 5 or 6 hundred lines, which would not bear separate publication, yet might be advantageously interspersed with the 4 vols of Miscellaneous Poems. These ought to be considered in the bargain—as there are many periodical publications that would pay me handsomely for them. But I never publish thro' those channels. The Continental Memorials and Ecc^l Sketches would also be added.

It has sometimes struck me the matter of my Misc^ous Poems might be [so] arranged (if thought advisable) as to be sold in separate Vols.—One Vol we will say of local Poetry, to consist of the river Duddon, the Scotch Poems with additions, the Continental pieces, and others. A Vol of Sonnets, perhaps, etc. I throw this out merely as a hint, being persuaded that many are deterred by the expence of purchasing the whole who would be glad of a part. Yet I am aware there might be strong objections to this.

Pray let me have an answer at your earliest convenience.

My friend Mr Robinson tells us he had the pleasure of seeing

---

¹ i.e. Servant.   ² *Word dropped out.*

your Sister not long ago, *well*. Give our best remembrances to her, and accept them yourself, and let us know how you are and have been. Where and how Sharp is? and what he reports of Italy and Italian scenery.

Poor Monkhouse is removed from Devonshire to Clifton, dying, it should seem, as slowly as ever any one did in such a complaint.

Mrs W. Dora and I had a delightful ramble last summer thro' North and part of S. Wales. I had not seen N.W. for more than 30 years. The scenery is much finer than my memory represented. I wish you had been with us.

> ever faithfully yours
> [*signed*] Wᵐ Wordsworth

161. W. W. to JACOB FLETCHER

Address: To J. Fletcher Esqʳᵉ, Allerton, nʳ Liverpool.
Stamp: Kendal Penny Post.
MS. Cornell.
K (—). *LY i. 183.*

[*In M. W.'s hand*]

Rydal Mount Febʳʸ 25ᵗʰ [1825]

My dear Sir

Many pressing engagements have prevented an earlier acknowledgment of your last letter, in the way I wished: since it reached me I have carefully perused the whole essay[1] with much pleasure—but neither by the remarks, nor by the explanation in your letter, have I been able to gain a distinct understanding of your notion of the picturesque as something separate from what is suited to the pencil. But first let me correct an error respecting my own meaning, into which I have led you. When I observed that many objects were fitted for the pencil without being picturesque, I did not mean to allude, as you infer, to the Dutch School—but to the highest order of the Italian Artists, in whom beauty and grace are predominant; and I was censureably careless in not marking, that my eye was less upon landscape than upon their mode of treating the human figure—in their Madonnas, Holy families, and all their pieces of still life. These materials as treated by them, we feel to be exquisitely fitted for the pencil—yet we never think of them as picturesque—but shall I say as something higher—

---

[1] On the picturesque: see L. 154 above.

something that realizes the idealisms of our nature, and assists us in the formation of new ones. Yet I concur with you that the Dutch School has made excellent use of Objects which in life and nature would not by a superficial Observer be deemed picturesque, nor would they with any propriety, in popular language, be termed so—this however I suspect is, because our sense of their picturesque qualities is overpowered by disgust which some other properties about them create: I allude to their pictures of insides of stables—dung carts—dunghills and foul and loathsome situations, which they not infrequently are pleased to exhibit. But strip objects of these qualities—or rather take such as are found without them, and if they produce a more agreeable effect upon canvas than in reality, then I think it may be safely said, that the qualities which constitute the picturesque, are eminently inherent in such objects. I will dismiss this, I fear tedious, subject with one remark which will be illustrated at large, if I execute my intention—viz—that our business is not so much with objects as with the law under which they are contemplated. The confusion incident to these disquisitions has I think arisen principally from not attending to this distinction. We hear people perpetually disputing whether this or that thing be beautiful or not—sublime or otherwise, without being aware that the same object may be both beautiful and sublime, but it cannot be felt to be such at the same moment—but I must stop—let me only add, that I have no doubt the fault is in myself and not in you that I have not caught, as clearly as I could wish, your meaning.

I do not relish the notion of interfering with any use you might be disposed to make of your interesting MS.—my own plan is so uncertain that you ought not to cede anything to it—my first view was as I have said, to analyze the regions of Snowdon and Cader Idris, with a glance at some more remote river scenery in N.W.—I have since taken up another thought, and feel inclined to make Snowdon the scene of a Dialogue upon Nature, Poetry, and Painting—to be illustrated by the surrounding imagery.

Notwithstanding the particulars which make you averse to send your MS. on Scotland, I have a strong wish to be favoured with a sight of it. If you think proper it might be sent by Coach—or if you preferred, by some private hand to Kendal—'to the care of Mr Cookson, Kent Side—Kendal', who would be sure to forward it in the safest way immediately.

I wish your Tragedies[1] had been more successful, particularly if

---

[1] See L. 167 below.

you are likely to be discouraged from a second adventure—tho' I am the last person to press publication upon any one, and I think it for the most part very prejudicial to young writers. I have not seen your Plays—from which no inference can be drawn to their prejudice—very few Modern publications find their way to me—we have no Book clubs in this neighbourhood—and when I am from home, in Spring and Summer, my eyes are so apt to be inflamed that I am able to profit little by any thing that falls in my way.

With many thanks, and sincere respect

Believe me to be truly your's

[*signed*] Wm Wordsworth

162. M. W. to LADY BEAUMONT

Address: To Lady Beaumont, Coleorton Hall, Ashby de la Zouche. *Single Sheet.*
Stamp: Kendal Penny Post.
MS. Pierpont Morgan Library. Hitherto unpublished.

Rydal Mount Feb^{ry} 25th [1825]

My dear Lady Beaumont,

We are all much moved by the manner in which dear Miss Wills[1] has received the verses[2]—particularly W^m who feels himself more than rewarded for the *labour*, I cannot call it, of the composition—for the Tribute was poured forth with a deep stream of fervour that was something beyond labour—and it has required very little correction. In one instance a single word in the 'Address to Sir George' is changed, since we sent the copy—viz 'graciously' for 'courteously' as being a word of more dignity. The additional Stanza *last sent* is intended to close the address—which I rather think you have placed with the inscription. I will however re-transcribe the whole and shall be gratified if Miss Wills will accept the Copy from me.—To fit the lines, intended for an Urn for a Monument W. has altered the closing stanza—which (tho' they are not what he would have produced had he first cast them with a view to the Church) he hopes you will not disapprove.

Nothing would have been more agreeable to my Sister Sarah, (indeed so she expressed herself, when I applied to her, in the absence of Mr Barber, about the flowers) than to have taken a

[1] Lady Beaumont's sister, Miss Anne Willes.
[2] *Elegiac Stanzas* (*Addressed to Sir G. H. B. upon the Death of his Sister-in-law*).

journey to Coleorton to see you, and plant your flower borders, had she not been bound to her present sacred and melancholy duty. I hope however that the hints she has given may at present be of use to Barret.[1] I will now transcribe the verses I once mentioned to you on this subject. But read them at your leisure.

Southey's visit is yet delayed, but we still expect him.[2] Sir G. Dance's[3] letters shall be taken care of. We are sorry that Mr Price's activity has received such a check. God bless you d[r] Lady B. With best love from all,

ever gratefully and aff[ly] yours
M. Wordsworth.

[*There follows* A Flower Garden, *as in PW ii. 126, except that in ll. 26–7 read* . . . is the eye . . . It sees . . . suspects.]

This garden is made out of Lady Caroline Price's[4] and your own, combining the recommendations of both.—Like you I enjoy the beauty of flowers but do not carry my admiration so far as my Sister, not to feel how very troublesome they are. I have more pleasure in clearing away thickets, and making such arrangements as produced the Winter Garden and those sweet glades behind Coleorton Church.

[*Then follows* To Sir Geo H. Beaumont Bart., *as in PW iv. 269; and* The Inscription, *PW iv. 255, except that for* Tablet *in l. 7 read* Cenotaph—or Sacred Stone, *M. W. adds*]

163. D. W. to CATHERINE CLARKSON

Address: Mrs Clarkson, Playford Hall, Ipswich, Suffolk.
Postmark: 14 Mar. 1825. *Stamp*: Kendal Penny Post. *Endorsed*: Account o Mr T. Monkhouse's Death.
MS. British Museum.
LY i. 185.

Thursday March 10th [1825]

My dear Friend,

I can wait no longer without inquiring after you. About five weeks ago in a letter from Henry Robinson we were told that your

---

[1] Sir George Beaumont's gardener.
[2] According to D. W.'s MS. Journals, Southey arrived on 7 Mar.
[3] M. W. presumably means *Mr.* George Dance, R.A., the architect of Coleorton Hall, who had died on 14 Jan.
[4] Wife of Uvedale Price. She was Lady Caroline Carpenter (1754–1826), fourth daughter of the 1st Earl of Tyrconnell.

son was 'seriously ill' at Playford.—I know that he has had many
serious illnesses, and still expected to hear from you—that he was
as usual getting better with country air, exercise, and your good
nursing, and would soon be able to return to his London confinement and Labours. Such I hope has been the case—no news is
generally good—and yet it *may* be otherwise; and I do entreat you
to write. I have within the last few days been really very uneasy; for
I had thought you would certainly write as soon as you heard of our
good Friend's Death, and cannot help fearing that home anxieties
have prevented you—yet why should I? Perhaps you only shrink
from a painful task as I myself have done. You will have learned
from the newspapers, if not from Henry Robinson or some other
Friend, that Thomas Monkhouse breathed his last at Clifton on
Saturday (the 26th I believe) of February. His removal from
Torquay (at the suggestion of his Brother who visited him there
about six weeks ago) was a happy one. He never liked the place,
not being benefitted by the warm climate, and feeling himself so far
from his Br and Sr. The journey refreshed him, he was pleased with
Clifton, walked out daily when weather allowed, rose as usual
before nine o'clock in the mornings, and looked forward to going
on to the Stowe at the end of March.—And perhaps even—in six
weeks more—coming to Preston and Westmorland. The latter
journey was not expected by any of his Friends—except perhaps
his poor wife who always deceived herself with hope; but his end
was at last sudden; and after the first shock was over those to
whom he was nearest and dearest must have felt that it was a
merciful Dispensation of Providence.

He went to Bed as usual on the Friday night and at 3 o'clock in
the morning, in consequence of some inward rupture there was a
rising of phlegm or matter—almost to suffocation. This passed
away and Major [?Bleamire][1] (who fortunately happened to have
gone to Clifton to stay with him and was present at the last)
informed us that his Death was the most 'tranquil possible' and
Sara Hutchinson says 'it was like the sleep of an innocent child',
and that his countenance, at that awful time, resembled most the
pictures she has seen of our Saviour. This morning we received
a letter from Joanna from the Stowe. The funeral took place at
Clifton last Friday. On Saturday the afflicted family (including
Miss Horrocks and John Monkhouse who had gone to them) set
off for the Stowe and arrived there the same night. Mrs M. had

[1] *MS. obscure*—but the reference is evidently to 'the Major' mentioned in
SH, p. 295.

borne up wonderfully and was perfectly resigned—but when a fresh exertion of strength was called for in the journey—poor Thing! she was hardly equal to it, and Joanna says she has a cough, is miserably thin, and they are very anxious about her. She says Sara H looks very much worn. Mrs Hutchinson more composed after the meeting.

You will be glad to hear that our lamented Friend has left not only ample provision for his wife and child, but the Sebergham Estate[1] to his Brother—and a legacy of seven thousand Pounds, with three thousand Pounds to his Sister—and besides this—three thousand between the Brother and Sister, recommending it to them to take *suitable* care of his Brother Joseph's natural son. That sum was originally left to Joseph who died in the West Indies, and had previously sent over the child (a half-cast) to England. He is at school with George Hutchinson.[2] I have neither the time nor the space for particular inquiries—but tell me everything concerning everyone of your Family and Friends—and earnestly hoping for good news believe me ever my dearest Friend   yours

D. W.

Mrs Luff is quite well, lodging at Spring Cottage and daily visiting her grounds at Fox Ghyll—her spirits very good. Mrs Monkhouse is coming to Preston with Miss Horrocks as soon as she is able.

We are all well, yet William is thinner than we ever saw him. Mary has suffered much for her Cousin's Death and looks ill. Southey has been here since Monday. He does not look well and cannot cast off his cough, which indeed is not much—but one cannot be easy about it. He says he intends to run away from it, southward in May.

[1] A property that had come down in the Monkhouse family from Thomas Monkhouse's unmarried great-uncle William (1705–70), through his grandfather, John Monkhouse (1713–96), the Penrith attorney. Sebergham is a small village near Caldbeck. See also *MW*, pp. 27–8.

[2] George (1818–76), second son of Thomas and Mary Hutchinson.

164. W. W. to SAMUEL ROGERS

Address: To Sam¹ Rogers Esqʳᵉ, St James Place, London.
Postmark: 26 Mar. 1825. *Stamp*: Kendal Penny Post.
MS. Sharpe Collection, University College, London.
Rogers. K (—). *LY i.* 187.

[In M. W.'s hand]

Rydal Mount March 23ᵈ [1825]

My dear Friend,

I am much obliged by your kindness in taking so much trouble about my Poems, and more especially so by the tone in which you met Mr Murray[1] when he was disposed to put on the airs of a Patron. I do not look for much advantage either to Mr M. or to any other Bookseller with whom I may treat; and for still less to myself, but I assure you that I would a thousand times rather that not a verse of mine should ever enter the Press again, than to allow any of them to say that I was to the amount of the strength of a hair dependant upon their countenance, consideration, Patronage, or by whatever term they may dignify their ostentation and selfish vanity. You recollect Dʳ Johnson's short method of settling precedence at Dilly's,[2] 'No Sir, Authors above Booksellers.'

I ought to apologize in being so late in my reply—and indeed I scarcely feel justified in troubling even so kind a friend about an affair in which I am myself so indifferent, as far as inclination goes. As long as any portion of the Public seems inclined to call for my Poems, it is my duty to gratify that inclination, and if there be the prospect of pecuniary gain, tho' small, it does not become me to despise it, otherwise I should not face the disagreeable sensations, and injurious, and for the most part unprofitable labours in which the preparing for a new edition always entangles me: the older I grow, the more irksome does this task become—for many reasons which you as a pains-taking Author will easily divine, and with which you can readily sympathize. But to the point.

---

[1] On receiving W. W.'s letter of 19 Feb. (L. 160 above), Rogers approached John Murray (1778–1843), but the negotiations were slow to get under way, as he reported in an undated letter of this period: 'I applied instantly to Murray, and for above a month have been expecting his answer. I have called and called about it at least a dozen times; and whenever I get access to him, he promises me a letter in a day or two. When he shakes his head, and expresses his desire to serve you and talks of his respect, his admiration, I assure him that we come to ask no favour and he concludes with saying he is cogitating about your material interest.' (*WL MSS.*)

[2] A bookseller to 'whose hospitable and well covered table in the Poultry' Boswell took Johnson to meet Wilkes. (De Selincourt's note.)

I have seen Southey lately; he tells me that Murray can sell more copies of any book that will sell at all, than Longman—but it does not follow from that that in the end an Author will profit more, because Murray sells books considerably lower to the Trade, and advertizes even more expensively than Longman; tho' that seems scarcely possible. Southey's Book of the Church cost £100, advertizing 1st Ed. This is not equal to my little tract of the Lakes, the first Ed. for which *I* got £9 8. 2 was charged £27 2s. 3 adverg. The 2d Ed: is already charged to me, £30 7. 2. the immense profits are yet to come. Thus my throat is cut; and if we bargain with M. we must have some protection from this deadly weapon. I have little to say; the books are before the Public, only there will be to be added to the Miscellaneous vols. about 60 pages of new matter, and 200, viz the Memorials and Ecc. Sketches not yet incorporated with them and the Ex: to be printed uniform with them in one volume. I mean to divide the Poems into 5 Vols in this way.

1st Vol as at present, to consist of Childhood and Early Youth, Juvenile Pieces, and Poems of the Affections, withdrawing from it the blind Highland Boy (to be added to the Scotch Poems), and Ruth, Laodamia, Her Eyes are wild etc, to be added to those of the Imagination.

2d Vol. to consist of poems of The Fancy and Imn, as now—the Scotch Poems to be subducted and their place supplied as above—with the Ode to Enterprize, and others.

3d Vol. Local Poems—the River Duddon, Scotch Poems, with some new ones—The Continental Memorials and Miscellaneous pieces selected out of the 4 vols—with some additions—Those on the naming of Places, and the Waggoner.

4th Vol. to consist of Sonnets, political and Eccl, meaning the Sketches and Miscous, with the Thanksgiving and the other political odes.

5th Vol. White Doe—Poems of Sentiment and Reflection, Elegies and Epitaphs, Final Ode etc.

6th Vol. The Excursion.

Now these vols I conjecture will run about 340 pages each, and the 'Excursion' 450. Of the Mis: two vols.—viz: the local Poetry and the Sonnets might perhaps be sold separately to advantage. The others cannot be divided without much injury to their effect upon any reflecting Mind.

As to your considerate proposal of making a Selection of the most admired, or the most popular, even were there not insuperable objections to it in my own feelings, I should be utterly at a loss how to proceed in that selection. Therefore I must abide by the above arrangement, and throw the management of the business upon your friendship.

I shall not be in Town this year, nor can I foresee, since the loss of Mr Monkhouse, when I shall revisit London; the Place does not suit me on account of the irritability of my eyes—I must look for you and other friends here. Pray come down this Summer—I could let you have a quiet room, this House having lately been added to in a small way.[1] Mr M. is not only a loss to his Friends and Kindred but to Society at large, as in all his dealings and transactions he was a Man of perfect integrity and the most refined honour—he was not bright or entertaining, but so gentle and gracious, and so much interested in most of what ought to interest a pure mind, that his company was highly prized by all who knew him intimately. You say nothing of your Sister, nothing of Sharp, but you Londoners have so many notes and letters to write that this must be excused. I often read your Italy, which I like much, though there are quaint-nesses and abruptnesses which I think might be softened down, and in the versification I would suggest that with so many Trochaic terminations to the lines, the final pauses in the middle of the verse should be more frequently on firm syllables on that account. With best remembrances from all, ever your obliged Friend,

[signed] Wm Wordsworth

Pray read what part [you like][2] of the above to Mr Murray; you will then hear what he has to say, and I leave it to you to proceed accordingly.

165. W. W. to JOHN WORDSWORTH

MS. Mr. Jonathan Wordsworth. Hitherto unpublished.

[late Mar. 1825]

My dear Nephew,

Your account of your dear Father and the few lines which he was good enough to add depressed us for we were unprepared for a Relapse. I wrote to him immediately and begged he would thank you in my name for your attention in writing. I have since received, directed by your hand, a Cambridge newspaper from which I learn

---

[1] Probably at the rear and on the east side of the building.
[2] *Words dropped out.*

with much pleasure that you are elected Scholar of your College.[1] You spoke of your health not having been good; I hope, and earnestly wish that it may improve, and then I have no doubt that your talents and well-directed application will carry you prosperously forward in your University Career.—But to return to your Father. —As I have not heard of him since the Receipt of your Letter I trust that he is no worse, and would gladly believe that by aid of the milder weather he is getting the better of his Complaint. Do not fail to write [as][2] soon as you have reason to believe that a favorable change is taking place—should, which Heaven forbid, the disease assume a more formidable shape, on no account forbear to let us know. I am so deeply interested in whatever befalls your Father, that I must not be left in ignorance. My hopes I assure you would be much less checquered with apprehension if it were not for this interest. We had lately a case under my own roof that of Miss Hutchinson who was reduced to *extreme* weakness by an irritation in the bowels, that continued several weeks—she is now quite well and strong. I mentioned this to your Father. . . .

[*cetera desunt*]

166. D. W. to JOHN MONKHOUSE

Address: To John Monkhouse Esq., 21 Budge Row, London.
Postmark: 7 Apr. [?1825]. *Stamp*: Kendal Penny Post.
MS. WL.
LT i. 190.

Rydal Mount April 3rd [1825]

My dear Friend,
    I wrote to Sara Hutchinson yesterday with one or two commissions for you, and forgot yet another, which we are desirous to have executed, and I cannot in conscience charge her with the postage of another letter; yet perhaps to repair one fault, I may be committing a greater in troubling *you*, who have at present too much distressing labour for your eyes, your head, and your feelings —but as you like to hear of your Friends at all times—and used to like to receive a letter—I will venture;—writing wide that I may not give you overmuch—and as legibly as I can that your eyes may not be strained. The forgotten commission was this. Sara sent a

---

[1] John Wordsworth had been awarded the Bell Scholarship at Trinity.
[2] *Written* when.

parcel for us to Budge Row[1] before she went to Hindwell, which was to wait for some opportunity—none has hitherto occurred; but in two or three weeks Miss Southey will be coming home and she will bring it, therefore be so kind as to send the parcel directed for Mrs Wordsworth to the care of Miss S. enclosed in a cover directed to Miss Southey at Joshua Stanger's Esq[r][2] no. 4 Lansdown Place, Guilford Street. I will repeat my Brother's requests already transmitted to Sara. First that you will take the trouble to look out among your poor Brother's papers for a Power of Attorney for the selling out of his French Stock, and secondly that you will talk with Mr Addison[3] concerning the Mortgage on which your Brother lent a sum of money to my Brothers (Wm and Cr) as executors to my Brother Richard. Is the property likely to be saleable now that the times are improved? William begs Mr Addison will settle this mortgage affair if possible. We heard from Sara yesterday and at the same time from you for she was so good as to send your letter, knowing that we were chiefly anxious to hear from her on your account. We were very sorry to hear that the time of your return to Herefordshire was still uncertain, I hope however as the points to be decided are neither complex nor numerous, that when you do return to your own home you will, at least, be free from anxiety and perplexity and, in the meantime, it is a comfort that you have some home blessings when the day's labours are ended among your tried and faithful Friends of the Old Times—Pray remember us kindly to Mrs Addison and Miss Hindson.[4] Miss H. was my good Mother's bridesmaid, and I believe dressed for me the first doll I ever possessed. Thus I prove her to be even a very old woman—for I have lived more than half a century—yet when last in London I was surprized to see her move with as much activity as many young ones.

Your letter brought one piece of news which gave us true satisfaction, that Charles Lamb was free from the India House.[5]

This happy change, I suppose must have been effected through the interest of Friends—He is not surely among the super-annuated? If you see him pray congratulate him for us—I could fancy him with

[1] Thomas Monkhouse's place of business, where John Monkhouse was now settling his late brother's affairs.
[2] Joshua (1801–54), son of James Stanger of Keswick (see L. 42 above). He had married Dora W.'s schoolfriend, Mary Calvert (1804–90), in Aug. 1824.
[3] Richard Addison, the London solicitor, formerly R. W.'s partner.
[4] John Monkhouse's mother-in-law, formerly Jane Hindson, and her sister. See *EY*, pp. 404–5.
[5] Lamb was 'superannuated' on 29 Mar., with a pension of £450. See 'The Superannuated Man' in *Essays of Elia* and L. 168 below.

almost boyish glee beginning life again—then follows a sigh and a sad thought.—But I will not go on in this strain—and indeed in mercy to your eyes I would not *fill* my paper but that you might say this is no Rydal letter if there was not a word said of Rydal or Rydal Folks. William is well but much thinner than he used to be, and this makes him look old. He is thinking about a new Edition of his Poems (including the Excursion) in six Volumes. Mary has been on the whole very well since her return from Wales, but at the termination of our anxieties for your dear lamented Brother she was very much shaken, though, as one might have thought, entirely prepared for the event; and she has lately had a severe cold, so that I am sorry to say I have seldom seen her look worse. Doro is active and industrious and in good health and spirits, Poor Girl she has been a true mourner and carries about with her most tender remembrances of our dear Friend. She often talks with me about *you*, and would send her love if she knew of my writing. We were much surprized that Mrs Monkhouse should chuse to return to Clifton——I cannot think she will stay long there, though Miss Alice H.[1] tells me that her sister Sarah[2] thought she would be more happy at Clifton at present than anywhere else. Some people love to feed on sorrow; but that is not in her character, therefore one would have thought she would have far rather fixed on any other place. If you have as fine weather as we have it will make London more tolerable to you. We do not remember a finer season here. William and Mary beg their kind love. Believe me your affectionate Friend

Dorothy Wordsworth.

I wish my pen had been better; for in spite of good resolutions, I fear this letter will be very troublesome to your eyes.[3]

---

[1] Alice Horrocks, later Mrs. Master.
[2] Sarah Horrocks, later Mrs. St. Clare.
[3] This letter is written in a large round hand, for the sake of John Monkhouse's eyes.

167. W. W. to JACOB FLETCHER

Address: J. Fletcher Esqre, Allerton, n^r Liverpool.
Stamp: Kendal Penny Post.
MS. Cornell.
K (—). *LY i. 192.*

[*In M. W.'s hand*]

Rydal Mount Apr^l 6th [1825]

Dear Sir

I fear you may have been uneasy about the arrival of your Parcel, especially as you have no copy of the M.S.[1] and I ask your pardon for not acknowledging earlier your kindness, for which omission I have no excuse except the fine Spring weather, and a wish to sit down to write at some length upon an urgent subject of a public nature. This I regard as my most pressing engagement and unfortunately, without being itself got rid of, it has prevented me discharging my agreeable duty to you. And first, for your obliging invitation, I should be well pleased to avail myself of it, but my visit to Wales in the course of next Summer, depends entirely upon a Friend[2] who being advanced in life cannot of course be depended upon, and at all events, my motions must be regulated by his.

Your Tragedies I have read with much pleasure, they are in language, versification, and general propriety both as to sentiment, character, and conduct of story, *very much* above mediocrity—so that I think every one that reads must approve in no ordinary degree. Nevertheless I am not surprized at their not having attracted as much attention as they deserve. First, because they have no false beauties, or spurious interest, and next (and for being thus sincere I make no apology) the passions, especially in the former, are not wrought upon with so daring a hand as is desireable in dramatic composition. In the first play the tragic character of the story would lead you to expect that the interest would settle upon the Father, who, in his joint character of Magistrate and Father became the Judge and executioner of his own Son—but it does not —the Lady attached to Giovani undergoes the most dramatic feelings of any one in the Piece, there is a conflict in her mind in more than one scene that is sufficiently animated; but the incident which is the hinge of the whole, viz the death of Giovani, is produced without design, and the Play moves throughout with too little of a

---

[1] Fletcher had written on 10 Mar. (*WL MSS.*), sending his MS. tour of Scotland based on a series of letters, and a copy of his plays.

[2] i.e. Robert Jones.

prospective interest—so that you do not hang trembling upon the course of events, in part foreseen. The 2ᵈ Play, tho' less poetical and elegant, has I think much more of *dramatic* interest—some of the situations are pregnant with anxiety and strong emotion, in particular the point where the youth arrives unexpected[1] by his Mother, and he himself being safe, has to blast her congratulatory joy by being the bearer of such miserable news as his Father's death. This is a fine reverse. The foster Brother's situation is also well suited to Tragedy, and indeed the general course of this story which involves in its nature a plot, things being done by design—an advantage in which, as I have already observed, I think the other deficient.—I am well pleased to possess your book, and more especially as coming from yourself.[2]

Now for your M.S.—I find no fault with your Scotch Tour, but that you have given us too little of it. I am reconciled to your comparative judgement of the two Countries—now understanding it, which I did not before. I have seen much more of Scotland than you notice and particularly regret your silence upon Loch Linne, Glencoe, the Fall of Foyers, and those upon the river Bewley, with all of which I was delighted—but the pleasure given by these several Scenes depends absolutely upon the weather, and upon accidents. When I wished to see the sublime Mountains of Glencoe a 2ᵈ time they were hidden by vapoury rain—Loch Linne, which looking seaward from Portnacreuch (excuse bad spelling) had presented to my eyes one of the most beautiful visions I ever beheld —appeared upon a second visit many years after, from a changed state of atmosphere only, with its islands and shores—cold, spotty, dreary, and forbidding. Waterfalls and close River scenes are full as much as extensive landscapes, dependent upon accident—you may have too much, or too little, water. Those of Foyers and Bewley I have only seen once—and in perfection.

You have been successful in clearing up my doubts as to your meaning upon the picturesque:—it would occupy more paper than I have before me, and require more exertion than this languid *Summer's day* in April—(for such it is, the heat reverberated from our Mountains) would allow to establish my position—'the sublime and beautiful cannot be felt in the same instant of time'—

[1] *Written* unexpectedly.
[2] Fletcher wrote again on 9 May: 'I scarcely expected that you would have read my plays, and I perfectly agree in your estimate of their defects. Chance gave my pen that direction, and I have only learnt my weakness when it is too late. It still indeed excites my wonder at times, how Gifford could have so vehemently extolled, and Murray so fearlessly published them.' (*WL MSS.*)

attaching such meaning to the words as I think they ought to bear. One is surprized that it should have been supposed for a moment, that *Longinus* writes upon the Sublime, even in our vague and popular sense of the word—What is there in Sappho's ode that has any affinity with the sublimity of Ezekiel or Isaiah, or even of Homer or Eschylus? Longinus treats of animated, impassioned, energetic or if you will, elevated writing—of these, abundant instances are to be found in Eschylus and Homer—but nothing would be easier than to shew, both by positive and negative proof, that his υψος when translated sublimity deceives the english Reader, by substituting an etymology for a translation. Much of what I observe you call sublime, *I* should denominate grand or dignified. But as I wrote before we shall never see clearly into this subject unless we turn from objects to laws—I am far from thinking that I am able to write satisfactorily upon matters so subtile—yet I hope to make a trial[1] and must request your patience till that time.

I cannot conclude without expressing a hope that the beauties of our Lakes may tempt you to revisit them, when you will receive a kind welcome from myself and family at any time—I am a little too old to be an active guide for things at a distance, but I would lead you to the most interesting points in my own neighbourhood with great pleasure.

ever sincerely I remain d^r Sir etc
[*signed*] Wm Wordsworth

I hope to be able ere long to return your M.S. thro' a private channel.

168. D. W. to H. C. R.

Endorsed: 12th April 1825, Miss Wordsworth, An^d 6th June, My Quart. Rev.
MS. Dr. Williams's Library.
K (—). Morley, i. 135.

Rydal Mount April 12th [1825]—

My dear Friend

I think we should have heard from you ere this had not the same causes prevented you, that kept me from writing—When our dear Friend[2] was taken for ever from us—I shrunk from the task, and

---

[1] In this and previous letters to Jacob Fletcher, as Owen and Smyser note, W. W. repeats the main points of his fragment on 'The Sublime and the Beautiful', as if he were thinking of taking up the same issues again. See *Prose Works*, ii. 131–2, 349 ff.   [2] Thomas Monkhouse.

persuaded myself that you, (sympathizing so truly with us as I know you do) would write to some of us—Then came the happy tidings of Charles Lamb's Freedom[1]—and again I thought every post would bring a report from you of the effect upon him and his good Sister—of some pleasant evening you had spent together in their quiet home. I expect in vain, and the opportunity of sending a packet to London tempts me to break the silence though with little to say of ourselves, and why should I dwell on regrets for a loss which Time can never repair to us?—We feel it daily—though so far distant from the house which he inhabited, that was a hospitable home ever ready for us.—No doubt you have heard what an easy death he had—he was prepared for it thoroughly— yet no one through the course of a long illness perhaps ever clung more fondly to life. Probably his exemption from severe pain might in part contribute to this, then he had been a fortunate and a happy man; and was deeply attached to family and Friends. Miss Hutchinson was with him at the last, though unfortunately not the few days preceding his death, she being on a visit to Mr and Mrs Gee.[2] Her health seemed, from all accounts, to have suffered from anxiety and distress when all was over. She accompanied Mrs Monkhouse and Miss Horrocks, to Mr Monkhouse's house (the Brother) in Herefordshire; She Miss Hutchinson, is now pretty well again and looks forward with pleasure to returning to Rydal in summer. Mrs Monkhouse and Miss A. Horrocks after a few weeks' stay at Mr M's, return to Clifton. Mrs M. has had a bad cough after her husband's death and, as might be expected, was much weakened by what she had gone through, they therefore thought the air of Clifton might be salutary—and Miss H. writes to me that her Sister is much better. They are coming to Preston before the end of this month. The Child is perfectly well, and Miss H. says, is a great comfort to her Mother, who is resigned to God's will, and bears her affliction much better than could have been expected.—Before I turn to other subjects I must mention one grievous circumstance—Our poor Friend made his own Will—in consequence of which his intentions towards his Brother will in some degree be frustrated. He had left him his Estate (in Cumberland)[3] but having only two witnesses to the Will—the Estate will

[1] From the India House. At the end of March Lamb wrote to H. C. R., 'I have left the d——d India House for Ever! give me great joy . . .', and the latter endorsed his letter, 'As an Autograph curious being characteristic' (*Dr. Williams's Library MSS.*). See also *HCR* i. 318.
[2] At Weston-super-Mare.
[3] At Sebergham. See L. 163 above.

go to the Child. This is the more to be regretted, as when she comes of age, her fortune will be large far beyond the needs of any woman of her rank; and the Uncle, owing to bad times for farming, is in rather confined circumstances; he, however, only laments the circumstance as defeating his lamented Brother's wishes—not at all on his own account. He and Mrs Hutchinson, the Sister, will each have a handsome legacy.

A few days ago, my Brother had a most interesting letter from Charles Lamb.[1] He feels Thomas Monkhouse's death just as I thought he would feel it. Oh! that I could flatter myself that this release from the necessity of remaining in, or near London would ever bring us the happiness of seeing them here—and, above all, of having them stationary near us for a few months—a whole winter —or a whole summer! This I fear can never be.

The Quarterly Review is now in the House. My Brother has read your Article[2] with great pleasure, and says you think too humbly of the style in which it is done. He thinks the matter excellent—the style good enough. I have not yet had an opportunity of reading it.

A letter from Mrs Clarkson gives a tolerable account of herself and Husband—and a good one of Tom.

My Sister has had a very bad cold—a sort of Influenza—and looks thin and ill; but will, I hope, soon regain what she has lost. On the whole she has had a healthy winter—So have we all. My Brother's eyes are at this time better than we have seen them for some years. He often reads several hours in the course of the day, yet cannot use them at night. He will soon be sending out a new Edition of his poems—in six volumes—the Excursion included.— I never have thanked you for the valuable notes you were so kind as to add to my journal of our Tour—not I assure you because they were not prized, but because, except one, I did not discover them till the other day, when glancing my eye over it, on lending it to a friend. As to compressing—or re-writing I shall never do it—My plan would be—make another Tour, and write a better journal— that is,—in some respects more comprehensive—in others less so. —Not that I regret that this is as it is: for it well answers the purpose intended, of reviving recollections.—

I do not think my Brother will stir far from home this Summer, he was so much of a wanderer the last, and the preceding;—indeed

---

[1] For Lamb's letter of 6 Apr. to W. W. giving his first thoughts about retirement and paying tribute to Thomas Monkhouse, see *Lamb*, ii. 466.

[2] 'Prussian Reforms', *Quarterly Review*, xxxi (Mar. 1825), 327–41. Southey had asked H. C. R. to write the article, which deals with social and economic reform in Prussia and its effect on popular sentiment.

we shall most likely all stay at home—so pray contrive to peep in amongst us in your way to some other quarter of his Majesty's Dominions—or, come on purpose, and stay as long as you like. We cannot hope to see you if you have a Continental scheme.

Give our kind love to C. and M. Lamb when you see them—My Brother has written our congratulations.[1] Forgive this poor scrawl and believe me your faithful and affectionate Friend

D Wordsworth.

In what an admirable point of view is your Friend Flaxman's[2] Character set forth, in Hayley's Life![3]

How is your Sister?

169. D. W. to ELIZABETH CRUMP

Address: Miss Elizabeth Crumpe, Liverpool.
MS. WL.
LY i. 195.

Friday Morning [late Apr. 1825]

My dear Elizabeth,

Mr Wm Jackson brought me your letter yesterday morning he having met with your Brother at Ambleside on his way from Mr John Wakefield's where he had been spending one night. I hope John[4] will be able to come to see us to-day, as Mr Jackson goes in the afternoon, but he said he was so busy that he could spare but little time; however he will certainly not set off for Liverpool without looking in on us, at least, at Rydal Mount, therefore I prepare a few lines for you, to be ready.

Jane Harden has told us that you were likely to be here on your way to Scotland and I cannot tell you how much I was pleased with the expectation of seeing you, and my disappointment was very great on learning from yourself that the journey was put off for another year. I have often thought of your kindness and of the quiet

---

[1] This letter is untraced. According to *HCR* i. 319, it included some discussion of H. C. R.'s article.

[2] John Flaxman, R.A. (1755–1826), the sculptor. See also L. 97 above.

[3] *Memoirs of the Life and Writings of William Hayley, Esq. the Friend and Biographer of Cowper, written by himself.* . . . Ed. John Johnson, 2 vols., 1823. Southey, a friend of William Hayley (1745–1820), the poet and biographer, had reviewed this work in the *Quarterly* for March (xxxi. 263–311), quoting the letter which Flaxman wrote to Hayley when the latter entrusted his son to the sculptor for instruction (p. 302).

[4] John Crump, the Liverpool wine merchant.

time we spent together two years ago. The same season of the year brings back vividly my recollections. Thank God, I am in much stronger health than at that time. When the air is clear I can walk nine or ten miles or more with as little fatigue as ever I did in my life. My Sister has had a very bad lingering cold, and has lately looked very ill. She is however now quite recovered and has enjoyed the delightful spring as much as any of us, though she is not yet able to take what I call a long walk. Poor Dora looks very ill, she has been worried with the toothache and at last had a tooth drawn. Since that time her appetite has been wretched and her stomach not in proper tone, yet she always *says* she is well, being, as you know, no complainer. She has an immense family of Chickens, Ducks, and Turkeys—of great use at present as inducements to exercise without fatigue, walking does not at present suit her, and her pony has been lame. We hope it is almost well, and that *daily* rides will soon set her right.

My Brother's eyes are certainly better. He can read by daylight. He is well and in good spirits. Willy just as usual as to liveliness and activity and his health good all winter. John left us on Wednesday for Oxford. In six weeks he will return with Miss Hutchinson who will meet him at Birmingham after an absence of two years and a half. She is at present assisting Mrs Hutchinson to settle in her new house, Brinsop Court, near Hereford. You know what a melancholy duty she had to perform in the autumn and winter attending our lamented Friend Mr Thomas Monkhouse. Mrs Monkhouse is now, I suppose, about to return to her Father's house at Preston. She and Miss Horrocks have been for some weeks at Clifton, where Mr M. died. They accompanied Miss Hutchinson to Mr Monkhouse's (The Stowe) in Herefordshire immediately after the funeral, and after three weeks stay there the poor widow went with Miss Horrocks and her child back to Clifton.

I wish, my dear Elizabeth, you could see how pretty the chapel tower looks from my bedroom, where I now write, and how charming the prospect. It would chear your spirits which I am grieved to find are so drooping—indeed my dear Friend, your letter has given me much pain, along with the pleasure of hearing from you. But why not rouze yourself? Why lament for the Past? Rather should you rejoice in your escape for which I know you are thankful.[1]

---

[1] Elizabeth Crump's engagement to the doctor (see L. 110 above) had been suspended the previous autumn. '*Shall* I or shall I *not* congratulate you on your escape (at least for the present) from a voyage to India?' Dora wrote on

Late April 1825

We are very sorry to part with Mr Jackson so soon. He seems to enjoy the quiet of this place and release from labour, yet is too zealous in the performance of his duties to consent to stay longer away from them. He is thin; but looks remarkably well, and we all think his health much improved. Mrs Luff is very busy beautifying Fox Ghyll. It will be a very pretty place, but nothing would have tempted me to undertake so much care, labour, and anxiety, were I, at my time of life, put into a situation similar to hers. I would have housed myself in a Lodging and been free to visit my Friends whenever I pleased. I must say however for Mrs Luff that she has an admirable talent for contrivance of Buildings etc, which I have not. She likes overlooking workmen—I detest it. My dear Elizabeth, this is another bad scrawl. I expect every moment to be summoned to walk with Mr Jackson to Spring Cottage where Mrs Luff now lodges. He is going to settle with her about the time of her going to Whitehaven to order furniture.

Mrs John Harden was much shaken by her Sister's death, and has since been very ill and looks wretchedly. The old lady[1] too is far from well. Mr Harden as gay as usual. No doubt you have heard of the decamping of their last tenants and of some of Mr Douglas's[2] swindling tricks. You do not mention Louisa's health. How is she? and how are her spirits? Give my kindest love to your dear Father and Mother and to all your sisters. I hope John's health is pretty good, God bless you dearest Elizabeth, Believe me ever your affectionate Friend,

D. Wordsworth.

I am sorry I have no hope of the school succeeding at Ambleside, as a Boarding School. Hartley[3] has no concern in the Establishment

27 Dec. 1824: '. . . Putting self out of the question I feel convinced it is for the best. You say you did *not love* him, and to make one *happy* or even *able* to leave Father, Mother, Sisters, and Brothers, for such a length of time and such a length of distance! must require no common degree of love and affection.' (*WL MSS.*)

[1] John Harden's mother, formerly Jane Webster (1749–1829), who had a cottage at Rotha Bridge (see *SH*, p. 331).

[2] Presumably Mr. Harden's tenant at Brathay Hall.

[3] Hartley had written to Elizabeth Crump on 9 June 1824: 'I am fagging on in the regular jog-trot line of my business, which is about poetry instead of writing it, without much hope or fear as to my present existence, the happier for not expecting much happiness. I am, I think cured by this time of a very common and plausible but very dangerous error, that of expecting positive pleasure from the performance of ordinary duties. All we have a right to *look* for, is an exemption from the haunting pain which avenges their infraction. Moralists, those especially who write for youth, are too apt to hold out deceitful lures to good conduct, promising a sort of peace of mind, an inward

340

except as classical teacher that is—he is to pay for his Board, and to
be paid for his own scholars. This is well. No time to read what I
have written, so excuse all blunders, etc. etc.

170. W. W. to SAMUEL ROGERS

Address: Sam¹ Rogers Esqʳᵉ.
Endorsed: not to be published *S.R.*
MS. Sharpe Collection, University College, London.
Rogers. LT i. 197.

[*In M. W.'s hand*]

[3 May 1825][1]

My dear Rogers,

Pray forward the enclosed to Murray[2] when you have looked it
over. Copying from your letter, as you will observe, I have
confined myself to the words 'responsible for the *loss*', without using
the word expence—ultimate loss I believe there will be none, but
there will be a heavy expence which the Sale of the books, if M.
does not push, and the leading reviews and periodicals should not
take a fit of praising, may be some years in discharging. When am
I to become answerable for this?—this question I did not like to
put directly to M. for it was suggesting a demand sooner than he
might otherwise have been disposed to make it—and the new
bargain will not eventually be advantageous to me, if I am to
advance money and be long out of it.

satisfaction, which experience does not justify them in holding forth as a
necessary effect, even of the highest Virtue, I mean in this world. Most persons
have felt the wretchedness of self-reproach, and hence readily imagine that
there must be an express enjoyment in self-approbation, but I am inclined to
think that neither the pain nor the enjoyment, where it exists, are safe criterions
of the moral sense, often deriving their weakness or intensity from the physical
constitution and being often inseparably confounded with fear, shame, vanity . . .'
The recent introduction of boarders into the school had led to a renewal of
anxiety about Hartley among the Wordsworth circle, from which he cut himself off for long periods; and Sara Coleridge, writing from Rydal Mount on
15 Apr., had felt impelled to reassure Elizabeth Crump about the extent of
her brother's responsibilities: 'You must understand, ma chère, that he will
have nothing to do with the *boarding* part of the concern: that would not be
advisable for him for reasons that you will readily perceive from your knowledge of my dear brother's character.' (*WL MSS.*)

[1] Dated by P. S., taken in conjunction with the next letter.
[2] The negotiations with John Murray for a new edition of W. W.'s poems
(see L. 164 above) were so far proceeding satisfactorily. On 22 Apr. Rogers
had written, 'I have seen Murray several times and he agrees to all you wish,
or rather, I should say, to all I wish.' (*WL MSS.*)

Many thanks for your kindness on this occasion—I have been slow to reply, not from being insensible of your services but from the extreme dislike which I have ever had to publication, as it is then that the faults of my writings, to use a conversational expression of your own applied to beauties, 'shine out'. How came I by this expression? Sir George Beaumont can tell.

You are as mute as a mouse about coming here, and everything else, except a brief remembrance from your Brother[1] and Sister. I forgive you. A man so prompt in deeds may be sparing in words.

God bless you! and long may you be healthy and happy in your delightful habitation, which is distinctly before my eyes.

ever faithfully yours
[*signed*] Wm Wordsworth

[*W. W. adds*]

Yesterday I had the honor of receiving a book dedicated to my dear Self—by a Lady, a fair one I hope, but I have never seen her or heard of her before. She is clever—adieu.

171. W. W. to MARIA JANE JEWSBURY[2]

MS. untraced.
The Times, 5 Oct. 1931. Gillett, p. xxi. LY i. 198.

Rydal Mount.
May 4th, 1825.

Madam,

Two days ago I received, and have since read your volume, in which I find so much to admire that it would have afforded me great pleasure to thank you for it under ordinary circumstances; but the accompanying letter and the avowal of your obligations to me in the Dedication,[3] call for an acknowledgement which I should

---

[1] Presumably Rogers's youngest brother Henry, who had until recently run the family banking business.

[2] Maria Jane Jewsbury (1800–33) began to contribute to the *Manchester Gazette* in 1821, and with the help of her friend Alaric Watts (see L. 144 above) published *Phantasmagoria, or Sketches of Life and Literature*, 2 vols., 1825, dedicated to W. W. She sent him an advance copy of the first volume in May with a letter of 'respectful admiration' (quoted by Gillett, p. xix, from *WL MSS.*), to which this letter is the reply. Her close friendship with the Wordsworths continued until 1831, when she married the Revd. William Kew Fletcher, and went out with him to India, where she died of cholera two years later. See Eric Gillett, *Maria Jane Jewsbury: Occasional Papers, selected with a Memoir*, 1932.

[3] It referred to the 'grateful feeling for the high delight and essential benefit' which she had derived from the poet's works.

find difficult to express in terms suitable to my feelings. The honour you have done me puts me unavoidably on thinking a little about myself, which it would be spurious humility to say I should be averse to on such an incitement, did not the occasion seem to require that I should *say* something of myself also—but on this point a word shall suffice. I am not altogether free from reflections natural to my time of life, such as, that I have lived and laboured to little purpose, —assurances like yours are correctives of this mistake, for how can it be other than one, when I receive blossoms of such promise with declarations so fervent, yet evidently sincere!

I am afraid that it may give you some little pain to be told, that upon the whole, I prefer your Prose to your Verse; but the lines 'to Love' are so excellent that you need not be discouraged even should you coincide with me in thinking this opinion is just. In this Poem is a Couplet that is obscure 'And I know what all have known' should be 'I shall know' etc.—the rest is admirable, both in thought and expression, and the conclusion from 'Bright-winged wanderer etc.' appears to me quite original. In the Lines to Death there is much strength, but I will point to your notice a faulty Couplet for the sake of summoning you to rigorous examination, which I look upon as indispensable in verse—

> Death thou art half disarm'd and even I
> Could find it then less terrible *to die*

There is confusion between *the person of Death* and *act of dying*— the process under two conflicting views—it ought to be, to meet thy dart—or, to submit to thy might—or something of that kind. But I might have spared these notices, since you describe yourself as deeply regretting defects and imperfections. Though I wished in this letter to benefit you in another way than my writings have yet done—a thousand times more agreeable to me is it to express my admiration of the good sense, the vivacity, the versatility and the ease and vigour diffused thro' your very interesting volume. The Critical Essays, and those that turn upon manners and the surface of life, are remarkable; the one for sound judgment, and the other for acute observation and delicate handling, without exaggeration or caricature, and the episode 'the Unknown', highly to be com- mended for the conciseness and spirit of the style (as indeed is all you have written), shews an acquaintance with the human heart and a power over the feelings from which no common things may be augured. Yet while I express myself thus, let me caution you, who are probably young, not to rest your hopes or happiness upon

Authorship. I am aware that nothing can be done in literature without enthusiasm, and therefore it costs me more to write in this strain—but of even successful Authors how few have become happier Men—how few I am afraid have become better by their labours. Why should this be? and yet I cannot but feel persuaded that it is so with our sex, and your's is, I think, full as much exposed to evils that beset the condition. It is obvious that you have a just sense of what female merit consists in—therefore I hope for you in a degree which I could not venture to do without this evidence of the depth of your feelings and the loftiness of your conceptions.

I am glad that Mr A. Watts is interested in your Publication, his Poems have the stamp of genuine sensibility, and his opinions, as far as I am acquainted with them, are sound.

I am afraid that having entered so far into detail in this letter, I ought to have gone farther—not to have said so much, or to have said more—at all events I shall have proved that I am sincerely interested in your welfare. I shall look for your second volume with some impatience and remain meanwhile, Madam,

Your oblig^d Friend and Servant,
Wm Wordsworth

172. D. W. to CATHERINE CLARKSON

Address: Mrs Clarkson, Playford Hall, Ipswich, Suffolk.
Postmark: 9 May. *Stamp*: Kendal Penny Post.
MS. British Museum.
K (—). *LT i. 200.*

Rydal Mount, 4th May [1825]

My dear Friend,

An unusual event, a letter from Coleridge, impels me to take the pen immediately. He begins by requesting in the most earnest language that I will use my interest with the Hoares of Hampstead, if I have any, and with Mr Clarkson, to promote an object that he has very much at heart. He then states that a Mr Harrison,[1] a Quaker, is coming to settle at Highgate, and that he is most anxious that his friend, Mr Gilman,[2] should be recommended to the said Mr Harrison, as his medical attendant. Now this matter, as nakedly stated to us, at this distance from Highgate, might seem of little

---

[1] George Harrison, of Lincoln's Inn, a barrister; formerly of Hampstead.
[2] James Gillman (1782–1839), later S. T. C.'s biographer.

importance; but to dear Coleridge, from his extreme earnestness, it is evident few things at this present time are of more. I will quote from his letter, and you shall judge for yourselves. But, by the bye, I must first explain that the letter (except the introductory sentence) was originally addressed to another Friend, who, he afterwards found, had no acquaintance with Mr Harrison; and Coleridge, not having time to write another letter to me, forwarded that which had been intended for his male friend.[1]

'I hear that a neighbour of yours is coming to settle at Highgate, and I will venture to entreat you, in my own name, and as an act of friendship to me personally, that you would use your interest in recommending Mr Gilman as his medical attendant.' Coleridge then goes on to speak in high terms of Mr G.'s medical skill, and of his excellent moral character; and states that a Mr Snow[2] has been recommended to Mr Harrison by one of the 'Religious'; and, from what C. says, it appears that he is apprehensive of a formidable Rival in this Mr Snow, who is favoured by certain denominations of religious persons. And this will throw some light upon Coleridge's wish that his Friend should attend Mr Harrison's Family. We live in a strange world. What can be so stupid as to choose a medical adviser from any other considerations than professional skill, humanity, and integrity! To these points Coleridge speaks decidedly in Mr Gilman's favour, and all Coleridge's friends think highly of him. Therefore Mr Clarkson (being ever ready to serve worthy people) will I am sure if he have the means, and can use them with propriety do his utmost to recommend Mr Gilman to Mr Harrison. Coleridge speaks of Mr Snow, as a man not respectable in private life—and very ignorant—but of this part of C's communication it would be improper to take any notice.

And now my dear Friend a word or two concerning ourselves—but I am much hurried—This letter must go off to-day to prevent loss of time. We are all well—William's eyes better than for years past—He reads often for hours by day-light. Willy strong and lively—but poor thing! his mother is often haunted by inward fears, and I cannot get rid of them. He is pale with a yellowish hue—and thin—and does not grow much—and wakes every morning with a sour taste in his mouth, and the tongue streaked down the middle with one broad dark coloured line. Does not this indicate that all is not right within? I fear a disarrangement of the Liver. God grant there may be no organic disease. He studies under

[1] See also his letter to John Taylor Coleridge, Griggs, v. 432.
[2] Benjamin G. Snow, surgeon of Highgate.

Mr Carter (the clerk).[1] Dora has been poorly but now is well and recovering better looks. John returned to Oxford. Mrs Coleridge and Sara went home 10 days ago after 3 weeks and 3 days happy stay[2]—They both enjoyed themselves much. Sara's translation of Bayard's Life[3] is published; the style and execution very good. She is to go to London in Autumn. Her eyes not worse, but no better. Mrs Coleridge was very pleasant. Worrying is of no use with her Children; and she is now satisfied to be quiet, and does not fret and flurry as she used to do. Adversity is the best school, I believe, for the best of us; and poor Mrs Coleridge has had enough of it, in the shape of humiliation and disappointed hopes concerning the talents of her Sons. Dear Sara is a sweet creature, so thoughtful and gentle, patient and persevering—and in conversation not disputatious as she used to be. Southey in May goes to Holland—Bertha is coming home; and Edith will perhaps stay in the South till her Father returns. Mrs Luff and Mary are just passing across the front 'What message to Mrs Clarkson?' 'Say that I am in a peck of troubles', says Mrs Luff. Dear Soul! I believe she many a time wishes she had never meddled with these troubles; but as it has been all her own doing she bears up wonderfully—Her strength is surprizing—yet sometimes she almost sinks, after a long day of labour—interspersed with vexation—workmen going away—fresh jobs rising up—etc. etc. etc. We do all we can to chear her—praising most sincerely the beauties of her little plot of ground and the fresh proofs of her skill which appear almost daily—She is an admirable contriver—I only wish she had a purse of a thousand guineas—but if I had such a purse I would employ it differently. The Farquhars kindly offer her all needful assistance. It is very long since we have heard from you—Pray do write—My letter is called for, so I must ask no questions, but you know that all you can *tell will be interesting* My dearest Friend ever your affectionate

D. W.

Love to Mr Clarkson.

[1] i.e. John Carter, W. W.'s clerk.
[2] See *Minnow Among Tritons*, pp. 119–20.
[3] See L. 149 above.

173. W. W. to LORD LONSDALE

Address: The Earl of Lonsdale, Charles Street, London.
Postmark: 9 May, 1825. *Stamp*: Kendal Penny Post.
MS. Lonsdale MSS.
K (—), *LY i. 206* (—).

Rydal Mount
May 5th [1825]

My Lord,

Excuse me for troubling you with the Enclosed[1]—it is a concern of my own, and I do not like to call upon Mr Rogers to pay double Postage. Pray have the goodness to direct your Servant to put it into the Twopenny Post.

I am glad of this occasion to say a few words to your Lordship on the Catholic Question. It rejoices me to see the Lowther names and Lowther interest in the minority.[2] I have not seen the Reports of the Evidence before Parliament,[3] only certain Extracts in Newspapers, and passages quoted in the Debates. But whatever may be the weight of such evidence, it cannot overbalance in my mind all that I have read in history, all that I have heard in conversation, and all that I have observed in life; besides, as far as I can learn it is in a great measure ex parte. But were not this so, I must own that in a complex and subtle religious question as this is, I should reckon little of formal and dressed up testimony, even upon oath, compared with what occurs in the regular course of life, or escapes from people in unguarded moments. Little value then can be put upon Committee Evidence contradicting as here men's opinions in their natural overflow. From what may be observed among the Irish and English Romanists, it is justly to be dreaded that there is a stronger disposition to approximate to their Brethren in Italy, Spain, Portugal, and Elsewhere than to unite in faith and Practise

---

[1] i.e. L. 170.

[2] On the second reading of the Roman Catholic Relief Bill (see L. 158 above) on 21 Apr. There were four 'Lowther' members in the House of Commons; Lord Lowther and Col. Lowther representing Westmorland, Lord Lonsdale's brother Sir John Lowther, Bart. (see *MY* ii. 581), one of the members for Cumberland, and John Henry Lowther his son, later 2nd Bart., who represented Cockermouth, 1818–26.

[3] A petition against the Bill to suppress the Catholic Association (see L. 158 above) had been drawn up, and a deputation, which included O'Connell, took it to London. When the Roman Catholic Relief Bill (in which O'Connell may have had a hand) was introduced, committees of both Houses were set up to inquire into the state of Ireland, and O'Connell appeared before them to set out his views on tithes, education, the Orange societies, the condition of the peasantry, the electoral franchise, the endowment of the clergy, and the administration of justice.

with us Protestants. Not long ago, for instance, application was made in the case of the Jerninghams[1] of Norfolk for one of their Family being admitted to Trin: Coll. Cam; but it was first asked whether his attendance at Chapel would be required; the answer being yes, the Youth was not sent, their Priest would not sanction the step. This I had from the Master.

The Question is a most melancholy one, and I shall ever regard the division in the Cabinet in favor of concession, as the principal cause of the boldness with which the claims are now urged, and therefore one of the greatest misfortunes that has befallen this Country for some time. The Majority of the people of England are against concession, as would have been proved had they been fairly appealed to, which was not done because the Laity were unwilling to take the lead in a matter which is (notwithstanding all that has been said to the Contrary) eminently ecclesiastical, and the Clergy are averse from coming forward except in a corporate Capacity, least they should be accused of stirring up the people for selfish views: and thus the real opinion of the nation is not embodied.

I ventured to originate a Petition from the two Parishes of Grasmere and Windermere, including the Town of Ambleside; there were not half a dozen dissenting Voices—the names were annexed to the Petition from Kendal.[2]

I see that Mr Satterthwaite[3] has closed his long career. I hear nothing of the Dr. and am afraid he is unwell, as I begged him to write some time since.

Ever my Lord most faithfully
your Lordship's obliged Serv[nt]
Wm Wordsworth

[1] The family name of the Lords Stafford, of Cossy Hall, nr. Norwich, who were connected with the Dukes of Norfolk. The 1st Baron Stafford was found guilty of treason on the evidence of Titus Oates, forfeited all his honours, and was beheaded in 1680. His descendant, Sir George William Stafford Jerningham, 7th Bart. (1771–1851), obtained the reversal of the attainder of his ancestor in 1824, and successfully laid claim to the barony of Stafford the following year.

[2] Presented in the House of Commons by Lord Lowther on 25 Apr.

[3] Probably Col. J. C. Satterthwaite (see *EY*, p. 616) of Papcastle, nr. Cockermouth, Dr. Satterthwaite's father; formerly M.P. for Cockermouth, Carlisle, and then Haslemere.

174. W. W. to ROBERT W. BAMFORD[1]

Address: The Revd R^t Bamford, Sherbourn House, nr Durham [*In M. W.'s hand*]
Postmark: 29 May 1825. *Stamp*: Kendal.
MS. Trinity College, Cambridge. Hitherto unpublished.

Rydal Mount
May 28—1825.

Dear Sir,

I sincerely congratulate you upon the testimony you have received of the esteem of so eminent a person as Dr Bell. It gives me great pleasure to have been the occasion of introducing you to him;—for the result you are indebted to your own desert—nevertheless I cannot but be gratified by your acknowledgements. That you may long live to enjoy the reward which you have earned is the sincere wish of yours faithfully

Wm Wordsworth

175. W. W. to SIR GEORGE BEAUMONT

Address: Sir Geo Beaumont Bart, Grosvenor Square, London. [*In M. W.'s hand*]
Postmark: 31 May 1825. *Stamp*: Kendal Penny Post.
MS. Pierpont Morgan Library.
K. LY i. 203.

May 28th[2] [1825] Rydal Mount

My dear Sir George,

It delights me indeed to receive a Letter from you written in such a happy state of mind. Heaven grant that your best wishes may be realized; and surely the promises from this alliance[3] are of the fairest kind. What you say of George gives me great pleasure; I hope he will enter into your feelings and Lady Beaumont's in respect to Coleorton, with a becoming spirit; so that your views may not be frustrated. This I have much at heart. The

---

[1] See *MY* ii. 7. On leaving Grasmere Bamford remained in close association with Andrew Bell, and served for a time under William Johnson at the Central School in London. Thereafter he taught for a short time in Liverpool until he was ordained and appointed chaplain of Sherburn Hospital, Durham, and general inspector of the Durham diocesan schools.   [2] Dated by M. W.
[3] Sir George's letter of 24 May referred to 'the alliance about to take place between us and the Bishop of London . . . it relieves my mind from a world of cares, and even extends its influence to hopes and expectations beyond the grave. . . .' (*WL MSS.*) His cousin and heir, George (1799–1845), later 8th Bart., was about to marry Mary Anne (d. 1834), eldest daughter of W. W.'s friend William Howley, Bishop of London (see *MY* ii. 557). See also next letter.

Place is worthy of the pains you have taken with it, and one cannot breathe a better wish for him, as your Successor, than that his duties there should become his principal pleasure. How glad should we be to hear that Lady Beaumont is tranquillized; I wish we could transport her hither for a week at least under this quiet roof, in this bright and fragrant season of fresh green leaves and blossoms. Never, I think, have we had so beautiful a spring; sunshine and showers coming just as if they had been called for by the spirits of Hope, Love, and Beauty. This spot is at present a Paradise, if you will admit the term when I acknowledge that yesterday afternoon the mountains were whitened with a fall of snow.—But this only served to give the landscape, with all its verdure, blossoms, and leafy trees, a striking Swiss air, which reminded us of Unterseen and Interlaken.—

Most reluctantly do I give up the hope of our seeing Italy together; but I am prepared to submit to what you think best. My own going with any part of my family must be deferred till John is nearer the conclusion of his University studies; so that for this summer it must not be thought of. I am truly sensible of your kind offer[1] of assistance, and cannot be affronted at such testimonies of your esteem. We sacrifice our time, our ease, and often our health, for the sake of our Friends (and what is Friendship unless we are prepared to do so?). I will not then pay *money* such a Compliment, as to allow *it* to be too precious a thing to be added to the Catalogue, where Fortunes are unequal, and where the occasion is mutually deemed important. But at present this must sleep.

You say nothing of Painting. What was the fate of your Mont Blanc?—and what is the character of the present annual exhibitions? Leslie,[2] I hear, has not advanced. John Bull is very bitter against poor Haydon[3] who, it is to be apprehended, is not making progress in the art.—

---

[1] Sir George offered W. W. another £100 to add to Mrs. Fermor's recent gift: '. . . I hope you will not be offended at the offer when you consider of what use you have been to my mind by your poetry and by your friendship and kindness on various occasions to my body. Your friendship has been one of the chief blessings of my life and I shall remain deeply in arrears.' (*WL MSS.*)

[2] For C. R. Leslie the artist, see L. 139 above.

[3] Haydon's recent portraits—which he detested himself as bread-and-butter work—had been on exhibition at the Suffolk Street Gallery this month, and had come under fire in *John Bull*. 'I do not believe any portraits ever made more uproar,' he confided to Miss Mitford, one of his sitters, on 16 Apr.; 'There has been a regular yell, but it is dying off.' (Haydon, ii. 95.) But at the end of the year he spoke sadly of 'being deprived of my bread by the abuse of the press' (*Diary*, ed. Pope, iii. 73). Not all the reports were unfavourable, however: for the review in the *Examiner*, see *Diary*, ii. 423–4.

I never had a higher relish for the beauties of Nature than during this spring, nor enjoyed myself more. What manifold reason, my dear Sir George, have you and I to be thankful to Providence! Theologians may puzzle their heads about dogmas as they will; the Religion of gratitude cannot mislead us. Of that we are sure; and Gratitude is the handmaid to Hope, and hope the harbinger of Faith. I look abroad upon Nature, I think of the best part of our species, I lean upon my Friends, and I meditate upon the Scriptures, especially the Gospel of St John; and my creed rises up of itself with the ease of an exhalation, yet a Fabric of adamant. God bless you, my ever dear friend! Kindest love to Lady B.

W. Wordsworth.

176. DORA W., D. W., and M. W. to S. H. and MRS. THOMAS HUTCHINSON

Address: M^{rs}. Hutchinson, The Stow, near Hereford.
Stamp: Kendal Penny Post.
MS. WL. Hitherto unpublished.

Rydal Mount
Friday [28 May 1825]

My dearest Aunt Sara,

You are kind enough to say that it is long since you have heard from me, it is true, but I feel it foolish for me to fill a sheet of paper with trash, when the house affords such able Correspondents as my Mother and Aunt. Your last letter threw a melancholy gloom over us all. I do trust that the quiet of the Stow has by this time done much towards restoring my dear Aunt Hutchinson's health and strength and that *your* Spirits are better. Are you in better heart about Brinsop and can you *now* think it will ever be comfortable?

My Father is gone over by coach to see Mr Southey this morning. He and my Aunt started yesterday but when they got to the top of the Raise my Father found himself 'too weak' to proceed. They spent the day in the Fields at Grasmere and reached home to a latish Tea. He as you can guess was working the whole time. I suppose Bertha S. is at home by this time—we heard she was to come down with the Stangers who were to leave London last Tuesday. Edith remains in Town until her Father's return from the Continent.[1] Her opinion of London must be altered since we

---

[1] Southey was about to leave for his tour of Holland.

saw [her], or she could have found her way to Keswick long ago.
We have all been busy about the Ivy Cot. for the last day or two—
my Mother and Aunt settling Mr Elliott's and Mr Tillbrook's
affairs and arranging old China, shells etc, which have just come
from London. His HouseKeeper says 'Aye, dear, he has a deal of
old Bachelor's nicknacs but not quite as bad as Mr Barber neither.'
The Webbers' Servants come on Monday and themselves on
Wednesday. They must be *Grandees* for Mrs W. said in a note to
Margarite 'I shall send over the Butler to order in coals etc.' They
have bespoken a bed out of the house for the Groom and footboy.—
and where the family who require so many Servants are to be
packed we cannot divine.

   We had an amusing concordance from Preston yesterday.
Mrs Monkhouse in a note to my Mother says 'I have been so
tormented with violent head ache for the last fortnight I have been
unfitted for exertion of every kind'—this in excuse for not having
answered my Mother's letter sooner. Miss H[1] in a letter to my
Aunt in the same frank says 'Jane is wonderfully altered, she is not
I think as strong as any of the family'. By the advice of her own
relatives, on account of her health, Mrs M. returns to Clifton in
Septr. She will be with her friends M^rs and Miss Lewis[2] for some
time and then go into lodgings. Alice H was to be married yesterday. Mrs M. and dear little Mary went down to the sea side to be
out of the bustle. I must correct a mistake which my hand made.
Mrs M. said she had heard from none of her husband's family
except *Mr Monkhouse* and *Mrs Hutchinson*. Little Mary M. was at
Church last Sunday. She told her Mamma when she got home the
Clergyman said 'The *Geese* of our Lord—Our Father' and a man
played 'the Ding Dongs.' I was prevented yesterday finishing my
letter by the arrival of a party of young ladies from Miss Dowling's
to tea—Julia among them. She is much improved both in *body mind*
and *disposition*. She enquired anxiously as to the time of your return
and said 'I do think, Dora, Miss Hutchinson will think me altered.
I feel quite different.' The Miss Dowlings are much pleased with
her conduct this half year. Mrs Carr was at our Chapel this morning.
She saw Mrs J. Stanger and her good man yesterday for two
minutes on their way to Keswick. I hope to be able to ride over
some day this week to *pay my respects* to them. Bertha Southey is
not come down with them.

[1] Sarah Horrocks.
[2] The Clifton friends who had been very helpful in securing lodgings for
Thomas Monkhouse the previous February. See *SH*, pp. 297, 299.

28 May 1825

[*D. W. writes*]

Sunday ½ past four—just come from church—and not for your sake but Dora's I take the pen. *Her* letter will be much more of a treat than mine—as to variety of matter, and had she not been a little poorly—as well as a little lazy I should have turned a deaf ear to her entreaties. I hope, and believe, that her ailments will be entirely removed by regular horse exercise—and speedily; but she is far from being in 'flourishing health'—to use one of Father's expressions, yet it is difficult to say what is amiss in her—except want of appetite—and restlessness at nights. Her spirits are excellent, and though she is not able to match with me in a long walk (and indeed I never try her) she uses exercise enough among her poultry to satisfy cravings more than equal to mine. The pony's lameness has lasted three months, and still it is not fit to be ridden, but we keep hoping for perfect amendment and the first ride is to be to Keswick. A letter is come with the Cambridge post-mark (no doubt from E. Brydges) to Mr Quillinan—but that is no proof of his present intention to come. The letter may have been written in consequence of Q's plans before he visited you. William desired Dora to rally her 'dear Aunt Sara' out of her cowardly fear respecting a *meeting* at Birmingham. I see she had not done so, and I should be inclined to take the office, were I not sure that, if you had not felt there were other obstacles to your leaving your friends so soon as at John's breaking-up you would not have shrunk from our proposal. I trust that the pure air and quiet of the Stowe have already restored dear Mrs Hutchinson's health, but, even in that case, perhaps it is not likely that you can make up your mind to come away so soon as it would be after her settling at Brinsop, especially as you have seen so little of each other. John talks of the 15th for the *general* departure from New College; but *his* cannot be fixed on account of the Collections, and the Warden[1] talked of his staying a few days longer on account of his late going up; but most likely he will not be detained at all after his examination. We have proposed to Mr Tillbrook to come to Rydal by Herefordshire to escort you hither. Little enough I am sure for all you have done for him—and if any thing comes of the proposal he is to write to you. I know nothing that I have to say to you except that the end of this Spring-time is as delightful as the beginning, and Rydal more beautiful than ever.—Lilacs, Laburnums, and Roses all in full bloom

[1] The Revd. Philip Nicholas Shuttleworth, D.D. (1782–1842), Fellow of New College, Oxford, 1800–22; Warden, 1822–40; Bishop of Chichester, 1840–2.

around the Court. I write at Dora's room window looking up the Terrace—the pink line of London pride is in perfection. Mr Jones tells us that he cannot leave home till after Whitsunday (today) so we expect him about Wednesday. I wish Q. may not come while he is here; for both cannot be entertained in the same way, and poor Jones has no pleasant recollections of the bustle of his last visit.

A note from dear Lady Beaumont! one of her own little Bits came yesterday to impart her happiness. George Beaumont is to be married to Miss Howley!![1] I think it is almost the first time I have ever heard of a good and unintriguing woman accomplishing her wishes in that line.—All that was amiss in the young man seems now to be done away with. Sir G., Lady B. and he understand each other —and they are quite satisfied in the change that has taken place— so we gather from her brief note—and she tells of 'comfort [? for our][2] latter days.' God grant that her virtuous hopes may be [rewarded]! I have always heard that G had no vice, and was very good [natu]red. Good nature may do much if his clever and amiable wife gets the ascendancy—leading without moving to do [right]. —But that same good nature—for he has not a strong understanding —can be but too likely to subject him to worse influence. We glory in our Bishop's thankful defence of the protestant faith[3]— and for my part I think the House of Lords puts the Commons to shame, ending the matter so at once and compressing all there was of sense uttered before in so many nights, into one debate.

Mary is come and I leave the rest of the paper for her. We expect Wm at home tomorrow. He and she have had a hard tug at the Excursion, and have gone through with it. I begin tomorrow to read it over. The curtailments in *some* parts are considerable—no other alterations except trifles. This letter will be opened by Mrs Hutchinson. She must not think me unkind for not addressing a word to her. She will give the God mother's Love and Blessing to Elizabeth,[4] and say kind words for me to the rest of her dear children, with best love to her Brothers—adieu, dear Sara

Yours ever,
D Wordsworth.

[*M. W. writes*]

This letter, dearest Mary, was to have been begun by D. to Aunt S. and finished by me to you, to whom Sara begged we would

---

[1] See previous letter.   [2] *Hole in MS.*

[3] In the debate in the Lords on 17 May on the Roman Catholic Relief Bill. The Bishop of Chester (in which diocese large parts of Westmorland were at this time included) was Charles James Blomfield, for whom see *MY* ii. 37.

[4] Elizabeth Hutchinson (1820–1905).

direct. So far being written, much matter cannot remain for me. Only I must add my entreaties to those no doubt express'd above, that you will relieve our anxiety concerning your health by writing very soon. I would gladly hope that rest is all you need to restore it. I often wish that my visit had been deferred till this Spring— that I might have been useful to you and seen how all your arrangments were completed. Yet there are reasons that make me thankful it was not delayed. Sarah says that if quiet and the Stow does not set you to right, further change of air must be tried—if sea air is not what is recommended, your natural plan will be to accompany Sarah hither. Could this be managed?—But I will not look to such a necessity, knowing that it must be a *necessity* that would urge you from home so soon after your removal. Dearest Mary do think of yourself, and of others thro' yourself. Amongst all Sarah's means it will be hard if she can get none to escort her brother. John dare not trust himself an hour out of his beaten track, or he would think nothing a trouble to accommodate his Aunt Sarah, who is his prime favourite and whom he longs to see here. But he thinks, with her, that they would make 'a jumble of it,' if they were to attempt a meeting upon the road. The father is vext at *such imbecility*— however John's uncertainty throws cold water upon the Scheme— and I doubt she must trust to some other,—as soon as *you* are well and can spare her (for our being uncertain of remaining in this dear spot beyond the year, upon which alas we have entered makes me very desirous she should be here). Till Lady F. returns from London we cannot know our doom.[1] Great preparations are making for her return (in about a month) and to give a reception to the Bishop, whose visit I fear will be no little disappointment. She knows not the value of time to a Bp. on his tour of visitation—for she is arranging as if she expected he was merely going to pay a complimentary visit to Rydal Hall! Sarah's accts. of the Darlings are delightful and we are very thankful that the Tutor answers so well. My Aunt will have seen in the Papers the death of old Mrs Satterthwaite[2]—we have never heard from the Dr. I shall not wonder if you shall see Southey in his wanderings—for I think he talked, when he was here, of including Wales in his plan. If so, and he came near, he meant to find you all out. I do not mention the Preston Ladies—tho' I do long to see that darling Mary and I so expressed myself to her mother (Miss Horrocks giving a hint that letters from her husbands relations were looked for) in answer to which Mrs M. said 'She should like us to see Mary, but she could

[1] See L. 180 below.   [2] Probably Dr. Satterthwaite's mother.

not bring herself to part with her to send her to R.M.'—How could any widowed mother require that such an expectation should be dreamt of? So I have told my brother and asked her to bring the child over—for Dorothy though, as invitations were thus fished for—but I added I had no accommodation for a Servt.—that Dora could with pleasure attend to Mary's needs—for truly we would have none of those prying Abigails here.

Mrs Luff is at her wits end and will soon be at the bottom of her purse. She has involved herself with so much work at Fox Gyll—and she is purchasing furniture as if she was a Jewess.

Best love to dearest John and kisses to the Darlings one and all, even to manly Tom. Ask John if he has heard any acc^t. of the Power of Att^y. that was enquired after once before—and also if Mr Addison has mentioned any thing about the Mortgage.[1] Sara will explain. I must be done or they will pull down the bell by calling me to tea.

farewell,
M. W.

177. D. W. to SIR WALTER SCOTT

Address: To Sir Walter Scott Bart, Abbot's Ford, Melrose, Scotland.
[*Readdressed to*] Edinburgh.
Postmark: 3 June 1825. *Stamp*: (1) Kendal Penny Post. (2) Melrose. *Endorsed*: Miss Wordsworth.
MS. National Library of Scotland.
LY i. 205.

Rydal Mount near Kendal May 30th 1825.

My dear Sir Walter Scott,

My vivid remembrance of your kind reception of me, along with my Brother, at Liswayde,[2] above twenty years ago, of our meeting under the Matron's Roof at Jedbergh, and of our pleasant travels together afterwards on the Banks of the Tweed makes me feel that I have still some claim upon your kindness, and, though it is many years since I had last the pleasure of seeing you I count on your not having forgotten me, and shall therefore make no apology for this unexpected intrusion, especially as you are the only person now in existence who can solve a dispute—(be not alarmed, it is not of a very serious nature) between my Brother and myself.

---

[1] See L. 166 above.
[2] i.e. Lasswade. D. W. is referring to the Scottish tour of 1803. See *DWJ* i. 387 ff.

30 May 1825

It is, I think, sixteen years since you visited us at Coleorton[1] in Leicestershire;—we were then residing in a house belonging to Sir George Beaumont—you were going to Lichfield and do you not remember that my Brother and I accompanied you thither? Now we come to the point in dispute—Did we go with you to Miss Seward's[2] house? Did we see Miss Seward? If your memory enables you to give a decisive answer to these questions, perhaps you may also recollect some other little circumstances in connexion with the half-hour—for I think it was not more—that we spent together at Lichfield, and if so, you will take the trouble of noting *them* also in your answer, which may help to clear up the recollections of the one of us twain that are at present mistified.

We hear of you and yours from time to time, but how long is it since you travelled this road! We were then[3] living at Grasmere. My Brother and Sister beg me to say that it would give them great pleasure—so it would me too—and others of the Family, whom you have only seen as children, if you would yet again halt among the Lakes on your way southward—or come on purpose—with Lady Scott or any part of your household at liberty to accompany you.

Probably you have heard that my Brother has of late years suffered much from weakness and occasional inflammation of the eyes—I am happy to tell you that for many months past his eyes have been much stronger in general, and he has had no attack of inflammation. He begs to be most kindly remembered to you, and adds again 'how glad I should be to see Sir Walter Scott here and any of his Family'.

Pray present our united regards to Lady Scott, and believe me, dear Sir Walter

Yours faithfully and with great respect

Dorothy Wordsworth

[1] It was in fact in Mar. 1807. See *MY* i. 139.

[2] Anna Seward (1747–1809), known as the 'Swan of Lichfield', an indefatigable correspondent of Scott's, to whom she bequeathed her poetry. Scott superintended its publication in three volumes, 1810, and composed the prefatory memoir.

[3] i.e. in Aug. 1805. See *EY*, p. 621.

178. W. W. to SIR ROBERT INGLIS[1]

MS. WL.[2]
LY i. 208.

[*In M. W.'s hand*]

Rydal Mount June 11th 1825.

Dear Sir Robert

Without recollecting that I had ever the honor of being introduced to you, I was strongly inclined, when I read the report of your excellent Speech[3] in the Newspapers—to thank you for it by letter; and was only prevented from doing so by apprehension that I should seem to be setting too great a value on my own good opinion. The arrival of your Packet[4] by this morning's Post, allows me to repeat the acknowledgments which I begged Mr Southey to make in my name, and calls upon me to thank you for this agreeable mark of your attention.

I have re-perused the Speech; if possible, with additional conviction that it is unanswerable—and I ardently wish that, along with other productions to the same effect, it might be universally read. The fate of the Bill in the House of Lords had afforded time for the eyes of the ignorant being opened, and for Zeal being

[1] Sir Robert Harry Inglis, 2nd Bart. (1786–1855), an old-fashioned Tory of strong views, and a staunch churchman, who entered the House in 1824 as M.P. for Dundalk. In May 1825 he strenuously protested against the third reading of Burdett's Roman Catholic Relief Bill; in Feb. 1828 he opposed Lord John Russell's motion for the repeal of the Test and Corporation Acts; in 1829 he beat Sir Robert Peel as parliamentary candidate for Oxford University and again spoke against the third reading of the Catholic Relief Bill; in 1831 he opposed ministerial plans for parliamentary reform; in 1833 he protested against the Bill for reform of the Irish Church, and in 1834 against a Bill for Jewish relief; in 1845 he opposed the Maynooth grant and the establishment of the Queen's Colleges in Ireland as 'a gigantic scheme of godless education'; in 1851 he supported Lord John Russell's Ecclesiastical Titles Assumption Bill. In later years W. W. visited Inglis at his home at Battersea Rise, Clapham, where he met some of the distinguished churchmen of the day; and Inglis returned the visits at Rydal Mount (*RMVB*).

[2] This is a copy of the letter actually sent, apparently made for Lord Lonsdale's benefit (see L. 180 below), but also possibly with a view to eventual publication.

[3] On the third reading of the Roman Catholic Relief Bill on 10 May. In his speech Inglis attacked the current assumption that there had been some change in the principles and character of the Church of Rome. 'I contend, on the contrary, that the church of Rome is not merely unchanged, but unchangeable.' He maintained that the British constitution, by its exclusions, was specifically designed to withstand the practical evils of the Roman system, and he denied that, either under the treaty of Limerick or under the articles of the Union, the Catholics had any claim whatever to relief.

[4] Sir Robert Inglis's speech was published immediately after the debate.

awakened in the minds of the indifferent; and I earnestly hope that the opportunity may not be lost. The ground of a mitigation in the bigotry of the Romanists is not tenable, nor is any answer attempted to your proof of this, from facts of which neither the evidence was to be denied, nor the force to be eluded; and as a question of expediency you shewed that regulating our expectations of Men's future conduct by their past, there was no ground for hoping that the discontented in Ireland would be satisfied with the proposed concessions—from their own declarations, it was clear that they would not.

With many classes among the Friends of this bill, it seems to be of no use to argue—for they treat the matter merely as Party Advocates; but certain Individuals from the Offices they hold, can only, one would think, be interested in it, as a great State question; and surely it is not too much to expect from them to treat it fairly and candidly: with sorrow must we observe this has not been done —and that the dangerous principle of the end justifying the means, has had its full influence over Men who ought to have been above its reach. How, otherwise, could we have seen a Minister of State[1] attempting to reconcile us to Papacy, by endeavours to prove that in points of Faith and practice, Protestantism stands pretty much upon a par with it—or another Person in Office roundly asserting, that it was absurd to expect the Reformed religion would gain upon the Unreformed by any measures that could be adopted. No opinion dropt in the whole debate was, I humbly think, so ominous as this. Are not the same Arguments that induced our Forefathers to withdraw from the Roman faith 300 years ago still applicable? And if they were able to produce such effects then, what may we not expect from them now, strengthened by 300 years experience of the superiority of one faith over the other, as demonstrated by the condition of Roman Catholic, as contrasted with Protestant Countries—in Arts, in Morals, and in general prosperity.

Were we to abandon the hope of gaining upon the Romanists, we must be prepared to admit the evil of their gaining upon us. Protestant Ascendancy must be renounced, and sooner or later will be substituted Catholic domination—the two religions cannot coexist, in a Country free as our's upon equal terms. For my own part while I condemn as founded in ignorance, I reprobate as of the most injurious tendency, every Measure that does not point to the maintenance of Protestant ascendancy, and to the diffusion of

[1] i.e. Canning, speaking during the debate on the second reading of the Catholic Relief Bill on 21 Apr.

Protestant principles: and this doctrine I hold not more as a friend to Great Britain, than to Ireland.

Papacy is founded upon the overthrow of private judgement—it is essentially at enmity with light and knowledge; its power to exclude these blessings is not so great as formerly, tho' its desire to do so, is equally strong; and its determination to exert its power for that effect to the utmost, is not in the least abated. But persecution must go hand in hand with ignorance—a sincere Romanist is *by duty* a persecutor. The ambition of the papal priesthood, pursuing their own ends by the exclusion of knowledge, might have been far more successfully opposed than it has been by the very *Members* of that Church, had not the Church contrived to enlist the disinterested passions of human nature on its side by establishing a conviction that there is no safety out of the pale of that Church:—hence humanity is abused, if I may say so, to make Men inhuman.

I have met with many Persons who thinking as unfavourably as you and I do of Papacy, and acknowledging that what the Romanists are now seeking can neither be required upon principles of abstract justice, nor positive convention, are nevertheless persuaded, that by excluding them from political power we make them more attached to their religion, and unite them more strongly in support of it. Were this true to the extent insisted upon, we should still have to balance between the unorganized power which they derive from a sense of injustice, real or supposed, and the legitimate organized power which concession would confer. But it is a deception and a most dangerous one to conclude that if a free passage were given to this torrent it would spread and lose by diffusion its ability to do injury. The checks, which after a time are necessary to provoke other Sects to activity are not wanted here; this Church stands independent of them thro' its Constitution, so exquisitely contrived, and thro' its doctrines and discipline which give a peculiar and monstrous power to its Priesthood. Take the injunction of Celibacy alone, backed by auricular Confession, Indulgences, Absolution and penance;—the Celibacy separating the Priesthood from the body of the Community, and the practise of Confession—making them Masters of the conscience, while the doctrines give them an almost absolute power over the will. To submit to such thraldom men must be bigotted in its favour, and that we see is the case in Spain, in Portugal, in Austria, in Italy, in Flanders, in Ireland and in all Countries where you have Papacy in full blow: and does not History prove, that however other Sects may have languished under the relaxing influence of good fortune—Papacy has ever been most fiery and rampant when most prosperous.

What then must be done, if from these, and other causes, Concession is to be resisted? The difficulties on that side it did not fall within your plan to treat, nor did you give the sanction of your judgment as to the course to be pursued. Allow me to submit a few thoughts upon this part of the subject to your consideration, with a hope of being corrected, if my views appear to you erroneous. The condition of Ireland is, and long has been wretched; lamentable is it to acknowledge that the mass of her people are so grossly ignorant and from that cause subject to such delusions and passions that they would destroy each other were it not for the restraint exercised upon them by England; this restraint it is that protracts their existence in a state which otherwise the course of nature would provide a remedy for, by reducing their numbers thro' mutual destruction. So that English civilization may fairly be said to be the Shield of Irish barbarism. If then these swarms of degraded people could not exist but thro' us, how much does this add to the awfulness of the responsibility under which our Govt. lies in respect to that unhappy Country; and how much more strongly does it call for every exertion that can be made, for removing those evils of which its own misapplied power is in so great a measure the source.

The chief proximate causes of Irish misery and ignorance are twofold—Papacy and the tenure and management of landed Property; and both these have a common origin, viz, the imperfect conquest of the Country. There are two ways in which a Country may be improved by being conquered. The Countries subjected by the ancient Romans afford striking instances of the one, and those that in the Middle Ages were subdued by the Northern Nations of the other. The Romans from their superiority in Arts and arms, and—in the earlier period of their History—in virtues, may seem to have established a moral right to force their Institutions upon other Nations, whether declined or existing in primitive barbarity; and this they effected, as we all know, not by overrunning Countries as Eastern Conquerors have done, and Buonaparte in our own days, but by completing a local and regular subjugation, with military roads and garrisons which were centres of civilization for the surrounding district: and I am not afraid to add, tho' many would catch at the fact as bearing strongly against the general scope of our argument, that both Conquerors and Conquered owed much to the participation of civil rights which the Romans liberally communicated. The other mode of beneficial conquest, i.e. *that* pursued by the Northern Nations—as the Franks in Gaul, the Goths in Spain, the Huns in Italy, the Normans—first in Normandy, and afterwards in England and Sicily, brought about its beneficial effects by the settlement of a hardy and vigorous people among the distracted and effeminate Nations against whom their incursions were made: the conquerors brought along with them their independent and ferocious spirit, to animate exhausted communities, and in their turn received a salutary mitigation, till in process of time the Conquered and Conqueror were lost in each other. To neither of these modes was unfortunate Ireland subject, and her insular territory by physical obstacles, and still more by moral influences arising out of them, has greatly aggravated the evil consequent upon independence lost as hers was lost. The writers on the time of Queen Eliz.[1] have pointed out how unwise it was to transplant among a barbarous people, not half subjugated, the institutions that Time had matured among those who considered themselves as the Masters of that People.

It would be trespassing on your time, and presumptuous to advert in detail to the causes of the exacerbations and long-lived hatreds which have prevented the development of morality in Ireland,—obstructed religious knowledge and prevented a participation in English refinement and civility. It is enough to observe that the Reformation made little progress there, and that the soil became, thro' frequent forfeitures, mainly the property of Persons whose hearts were not in the Country.—As we have hitherto chiefly considered the evils produced by the religion of Ireland, I will dispose of that part of the subject, by submitting to you my notion of what is called for here, discarding as unworthy of notice the commonplaces, not to say cant, about the cruelty and injustice of hindering Persons from worshipping God in their own way. I concur with those who maintain that the Romanists, in matters of religious liberty have no grounds for complaint whatsoever— but I go further and contend that the liberty which the Ministers of the religion have, and the powers which they exercise far exceed those allowed to the Functionaries of the Protestant Establishment. For the benefit of the Roman Catholics themselves, I would abridge

[1] Principally Spenser, in his *View of the Present State of Ireland* (written 1596); but also perhaps Meredith Hanmer (1543–1604) in his *Chronicle*, and Edmund Campian (1540–81), the Jesuit, in his *History*. All three works were published by Sir James Ware, *The Historie of Ireland, Collected by Three Learned Authors . . .*, Dublin, 1633, a collection which W. W. may have known; and later, in *Ancient Irish Histories*, 2 vols., Dublin, 1809. See also *EY*, p. 378, and *Cornell Wordsworth Collection*, no. 2265.

this power, if it be found to be as grievous a burthen as many temperate Observers are persuaded that it is. Parliament ought to enquire into the real character of Penance, as now administered in these Realms under the Popish Clergy—What restrictions they exercise over the body, and to what pains they subject it. How far it is possible for legislation to interfere for the punishment of those who abuse the power of inflicting spiritual terrors I do not enquire, —being well aware how delicate is such a matter. But the grosser parts of their discipline are surely fit subjects for public investigation. The Popish priesthood ought to be prevented from punishing such of their Flock as they may find possessed of the Holy Scriptures, or putting themselves in the way of deriving knowledge from attending Protestant places of worship, or communicating for religious instruction with those whom they call Heretics. If Nunneries are to be allowed at all, no one ought to be received under the age of 21 at the least; nothing can be more cruel than to take advantage of the inexperience of a Child, to entrap her into a course of life by which Nature is counteracted and religion distorted. I do not insist upon this so much for the sake of saving the poor victims, as from the indirect influence these sacrifices have in giving undue value in the eyes of the multitude to that Faith for which the sacrifice is made; of this influence the Romish Priesthood (wise men in their generation compared with the liberalists in our house of Parliament and to those out of it) are thoroughly conscious. In these and divers other points the power of that Church ought to be curtailed. A measure very different from that of supporting the Priesthood by Parliamentary grant in the plenitude of their present usurpations over the dignity of human Nature. This course would lead to placing us firmly upon the true ground which some have been weak enough to abandon. As a most important measure of the same tendency, we ought actively to set about breaking up as far as possible, that consolidation of Parishes, which by withdrawing Protestant Clergymen altogether from large tracts of the Country, has removed an obstacle to the increase of Popery, and furnished an opening to the lowest order of Priests, who find even poverty, inasmuch as it is favourable to ignorance, favourable to their views,—for no one is so poor but, if superstitious, he will spare something to his Priest. If the stipends of the protestant parochial Clergy have been dilapidated so as not to allow of their Ministers being distributed over the Country with an adequate maintenance, what belongs to the Church by just right, should be recovered wherever possible; whatever clamor this might occasion it would be a much more salutary expedient than that of paying out of the public purse popish priests for inculcating doctrines which as Christians we condemn, and by such enactment creating a political Monster with two heads that must in time throw out as many as the Hydra herself. By these means—by correcting all the abuses in the Irish Protestant Church—by a distribution of its dignities upon patriotic principles—and strictly enforcing Residence upon all Ecclesiastics and by the establishment and judicious regulation of Protestant Schools, we may confidently expect that Protestantism may be seen gaining ground upon Papacy in Ireland.

But when I look to the one religion gradually supplanting the other, which I trust is the intention of Providence, I place no dependance upon any thing that has thus far been recommended unless in conjunction with political arrangements—the first step must be to place Person and Property in security. The Advocates for the relief bill tell you that this will be effected by removing civil disabilities, and that content and tranquillity will be the result. These men dread nothing from the aversion of the Papists to the Protestant establishment, which if civil equality was established, while they insist upon the disproportion in the several numbers of the two communities—and in the wealth of the respective Churches with regard to those numbers they forget that that disproportion must be the same and possibly much increased after their object is gained. But enough of this—especially to you. Tranquillity in Ireland is not to be secured by aiming at Conciliation in this way. We must have in Rulers competent to conduct this arduous business —No luxuries of sentiment—none of those persuasions that flatter the feelings at the expence of the understanding—no self-applauding liberality that fixes a doating gaze on one side of the question, and will not vouchsafe a glance at the other. We require Men that can look steadily and sternly at both—in a word, it is vigour and not indulgence that must serve us.

The path recommended by the Concessionists is according to their view, so very smooth, easy, and flowery that to continue the alle-gorical strain one is surprized they have never suspected that it must mislead and terminate in a quagmire or a precipice. Great embarrassments can never be got out of, by easy courses—Persons and property then must be placed in security in Ireland at whatever cost, whether of civil Police, or, if necessary, of military Power; without the said protection the Absentees cannot be expected to return nor can we require Proprietors to look after their lands and to remodel the occupation of them. Under this protection the rents of Ireland would in a great measure be kept in the Country—and English Capital would flow into it, with English Persons to manage and apply it—English Arts, Manners, refinements and aspirations —thus would the grovelling Peasantry be raised, they would become discontented with, and ashamed of their nakedness and raggedness—of their peatbogs, and their hovels; and the destitution of household accommodation, in which they *breathe* rather than live.

It is not then upon the purity of the reformed faith merely that I rely for making its way into the hearts of these oppressed Creatures —but upon the manifestation which may in course of time thus be given them of the social blessings which Protestants have acquired by being delivered from Spiritual thraldom. In proportion as a disposition was thus excited to accumulate property, the Irish Peasantry would be less and less liable to become the tools of agitators and aspirants, whether political or religious—they would be attached to tranquillity. The increase of vicious population would be stopped, and here I would observe, that instead of reversing [?] course of grounding a demand for political power upon numbers merely, without regard to property or condition, we ought to reckon the very existence of such swarms, as one of the greatest evils of the Country and every political inducement for keeping up, or adding to those numbers should be removed as far as possible. Part of the population now existing might for its own benefit be got rid of by extensive schemes of colonization, which would allow space, and opportunity for the people of the two Countries intermixing, for mutual advantage. Knowledge Industry, Riches, would spread accordingly, and along with these dispositions to loyalty and good order.

What the contrary course may lead to, it is impossible to foresee, but I entirely agree with you, that we risk far too much in entering upon it—much of the evil which we forbode may, thro' the blessings of Providence be prevented; and Concession may possibly after all be the best course to take; but, sure I am that it is not justifiable by the reasons which in Parliament have been brought forward in support of it. Providence will prevent evil and deduce good by agency hidden from our limited faculties. Happily for us Protestantism is at present paramount, and while it is wanton by our laws to attempt the subjugation of the Protestant succession, we have the satisfaction of knowing that in defending a Government resting upon this basis, which say what they will, the other Party have abandoned, we are working for the welfare, and supporting the dignity of Human Nature.

[*unsigned*]

179. D. W. and W. W. to SIR WALTER SCOTT

Address: Sir Walter Scott, Bart., Abbotsford, near Melross, Scotland. *[In M. W.'s hand]* *[Readdressed to]* 39 Castle St. Edinburgh.
Postmark: *[?17]* June 1825. *Stamp*: (1) Kendal Penny Post. (2) Melrose.
  Endorsed: Wordsworth and Miss W.
MS. National Library of Scotland.
LY i. 216.

Rydal Mount, near Kendal
June 13th, 1825

My dear Sir Walter,

Accept my best thanks for your speedy reply[1] to my questions. On that score my pleasure was great on breaking the seal of your letter, and in reading it I was truly gratified by your kindness towards us, the inmates of Rydal Mount, and by your interesting communications respecting yourself and Family;—Yet we should have been better pleased had you held out hopes that your travels this summer might have led you into Westmorland. Should you, on your return from Dublin, land at Liverpool, this might be; but one can hardly hope you will chuse that route, the Steam-boats of Glasgow bringing you so near home. We had heard of your Son's marriage;[2] and, but a few days after you had told us of your intention of going to see him, we had the pleasure of meeting with a record in the newspapers of his gallantry and courage in saving the Life of an individual at the risque of his own—*him* I saw a Boy in petticoats at Liswayde. For the sake of that remembrance I was the more gratified by this honorable mention of the young man, your Son, though perhaps, when you hear the whole history of the Seward Dispute you will say I have little cause to rely upon my memory as a helper to present gratifications.

And now to the point. A few days before I wrote to you, in conversation with my Brother I chanced to say 'When you and I saw Miss Seward at Lichfield'—nothing doubting; when he exclaimed—'Saw Miss Seward! I *never* saw her!' Observe, Mrs Wordsworth was present, and she declared that the impression on her mind was that we *had* called on Miss S. with you. As for myself, never did I seem to recollect any thing more distinctly, except the subject of conversation, which, as the visit was short, could hardly have been important—the room in which we sate—upstairs—not

---

[1] See L. 177 above. Scott's reply of early June (*WL MSS.*) is printed in *The Letters of Sir Walter Scott* (ed. Grierson), ix. 128.
[2] Walter Scott, who had married Jane Jobson of Lochore, Fife, on 3 Feb., was now with his regiment in Ireland. On 31 May he was reported to have rescued a young woman from the canal near Portobello, Dublin.

a large room—Miss Seward's appearance—rather a short woman when I had expected to meet a tall one—disappointed in her beauty—for I had gone with that foolish forgetfulness that Ladies whom we hear spoken of as very handsome do not remain the same during their whole lives—her manners lively—but not extravagantly complimentary, as I had expected they would be—her dress —I *think* a white gown—certainly a small black Bonnet. We were mortified that our visit was so short; had not time to enter the Cathedral—looked in at the West door—which I think was fastened within by a little Gate, otherwise we should have not seen up the Centre to the painted window or would certainly have gone forward. The whole appearance of the Building struck me much, and this is all I recollect—except wall-flowers growing on the old walls in the town—and a general pleasing effect of antiquity. Your letter finds me with these impressions fixed on the mind, yet my Brother's testimony—so different, and yet so clear—at times made me fancy the whole (as far as relates to the *interview* with Miss Seward) but a dream—made up of some real dream and of reports and descriptions concerning that celebrated Lady. I now try to believe it so—So it must be. Yet the conclusion is mortifying, and will principally tend to make me doubt my internal testimony respecting past events connected with external objects.

I wish your recollections had been more distinct. We certainly did go to Lichfield—as my Brother will convince you. There are yet one or two questions which I must put to you. Was Miss Seward accustomed to sit in an upstairs Room? Was the Room not a large one? Was the entrance by a Door at the left hand near the head of the Stairs? Now if your answers to the above Queries are discordant with my supposed recollections, the evidence will be conclusive against me, and *therefore* most satisfactory to my mind; but if on the contrary, Miss Seward *did* sit in an upstairs room—with a door on the left hand, etc, etc. I may have heard these particulars from some one who had visited her, and I must still be turning to this subject, haunted with a troublesome obscurity and doubt.

I beg your pardon for having taken up so much of the Paper, which I ought to have left for my Brother: but cannot conclude without heartily thanking you and Lady Scott (to whom I beg to be kindly remembered) for your friendly invitation to which my Brother will reply particularly, only I must add that I should be loth to be left at home if a Party were going from Rydal Mount to Abbotsford.— I remain, dear Sir Walter, with great Respect, your obliged Friend,
                                    Dorothy Wordsworth.

[*W. W. writes*]

My dear Sir Walter,

There can be no doubt that we went with you as far as Litch-field. There was a talk of our waiting along with you on Miss S.—but it went off, as you say. I remember your saying that Mr Southey would be a much more welcome visitor than either you or me, for she was his enthusiastic admirer. But though I was averse to intruding, the reason why we did not see Miss S. was this: The Post Boy insisted on returning to Tamworth to bait his Horses, and allowed us only $\frac{1}{4}$ of an hour to stay in Litchfield, to our great disappointment, as we were particularly desirous to inspect the Cathedral, of which, as my Sister says, we had only a glimpse. Your testimony though negative only, and inferential tends to establish the truth of my recollection, which is that we did *not* see Miss S. You must have seen Tutbury when you had left Lich-field, on your way northward. The Castle stands on a bold situa-tion overlooking the vale of the Dove.—In one point of your Letter your admirable memory has failed: it was not Southey, but Sir Humphrey, then Mr Davy, who went with us from Patterdale to the top of Helvellyn, where he left us and hastened on to the vale of Grasmere. You say you are not so active for Climbing as you then were, I should much regret this did you not add that your health is so excellent. Being very thin I am able as ever to mount Helvellyn, but in many things I am admonished of the Non sum qualis eram; particularly my eyes. I do not require spectacles except for Maps, my sight not being worn as most people of my age find them: but the organ with me is very irritable, and hot rooms, candlelight, and much reading I cannot bear. May you be blest, like your good mother, with power to read as late in life as she could. Thanks for your invitation to my children, who will be proud at some time or other to avail themselves of it. I have but three; one at Oxford; a girl, *now*, I ought to say a Woman, at home; and a Boy who was some years at the Charterhouse where his health failed, and is now with me preparing for Oxford. Though you overlook my invitation to West[nd1] which would shew you Southey also, I live in hope of seeing you one day at your own abode of which I have heard much. Most distinctly do I recollect it and the then state of the grounds, as shewn by your delightful

---

[1] As D. W. anticipates at the beginning of this letter, Scott did in fact return from his Irish tour by way of Holyhead and the Lakes, and met W. W. and Southey again at the colourful gathering at Storrs Hall on Windermere in August. See L. 187 below.

daughter, now Mrs Lockhart;[1] in particular the filial pride with which she conducted me to a well, decorated with architectural Fragments from Melross.

With kind remembrances to Lady Scott, in which Mrs W unites,—I remain my dear Sir Walter, most cordially your Friend,

W. Wordsworth

180. W. W. to LORD LONSDALE

Address: The Earl of Lonsdale, Charles St., Berkley Sq^re. London.
Postmark: 18 June, 1825.
MS. Lonsdale MSS.
K (—). *LY i.* 207 (—).

June 15th [1825]

My Lord,

I shall be glad to see the Evidence before the Com:^s[2] if not inconvenient to your Lordship to bring it down; and should have written immediately upon your Lordship's obliging offer, but I thought, if I waited a little, something might occur to make my Letter worth reading—but I am disappointed.

The decision of the House of Lords on the Relief Bill[3] will afford an opportunity for opening the eyes of thousands to the true state of this Question. In the course of the summer I shall request the favor of your Lordship's perusing the Copy of a long Letter[4] which I have just written to Sir Robert Inglis, occasioned by his excellent Speech in the House of Commons, against the Bill. I am anxious for the benefit of your Lordship's observations.

I hear nothing of West^nd politics, except that an attempt appears to have been made at Kendal to pay off the debt of the old Election[5] by subscription. It is reported to have failed—the sum required said to be £6,000—and only a few hundreds could be raised. Mr i.e. Lieutenant Lutwidge[6] who lives at Ambleside, knew both the Tuftons[7] for upwards of ten years while they were all fellow prisoners at Verdun. He tells me that the present Lord troubled

---

[1] Sophia, Scott's eldest daughter, had married J. G. Lockhart in Apr. 1820.
[2] i.e. the Parliamentary Committees on the state of Ireland. See L. 173 above.
[3] See L. 158 above.   [4] i.e. L. 178 above.
[5] The Westmorland election of 1820. See *MY* ii. 590.
[6] Commander Henry Thomas Lutwidge, R.N. (1780–1861), later of Holmrook, nr. Ravenglass, a Lowther supporter.
[7] i.e. Lord Thanet (see L. 158 above), and his brother, the Hon. Henry Tufton (1775–1849), later 11th Earl: M.P. for Appleby, 1826–32.

himself very little about politics; but that his younger Brother was a hotheaded Zealot, a fierce Bonapartist and Jacobin—characters that go much together.

Lady *le* Fleming as she styles herself leaves London next Monday as we hear; she is become to me an important Personage; for I am in the last year of the Lease[1] which Lady Diana was so kind as to grant me of this pleasant Habitation; it would almost break our hearts to be forced to quit it; but I hope Lady F. will be so considerate as not to require of us such a sacrifice. Sir Richard goes on worse and worse—and I regret to say that this whole neighbourhood is in sad disorder from the habit of excessive drinking, becoming more and more prevalent. Many causes contribute to this, the high wages, and otherwise prosperous condition of the humbler ranks—bad example of some of the Clergy and want of zeal in others; the Resident Gentry having little influence or interest in the state of the neighbourhood as not being Proprietors, or only so in a trifling degree; the want of a Magistracy at Ambleside—the expenses in improving the roads and the number of Labourers from a distance—and I take this occasion of mentioning, that certain verdicts of acquittal in the cases of men charged with murdering their Wives have had, I am confident, a pernicious effect in this neighbourhood. You probably recollect the instance of Towers[2] the Surgeon of Kendal who shot his Wife, and on the ground of delirium produced by liquor, was found guilty only of Manslaughter; a person at Liverpool who was connected by marriage with this neighbourhood destroyed his Wife pretty much under the same circumstances and was acquitted. One of the Drunkards of Ambleside drowned himself the other day, after having a short time ago nearly killed his Uncle; and I have at this moment three persons in my eye, who are daily in the habit of seizing dangerous weapons and threatening their wives or those around them with instant destruction through frenzy produced by liquor. Surely this subject merits judicial consideration.

I was truly glad to hear of young Peele's[3] success. His merit must be very great. I observe he is in the first Class, at the College Examinations; which proves his application to Mathematics also.

---

[1] See L. 206 below. [2] See *MY* ii. 446.
[3] The Revd. Thomas Williamson Peile, D.D. (1806–82), eldest son of John Peile, proprietor of the *Cumberland Pacquet* and Lord Lonsdale's principal agent at Whitehaven, had been educated at Shrewsbury, and went on to a brilliant career at Trinity, where he had just been awarded the Davies Scholarship. He was elected Fellow in 1829, and was then successively headmaster of the Liverpool Collegiate School, tutor at the new Durham University, headmaster of Repton (1841–54), and vicar of Luton.

The Master of Trinity tells me, that Dr Butler[1] knows better than any Body how to prepare his Scholars for Cambridge Examinations and also takes more pains.

With respectful regards to Lady Lonsdale, I remain

> my Lord
> your Lordship's
> ever most faithfully
> W Wordsworth

I hear that Mr Marshall is a member of the Lon. Coll. Committee[2]—and active in all the *improvements* now going forward.— It cannot be doubted that a main motive with the Leaders of this and similar Institutions is to acquire influence for political purposes. Mr Brougham mentions[3] as a strong inducement for founding the proposed College that it will render medical Education so much cheaper. It is already cheap enough. We have far more Doctors than can find Patients to live by, and I cannot see how Society will be benefited by swarms of medical Practitioners starting up from lower classes in the community than they are now furnished by. The better able the Parents are to incur expense the stronger pledge have we of the children being above meanness and unfeeling and sordid habits.—As to teaching Belles Lettres, languages, Law, Political Economy, Morals etc. by Lectures it is absurd. Lectures may be very useful, in experimental Philosophy, Geology, and natural History, or any art or science capable of Illustration by experiments, operations, and specimens—but in other departments of knowledge they are in most cases worse than superfluous. Of course I do not include in the above censure College *Lectures* as they

---

[1] The Revd. Samuel Butler, D.D. (1774–1839), S. T. C.'s contemporary at Cambridge (see Griggs, i. 45–7, 82), and headmaster of Shrewsbury for 38 years from 1798: vicar of Kenilworth, 1802, Archdeacon of Derby, 1822, and Bishop of Lichfield and Coventry from 1836: editor of Aeschylus.

[2] i.e. the London College Committee, set up in May. Since 1820, when the poet Campbell first mooted the idea of a non-denominational university in London to break the monopoly of the Established Church over the ancient universities of Oxford and Cambridge, the movement had been gathering strength as the various interested parties came together, and by 1824 Brougham had put himself at their head. In May 1825, fearing that a royal charter might be refused for the new institution, he sought to promote the cause through a parliamentary bill, which he subsequently dropped for fear the Lords would throw it out; and a promotion committee was set up instead. The University was inaugurated the following year, the Prospectus being drawn up by Brougham and Sir James Mackintosh, and it was open to all including Dissenters and Jews; but Evangelicals and High-churchmen combined together to oppose the idea of a university without religion. See Chester N. New, *Life of Henry Brougham to 1830*, 1961, pp. 359 ff.

[3] During discussion of the London College Bill in the Commons on 3 June.

are *called,* where the business consists not in haranguing the Pupils, but in ascertaining by Examination what progress they have made.

181. D. W. to H. C. R.

Address: H. C. Robinson Esqre, 3 King's Bench Walk, Temple, London. *Single.*
Stamp: Kendal Penny Post. *Endorsed*: 2^d July 1825, Miss Wordsworth travell^g projects.
MS. Dr. Williams's Library.
K (—). *Morley, i. 139.*

July 2nd 1825
Direct Rydal Mount—Kendal

My dear Friend,

I have spent a full hour in seeking for your letter and must answer it without re-reading which I was anxious to do lest I should forget to reply to some part where a reply is called for. The letter must be at Kendal. I have been there spending a week, and took it along with me for the comfort and amusement of a sick friend, a young woman, the Daughter of Mrs Cookson at whose house you were with me who has for three years been confined to her Chamber—almost to her Bed. I need give no better proof that your letter and its heart-reaching truths,[1] which you are pleased to call trite and commonplace interested me; and do not suppose that though I have been so careless as not to bring the letter home with me, I shall neglect to have it restored; but (knowing my weakness—my disposition to go on procrastinating—when once I begin) I think it better to seize the present half-hour of leisure than to wait a few days longer for the benefit of a fresh perusal of your letter, yet I have little to communicate that is new.—Though my Brother is preparing for the Press he has not yet even fixed upon a Publisher, so it will be some time before the poems are out.—He has had so little profit in his engagement with Longman, that he is inclined to try another, and he (Longman) after assuring him that it would not answer for the Concern to allow a larger share of profits—or, in other words, more than half (my B^r being secured from loss) assured him that they should not think themselves unhandsomely used if he applied elsewhere (as he had proposed to

---

[1] In his letter of 7 June (Morley, i. 138), H. C. R. had paid tribute to Thomas Monkhouse. 'He has left few equal to him in purity generosity and dignity of character.'

do.) After all, I think, it will prove that he is not likely to MEND
HIMSELF; and perhaps he may turn again to the Longmans, from
whom if he parts, he parts on friendly terms. I wish he had made up
his mind, and for my part, am sorry that he has ever entertained
a thought of change; for *his* works are not likely to be much aided
in the Sale by exertions even of the most active publishers.—Do
not mention this matter nor speak of it in reply to me: for I believe
no one has heard of it except the person employed as a negotiator,[1]
and, I assure you there has been no great encouragement.—I hope
we may see you here some weeks before the poems *can* be printed;
for if you go into Ireland you will certainly not refuse a Berth in
one of the Steam packets to Glasgow—thence to the Hebrides, and
you will come home by *Rydal Mount*—to say nothing of the inducement of the Lakes. My Brother would gladly accompany you and
make me one of the party—He would do so were money no
object—nor indeed would he *make* it an object in the present case,
had he not a much grander scheme in view, for which all our savings
must be heaped up—no less than spending a whole winter in Italy,
and a whole summer in moving from place to place—in Switzerland
and elsewhere, not neglecting the Tyrol. John Wordsworth will
have finished at Oxford at the close of the year 26—and we talk,
if it can be accomplished, of setting out in the Spring of 27—and in
our day-dreams you always make one of the Company.—I really
speak seriously—Such is our plan—but even supposing life health
and strength are continued to us, there will still be difficulties—
the Stamp-office—the house, home, and other concerns to be taken
care of etc. None of the difficulties, however, appear to be insurmountable; so you *must* go to the Highlands on purpose to come
back by this road to plan with my Brother—to give us estimates of
expenses—and to enable us to settle a hundred things. My Brother
fancies that he might almost make the journey cost nothing by
residing *two* years abroad,—but that is too long a period to enter
into the first scheme, especially for a Gover[n]ment Agent. I trust
before 1827 you will be quite satisfied of the propriety of retiring
from the Law,[2] and that in the meantime you will have continued
to you the chearful spirits which make even the *Drudgery* of your
London Life no misfortune. We keep our scheme entirely to our-

[1] Samuel Rogers.
[2] In his (unpublished) reply of 10 Aug., H. C. R. wrote: ' . . . could I
creditably exercise the office of a regular leader of a circuit—even so poor a
one as the Norfolk—I shall probably be convinced that I ought not to renounce
a situation so profitable and honourable, even for the sake of being a party in the
proposed journey.' (*Dr. Williams's Library MSS.*)

selves—You only (as a destined Sharer in it) are made acquainted with it:—and for various reasons—especially the delicacy required in managing any Business of this kind with the Rulers of the Stamp-office, we shall not speak of it till it is needful to make arrangements for effecting our purpose; therefore give no hint to any one. Surely amongst so many, we might make up a Tour print and publish that would at least have enough of originality in the manner of it to insure some profit—but we must see our way clearly before us without any help of that kind. But no more of this—I cast my eyes with fear and trembling on what I have just been writing. Of the party from this house, one only (my Niece) is young—The youngest of us elder ones will have numbered 54 years next Christmas.—This thought leads me to your poor Sister,[1] who may I fear, before her final release have much pain to endure. If she be still near you pray give my kind regards to her—and sincerest good wishes.—It would give us great pleasure to hear of Charles Lamb's having got through his troublesome businesses and being again able thoroughly to enjoy his liberty. When you wrote he had a sort of nervous feverishness hanging upon him. A long journey, I find, is not to be thought of; but I hope his Sister and he will make one of their little trips before the summer is over.

Have you heard of the Clarksons lately? I have twice written to Mrs C since I had a letter from her and as she is generally a more faithful correspondent than I am her silence makes me uneasy. Miss Hutchinson is not yet arrived—She *was* to have come with John W. who went into Herefordshire to fetch her on his way from Oxford; but found her obliged to attend her Sister-in-law to Harrowgate, who after having suffered a good deal for many weeks, from indigestion had, the day before John's arrival been advised to try the Harrowgate waters. God grant that Sarah Hutchinson may not have to go through anxieties similar to what she endured last winter! Mrs Thomas Hutchinson is the only Sister of our poor departed Friend Thomas Monkhouse and there is a fraternal resemblance between the bodily constitutions of the Brother and Sister. This makes the Family very anxious—though there are at present no dangerous symptoms. *Her* disorder is taken at the beginning, which *his* was not, but the first symptoms are the same in both—indigestion and extreme leanness; he, however, had many anxieties to struggle with which she is free from—besides the cares attending his business—and much bodily fatigue. I do not wonder at Sarah Hutchinson's extreme anxiety; but for myself I hope there is

[1] Mary Robinson, suffering from cancer.

little cause for alarm, tho' much for caution and that two or three weeks at Harrowgate will set all right.—I know no one who could be worse spared—She is as good as was her dear Brother—an excellent Wife and Mother—and in manners and deportment an example for all who have the happiness of knowing her.—We are sadly out of the way of Magazines—This I say only for Charles Lamb's sake. I begin now to despair of seeing any of his late papers till they are published all together—yet if Mr De Quincey ever does find his way back to Rydal, we can borrow the Magazines from him. With all this scarcity of Magazines, novels from our Lady Friends have poured in upon us so fast that we are muddled among them, and can never attempt to get through all.—Besides, I am deep in Madame de Genlis's life[1]—a hundred times more entertaining than the best of our now-a-days novels—and how much more surprizing!—If you have not read this Book pray do.—I ought to have told you that after three weeks' stay at Harrowgate, we hope to have Miss Hutchinson at Rydal—and certainly shall if Mrs Hutchinson is tempted according to our expectation, by the Harrowgate Waters. When you see the Lambs tell them about her.—They also, I believe, know Mrs H. and her only surviving Brother, that excellent man, John Monkhouse—My Brother and Sister beg their kindest remembrances—and Dora too, who in spite of your sauciness, will be very glad to borrow your arm on the Italian precipices. Now say in your next that Ireland and Scotland are your choice for this year—and that you will come and plan with us for Italy—I wish this letter were not half so long; for I give you but little matter and a large share of plague for the eyes—but I know your good-nature too well to fear that you will be angry—or even a little cross—God bless you

ever your affecte. Friend
D Wordsworth

[1] *Mémoires inédits sur le XVIIIe siècle et la Révolution française*, 1825 (English trans., 1825–6). Stéphanie Félicité, Comtesse de Genlis (1746–1830), prolific writer of popular romances, lived through the Revolution, in which her husband was the first of the Girondins to be beheaded, and on into the Restoration. In this work she painted a fairly scandalous picture of the society of her day.

182. W. W. to ALARIC WATTS

MS. untraced.
Alaric Watts, i. 281. K (—). *LY i. 220* (—).

Kent's Bank,[1]
August 5, 1825.

Dear Sir,

The interest which you kindly take in the publication of my poems, as expressed by Miss Jewsbury,[2] encourages me to trouble you with a letter upon the subject. A proposal was made to Mr John Murray, the publisher, by Mr Rogers, to print seven hundred and fifty copies of six volumes, including *The Excursion*, the author incurring two-thirds of the expense, and receiving two-thirds of the profits. Upon Mr Murray agreeing to this, I wrote him to inform me what would be the expense; but to this letter, written three months ago, I have received no answer; and therefore cannot but think that I am at liberty, giving due notice to Mr Murray, to make an arrangement elsewhere. Could a bookseller of spirit and integrity be found, I should have no objection to allow him to print seven hundred and fifty or a thousand copies, for an adequate remuneration, of which you would be a judge on whom I could rely.

My daughter will have thanked Miss Jewsbury in my name for her two interesting volumes, *Phantasmagoria*. Knowing the friendship which exists between you and that lady, it would gratify me to enlarge upon the pleasure which my family and I have derived

---

[1] On the north side of Morecambe Bay, where W. W., M. W., Dora, and Willy had been staying in a small cottage for about a month for the sake of Dora W.'s health. D. W. remained at Rydal Mount except for an overnight visit on 19–20 July, as recorded in her MS. Journal: '19th. Up—10 minutes before 4—Off to Kent's Bank before 5—Wet meadows—clear air—very hot— at Kent's Bank ½ past one—Dora improved—all but me bathe—unpack, arrange etc etc.—To bed after dinner—Ladies arrive from Lancaster to tea—climb hill. Mountains hazy—ruffling breeze . . . Wednesday 20th. Very hot—I depart at ½ past 5 . . . Home at 12.' (*WL MSS.*)

[2] Since her first letter to W. W. in May, Maria Jane Jewsbury's friendship with the Wordsworths, and especially with Dora, had gone from strength to strength. On 23 May she called at Rydal Mount and made a very favourable impression, and in the middle of July she was invited to stay with them at Kent's Bank, where she recorded their holiday activities in a newsheet called the *Kent's Bank Mercury* (see Gillett, pp. 98–108). It was during this visit that Miss Jewsbury, learning that W. W. was seeking a new publisher, suggested that Alaric Watts might be able to arrange suitable terms with Hurst and Robinson, publishers of the *Literary Souvenir* and of her own *Phantasmagoria*. She appears to have written off to Watts straightaway, since he replied to W. W. on 1 Aug. (*WL MSS.*) with lengthy advice and warnings about the ways of publishers.

from her society, and to express our high opinion of her head and heart. It is impossible to foretell how the powers of such a mind may develop themselves, but my judgment inclines to pronounce her natural bent to be more decidedly toward life and manners than poetic nature. Yet it would not in the least surprise me if, with favourable opportunities for cultivating feelings more peculiarly poetical, Miss Jewsbury should give proof of capabilities for productions of imaginative enthusiasm.

If I have ever the pleasure of seeing you at Rydal Mount, I should be happy to converse with you upon certain principles of style, taking for my text any one of your own animated poems, say the last in your *Souvenir*,[1] which along with your other pieces[2] in the same work I read with no little admiration. With many thanks and high esteem,

I remain
your obliged servant,
Wm Wordsworth

183. W. W. and DORA W. to
MARIA JANE JEWSBURY

MS. Historical Society of Pennsylvania.
LY. i. 221 (—). Letters of Dora Wordsworth, ed. Howard P. Vincent, Chicago, 1944, p. 21.

Dear Miss J—   [6 Aug. 1825]

A thousand thanks for your services[3] towards procuring me a fair remuneration through Mr Watts for my labours—You know how ignorant I am in these matters, and still better how experienced your Friend is—so that I regard this opening as very promising—ever most faithfully yours.

[*Dora W. writes*]   W. W.

My very dearest Friend,

My best thanks for the half letter[4]—we are all much disappointed that your Friends did not think you looking better. I am sure you

[1] *The Sleeping Cupid.* (K's note.)
[2] *The Death of the First-Born*; *Kirkstall Abbey*. (K's note.)
[3] See previous letter.
[4] The other half, along with the second volume of *Phantasmagoria*, was addressed to W. W. 'I was proud and happy, when I only knew and appreciated you as a poet. What then are my feelings, now that I am emboldened to look up to you as a friend!' (*WL MSS.*)

were growing quite rosy before you left this place and it is the worry and bustle of Manchester that has thrown you back—and your poor dear Sister[1] we most sincerely hope to have more favorable reports of her health.

My father has spoken for himself so that it is unnecessary for me to repeat how much he is obliged to you—he is just come to tell me that he '*has disposed of Mr Murray*', meaning he has written to him[2] to say that in consequence of his not answering a letter sent three months ago he, my Father, feels himself at liberty to make other arrangements. This delights my Mother and myself, and I am sure it will my Aunt, more than we can tell—and we shall be for ever obliged to you for being the means of my Father's having *naught* to do with that vile John Murray.[3]

My Father leaves us tomorrow—and does not intend returning to Kent's Bank as he thinks he might as well pay his visit to Lowther now that he is on the wing. My Mother Willy and I remain here—till the 16. Aunt Hutchinson[4] also if the situation agrees with her but I am grieved to say she has not been at all well these two last days—Miss Barlow[5] too, will most probably not go home until the 16. Oh dear me, I am so thankful for an excuse to get into my own room to think of my dearest Friend. I contrive to have some-thing to do or to write every day—but indeed I behave very *prettily*, and I do *like* Miss Barlow but the 'attachment' is at its height—it will never get beyond *liking* I fear.

The weather is so changed that we are all gathering round a bright warm fire in the hall, and the trees in the garden are all but stripd of their leaves. Let me correct a mistake which I led you into, the tree which you long for is a *Poplar* not a *Pear* tree. My dear Daddy set me to rights about it—but I was so convinced that it was a pear tree he had some difficulty in making me confess I was mistaken—My dear we are now quite splendid! An elegant Grecian Couch in the Drawing Room, new fire Irons and all sorts of gay things, purchased by Mrs Ashburn at a Sale near Levens. We have

[1] Geraldine Jewsbury (1812–80), later a popular novelist, and friend of the Carlyles.　　　　　　　　　　　　　　　　　　　　　　　[2] See next letter.

[3] So called, not only on account of his dilatoriness, but also because he was Byron's publisher.

[4] Mary Hutchinson, who had been forced to leave Brinsop while the renovations were in progress.

[5] According to K, Fanny Barlow of Middlethorpe Hall, York, who married 1. the Revd. Edward Trafford Leigh (1798–1847), rector of Cheadle, Cheshire, from 1829, and 2. Dr. Eason Wilkinson of Manchester. Her name appears frequently along with Mrs. Barlow's in D. W.'s MS. Journals, and they often visited Rydal Mount.

a black Cat at home. I shall make up to it as soon as I get back to Rydal, that I may have a pet like yours, and when I am looking at it I shall fancy you too looking at the same thing. It must not be admitted into my Sanctum as the Doves and it would not agree well together. Aunt sends word the sitting goes on prosperously.

You bid me tell you exactly how I am—*quite well* except for the tooth ache. I am thinking of going as far [as] Kendal tomorrow with my Father, to have it drawn—if when the time comes I dont turn coward for even now I feel nervous about it.

Neddy is quite well, but not in high favor—he *will not go* for any body. My Mother has mounted him several times, but if we want to stand still for a second or two his Honor does not relish it and immediately lies down. He wants you again . . .

[*cetera desunt*]

184. W. W. to JOHN MURRAY

Address: John Murray Esqre, Albermarle St.
Endorsed: Aug. 6 W. Wordsworth.
MS. Yale University Library.
LY i. 221 (—).

[*In M. W.'s hand*]

Rydal Mount near Kendal[1]
Aug. 6th [1825]

Dear Sir

Upwards of 3 Months ago I think, in consequence of a letter from Mr Rogers expressing the terms upon which you would print 750 copies of my Poems in 6 vols, I wrote to beg you would inform me what would be the cost of printing etc, as without that knowledge I would not close the bargain. Having waited so long for your answer, I conclude it is not convenient for you to enter upon this undertaking; and therefore feel myself at liberty to make other arrangements if an opportunity should occur.

Some time ago I was much concerned to hear thro' Mr Southey that you had been unwell but were then recovered; had it not been for this indisposition, I should have written to you sooner.

I remain Dr Sir
faithfully your's
[*signed*] Wm Wordsworth

[1] Written from Kent's Bank—see previous letter.

185. W. W. to UNKNOWN CORRESPONDENT

MS. Pierpont Morgan Library.
LY i. 222.

Lowther Castle near Penrith
August 11th 1825

Dear Sir,

Relying upon your formerly experienced kindness I am about to address you rather abruptly—This day I have met Mr Courtenay who tells me that the Rock[1] shares have fallen to 4.15—and that the office is now closed—I have not an opportunity of consulting at this place the letter you were so good as to address to me upon this subject, but according to the best of my recollection it instructed me not to look for such an event as the closing of the office for sale of these shares till about the Autumn of 1826—But perhaps I am mistaken in this—

May I presume so far as to beg you would favour me with the Letter, letting me know whether Mr Courtenays information be accurate—or any thing you deem likely to be useful to me in my concern with this office. As soon as I return to Rydal Mount I shall consult your Letter which is there.

Hoping you will excuse this Liberty I remain my dear Sir
Your very obliged
Ser^{nt}
Wm Wordsworth

P.S. Be so good as to address me under cover—to the Honble —Col^{nl} Lowther M.P.
Lowther Castle
near Penrith
Cumberland.

186. W. W. to ALARIC WATTS

MS. untraced.
Alaric Watts, i. 283. K (—). LY i. 222 (—).

Lowther Castle, Penrith,
August 13, 1825.

My dear Sir,

Your very kind letter[2] has been forwarded to me. I return you sincere thanks for the trouble you have taken on my account. I do

---

[1] Rock Life Assurance Company. [2] Of 1 Aug. See L. 182 above.

not wish to dispose of the copyright of my works. The value of works of imagination it is impossible to predict; and it would be more mortifying to dispose of the copyright for less than might prove its value, than it would gratify me to sell it at a price beyond its worth. I would therefore wish to dispose of the right of printing an edition at a given sum. I therefore authorise you to treat with Messrs. Hurst and Robinson for a new edition of my poems, including the *Excursion*, in six volumes.

> I remain, with great respect,
> Your faithful and obliged servant,
> Wm Wordsworth

187. W. W. to SAMUEL ROGERS

Endorsed: not to be published S. R.
MS. Sharpe Collection, University College, London.
Rogers. LY i. 223.

> Lowther Castle
> August 15th [1825]

My dear Rogers,

Month after month elapses and I receive no answer from the grand Murray. I will not pay him the Compt. to say I am offended at this; but really it is so unpromising for my comfort in carrying six vols through the Press, and also for the question of ultimate profit, that I have determined not to proceed in the Arrangement; and now write to thank you for your kind exertions which have proved so fruitless. I have sent off a Letter to Murray telling him that I have given up the arrangement with him; and shall look out elsewhere.—I am persuaded that he is too great a Personage for any one but a Court, an Aristocratic or most fashionable Author to deal with. You will recollect the time that elapsed before you could bring him to terms—for the pains you then took I again thank you. And believe [me], my dear Rogers,

> faithfully your obliged Friend
> Wm Wordsworth

If I succeed in another quarter I will let you know. Everybody is well here.—[1]

---

[1] Shortly after this, W. W. left Lowther for the three-day festivities at Storrs Hall, John Bolton's residence on Windermere, in honour of Canning and Sir Walter Scott. (The former had been there since 7 Aug.: the latter

188. W. W. to JOHN TAYLOR

MS. Cornell. Hitherto unpublished.

Lowther Hall near Penrith.

[? *c.* 15 Aug. 1825][1]

My dear Sir,

Having an opportunity of sending you a Letter without putting you to the expense of Postage, I cannot deny myself the pleasure of letting you know that our object has been thoroughly answered by the Paragraph in the Evening Mail; and that I am quite in favor with the person for whose perusal it was intended.—

I have also to thank you for your kind intention of making honourable mention of me in the Sun; which perhaps you may have already done; but as I do not regularly see that Paper, I am ignorant whether your intention has yet been fulfilled.

I am at present at Lowther Hall, the seat of Lord Lonsdale; and have the satisfaction of having Sir George and Lady Beaumount Co-inmates with me in this delightful place. They are both well; Sir George often speaks of you with great pleasure. Excuse the abruptness of this conclusion as I am called to breakfast, and believe me most truly and sincerely

Yours,

William Wordsworth

arrived from his Irish tour on the 20th.) On the 21st they were guests-of-honour at a dinner attended by W. W., Lockhart, Professor Wilson of Elleray, Lord and Lady Bentinck, and Sir James Graham. Three of Canning's political associates—Charles Ellis, M.P., leader of 'the West Indian interest', John Denison, M.P., later Lord of the Admiralty and Speaker of the House, and the Hon. William Harvey—were also of the party, as well as several prominent members of the Bar. The next day there was a grand procession of boats on the lake, followed by a regatta. On the 23rd Scott, accompanied by Lockhart and Wilson, breakfasted at Rydal Mount, and afterwards went on with W. W. and Dora W. to visit Southey at Keswick. Sara Coleridge noted in a letter to Derwent of 30 Aug., 'Sir Walter looks like an old lame, fat, honest, good-natured Admiral . . .' (*University of Texas MSS.*). On the 24th they moved on to Hallsteads, whence Scott went on alone to Lowther. On the 26th Bishop Blomfield arrived at Rydal for the consecration of the new chapel. (See *Carlisle Patriot*, 2 Sept. 1825; Lockhart, *Life of Scott*, vi. 78–9; *Letters of Dora Wordsworth*, pp. 23–4; and D. W.'s MS. Journals.)

[1] This letter cannot be dated with any certainty, nor can the various references in it be fully explained: it must have been written before the end of 1825, when John Taylor ceased to be proprietor of the *Sun*, and may belong to the August of that year when W. W. and the Beaumonts were guests together at Lowther.

189. W. W. to ALARIC WATTS

MS. untraced.
Alaric Watts, i. 283. K (—). LY i. 223 (—).

My dear Sir,   September 5, 1825.

The offer of Hurst and Robinson[1] is anything but liberal, and, sharing your opinion, I decline it. Mr Longman, on his recent visit,[2] opened the conversation by observing that Messrs Hurst and Robinson were about to publish my poems. I answered no; that, through a friend, I had opened negotiations with them, but that their offer had not satisfied me. He asked me to name a sum; and I told him I could not incur the trouble of carrying the work through the press for less than £300 for an edition of a thousand copies, twenty to be placed at my own disposal. He made no objection, and proposed to lay my offer before his partners. Mr Longman behaved perfectly like a gentleman, and had I to deal with him alone there would be no obstacle.

It is now high time to thank you again for all the trouble you have taken. I wish I could make you an adequate or any return; and particularly regret that I am under general restrictions which prevent me contributing a small poem to your own next publication.

I am, dear sir,
Your obliged friend and servant,
Wm Wordsworth

190. W. W. to ALARIC WATTS

MS. untraced.
Alaric Watts, i. 284. K. LY i. 224.

My dear Sir,   Rydal, September 5, 1825.

Allow me to introduce to you Mr Quillinan, a particular friend of ours, who is just leaving us. He is merely passing through Manchester, but I think you will be pleased with each other, however short the

---

[1] Watts had sent another long letter of advice on 30 Aug., including details of an offer from Hurst and Robinson. 'They have the assurance to offer only £200 for an edition of 1000 copies with a reservation too that if successful they shall be allowed hereafter to print another edition upon similar terms. The proposition appears to me so illiberal that I told them I should not care to communicate it to you . . .' (*WL MSS.*). They made a better offer later (see L. 196 below), and negotiations continued till the following January.

[2] Longman had recently visited Rydal Mount with his wife and daughters in an attempt to reopen negotiations with W. W., and he wrote on 10 Oct. offering new terms (see L. 196 below).

interview. I forgot to thank you for the favourable notice you took of the intended edition of my poems in your journal. I have this moment received my annual account from Longman. The *Excursion* has been more than a year out of print, and none of the *Poems* are left. I find that for forty-nine copies of the four volumes I have received £25-14-6 net profit, great part of which would have been swallowed up in advertisements if I had not forbad them a year ago.

Ever most faithfully,
Your obliged friend and servant,
Wm Wordsworth

191. W. W. to MESSRS. LONGMAN AND CO.

MS. Mr. W. Hugh Peal. Hitherto unpublished.

Rydal Mount
25 September [1825]

Dear Sirs,

In your last annual Account you mention a spoiled or imperfect copy of the Miscellaneous Poems, this would be very useful to me in preparing the new Edition, pray be so good as to let the Bearer Mr Strickland Cookson have it, to forward to me.

I am your obed^nt Servt
Wm Wordsworth

192. W. W. to JOHN BREWSTER[1]

Address: To the Revd John Brewster Greatham—
MS. Cornell. Hitherto unpublished.

Rydal Mount
26th Septr 1825

My dear Sir,

It gives me great pleasure to comply with your request by sending You my Autograph; I have only to regret that the penmanship is not a more worthy Memorial of One who is with great respect

sincerely your's
Wm Wordsworth

[1] The Revd. John Brewster (1754–1842), author of the *Parochial History and Antiquities of Stockton upon Tees*, 1796, and of a number of devotional works: vicar of Greatham-on-Tees and Stockton-on-Tees, and then rector of Egglescliffe from 1814. The reference is almost certainly not to his son, of the same name, who was vicar of Greatham, 1818–22, but thereafter moved to a living at Laughton in Lincs.

193. D. W. to WILLIAM PEARSON

MS. untraced.
Pearson (—). *K* (—). *LY i. 224* (—).

Rydal Mount,
Sept. 30th, 1825.

My dear Sir,

My brother is much interested by your simple and affecting report, concerning the character of Mr Smith's[1] deceased wife, and desires me to say that he is not hopeless of being able to throw off a few lines at some time or other, in contemplating so interesting a character; yet he can by no means promise for himself. There are, however, two points which you have omitted to name, and which are essential in the composition of an epitaph—namely her age and the date of her decease; therefore, be so good as to inform us of these particulars by the next post after your receipt of this. The day of my brother's departure[2] is not fixed; but I think it will not be later than Thursday, and I very much wish to hear from you before that time, as during his journey, it is not unlikely that his thoughts may take the turn which might lead to the accomplishment of his and your wishes. . . . I must not omit to tell you that we have read your journal[3] with great pleasure. There are two or three passages which throw light upon some imperfect recollections of my own, which I shall, with your permission, take the liberty to copy. . . .

and believe me, Dear Sir,
Yours respectfully,
D. Wordsworth, Senr.

[1] William Pearson's intimate friend, Thomas Smith of Gorton, a silk-weaver and fellow admirer of Wordsworth, had lost his wife in July less than a year after marriage. He had applied to W. W. through Pearson for a epitaph. There is no evidence that it was ever completed.

[2] For Coleorton.

[3] Probably of his Scottish tour in summer 1822.

Address: The Revd. Robert Jones, Llan Fehangel—Glyn Myvor, Caery druidion North Wales.
MS. WL transcript.
LY i. 225.

Rydal Mount near Kendal.
October 7th. 1825.

My dear Mr Jones,

My Brother has commissioned me to write to you respecting a matter in which he supposes there may have been some mistake; but which I solve otherwise; however I am not sorry for the opportunity it gives me of inquiring after you, and of telling you something of our goings-on. But first to the point in question. Did you, or did you not remit to Masterman and Co the little sum (I believe about £8) which you owed my Brother? If you *have* done so there is an error in our Banker's accounts for no mention is made of it in my Brother's last half-yearly statement from them. I tell him (but he is not satisfied with my explanation) that surely enough the money has never been paid—that you are no more of a man of business than himself—and that you have intended coming this summer, and settling all in a much pleasanter and more convenient way than through the medium of Bankers—yourself by the fireside at Rydal Mount.—Well, however this may be, I hope it will secure us the pleasure of a letter from you—by *us* I mean my Niece and myself; for she and I are now sole housekeepers, and her Brother William is our only companion. John set off for Oxford this morning, with his Father and Aunt (Miss Hutchinson)[1] who are to meet Mrs Wordsworth[2] at Sir George Beaumont's in Leicestershire; where they will all stay a full month, except that my Brother talks of taking a week out of it for Cambridge, leaving my Sister and Miss H. at Coleorton; but I think it is more likely they will all go the round together, which, if it be done, will a little prolong their absence. The whole party are in good health, only my Brother's eyes not quite so well as during the summer. Your Friend Dora was much out of health in the spring and summer, but is now as stout and strong as ever I saw her. We hope you will take next *spring* for your long-promised visit to us—arrange for the supply

---

[1] After the death of Thomas Monkhouse, S. H. had spent some time at Hindwell and Brinsop, and finally returned to Rydal Mount after her long absence on 5 Aug.

[2] M. W. had accompanied her sister-in-law Mary Hutchinson on a visit to Harrogate for the sake of her health. See *MW*, pp. 122–3.

of your Church in good time, and come as early in May as possible. We really were not sorry that you did not arrive in the course of last *summer*; for you would have had no *quiet* enjoyment, and you are not made for *bustling* pleasures. We never in our lives had so many visitors. The newspapers (for I suppose newspapers are not excluded from the Valley of Meditation) will have announced to you the names of some of them—Mr. Canning, Sir Walter Scott[1] etc. etc.; but if we had kept a private register of the names of others of less note you would really have been astonished with their numbers. Dora regrets that she did not do so. Many thanks for your kind wish to see me in N. Wales. It is a country wholly unknown to me, [   ]² you, if ever my wish of seeing it be gratified. [? It would be] no small addition to my pleasure to visit you, and your good Family at Plasy-llan—a place of which I have heard so much in the days of my youth. My Brother has promised me, if all be well, and if no other scheme of travelling elsewhere prevent him, that he will take me the round of Snowdon next summer; but it is too soon to talk of this. We shall hope to see you in the spring, and then perhaps some arrangement may be made.

Dora begs her love to you, and kind remembrances to all her Friends in North Wales. Believe me, dear, Sir,

Yours faithfully
D. Wordsworth.

Will you trust yourself again to my guidance to the Top of one of our Mountains? Or did I give you too much of it the last time? For myself—and I am thankful for the blessing—I can walk as well as when but twenty years old, and can climb the hills better than in those days. The pure air of high places seems to restore all my youthful feelings.

¹ For the festivities at Storrs at the end of August, and the subsequent visits of Canning and Scott to Rydal Mount see L. 187 above.
² *MS. torn.*

195. DORA W. and D. W. to EDWARD QUILLINAN

Address: Edward Quillinan Esq., Pall Mall, London.
Postmark: 20 Oct. 1825. *Stamp*: Kendal Penny Post. *Endorsed*: 1825. Dora
    Wordsworth Oct^br 17. Rydal.
MS. WL. Hitherto unpublished.

Rydal Mount.
Octr 17th [1825]

My dear Mr Quillinan,

Many thanks for your long looked for letter. We are grieved
to hear that you are under medical care. Do be obedient and good
and soon get well. Aunt Wordsworth, Willy and myself are all
that are left at Rydal Mount. We have heard of the safe arrival of
the party at Coleorton—and of the great improvement in dear
Aunt Hutchinson's health. She bore her journey as far as Coleorton
wonderfully—was in excellent spirits and *much* fatter. Mrs Luff too
has reached her destination and found Lady Farquhar better but
very weak. John has not yet condescended to write to us—nor do
I suppose he will unless to inquire about his fair Friend whom I
have never seen since his departure. She had a gay ball the other
day and poor Willy is highly indignant that he was not invited
younger boys than he being of the party. I fear I shall make it more
stupid than ever. The *Lakers* are nearly over. Sir James[1] and Miss
Mackintosh are the only strangers we have had since my Father
left us. They took luncheon with us yesterday. We have seen
a good deal of poor Barber and yesterday he seriously invited us
to go and spend a week with him—and was by no means pleased
with me for telling him it was the most absurd scheme I ever heard
of. Your account of his taking you for Mr De Quincey amused us
not a little. How I should have enjoyed seeing you personate the
Opium Eater. By the way, the poor little man is returned—he
reached the Nab Thursday last.

We are delighted to hear your Darlings are so well. Shall we
ever have them at Rydal again?—But if they were only to remain
a few months I would almost rather not see them. I *now can* live
without them, but if they were once to come among us again
parting from them would be *dreadful*. I fear your illness will pre

---

[1] For Sir James Mackintosh, the historian and philosopher, see *MY* i. 265
and *MY* ii. 45. Since his return from India in 1811 he had embarked on a
political career as M.P. first for Nairn (1813), and then for Knaresborough
(1819); and from 1818 to 1824 he was Professor of 'law and general politics'
at Haileybury. His most considerable philosophical work, the *Dissertation on
the Progress of Ethical Philosophy*, written for the *Encyclopaedia Britannica*
appeared in 1830.

ent your visit to Brinsop—and then you will not get your odious
green collar and some other things which were left here and which
were sent by Uncle Henry.[1] 'The Cuckoo and the Nightingale'[2]
was put into the parcel—we found it in my Aunt's large Bible
a day or two after you were gone.

I think my Father will be in Town before he sees Rydal Mount
again. He will certainly go to Cambridge, and being so near, he will
get upon a coach and pop over, if he had no other notion than seeing
his lover Rogers. Then perhaps he may be lucky enough to catch
a glimpse of you. My Mother and Aunt Sarah intend to remain
quietly at Coleorton. On their return they stay a day or two at
Manchester to see Miss Jewsbury and Mr Watts.[3] You never
mention what you thought of and how you liked my Friend Miss J.
—and I was very very desirous to know she was so charmed with
you that she bids me not only tell her how you are whenever I write,
but when I or any of us writes to you she begs us to add her
respects and she 'will pocket the improprieties.'

They have got the hooping cough at Keswick and poor dear Sara
Coleridge is suffering from it very much. Edith has hitherto escaped
and I so trust she will not take it at all. The children have it very
mildly. Mr Southey's foot is no better. Aunt and Willy join with me
in kindest love and sincere wishes for your recovery and kisses to
the dear Darlings when you see them, and believe me ever your
grateful and faithful Friend.

Dora Wordsworth.

D. W. writes]

My dear Friend,

Dora says she has written a stupid letter and wants me to make
amends; but that I cannot do being stupid enough—though without
any thing to complain of, except Damp heat, which always makes
me weak and powerless. Today, however, we have October
chilliness, and though with flying showers, I am getting back my
walking powers.

Your illness grieved us heartily and I must pray you to write
to tell us how you are.—I hope recovered—but whether or not,
pray write. Remember the comfort of loving words—lively news
(if it can be sent) to two poor deserted families. We are however

---

[1] Henry Hutchinson, M. W.'s sailor brother.
[2] *PW* iv. 217, written in 1801, but unpublished until 1841. See *DWJ* i. 89.
[3] They also met Mrs. Watts, formerly Priscilla Wiffen, of a Quaker family
at Woburn in Bedfordshire, who gives a striking account of the poet's conversation. See *Alaric Watts*, i. 238–41.

very comfortable—Willy well and Dora in spirit and healthy looking—it would delight you to look on her. God bless you

Ever yours
D W

Do come again to see us very soon. You were much missed and much regretted when you were gone. I am happy your dear little Girls are so well. God bless them and you! My best Regards to Captain Barret. How much do I regret that you had ever so close a connexion with Mr Gee! Better to have been deceived by his liberal gentleman-like manners at a distance—and his Kindness in the common Round of familiar intercourse! Adieu. Do write.

196. W. W. to ALARIC WATTS

MS. untraced.
Alaric Watts, i. 285. K. LY i. 227.

Coleorton Hall, Ashby-de-la-Zouche
October 18, 1825

My dear Sir,

Messrs Longman and Co. declining my proposition, offer £100 on publication, £50 when an edition of five hundred copies shall have been sold, and the printing of five hundred more to be optional on the same terms. This I have declined;[1] but have proposed to allow them to print an edition of five hundred copies they paying me on publication £150, and placing twenty copies at my disposal. Mr Longman acknowledges that there is no doubt of a thousand copies being ultimately sold, but he says that the last edition of five hundred copies took five years to go off. This is not quite accurate. The *Poems* and *Excursion* were both ready for publication in the autumn of 1820, and, if I am not grossly mistaken

---

[1] Longman wrote again on 22 Oct. offering a small modification in the terms set out in his letter of the 10th, namely, an advance on the estimated profit *before* publication. 'If these terms be not agreeable to you, we must wholly despair with great regret that it is out of our power to make them so.' (*WL MSS.*) But Watts had already, on 11 Oct., cast doubt on Longman's latest overtures: '. . . I was astonished beyond all reason at the sum you mention having received on account of the last edition of your poems, and have no hesitation in declaring that you have been most grossly imposed upon . . .' And he wrote again on the 25th recommending Hurst and Robinson: 'Longman and Co are I fear a very mean . . . set, and their conduct throughout has been so disgusting that I do most sincerely hope you will have nothing further to do with them . . .' (*WL MSS.*)

390

they cleared the expense of printing in less than a year; and in June, 1824, there were none of the *Excursion* on hand, and only twenty-five copies of the *Miscellaneous Poems* remaining. Mr Longman says that six volumes cannot be sold for less than £2-8s.

I am desirous to hear something of your *Souvenir*. I should be very insensible not to be wishful for its success, and sincerely regret that the restrictions under which I am, do not allow me to make an exception in its behalf, without incurring a charge of disingenuousness.

I remain, my dear sir, very sincerely,
Your obliged friend and servant,
Wm Wordsworth

197. D. W. to CATHERINE CLARKSON

Address: Mrs Clarkson, Playford Hall, Ipswich, Suffolk.
Postmark: 20 Oct. 1825. *Stamp*: Kendal Penny Post. *Endorsed*: Miss Wordsworth. Oct. 18.
MS. British Museum.
LY i. 228.

October 18th Tuesday. [1825]

My dear Friend,

After your last letter full of interesting intelligence—happy and mournful—I ought not to have been so long silent—nor should I had I thought *inquiries* were necessary. I satisfied myself that if any important change should take place in your poor Niece's state you would write. As I have heard nothing I feel no doubt of her being still among the living; but cannot hope that she is likely to be restored to her Family, for you would have been ready to make me a sharer in your hopes. The last news we have had of you was through my Brother, who as Tom[1] will have told you, had a hearty shake of his hand in Carlisle Streets—a few hasty words and both were off. Then again they met at Dinner (I believe at Rose Castle[2]) —were at different parts of the Table—drank a Glass of wine together—and when my Brother looked about for him at the stirring of the Party—lo! Tom had disappeared and he never saw him again. My Brother thought he looked harassed and pale, and he said that the heat affected him a good deal with the bustle of the Circuit.

---

[1] C. C.'s son, now a barrister.
[2] Residence of the bishops of Carlisle since the thirteenth century. But according to C. C.'s letter of 25 Dec. (*WL MSS.*), the meeting took place at *Lowther* Castle.

I was on the look-out for T's appearance after the Lancaster assizes
—John W and I were then the sole housekeepers—William, Mary,
Dora and Willy had been a month by the sea-side.[1] He (my
Brother) left them there, and they in the mean time came home
with Mrs Hutchinson, who stayed a month here—then Mary W
accompanied her to Harrowgate, where the Invalid threw off her
maladies. Mary W and she travelled together to Derby. There my
Brother and Sara Hutchinson met them, and the whole party proceeded to Coleorton where they found Thomas H ready to escort
his Wife home, after two whole days spent with our good Friends,
Sir G. and Lady Beaumont. Sara writes in excellent spirits concerning Mrs H. She says she looks quite well and is growing fatter.
It will be a fortnight on Thursday since Dora and Willy and I
were left alone—thoroughly alone—for Mrs Luff accompanied
them to Manchester on her way to London, summoned thither by
the dangerous illness of Lady Farquhar. She found her out of
danger; but very weak, as all persons must be in recovery from a
violent fever. John went to Oxford at the same time.

You will be truly glad to hear that Dora is now in perfect health.
We were very anxious about her in the summer, but the right
course was hit upon—change of air and horse-exercise. Willy has
taken to growing and has no symptoms of derangement except a
pale face—and a black tongue at waking in the mornings. I wish
that appearance of the tongue could be satisfactorily explained. We
have had the finest weather, and the most bustling summer ever
remembered. No dinner-parties, it is true, except such as have been
made up of chance comers and our own Family; but *that* has often
been large. Callers innumerable. I have never been from home
except on a few days excursions—and for a week[2] at Mr Marshall's
beside Ullswater. I then called at Eusemere. How I wished for
you! The place is very pretty—nothing wanted but the axe. In
some places it would be very useful in bringing out the good trees—
in others, having been so much neglected, it would not do much
good. I saw Betty Wilson and *Hannah* Walker, for the first time—
What a beauty Hannah is! She is a perfect specimen of beauty in
old age. They talked much of Tom (whom they had just seen) and
of all of you—and of old times. Miss Honeyman[3] has been staying

[1] At Kent's Bank.
[2] Sometime during September—but the exact date cannot be determined as
there is a gap in D. W.'s MS. Journals at this point.
[3] It was to Mrs. Honeyman that Sarah Green was sent to lodge for three
years on leaving the Wordsworths in 1810. See D. W.'s *George and Sarah
Green, A Narrative*, ed. E. de Selincourt, 1936, p. 32. (De Selincourt's note.)

with us a fortnight—very happy—She has had a whole summer of quiet rambling, and returns with pleasure to her winter duties at Penrith. She has a small house there—has a comfortable independence of her own making, and is able thoroughly to enjoy it. Her good religious and moral principles, and her great desire to be useful provide her with constant employment, so she is not like one put out of place by relinquishing the labours of her Business. Dora and I find her an excellent companion.

I think we had the last of our Lakers on Sunday. The weather is now so unsettled, that none will now be tempted to linger. Sir James Mackintosh[1] and his Daughter called on Saturday—and on Sunday came to sit with us at Chapel and stayed *their* Luncheon— *our* dinner—a cold one—set out while we were at Chapel. Sir James looks wonderfully well, considering the wearing life he has led—politics—Law—India—house of Commons wrangling! Miss M is very pleasing—a little woman [with] spectacles. Dora took much to her, she [was] so natural and unaffected—with very good sense. No doubt you want to hear of Mrs Luff's cottage[2]—I can only say it is as pretty as it can be and as well contrived—but it is not made for an income of £150. It is a good thing for women in general to have a *master*, and Mrs Luff should always have had one —I mean a *legal master*; for she *will* have her own way now that he is gone who had the sole *right* to manage her. Through her kind Friends the Farquhars I trust she will never suffer any serious privations for having involved herself in the cares of keeping up a house that must necessitate more expense than was needful for her. God Bless her! She is a good and charitable creature and has so much pleasure in doing kind actions that I chiefly grieve that she has deprived herself of the power of feasting in that way—in a hundred instances where the privation will cause positive pain. My dearest Friend this is a rambling dull letter—and no word of inquiry or congratulation. You will supply this want and tell me everything that concerns you and yours. Mary Clarkson[3] will be a delightful Daughter for you, and I am sure an excellent wife for your Son. They must know each other thoroughly—faults and failings no less than excellences. My best Love and best wishes attend them. How is dear Mr Clarkson? and pray speak particularly of your own health. Sara Coleridge has the hooping cough severely

---

[1] See L. 195 above. [2] Fox Ghyll.
[3] Mary Clarkson, C. C.'s niece, who married her cousin Tom in 1829. In 1843—six years after his death—she married the Revd. W. W. Dickinson, icar of Playford. She was the daughter of Thomas Clarkson's younger brother, Lieut. John Clarkson, R.N. See *EY*, p. 527.

—Edith has not caught it—All the younger have it slightly Hartley's school is done up. He writes for Magazines[1]—at Amble side. Adieu dearest Friend,

Ever yours D. W.

198. D. W. to MARY LAING

Address: To Miss Laing, at Wm Laing's Esqre, Lauriston, Edinburgh.
Postmark: 4 Nov. 1825. *Stamp*: Kendal Penny [Post].
MS. Edinburgh University Library.
The Wordsworth–Laing Letters (—).

Rydal Mount, near Kenda
Novr 3rd 182£

My dear Miss Laing,

If you have ever turned your thoughts to Rydal Mount—(and I believe you have very often) you must have set me down as one of the most negligent or ungrateful of human Beings. Such a charge *indeed* I do not deserve; for I have wilfully offended against the admonitions of conscience, and have often keenly suffered from its reproaches. I will make neither apology nor explanation, for nothing in the world is so tiresome to the reader, only I must assure you that so far from having forgotten you, I think of you very frequently, and it would give me the greatest pleasure to see you again.

You were about going to London when I last heard from you—a second visit I mean—not with your amiable Friends and protec toresses. Did you get the visit accomplished or not? My Niece was at that time at Hendon, and afterwards, in April (1824), I was in London with my Brother, and she spent a month with us in Gloucester Place. At Christmas she had spent a fortnight there—and these two short visits included the whole of her stay in the Metropolis.

After a visit to the neighbourhood of Canterbury, we all went to Cambridge, stayed a fortnight at Trinity Lodge,—the Father and Daughter returned to Rydal—and I after a short stay with

---

[1] With the failure of Mr. Dawes's school at Ambleside, Hartley Coleridge turned to supporting himself from contributions to the reviews and annuals His cousin John Taylor Coleridge had succeeded Gifford as editor of the *Quarterly* late in 1824, and he was anxious to make use of Hartley's service as a reviewer; but he resigned his editorship in Nov. 1825 on the grounds that it interfered with his legal practice, before Hartley could benefit from the offer See *Letters of Hartley Coleridge*, pp. 88 ff.

M^r and Mrs Clarkson at Playford Hall near Ipswich came home, where I have been almost stationary ever since. The rest of the Family have been somewhat of Wanderers. Last Autumn Dora accompanied her Father and Mother to see their Relatives in Herefordshire and Radnorshire.

Your Friend, Miss Joanna Hutchinson, happened to be in the North at that time, and stayed a while with me; but not long—her visit was to Kendal where she was in attendance upon a sick Friend, a young Woman[1] who has been nearly confined to her Bed for three years. Benevolent and kind creature as she is, she had no other object but to chear and help to nurse her Friend; however she continued to make a voyage to the Isle of Man with one of her Brothers. I would gladly have been of the Party, but, being sole house-keeper, could not leave home. Joanna came home delighted with the little Island. We often talked of you—and of a longer Voyage with you—to Staffa and Skye and all the Isles to which Steam-Boats can carry us; but now alas! the dreadful Fate of *the Comet*,[2] casts a gloom over all Dreams of Steam-boat expeditions. I hope no Friends of yours were among the Sufferers. My Brother and Sister are at Sir George Beaumont's in Leicestershire. It is nearly 8 weeks since *she* left home, to accompany an invalid Sister-in-Law to Harrowgate. After three weeks stay at Harrowgate she joined her Husband in Leicestershire. Dora is at home with me and your Friend Willy. I am happy to tell you that both are in good health. John is at Oxford. Mr Hartley Coleridge is still living at Ambleside. He has given up his school; and is employed in writing for the Press. He dined with us yesterday; and spent the evening, joining our young People in a merry game at cards. Two of the Misses Southey (Bertha and Kate) have been a fortnight at Rydal Mount. They are delightful Girls. Bertha (of whom I had known but little before) is an especial favorite of mine. We talked about you last night, and I [was p]leased[3] to find that they both re-member you [with great] delight. They reported your opinion of their Skulls, etc. etc. All Mr Southey's Children except Miss Southey have had the Whooping-cough, but are nearly well again. Not so poor Miss Coleridge, who has had the disorder violently. She is, however, recovering. My dear Miss Laing, this is a poor scrawl after so long a silence, but, having taken the resolution to

---

[1] Elizabeth Cookson.

[2] According to the *Annual Register* for 1825, the steamboat *Comet* was run down off Kempock Point between Gourock and the Clouth Lighthouse by the steamboat *Ayr*. The *Comet* went down almost instantaneously. Eleven only were saved out of more than eighty.　　　　[3] *MS. torn.*

write, I am determined not to lose another Post and the Girls are hurrying me to be done, that I may go with them to the Waterfall during a sunny gleam after a heavy shower.

I will not trouble you with particular inquiries being assured that you will give me credit for being interested in all your Family concerns—Father, Mother, Brothers and Sister—to all of whom I beg my kind remembrances. I hope your good Mother is pretty well. I shall never forget her kindness to my Friend and me. When shall you again travel along this Road? Rydal Mount is just as pretty as ever and the village beautified by our new Chapel which is a great comfort to us. We should all be very glad to see you here or either of your Brothers.

Adieu, believe me, dear Miss Laing

Your affect^e Friend

D Wordsworth

199. D. W. to H. C. R.

Address: H. C. Robinson Esqre, 3 King's Bench Walk, London.
Postmark: 10 Nov. 1825. *Stamp*: Kendal Penny Post. *Endorsed*: 8 Novr 1825, Miss Wordsworth.
MS. Dr. Williams's Library.
K (—). *Morley, i. 143.*

Rydal Mount near *Kendal*

November 8th—[1825]

My dear Friend,

My original intention was to meet you with a note of congratulation on your return[1] to the lonesome Chambers in King's Bench Walk; but I have just heard of poor Mary Lamb's illness and this is a matter of sincere condolence. I write then chiefly to *inquire* after her and her Brother—and next to plead for a continuation of your journal, the first part of which was duly received and read by all of us with very great pleasure—It made me wish to touch at those agreeable Islands[2] the next voyage we take—if ever we are destined again to wander beyond the shores of Britain.—My Brother and Sister and Miss Hutchinson have been a month at Coleorton, and it is from there that we, at home, have received the distressing tidings of Miss Lamb's illness, brought to them by the Master of Trinity, who has also been at Coleorton—Now my good Friend, I pray you write as soon as you receive this. I hope you may

---

[1] From France.   [2] The Channel Islands.

be able to say that the present attack is of the milder kind, as they have lately been, and that she is in the way of recovery. Besides, tell us particularly how Charles is himself. I learn that the supposed cause of the Sister's illness, was his having had a relapse after a nervous fever.—Beyond this at present I require no more than to know that you are safe and well after a journey, which I trust has been pleasant; for you have the happy art of enjoying wherever there is a possibility of finding anything to enjoy. Leave all particulars, only do not retract your promise.—I have stayed at home all summer and have had an agreeable lot—the weather has been better than was ever known and I have had health and strength to allow me to take long walks—which (especially upon the mountains) are as delightful to my feelings as ever in my younger days— My Sister has been ten weeks absent—She accompanied Mrs Thomas Hutchinson to Harrowgate, stayed some time there, and met her Husband and Sister at Sir G. Beaumont's.

My last report to you on the state of my Brother's eyes was very cheerful—We were in hopes that he was going to outlive that troublesome weakness; but alas! ever since he went to Coleorton he has been suffering from inflammation, especially in *one* of his eyes. Mrs Wordsworth is quite well. We expect them at home about the middle of next week.

Nothing is yet done towards the printing of the Poems except a bargain made with Hurst and Robinson. Longman was at Rydal with his Family—my Brother made his proposals to him, which he has no doubt would have been chearfully acceded to by *him*: but the jewish *Concern* could not agree to them. Alaric Watts has been the agent with Hurst etc, and they give all that the Author required from the Longmans. I have always believed that they never pushed the Sale—If this belief be well founded there can be no doubt of my Brother's being a gainer by the change. I am right glad he has nothing to do with Murray. When he is at home again, we shall be kept very busy for a while—A new arrangement is to be made—and till the work is printed he will always be attempting to correct faults.

I have this moment received a letter from Miss Horrocks telling me she is going to be married, with the approbation of her Father and of all her Family. Her intended Husband is a physician of the name of St. Clair,[1] resident in Preston. She has known him intimately

---

[1] Sarah Horrocks married William St. Clare (b. 1784) of Blackburn in Jan. 1826. He was educated at Christ Church, Oxford, and took his M.D. in 1812.

for 15 years.—Mrs Monkhouse and her Daughter are come back to Preston—She departed thence in August, to Clifton, where she had *lodgings* I believe, and intended spending the winter there, physicians having pronounced the Climate of the North too cold for her. These said physicians now decide differently—They tell her her lungs are quite sound and she may live wherever it suits her best.—For myself I have little doubt that both opinions have had the same foundation, inclinations discovered on the part of the Consulter—This, I am sure, is the trick of South-country physicians.

At present Mrs Monkhouse intends to reside a year with her Father. This arrangement, no doubt was in consequence of the intended marriage. There will, when Miss Horrocks resigns her name, only be the youngest (Anne Eliza) unmarried.—My niece Dora, and William are both well. Dora sends her kind remembrances—Two Miss Southeys are staying with us, so we are a lively party. All the Southeys (except the eldest) have the hooping-cough—and Sara Coleridge, who has been very ill, but is now recovering. I am sorry to tell you that Southey's foot does not get well, but I am forgetting that you have been out of England and may not have heard of his confinement at Leyden with the Bite of a Bug. The foot inflamed very much and the Erysipelas has since fixed in it and is very troublesome, though not much if it were in any other part. He can only take very short walks: his health is, however, good in other respects. The air of Flanders and Holland quite cured his cough.—Again I entreat for a letter immediately.—Believe me ever, Your affectionate Friend

D Wordsworth.

200. W. W. to RICHARD HEBER[1]

Endorsed: Wordsworth.
MS. Bodleian Library. Hitherto unpublished.
[*In M. W's hand*]

Rydal Mount, Kendal
Nov.ʳ 21ˢᵗ [1825]

My dear Sir,

It has been recommended to my Son, who is a Gent Comm.ʳ of New Coll: to endeavour to obtain a Fellowship at Merton. You know unquestionably the principles that govern the election in this

---

[1] See *MY* ii. 152. Richard Heber had been M.P. for Oxford University since 1821.

Society, and bearing in mind the relation in which you stand to that University it is not without much Scruple that I even mention the Subject to you—but relying on your friendly regards, I have ventured to do so; not soliciting your interposition with the Electors (the Warden and Fellows) in any way that might in the slightest degree embarrass you. To spare you the trouble of consulting the Oxford Callendar, I enclose a list of the Electors by the friend who encouraged us to this pursuit. Trusting you will excuse the liberty I have taken, I remain dear Sir with high respect faithfully yours

[*signed*] Wm Wordsworth

Warden Dr Vaughn[1]	*Mildmay*[2]	*Buckley*[3]
Capel, Honble[4]	*Cockerell*[5]	*Bridges*[6]
Griffith[7]	*Hammond*[8]	*Tierney*[9]
Oglander[10]	*Bouverie*[11]	
Marsham[12]	*Grey*[13]	
Addington[14]	*Rooke*[15]	

[1] Peter Vaughan, D.D. (1770–1825), Fellow of Merton from 1794, Warden from 1809, and Dean of Chester from 1820. He had in fact died the previous April.

[2] The Revd. Charles William St. John-Mildmay (1793–1830), son of Sir Henry St. John-Mildmay, 3rd Bart.: Fellow from 1816, perpetual curate of Holywell, Oxford, 1823, and then rector of Shorwell and Mottistone, Isle of Wight.

[3] The Revd. Henry William Buckley (1800–92), Fellow, 1821–32, thereafter rector of Hartshorne, Derbs.

[4] Major-General the Hon. Thomas Edward Capell (1770–1855), brother of George Capell-Coningsby, 5th Earl of Essex (1757–1839).

[5] Samuel Pepys Cockerell (1794–1869), barrister: Fellow, 1816–69.

[6] Brook-Henry Bridges (1799–1829), nephew of Sir Brook-William Bridges, 3rd Bart., of Goodnestone, nr. Canterbury; barrister and Fellow from 1824.

[7] The Revd. Edward Moses Griffith (1767–1859), Fellow, 1798–1859.

[8] George Hammond (1797–1882), barrister: Fellow, 1818–82.

[9] George Tierney (1800–83), Fellow from 1823, and a commissioner of Greenwich Hospital: son of George Tierney, the Whig politician (see *MY* ii. 529).

[10] John Oglander (1778–1825), Fellow, 1800–25; brother of Sir William Oglander, 6th Bart. (1769–1852), of Nunwell, Isle of Wight, M.P. for Bodmin, 1812. John Oglander had in fact died on 30 Oct.

[11] The Revd. William Arundell Bouverie (1797–1877), Fellow from 1820: rector of West Tytherley, Hants, 1829–39, thereafter rector of Denton, Norfolk, and Archdeacon of Norfolk, 1850–69.

[12] Robert Bullock-Marsham (1786–1880), a cousin of Charles Marsham, 2nd Earl of Romney (1777–1845): barrister, Fellow from 1811, and Warden from 1826 in succession to Dr. Vaughan.

[13] Matthew Robert Grey (1797–1850), Fellow from 1818.

[14] Haviland John Addington (b. 1787), son of the Right Hon. John Addington, M.P. for Harwich, 1803–18, and a Lord of the Treasury: barrister, Fellow from 1813.

[15] The Revd. George Rooke (1797–1874), Fellow, 1821–31: vicar of Embledon, Northumberland, from 1830, Hon. Canon of Durham, 1852.

Whish[1]   *Seymour*[2]
Compton[3]   *Pigou*[4]
Herbert[5]   *Tindall*[6]
Mills[7]

201. W. W. to ALLAN CUNNINGHAM

Address: Allan Cunningham Esqre, 27 Lower Belgrave Place, Pimlico, London.
Postmark: 25 Nov. [?1825]. *Stamp*: Kendal Penny Post.
MS. University of Virginia Library.
K (—). *LY i. 126* (—).

[*In M. W.'s hand*]

Rydal Mount Novr 23^d [1825][8]

My dear Sir,

On returning from Leicestershire a few days ago, I had the pleasure of finding in its destined place the Bust of Sir Walter Scott. It is, as you say, a very fine one; and I doubt not you have been equally select in the one which you have sent *of* me to Sir Walter. I will take care that my debt to you on this score shall be speedily discharged. And here I am reminded of an obligation of the same kind which I am afraid has not been met as it ought to be. Pray, has Mr E^d Coleridge[9] paid for the Cast of my Bust which at his request was forwarded to him at Eton? Bear in mind that I am ultimately responsible for it. I am already in possession of a cast of Mr Southey—a striking likeness, as to feature, but so ill executed in point of character and expression, that I must defer placing a likeness of that honored friend in company with this fine one of

---

[1] The Revd. Henry Francis Whish (1787–1867), Fellow from 1813, and curate of Birchington, Kent.

[2] The Right Hon. Sir George Hamilton Seymour (1797–1880), grandson of Francis Seymour, 1st Marquess of Hertford (1718–94): Fellow, 1821–32: Ambassador at St. Petersburg and then Vienna, 1855–8.

[3] John Combe Compton (b. 1792), of Minstead, Hants, Fellow, 1814–29.

[4] Robert Richard Pigou (b. 1768), Fellow, 1795–1823.

[5] Algernon Herbert (1792–1855), brother of Henry George Herbert, 2nd Earl of Carnarvon (1772–1833): barrister, Fellow, 1814–31.

[6] The Revd. George Tyndall (1798–1848), Fellow, 1823–40: rector of Lapworth, Warwicks., 1839.

[7] Francis Mills (1793–1854), Fellow, 1816–46: son of William Mills of Bisterne, Ringwood, Hants, M.P. for Coventry, 1808–12.

[8] *1823* added in a later hand: but the date must be 1825 as W. W. was not at Coleorton in Nov. 1823.

[9] For Edward Coleridge, see L. 126 above.

Sir Walter, till I can procure one from the hand of Mr Chantrey, who I hope will one day undertake a work which would redound to the credit of both Parties. I am not without hope also that Mr Chantrey may be induced to transmit to posterity the magnificent forehead of one of the first Intellects that Great Britain has produced.—I mean that of Mr Coleridge, and proud should I be to place this triumvirate of my Friends in the most distinguished stations of my little mansion.

Many thanks for your letter. The interest which yourself and family take in my writings and Person is grateful to my feelings —testimonies of this kind are among the very pleasantest results of a literary life. The ground upon which I am disposed to meet your anticipation of the spread of my Poetry is, that I have endeavoured to dwell with truth upon those points of human nature in which all men resemble each other, rather than on those accidents of manners and character produced by times and circumstances; which are the favourite seasoning, and substance too often, of imaginative writings. If therefore I have been successful in the execution of my attempt, it seems not improbable, that as education is extended, writings that are independent of an over—not to say vicious—refinement will find a proportionate increase of readers, provided there be found in them a genuine inspiration.

The selection you again advert to will no doubt be executed at some future time. Something of the kind is already in progress at Paris, in respect to my Poems in common with others. The value of such selections will depend entirely upon the judgement of the Editor. In this case Mr Washington Irvin,[1] whose taste I have no great opinion of, if I may judge from his Sketch book, which, tho' a work of talent, is disfigured by abundance of affectation. In the mean while I am going to press (at last) with a re-publication of the whole of my Poetry, including the Excursion, which will give me an opportunity of performing my promise to you, by sending you the whole, as soon as it is ready for delivery.

The collection of Songs[2] which you announce I had not heard of; your own poetry shews how fit you are for the office of editing native strains; and may not one hope that the taste of the public in

---

[1] Washington Irving (1783–1859) published Knickerbocker's comic *History of New York* in 1809, travelled in Europe and visited Scott at Abbotsford (1817), and published the *Sketch Book* in London in 1820, and *Bracebridge Hall* in 1822. Thereafter he was in Paris, 1823–5, working for Galignani's where he was in much demand as an editor; and then in Spain, before his return to London in 1829. He went back to America in 1832.

[2] *The Songs of Scotland, ancient and modern . . .*, 4 vols., 1825.

these matters is much improved since the time when McPherson's[1] frauds met with such dangerous success, and Percy's[2] Ballads produced those hosts of legendary Tales that bear no more resemblance to their supposed models than Pope's Homer does to the work of the Blind Bard. Do not say I ought to have been a Scotchman. Tear me not from the Country of Chaucer, Spencer, Shakespeare and Milton; yet I own that since the days of childhood, when I became familiar with the phrase, 'They are killing geese in Scotland, and sending the feathers to England' which every one had ready when the snow began to fall, and I used to hear in the time of a high wind that

> Arthur's Bower has broken his band
> And he comes roaring up the land
> King of Scotts wi' a' his Power
> Cannot turn Arthur's Bower,

I have been indebted to the North for more than I shall ever be able to acknowledge. Thomson,[3] Mickle,[4] Armstrong,[5] Leyden,[6] yourself, Irving[7] (a poet in *spirit*), and I may add Sir Walter Scott were all Borderers. If they did not drink the water, they breathed at least the air of the two countries. The list of English Border poets is not so distinguished, but Langhorne[8] was a native of West[d], and Brown, the author of the Estimate of Manners and Principles, etc., a Poet as his letter on the vale of Keswick, with the accompanying verses, shows—was born in Cumberland.[9] So

[1] James Macpherson (1736–96) published two epic poems *Fingal*, 1762, and *Temora*, 1763, which he alleged were translated from Ossian. See also *Prose Works*, iii. 77.
[2] Thomas Percy (1729–1811), Bishop of Dromore, published *Reliques of Ancient English Poetry*, 1765.
[3] James Thomson (1700–48) was born at Ednam, Roxburgh.
[4] William Julius Mickle (1735–88), born at Langholm, Dumfries, the translator of *The Lusiads*, 1775. His Poems appeared in 1794; the chief of them, 'Sir Martyn' (1778), W. W. knew so well that on visiting Langholm with D. W. in 1803 he was able to quote it from memory. (De Selincourt's note.)
[5] John Armstrong (1709–79), born at Castleton, Roxburgh, physician and poet, author of *The Art of Preserving Health*, 1744.
[6] John Leyden (1775–1811), born at Denholm, Roxburgh, physician and poet, assisted Sir Walter Scott with the earlier volumes of the *Border Minstrelsy*, 1802. Scott pays tribute to his 'tuneful strains' in *The Lord of the Isles*, iv. xi.
[7] i.e. Edward Irving, the preacher. See L. 106 above.
[8] John Langhorne (1735–79), born at Kirkby Stephen; best known as co-translator with his brother of Plutarch's *Lives*, 1770. His Poems, very popular in his day, appeared in two volumes in 1766.
[9] Dr. John Brown (1715–66) was born in Northumberland, but educated at Wigton, Cumberland, where his parents went to live while he was still an infant: he was first a minor canon of Carlisle, and then rector of St. Nicholas's

also was Skelton,[1] a Demon in point of genius; and Tickell[2] in later times, whose style is superior in chastity to Pope's, his contemporary. Addison and Hogarth were both within a step of Cum^d and West^d, their several Fathers[3] having been natives of those counties, which are still crowded with their name and relatives. It is enough for me to be ranked in this catalogue, and to know that I have touched the hearts of many by subjects suggested to me on Scottish ground; these pieces you will find classed together in the new Ed^n. Present my thanks to Mrs C. for her kind invitation. I need not add that if you, or any of yours, come this way we shall be most happy to see you.

Pray give my congratulations to Mr Chantrey on the improvement in Mrs C.'s health; they have both our best wishes; and believe me, my dear sir,

Very faithfully yours,
[*signed*] Wm Wordsworth

202. D. W. to H. C. R.

Address: To H. C. Robinson Esqre, 3 King's Bench Walk, Temple, London.
Postmark: 29 Nov. 1825. *Stamp*: Kendal Penny Post. *Endorsed*: 26 Novr 1825, Miss Wordsworth.
MS. Dr. Williams's Library.
K (—). *Morley, i. 146.*

Rydal Mount near *Kendal*
This is our address
Novr 26th—1825

My dear Friend,

On telling my Brother that I was going to write to you, with a question 'have you anything to say to him?' his reply was 'A hundred things'—'Tell him I wish I were as strong as he—that

Newcastle, from 1761. His 'inestimable' *Estimate of the Manners and Principles of the Times* appeared in 1757. In 1770 he published his *Description of the Lake at Keswick . . . by a Late Popular Writer* (see *Prose Works*, ii. 193, 400).

[1] John Skelton (?1460–1529), the satirist, was descended from an old Cumberland family.
[2] Thomas Tickell (1686–1740), born at Bridekirk, Cumberland, the friend of Addison. He edited Addison's *Works*, publishing in the first volume his celebrated elegy *To the Earl of Warwick on the Death of Mr Addison*.
[3] Lancelot Addison, D.D. (1632–1703), Dean of Lichfield, was born in the parish of Crosby Ravensworth, Westmorland, and educated at Appleby Grammar School. Richard Hogarth, the artist's father, was born at Bampton, nr. Kendal, and educated at St. Bees. His uncle, Thomas Hogarth, a rustic poet, came from Troutbeck.

I half envy him his joyous spirits—that I should have liked to have gone with him, or to go with him to the Tyrol—to Italy—or any where' and he added many more of the hundred things—which I have now forgotten, and your fancy must supply:—and now, setting aside wishes, which for at least two or three years *cannot* be gratified (College expenses and others being so great) I must tell you the simple truth that your letter has interested us very much, and I return you a thousand thanks not only for gratifying my wishes in the most agreeable manner possible; but for even anticipating them.—I did not venture to expect the journal for weeks to come, yet it arrives before my request reaches you, and at the same time your account of Charles and Mary Lamb[1] allays our anxiety, though, till we hear from you again, we cannot be satisfied: —yet I hope he has had no second relapse, and that she has been restored to herself and her good Brother at the accustomed period, but, after all that is passed, there must [be] a heavy struggle with sadness and depression of spirits before they are re-instated in their usual comforts. Pray give our kindest regards to them: and write as soon as you have leisure to tell us exactly how they are going on; and mention also your poor Sister, whether she still continues to suffer less than is usual in her afflicting malady, and if you think it will not give her pain to be reminded of those times when I have seen her—or of one whom she will never meet again in this world, will you give my Love to her, and add that I frequently think of her—

I know not that I have any thing new to tell you—It will be a fortnight on Thursday since my Brother and Sister and Miss Hutchinson returned to Rydal Mount—They spent above a month at Coleorton, and with *Stops* on the road, were six weeks absent— that is, my Brother and Miss H., but Mrs W.'s absence had extended to ten weeks and a half when she reached home, and truly happy she was to settle herself again. She is in good health, and her Husband also, which I hardly looked to: for, during the whole of his stay at Coleorton, he suffered grievously from his eyes, having more *pain* and distressful weakness in the eye-*balls* than he had ever had before. In this state he set forward, alone, in a pony-chaise!—I knew of his intentions and was very anxious—but, as he

[1] In his (unpublished) letter of 2 Nov. (*Dr. Williams's Library MSS.*) H. C. R. had written: 'He was a distressing subject. He was slowly recovering from an alarming disease and at the same time suffering on account of his poor Sister. Now I have the pleasure of saying that he is recovered and tho' Mary L. is still very ill, yet the periodical nature of her complaint and her regular recovery render her situation less a subject of anxiety.'

foretold, the journey proved a great relief—almost a cure—
though the weather was sometimes cold and stormy. In fact he
always finds the fresh air more beneficial than any thing else; but
my fears were grounded on the long-continued exposure to all
changes.

My Sister and Miss H. travelled per coach, waited his arrival at
Manchester, and stayed with him there two days,—saw some
pleasant well-informed people—and one most beautiful picture—
for which seven thousand pounds had been refused. I forget the
Master's name, the subject is The Holy Family—the Virgin, they
tell me, a striking likeness of Sara Coleridge—This picture belongs
to a Manchester Merchant, who had it from abroad in lieu of a
bad Debt.—Now while I speak of Manchester let me say a word
in favour of a Friend of Dora's, a Miss Jewsbury, who has written
for 'the Souvenir' and for several other periodicals, under the
signature M. J. J. She is a young woman of extraordinary talents,
is a good Daughter, and a good Sister to a numerous Family at the
head of which she was left, by the Death of her Mother, at the age
of 15. We became acquainted with Miss Jewsbury last summer, and
she spent above a week under our roof; and the Party were with
her at Manchester, and were all much interested by, and for her.
Mr. Alaric Watts has encouraged and persuaded Miss Jewsbury to
publish a volume in prose and verse—miscellaneous—(sketches—
short Essays etc)—and there is one pretty long Tale, ('The
Unknown') which is, to me affectingly told.

The Title[1] of the volumes is *Phantasmagoria*[2]—a title which
would not be very taking to me were the Author a Stranger. I
mention it, however, in order that if you have leisure you may
glance an eye over the Book, and, as you are sometimes a Dabbler
in Reviews, you may have an opportunity of serving the Authoress,
or perhaps Charles Lamb could slip a favorable notice into one of
the Magazines. I cannot ask either of you to *review* the volumes,
though if you would do so and could in conscience speak favorably
it would be a great kindness done to a deserving person and gratefully received.—I think I told you that Hurst and Robinson are to
publish for my Brother; but preliminaries are, I find, not yet
entirely settled—our work is not begun—I much fear that the
printers will not get through in time for the Spring Sale, and if so,
it is the loss of another year.

To return to your Tour,—Guernsey and Mont St. Michel set
me upon wishing—for it would neither be difficult nor expensive

---

[1] *Written* Tittle.   [2] *Written* Phantasmogria.

to accomplish a circuit thereabouts, if we happened to be in the
South of England—As to re-visiting those Vales of the Alps where
you have been tracking our steps—it is so large a scheme—that
now—in this time of impossibility—I go no further than an ex-
clamation—'if it ever *could* be how delightful!—We had just such
bright weather as you describe in your passage from Meyringhen
to Grindelwald[1] when we travelled the contrary way—excepting
a thunder shower while we rested at the Chalet, and ate our dinners
under the shed at the Door opposite to the Wetterhorn, alternately
hidden and revealed by driving clouds and flashing sunbeams. You
ask for an Itinerary of our route[2] from Frankfort to Lucern—
Frankfort — Darmstadt — Heidelberg — Bruchsal — Carlesruhe
— Radstadt — Baden-baden — Offenbach — Hornberg — through
a beautiful valley—ascended from it through Black Forest—to
Villinghen-Donneschingen (where is the Source of the Danube)—
Schaffhausen—Zurich, along the Banks of the Limmat to Baden
standing close to that River—Lenzberg-Murgenthal (It was here
we met with the two handsome Maidens who danced with poor
Thomas Monkhouse). Herzegenboschie, (here we slept in our
Carriages) Berne — Thoun — Interlachen — Lauterbrunnen —
Grindelwald, Meiringhen—Handek—Back to Meiringhen—Over
Brunig to Sarnen, Engelberg—Back again next day to Stanz—
Embarked at Stanzstadt—crossed that part of the Lake to Winkeln
—walked thence to Lucern. I spell wretchedly; but a young Friend
of mine has begun to re-copy my journal (with omissions—In the
way of abridging I can do little) and I will endeavour to correct
spelling by[3] [you] and other good [autho]rities and shall insert
all the notes y[ou] were so good a[s] t[o] make—besides correcting whatever [errors] you have pointed out. For this fair Copy[4]
I wish, before it is bound to procure a Set of Swiss Costumes, and
hope by your kindness to be enabled to do so.—Perhaps some
Friend of yours may be going in to Switzerland—or perhaps they
may be purchased in London at no very great expense. Should the
expence be moderate; we should like two Sets (one for my Sister's
Tour also) but as hers is already bound it is of less consequence,
because the prints could not perhaps be inserted without injury to
the Binding.—I have been so bad a payer that you would have good
cause to fear my getting further into your debt—I owe you for

[1] *Written* Grindelwald to Meyringhen *and marked for transposition.*
[2] On the tour of 1820.
[3] *MS. torn.*
[4] This copy (*WL MSS.*), in an unidentified hand, is now the only surviving
MS. See *DWJ* i. xvii.

Razors and needles, which Debt I have always forgotten at the proper time—and will now discharge the whole together, for I hope you may be able to get the prints, and this discharge I hope may take place at Rydal Mount next summer.—Remember the Hebrides—which you have not seen, and we are in the way to or from Ireland. I wrote a few weeks ago to Mrs Clarkson and am surprized[1] I do not hear from her. Pray when you see Tom, ask how Cousin Emma is[2] and how his Father and Mother are going on. My Brother and Sister saw Mrs Monkhouse at Preston—She was well and chearful, and the Child is remarkably healthy.— Miss Horrocks is very soon to be married. God bless you.

Ever your affectionate friend
D Wordsworth.

What would I not have given to have heard the Avalanches with you!

If the price in London of costumes is beyond what you like to venture unauthorized, pray tell me what it is, and I will say buy— or not buy. Should you be able to procure the Costume by the middle of January a Friend of mine will bring the parcel.

203. W. W. to LORD LONSDALE

MS. Lonsdale MSS. Hitherto unpublished.

Rydal Mount
29th Nov^{br} 1825

My Lord,

The enclosed for Lady Frederic enters into particulars, which I hope she may have the opportunity of reading to you, respecting a matter in which I may probably profit by your Lordship's so often experienced kindness.

My Son is of New Coll: Oxford, but not being a Winchester Man he has no prospects there beyond his education.

He has been advised to try to obtain a Fellowship at Merton; a situation procured mainly through friendly interposition with the Warden and Fellows in whom the election is vested. I beg leave to enclose you a list of them, with some notice of their supposed connections as furnished me by a Friend. The name of Dr Good- enough[3] Head Master of Westminster occurs through the Bishop of

---

[1] *Written* susprized. [2] is *written twice.*
[3] The Revd. Edmund Goodenough, D.D. (1785–1845), headmaster of Westminster School, 1819–28, and Dean of Wells from 1831.

Carlisle,[1] and I venture to hope that it may not be disagreeable to your Lordship to express a wish in that, or some other quarter, that could not but be of eminent service upon this occasion. The situation is an enviable one on every account; and I am particularly desirous that my son should obtain it, as he is regular and studious, and I am sure he would profit greatly by continuing his studies at Oxford which a Fellowship would enable him to do, after he has taken his degree.

I left Sir George and Lady Beaumont in excellent health, Lady B. particularly.

Repeating on this occasion my respectful regards to Lady Lonsdale, I have the honor to be

> my Lord
> your Lordship's
> obliged Ser^vnt
> Wm Wordsworth

[List of Fellows of Merton and their connections][2]

Capel Honble Brother to Ld. Essex—Greville Howard[3] of Levens Park his intimate Friend

Griffith—resident at Merton his Friend the Bishop of Oxford.[4]

Oglander. Sir Wm Oglander and Lord de Dunstanville[5]

Marsham—Lord Romney and Dr Marsham[6] Rector of Kirkby Overblow—a connexion of Ld. Egremont[7]

Addington Lord Sidmouth[8]

Whish In the War Office—his Friend Lord Folkestone[9]

---

[1] Samuel Goodenough (1743–1827), famous as a botanist: Dean of Rochester, 1802, and Bishop of Carlisle from 1808.

[2] See also L. 200 above.

[3] Col. the Hon. Fulke Greville Howard (1773–1846), of Levens Hall, nr. Kendal, and Ashstead Park, Surrey: M.P. for Castle Rising, Norfolk.

[4] The Hon. Edward Legge (1767–1827), son of William, 2nd Earl of Dartmouth (1731–1801); Dean of Windsor, 1805, Bishop of Oxford from 1815, and Warden of All Souls from 1817.

[5] Francis Basset, Baron de Dunstanville and Basset (1757–1835), of Tehidy, nr. Redruth, Cornwall.

[6] The Revd. Jacob Marsham, D.D. (1759–1840), of Kirkby Overblow, Yorks., Bullock-Marsham's father, and uncle of the 2nd Earl of Romney: prebendary of Wells and Rochester, Canon of Windsor from 1805.

[7] Charles, 1st Earl of Romney (1744–1811), Dr. Marsham's brother, married Lady Frances Wyndham, daughter of Charles, 2nd Earl of Egremont.

[8] Addington's uncle, Henry Addington, 1st Viscount Sidmouth (1757–1844), the Tory statesman: Home Secretary 1812–21.

[9] William Pleydell-Bouverie, Viscount Folkestone (1779–1869), Whig M.P. for Salisbury, 1802–28: friend of Cobbett and supporter of radical causes; succeeded his father as 3rd Earl of Radnor.

Compton A Hampshire Family[1]
Herbert His Brother Lord Carnarvon—his Friend Lord Pembroke[2]—his uncle Ld. Egremont[3]
Mills—
Mildmay Friend Ld. Folkestone[4]
Cockerell—Sir John Leach[5] and Dr Goodenough
Hammond His connexions in the diplomatic line
Bouverie Lord Folkestone
Grey—
Rooke Sir Harry Burrard[6]—Revd G. Burrard
Seymour The Sergeant at Arms[7] to the House of Commons
Pigou and Tyndall Both Barristers
Buckley Lord de la Warre[8]
Bridges A Kentish family
Tierney G.

Warden Dr Vaughan

[1] John Compton was related to Henry Combe Compton (1789–1866), of Minstead, nr. Lyndhurst, High Sheriff of Hants, 1819, M.P. for S. Hants, 1835–57, who was married to Francis Mills's sister.
[2] George Augustus Herbert, 11th Earl of Pembroke and 8th Earl of Montgomery (1759–1827), of Wilton House, Salisbury. The 'Carnarvon' branch of the family was descended from the 8th Earl of Pembroke.
[3] His mother was Lady Elizabeth Wyndham, daughter of Charles, 1st Earl of Egremont.
[4] The two were actually brothers-in-law, since Lord Folkestone married as his second wife (1814) Judith, daughter of Sir Henry St. John-Mildmay, 3rd Bart.
[5] Vice-Chancellor of England. See L. 16 above.
[6] Admiral Sir Harry Burrard, 2nd Bart. (1765–1840), in command of the Mediterranean fleet: M.P. for Lymington for 46 years. He was succeeded as 3rd Bart. by his brother, the Revd. George Burrard (1769–1856), chaplain-in-ordinary to four successive sovereigns. See also *MY* i. 267. Their sister was married to Sir Giles Rooke, a Judge.
[7] Seymour's cousin, Admiral Sir George Francis Seymour (1787–1870), another grandson of the 1st Marquess of Hertford.
[8] Buckley's father, Col. Edward Pery Buckley (1760–1840) of Woolcombe Hall, Dorset, groom of the bedchamber to George III, married Lady Georgiana West (d. 1832), eldest daughter of the 2nd Earl De La Warr. George John Sackville-West, 5th Earl De La Warr (1791–1869), Lord Chamberlain 1858–9, was therefore Buckley's cousin.

204. W. W. to LORD LONSDALE

MS. Lonsdale MSS. Hitherto unpublished.

Rydal Mount
8th Dec^br 1825

My Lord,

I am infinitely obliged by your kindness in regard to the Merton Fellowship.[1] The enclosed Letter from the Bishop of London will shew that he does not consider the case as hopeless.[2] I expect speedily to ascertain this point—and if the inquiry does not terminate unfavorably I shall be emboldened again to trouble your Lordship and my other Friends. The Fellowships of Merton are in great request, and cannot be procured without strong interest put forth in good time.

You will not be displeased to hear that local politics are taking a favorable turn in this quarter. Good dispositions exist, though nothing is more difficult than to turn the Yeomanry out of their course which cannot be abandoned without humiliation. I was brought much into contact with them during the late enclosure affair,[3] and could then see clearly how well disposed the Blues were towards your Lordship, and the house of Lowther. The gracious manner in which their wishes were then met by the Lord of the Manor made a most favorable impression upon them, which I hope may be turned to account. They dislike also indulgencies to the Catholics. Mr David Huddles, formerly of the Bank of Kendal, is the Person on whom I rely. He has promised me to visit all the Grasmere Blues. I shall hear his report, and proceed accordingly. My own situation as a Government officer prevents me from acting openly in person, from fear of prejudicing the cause.[4] I have the honor to be ever your Lordship's

most obliged Friend and Ser^vnt
Wm Wordsworth

[1] Lord Lowther had written on 5 Dec. to say that his father had approached Lord Sidmouth, and that he himself was following up one or two other lines (*WL MSS.*).
[2] The point at issue was whether candidates from the Diocese of Chester were eligible. Dr. Howley, to whom W. W. had applied for help, had already written on 25 Nov. (*WL MSS.*) to explain that he was unfortunately supporting another candidate; and he wrote again on 6 Dec. lamenting W. W.'s disappointment, but at the same time questioning whether there was any direct exclusion of the Diocese of Chester in the Statutes of Merton (see L. 206 below). [3] See L. 155 above.
[4] The controversy over the St. Bees School Charity (see *MY* ii. 485 ff.) was still renewed from time to time in the local press. Lord Lonsdale and 'the poetical distributor of Stamps' came under fire in the *Kendal Chronicle* for 3 Dec., in an article reprinted from the *Whitehaven Gazette.*

205. W. W. to CHARLES WILLIAM PASLEY[1]

Address: To Lt Col. Pasley, Chatham.
Franked: Geo: Harrison.[2] *Postmark*: 12 Dec. 1825.
MS. Henry E. Huntington Library.
LY i. 231.

9th Dec^{br} 1825
Rydal Mount
near Ambleside

My dear Sir

It gives me great pleasure to learn that you are about to publish, —a pleasure which is encreased by your kind remembrance of me on this occasion.

Your Book[3] will not be long in reaching me if addressed to Messrs Longman for Mr Southey, with an under Cover, for me. —I waited a day or two for the opportunity of a Frank or you would have heard from me instantly on the receipt of[4] yours

Believe [me] with
sincere regard
faithfully yours
Wm Wordsworth

206. M. W. to LADY BEAUMONT

Address: Lady Beaumont, Coleorton Hall, Ashby de la Zouche.
Stamp: Kendal Penny Post.
MS. Pierpont Morgan Library.
K. LY i. 163 (—).

Rydal Mount, Dec. 9th [1825].

My dear Lady Beaumont,

I lose not a moment to tell you that W[illiam] has made up his mind to avail himself of your proposal that the carriage shall be turned over to you, on the ground that the money which was to pay

---

[1] See *MY* i. 370. After a distinguished military career, Col. Pasley was for nearly 30 years (1812–41) Director of the Royal Engineers' Establishment at Chatham, where he introduced the methods of Bell and Lancaster into military education, and wrote numerous works on military engineering.

[2] George Harrison (d. 1841), legal writer: auditor of the Duchy of Cornwall from 1823, and of the Duchy of Lancaster from 1826. He was knighted in 1831.

[3] Apparently *An Inquiry into the system of general or commissariat contracts for supplying his Majesty's forces in Great Britain with bread and meat, as compared with that of regimental purchases: with a recommendation that the former should be entirely abolished*, [privately printed], Chatham, 1825.

[4] *Written* for.

for it (viz part of the produce of the new Edition) is gone in another direction—the purchase of the field.[1] We all earnestly hope with you that the time for building will never arrive, but it is an amusement to talk of, and when spring comes the employment of planting upon *his own land* (though under such a tenure it can scarcely be called so) will be a great amusement to W[m], and stand him in the stead of driving one or two of us in the carriage, which I am sure, under existing circumstances, it is prudent to give up, as your kindness allows us to do so. The field was an extravagant price, but, lying where it does, it cannot be a loss in the end. And we did hope that the possession of it might be the means of our being permitted to remain at Rydal Mount. I fear we herein have judged wrong.

You take the right view of making the best of our disappointment (if aught so uncertain can be called one) in regard to Merton.[2] Yet from the Bishop of London's opinion we have gathered hope that the thing is not impossible. He says, 'I can hardly conceive that there can be any direct exclusion of the diocese of Chester in the Book of Merton. If there be, it must be of recent enactment, that diocese having been formed out of parcels of York and Lichfield, which one would think would have continued to enjoy their ancient privileges notwithstanding the change of jurisdiction.' We have, therefore, in conformity to the good Bishop's suggestion, made application at Oxford, and the result will settle the point. If, unexpectedly, it prove favourable, W. is determined that the apparent difficulty of the pursuit shall not discourage his efforts; and, indeed, from every letter we have received we have good hope of success *eventually*. Lord Lonsdale had *procured us the vote* of Gen[l] Capel;[3] and Mr Canning[4] and many others—whose interest

---

[1] The field situated just below Rydal Mount and known as 'the Rash', and later as 'Dora's Field'. It was left to the National Trust by Gordon Wordsworth on his death in 1933. Lady le Fleming had proposed that the Wordsworths vacate Rydal Mount in favour of her aunt Mrs. Elizabeth Huddleston of Hutton John, and on the first hint of this possibility W. W. bought the land for building, and by the following May (see *SH*, p. 318) had plans drawn up by George Webster, the Kendal architect, for a substantial residence in a free Tudor style. These plans, complete with elevations and specifications for the proposed building, have now been presented to the *WL*. In the event Mrs. Huddleston declined to move, and the Wordsworths were allowed to remain where they were. See *Composed when a probability existed of our being obliged to quit Rydal Mount as a residence* (*PW* iv. 381).

[2] i.e. the Merton fellowship. See L. 204 above and next letter.

[3] See L. 200 above.

[4] Canning wrote on 26 Nov.: 'I see two names on the List of Voters which you have enclosed to me, with whom it is *possible* that, if not pre-engaged, the expression of my wishes in your Son's behalf may have some weight . . .' (*WL MSS.*).

could not be questioned—expressed not only willingness, but *pleasure*, at the opportunity given them to hope they might be of service to W. This is gratifying, if nothing else comes of it; in which case many considerations are at hand to persuade me it is best it should be so. Under any consideration it would be most satisfactory to us if John's thoughts should rest upon the Church; but this is a delicate subject, and unless his own mind—in conjunction with our own wishes, which are not unknown to him—led him thither, we should think it wrong to *press* him into the sacred profession merely to gain a worldly maintenance. The Army is out of the question—he knows that—and, strong as his bias towards the profession seems to be, at his age, and in times of peace, he would not give way to it. You are very good to be interested, and allow me to write to you, about him.

This subject leads me to another, which you will not be sorry to hear has ended as it has done. The Bishop of Chester[1] cannot ordain J. Carter[2] consistently with the rules he has prescribed to himself, not to ordain any who have not been from the first educated for the ministry, i.e. those who have followed other business, or who have not been at the University or at St Bees.[3] J. C. is too honorable to seek for ordination in any other diocese after this declaration, and has given up the thought of going into the Church. I should have been sorry, did I not believe that some other means of advancing himself—more useful to others, as well as more profitable to himself—may without difficulty be hit upon; in the meanwhile he is invaluable where he is.

We have had some few mild days, but the winter has set in very fiercely. From Herefordshire we hear wonderful reports of the fineness of the Season, and good tidings of Mrs Hutchinson, which you will be glad to learn. I conclude that Lady Susan Percy[4] has left; Coleorton, as you mention, being shut up for the winter. I enjoy, in imagination, the quiet of your fireside. I am to send you a corrected copy of the sonnet suggested by you; therefore, dear Lady B., with best love and respectful remembrances from all,

Believe me ever to be affectionately yours,

M. Wordsworth.

[1] Charles James Blomfield (see *MY* ii. 37).
[2] John Carter (1796–1863), W. W.'s clerk for some fifty years. After W. W.'s death he moved to Loughrigg Holme. He was buried in Grasmere churchyard.
[3] The chancel of St. Bees church had been repaired in 1819 and adapted as a training college for those ordinands who could not afford to go to Oxford or Cambridge.
[4] Younger daughter of Algernon, 1st Earl of Beverley (1750–1830).

Lady, what delicate graces may unite
In age—so often comfortless and bleak!
Though from thy unenfeebled eye-balls break
Those saintly emanations of delight,
A snow-drop let me name thee; pure, chaste, white,
Too pure for flesh and blood; with smooth, blanch'd cheek,
And head that droops because the Soul is meek
And not that Time presses with weary weight.
Hope, Love, and Joy are with thee fresh as fair;
A child of winter prompting thoughts that climb
From desolation towards the genial prime:
Or like the moon, conquering the misty air
And filling more and more with chrystal light.
As pensive evening deepens into night.

207. W. W. to UNKNOWN CORRESPONDENT

MS. Cornell. Hitherto unpublished.

Rydal Mount
Decr 22^d. [1825]

[*In M. W.'s hand*]

Sir,

The letter of the Warden of Merton which you have so obligingly
forwarded to me, by explaining so satisfactorily the ground upon
which the exclusion of Natives of the Diocese of Chester, and
others similarly situated rests, has reconciled me to a disappointment which otherwise might have hung upon my mind. May I
beg of you to accept my Sincere thanks for the trouble you have
taken upon this occasion, and to present at your convenience the
same to Dr Vaughan[1] accompanied with my acknowledgments for
the expressions of good-will which gave additional value to his
communication.

I have the honour to be with
high respect
Your obliged and obed^t S^t
[*signed*] Wm Wordsworth

[1] W. W. seems to be in some confusion here. Dr. Vaughan had died the
previous spring, and the reference must surely be to a letter from the acting
Warden of Merton.

208. D. W. to JANE MARSHALL

Address: Mrs Marshall, Headingley, near Leeds.
Stamp: Kendal Penny Post. *Endorsed*: 1825 Criticism of Mr Waterton's book.
Threatened removal from Rydal Mount.
MS. WL.
K (—). *LY i. 231* (—).

Rydal Mount, December 23rd [1825]

My dear Friend,

A few days ago I should have saved you the expence of Carriage to Halifax had my Brother then done with Mr Waterton's Book.[1] When I wrote to Mrs Rawson by her Nieces, I did not think he would have so speedily looked it over again; otherwise I should not have troubled her with a long message to you, which probably you may not receive for some time after the arrival of the parcel.

I was very much obliged to your Sister for her letter, and to you for the Book, which has interested us very much. I only wished that the narrative had been a little tighter bound together; but probably had the Author been more of an Author his Book would have been less interesting. The interspersion of Yorkshireisms—and occasional incorrectness of style did not at all disturb us. Had he been afraid of these he would not perhaps have written so eloquently as he has often done. His enthusiasm as a traveller, his simple undisguised manner of displaying his sentiments and feelings—and the accuracy and spirit of his descriptions of Birds and other animals are not seldom really delightful.

I wish we could have helped Mr Waterton to a favorable Review; but we think it would be too bold to send a Book to Southey for that purpose in which he is so severely abused.

While writing the last sentence, a thought has struck me. Perhaps Mr de Quincey (who after a long absence is returned to Rydal) will review it. No one is more able to do it well—or more likely to discern Mr Waterton's merits; but he is a sad procrastinator, and, however willingly he may promise, I cannot depend upon him—but I will limit him as to time, and with a hope that the work may be done I will not send the parcel with this letter, as I intended when I began to write to you.

[1] Charles Waterton (1782–1865), of Walton Hall, Yorks., traveller and naturalist, had just published his *Wanderings in South America, the North-West of the United States and the Antilles in the years 1812, 1816, 1820, and 1824.* Sydney Smith reviewed it in the *Edinburgh Review* for Feb. 1826. Whether De Quincey reviewed it or not, he referred to it in his *English Mail Coach* (*Works*, ed. Masson, xiii. 288). Waterton adopted a somewhat racy and colloquial style, modelling himself on Sterne.

Have you heard the sad news of our intended Dismissal from Rydal Mount? I think you will recollect my telling you when last at Hallsteads, that another year had been granted, though at the same time with a warning that Mrs Huddlestone might want the place. This we thought little of and considered it as almost as good as secure possession, Mrs Huddlestone having expressed that she neither wished to leave Temple Sowerby nor to live here. But through the Crackanthorps,[1] (not to speak of general rumour), we had been informed that Mrs Huddlestone did really intend to live at Rydal Mount. My Brother took his resolution immediately (he and all of us being so unwilling to leave Rydal) and purchased a piece of Land on which to build a house—and the next morning wrote to Lady le Fleming to know if the reports were true and informing of his intentions, in case it was true that R Mount would, as was reported, be wanted for Mrs Huddlestone. He then told her he should much prefer staying here, apologised for applying so long before the time, and added that his excuse must be the necessity for making preparations for building—that his family might not be without a house to remove to. Lady Fleming's answer was a verbal one, that Mrs Huddlestone was coming in 1827.

The piece of Land which my Brother has bought is just below Rydal Mount, between the Chapel and Mr Tillbrook's—commanding a view as fine as from our Terrace (Mary Anne[2] will recollect the view—she sketched the same from the wall of Rydal Mount *Field.*)

Well! if the Dwelling which Dora has already sketched upon paper would '*rise like an exhalation*' without expense or trouble I should comparatively be little distressed at the thought of leaving Rydal Mount. We should still have the command of most of those objects so long endeared to us. But the expense, the anxiety, and the trouble are *awful*—yet I tell Wm, (the Patterdale estate[3] paying such poor interest for the money it cost) if he could sell *that*, he might feel himself not much poorer (considering the present Rent of Rydal Mount) than at present. It strikes me as possible that Mr Marshall might buy this little Estate as lying near his Property in Patterdale. Pray, with my kind regards, mention this hint to him. I am sure my Brother would be willing to sell if it could be done advantageously. Still, however, we have a hope that

[1] For William Crackanthorpe of Newbiggin Hall, D. W.'s cousin, see *MY* ii. 82, 405.

[2] Mary Anne (1799–1878), Jane Marshall's eldest daughter, who married as his second wife, Thomas Spring Rice, Lord Monteagle (see *MY* ii. 394).

[3] The Broad How estate. See *MY* ii. 3.

we may be allowed to stay where we are—that Mrs H. (who we know must have unwillingly yielded to importunity in giving her consent) may change her mind—that her Son may dissuade her—or that something may happen to prevent her coming. We think that in such case Lady Fleming can not be so cruel as to turn us away: besides, even if she has a particular dislike to us as tenants, it would not be less disagreeable to have us as neighbours, in a house of our own, so close to her Chapel and her Hall.

It is good policy, as you will see, in this state of the matter, to say as little as possible, therefore we do no more, when any one makes inquiries, than just state that my Brother intends to build unless Mrs Huddlestone and Lady Fleming change their minds, in which case we should much prefer staying at Rydal Mount.

My dear Friend, you must forgive this long story. You will I am sure do so, being in[te]rested in whatever concerns our comfort and happines[s].

I am anxiously expecting news from Halifax of the settlement of anxieties among the Bankers and Merchants. I hope, as it is not likely that Mr Marshall is immediately connected with any of the failing Banks, that his Loss may not have been serious, and I have the like hopes for our Friends at Halifax. There has been a Run upon Kendal;[1] but fears are subsiding here. All in this Family are well. My Brother's eyes continue better.

Tomorrow I begin keeping Christmas by dining with our Friend Mrs Elliott, who is at Ambleside.

I was sorry to hear of poor Thomas Cookson's[2] illness, which I fear may make his return to Leeds undesirable. Dora begs her Love to you all, especially to Cordelia. Give my best regards to your Sisters. I will write soon to Miss Pollard.

Do not forget my message to Mr Marshall. It would, indeed, be a relief to my mind, if (in case my Brother *does* build) that property were sold to meet the expense.

Adieu, my dear Friend. Wishing you and yours a merry Christmas and a happy New-Year. I am ever your affect^e

D. Wordsworth

My Brother and Sister and Miss Hutchinson beg their best regards to you all—

Excuse haste in penmanship with a bad pen——

[1] The run on the Kendal banks of Messrs. Wilson, Crewdson, and Co., and John Wakefield and Son continued into the following February, when a number of public figures in the town were forced to issue a notice guaranteeing their deposits. [2] Son of the Cooksons of Kendal.

209. M. W. to ALARIC WATTS

MS. untraced.
Alaric Watts, i. 286. K. LY i. 234.

Rydal Mount,
December 27, 1825.

Dear Sir,

From your continued silence, we cannot but be apprehensive that some demur, which is causing you trouble on the part of Messrs Hurst and Robinson, has taken place. At the same time Mr Wordsworth feels it his duty to request that he may be informed how the matter stands, it being both disagreeable and *very* inconvenient to remain in this state of uncertainty. I feel the more sorry thus to trouble you, having heard through Miss Jewsbury how very much you had been harassed; and nothing short of the peculiar injury which this delay occasions to Mr W., giving him time to exhaust himself by attempting *needless* corrections, at least what we presume to consider such, could justify my having expressed myself so strongly.

I need not tell you how much the enjoyment of the very pleasant day we passed with Mrs Watts would have been heightened had we been so fortunate as to have found you at home.

I remain, dear Sir, with high respect,
Your obliged servant,
M. Wordsworth.

210. W. W. to LORD LONSDALE

MS. Lonsdale MSS. Hitherto unpublished.

[late Dec. 1825]

My Lord,

Calculating on your leaving Lowther about the 12th Inst[nt], I took the liberty of addressing a Letter[1] to you at Cottesmore soliciting your interposition in favor of my Son's Election to a Fellowship at Merton Coll. Oxon. I have now to regret that I troubled you and my other Friends having strong grounds for believing him ineligible; how I came to entertain the contrary notion will appear if [your] Lordship will cast your eye over the enclosed[2] (which Mrs Wordsworth will be obliged to you to

---

[1] L. 204 above.   [2] Probably L. 207 above.

forward). Enclosed in my last was a Letter to Lady Frederic on the same subject, which it would be useless to forward. I shall trespass too much on your lordship's time if I do not hasten to subscribe myself

my Lord

your Lordship's

most obedient and obliged Serv^{nt}

Wm Wordsworth

211. W. W. to THOMAS KIBBLE HERVEY[1]

MS. Harvard University Library.
K (—). LT i. 235.

[? late 1825]

Sir

Your Letter, this moment received, reminds me of an un-performed Duty which I am happy to avail myself of this occasion to discharge, viz—that of thanking you for the agreeable present of your Vol: of Poems, which I received through the hands of Mr Southey some time ago. I read your Australia with much pleasure; it comprehends whatever is most interesting in the subject; and the verse is harmonious and the language elegant. The smaller pieces are not unworthy of their place.

A rule which I have invariably adhered to prevents me from complying with the request you make.[2] Mr Relph applied to me himself some time ago, and in language so creditable to the deli-cacy of his feelings, that I certainly should have made an exception in his case, could it have been done without hurting or offending old Friends who have interests of the same character.—My deter-mination has been thus far, to have no connection with any periodi-cal Publication—if ever I set it aside it will be probably in the instance of the Retrospective Review;[3] which if it kept to its title

---

[1] Thomas Kibble Hervey (1799–1859) entered Trinity College, Cambridge, in 1823 and began a poem for the Chancellor's Medal on the subject of 'Austra-lasia'. Changing the title to *Australia*, he published it, with other poems, in 1824: it was so favourably received that a second edn. appeared in 1825, of which he sent a copy to W. W. In the next year he took over the editorship of *Friendship's Offering*, an annual published by Lupton Relfe (see L. 243 below), and it was probably soon after his appointment that he applied to W. W. for a contribution. He resigned the editorship in 1827 owing to ill health. He was editor of the *Athenaeum* from 1846 till 1853.

[2] As later letters show, W. W. did not rigorously adhere to this rule in the future.   [3] Published from 1820 to 1854.

would stand apart from Contemporary Literature, and the injurious feelings which are too apt to mix with the critical part of it.

I am Sir
very sincerely your obliged Servant
Wm Wordsworth

212. W. W. to ROBERT JONES

Address: The Revd Robt Jones, Glynmyfyr, near Carig y Druidion, N.W. (by Salop).
Stamp: Kendal Penny Post.
MS. Mr. W. Hugh Peal.
LY i. 237.

[*In M. W.'s hand*]

Jany 2^d 1826.

My dear Friend

The warmth of your letter was highly gratifying to me. I thank you for it, and my acknowledgements would have been returned instantly could I have met your wishes and my own in regard to the proposal[1] it contained; but that was out of my power. In the first place I must mention what you will readily comprehend, that the political disturbances which Mr Brougham and his friends have created in our two Counties have much contracted the limits of my Friends' Patronage—they are obliged to look far more than otherwise would have been necessary, to local circumstances; so that no one who knows to the degree that I do how they are situated, would easily venture to request their interference in a matter of this kind. You are mistaken in supposing that Lord Lonsdale has property in Northamptonshire, at least none that I ever heard of—he lives a good part of the year in Rutlandshire,[2] but he *rents* the Place, so that no application could be made upon the ground you suggest. I have also very lately troubled my friends twice on my own account, therefore the time of your application was unfortunate. All that I could have done in the case would have been, had I been favoured with an opportunity, to mention it in conversation. With Mr Justice Littledale,[3] my acquaintance, tho' of long

---

[1] The exact nature of Jones's proposal is uncertain, but it clearly involved W. W. in approaching Lord Lonsdale on his behalf: perhaps he was seeking a favour for a relative.   [2] At Cottesmore Park.
[3] Sir Joseph Littledale (1767–1842), educated at St. John's College, Cambridge, had been Counsel to the University from 1813 until his appointment as a judge of the Court of the King's Bench in 1824. He edited Skelton's *Magnyfycence* in 1821.

standing, is not sufficiently intimate to allow me to address him by letter; besides as a quondam Fellow of his own College, and probably not unknown to him you will have a much better ground for applying to him in your own Person, which if it is not too late, might be done—though I cannot say with what prospect of success. I am much mortified that I cannot be of use on this occasion, as I am thoroughly aware of your excellent character both as a loyal Subject, a sound minded Politician, an orthodox Minister, and what is more than all these, a good and kind-hearted Man—to all these points and many more, most happy shall I be to speak whenever an occasion presents itself and with this sincere declaration, accompanied by regret which your own feelings will enable you to appreciate, I dismiss the Subject.

Mr Goulbourn seems determined to stand,[1] and the Master of Trinity supports him, with a view to the ultimate triumph of the Anti Catholic cause in that representation. I regret however that G. did not content himself with merely declaring his intention to come forward upon a future vacancy—which will take place on the elevation of Sir J. Copley either to the Chief-Justiceship or to the Woolsack. Some think it an objection to him as a Candidate that he is likely to be speedily removed but you will probably concur with Lord Lowther in deeming it a great advantage to connect a Person, having such prospects, with the University. Goulbourn I cannot but think ought, for the general interest of the cause, to have given way to him, who stood forth at the last Election and resigned his pretentions only to the Speaker and to Banks—who—having been already elected—has a strong claim. I hear with some little indignation that the Johnians with the Master[2] at their head—are

[1] With the approach of a general election, the question of the Cambridge University representation was again being actively considered (see above, Ls. 80 and 151). The sitting members were at present Palmerston and William John Bankes (d. 1855), the traveller and friend of Byron, and heir to the family estates at Corfe in Dorset, a descendant of Sir John Bankes, Lord Chief Justice in the time of Charles I. Henry Goulburn (1784–1856), at this time M.P. for West Looe and a staunch opponent of the Roman Catholic claims, was determined to stand, though the claims of Sir John Copley, the Attorney-General (see L. 31 above), and of Bankes were superior, in that the former had been one of the candidates (along with the Speaker) considered at the by-election of 1822, and the latter had actually been elected. In the event, Palmerston and Bankes were opposed by Copley and Goulburn, and Palmerston and Copley were elected, Copley becoming Lord Chancellor as Lord Lyndhurst. Goulburn was returned for Armagh, and two years later became Chancellor of the Exchequer under Wellington; he finally secured the Cambridge University representation in 1831. See also L. 226 below. C. W. had set out the claims of Goulburn at some length in his letter to W. W. of 21 Dec. (*WL MSS.*)
[2] Dr. James Wood (see *MY* ii. 653).

co-operating with the Trinity Whigs, to return Lord Palmerston.
But it is thought that this unnatural union will disgust so many that
they will be no gainers by it. Again I thank you for your vote.
Had *you* not taken that course, I should have hardly expected that
any Johnian would have had public spirit to do so.

We are all very well except for some floating colds—one of
which has fallen upon my Daughter; who never thinks of you but
with pleasure—On Saturday I was skating along with my Son upon
the edge of the lake [?but][1] to day we have a storm of rain.

[*In W. W.'s hand*]

With every good wish of the season, I remain my dear Jones
most faithfully yours   W. W.

all join in best wishes to yourself and family.

213. W. W. to SIR WALTER SCOTT

Address: To Sir Walter Scott Bart, Abbotsford, near Melross.
Stamp: Kendal Penny Post. *Endorsed*: Wordsworth March 1826.
MS. National Library of Scotland.
LY i. 236.

[*In M. W.'s hand*]

Rydal Mount Jan^ry 2^d '26.

My dear Sir Walter,

When I was in Leicestershire a few weeks ago, I received from
Alan Cunningham the agreeable notice that your Bust had been
despatched to Rydal Mount; and on my arrival here had the
pleasure of finding it in its place—a noble copy, done I have no
doubt with the best care that could be bestowed upon it. Do you
recollect where Mr Southey's stood, under an arch in the Book-case
at the end of the room in which you breakfasted? there you are—
Mr Southey being supplanted to make room for you. This will
startle you as being very unhandsome, and so it would have been
were there not, as the Lady says in the Play, very pressing reasons
for it. Your Bust is nearly twice the size of the Laureate's and therefore required the larger space; and in the larger apartment is seen
to better advantage, and it is so much better executed,—that as a
work of Art, it has a claim upon the best light. Mr Chantrey had
hopes a few years back that at some future time Mr Southey might

[1] *Seal.*

permit him to work upon his head—deeming him then too young for the purpose—happy should I be to add him and Mr Coleridge to what I possess from the same admirable Sculptor. On Christmas day my daughter decked the Laureate with the appropriate wreath —and stuck a sprig of Holly in your Mantle, and there it is 'with its polished leaves and berries red' among the other indoor decorations of the Season.

I have not seen Southey since my return from Leicestershire. My last news of him thro' Mrs Coleridge was that he was suffering, with others of his family, from a severe influenza—the plaguy erysipelas had left him.

On Saturday I was skating along with my eldest Son, on the margin of our Lake—yesterday the short-lived frost departed, and to day we have rain, and what in Cumberland and West^d, with the true old border spirit, is called 'Scotch mist'.

With the best wishes of the Season from this Household to yourself, Lady Scott, and all your family, I remain, my dear Sir Walter,

most faithfully yours

[*signed*] Wm Wordsworth

[*W. W. adds*]

My eyes having lately been much inflamed, I think still prudent to employ Mrs Wordsworth's pen, which you will excuse.

214. W. W. to [? THOMAS ROBINSON][1]

MS. untraced.
K (—). *LY i. 239.*

Rydal Mount,
17th January, 1826.

My dear Sir,

I reply to your letter instantly, because I am able to decide upon general grounds, long ago established in my mind. But first

---

[1] The late Gordon Wordsworth suggested that this letter was addressed to William Crackanthorpe of Newbiggin Hall. But as de Selincourt notes, the implication that the addressee had not a sufficient fortune makes this improbable, even though Crackanthorpe was certainly a suitor for Dora W.'s hand about this time. The 'cousin' is more likely to be one of the sons of Mrs. Mary Robinson, the Admiral's widow: most probably Thomas (see L. 23 above), a lieutenant in the navy. Some support for this identification is afforded by an unpublished letter of 3 Nov. 1825 from S. H. to John Monkhouse, which hints at a possible romance: '. . . Tom Robinson finds Rydal so attractive that he is a poor support to his Mother. This is news for Mary—but she need not fear any *taxation*, on the part of the Lady—Dora I mean—and the youth also is too wise. He sees enough of love in a Cottage at the foot of the hill.' (*MS. Jonathan Wordsworth.*)

let me thank you for addressing yourself directly to me. This procedure adds to the esteem which I have always entertained for you. My answer must be unfavourable to your wishes, as it would be to those of any one similarly circumstanced. The opinion, or rather judgment, of my daughter must have been little influenced by what she has been in the habit of hearing from me since her childhood, if she could see the matter in a different light. I therefore beg that the same reserve and delicacy which have done you so much honor may be preserved; that she may not be called to think upon the subject, and I cannot but express the hope that you will let it pass away from your mind.

Thus far I have been altogether serious, as the case required. I cannot conclude without a word or two in a lighter tone. If you have thoughts of marrying, do look out for some lady with a sufficient fortune for both of you. What I say to you now, I would recommend to every naval officer and clergyman, who is without prospect of professional advancement. Ladies of some fortune are as easily won as those without, and for the most part as deserving. Check the first liking to those who have nothing.

Your letter will not be mentioned. I have a wretched pen and cannot procure a better, or I should be tempted to add a few words upon Rydal topics; but I must content myself with adding my sincere and ardent wishes for your health and happiness. I remain,
Very faithfully your friend and cousin,
Wm Wordsworth

215. W. W. to ALARIC WATTS

MS. Cornell.[1]
LY i. 240.

[*In M. W.'s hand*]

Jan^{ry} 19 1826

My dear Sir,

In consequence of a Paragraph I have just read in the New Times the object of which is to correct some exaggerations, real or supposed, that had appeard in *The Times*—respecting certain acknowledged difficulties of the firm of Hurst and Robinson,[2]

---

[1] Xerox of manuscript in Preussischen Staatsbibliothek, Berlin, destroyed during the Second World War.
[2] Hurst and Robinson were the London agents of Constable, Scott's Edinburgh publishers. The financial ruin of both houses, and of Scott along with

I beg you would not proceed in going to the Press with the volume which I sent to Manchester by my Son yesterday to be delivered thro' Miss J.[1] to yourself. I do not know how far any thing that has yet past is binding in law or honour under the present change of circumstances, nor perhaps is it worth while to advert to this—it would be no satisfaction to me to accept the guarantee you so generously offered. My wish is that the business should be suspended till we see our way more clearly—and pray let me hear from you by return of post. Most likely the House in the present juncture would be glad to suspend the bargain—at least.

    I remain my dear Sir your much obliged

Friend and S^{vt}

[*signed*] Wm Wordsworth

216. W. W. to ALARIC WATTS

MS. untraced.
Alaric Watts, i. 287. K. LY i. 241.

January 23, 1826,

My dear Sir,

    Accept my cordial thanks for the care you have taken of my interests, and the prudent precautions your good sense and regard for me have led you to employ.[2] Be assured that I never imputed remissness or negligence to you, and I cannot but admire the delicacy of your reserve in regard to persons of whose insolvency you had no proof. Truly do I sympathize with your probable losses upon this occasion. I will not detain you longer than to express

---

them, was now impending. See *Journal of Sir Walter Scott*, ed. W. E. K. Anderson, 1972, pp. 38 ff. In answer to the anxieties expressed in M. W.'s letter of 27 Dec., Watts had written to W. W. on the 30th: 'I made before I left town a final arrangement on your behalf with Messrs Hurst and Robinson and have not the slightest reason for supposing that they wish one jot of it to be altered . . .' (*WL MSS.*)

  [1] Jewsbury.

  [2] See previous letter. Watts had written on 21 Jan.: 'Having for some time had my own strong suspicions that all was not well with Messrs Hurst and Robinson, I had determined not to make any final arrangements with them [until] one half the sum stipulated for the copy-right of your poems [was] in the mail, and the other half in such a bill at six months date as I could in the course of my business have turned into cash for you . . . The verbal agreement entered into . . . was of such a nature that provided they fulfilled their stipulation, you could be no loser, and if they neglected [or were] incapacitated from so doing, they had no claim upon you.' (*WL MSS.*)

a hope that the day may arrive when I shall be able to show, by something more substantial than words, in what degree

I am your sincere and obliged friend,

Wm Wordsworth

P.S.—Pray give our best regards to Mrs Watts.

217. D. W. to H. C. R.

Address: To H. C. Robinson Esqre, 3. King's Bench Walk, Temple, London.
Postmark: [?1826]. *Stamp*: [?Hereford]. *Endorsed*: 25 Feb. 1826, Miss
    Wordsworth.
MS. Dr. Williams's Library.
K (—). *Morley, i. 155.*

Brinsop Court, near Hereford. Febry 25th [1826].

My dear Friend,

I hope you have not set me down as an ungrateful one for not having sooner thanked you for your interesting letter, and Mrs Collier for her great kindness in sparing to me the valuable Memorials of her Tour, which, in course of time would I think become the more valuable for the cause which in some degree seems to reconcile you to the accepting them for me—namely that to her they are *now* become *melancholy* memorials—The assurance that, if her life be prolonged, she will hereafter cling with especial delight to the memory of those few weeks which cheered her declining husband's spirits makes me unwilling to deprive her of any thing that might assist her recollections, and if you feel as I do pray do not accept her Gift but return it to her with a thousand thanks from me.—I recollect Mrs Collier and her hospitable kindness, when she lived in Hatton Gardens[1]—I once dined there with you, at that time when I had travelled with you upon the Coach from Bury—Perhaps this circumstance may help her to recollect something about me.

My young Friend gets on slowly with the Journal[2] therefore the prints will not be wanted for a long time, however I will attend to your advice and have it bound with blank leaves so as to receive

[1] Where H. C. R. for a long time lodged at her house. She was Jane Payne (d. 1833), the much admired friend of Lamb and Hazlitt, and married John Dyer Collier (1762–1825), a journalist who edited the *Monthly Register* and the *Critical Review*, and who was on the staff of *The Times* and then the *Morning Chronicle*. He had died the previous November. Their son was John Payne Collier, the Shakespearian critic (see *MY* ii. 664). [2] See *L.* 202 above.

whatever prints I may be so fortunate as to pick up.—You all perhaps blame me for having taken so little pains in the curtailing. —I have done no more than cut out passages (sometimes pretty long ones) in giving it a hasty reading over.

It is time that I should explain the Date of this letter—Here I arrived yesterday week,[1] having parted from my Brother and his Daughter at Kendal just ten days before I halted a few days at Manchester with Miss Jewsbury, the Authoress of Phantasmagoria etc—and was even more pleased with her at home than abroad. Her talents are extraordinary; and she is admirable as a Daughter and Sister, and has, besides, many valuable Friends, to some of whom I was introduced. From Manchester I came by way of Worcester and the delightful Hills of Malvern to Hereford, where I was met by Mrs Wordsworth's Sister. Brinsop Court is six miles from Hereford—the country rich and climate good—far less rain than we have in Westmorland—but as I have always said our compensations do much more than make amends—our dry roads— where, after the heaviest shower, one can walk with comfort— and above all our mountains and lakes which are just as beautiful, just as interesting—in winter as in summer. Brinsop Court is, however even now, no cheerless spot—and flowers in the hedges, and blossoms in the numerous orchards will soon make it gay. Our fire side is enlivened by four fine well-managed Children—and chearful friends—and Mrs Hutchinson is one of the most pleasing and excellent of women, the Sister of our good Friend Thomas Monkhouse. She told me yesterday with tears that it was the anniversary of her Brother's death. I saw little Mary in passing through Preston—and Miss Horrocks (now Mrs St Clare) and her Husband Dr St Clare—but not Mrs Monkhouse. She was not well enough to meet me at the Inn.—I wished to find out a likeness of her Father in Mary; but could not. She very much resembles some of Mrs Monkhouse's Sisters. Mrs St Clare seemed in good spirits, but I thought her looking much older than when we parted in London—and *very* much older than when we travelled together on the Continent and the people more than once exclaimed 'Quelle belle Femme!—Her Husband did not take my fancy he is a stout, tall heavy man much older than herself.—I thought of a Gentleman's Butler at a well-covered Side-board.—the very opposite of our dear Friend, her Brother in law.—Yesterday I had a letter from Rydal

---

[1] According to her MS. Journal, D. W. left Kendal on 10 Feb. for Manchester, where she remained from the 11th until the 16th, before travelling to Brinsop on the 17th.

Mount with good tidings—Miss Hutchinson was seized with a dangerous illness soon after Christmas and recovered very slowly, which prevented my setting off so soon as intended—and at last I left her in a weak state; but she is now perfectly well again; and all the rest are in pretty good plight—My Brothers eyes in their better way. His poems are quite ready for the press; but no arrangement can be made till it is known whether Hurst and Robinson will go on or not—and even should they promise fair I hardly think it would be safe to conclude the bargain till the mercantile and bookselling world is a little more settled.—My Brother hitherto has been most fortunate—While people are suffering losses on all sides he has wholly escaped—and with respect to the poems he was particularly fortunate, for just before Hurst and Robinson stopped payment he had sent his first volume to Mr Alaric Watts to be forwarded to them, and he (Mr Watts) had the prudence to keep it back, having reason to suppose the House was tottering.

Probably you have seen the name of Hutchinson among the Bankrupts. One of the Partners of the Firm (The Tees Bank) is my Sister's eldest Brother[1]—the others are her first Cousins. Their misfortunes were entirely unexpected; and the blow has been a heavy one upon my Sister, Miss Hutchinson and all her Family. Happily the Females will lose nothing by the Tees Bank.

If you should write to me before all the Money alarms are settled (and I hope you will for there is no reason to expect a speedy settlement) pray tell me what you think of the Columbian Bonds—Here we see no newspaper but the Hereford journal and cannot form a notion of probabilities,—only I am sorry to tell you that one of Mrs Wordsworth's Sisters has had the imprudence to vest the greatest part of her property in the Columbians when at 90—and we have this day heard that the Dividends cannot be paid —while at the same time the price of Bonds is so low that she cannot possibly think of selling out—Much as we hear of losses and Bankruptcies I am more grieved for my kind Friend 'Joanna—that wild-hearted Maid'[2] than for anyone else whom I know.

Is your poor Sister yet alive?[3]—It is some time since I heard from Mrs Clarkson—Perhaps ere this Tom is married—but I have not seen it in the newspapers—And besides, our neighbour Mrs Luff (whom I think you have seen in Gloster place) is now in London and she told us Mrs Clarkson was expected there in February

[1] John Hutchinson of Stockton-on-Tees. See also *SH*, p. 313.
[2] See *To Joanna*, in *Poems on the Naming of Places* (*PW* ii. 112).
[3] Mary Robinson died on 4 Aug. this year.

and did not mention Tom's marriage. I hope you will have been with M^rs. C[? ollier]¹ already—if n[ot ?] tell her when you do see her where I am. Many thanks for the affecting verses by Mrs Barbauld!² and for your own delightful sketch of her character. I wish much to read her works as now collected, and shall try to get them at the Hereford Book Club—At Rydal we get no new publications except through Southey—and sometimes from the Watson's of Calgarth (the Bishops Daughters)—Poor Graham!³ what a wretched creature (though no doubt his heart is hardened, his moral sense utterly dead—and christian faith he had none) must he be! and I fear the end of his course will be the gallows in whatever country he is now seeking or begging his bread—No! I cannot add the sequel of his story to my journal—It is enough for me that the knowledge of it sullies my remembrances of our bewitching voyage on the Lake of Lugano when the hills were wrapped in green soft glowing light without shadows—and again the sun burst forth in all its brilliancy—But you had more to tell, and pray let me have it.—The story interested us all very much and indeed we had expected nothing good from him.

I shall remain in Herefordshire till May if nothing unforeseen happens. My Brother talks of meeting me in North Wales and going with me to the top of Snowdon; but I do not much depend on his being able to leave home. At all events, the *time* of his coming will be governed by the time of the general Election. If it be put off till Autumn it will probably be the *end* of May or beginning of June before he can come. That is the time when you Lawyers are busiest I believe, otherwise you might be tempted to join us. I should be no less glad of your support on Snowdon than on St Salvador. What is the price of Bishop Taylor's Works published by Heber?⁴ and can they be bought under the original price? Miss Hutchinson wants a copy, and will I believe when she knows the price trouble you to purchase it; but let *me* have the pleasure of your answer and I will write to her—adieu

Yours truly
D Wordsworth.

My best love to Charles and Mary Lamb—

¹ *MS. torn.*
² Writing to D. W. on 6 Jan., H. C. R. had mentioned the death of Mrs. Barbauld, and had paid tribute to her, quoting her stanzas to *Life*. See Morley, i. 150–1.
³ William G. Graham, swindler and ex-convict. See *HCR* i. 246.
⁴ Reginald Heber's edition of *The Whole Works of . . . Jeremy Taylor* appeared in fifteen volumes in 1822.

218. W. W. to WILLIAM PEARSON

Postmark: 6 Mar. 1826.
MS. untraced.
Pearson. K. LY i. 241.

Rydal Mount, Monday.
[6 Mar. 1826]

My dear Sir,

If I am not mistaken, I lent you some time ago, a copy of my little Tract upon the Lakes, which contains a corrected copy of a Sonnet upon Long Meg and her Daughters.[1] These alterations I want for the new edition of my poems. I should be glad if you would be kind enough to copy them for me, and send them.

Ever most sincerely yours,
W. Wordsworth

219. W. W. to THE COMMISSIONERS OF STAMPS

Address: The Hon'ble the Commissioners, Stamp Office, London.
Postmark: 28 Mar. [   ]. *Stamp*: Kendal Penny Post. *Endorsed*: William Words-
worth Esq. Rydal Mount Ambleside. 24 March 1826.
MS. Public Record Office. Hitherto unpublished.

[*In John Carter's hand*]

Rydal Mount, Ambleside.
24 Mar: 1826.

Hon'ble Sirs,

In reply to your letter of the 20th Inst: I beg to refer you to my letter of the 20th Decr 1824, in which (written in answer to an enquiry similar to the present one) I have stated the difficulty of obtaining a *punctual* return of *unregistered* Legacy Receipts, and that I am not aware that I possess any power to *compel* Parties to deliver back their Accounts.

I have the Honor to be
Hon'ble Sirs,
Your obedient Servant
[*signed*] Wm Wordsworth

---

[1] See *PW* iv. 47 and L. 3 above.

220. D. W. to MARY LAING

Address: To Miss Laing, Lauriston Place, Edinburgh.
Postmark: (1) 30 Mar. (2) 2 Apr. 1826. *Stamp*: Here[ford].
MS. Edinburgh University Library.
The Wordsworth–Laing Letters (—).

29th March 1826
Brinsop Court
near Hereford

My dear Miss Laing,

I had been from home some weeks when your Second letter arrived—and here I still am, and probably may remain till the end of June: for though it was my intention when I left Rydal to return at the end of May, I feel now, while amongst my kind Friends, that the time will be too short. This, however, will chiefly depend on my Brother's convenience, it being his intention to meet me in North Wales, and give me the pleasure of a Tour in the neighbourhood of Snowdon, and we are even ambitious enough to hope to reach its summit. Mr Hutchinson's Family have removed from Radnorshire into Herefordshire, (about 6 miles from Hereford). The Country is fertil and pleasant—open yet not flat—and we have a view of some of the Welsh Mountains. Miss Joanna H., as you know, lives with her Brother and Sister, and she is here at present. Her health has on the whole been much better since she was in Scotland, yet she is still delicate—not equal to me in walking—but we drive out together in a gig very often—and she is my chearful companion frequently on a short walk. We talk of Edinburgh with true pleasure, and of the kindness received from every member of your Family; and both wish we may be able to see you all there again—and we laugh over our Staffa and Isle of Skye scheme—not, however, as a scheme utterly hopeless and visionary —but years roll over our heads; and perhaps neither of us has much hope that it will ever be accomplished. I had begun to think you very slow in writing—not however blaming *you* but myself; for I had given you too much reason to suspect that you were forgotten. My dear Miss Laing, I am much concerned to hear that your health is still so indifferent. Perhaps you are to blame for confining yourself so closely to home. A little change is often very salutary— not that I would recommend a journey to *London* as the best cure for a delicate constitution—and perhaps you are right in refusing to go thither. In your former Letter very long ago—(so long I am ashamed to tell it)—you talked of your intention to go thither, and said you should be in Gloucester place. Was that intention set

431

aside? Or did you go? I was there in the Month of April [18]24 but have now no temptation to repeat my visit—our hospitable Friend[1] in G. place being dead. He was the Brother of Mrs Hutchinson, an excellent Creature, whose loss is deeply felt by every member of the Family. Mrs Hutchinson herself is delightful, and has four as good and as fine Children as ever I saw. Mr H. is an excellent Man. They have a Farm that promises to answer perfectly if times be tolerable; but though the rent is low, if produce should go on sinking, the profits will never repay for the labour and anxiety. At present Markets and Fairs produce nothing. The neighbouring Banks have either failed, or even, if they have stood the heavy Runs against them, the country people are suspicious—so that Business is almost at a stand, and prices, consequently, are sinking. Notwithstanding, I see nothing here but chearfulness and comfort. Poor Sir Walter Scott! I was indeed truly sorry to hear of his name in the Gazette[2]—I did not *see* it myself—and was still in hopes there might be a mistake on the part of my informer. (It was at Manchester where I stayed a few days ago on my road hither that I heard of it)—But the Sale of his furniture, Books etc etc, too clearly confirms the truth. How *could* it happen that he should have so entered into *trade* as to be involved in this Way— he a Baronet! a literary Man! a Lawyer?—I wish very much for particulars both respecting what has led to this calamity and his present condition. How does he bear the Change? I hope well— but am fearful that Lady Scott may not be fortified to the needful point having heard that she was a person fond of distinction and expence—but this may not be true. No doubt Sir Walter, having retained his offices, will still have a sufficient income for a plain gentleman; but does he retain his *Estates*?

A few Months ago my Brother and Sir Walter exchanged Busts. No doubt you have seen Sir Walter's? It is a fine work of art— a noble head—and an excellent Likeness. We prize it much at Rydal Mount, where it ornaments the Book-case in the dining-room. (By the Bye the dining-room has been enlarged since you were at Rydal and is now an excellent room). I wish my Brother's Bust may not have been subject to the stroke of the hammer; but I fear it may have shared the same fate as the rest of Sir W's moveables. Perhaps you have heard rumours of our leaving Rydal Mount:—*I* still hope that we may be suffered to remain there; but should we not, my Brother intends to build, being so unwilling to quit that beautiful Village, where, a church having lately been

[1] i.e. Thomas Monkhouse.   [2] As a bankrupt.

built, there is every comfort that should make us desire to end our days there. He has purchased a piece of Land adjoining the Rydal Mount property, which commands the same prospect as our own Terrace. I mean the *further* Terrace, which I call our own because my Brother made it—and caused that bit of ground to be added to the pleasure grounds belonging to the house. For my part, I can as little endure the thought of building as of quitting Rydal Mount; therefore let us turn from this unpleasant subject.

You will be glad to hear that all are well at Rydal. My Brother's eyes are much stronger than they were formerly, though still subject to inflammation in a slighter degree. My Niece is staying with Miss Southey and Miss Coleridge at Keswick. She is not hardy, and is grown very thin, and is subject to a cough; however there is at present no cause for anxiety, and I trust that in a few years her constitution will be established. William is quite well. John surprized us last week by his unexpected arrival from Oxford to spend the Easter holidays. He is in good spirits and looks very well. We have not his company now at Brinsop. He is staying with Mr Monkhouse,[1] Mrs Hutchinson's Brother, upon the Banks of the Wye, where I have also been. It is a pleasant country, and a pleasant house to stay at. Mr Monkhouse is a delightful Man. I shall go to see him again in May with Miss Joanna. John Wordsworth will return to Oxford in about a fortnight; and we shall see him here on his way thither. He is to finish at Oxford this year and will take [his] degree at the *end* of [?].[2]

I have thought of your good Father and Brothers in these disastrous times, and was truly glad to hear that the numerous Failures had not touched them. God grant that they may not hereafter suffer, for there seems not yet to be an end of the misery. My Brother has suffered nothing but a little inconvenience. He had prepared a new Edition of *all* his poems in five volumes, for the press; but the difficulties in which Hurst and Robinson have been placed have at present suspended the arrangement that he was making. My Sister will send you the Autographs before my return if she has an opportunity, which I think likely to occur, as some of our neighbours have connexions in Edinburgh. It would not answer to send them by the Carrier.

Miss Barker is still at Boulogne, and the Borrowdale house just as you left it, except that the furniture is restored to its place. I was not at Borrowdale last summer. Mr H. Coleridge is still at

---

[1] John Monkhouse.
[2] *MS. torn.* John W. took his degree later this year.

Ambleside. He has one pupil from Ireland at £100 per annum. Now, my dear Miss Laing, let me beg you to write to me here very soon. Miss J. H. will not be less glad to hear from you than I shall— and pray tell us all particulars—public and private. Have you seen Mr Wallace lately? I hope he will live as long as I do, for I can never expect any other Dentist to do me as good service as he has done—and as he is much younger than I am, I may calculate on his being the longer liver. Give our best respects to your Father and Mother and Brothers. How are your Mother's eyes? Believe me, dear Miss Laing, your affectionate Friend

D Wordsworth

221. D. W. to CATHERINE CLARKSON

Address: To Mrs Clarkson, Playford Hall, Ipswich, Suffolk.
Postmark: (1) 1 Apr. [   ]. (2) 3 Apr. 1826. *Stamp*: Kendal.
MS. British Museum.
LT i. 242.

Brinsop Court, near Hereford
April 1st [1826]

My dear Friend,

   You will have heard from Tom of my being at Brinsop and I am sure will be glad of some tidings of this good Family as well as of myself, and I have no chance of hearing from you if I do not write. Perhaps this last (selfish) motive may have some influence upon me; however the other has its weight. I left home on the 8th of February, stayed till the 10th at Kendal, where I found and left our young Friend Miss Cookson in the same state in which she has been for three years, nearly confined to her bed—yet I cannot think her case hopeless as she grows no worse. She was, before her illness, a good-humoured, sensible, pleasant Girl—rather too fat and stout —She is now perfectly elegant in her appearance, and her face is beautiful—her countenance angelic—and indeed her patience and chearfulness are an example for all who have an opportunity of seeing her. On the 10th I went to Manchester, where I stayed a few days with a Miss Jewsbury, who was introduced at Rydal Mount last summer—Dora and she became much attached to each other, and we were all exceedingly pleased with this young Lady—She is but four and twenty. Her Father[1] was a wealthy man, became

---

[1] Thomas Jewsbury, cotton spinner at Measham, Derbs., and then at Manchester.

a Bankrupt when Miss J. was but 15 years old, and about the same time her Mother died and she was left at the head of a large Family. She has remarkable talents—a quickness of mind that is astonishing, and notwithstanding she has had a sickly infant to nurse and has bestowed this care upon the rest of her Brothers and Sisters, she is an authoress. She has published two Miscellaneous volumes entitled Phantasmagoria—which, before she had seen my Brother, she dedicated to him. If they chance to fall in your way do read them. They shew uncommon aptitude in discerning the absurd or ridiculous in manners—rather too much of that—you would conclude her to be a very satirical person—yet without ill-nature—therefore pray read with charity and remember too—what I know to be true—that most of the things in those two volumes were written in ill health—Booksellers urgent—Children sickly so that she wrote in a sick room, and often sate up till three or four o'clock to enable her to do so.—I liked Miss Jewsbury at Rydal Mount, and still more at her own home at Manchester. This you will think much in her favor. She has many very valuable Friends at M—— But you are wanting to hear of Brinsop—so no more wanderings! I took the Coach from Manchester to Worcester where I slept—Next day travelled outside to Hereford—a delightful journey over the Malvern Hills—found Joanna Hutchinson waiting for me with a Cart, which brought us and my Luggage (six miles) to Brinsop. All the Family received me joyfully, and happy was I to find dear Mary Hutchinson plump (*for her*)—and healthy-looking—old Mrs Monkhouse able to stir about, to knit and sew, and enjoy a joke—the four Children delightful—they are all very small but perfectly healthy—steady at their Books in school hours and always interested in what they read at other times—yet remarkably fond of play—Be winter warm or cold it is all one to them—they run about and play lovingly together—never creep in to the fire—not a word of complaint do you hear—and when play-time is over they return chearfully to their Books. Their dear Mother is certainly the best manager of Children I ever saw, combining firmness and steadiness with the utmost tenderness. As to her health I know not what to say—I should pronounce her perfectly well if she were not with Child—but *she is*, and that may account for the entire cure which seems to be wrought at present of her stomach disorders. She is fat in the face—but that is natural to her—Her limbs and Body are still very thin, and it was a full gown (Company dress, for there happened to be a party on the day I came) which made her appear fat to me at first. As to *size*—no

one would suspect her situation—yet she is *at least* 5 months gone
with child—and there is a weakness about her which makes me
anxious. Every month she is threatened with miscarriage. So it has
been constantly since her return to Brinsop from Harrowgate.—
She went with me in a Gig to the Stowe 4 weeks ago—drove me
about there—was quite well—and at last we took a longer drive
than usual. It was 10 days before the time when she intended to
rest and lay by—The journey seemed not to fatigue her at all—
however the next day she was unable to quit her Bed—So continued for several days—Then came on her monthly discharge—
very severe—we both expected a miscarriage—Judge how uneasy
I was!—and how anxious after it went off to get her safe home.
Last Saturday we accomplished her return—without fatigue, and
she has since been strong, active, and perfectly well. She stirs about
the house as usual and takes daily a short walk—but will not venture again in a Gig—and at the month's end will keep herself
perfectly still. I hope a miscarriage will thus be avoided; but am
fearful of a sickly Child—And, for herself, poor Creature! perhaps
the stomach complaints may return—Yet she being so chearful, her
Friends naturally are chearful around her. All seem fearless—
and I put away my apprehensions as well as I can, knowing how
ignorantly we both hope and fear—and how very seldom it happens
that the thing we most dread comes to pass—or at least if it does
come, the means are totally different from what we have foreseen.—
Joanna is well—though anxious respecting her Columbian Bonds—
She was tempted by great interest and bought 1700£—6 per cents
at *92*!—There is I fear little chance of their ever rising so high
again; but she would be contented to sell out if they should come to
70 or 80; however, her present anxiety is chiefly on account of the
interest, but she is encouraged to expect regular payment in future.
—We do not know whether the Jersey Dividends are to be looked
for only from Goldsmidts assignees, or how it will be. Can you tell
us? I find Tom is a Holder of Columbians, so from him you may
perhaps know all about them, and if you can send her any comfort
I know you will. I must, however, do her the justice to tell you that
she is quite above fretting after money. The Stockton Bankruptcy[1]
is a sad affair—and I fear it will be very long before matters are
settled. Thomas Hutchinson likes his Farm very much, and he
cannot help doing well upon it—unless produce should go on
sinking. He says it is high enough now. He sold his Cattle at
Hereford fair on Wednesday at a fair price he says (He *breeds*

[1] See L. 217 above.

them)—but John Monkhouse (he *purchasing* cattle) was a loser—
Sold his, bought in Autumn, for 1 £ a head less than they cost—
and Oh! the grievous losses of Farmers! The other day he had
70 sheep worried by his Landlord's Dogs.—We spent our time
most agreeably at the Stowe—John Monkhouse is never dull,
notwithstanding his imperfect sight.—He is exceedingly fond of
reading—and that makes his chearfulness the more admirable—
he does, however, read a good deal—indeed I think he tries his
eyes too much in that way. You will be glad to hear that the
Failures of the neighbouring Banks have not affected him or the
Hutchinsons—*directly*. Every one who has any thing to sell—of
course feels the effects *in*directly.—Is it really the Son of Mr Wakefield, the Brinsop Steward, who ran off with Miss Turner?[1] Never
was there surely so horrible a case of the kind—Richly indeed does
Mr Edward Gibbon Wakefield deserve the severest punishment
that the Law can inflict. It must be an overwhelming distress to the
Father and Family. I do not know much of the Character of Mr
Wakefield himself, except that he has behaved very handsomely to
Mr Hutchinson—and in as much as he has done so, I am sure has
also been a just Steward to Mr Ricardo;[2] for Mr Hutchinson would
require nothing that would not in the end be a mutual benefit.
The house is excellent, and very convenient.

Mary desires me to say that she hopes you will come to see
her.—*You* were the first of your Family who promised her—when
she was Mary Monkhouse, and are the only one who has not been
under her Roof. She would be delighted to see you, and you would
be charmed with her and her Children. All well at Rydal Mount.[3]
There I hope we shall stay; for I have no pleasure even in *talking* of

[1] Ellen Turner, fifteen-year-old heiress to the estates of her father William
Turner of Shrigley Park, Cheshire, had been abducted from her school in
Liverpool by Edward Gibbon Wakefield, an official of the British Embassy in
Paris, who was son of Edward Wakefield, prospective parliamentary candidate
for Reading, and nephew of John Wakefield the Kendal banker. Helped by his
brother William, he carried her off to a forced marriage at Gretna, and they
then fled to the Continent; but they were overtaken at Calais before the
marriage could be consummated, and the plot was frustrated. Legal proceedings had now begun, and the affair was given much publicity in the newspapers.
The trial came on at Lancaster on 9 Aug.: the two brothers were sentenced to
three years' imprisonment, and the marriage was annulled by special Act of
Parliament. Edward Gibbon Wakefield became in due course an expert on
penal reform, drawing on his own experiences in Newgate. See Chandler,
Four Centuries of Banking, ii. 85–6.

[2] For Osman Ricardo, see L. 249 below.

[3] In her letter to D. W. of 25 Dec., C. C. had written: 'I rejoice exceedingly
to hear that a new edition of William's Poems is coming out. It is a symptom
of improvement in the age and an earnest of still greater improvements to
come.' (*WL MSS.*)

building. Others have, yet all partake with me in the desire to remain quietly at the Mount. I only differ with them in having more hope that it will end so, and in preferring any house to one of our own building. Not to speak of expense—the anxiety, trouble, and unrest are what I dread. William talks of meeting me in North Wales for a Tour about Snowdon—a most agreeable plan to me; but I hope he will put it off till June or even the beginning of July, as I feel I shall not be ready in May (the time we talked of) to bid adieu to my dear Friends here, and to this pleasant country. The weather is very cold—grass yellow that was green three weeks ago—in short all is wintry, but the garden borders and a few budding trees.

My dearest Friend, I have left no room for inquiries after you and yours—but you will tell me every thing I want to know. When is Tom to be married? and how is dear Mr Clarksons health? How do his limbs bear him in this cold weather? Joanna H. has got rid of Rheumatism—are you settled with Servants? Mrs Luff is I suppose now at Fox Ghyll—what a pity she should have spent so much money there! She *would* do it. Now, I pray you write immediately. God bless you—believe me ever your most affect^e   D W—

222. W. W. to H. C. R.

Endorsed: 6th April, 1826, Wordsworth, business.
MS. Dr. Williams's Library.
K (—). *Morley, i. 159.*

Rydal Mount 6th April [1826]
I have not time to read this over—

My dear Friend,

My Sister had taken flight for Herefordshire when *your* Letter, for such we guessed it [to] be arrived[1]—it was broken open—

---

[1] H. C. R.'s letter to D. W. of 20 Feb. is published only in part by Morley, i. 151. It also contains a long account of a visit to William Blake (see *HCR* i. 325 ff.), which W. W. does not refer to in this letter: 'I gave your brother some poems in MS by him and they interested him—as well they might, for there is an affinity between them, as there is between the regulated imagination of a wise poet and the incoherent dreams of a poet. . . . He has lived in obscurity and poverty, to which the constant hallucinations in which he lives have doomed him . . . He is not so much a disciple of Jacob Böhmen and Swedenborg as a fellow visionary. He lives as they did in a world of his own, enjoying constant intercourse with the world of spirits . . . I will not pretend to give you an account of his religious and philosophical opinions. They are a strange compound of Christianity, Spinozism, and Platonism . . . After what I have said Mr W: will not be flattered by knowing that Blake deems him the *only poet*

(pray forgive the offence) and all your charges of concealment and reserve frustrated—We are all, at all times, so glad to hear from you that we could not resist the temptation to purchase the pleasure at the expense of the peccaddillo for which we beg pardon with united voices.

—You are kind enough to mention my poems—let me touch first the business part of this question. In the publication I have had many disappointments. Rogers was kind enough to negotiate with Murray for the publication—three months elapsed before this personage could find leisure to settle the terms; and three months more without my being able to obtain any notice to a Letter I had addressed to him; upon which I took the thing out of his hands. Some time after, through the kind offices of Mr Alaric Watts, I effected a bargain, in my judgement, more favorable with Hurst and Robinson; but after a delay of many weeks the embarassments in their affairs prevented the fulfillment of it.—Mr Watts is now in London and has undertaken to ascertain whether they are likely to be able to proceed.—Now as I know that Mr Watts is very much occupied in his own affairs, it has struck me, that if you had a few spare moments, you might assist him in a negotiation in that quarter or some other. Mr Watts may be heard of at Robinson and Hursts, and this Letter would be a sufficient introduction. I have never had the pleasure of seeing Mr W. but he has given himself very much trouble about my affairs, and I cannot but think you would find him an amiable acquaintance, as he is undoubtedly a man of no common abilities—But pray attend to this suggestion or not, just as you find it agreeable—It is certainly to be regretted that the Poems have been and are likely to remain so long out of print.—

of the age nor much alarmed by hearing that . . . Blake thinks that he is often in his works an *Atheist*. Now according to Blake Atheism consists in worshipping the natural world, which same natural world properly speaking is nothing real, but a mere illusion produced by Satan . . . Dante lived and died an atheist —he was the slave of the world and time. But Dante and Wordsworth in spite of their Atheism were inspired by the Holy Ghost. Indeed all real poetry is the work of the Holy Ghost, and Wordsworth's poems (a large proportion at least) are the work of divine inspiration. Unhappily he is left by God to his own illusions, and then the Atheism is apparent. I had the pleasure of reading to Blake . . . the Ode on Immortality. I never witnessed greater delight in any listener and in general Blake loves the poems. What appears to have disturbed his mind . . . is the preface to the Excursion. He told me six months ago that it caused him a bowel complaint which nearly killed him. . . . I doubt whether what I have written will excite your and Mr W's curiosity—but there is something delightful about the man, tho' in great poverty, he is so perfect a gentleman with such genuine dignity and independence . . . that I have not scrupled promising introducing him and Mr W: together. . . . Coleridge has visited B. and I am told talks finely about him.' (*Dr. Williams's Library MSS.*)

Your valuable remarks about the arrangement I should not have acted upon had they reached me earlier—at present it is quite out of the question—as the 4 Vols have been carefully gone over and decided upon after the most mature consideration.—There is no material change in the classification—except that the Scotch Poems have been placed all together, under the Title of Memorials of Tours in Scotland; this has made a gap in the poems of Imagination which has been supplied by Laodamia, Ruth, and one or two more, from the close of Affections etc—But I need not trouble you with these minutiae—Miscellaneous poems ought not to be jumbled together at *random*—were this done with mine the passage from one to another would often be insupportably offensive; but in my judgement the only thing of much importance in arrangement is that one poem should shade off happily into another—and the contrasts where they occur be clear of all harshness or abruptness— I differ from you and Lamb[1] as to the classification of Imagination etc—it is of slight importance as matter of Reflection, but of great as matter of *feeling* for the Reader by making one Poem smooth the way for another—if this be not attended to classification by subject, or by mould or form, is of no value, for nothing can compensate for the neglect of it.—When I have the pleasure of seeing you we will take this matter up, as a question of literary curiosity—I can write no more. T. Clarkson[2] is going.—Your supposed Biography[3] entertained me much. I could give you the other side. —farewell.   W. W.

[1] 'Lamb observed there is only one good order—And that is the order in which they were written—That is a history of the poet's mind—This would be true enough of a poet who produced everything at a heat—Where there is no pondering and pausing and combining and bringing to bear on one point the inspirations and the wise reflections of years . . . In the last of the author's own editions intended for future generations the editor will say to himself . . .—How shall I be best understood and most strongly felt? By what train of thought and succession of feelings is the reader to be led on— his best faculties and wisest curiosity be most excited? The dates given to the table of contents will be sufficient to inform the inquisitive reader how the poet's mind was successively engaged.—Lamb disapproves (and it gave me pleasure to find I was authorised by his opinion in the decided opinion I had from the first) of the classification into poems of fancy, imagination and reflection—The reader who is enjoying for instance . . . the magnificent Ode which in every classification ought to be the last, does not stay to ask nor does he care what faculty has been most taxed to the production. This is certain that what the poet says of nature is equally true of the mind of man and the productions of his faculties. They exist not in "absolute independent singleness". To attempt ascertaining curiously the preponderance of any one faculty in each work is a profitless labour—' (Morley, i. 151–2).
[2] Tom Clarkson, who was to have delivered the letter.
[3] 'I assure you it gives me great pain when I think that some future commentator may possibly hereafter write—"This great poet survived to the

T. Clarkson was to have been the Bearer of this to you—but I find he will not reach London for three weeks, he will therefore get it franked—pray excuse the miserable scrawl—written in extreme hurry.[1]

223. W. W. to C. W.

Address: Rev^d Dr Wordsworth, c/o Revd Dr Walton, Birdbrook, near Castle Hedingham, Essex. [*Readdressed to*] Trin. Coll., Cambridge.
Postmark: (1) 11 Apr. 1826. (2) 13 Apr. 1826. *Stamp*: Kendal Penny Post.
MS. British Museum.
Elizabeth Wordsworth, William Wordsworth, 1891, p. 141 (—), *LY i. 246* (—).

Rydal Mount
9th April 1826

My dear Brother,

The account of the state of your health is melancholy, and gives us great concern; but the mild weather is now come, and we trust that you will feel the benefit of it:—I need not say how happy we should be to see you here, should so long a journey not be too much to undertake, or deemed hazardous at this early season. Our House is sufficiently roomy, having been enlarged since you were here.

I think the account of your malady would have depressed me more, if I had not recently seen an instance in my family of an illness, whose principal seat was the bowels. Miss Hutchinson was reduced extremely low by an irritation of this kind continuing for some weeks; so much so that she could not quit her bed—She is now active and strong—though the bowels are still somewhat deranged; and she had a relapse during the late severe weather. I do

fifth decennary of the nineteenth century, but he appears to have dyed in the year 1814 as far as life consisted in an active sympathy with the temporary welfare of his fellow creatures—He had written heroically and divinely against the tyranny of Napoleon, but was quite indifferent to all the successive tyrannies which disgraced the succeeding times—The Spaniards the moment they were under the yoke of the most odious and contemptible tyrant that ever breathed—ceased to be objects of interest—The Germans who emancipated themselves were most ungratefully neglected by their sovereigns and the poet—The Greeks began a War as holy as that of the Spaniards. He was silent —He had early manifested a feeling for the negroes and the poet did honour to his friend Clarkson—That source of sympathetic tears was dried up—A new field of enterprise was opened in America—The poet's eye was not a prophetic one—There is proof that he was alive abo^t 1823–4 when the new churches were built in London but otherwise he took no care about any of the events of the day . . ." ' (Morley, i. 153–4).

[1] This postscript has become detached from the rest of the letter, and Morley (ii. 846) prints it as a separate item with the endorsement '6 Apl. Autograph of the Poet'. But it seems to belong here.

not enter into the particulars of her case, not knowing how much it may differ from yours; but I mention it because our Surgeon appears to have treated [it] with judgement; and it proved to me that neither weakness nor pain nor duration of the disease, nor relapses, especially if obviously referable to severe changes of weather ought to occasion despondency in affections of this kind.

Pray thank dear John for his Letter; I need not trouble him with an answer myself. Present also my regards to Dr Walton[1] with thanks for his *Perilous Times*[2]—an energetic discourse, and proper both as to Place and Time.

Depend upon it, my dear Brother, that if it please God I should survive you, I shall not be wanting in rendering every service in my power to your Sons. It would be no less my duty than my Gratification to do so. They are fine young Men and I feel strongly attached to them.

I shall now bid you farewell, with best wishes, and earnest prayers for your being speedily restored to Health and Strength. Dora is at Keswick on a visit to Mr Southey's family—She returns next Wednesday; we will not sadden her visit by telling her how ill you have been.

In the above wishes and prayers Mary and Miss Hutchinson join, and believe me

My dear Brother ever most affectionately and faithfully yours
Wm Wordsworth

[*M. W. adds*]

Pray do not omit to write——

224. W. W. to H. C. R.

Address: H. C. Robinson Esqre, Temple, London.
Postmark: 29 Apr. 1826. *Stamp*: Kendal Penny Post. *Endorsed*: 27th Apl. 1826, Wordsworth, business.
MS. Dr. Williams's Library.
K (—). *Morley, i. 163.*

Rydal Mount April 27th [1826]

My dear Friend

I employ Mrs W's pen for your advantage and to spare my own eyes, which are plagued with irritability. Without wasting time on

[1] For Dr. Jonathan Walton, see L. 8 above.
[2] '*Perilous Times*': *a sermon preached before the University of Cambridge . . . on . . . Commencement Sunday, July 3, 1825*, 1826.

thanks, I will proceed to business. It was very unlucky that you did not see Mr Watts, as he could have told you every thing—He negociated for me last Autumn with H. and R. the terms, they to print one thousand Copies bearing every expence, and allowing me 25 Copies for my personal Friends—and 25 more Mr W. stipulated for, to be sent, at his direction—or mine, if I chose to interfere, to such literary Persons as might be thought likely to favour the sale of the work. The Ed: to be 5 Vols, including the Excursion—the Sum of £150 to be paid on delivery of the Copy to them, and £150 more when the Work was ready for Publication. With these terms I was satisfied—but before the work was prepared Mr W. had reason to suspect that all was not going well with the Firm, and prudently kept back—with great delicacy by the bye, exposing himself to some censure with me for procrastination, rather than incurring the risk of injuring them, whom he then only suspected. In consequence I stand wholly disengaged—I left Longman because the terms were very disadvantageous to me, viz; they incurring all the risk, which has been proved to me to be nothing, and I having ½ the profits—divided by themselves—when they had paid themselves. I proposed other terms, which they could not accede to, nor I to the new ones proposed by them. So we parted amicably. I looked about for a more liberal and a more active Publisher— Rogers concluded with Murray, after 3 months dancing attendance as one might call it—a verbal agreement—subject to my approval— 2/3ds of the profit to be mine I taking 2/3ds of the risk and expence, before *I* closed, I wrote to enquire of Murray what that expence would amount to? 3 months more elapsed without an answer; upon which I took leave of his High Mightiness. Observe this was before Mr W. kindly undertook the business.—*He* has had a great deal of experience, and totally disapproves of my taking any part of the expence; and I had found myself, that after the several Eds had paid the Expences, which was done in a great measure, or entirely, by a flush of sale on their first appearance, my moiety of the Profits was almost eaten away by subsequent Advertizing. The Excursion has been nearly 3 years out of print and the 4 Vols about a year and a half—they have been, as I know from several quarters a good deal enquired after—so that an active Publisher would have a probability of being speedily re-embursed. I know that the Trade is depressed, and *perhaps* I ought not to expect quite so much as £300, but I stickle for that sum as at the best but a poor repayment for the trouble I have been at in revising the old, and adding several new Poems—which, tho' individually of no great moment, amount on a rude guess to 800 or 1,000 verses. Besides I have a private reason for straining for that sum—Upon the strength of the Engagement with R and H. I was emboldened to give, for a field contiguous to my present Abode more than 3 times its value—for the sake of building upon it if I thought proper; this scrap of land the pastoral Jew of whom I bought it, as if he had known of my expectation would not yield up to me for less than £300 precisely. I have now done, and thank you again for your kind offer. As you say that Mr Watts has actually left Town, I shall look for a letter from him daily—he was charged with the first Vol. to commence printing immediately, in case he was successful in bargaining in some other quarter if necessary. I ought to have said that the last Ed: amounted only to 500 copies. Knowing how I am at present circumstanced—You can do nothing but make a trial where you think there is any chance of success, till we hear further from Mr Watts. As to what you say abt the negociations being in better hands than your own, I ascribe it only to a degree of modesty[1] —rare in all men of these days—and singularly rare in men of your profession—and of mine.—One word on the subject of arrangement—Lamb's order of time is the very worst that could be followed; except where determined by the course of public events; or if the subject be merely personal—in the case [of][2] Juvenile Poems, or those of advanced Age. For example I p[lace] the Ode to Enterprize among the Imaginative Poems, which class *concludes* with the Tintern Abbey—as being more admired than any other—according to my present arrangement the Enterprize immediately precedes it,—but this is objectionable. The Author cannot be supposed to be more than 6 or 8 and 20 when Tintern was written; and he must be taken for about 50 when he produced the other. So that it would perhaps be better placed elsewhere. I should like to *talk* this matter over with you for the sake of the general principle as affecting all the Arts, in individual composition.[3]

[1] 'I should feel myself honoured by being entrusted with any commission connected with the projected edition,' H. C. R. had written on 22 Apr., 'but—there is no affectation I assure you in what I am saying—I am satisfied that it is a negociation which ought to be in the hands of a person of *distinction*—and not of so exceedingly insignificant a man as I am . . .' (Morley, i. 161.)

[2] *MS. torn.*

[3] 'I assent to all you say about the principle on which the classification should be,' H. C. R. had written, '—The reader should be led on and trained as it were to the discernment and consequent enjoyment of the *poetical* character: I heard it well observed by a man of more poetical feeling than of indulgence in poetical study that you had shewn a fine tact in placing the line "Dear God! the very houses are asleep!" at the close of the Sonnet—At the beginning it would have been abrupt and almost offensive—And you would, where possible,

Do not go on to the Continent—You may carve out a much more interesting Tour by taking the best part of N. W.—a glorious country!—in your way to Ireland—and return from the North, having seen the Giants' Causeway, by Staffa and Iona, etc etc, to us. I am very disinterested in recomme[n]ding this wide Excursion as it will allow you less time for us. But the Steam boats make it irresistibly tempting, and few things would give me greater pleasure than being your Companion, along with my Sister who is as keen of travelling as ever. Your account of your own Sister is very melancholy—and we truly sympathize with you—but let us bear in mind, that to the really pious no affliction comes amiss—A religion like her's is worth all the other knowledge in the world a thousand times told. As to Italy—it seems to fly from me and mine as it did from Æneas and his Companions of old—if it can be effected we shall be right happy in your company—I say nothing of building, as not yet entered upon. Farewell. Mrs W joins in kindest regards. As soon as I hear from Mr Watts I shall write again.

Affectionately and faithfully
Yours Wm Wordsworth.

Very glad to have good news of the Lambs—our best love to them.

225. W. W. to LORD LONSDALE

Address: The Earl of Lonsdale, Charles St., Berkley Sq, London.
Postmark: 16 May 1826. *Stamp*: Kendal Penny Post.
MS. Lonsdale MSS. Hitherto unpublished.

[c. 15 May 1826]

My Lord,

The Persons who have applied in behalf of Fleming Coward[1] are all respectable Yeomen, Freeholders, and Friends, nor am I aware of any objection to their recommendation being attended to.—

I will take this opportunity of mentioning that there is in Rydal a family of the name of Fleming who begged me some time ago to solicit Lord Lowther's endeavours to procure a situation for one of their Sons in the Excise; as the family are very respectable, have been staunch Friends, and have three Votes, I replied that I

---

arrange the small poems as members of a whole and apply the remark on a great scale.' (Morley i. 162.)

[1] He became principal coast officer at Workington for the Customs House at Whitehaven.

certainly would name the thing to Lord Lowther on the first opportunity, adding at the same time that there were so many persons
applying for such situations, that they must not be sanguine in
their expectations of success. Lord Lowther need not notice this
till he comes into West^nd.

Sincerely do I congratulate your Lordship on the favorable aspect
of things.[1]

In this neighbourhood, I mean, in Ambleside, Rydal, Loughrigg,
and the two Langdales, 144 Votes have been reported to the Kendal
Committee; of these there are only 14 *decidedly* of the Blue Party and
of those who hang back and may *possibly* vote for them, there cannot
be at the utmost more than 16 additional Votes, which will leave
114 either decidedly for us, or persons formerly of the Blue party,
who will not vote at all.—If the change that has taken place in
favor of the present members, be at all correspondent, as we have
reason to think it is, in other parts of the County, to what has
occurred here, Mr B.[2] has not a shadow of chance, unless his new
created outlying Voters greatly exceed those of our side.—The
truth in this matter may be ascertained I suppose by reference to
the Land Tax, and the Registers of Annuities.—Lord Lowther has
been told that 40 new Votes had been made in Ambleside: almost
entirely for the Blue Party. I have inquired most carefully; nothing
like it can be true. If the Informant meant that the Freeholds lay
in or about Ambleside, he is utterly mistaken; no such change of
property has there taken place, if he meant that the Voters were
living in Ambleside he is equally so—nor are there any Persons in
Ambleside attached to the Blue Party of sufficient Property to have
made such a number of Votes by Annuity or otherwise, provided
they could have found persons at a distance whom they could
trust.

The falling off from the Blue Party is easily accounted for, among
the Resident Freeholders. 1st Their enthusiasm was too violent,
and founded upon too many illusions to last—and as it abated and
these illusions vanished common sense, and the natural ties of
interest resumed their power; not merely of downright self interest,

[1] In Westmorland. Henry Brougham, still M.P. for Winchelsea, was proposing to contest the county representation in the forthcoming general election
for the third and last time. On 20 Apr. Lord Lowther had written: 'It is
confidently stated that Lord Thanet will not spend any money, but it is added
that some of Brougham's friends have said, that he himself is so *insane* on the
subject of Westmorland, that he will spend all the money he has gained in his
profession in opposition. I have no apprehension upon this, he will think twice
before he embarks in it himself, and it is an assertion to encourage subscrip-
tions in his own behalf.' (*WL MSS.*)   [2] Brougham.

but ordinary social connections and obligations.—
2ndly. the inability of the Party to pay their debts.
3rdly. the Catholic Question which both as a cause and a pretext has hurt Mr B. in no small degree; several also in the upper classes of his adherents, do not much relish that sort of Education of which he is a Patron,[1] viz; Education without Religion, which they regard as Education in hostility to it or contempt of it; nor do they much approve of *pushing on* the scientific instruction of Mechanics etc etc. And lastly, it would be unpardonable to omit, a confidence from experience in the characters of the present members, and a reliance on the political discretion of the House of Lowther.—

Your Friends, my Lord, therefore cannot but anticipate a triumphant discomfiture of the opposite Party, if they venture, which some think not very likely, to come to the Poll. *As an Interest*, in Property, habit, station, the Yellows are immeasurably superior; as a *Cause*, they have equally the advantage or rather still more so, notwithstanding the Vaunts of their Opponents; for the Yellows are contending against a set of men whose aim is to form a precedent for altering the character of County Elections, by taking the decision from the genuine Freeholders, and placing it in the hands of the lowest of the Community, in conjunction with Voters from a distance, who know nothing about the County nor care any thing for it. Whatever be the issue, the real natural Freeholders will ever have grounds for this Charge against Mr B. and his supporters; for if the Yellow Party had not resorted to the same expedient of creating Votes, and fought their enemies with their own Weapons, they must have had a Representative *forced* upon them.

With sincere pleasure, I learned from Lady Beaumont, that Lady Lonsdale was perfectly recovered from the severe indisposition under which she had been suffering. I heard nothing of it till long after—Have the goodness to present my congratulations to her Ladyship, in whose health everyone must be interested who has the happiness of knowing her; and believe me my Lord

most faithfully your
Lordship's much obliged Servant,
Wm Wordsworth

[1] For Brougham's work for the London University, see L. 180 above. He had also put himself at the head of the movement for Mechanics Institutes, which were set up in Kendal, Carlisle, and Whitehaven in 1825, and he was already planning the Society for the Diffusion of Useful Knowledge, which was inaugurated in the autumn of 1826.

226. W. W. to ROBERT JONES

MS. Mr. W. Hugh Peal.
LY i. 246 (—).

[*In Dora W.'s hand*]

Rydal Mount
May 18th [1826]

My dear Jones,

I have been very busy about the threatened contest for West^d, that is no excuse for not writing to you earlier; in fact I have no hope of visiting Wales this spring or summer; we have received notice to quit Rydal Mount and I am entangled in preparations for building a house in an adjoining field purchased at an extravagant fancy price. I enter upon this work with great reluctance and w^d feign hope that some turn of fortune may yet prevent it going forward; if so I go into Ireland with a friend and perhaps my Sister, and if this be, we will have a peep at you going or returning —it is now time to express the regret of the whole family at not seeing you here this spring, we looked for you with no little confidence. How comes it to be so difficult to procure clerical substitutes in y^r part of the world? we have plenty of them in this—do come and see us, we are growing old and ought to make the best of our time to keep up long tried affections. My Sister is still in Herefordshire wishing to avoid the bustle of our approaching election; when she went thither in Feby our plan was that I was to meet her in the Vale of Clwydd at the end of this month as you know—but this is impossible both on account of the possible building, and the election.

Dr Wordsworth, you will be sorry to hear, has been seriously ill—he takes too much out of himself—studies hard and applies as sedulously to business, and both together are more than he can bear. Remember the Cambridge election, what a pity there should be three anti-Catholic candidates.[1] My Daughter is my amanuensis, an office she is pleased to perform as it brings her into the society of her old and much esteemed Friend. We often talk of you and your good nature at Barmouth—and your calm and even temper so enviable compared with mine.

Mr Brougham's support of the Catholics has done him harm among the electors of W^{std} and the nation seems opening its eyes upon this question.

---

[1] Sir John Copley, the Attorney-General (supported by the Lowther interest), W. J. Bankes, and Henry Goulburn. See also L. 212 above and L. 230 below.

We have had here dry weather for many weeks—the middle of the day hot, the evenings sharp and frosty, which has made colds too plentiful in this house and elsewhere—I am the last sufferer but am getting better—my eyes have felt the bad effects. Grass of course here makes little progress—corn has not suffered—we have little but oats and we sow late.

My son John is still at Oxford, reading I hope industriously—he takes his degree December next or rather goes up for examination—if he comes away a good scholar I shall be satisfied. I think we could have succeeded in getting him made fellow of Merton but he is not eligible on account of his birth-place, so that he will be thrown for advancement and maintenance upon his own exertions—my younger Son still continues with me—his constitution has been so shatter'd by maladies the foundations of which were laid at the Charterhouse, that I do [   ] He is however pretty well at present.

With kindest regards [   ] joins with my Daughter [   ] Jones your faithful Friend[1]

Wm Wordsworth

227. W. W. to CHRISTOPHER WILSON[2]

MS. Yale University Library. Hitherto unpublished.

Rydal Mount
Sunday 21st [?May 1826][3]

My dear Sir

Indisposition unluckily prevents me setting off as I intended tomorrow. Hoping to see you erelong, I remain

very sincerely yours
Wm Wordsworth

[1] The last part of the second sheet is torn away. A few words have been supplied from the *WL* transcript by Susan W.
[2] The Kendal banker and Lowther supporter. See *MY* ii. 417.
[3] It is impossible to date this letter with any certainty. 21 May fell on a Sunday this year, however, and the letter may refer to the gathering of Lowther supporters at Lowther Castle in late May and early June, at which W. W. was present.

228. W. W. to H. C. R.

Endorsed: May 1826
MS. Dr. Williams's Library.
K (—). *Morley, i. 168.*

[late May 1826]

My dear Friend

I have just received your 3rd letter:[1] your 2nd would have been answered long ago but I have been waiting in vain for a Reply to a couple of Letters addressed to Mr Watts—

The firs[t] question is—

Are Robinson and Hurst likely to go forward again, so as to make it expedient to recommence a negotiation with them?—

Coulburn[2] I have a mortal objection to, he is so impudent a puffer—Besides my pride boggles at submitting any proposal to so very slender a person as T. Campbell[3]—

Try for an interview with Mr Watt[s]—he is master of all particulars,—as [to?] the materials of the Vols, proposed mode of printing etc, etc, I will however mention that the intended Edition will make the 8th from the first in one Vol.—the number of Copies has varied from a thousand to 700—and 500—The last published in the autumn of 1820 was 500, paid its expenses instantly, but was not exhausted till 1824—. The Prose on the Lakes is not intended to be included, the Vols will be bulky enough without it.

I know not what more need be added. Mr Watts has the first Vol: in his possession corrected to go to press immediately, the rest are prepared also.

Truly am I sorry to give him and you and my other Friends so much trouble. The Poems the Excursion in particular have been far too long out of print; Rogers opinion is characterized by his usual good sense—

Mrs Ws Brother, who has conducted a Bank for nearly 45 years, with the highest confidence on the part of the public, has become a Bankrupt, through misfortune, the perfidy of a Partner, and over confidence in unworthy Persons. Miss H—has not suffered—nor

---

[1] Of 22 May. See Morley i. 166.

[2] Henry Colburn (d. 1855), publisher. In a previous (unpublished) letter of 6 Mar. (*Dr. Williams's Library MSS.*) H. C. R. had written: 'The most bustling active man in the trade now is said to be Colburn. Would you have no objection to see yourself jammed in an advertisement between my lady Morgan and the last fashionable novel-maker?'

[3] Colburn engaged Thomas Campbell to edit the *New Monthly Magazine* in 1820, and he remained editor for 10 years. He also seems to have acted as reader for the firm.

Mrs W—but some part of the family have,—in particular the late T. Monkhouse's estate would have sufferd but for the over liberality of his high minded Brother, who means to bear the loss himself. This you will the more admire if you bear in mind how Mr T. M's intentions towards him were frustrated by the informality of his will, made unluckily by himself. The Widow[1] is off to the Continent—

If I do not build, I will strain [?] a point to accompany you into Ireland etc.

Ever most faithfully W. W.

229. W. W. to LORD LONSDALE

MS. Lonsdale MSS. Hitherto unpublished.

[late May 1826]

My Lord,

Many thanks for your Lordship's obliging attention to my recommendation of the Individual for the Excise. His name is Leonard Fleming,[2] 22 years of age.

I take the liberty of enclosing a Letter received six or eight weeks ago from my Friend Mr Jackson of Whitehaven.[3] I think it will interest you as there are sentiments in it relating to his situation which redound greatly to his credit.—I am sorry to say that he still continues in a state of extreme debility. He fainted, when he returned from Distington, on getting out of the Chaise.

It was highly satisfactory to me to be authorized to put down the injurious Report of the Compromise.[4] No Friends mistrusted the House of Lowther; but as I observed to Lord Lowther, it was humiliating and mortifying to hear such a statement so confidently made, without a sanction for flatly contradicting it.—

A supporter of B.[5] in Troutbeck lately said to Captn Wilson[6]

[1] i.e. Mrs. Jane Monkhouse. [2] See L. 225 above.
[3] The Revd. William Jackson was about to return to Oxford as Bursar of Queen's.
[4] As early as 15 Apr. the *Kendal Chronicle* was reporting rumours that Col. Lowther would retire from the impending contest for Westmorland, and that Brougham would consequently be returned unopposed as the other member for the County; and the rumoured 'compromise' was mentioned again on 29 Apr. It was contradicted in the *Westmorland Gazette*—the Lowther paper—on 6 May. Brougham officially accepted an invitation to stand on the 3rd.
[5] Brougham.
[6] Capt. John Wilson, R.N. (1789–1870), of The Howe, on the Applethwaite side of the Troutbeck valley: only son of Sir John Wilson (1741–93), the Judge. His name occurs frequently in the *RMVB*.

that he believed along with many others, that B. had been paid for his upholding the Catholics. 'How then', said Capt[n] W. 'can you vote for such a Man?' 'Oh', replied the Grey-coat 'It is an awful thing to turn'.—No doubt this feeling of the awfulness of turning keeps some hundreds in ranks of which they are heartily tired. B. has already hurt himself much in West[nd] by his ardour in the Catholic cause, and the proposal for dispensing with the oaths at the time of voting cannot be made too public. A paper, however, has been put into circulation against the Romanists, by the Kendal Com: which strikes me as too harsh and opprobrious, and the more so, if what I was told by a respectable Person at Kendal be true; viz, that the Catholic Priest[1] in that neighbourhood has not exercised over his Flock any influence injurious to the present members; but rather the contrary, being of opinion that the ascendancy of the protestant Establishment is the best bulwark for general toleration. That a Catholic Priest should be so liberal, is not very probable, but under all circumstances, in papers issued under the authority of a Committee, it is best to be strong in facts (taking care that the statements are true) and mild and temperate in language.

A professional person of Kendal who has come over to the Yellows, was reproached the other day for deserting his principles; 'How can that be', he made answer, 'my principle is to take care of my family, and I am sure I am keeping to it by changing sides'.—

Brougham, I recollect, was very ill both in body and mind, about the time of Sir S. Romilly's death,[2] so much so, that he was restricted from all business and intellectual labour, by his Physicians.

We have to do with Men, who stick at nothing, but the information you give me, and all I can collect elsewhere, leads me to expect a signal triumph.

How could Sir James Graham express himself as he did at the London Meeting[3] on the subject of the views of your Lordship on

---

[1] For the Revd. Thomas Wilkinson, see L. 82 above.

[2] i.e. in the autumn of 1818, immediately after his first contest with the Lowthers. He was now reported to be ill again (in the *Carlisle Patriot* for 2 June) and unable to canvass. He finally arrived in Westmorland on 15 June, making a grand entry into Kendal to open his campaign.

[3] A meeting of Brougham's supporters at the City of London Tavern on 15 May: the speakers included Sir James Graham of Netherby (see *MY* ii. 536), the Hon. Henry Tufton, Henry Howard of Corby, and William Crackanthorpe, W. W.'s cousin. According to the *Carlisle Patriot* for the 19th, Graham had stated that the origin of the contest was to be found in the ambition of the Earl of Lonsdale, who was not satisfied with the fair exercise of his influence, by returning one member, but who would be pleased with nothing less than reducing the county to the situation of a close borough, and affixing

the representation of Cumberland? this was most reprehensibly disingenuous.

ever my Lord most faithfully
your Lordship's much obliged Servant
W. Wordsworth

230. W. W. to C. W.

Address: The Revd The Master of Trinity Coll., Trinity Lodge, Cambridge.
Postmark: 9 June 1826. *Stamp*: Penrith.
MS. British Museum. Hitherto unpublished.

Lowther Castle Friday
9 June 1826
(I send this by Post)

My dear Brother,
      The Bearer of this will either be the Revd Henry Lowther,[1] or Dr Satterthwaite.

I hope you have been able to succeed in pairing off, either with the Gentleman named or some one else. Things are going on well with us, but it is impossible to estimate of the secret strength of our Opponents—

The Cambridge Crisis is drawing nigh.[2] There is no prospect of 3 Anticatholic Members for Yorkshire—[3] a great disappointment— Could that have been affected and two for your University it would indeed have been a triumph for the cause. The more incumbent however is it on your University to do its duty. Save the principle if you can. If the Att^ny Gen: be decidedly above Palmerston and also above the other Candidates, as seems probable, cannot he be

the badge of servitude on the breasts of all the freeholders. The speech was attacked in the *Patriot* editorial (and in the *Westmorland Gazette* for 20 May) on the ground that it advocated a division of the County representation for the purpose of nullifying the rights and wishes of the majority of the freeholders.

   [1] The Revd. Henry Lowther (?1788–1874), rector of Distington from 1813. See also *MY* ii. 121.
   [2] The Cambridge election took place on 12–13 June. See also L. 212 above.
   [3] In Yorkshire Richard Fountayne Wilson (1783–1847) of Melton, nr. Doncaster, and the Hon. William Duncombe, later 2nd Baron Feversham (1798–1867), 'the friends of the Protestant cause', were standing against the two Whig candidates, Lord Milton, later 5th Earl Fitzwilliam (1786–1857), member for Yorks. in the previous parliament, and W. W.'s friend John Marshall. An independent candidate, Richard Bethell (1772–1864) of Rise, nr. Hull, and Watton Abbey, nr. Beverley, intervened early in the contest, but he announced himself in favour of emancipation, and withdrew on 12 June; so that the other four candidates were finally returned unopposed for the four vacancies.

prevailed upon to influence a few of his Benchers to give their second Vote to the other AntiCatholic who stands highest, or if Banks be much above Goulburn why cannot Goulburn shew his attachment to the Cause by giving up as many votes to Banks as would secure his return, or vice versa if Goulburn takes the lead of Banks, (which seems not however to be probable), let Banks make a surrender in his favor. Again I say let not the personal ambition of the Candidate be gratified at the expense of the Cause.

The Att^ny Gen: it is imagined will be decidedly at the head of the Poll—Doubt not that Goulburn is sincere in his opposition to the Catholics, but may he not have a leaning towards Palmerston, as a Brother Member of the Ministry;[1] and may not this indispose him to lend support to Banks, even if he should be convinced he has him self no prospect of success—

Pray consider all these things, and every thing that may influence a decision in favor of the cause at this crisis—

I am anxious to hear how you are in health—I cannot say yet how long I shall remain here.

Your most affectionate B^r
W Wordsworth

Since the above was written I have seen a printed Letter of Goulburn which leaves little hope that he will give way—and Banks I fear is equally resolved—

231. W. W. to S. H.

Address: Miss Hutchinson, Mr Cooksons's, Penrith.
MS. University of Tennessee Library. Hitherto unpublished.

Lowther Castle
Monday Mor
[5 *or* 12 June 1826]

My dear Sarah,

I cannot say when I shall be able to return, something new is daily springing up. All goes on as well as possible—There appears to be no foundation for the unfavorable Reports that had reached you.

I shall attend to your suggestions about the Pony which brought [me][2] perfectly well. Pray forward this to Rydal.

ever most affectionately
Yours W. W.

[1] Henry Goulburn had been chief secretary to the Marquess Wellesley, Lord Lieutenant of Ireland, since 1821.　　　[2] *Written* by.

[In unidentified hand, possibly Mrs. Cookson's]

Mr C. desires this may be kept as a Specimen of Wm's hand writing I mean the address is so excellent—He couldn't believe it was Wm's.

232. W. W. to ALARIC WATTS

MS. untraced.
Alaric Watts, i. 287. K (—). *LY i.* 248 (—)

Lowther Castle,
June 18, 1826.

My dear Sir,

I was from home when your last obliging letter arrived. Truly am I grieved to hear of your losses through Hurst and Robinson, and thankful for the prudent care you took of my interests. I will with pleasure speak to Mr De Quincey of your wish to have him among the contributors to your *Souvenir*; but, whatever hopes he may hold out, do not be tempted to depend upon him. He is strangely irresolute. A son of Mr Coleridge lives in the neighbourhood of Ambleside, and is a very able writer; but he also, like most men of genius, is little to be depended upon. Your having taken the *Souvenir* into your own hands makes me still more regret that the general rule I have laid down precludes my endeavouring to render you any service in that way.

The state of Miss Jewsbury's health gives me and all her friends very great concern. She is a most interesting person, and would be a great loss should she not recover.

I remain, my dear sir,
Your much obliged friend,
Wm Wordsworth

233. W. W. to LORD LONSDALE

Address: The Earl of Lonsdale, Charles st., London.
Postmark: 26 June [1826].
MS. Lonsdale MSS. Hitherto unpublished.

Appleby Thursday Noon.
22[1] June 1826

My Lord,

As there were Reporters upon the Hustings, from the Times, Morning Chronicle and other Newspapers, who were busy in

---

[1] *Written 23 by mistake.*

taking notes, your Lordship will obtain a particular account through those channels of what has passed at the Nomination.[1] I am happy to say there was no disturbance whatever, except from the *voices* of the Crowd indiscreetly employed, now and then, by the Partizans of the several Candidates in approbation of what was said—there was little other interruption;—and hissing occurred, I think, only once. The subject scarcely admitted of any novelty—Wybergh talked as usual of the domination of the House of Lowther—Mr Crackenthorp abused the Clergy (a tender point with him) and objected to the late Members as your Lordship's Sons, and besides the one a Placeman and the other a soldier. This was towards the conclusion, after he had declaimed about retrenchment, etc.: The only novelty and really important point in this morning's proceedings, was the nomination of the Col. by Mr Wilson of Dalham Tower—it was for him somewhat of a delicate office—but he did it in a manner wholly unobjectionable. He declared that in some points he differed from the Lowthers, but the sense of the County having been pronounced to be in their favour, and agreeing with them generally, in their political principles he was happy to propose the Col: as the best means of promoting the real independance of the County. Lord Lowther acquitted himself with his usual spirit and ability and the Col: surpassed himself.[2] Having had practice he speaks with more ease, his points were judiciously selected, and his expression often concise, terse, sharp and rememberable. He spoke like a gallant soldier, and an unpretending English Gentleman. Lord Lowther as a man of business and as became his Station.

Mr Brougham is said to look ill but certainly there was nothing in his voice or language indicating decayed power either of body or mind. His speech turned upon the old subjects—it was full of sophistry, but there was nothing in it of a marked personal or

[1] The Westmorland election opened at Appleby Castle on Thursday, 22 June and closed on Friday, 30th. (For full details see *Kendal Chronicle* and *Westmorland Gazette*, 24 June, 1 and 8 July; *Carlisle Patriot*, 23 June, 1 and 8 July.) At the Nomination on the first day, Lord Lowther was nominated by W. W. Carus Wilson (see *MY* ii. 419) and seconded by Edward Wilson (see *MY* ii. 493); and Col. Lowther was nominated by Col. George Wilson (d. 1853) of Dallam Tower, and seconded by T. H. Maude (see *MY* ii. 417). Col. Wilson made a surprise appearance, as he was reputed to have taken up a neutral stance in the election (see *Kendal Chronicle*, 20 May). Brougham was nominated by Thomas Wybergh (see *MY* ii. 442) and seconded by William Crackanthorpe.

[2] In his speech Lord Lowther defended the record of the previous administration, while Col. Lowther justified his intervention on the ground that he was the choice of the freeholders, whereas Brougham had already been chosen for Winchelsea and had no reason to stand in Westmorland.

inflammatory character. He complimented Mr Wilson of Dallam Tower for his Candour—yet contrasted the praise of him with the dispraise of others who had spoken. He began with noticing a question of the Colonel's who had said 'he (B) was in parliament—what would he move?' 'I will tell the gallant Col: what I would move—it is the independance of Westmorland, etc., etc.:' He then came to the merits of the question in general, and animadverted on what he called a Mistake of Mr Wilson of D.T.: that the majority of the Resident Freeholders had been with the Col: at the last Election and that the sense of the County was with him. The majority of Residents B. said was on his side, and as to the *sense* of the County—the sense of the clergy he owned was against him, so was that of the placemen, Receivers of Taxes, Distributors etc., and if it was true that the Gentry were not so numerous on his side, yet still there were other freeholders besides clergymen and gentry and that of these a majority supported him, as the last Poll Book[1] would shew. He then declaimed against the cry of No Popery—said that Mr Pitt, to whom the House of Lowther owed their titles etc., was a favorer of emancipation; that the King by his conduct in respect to Hanover[2] had showed what his sentiments were; that the University of Oxford had for its Chancellor[3] a favorer of Concession and that the University of Cambridge had just returned a pro-Catholic Representative.[4] But it is scarcely worth while to trouble you with these dry notices.

Crackanthorp let out that they were desponding—so did the tone of Brougham's speech. Crack: said 'as our difficulties encrease it becomes us to shew that our spirit and resolution keep pace with that encrease.—Brougham said if we are defeated a *third* time, a third will not be the last trial.' Sure I am that they have no hopes of success. They declaim against the new-created Votes—a plain proof that they are convinced we shall beat them at their own weapons. No notice was taken on either side of the *advertized* seceders amounting to 80.

Lord Lowther defended his adherence to the Ministry on the ground of their judgement their talents and their characters as the safest and best men to whom the rights and interests of the Empire could be entrusted. The composition of the new Votes on his side had been found fault with—he was sure, said he 'They

---

[1] For the election of 1820. [2] See L. 158 above.
[3] William Wyndham Grenville, Baron Grenville (1759–1834), Foreign Secretary, 1791–1801, head of 'All the Talents', 1806–7: Chancellor of Oxford University from 1809. His last speech in the Lords in 1822 had been in support of the R.C. claims. [4] i.e. Palmerston.

would not be found more objectionable as Freeholders of West^nd than a flight of Edinburgh Advocates,[1] Writers of the Signet, Reviewers, printers and printers Devils'—he was very happy in this retort. In short, the whole thing—though dull in this blotted letter went off, to the satisfaction of your Lordship's Friends.

7 o'clock Thursday afternoon,

I wrote thus far in the morning—and all is reduced to insignificance by a Strange proceeding of the Assessor[2] of which your Lordship will hear from quarters better able to give you an account. I will only add that at the nomination Wybergh attempted to speak a second time but could not gain a hearing—and Curwen[3] spoke a few minutes but what he said I know not having retired from the neighbourhood of the Hustings to some distance before he began. I am ashamed to send your Lordship such a blotted scrawl, but I have a wretched pen, and no convenience for writing; your kindness will excuse it.

Many think that the contest will soon be terminated for want of money. I fear not, as their expenditure is very stinted—at the risk of disgusting the Freeholders of their party John Wakefield the younger (but words are of little weight on these occasions) told me this morning that they would keep it up for ten days. His Father is not here, being ill of the Gout. I cannot but fear they will strain every point to protract the Contest in the hopes of tiring the House of Lowther out with expence—an unworthy proceeding which I trust the Gentlemen of the County will have the spirit to resent in the most emphatic way by taking on themselves no small part of the expense if not upon this occasion, upon some future one if any such should occur. Indeed whether Mr Brougham proceeds vexatiously or no it is high time for the County to be prepared to show by more than personal exertion that it considers the cause as its own.

Ever my Lord most faithfully your Lordship's obliged Friend and Servant

W. Wordsworth

[1] See next letter.

[2] John Pemberton Heywood (1756–1835), serjeant-at-law, appointed by the Hereditary High Sheriff, Lord Thanet. Contrary to his practice in 1818 and 1820, Brougham objected to the Yellow candidates having more than one attorney assigned to each voting booth to scrutinize voters' qualifications, on the ground that the interest of the two Lowthers was identical. This led to a warm discussion in the Assessor's Court between the lawyers on both sides, which was terminated by the Assessor upholding Brougham's objection.

[3] John Christian Curwen.

234. W. W. to LORD LONSDALE

MS. Lonsdale MSS. Hitherto unpublished.

Monday, 3 o'clock
26th[1] June 1826

My Lord,

Nothing has occurred worthy of particular notice since my last, except a scuffle and Row in the streets, which terminated in breaking windows, on Saturday, in each of the principal Inns, Yellow and Blue.[2]

In the earlier part of this morning the Blues gained ground—but they are now losing it fast. Today they intended to make a great push,—it has failed—and, for my own part, I cannot but think that they will give in earlier than was intended. I have conversed with a good number of intimate acquaintances of their party, and am convinced that not one of them entertain a hope of success—if the contest be protracted till the end of the week it must be merely to harrass the Candidates with expenses. The Defection tells heavily against the Blues and of new tendered Votes appearing in their favor, and the Votes not previously known to the Lowther Agents,—the number is small; if such exist it is high time *they* should make their appearance

Jeffrey Editor of the Edinburgh Review is here to vote for B.[3] with other Scotch advocates as is said; but Jeffrey is certainly here.

The Report in the Carlisle Patriot of what passed at the Nomination is very correct.

I write before the Poll is closed—the state of it will be sent your Lordship.

The weather is intensely hot—Brougham's health has nevertheless obviously improved—indeed he assured me on Saturday in the Assessor's Court that he was perfectly well at present, and that the heat agreed with him.

---

[1] *Written 27th by mistake.*
[2] According to the *Westmorland Gazette* for 1 July, a large body of Carlisle weavers—mostly Irish Catholics—were brought in by the Blues to cause trouble and lodged at Appleby Castle. On the Saturday, there was some skirmishing on the hustings: the Yellows took shelter in the King's Head and were attacked by the Blues, and then they in turn were attacked at their head-quarters, the Crown and Mitre, by the Yellows.
[3] According to the *Carlisle Patriot* for 1 July, Jeffrey's vote was set aside on the ground that his property in the county was insufficient to qualify him. Votes were disallowed when they resulted from a too minute subdivision of property, and this hit both sides who had created new 'mushroom' freeholds by this practice.

On the gross Poll the Col: is at this moment 91 ahead—half past three.

Ever most faithfully your Lordship
W. Wordsworth.

235. W. W. to LORD LONSDALE

Address: The Earl of Lonsdale, Charles Street, London.
Postmark: 30 June 1826. *Stamp*: [?Kendal].
MS. Lonsdale MSS. Hitherto unpublished.

Wednesday Morning
Ten o'clock
28th June 1826

My Lord,

I fear that I may have innocently [been] the cause of your Lordship not hearing as particularly of the state and course of things here, as you might have wished, for Mr Beckett[1] tells me he has understood that I should write often. This I should have done with pleasure had I not been told that your Lordship was daily informed of the state of the Poll at the close, and the Letters are sent off at five o'clock when the proceeding of the Hustings terminate—a moment which renders it impossible to give an account of the proceedings of the day.

I enclose an Address[2] which Mr B's Committee have this morning put into circulation. It is in a desponding tone—a note of preparation for his retiring.

Since Saturday, excepting a few squabbles about the Booths there has been no disturbance. Mr Perrin,[3] of the Carlisle Patriot, is taking an hourly account of all the events of the Election, as far as he can collect them, and to this your Lordship may be safely referred as I can bear testimony to his accuracy.

The *words* of our opponents are not to be trusted, and it perhaps is not worth while to mention that in reply to a question of mine,

---

[1] John Beckett, Lord Lonsdale's son-in-law.

[2] 'Independent Freeholders,—Your cause is safe, if you will exert yourselves for it . . . I am doing every thing in my power to win the day for you; but if you do not come to my assistance, it must be in vain. The cause is your own; let every man reflect that upon his own conduct, at this moment, it depends whether the county shall be free for ever, or for ever dependent upon a single family. . . .' (*Carlisle Patriot*, 1 July.)

[3] Robert Perrin, editor of the *Patriot*. See Aspinall, *Politics and the Press*, pp. 364 ff.

John Wakefield told me they intended to poll out the County, if so, we shall be detained till Friday Morning, or perhaps later.

The most important features of Mr B's speeches from the hustings is his attempt to fasten the origin of Mushroom Votes upon the Lowthers. Nothing can be more untrue. To this he confines himself, and to putting the best face he can upon the unfavorable state of the Poll. He avoids altogether the discussion of public principles with the exception of the Catholic Question on which he occasionally glances.

The friends of the Lowther Cause whom I meet have manifested the best spirit, whether Residents or from a distance.[1] I have seen Londoners persons from Manchester and from Liverpool in numbers all declaring their resolution to stand by the cause.

The fate of *this* Election is secure but the future must be looked at: before we part I hope for an opportunity of stating to Lord Lowther and the Col: my views without reserve. This may be done without presumption, from the opportunities I have had of the temper and opinions of our opponents.

Ever most faithfully
your Lordship's etc,
W. Wordsworth

Two o'clock. Every manoeuvre is resorted to to keep down the Lowther Votes by sending them to the Assessors Courts—in order to give a shew of strength to their nearly exhausted party.

236. W. W. to LORD LONSDALE

MS. Lonsdale MSS. Hitherto unpublished.

Thursday, half past one
29th June, 1826

My Lord,

I am not aware of any thing of importance occurring yesterday except a decision in the Assessor's Court which will set aside a great number of the Lowther Votes. It was made in consequence of an opinion of Mr Scarlet,[2] just received that the class of Votes were strictly Annuitees and as such ought to have been registered—

---

[1] Among the non-resident voters were Thomas Hutchinson, who—according to D. W.'s MS. Journal—left Brinsop for Appleby on the 22nd, Henry Hutchinson, and John Monkhouse of Stow.

[2] Sir James Scarlett, 1st Baron Abinger (1769–1844); at this time M.P. for Peterborough and the most successful advocate on the northern circuit: later Attorney-General, and Lord Chief Baron of the Exchequer from 1834.

and as they were not, the Votes were invalid. A considerable number of these Votes had been tendered and admitted before this legal opinion was received, and though the decision precludes the tendering [of] a large number which otherwise would have been deemed good, it is of little consequence as to the present election; the fate of which is as good as decided. At one oclock this day the Col: was 276 ahead upon the gross Poll; and I have this moment learned that Mr B. has polled only six during the last Hour.—The whole proceedings of this last Contest have [been] strange and unaccountable on the part of the Blues, since the first publication of the Requisition to Mr B. yet hopeful to the Lowther Cause as they indicated indecision and embarrassment.—On the Hustings Mr B. as usual avoided yesterday the discussion of public topics—he exulted in the discovery of this flaw in so large a number of the Lowther Votes—he dwelt upon the illiberality of tendering the long oath to the Catholics—and condescended to say that he held in his hand a Letter of a confidential Agent of your Lordships who in the year 1802 on your part did in that Letter request of Mr Howard[1] to propose Mr Lowther now Sir John[2] as member for the County. Mr B. then affirmed that if Mr Howard should appear to tender his Vote, the recollection of this fact would make it impossible that the long oath should be put to Him. Little credit does it reflect on Mr. H. to have put this Letter into Mr B's hands—for such a purpose and as little on Mr B's to employ it. What has this to do with the Question; or in what respect ought any proceeding of your Lordship's in 1802 to bind the Candidates for the Representation of West^d [in] 1826. Well would it be to confront this Letter with those of Mr Wilberforce and Mr B addressed to your Lordship with the proposal of a seat being given him etc[3]—How strangely do men of Mr B's Stamp forget themselves—Latterly I have not found myself of much use here. My thoughts and exertions have been mainly directed to the future—collecting the opinions of different persons, and endeavouring to open their eyes to the true character of this Contest—as affecting West^d and the whole Kingdom.—

Mr Leach[4] was called to the Assessors' Court yesterday to give evidence on the quality of the Vote of a Schoolmaster; Mr Leach being Trustee for the School—Unfortunately, though with the best intention Mr Leach instead of answering a plain question in a

[1] i.e. Henry Howard of Corby, a Roman Catholic (see also *MY* ii. 610).
[2] Lord Lonsdale's brother, Sir John Lowther. See *MY* ii. 581.
[3] See *MY* ii. 411.   [4] The Revd. John Leach, vicar of Askham.

plain way took to prating; and in consequence Mr Holt[1] seeing
that the Vote was thereby endangered, called Mr Leech a Coxcomb
in open Court. Mr Holt was not aware at the time who the Individual was, whom he was thus designating—Poor Leach was in
a most dreadful fume, and Mr Brougham with apalling minuteness
told the fact of the Rev.[d]. Divine being called a Coxcomb, from the
Hustings, making it an occasion of contrasting such rudeness with
the Civility and respectful demeanour of himself and his friends to
Gentlemen of that cloth. Again may it be said how strangely does
this man either forget himself, or speak in disregard or contempt
of facts!

Mr B. went last night to Kendal—I suppose to stimulate his
friends there—we shall soon see the Result of this Expedition from
which I dread little.—

Ever faithfully your Lordship's

W. W.

237. W. W. to LORD LONSDALE

MS. Lonsdale MSS. Hitherto unpublished.

Appleby
Friday Noon
30th June, 1826.

My Lord,

Lord Lowther justified yesterday from the hustings his determination to put the oath of supremacy, to the Catholics, on the
ground that faith had not been kept with him on a former occasion
when objections were made to his Catholic Votes after an agreement to the contrary; Besides, some fifty or sixty Catholic Votes
had been manufactered by his Opponents; and the obstructions
thrown in his way had been so many and so vexatious that he
thought himself justified in turning to his advantage every power
which he possessed by Law. He had been asked whether if Mr
Howard of Corby appeared he would have the oath tendered to
him. *Certainly*, was his reply, uttering the word with a marked
Emphasis, for it would be impossible to draw a line of distinction—
how could the oath be imposed for instance on Mr Petre[2] if not
offered to Mr Howard.—

[1] Francis Ludlow Holt, K.C. (1780–1844), Vice-Chancellor of the Duchy
of Lancaster, 1826–44, and legal writer: counsel for the Lowthers in the
Assessor's Court.

[2] Henry William Petre (1791–1852), Henry Howard's nephew, and a
grandson of the 9th Baron Petre.

Mr B. finding the majority of new votes running so high against him, confined himself yesterday to dwelling upon his majority of Resident Freeholders as manifested by the Poll of the last Election and to an endeavour at showing the superior quality of his own new Votes—which he contended, even where they came in Batches, consisted of independent Gentlemen, who of their own free will have united to liberate this County from domination. Contrast, he said, these men with the Shipwrights of Mr Bolton,[1] and the mechanics dependent upon other Gentlemen—in this part of his speech he shewed his usual lack of discretion, as he was placing operatives in a disadvantageous point of view in comparison with the upper classes; which was not at all to the taste of his audience.—

It is now twelve oclock and the Poll languishes so much on Mr B's part without slackening at all on the Lowther side, that it can be prolonged only either out of spite, or from the ungenerous, and I will add impolite motive of creating expense. The Col: yesterday affirmed from the Hustings that every additional days Poll would add 100 to his majority—and he is likely to prove a true prophet.— The opposite Party proceed now so languidly, that their inclination for disturbance seems to have died away—all is flat and spiritless.

Mr Alderson[2] is to be in London, on Monday—nevertheless no one seems confident that the Poll may not be kept open till that Day. One would fain hope, not—should it be so, it will be mainly, I think, on the instigation of James Brougham,[3] who is more actuated by petty malice than his Brother.—

I do not expect to have any thing of importance to add to this Letter. We are all as your Lordship will conceive anxious to be off —the weather has been insupportably hot, and yesterday Mr Holt was off his work, being taken with violent vomiting, and sharp attacks of spasm which terminated in several fainting fits.

I had a private conversation with Mr Chairman Wilson[4] yesterday on the future course which this opposition may take and the way in which it is to be met—He thought that the Gentlemen of the County would be ready to make votes, but not to subscribe. I hope he is in some degree mistaken, but when I have the honor of seeing your Lordship in the North, I will enter into particulars,

[1] John Bolton of Storrs.

[2] Edward Hall Alderson (1787–1857), Fellow of Caius College, Cambridge (1809–23), Counsel to the University (1825–30), a Judge (1830) and Baron of the Exchequer from 1834: counsel for Brougham in the Assessor's Court.

[3] Henry Brougham's brother (see *MY* ii. 420), who had been actively canvassing the county since the previous month. He had just been returned for Tregony, Cornwall.

[4] Christopher Wilson of Abbot Hall.

upon this most important struggle, in which every rational Englishman must feel himself obliged deeply to the House of the Lowthers.

> I have the honor to be
> most faithfully your Lordship's
> Friend and Ser^nt
> ## W. W.

4 oclock—the Enemy are in utter confusion—their Committee
disputing and quarrelling—some for giving up today, other not—
Brougham in the Sulks, and won't take the decision upon himself,
as urged to do by Alderson—but as he has not polled his Committee, and Mr Atkinson[1] was told by one of them that they had
no orders to poll today, and as it is now so late, there is too much
reason to fear we shall be detained another day.

238. W. W. to LORD LONSDALE

MS. Lonsdale MSS. Hitherto unpublished.

> Lowther Castle
> Sunday afternoon [2 July 1826]

My Lord,

Before this reaches London you will have had viva communications in abundance and have been made acquainted fully with all
particulars of the late victory.[2] Lord L. and the Col. were brief
in their addresses at the close of the Poll, and I was so placed that
I did not hear a syllable of their speeches. The Blues were in ill
temper, and as I was something of a marked man I thought it
prudent to place myself in a House, that of Mrs Dent, on the side
of the Street opposite the Hustings, and somewhat higher up.
From my Station I could hear Mr B. pretty distinctly, he spoke
loud and exerted himself vehemently. He acknowledged that if he
had been induced to stand forth in the first of these Contests by
personal ambition, the state of the Poll at the close of this third
effort would have produced in his mind feelings of disappointment,
peradventure of mortification. He stated that it was only after
repeated refusals on his part that he was at last prevailed upon to
undertake the liberation of the County and as he had been slow to
begin, he would be more slow to retire. He spent some time in

---

[1] Matthew Atkinson of Temple Sowerby (see *MY* ii. 474).
[2] When the Poll closed on Friday, 30 June, the Lowther brothers were
returned with 1,925 and 1,851 votes respectively, to Brougham's 1,353.

exculpating himself from the charge of acting as misbecame his fortune his rank his profession and station in having listened to a call so urgent; and said that it was not his ambition to be a County Member that influenced him but his desire to frustrate the aims [of] those who would make, not a County but a Borough of old Westmorland. He then guarded himself from an imputation of not paying due respect to property, and somewhat boastfully, and most inconsistently, in the estimation of those who recollected his language in the first Contest, spoke of the Thanet Estate in Westmorland as pledged or at least interested in his support, and pointed also to the property of the Wakefields, not however naming them, and other wealthy persons in the Kendal Ward, who had done their utmost for his cause. He then gave his views how property ought to be represented, not merely in large masses, but in its smallest divisions. I admit, said he, that it ought to have its preponderance, but he conceived that three thousand freeholders having ten pound a year each, had an equal right to have their property represented as one Individual with his Thirty Thousand a year. Recurring to the majority against him at the close of this third but not the *last* Contest, (and on the word *last* he dwelt with great bitterness of emphasis) he entreated his adherents not to be disheartened. He himself had never been discouraged in parliament by majorities against him, had it been so how could he and those with whom he had the honor of acting, have effected a reduction of 20 millions of taxes? Had they submitted to majorities they never could have brought the government, the half liberal ministry as he had called them one day before, to adopt the principles of free trade, and of that enlightened policy by which their measures were at present, and had been for some time governed.

He then came to the Declaration,[1] which has made so much noise. He denied that they who had signed were actuated by the pretended motives; and singling out several individuals imputed to them severally motives entirely selfish, or charged them with the greatest inconsistency. Under the latter head he placed Dr Adamthwaite,[2] and the Minister of Newbiggin he roundly asserted

[1] The Declaration signed by a number of Brougham's supporters announcing that they had abandoned his cause in consequence of his conduct on the Catholic Question. It was published in the *Westmorland Gazette* for 10 June.

[2] The Revd. John Adamthwaite, D.D., rector of Winton, nr. Brough, staged a dramatic entry into Appleby at the head of a company of freeholders from the East Ward—a Thanet preserve—towards the close of the election. He stated that he had formerly supported Brougham because he had befriended the Queen, but that he could not go along with him in supporting Catholic Emancipation. In his closing speech Brougham criticized Adamthwaite and the

signed the paper because Mr Crackenthorp had no better living to give him. Then came the Perroration which need not be particularised as it was commonplace enough. Lord Lowther has just come in and tells me that you will have all this in the Papers before my Letter reaches your Lordship—I will however send it—with a chance of some expression being preserved in this slight sketch which may not be found elsewhere.

From all that I can collect I am convinced that the opposite Party have no hopes but that the house of Lowther may be tired out with the expense—they are prepared to undergo defeat after defeat, consoling themselves with the expectation that at last the Lowthers will be sick of their own victories so dearly bought. Such is their present temper of mind—how it may change with circumstances one cannot say. I fear county elections cannot be *won* without many expences, or rather enormous cost. But I am anxious that the Country gentlemen should do more than make votes, that they should show that they deem the cause their own subscribing according to their means which would do more than any thing to daunt the Enemy, as it would both favor an economical application of the money subscribed, and of the major expenditure as proceeding from the House of Lowther, if this Contest is to be renewed. The Blues appear to have had from 8 to 10 thousand pounds, and scarcely I think can have spent more than the latter sum. They never can win the prize at this rate of expenditure and they know it—but they contrast this sum coming from a hundred different quarters with the much larger which it costs the Lord Lieutenant as one Individual, and on this and this alone their hopes are built of ultimate success. It is obvious also, that it is not against two of the *name and family* of Lowther merely that (in their passions at least) they are contesting, but against two members returned by Lowther influence. What a strange thing, said John Wakefield to me, that Mr Wilson[1] of Dalham Tower should have identified himself with the House of Lowther—we should have looked to him as *our* Representative for the future *now*, having taken this part, he never can come in for the County without a contest. The Letter Bag is making up and I must conclude abruptly,

ever most faithfully your Lordships
obliged friend and servant
W. Wordsworth

rector of Newbiggin, the Revd. John Robinson, for opposing emancipation; but Adamthwaite had the last word, and spoke at length from the hustings about Brougham's political career and character. [1] See L. 233 above.

239. W. W. to LORD LONSDALE

MS. Lonsdale MSS. Hitherto unpublished.

July 5th 1826

My Lord,

My Letter of Sunday from Lowther was concluded abruptly—it was with the hope of a brief conversation with Lord Lowther when at leisure that I returned from Appleby by way of Lowther; that conversation I have had, and received his judgment as to what is best for the future. It is not safe to differ from Lord Lowther in practical matters; his experience is so extensive, and his notions so well-weighed. He thinks, notwithstanding all reasons for a contrary opinion, that the Blues expected to win; however this might be is not of much consequence; the main question is, what is to be done for the future? Lord L. is of opinion, in which his Friends will all concur, that the attached Supporters of the cause should make as many votes as can be trusted among their *Resident Connections*; but that a subscription in money is not to be expected towards the expenses of any future contest. Few can afford it, and those that can will not probably be inclined and certainly the policy of aiming at a support of this kind may be questioned; for though it would discourage the opposite party it might also slacken the zeal of friends, who would be afraid of being subject perhaps to repeated calls of the same turn. It might be thought that so large a majority against them would compel our Adversaries to abandon the attempt—it may be so, but there is no depending on this; and all that I hear from both parties confirms me in the belief, that all their hopes of ultimate success are grounded on the comparison of expense. Therefore again and again may it be said, let economy be studied as far as can be without injury to the cause. Great improvements have been made in this department during the last contest. The opposite Party in their Imaginations exaggerated the Lowther expenses, which is to be regretted as such a delusion encourages them—it would not be politic that they should know by what course of management the Yellows make their money go the farthest, but it certainly is advisable that they should not entertain such extravagant notions of the expense which your Lordship is put to.

In the course of my hurried Letters from Appleby, I neither adverted to the military being moved from Carlisle[1] nor to News-

---

[1] Forces were moved in the direction of Appleby at the start of the election for fear of violence.

paper Comments on the words of the Colonel[1] which induced Mr B. to demand an explanation. I was not sufficiently acquainted with the particulars of either of these occurrences to deem myself justified in entering upon them at all. The Words used by the Col. I distinctly heard; they are faithfully reported in the *Carlisle Patriot*; verbatim as Mr Perrin assured me and I believe. The impression on my mind when I heard them was, those words if applied to any other Individuals than Mr B. would have no meaning or character, but that of a fair and unobjectionable common-place retort; but as applicable to Mr B. whose personal courage, though unjustly perhaps, has been brought into question they have the air of being pointed, and might be taken up to his prejudice. With the Col. or Lord Lowther I had no conversation on the subject, and do not feel myself entitled to say anything further than that I am not aware of any fault on the part of the Col. except a want of caution in giving an answer to Mr Strickland,[2] without a Friend of his own being present at the time.

Mr Leach has made up his quarrel with Mr Holt,[3] and I found him on the Sunday quite in good humour with the state of the affair.

Lord Lowther will be at Rydal Mount either this evening or tomorrow. As he did not canvass this part it will be well he should show himself, for however short a time in the neighbourhood.

Mr Southey will be at Keswick next Friday; he does not frank his Letter, so that I infer he is not yet decided to accept the honor[4] which has been thrust upon him.

Sir Richard Fleming[5] lingered at Kendal till he was too late for the Poll—two other Grasmere Voters would have attended, but they are infirm, and the extreme heat rendered it hazardous to go. This neighbourhood has done its duty.

Ever most faithfully your Lordship's

W. W.

[1] The reference is apparently to Col. Lowther's speech at the Nomination: 'Mr Wybergh has thought proper to sneer at my want of eloquence, and to compare me, in that respect, with Mr Brougham. Gentlemen, I do not pretend to eloquence. Every man to his trade, you know, and perhaps Mr B. may want as much of my trade of fighting, as I do of his trade of talking.' (*Carlisle Patriot*, 23 June.)

[2] Brougham had taken exception to Col. Lowther's remarks as reported in the *Courier*, and had sent Mr. Strickland—one of his most trusted supporters —to demand an explanation: whereupon the matter was satisfactorily concluded.

[3] See L. 236 above.

[4] Southey had been returned for Downton, a borough in the gift of the Earl of Radnor. See Southey, v. 261–5. He declined the honour, on the ground that, being Poet Laureate and in receipt of a salary from the Crown, he was ineligible to stand.   [5] Rector of Grasmere.

240. W. W. to LORD LONSDALE

MS. Lonsdale MSS. Hitherto unpublished.

Rydal Mount
Tuesday[1] 7th July 1826

My Lord,

I had entrusted the Documents respecting Mr B's application through Mr Wilberforce[2] to Mr Gee. He is this moment come to Rydal Mount, having these with him. They consist of three papers, Mr B's note, Lord Lonsdale's reply to Mr Wilberforce, and Mr Wilberforce's rejoinder; but Mr Wilberforce's first Letter enclosing Mr B's note to Lord Lonsdale does not form a part of these Papers—there is only a memorandum of the heads of it.

Many of your Lordship's Friends, myself included, were desirous that these Papers should have been published on a former occasion;[3] how far it might be proper to send them forth, now that the Contest is over, may admit of a doubt, as they might be reserved for a future demand.

Having dwelt so much upon the comparative expense of the two Parties as a principal ground of hope for our opponents, it gives me the utmost pleasure to congratulate your Lordship on the fact that, as far as conjecture can at present be formed, expenses are much less than was apprehended[4] when the great additional number of Voters which were actually polled, is considered, and the distance from which many of them were brought. Mr Gee says that in his own department, the Constabulary force, and that of Persons employed to protect our Voters at the Poll-Booths, the expense does not amount to half of what it did last time. In the victualling department also, notwithstanding the very much great number that were fed, (the fine weather being also in that respect much against us) the expense is considerably less. Nevertheless the cost on the Lowther side has been so much greater (every thing being admirably conducted) that one cannot but be anxious that every thing should be done for the future to take away from our Adversaries that ground of hope. If one may

---

[1] The 7th was a Friday.　　　　　　　　　　[2] See above, L. 236.
[3] During the 1818 election. See *MY* ii. 411, 452, etc.
[4] Among the *Lonsdale MSS.* is a record of the election expenses for the 1818 contest, which gives some idea of the sums involved. The gross expenditure was over £21,000 and included £6,000 to innkeepers at Appleby, £4,520 to innkeepers in other parts of the county, £3,000 for stage-coaches and conveyances, £2,800 for lawyers' fees, and £1,000 for music and constables.

allude to one particular, what necessity for so much music? It was very harrassing and troublesome to protect them; it was difficult to keep them in order, occasionally they threw impediments unavoidably in the way of Polling; and frequently instead of chearing the spirits, the noise they made was enough, in that hot weather, to distract one.

When I have the pleasure of seeing your Lordship, I will mention the facts, *pro* and *con,* that have come to my knowledge respecting the Dispositions of the Country Gentlemen to take a part in the expense upon themselves should the Contest be renewed hereafter. It will be difficult to encrease the Muster of Resident Voters, who can be trusted, but your Lordship's friends will I hope do their utmost, then we may, for credit's sake, be as little dependent as possible on beds of mushrooms,[1] come from what quarter they may.

Lord Lowther arrived here on Wednesday Evening along with Mr Holmes.[2] They departed yesterday after an early dinner; Lord L. called on all the Gentlemen of his Committee. Lady Fleming pleaded indisposition for not seeing him; as I heard; for Lord L. had kindly undertaken a little negotiation with her Ladyship on my behalf—the purpose of it to let her allow me to remain at Rydal Mount; or if that could not be, to enfranchise me in the field I had purchased, with a view to building in the last necessity.

Mr Edmonds,[3] B's active Partner, died this morning in consequence of having broken his leg by a fall from a Gig, while canvassing a few weeks ago. He has left a large family.

Ever most faithfully your Lordship's
W. W.

[1] i.e. mushroom votes, created by the subdivision of property.
[2] William ('Billy') Holmes (1779–1851), Tory whip for some thirty years: at this time M.P. for Bishop's Castle, Shropshire, and Treasurer of the Ordnance. See Henry Thomas Royall, *Portraits of Eminent Conservative's and Statesmen*, [1836, etc.].
[3] John Edmunds, a signatory of Brougham's Requisition. See also *MT* ii. 515. His accident was reported in the *Carlisle Patriot* for 23 June. He died thereafter, following an amputation.

241. M. W. and W. W. to JOHN KENYON

Address: John Kenyon Esqre Bath.
MS. WL and Mr. Robert H. Taylor. Hitherto unpublished.

Rydal Mount July 25th [1826]

[*M. W. writes*]

My dear Sir,

A fortnight ago your very friendly letter (Mar: 7th) reached us—I sat down instantly and wrote ½ a page in reply; when upon asking W. what he had to say to you, he (being in the bustle of starting for a book-sale with Mr Gee at Kendal) cut me short with 'how can I in this hurry think of what I have to say to an old friend with whom we have had no communication for so long?'—or something to this purpose. In this season of idleness I make a second attempt, but with a worse grace, to thank you for your letter which was most welcome—for we had often talked of, and wondered what was become of you. How could we but be reminded of you, who used so much to enjoy the *idleness* of the Mount, during such a Summer as this has been? The 'months' that you speak of as intending to remain at Bath may be passed away since your letter was written and this may not find you there, but it must take its chance;—and as you give us no hope of seeing you in the North, I fear it will yet be long before we have the pleasure of being made known to Mrs Kenyon, as we are likely to remain stationary during the Autumn. Miss W. has been in Herefordshire since Feb^ry—a long absence—we look however for her return next month. The rest of us are all at home—and except that W. has occasional attacks of inflamation in the eye-lids, and poor Dora of late almost constant tooth-ache, we all enjoy excellent health.

I do not like to touch upon the disagreeable prospect that lies before us—viz, that we are likely to be driven from our pleasant habitation next spring. If W. chooses to recur to the subject, and speak of the field he has purchased with a desperate intent to build, I leave the other page for him to do so. We all however *hope* that we may not be driven to that necessity; but that he may be left to build his most lasting edifices in the dwelling we so much love, and where we would fain hope to be permitted to receive you and yours once again.

We are very glad to find your Brother was well, and thinking of coming back to England. When you write pray remember us to him.

It will grieve you to hear that Mr and Mrs Southey have just

472

lost their youngest Daughter.—You must remember the beautiful
Isabel. She has been taken from them very suddenly, and they are
at this time in deep affliction. Sara Coleridge, under the protection
of Mr Gee (who is now our guest) sets out tomorrow for London[1]
—to visit her Father and other friends. As she will make a long
stay there you probably may meet with her. I wish I could give a
good report of Hartley for whom you kindly enquire—but we have
no hope that he will ever act worthy of himself or of his friends—he
is at Ambleside, but doing nothing.

I must not fail to notice your intended friendly present—which,
come when it may, will be very acceptable for its own sake, and
still more so as a token of your regard; and now my dear Sir I
will only beg you to present my kindest remembrances to Mrs K,
trusting that you will believe them ever to remain with yourself,
and pass the sheet to W. who I hope will make amends for this
stupid letter.

Ever very sincerely yours
M Wordsworth

[*W. W. writes*]

My dear Friend,

Notwithstanding the unparallelled drought which had parched
every blade of grass, and dried up the green leaves and fruits, it
was no bad season which bore a letter from you—and one as warm
and cordial as ever. I did check Mrs W as she has said—and now
when I have leisure and the pen is in my hand, I know not how to
make amends for the interruption, being under all circumstances a
poor Epistolarian, and feeling this disability the most after long
intervals of silence; which I believe are somewhat perplexing even
to experienced Letter writers.—But be assured if you were here
on this bright Sunny day, while a brisk breeze is rusling en-
chantingly among the trees, I would talk to you at a [?   ]
rate; not unwilling to listen as readily and as long.

You enquire after my Poetry. I have a poor account to give of
my progress in Composition since I saw you. I cannot get over the
idea which long ago haunted me, that I have written too much
in common with almost every writer of our time.—Of Publication
I have only to say that I have been desirous to send forth a new
Edition of all my Poetry that has seen the Light including the
Excursion, and several small additional Pieces—one, a fragment

---

[1] Sara Coleridge did not in fact reach Highgate until 17 Sept. (see *SH*,
p. 322). She had recently become engaged to her cousin Henry Nelson Coleridge (see L. 341 below).

of the Recluse, viz an address to the Clouds[1] [? from] which you may judge if any Spirit be left in me.—but this scheme has been frustrated by the failures among the Booksellers—so that the Poems and Excursion which have been long out of print are likely to remain so. Already have I reached the end of my paper; [   ] I was somewhat afraid of beginning a scrawl which [   ]— farewell—let us hear from you again—ever most faithfully yours
W. W.

[2]A thought has struck me, that as my Friend Mr Gee tomorrow sets out for London from this place you may have a double Letter without the expense of Postage—I will therefore send you a Copy of Verses, part of which were written this very morning in the delightful wood that borders our garden on the side towards Rydal Water—You may be inclined to think from these verses that my tone of mind at present is somewhat melancholy—it is not by any means particularly so except from the shade that has been cast over it recently by poor Southey's afflictions.—I laugh full as much as ever, and of course talk more nonsense; for, be assured that after a certain Period of life old sense slips faster away from one than new can be collected to supply the loss. This is true with all men, and especially true when the eyes fail for the purposes of reading and writing as mine have done.—But now for the verses which are for yourself and Mrs Kenyon—and not for miscellaneous ears. Pray attend to this as they are not likely soon to be published —Again farewell—O Kenyon gerando ego te aspiciam, quandoque licebit etc.
W

I have not spoken about my House, for I hate care. Mrs W. said of Hartley that he is doing nothing. She errs in this unless she meant to say that he is engaged in no regular way of maintenance. I believe he writes a good deal, and always what is clever and interesting. The fault is not that he is doing nothing but often worse than nothing, viz getting drunk in low company, and running away from every engagement to skulk in pot houses. Alas for humanity!—My daughter, Dora by name, is now installed in my House in the office of regular tea maker, why cannot you come and swell the chorus of praises she draws forth for her performance of that important part of feminine duty? Once more—adieu—
W. W.

[1] *PW* ii. 316. The poem, apparently composed in 1808, was not published till 1842.
[2] This part of the MS. is in the possession of Mr. Robert H. Taylor.

[*There follows in S. H.'s hand* Once I could hail (howe'er serene
the sky) *as in PW iv. 163, except that l. 25 reads* And when aloft
I marked . . .]

242. W. W. to BASIL MONTAGU

Address: Basil Montagu Esqʳᵉ, Bedford Sq., London. [*In M. W.'s hand*]
Postmark: [?31 July 1826].
MS. Bodleian Library.
LY i. 248.

July 25 [1826]

Dear Montagu,

Your valuable present of 4 vols: of your advancing Edition of
Lord Bacon's Works[1] was brought me by my excellent young
Friend, Strickland Cookson, during the hurry of the Westⁿᵈ
Election; but he carried it on with him to Kendal, and I did not set
eyes upon the Book, till my return from that scene of bustle and
noise to this quiet abode. It is a beautiful Book, the Paper and
print excellent, and promises to be every way worthy of its
illustrious Author. It was particularly acceptable to me as an
evidence of the leisure which your busy profession allows you, and
of the dignified manner in which you employ it.—The only
collection I have access to of Lord Bacon's work belongs to
Coleridge. I possess indeed many of his best things in separate
shapes, but I have long felt uncomfortable at having no complete
Collection of my own; your Book will supply this deficiency and
in the most agreeable way.

You have heard most probably of Southey's late affliction in
the loss of his youngest Daughter,[2] a most beautiful and delightful
child, who made a pair with her next Sister, being in fact somewhat
taller. They were the admiration of every one who saw them; and
the envy, I do not use the word in an unfavorable sense, of all
Parents who looked upon them. One is fled—and with her more
than half the attraction, and I fear all the security that in the
parents' minds hung about the other. Southey is a Christian, and
cannot want consolation. Farewell. God bless you

faithfully your obliged friend
W Wordsworth

---

[1] Montagu's edition of Bacon's works was published 1825–34 in sixteen
volumes, of which the first four had lately appeared.
[2] Isabel Southey (b. Nov. 1812) died on 16 July: the 'next' sister, Bertha,
had been born in 1809. See also previous letter.

243. W. W. to LUPTON RELFE[1]

Address: L. Relfe Esqre, 13 Cornhill, London. [*In M. W.'s hand*]
Postmark: 31 July 1826. *Stamp*: New St.
MS. Cornell.
LY i. 249.

Rydal Mount
25th July 1826

Dear Sir,

I have to thank you for an elegant large Copy of your Friendship's Offering, and for an accompanying letter dated far back,
though I only received the parcel a week or two ago, and have
since been too much engaged to do justice to a work of such promise.
I have however read most of the Poetry, and have been much
pleased with several pieces both of the Editor[2] and the Contributors. Your Book is designed principally for the sofa Table,
and appears to me admirably adapted to that purpose—both in its
embellishments and the mode in which the Authors have executed
their part of the Task. It would be, as you will conjecture, something more to my particular taste, if it were less for that of the
fine world—if it pressed closer upon common life—but this would
not suit the market—therefore you will do well to go on as you
have begun under the auspices of the present able Editor. Will he
excuse me if I mention that the arrangement of miscellaneous
poems is of consequence—it either may greatly aid or much spoil
their effect—For instance, Mr Montgomery's serious and even
solemn Lines are unluckily followed by a smart jeu d'esprit of one
of the Smith's, and the two poems,[3] though both very good in their
several ways, strangle each other. Another Poem, one of Mr
Hervey's, has many sweet lines, but it is unfortunately entitled on
a Picture of a *dead* Girl—instead of a Girl since dead. Such a title
reminds one of Pictures of dead Game—these are trifles, but of most

---

[1] The publisher of *Friendship's Offering*.
[2] The editor was T. K. Hervey (see L. 211 above), who included nine of his
own poems in the volume. Among the contributors were L. E. L., Bernard
Barton, W. L. Bowles, Miss Mitford, 'Barry Cornwall', Southey, Galt, Mil-
man, Jane Porter, Allan Cunningham, and Tom Hood ('I remember, I remember'). (De Selincourt's note.)
[3] 'Questions and Answers', by James Montgomery. The poem ends

Q. O death where ends thy strife?
A. In everlasting life.
Q. O grave, where is thy victory?
A. Ask HIM, who rose again for me.

It is followed by Horatio Smith's 'Discretion the better part of Valour'. (De
Selincourt's note.)

476

importance to the class of readers whom your Book will best suit.
With many thanks for this obliging token of your remembrance
I remain dear Sir

faithfully yours
Wm Wordsworth

244. W. W. to H. C. R.

Address: H. C. Robinson Esq., Barrister on the Norfolk Circuit [*readdressed to*] London. *Left Norfolk.*
Postmark: 31 July, 1826. *Stamp*: Kendal. *Endorsed*: Aug[t] 1826, Wordsworth, Objects on tour in Wales.
MS. Dr. Williams's Library.
K (—). *Morley, i. 169; ii. 845.*[1]

[*c. 30 July 1826*]

My dear Friend,

I know not what chance there is of this Note reaching you; but as it will only cost you twopence I send it at haphazard merely to say, that the hope I had encouraged of being able to tour with you in Ireland is vanished. You need not be troubled with particulars but the sum is I cannot get my Neighbour Lady le F. to assure me that in the event of her Aunt not coming to Rydal Mount which the aunt does not wish to do, we may be permitted to remain.

As to your tour in N. Wales it would be impossible to chalk one out without knowing what time you have at disposal, or where you would enter upon the principality. My Sister seems to have some hope of seeing you in Herefordshire. In that case, you ought to go up the Wye as far as Rhaidwr Gorvy,[2] there fall in with the Aberystwith Coach, and proceed to an Inn within four or five miles of the Devil's Bridge, I forget its name, turn down thence to Hafod on foot, from Hafod to the Devil's Bridge—which thoroughly to see with the Waterfalls of the 2 Streams would detain you two Hours. From the Devil's Bridge to Machynlleth is a horse track of 20 miles over a desolate Country, (for Aberystwith though a pleasant Bathing place is not worth going to see). From Machynlleth to Tal-y Llynn where you might ascend Cader Idris, and thence drop down on Dollgelli whence to Barmouth or to Harlech and over Traeth Mawr to Pont Aberglaslynn and Bedd Kelert— And now comes a difficulty, you are in the neighbourhood of Snowdon, but the finest outline of this mountain and almost of any other, is to be seen from the Garden of the Inn at Kepel Kerrig

[1] The two parts of this letter have become separated in Morley, but they appear to belong together.
[2] Rhaiadr Gwy, the waterfall of the Wye.

—If you could sacrifice this view I should say at once take the road from Bedd Kellert towards Kepel Kerrig and pursue it till within 4 or five miles of the Latter place and then turn off along a faint Horse track to the left for Llanberrys.

This walk would shew you some of the most exquisite scenery in Great Britain.

[In Dora W.'s hand]

From Llanberris mount Snowdon and descend to Dolbarden Inn in the vale of Llanberris, and by the lake to the romantic villiege of Cwm y Gloed whence to Carnarvon Bangor and Holy Head for Ireland, this will have shewn you most of the finest things in N. and S. Wales but observe with the exception of Conway Castle a most magnificent thing and the whole line of the great road to Ireland from Llangollen including Capel Kerrig to Bangor which would leave your knowledge of N.W. very imperfect but this might easily be taken at some future time when you come into the north of England by coaching through Llangollen to Bangor thence walking to Conway and so on by Abergelly to [?Holyw]ell[1] from within two miles of which place is a daily steam boat to Liverpool as there is one also from Bangor to L—a most delightful voyage of eight or nine hours.—Of Ireland I can say nothing but that every body sees Killarney there are some fine ruins of monasteries, etc not far from Limerick the Vale of the Dargle and the Wicklow Mountains would lie in your way from Killarney to Dublin supposing you to start from Dublin you would go by Limerick and return by the Wicklow country but to one who should leave Wales out the best way of seeing Ireland from London would be to go from London to Bristol and thence to Cork Killarney and Dublin and the Giants Causeway. From Belfast there will no doubt be a Steam Boat to Glascow and so on by Steam to Iona and Staffa and as much of the West of Scotland as you could conveniently see returning by West^d. I have given up all hopes of succeeding in a bargain for my poems so they may rest. Poor Southey has lately lost his youngest Daughter a delightful Creature of fourteen. Farewell

Believe me with love from this household your faithful Friend *[signed]* Wm Wordsworth

[W. W. adds] My Daughter has been my amanuensis for this half-sheet. I find from Mrs W. that I must direct to you on the Circuit.—

---

[1] *MS. torn.*

245. D. W. to JOHN MONKHOUSE

MS. WL.
LY i. 250 (—).

[Brinsop]
[4 Aug. 1826][1]

My Dr. John,

I must confess I never expected much from the Ballingham seminary[2] and have been anxious for some time that G. should be removed, but did not like to interfere.

Mary calls on me to finish—I calling on her to read a letter from Sara, which I have just brought home with the Turtle Doves.

The *packet* (written since that letter) came a few days ago—it will tell the sad story to you of poor Isabel Southey's death. It was somewhat of a relief to my mind, I confess, when I found that it was not the Boy that had been taken away—which I had supposed—yet I know not whether the Father and Mother will not be more afflicted that the fair knot of Girls is snapped. Southey has always looked on the Boy as but *lent* to him for a short time.

To take up Mary's story—not with her instructions, but from my own head. There is a school at Richmond in Yorkshire of which we have the Advertiz[mt]. We hope much from it and I shall make inquiries in my next letter; but perhaps may not have satisfactory answers; however depend on it, when I go to Rydal I will hunt out a true character of the school.

We shall be right glad to see you next week. I have at length fixed to leave dear Brinsop on or about the 21st and *fear* I shall not see you again at the Stowe. At all events it must be a week taken after the 21st if I can manage it at all. Adieu my dear Friend —ever your affectionate

D. W.

Mary sends you poor M[rs] Donaldson's[3] affecting letter. She begs you will, without fail, send it to Hereford tomorrow directed to be left at the Greyhound. She wants to forward it to Sara in a frank which Mr Morgan[4] will provide and Sara must forward it to Joanna, if gone from Rydal.

---

[1] Dated by reference to D. W.'s MS. Journals.
[2] The local school near Hereford where George Hutchinson was a pupil. D. W. had visited him there in April.
[3] A local friend.
[4] George Gould Morgan (1794–1845), M.P. for Brecon: younger brother of Sir Charles Morgan-Robinson, 3rd Bart., 1st Baron Tredegar. See also L. 249 below.

246. W. W. to MARIA JANE JEWSBURY

MS. untraced.
The Times, 5 Oct. 1931. Gillett, p. xxx. LY i. 251. Letters of Dora Wordsworth,
p. 30.

Marston Moor.[1] [early Aug. 1826]

My dear Miss Jewsbury,—

Having an opportunity of a Frank which rarely occurs here but at this season, I write a few words to congratulate you upon the turn of the tide of health in your favor. It gave me I assure you inexpressible pleasure to learn that a streak in the East was appearing after the long night of sickness. Two days ago Mrs W. and I were at Mrs Barlow's, and through her we learned from your excellent Friend Miss Bayley that you were gaining strength, and as you have yet so much summer before you much may be hoped from warm weather—Heaven grant it may restore you!

Dora will give you the little news that occurs here. A book was put into my hands the other day, entitled 'Diary of an Ennuyée'[2]— it purports to be the work of a Lady deceased, though many passages lead me to suspect it is a forgery; and I mention it merely for the peculiarity that the Author, whoever She or He may be, seems as familiar with my Poems as yourself, quoting them at every instant. Perhaps when you are sufficiently recovered to be able to read books of mere amusement, it might be worth your while to turn it over.

Does your health allow you to communicate occasionally with Mrs Hemans?[3] if so, pray tell her how much I regret having been prevented from fulfilling my intention of visiting North Wales. I should have made a point of seeing her had I gone; but I was engaged in the turmoil of a County Election, and harassing speculations, of which the text was—'To build or not to build' etc.

I will now release you from this Scrawl penned with glimmering

[1] Between Wetherby and York. W. W. was perhaps visiting his Robinson relatives, or one of the Lowther Castle circle (he had recently met Sir John Copley and Dr. Vernon Harcourt, the Archbishop of York, at Lowther: see *SH*, p. 321).

[2] By Anna Brownell Jameson (1794–1860), published 1826. Her best-known work was probably *Sacred and Legendary Art*, 4 vols., 1848–52. See also *MY* i. 331.

[3] Felicia Dorothea Hemans (1793–1835), writer of numerous volumes of popular verse, including *Lays of Many Lands*, 1825, *Records of Woman*, 1828, and *Songs of the Affections*, 1830. She lived in North Wales until 1828, and then at Wavertree, Liverpool, till 1831, when she moved to Dublin.

eyesight, and a little of an achey head—Heaven bless you my dear
Friend, and believe me with prayers for your recovery,

most faithfully yours,
W. Wordsworth

247. D. W. to JOHN MONKHOUSE

Address: To John Monkhouse Esqre, Stowe, near Hereford.
Postmark: 15 Aug. 18[?].
MS. Jonathan Wordsworth. Hitherto unpublished.

[Brinsop]
Monday Evening.
[14 Aug. 1826]

My dear Friend,

We have not curiosity after Mr Wakefield's trial[1] sufficient to
have led us to Lancaster had we been in the neighbouring country.
We have sufficient portion of that female infirmity to wish for a
fuller detail than our newspapers will afford. Therefore we beg
you to be so good as to send us your paper or papers with the
account of the Trial.

Thomas set off this morning for [? Gwerndovenant].[2] After you
were gone he was sorry he had not accompanied you.—We have
had [no] letters, therefore at present I think only of leaving my
good Friends and this pleasant place on Tuesday morning. I hope
nothing will prevent your riding over to see us unless you should
hear that I stay a week longer. If I do I will write again.

adieu,
Yours ever truly
D Wordsworth

248. D. W. to JOHN MONKHOUSE

Address: John Monkhouse Esqre, Stowe, near Hereford.
MS. WL. Hitherto unpublished.

[Brinsop]
Thursday Evening.
[24 Aug. 1826]

My dear Friend,

I have determined not to go from Brinsop till Thursday the 31st
of this month, therefore if it be inconvenient to you to come on

[1] See L. 221 above.
[2] MS. illegible: reading supplied from D. W.'s MS. Journal. Gwerndovenant, or Gwerndyffnant, was the small farm nr. Hindwell owned by Thomas
Hutchinson. D. W. had visited it on 10 May.

Sunday, as you kindly said you would do should I abide by my original intention, it is not necessary. I may possibly get over to see you at the Stowe—or you may have a more convenient opportunity.

Thomas and Mary intend to go to Mr Field's[1] on Wednesday. Probably you may have been informed of this, and may intend to meet them there.

I have had a letter from Rydal. You will be sorry to hear my Brother's eyes had been inflamed—all else well. The Farquhars expected at Fox Ghyll—Walter F. already arrived. Sara H. talks of accompanying E. Cookson to Bristol, and visiting the Gees. In that case no doubt you will see her. I do not quite like her leaving Rydal again so soon after my return.

Joanna and Henry were to sail for the Isle of Man last Wednesday week—both in good spirits, and [? went] from Whitehaven where they were detained two days.

I see cheering paragraphs concerning [? Columbians][2]—at least as far as honest intentions go—or promises of such.

Adieu, believe me your affect<sup>e</sup> Friend
D Wordsworth

There may be an opportunity for the Journal without sending on purpose.

249. D. W. to JOHN MONKHOUSE

MS. WL. Hitherto unpublished.

[Brinsop]
Sunday afternoon.
[27 Aug. 1826]

My dear Friend,

I did expect you at breakfast this morning—and again at our return from Church expected to find you here. The Basket of beautiful peaches, your letter, and the newspapers have not quite reconciled me to the disappointment: however I shall (God willing!) see you again at the Stowe. In hopes of meeting at least Mr (perhaps *Mrs*) Gee at Malvern I have deferred my departure (from Brinsop) till Tuesday the 5th.[3] We are to dine at

---

[1] A local acquaintance: see next letter.   [2] i.e. Columbian Bonds.
[3] In fact D. W., accompanied by John W., left Brinsop on 9 Sept., visited Miss Willes at Worcester, and arrived at Malvern on the 12th *en route* for Leamington, where she saw Miss Jewsbury, and Coleorton.

Brinsop Court.

BRINSOP COURT, HEREFORDSHIRE
from a drawing by Sara Hutchinson jnr., c. 1855

Mr Morgan's[1] on Wednesday next (—I hope he will invite you to meet us). I intend to sleep at his house and shall the next morning proceed on foot to the Stowe, and stay with you till Saturday, and I hope that on that same day you will come hither and stay over Sunday.

I wish I had not been so dutiful as to write that note which prevented your coming last Saturday—or that I had chanced to mention that Mr Fièld was from home. You would be disappointed at finding only the Lady and her young brood etc. What is worse, your visit would not *tell, as* a visit. How much better had you been with us! Besides I think we should have coaxed you to stay to see the young Landlord. He arrived on Monday morning on horseback —with a servant—the lease, a brown paper parcel, in his hand— Stayed ½ an hour, and promised to return to Breakfast next morning with Mrs Ricardo[2] at Seven o'clock. He and she arrived punctually with Lawyer James—the Lease was signed, and at one o'clock Mr Ricardo, his beautiful Wife, and Thomas and Mary set off on horseback to Lady [? Lift][3] and Raven's Causeway. I, alas! was ill in bed—able, however, to rise to dinner. We were all much pleased with Mr and Mrs R. and they, I *believe*, were not less so with their Tenants. They stayed all night.

Future Repairs and all other matters were settled to mutual satisfaction. I think you will not see Thomas and Mary tomorrow. They will be anxious to be at home again. We have gone on very comfortably—the children tractable and good and your Aunt pretty well. My complaint was the prevalent one, and went off in two days.

I enclose a letter from Mary W. and from Joanna. Your Aunt had one last night from J. written in very good spirits. She was quite well, had got cheaper Lodgings, and they hoped to make their Income answer. I cannot send that letter as Thos. and Mary have not seen it.

[*cetera desunt*]

[1] See L. 245 above.
[2] Osman Ricardo (1795–1881), eldest son of the celebrated economist David Ricardo (1772–1823), inherited the estate of Bromesberrow Place, nr. Ledbury, Worcs., and was M.P. for Worcester, 1847–65. In 1817 he had married Harriet, daughter of Robert Mallory of Woodcote, Warwickshire.
[3] A picturesque hill between Hereford and Weobley.

250. W. W. to [? JOHN GREGORY CRUMP][1]

MS. Brown University Library. Hitherto unpublished.

Clappersgate
Monday Noon [? 11 Sept 1826]

Dear Sir,

I am very sorry that I cannot have my wish in calling on you this morning—I do not return through Ambleside as I expected; being carried off in another direction, which will make it impossible for me to be at Grasmere in Time for the Wedding dinner, if I go to Ambleside. Pray excuse me and believe me in extreme haste faithfully your

much obliged
W Wordsworth

251. W. W. to UNKNOWN CORRESPONDENT

MS. Carl H. Pforzheimer Library. Hitherto unpublished.

[? Sept. 1826]

. . . I have no news from this Quarter, but that our trees are of foliage this year unusually luxuriant; so much so, that many of the Dwellings of this neighbourhood seem packed in green leaves like precious Trinkets in cotton. Every thing about us looks bright, clear, soft, sheltered and peaceful; for the weather has been quite heavenly for many weeks . . .

W Wordsworth

252. W. W. to JANE MARSHALL

MS. untraced.
LY i. 253.

Keswick
Friday [22 Sept. 1826][2]

Dear Mrs. Marshall,

Many thanks for your obliging letter. My visit here was to Mr. Southey, whom I had not seen before since the death of his

---

[1] The Liverpool attorney, of Allan Bank. This letter appears to refer to the wedding of one of Crump's younger daughters, mentioned by *SH*, pp. 324, 329.

[2] For date see *Rogers*, i. 434–5.

child. But Sir G. Beaumont and Mr Rogers[1] are both here, and I
am committed with them and Mr. Southey, to-day we go to
Buttermere, and I could not get off an engagement to-morrow.
I shall however call at Halsteads towards the latter part of next
week, and then perhaps we may settle when I can have the pleasure
of paying a visit in which I have been thus far disappointed. Dora,
I am happy to learn, is considerably better, so that I hope she may
be trusted over the mountain.

I am truly sorry for Mr. Marshall's accident particularly so in
this most beautiful weather.

I promise myself a good deal of pleasure in [   ] the neighbourhood of Buttermere.

I remain dear Mrs. Marshall
faithfully your obliged
W. Wordsworth

My sister is at present at Sir G. Beaumont's.[2]

253. W. W. to BENJAMIN DOCKRAY[3]

Address: Benjamin Dockray Esq[re], Lancaster.
MS. Haverford College.
LY i. 252.

17th Oct[r] 1826

Dear Sir,

I am much obliged by your Letter, and will not fail to set the
matter right in another Edition.—What I have asserted was upon
the authority of a near Relative of Mr. Walker, but certainly the
expression is very inaccurate.[4] As you justly observe *to refuse* to be
distrained upon was what they could not have done; the thing
would have [been] nugatory. But allow me to observe, that

---

[1] Sir George Beaumont and Rogers had arrived at Ambleside on 8 Sept.,
dined at Rydal Mount on the 10th, and moved on to Keswick on the 15th,
where W. W. joined them—as Southey's guest—on the 19th. See also *SH*,
p. 324.   [2] i.e. at Coleorton.
[3] Benjamin Dockray (1786–1861), a Quaker, belonged to a family with
manufacturing interests in Lancaster and Manchester, but he does not seem
to have engaged in active business himself. He visited W. W. at Rydal Mount
in 1831 (*RMVB*).
[4] In his memoir of Robert Walker in the 1820 edition of *The River Duddon*
W. W. had written of the Quakers: 'certain persons . . . had refused to pay, or
be distrained upon, for the accustomed annual interest due from them among
others, under the title of church stock.' In consequence of Dockray's letter this
was altered to: 'certain persons . . . had refused to pay annual interest due under
the title of Church-stock', and a note appended, as in *PW* iii. 519.

though the expressions I have reported are lax, the spirit of the fact as mentioned by me is not thereby affected.—Dues that could not be had from a Brother Christian without the intervention of legal process, a clergyman of Mr. Walker's temper would not desire however necessary for his maintenance.—It was to place this feature of his character in full light, that the circumstance was introduced; and I thank you for a communication that will enable me to do it with less injustice to a body of Christians for whom I entertain a most high respect.

It gave me pleasure to hear that any Persons of sensibility have visited the Duddon among its mountains. No one who has not done so has an adequate idea of the varieties of this district of the Lakes—Wastdale should be seen also by every one who has time and strength to spare—

I remain very sincerely
Your obliged Friend,
W. Wordsworth

254. W. W. to UNKNOWN CORRESPONDENT

MS. St. John's College, Cambridge.
The Eagle, xli (1920), 225. LY i. 253.

[In M. W.'s hand]

Rydal Mount Octr. 17th. [?1826][1]

Sir

In reply to your letter received this morning I have to say that my intention was to point out the injurious effects of putting inconsiderate questions to Children, and urging them to give answers upon matters either uninteresting to them, or upon which they had no decided opinion.

I am Sir your obed^t Servant
[signed] W. Wordsworth

---

[1] It is impossible to date this letter with any certainty. The reference is to *Anecdote for Fathers* (*PW* i. 241), which, until 1845, had the sub-title 'Shewing how the art of lying may be taught'.

255. W. W. to ALARIC WATTS

Address: Alaric A Watts Esq., no 8 North Bank, Regent's Park London.
MS. Wesleyan University Library, Middletown, Connecticut.
Hitherto unpublished.

Rydal Mount
Oct^{br} 22nd 1826

My dear Sir,

I hope the Gentleman, Mr Cookson[1] of Kendal, who is the Bearer of this will be able to deliver it himself; if so, may I beg you to entrust him with the Vol: of Poems which I sent some time ago as revised for the Press.—I am induced to wish for it again, seeing no prospect of printing in a way at all satisfactory.—If Mr Cookson should not be fortunate enough to meet with you, he will leave directions to what place in London he would have it sent, so that he may bring it down to me.

I have lately seen Mr Robinson, and I told him I would trouble you with a request to let him have the Vol: as he was likely to have an opportunity of forwarding it to me; in case you should not yourself have one.—But it will be much the best to send it by Mr Cookson.—

I am truly sorry you should have been so often called upon to think about this unpleasant concern.

Pray how have you got out of the hands of Hurst and Robinson;[2] —and how goes on the Souvenir. I ask being sincerely interested in your success.

With kindest regards to yourself and Mrs Watts from all here I remain

my dear Sir
your obliged Friend and Ser^{vnt}
Wm Wordsworth

[1] i.e. Strickland Cookson.
[2] See L. 232 above.

256. W. W. to HENRY TAYLOR

Address: Henry Taylor Esqr, Colonial Office.
MS. The Royal Library, Windsor Castle. Hitherto unpublished.

Rydal Mount
23^d Oct^br 1826

Dear Sir,

The Bearer of this is Mr James Houtson, Brother of the late Mr John Houtson[1] who died on the 1st May last at Accra on the coast of Africa, and I am induced to trouble you on his behalf, being persuaded that you will be interested in the affair. His late Brother was the Person who buried Belzoni,[2] and who conducted the African Mission under Captn Clapperton,[3] 5 or 600 miles to Katunga the Capital of Eyoe, by the request of Government as I understand; and was in communication with Earl Bathurst[4] on the entire abolition of the Slave trade on this side the Equator.

The point upon which the Brother of the Deceased wishes for assistance from the Colonial office he will explain himself to you if you will be kind enough to allow him, and to give him the benefit of your advice as to his mode of proceeding, and also such futherance as it may be in your power to lend him.—

Mr James Houtson is not kn[own][5] to me, but I make this

---

[1] An English merchant and friend of William Pearson. After John Houtson's death, his brother had difficulty in recovering his property and sought Pearson's help in approaching W. W., who undertook to write to Henry Taylor. See Pearson, pp. 30–1.

[2] Giovanni Battista Belzoni (1778–1823), Italian showman, engineer, and explorer of Egyptian antiquities, came to London in 1803 and gave highly popular displays at Bartholomew Fair and Astley's Amphitheatre; later, he excavated at Abu Simbel and Karnak and published a *Narrative* of his discoveries (1820). Three years later he set out for Timbuktu, but died at the village of Gwato, nr. Benin, Nigeria, on 3 Dec. 1823. For W. W.'s admiration of Belzoni, see De Quincey's *Works* (ed. Masson), v. 325; and J. R. Findlay, *Personal Recollections of Thomas De Quincey*, 1886, p. 48: 'Wordsworth thanked God that there was only one man in England he would go out of his way to see, namely, Belzoni. De Quincey remarked on the beggarly idea of renown Wordsworth entertained in regarding as nothing all the intellect and worth of England as compared with a man seven feet high, who could walk about with a living pyramid on his shoulders.'

[3] Captain Hugh Clapperton (1788–1827), Scottish explorer, published in 1826 (with Major Dixon Denham) a *Narrative of Travels and Discoveries in Northern and Central Africa, in 1822, 1823, and 1824*. He conducted a second expedition in 1825 at the request of the Colonial Office, accompanied by Houtson and Richard Lander (who later wrote an account of the journey), and reached Katunga on 15 Jan. 1826. Clapperton died the following April, while tracing the course of the Niger.

[4] Henry, 3rd Earl Bathurst (1762–1834), President of the Board of Trade, 1807–12; Secretary of War and Colonies, 1812–27; President of the Council in Wellington's administration, 1828–30.   [5] *MS. torn.*

application upon the representation of a Friend of mine, who was particularly attached to his deceased Brother; a Man very amiable in private life, and certainly not uninteresting to the Public.— With kind regards from Mrs Wordsworth and Miss Hutchinson, I remain dear Sir

very sincerely yours
Wm Wordsworth

257. W. W. to FREDERIC MANSEL REYNOLDS[1]

MS. British Museum.
LY i. 255.

Halsteads Oct^{br} 24th [1826][2]
near Penrith.

My dear Sir,

I deferred answering your very obliging Letter till my visit to this place would give me an opportunity of a Frank.

I am truly sensible of the kindness of your enquiries, and of the interest which you take in my case.—It gives me great pleasure to say, which I do with gratitude, that I have derived, I am persuaded, great benefit from your remedy. The Blue stone was applied by Mrs W. to my eyes, five or six times; it distressed them not a little for the time; but they have not been any thing like so well for many years as since. It is but justice to ascribe this to the virtues of the Stone; though it is proper to say that my having about the same period entirely left off wine (fermented or spirituous liquors have never made a part of my beverage) it is probable that this change may have concurred in producing the beneficial effect. At all events I am thankful, and shall always feel greatly indebted to your advice. If my Life were thoroughly regulated as to diet, and exertion of body and mind, I have reason to think that I should henceforth have comparatively little reason to complain of my eyes.— If they become deranged again, depend upon it I will persist in the use of the Blue Stone, and this will be the best way of acknowledging my obligation to you.

[1] F. Mansel Reynolds (d. 1850), son of Frederic Reynolds the dramatist, edited *The Keepsake*, a Christmas annual, 1828–35 and 1838–9.
[2] The year of this letter is established conclusively by S. H. to E. Q., [28 Sept. 1826]: '. . . Mr Wordsworth's eyes have been cured by one of our visitors Mr F. Reynolds . . . who prescribed the touching them with the blue stone [i.e. copper sulphate]—which acted like magic upon them . . .' (*SH*, p. 329).

I am further obliged by your offer of service in[1] London, which
I shall not scruple to accept should there be occasion. Let me add
that I shall always be glad to see you, if you are again tempted to
visit Westmorland. And believe me with best Compts from Mrs **W.**
most sincerely your obliged friend and Servt
W. Wordsworth

258. M. W. to JOHN KENYON[2]

Address: John Kenyon Esqre, Bath.
MS. untraced.
Transactions of the Wordsworth Society, no. 6, p. 89. K (—). LY. i. 256.

Oct 27th [1826]

My dear Sir,
   Your friendly and very acceptable present arrived at Rydal
Mount yesterday. I have not yet opened the Cask, but doubt not
that the sugar is in excellent condition; and it could not have come
more opportunely than now, when we are threatened with a
serious rise in the price of an article, which, as Christmas-pies will
ere long be called for, must be in great requisition. I lose no time
in thanking you for this your kind remembrance, though, barren
as a letter just now from me will be, I should have been loth to
trouble you with one, had I not the temptation of procuring a
frank, and probably an additional note from William, who is at
present either at the house of the Member for Yorkshire, Mr
Marshall, or at Lowther.
   W. is paying his last summer visits for this season—our latest
lingerers after pleasure have departed, Miss Wordsworth we
expect at home (she having been an Absentee for 10 months) in the
course of the next fortnight[3]—so that after the rejoicings for her
return are over we look forward to a quiet and industrious winter
—without any harassing fears that we are to be turned [out] of our
favoured Residence—a fear that haunted us, if I remember right,
the last time I had the pleasure of writing to you.
   I can now look forward to the hope that, as soon as you like after
the Cuckoo arrives, you will not let another season pass without
introducing Mrs Kenyon to us—if not, I shall begin to suspect that
you think the influence of *Idle* Mount may interfere with, and have

---

[1] *Written* of.   [2] Evidently enclosed with the next letter.
[3] D. W. returned to Rydal Mount on 6 Nov.

a bad effect upon the more industrious habits of your good wife, and that you had best keep her out of the way of that Castle of Indolence.

Dora has had a long illness, a sort of bilious fever, which has left her looking ill and very weak; but we consider her as convalescent. She and my sister Sarah and Willy join me in best remembrances to yourself, Mrs K. and to your good Br when you write to him—and believe me, my dear Sir, ever to remain very sincerely yours,

M. Wordsworth.

259. W. W. to JOHN KENYON

Address: John Kenyon Esqʳ, Bath [*readdressed to*] Exmouth, Devon.
Franked: Whitehaven thirty first October 1826 Lonsdale.
Postmark: 2 Nov. 1826. *Stamp*: (1) Whitehaven. (2) Bath.
MS. Mr. W. Hugh Peal. Hitherto unpublished.

Rydal Mount
[*c.* 29 Oct. 1826]

My dear Friend,

This letter has been prematurely sent to Lowther, and returned to me at this place. I have just a moment to shew you my beautiful handwriting and to add my thanks to Mrs Wordsworth's for your kind present.

—We have lately had a high gratification in the sight of our old Friend T. Pool[1] on his return from Edinburgh.—I took him a long ramble among our hills with which he was greatly delighted. I chose the rocky wildness of Loughrigg Fell and Langdale, as they have nothing of the craggy in Somerset; we returned by Grasmere. I wish heartily he could have stayed a week with us.[2]

We have had an enchanting summer and Autumn. The leaves remain longer with us . . .

[cetera desunt]

[1] i.e. Thomas Poole.
[2] Poole wrote on 12 Nov. about his recent visit, praising W. W.'s descriptions of Lakeland in his *Guide*: 'The Country is an exquisite *Skeleton* of Poetry and in that little Book you have accurately copied the *Form* and have transferred therein a Part of yourself—a living Soul.' (*WL MSS.*)

260. D. W. to THOMAS DE QUINCEY

Address: To Thomas de Quincey Esqre, at Professor Wilson's, Edinburgh.
Postmark: 17 Nov. 1826. *Stamp*: Kendal Penny Post.
MS. Harvard University Library.
K (—). *LY i. 257* (—).

Rydal Mount,
Thursday, 16th Nov^r ⌈1826⌉

I have broken the seal of my letter to add to the last page.

My dear Sir,

A letter of good tidings respecting Mrs de Quincey and your
Family cannot, I am sure, be unwelcome,[1] and besides, she assures
me that you will be glad to hear of my safe return to Rydal after
a nine months' absence. I called at your cottage yesterday, having
first seen your Son William[2] at the head of the school-boys; as it
might seem a leader of their noontide games, and Horace[3] among
the tribe—both as healthy-looking as the best, and William very
much grown—Margaret[4] was in the kitchen preparing to follow
her Brothers to school, and I was pleased to see her also looking
stout and well, and much grown. Mrs de Quincey was seated by
the fire above stairs with her Baby on her knee—She rose and received me chearfully, as a person in perfect health, and does indeed
seem to have had an extraordinary recovery; and as little suffering
as could be expected. The Babe looks as if it would thrive and is
what we call a nice Child—neither big nor little.—

Mrs de Quincey seemed on the whole in very good spirits;
but, with something of sadness in her manner, she told me you
were not likely very soon to be at home. She then said that you
had at present some literary employments at Edinburgh; and had,
besides, had an offer (or something to this effect) of a permanent
engagement, the nature of which she did not know; but that you
hesitated about accepting it, as it might necessitate you to settle
in Edinburgh.[5] To this I replied, 'Why not settle there for the time

---

[1] Since his marriage in 1817 De Quincey had become estranged from the
ladies at Rydal Mount; but on 16 July 1825 he had written to D. W. in great
distress from London, begging her to visit his wife, who was in a state of
anxiety and depression (see Jordan, pp. 330–2). Doubtless D. W. went—and
this letter records another visit, made within ten days of her return home.
Mrs. De Quincey and her children had returned to live at Dove Cottage the
previous year when Mrs. Luff took possession of Fox Ghyll.

[2] De Quincey's eldest son: d. 1835 of brain disease.

[3] Later an army officer, serving under Sir Hugh Gough in China (d. 1842).

[4] Later Mrs. Robert Craig (d. 1871).

[5] De Quincey was about to contribute to *Blackwood's Magazine*, xxi (Feb.

at least that this engagement lasts. Lodgings are cheap at Edinburgh, and provisions and coals not dear. Of these facts I had some weeks' experience four years ago.' I then added that it was my firm opinion that you could never regularly keep up to your engagements at a distance from the press; and, said I, 'pray tell him so when you write.' She replied, 'Do write yourself.' Now I could not refuse to give her pleasure by so doing, especially being assured that my letter would not be wholly worthless to you, having such agreeable news to send of your Family. The little cottage and every thing seemed comfortable.

I do not presume to take the liberty of advising the acceptance of this engagement, or of that—only I would venture to request you well to consider the many impediments to literary employments to be regularly carried on in limited time, at a distance from the press, in a small house, and in perfect solitude. You must well know that it is a true and faithful concern for your interests and those of your Family that prompts me to call your attention to this point; and, if you think that I am mistaken, you will not, I am sure, take it ill that I have thus freely expressed my opinion.

It gave me great pleasure to hear of your good health and spirits, and you, I am sure, will be glad to have good accounts of all our Family except poor Dora, who has been very ill indeed—dangerously ill; but now, thank God, she is gaining ground, I hope daily— Her extreme illness was during my absence, and I was therefore spared great anxiety, for I did not know of it till she was convalescent. I was, however, greatly shocked by her sickly looks. They improve, however, visibly, and she gains strength and has a good appetite. Whenever weather permits she rides on horseback. My Brother's eyes are literally quite well. This surely is a great blessing, and I hope we are sufficiently thankful for it. He reads aloud to us by candle-light, and uses the pen for himself. My poor Sister is a little worn by anxiety for Dora, but in other respects looks as well as usual, and is active and chearful.

I cannot express how happy I am to find myself at home again after so long an absence, though my time has passed very agreeably, and my health been excellent. I have had many very long walks since my return, and am more than ever charmed with our

1827), 199–213, the first part of *On Murder considered as one of the Fine Arts*. In summer 1827 he began his contributions to the *Edinburgh Saturday Post* and the *Edinburgh Evening Post* (see Stuart M. Tave, *New Essays by De Quincey*, 1966).

rocks and mountains. Rich autumnal tints, with an intermixture of green ones, still linger on the Trees.

My Brother and Sister do not know of my writing: otherwise they would send their remembrances.

Make my Respects to Mr and Mrs and Miss Wilson, and believe me, dear Sir,

Yours affectionately,
D. Wordsworth.

Excuse a very bad pen and haste.

One o'clock Thursday.—I have been at Grasmere, and again seen your Wife. She desires me to say that she is particularly anxious to hear from you on her Father's[1] account. The newspaper continues to come *directed* to my Brother, though before Dr Stoddart left England my Brother wrote to request that it might not. The new Editors[2] no doubt have wished to continue the connection with you; but we think that it would be much better that Mrs de Quincey should write to order it not to be sent, at least until your return to Grasmere, especially as at present you are not likely to contribute anything to the paper. She agrees with me in thinking it right so to do; and will write to the Editor, unless you order to the contrary. Perhaps you will write yourself. Pray mention this matter to him when you next write to him. My Brother is uneasy about it, fearing a Bill may be sent to you or to him.

261. W. W. to JOHN TAYLOR

MS. Harvard University Library.
K (—). LY i. 259.

Rydal Mount
21st Nov^{br} 1826

My dear Sir,

Having an opportunity of a Frank by this Post I avail myself of it to thank you for your obliging Letter, this moment received. It gave me much concern to hear from Sir G. B. how ill you had been used—it is some consolation however when one supposed Friend[3] has betrayed you to find that he has created an opportunity for so many true ones to give proof of their good wishes. I shall be

---

[1] John Simpson of the Nab.

[2] Stoddart's connection with the *New Times* ceased this year with his appointment as Chief Justice in Malta.

[3] Taylor had sold his paper *The Sun* the previous year to a journalist named Murdo Young, who changed its politics. The reference may be to him, or possibly to an unsatisfactory business partner of Taylor's.

glad and proud to have my name enrolled in this list,[1] upon the present occasion. It becomes me also to thank you for your obliging Letter and the elegant Sonnet with which you have honored me: My Vols[2] have long been out of print, but I believe a few Copies of the Quarto Edit: of the Excursion are in Mr Longman's hands, and it is my wish to present you with one—be so kind therefore as to forward to Mr L. the slip of paper on the opposite page, and I have no doubt that he will readily comply with my request.

I had the pleasure of seeing much of our common Friend Sir G. B. who (along with Mr Rogers) was down here last Summer. He was wonderfully well, and enjoyed his old haunts with a freshness most enviable.—

Believe me, my dear Sir, with kindest regards in which Mrs W. unites

very faithfully yours
Wm Wordsworth

262. W. W. to MESSRS. LONGMAN AND CO.[3]

MS. Amherst College Library. Hitherto unpublished.

Rydal Mount
22nd Nov^{br} 1826

Be so kind as to let Mr Taylor have one of the remaining Quarto Copies of the Excursion.

I am Gentlemen
sincerely yours
Wm Wordsworth

263. W. W. to RICHARD SHARP

MS. untraced.
Bookseller's Catalogue.

Rydal Mount,
22 Nov. 1826.

. . . Italy is seldom out of my mind—I talked much with Rogers about it and with Sir George—but I have taken no step yet. . . .

[*cetera desunt*]

[1] i.e. the list of subscribers for his *Poems on Various Subjects*, 2 vols., 1827.
[2] The *Miscellaneous Poems*, 4 vols., 1820.
[3] Originally attached to the previous letter.

264. W. W. to JOHN MURRAY

MS. untraced.
Samuel Smiles, A Publisher and His Friends, Memoir and Correspondence of the late John Murray, 1891, ii. 245.

Rydal Mount, near Ambleside,
December 4th, 1826.

Dear Sir,

I have at last determined to go to the Press with my Poems as early as possible. Twelve months ago they were to have been put into the hands of Messrs. Robinson and Hurst, upon the terms of payment of a certain sum, independent of expense on my part; but the failure of that house prevented the thing going forward. Before I offer the publication to any one but yourself, upon the different principle agreed on between you and me, as you may recollect, viz: the author to meet two-thirds of the expenses and risk, and to share two-thirds of the profit, I think it proper to renew the proposal to you.[1] If you are not inclined to accept it, I shall infer so from your silence; if such an arrangement suits you, pray let me *immediately* know; and all I have to request is, that without loss of time, when I have informed you of the intended quantity of letter-press, you will then let me know what my share of the expense will amount to.

I am, dear Sir,
Your obedient Servant,
Wm Wordsworth

---

[1] The previous summer W. W. had reopened negotiations with Murray, who consulted Lockhart, and some preliminary arrangement seems to have been arrived at on the terms previously agreed by Rogers. When, however, Murray failed now to reply promptly to this letter, W. W. interpreted his silence as a refusal, and offered the proposed edition of 750 copies on these same terms to Longman, who accepted on 27 Dec. (*WL MSS.*)

265. W. W. to EDWARD MOXON¹

Address: Mr. Edward Moxon, Messʳˢ Longman and Co, Paternoster Row.
Postmark: 8 Dec. 18[   ].
MS. Berg Collection, New York Public Library.
Mem. K (—). *LY i. 260.*

[*c.* 7 Dec. 1826]

Dear Sir,

It is some time since I received your little Vol: for which I now return you my thanks, and also for the obliging Letter² that accompanied it.

Your poem I have read with no inconsiderable pleasure; it is full of natural sentiments and pleasing pictures. Among the minor pieces, the last pleased me much the best, and especially the latter part of it.—This little Vol., with what I saw of yourself during a short interview, interest me in your welfare; and the more so, as I always feel some apprehension for the destiny of those who in Youth addict themselves to the Composition of verse. It is a very seducing employment; and though begun in disinterested love of the Muses is too apt to connect itself with self-love and the disquieting passions which follow in the train of that our natural infirmity. Fix your eye upon acquiring Independence by honorable business, and let the Muses come after rather than go before.—Such lines as the latter of this Couplet

> Where lovely woman, chaste as Heaven above,
> Shines in the golden virtues of her love,

and many other passages in your Poem give proof of no commonplace

---

¹ Edward Moxon (1801–58) had been introduced to W. W. by Lamb the previous Sept. (*Lamb*, iii. 56–7): '. . . pray pat him on the head, ask him a civil question or two about his verses, and favour him with your genuine autograph'. His 'little volume' *The Prospect and other Poems* appeared this year, dedicated to Rogers. He had been in Longman's business since 1821, but in 1830 Rogers advanced him £500 to start publishing on his own account in New Bond St. In 1833 he moved to larger premises at 44 Dover St. The same year he married Lamb's adopted daughter Emma Isola. In 1834 he brought out a selection of W. W.'s poems, and in 1835 published for W. W. jointly with Longman; in 1836 he became W. W.'s sole publisher. In 1830 and 1835 he published his own sonnets, dedicating the second volume, 1835, to W. W. For the history of their relationship, see H. G. Merriam, *Edward Moxon, Publisher of Poets*, New York, 1939, pp. 130 ff.

² Moxon had written enthusiastically on 12 Oct. about his recent visit to Rydal Mount: 'The Autumn of eighteen hundred and twenty six is an era in my Life never to be forgot . . .', signing his letter 'Your devoted Servant and admirer' (*WL MSS.*).

sensibility. I am therefore the more earnest that you should guard yourself against this temptation.

Excuse this freedom; and believe me my dear Sir very faithfully
Your obliged Ser^{vnt}
Wm Wordsworth

266. D. W. to H. C. R.

Address: To H. C. Robinson Esqre, 3. King's Bench Walk, Temple.
Postmark: 26 [? Dec.] 1826. *Endorsed*: 18 Decr 1826, Miss Wordsworth.
MS. Dr. Williams's Library.
K (—). *Morley, i. 170.*

Rydal Mount Decr 18th [1826]

My dear Friend,

I have little to say but thanks for your lively and very interesting sketch of your Irish Tour.[1] My Brother is much pleased with it; and you will not doubt, knowing my delight in travelling, that the dreary tracts you sometimes passed through did not deter me from a wish, at some period, to visit the Giants' Causeway and the Devils' Haunts—the soft Lakes of Killarney—the towers—the ruins etc etc I enter entirely into your notions of Dublin in comparison with Edinburgh; and can even sympathise with your pleasure in O'Connell's society, and think *your* loss was gain in travelling by the wrong road, thereby securing an eight-hour's discuss with that Champion of the Papists—and of LIBERTY, you will say,—Well let that pass—I will not inquire after the treason you talked—nor, if you should in an unguarded moment let it out will I inform against you—and if ever we *should* go to Ireland should like very well to be introduced to the Domain of Darinane[2]— and have no horror even of the Mansion and the Priest under the sanction of your guidance and my Brother's protection. But Ireland, and even North Wales do not make any part of my present travelling wishes,—nor have I any that can be absolutely termed *hopes*; for my dear Nieces long-delayed recovery keeps us still anxious and watchful—not that we apprehend danger if proper means be used; but it seems nearly certain that change of air and scene will be required as soon as weather will permit in the Spring,—and this

[1] For H. C. R.'s Irish tour the previous summer, and his meetings with Daniel O'Connell, see Sadler, ii. 331 ff. He had returned home through Ambleside early in October. (see *HCR* i. 339–40), while D. W. was at Coleorton.

[2] Derrynane, O'Connell's residence in Co. Kerry, where H. C. R. stayed 16–18 Aug.

conviction prevents us from looking at, or contriving any thing disconnected with her state of health. *She* talks with glee of Italy, but such a journey could not be accomplished without strength to begin with;—and a salutary change for her may be procured at much less expence. Most likely she will be taken into Somersetshire by her Mother, and that expence would make us less able to face a greater.—Such are my feelings and opinions at present and I go still further—thinking that Funds would be wanting for a Family journey to such a distance, yet my Brother *talks* of it—and it is well, if only for an amusement.—You will be glad to hear, that a physician of great practice whom we have consulted agrees with our Apothecary in opinion that there are no consumptive symptoms in Dora—that she is only debilitated by the several severe attacks she had in the Autumn, which a previous derangement of stomach rendered her peculiarly unable to resist.—She is very much better within the last three weeks, and rides on horseback whenever we have a fine day.

What do you know or hear of the Clarksons? I wrote to Mrs C. before leaving home in February, wrote again from Herefordshire —and yet once more since my return, begging for an answer immediately, and no answer arrives. I fear she is sick, or at least in a languid and depressed state of mind, for though not given to frequent letter-writing, I never knew her slow to answer inquiries.— Miss Hutchinson had one letter from her during my absence. She was then tormented with the Erysypilis (I always forget how that word is spelt) and I fear it is still hanging upon her—or that Mr Clarkson may be ill. Do tell me all you know—I include Tom's condition in the inquiry.

We expect John from Oxford this week. He was to take his degree today, wrote in good spirits after passing the examination, and the same post brought a satisfactory letter from his Tutor, lamenting his illness in the summer, and consequent inability to study having prevented him from going up for honours, which, 'from the manner he passed the examination,' he had 'no doubt he would have attained'.

What do you say to the War?[1] It seems there never was one which so few voices were raised against. I am afraid of the French proving false, that is, of their seeking occasion to quarrel with us— if we once begin to fight with them again, farewell to Peace—

When you see Charles and Mary Lamb, give our kindest regards to them—I wish they would now and then let us see their handwriting—A single page from Charles Lamb is worth ten postages—

[1] The French army was still in Spain. See L. 87 above.

however, it is well to hear good tidings and we have no right to complain of their silence. Your assurance that they were well and in good spirits gave [us]¹ great satisfaction.

My Brother does really intend, by the same Lady who conveys this to London, to write respecting the publishing of his poems— *to Longman.* I heartily wish that an agreement, and speedy printing may follow. He has lately written some very good Sonnets. I wish I could add that the 'Recluse' was brought from his hiding-place.

The eyes continue well, and as active and useful as any eyes in the house.—I will conclude with begging you to send your Extract concerning Goddard² as soon as you can; but not till you can add to it a *letter*—though but a little one—however the longer the better—You cannot think what pleasure we have in hearing from you. Excuse my penmanship, and accept the good old wish 'A merry Christmas to you and a happy new year!' from your grateful and affectionate Friend D Wordsworth

Have you chanced to see Miss Coleridge? She is in London. The Southeys are well—Mrs Coleridge in sad spirits about her son Hartley. He has been on his wanderings nearly a month.³ Derwent has a Curacy⁴ in Cornwall. Report speaks well of his performances in the pulpit.

My Brother, sister, Miss Hutchinson, Dora and Willy all beg their kindest remembrances.

267. W. W. to WILLIAM STRICKLAND COOKSON

Address: W. Strickland Cookson Esqʳᵉ, 6 Lincoln's Inn. [*In M. W.'s hand*]
Postmark: 26 Dec. 1826. *Endorsed*: W. Wordsworth. 26 Decʳ 1826.
MS. Yale University Library.
LY i. 261.

[*c.* 22 Dec. 1826]

My dear Sir,
     Thanks for the Inscription,⁵ it had need to be taken care of, being so expensive.—

¹ *MS. torn.*
² See L. 47 above and L. 279 below. The reference is to H. C. R.'s note placed in 1827 before the *Elegiac Stanzas* (*PW* iii. 193).
³ '. . . Hartley after a long course of vagabondism is now lodged at the Red Lion, Grasmere. . . . We hear bad reports of Sir Rᵈ [le Fleming]—his Lady has a good character for judicious management of him, but I suppose he is beyond her power to keep in decent order. Hartley is his occasional visitor.' M. W. to William Jackson, 15 Jan. 1827 (*Cornell MSS.*).
⁴ At Helston.   ⁵ i.e. the registration of one of W. W.'s share holdings.

I am quite at a loss to know what I have gained by the Bonus of which so much used to be said—It would be adding to the many obligations I owe you if at your perfect leisure and convenience you could learn this, and state it to me in a way that would be intelligible to one of my slender comprehension for things of this sort.

We expect John in two or three days. He was to take his degree last Monday, having passed his Examination ten days ago with much credit. You perhaps know that the failure of his Health, when he returned to close study last August, rendered it necessary that he should give up aiming at Honors, which we are assured he would otherwise have attained, so that we are quite satisfied with his University Career.

Miss Hutchinson has just returned from a visit of a month to Kendal.

Dora who has long been in a poorly way, we hope is better; but still very weak and incapable of exertion, and wholly unfit for any kind of exposure—

With many thanks for your attention and all the kind regards of the season from all here I remain

my dear friend
faithfully yours
Wm Wordsworth

268. W. W. to MRS. RICHARD WORDSWORTH[1]

MS. WL. Hitherto unpublished.

[? early 1827]

Dear Mrs Wordsworth,

I have just received your Letter. I hope that the apprehensions respecting the irregularity of Mr Slee's[2] account in the case of Wilkinson are more than the occasion calls for.

Some time since Mr Carter returned to you Mr Slee's account with remarks upon it respecting points which required elucidation, with an earnest request to Mr Slee for Mr Drury's[3] banking account; which request I have myself repeatedly enforced. This day

[1] This letter about the administration of R. W.'s estate cannot be dated exactly, nor can all the persons mentioned in the business transactions it refers to, be identified.

[2] Isaac Slee, land agent at Tirril, nr. Penrith (see *MY* ii. 383).

[3] Perhaps Joseph Drewry, grocer, of the Market Place, Penrith.

Mr Slee will again be written to in such terms that I hope the result will be an immediate production of the Account. Should this not be so or the account prove unsatisfactory Mr Carter will go over to Penrith, and examine every thing to the bottom.

The interest that has been paid on my Brother's bond to me is 100 pounds. Mr Slee is in no arrears either upon that Bond or to Miss Knott.[1] I have ordered the £100 accruing from Mr [? Rushworth's] debt to be paid over to me which of course will relieve my demand of interest next year.

I am very sorry to hear that you have had so much sickness and sorrow in your Family. Dora continues far from well; indeed she has been looking ill for upwards of two years. She has never cast off the late feverish complaint, so . . .

[half a page torn away]

. . . eleven hundred pound has been paid to me upon the Bond—what was paid to Mr Hutchinson I do not know, but of course there are no arrears there, nor to Miss Knott,—her interest was received I believe through Mr A. Harrison.[2]

269. W. W. to MESSRS. LONGMAN AND CO.

MS. Harvard University Library.
LY i. 262.

Kendal. 2nd Janry 1827

Gentlemen

I have sent by this night's Manchester Mail, Swan with two necks, Lad Lane, a parcel, containing the 1st Vol: of my Poems,[3] and a portion of the Excursion and a Letter for you—Should it not come punctually be so good as to inquire after it.

sincerely yours
Wm Wordsworth

[1] See *MY* i. 464–5.
[2] Anthony Harrison, the Penrith attorney.
[3] Having accepted W. W.'s terms, Messrs. Longman were now printing the 5-vol. edition of 1827, the first complete edition to include *The Excursion*; and W. W. was busy this month preparing the copy. M. W. wrote to William Jackson on 15 Jan.: 'W's eyes are famous—and I hear his voice below murmuring over the work he is about to forward to the press; but tho' able to read himself he still requires a help-mate—and as soon as I have done scribbling to you I must join him' (*Cornell MSS.*).

270. D. W. to H. C. R.

Address: To H. C. Robinson Esqre, 3 King's Bench Walk, Temple, London.
Postmark: 9 Jan. 1827. *Stamp*: Kendal Penny Post. *Endorsed*: 6th Jany, 1827.
Miss Wordsworth.
MS. Dr. Williams's Library.
K (—). *Morley, i. 173.*

Rydal Mount 6th Jan^ry. [1827]

My dear Friend,

I took the opportunity of a private hand to send you our Christmas good wishes, which partly reconciles me to putting you to the expence of postage, for another letter of as little worth as the former, as far as regards yourself; however, as you have no greater pleasure than in obliging your friends, I know not but that you may be thankful even for this poor scrawl, the object of which is to point out a means by which you may possibly do a service (not a very important one I grant) to a person whom we have long known and esteemed.

You once met, at Southeys, a Mr Kenyon, and, having met, I think cannot have forgotten him—Oh no! *that* you *cannot*, for it has just come into my recollection that he dined with us in Gloucester place, in 1820—when the wedding-cake was cut—a sort of Christmas feast before its time—when poor Thomas Monkhouse Charles Lamb, my Brother and you made a company of Sleepers after dinner—Was he, or was he not there? When I began this sentence I surely thought he was;—but my Sister, who sits beside me, says not—and now I begin to doubt. Well this same Mr Kenyon has written to my Sister for the family interest, and I will, as the easiest mode of explaining, quote from his own letter 'The fact is, I am desirous (I will not say anxious—the word would be untruly strong!) to be a member of the Athæneum Club,[1] and am to be balloted for on Monday, the 5th of February. On looking over the List of Members I see some names of your Friends. Amongst them that of H. C. Robinson, your travelling companion, and Allan Cunningham. If these Gentlemen are likely to be in London at that time, perhaps I might be allowed to ask your interest with them to give me their votes and their interest—on this occasion. You may venture to represent me as a Man who will not steal the silver spoons, who do not wear creaking shoes,— and as a good listener' etc. He adds, 'Sir George Beaumont and

---

[1] The Athenaeum had been founded in 1823, largely through the efforts of John Wilson Croker. See Croker's *Correspondence and Diaries* (ed. Jennings), i. 253 ff. H. C. R. was one of the first members (see Sadler, ii. 275–6).

Rogers, I see, both belong to the Club—but these are old Men not to be teized to think of trifles, or to go out on a February Even^g.'

I need say no more on this subject except (which I suppose may not be necessary for you to know) that Mr Kenyon's address is, No 7 Upper Church Street, *Bath*, but if you *should* have any thing to say on the matter I am sure he would be glad to hear from you.

Since I last wrote we have heard from Mrs Clarkson. I need not repeat the distressing contents of her letter. No doubt you are acquainted with poor dear, Mr Clarkson's past and present state. She had undergone great anxiety; but at the time of writing seemed to consider him as out of danger, and the symptoms of mortification (in the Leg) stopped; the whole, however, was sad news, for we cannot but fear an entire breaking up of that good Man's constitution.

—I was happy to hear of Tom Clarkson being in perfect health, with encreasing business—and why does not the marriage[1] take place? Thus people wait till 'All the life of life is gone'—

I have the same good tidings for you of my Brother's eyes. We have now no dread of proof sheets; but are *hoping* for their arrival before the end of next week. Longman has agreed to his Terms, and the poems were to go to press immediately, and proceed with all possible speed.

My dear Niece's health is very much improved—She gains strength and flesh. True, she is still invalidish and will probably be so through the winter; but there seems to be no present cause for anxiety, and, through God's blessing, we trust to the Spring for perfect restoration.

The weather is now as wintry as it can be. Ponds are all frozen and thronged with Skaters and Sliders—the Lakes not yet frozen. Strong winds have prevented this. My Brother is Christmassing at Sedbergh with his Son John at his (John's) old Schoolmasters'. We expect them at home again on Monday.

I have today received a letter from my Nephew John (of Cambridge) he says 'You will be pleased to hear that my Father is gradually gaining ground, in spite of the troubles and anxieties of his Vice-chancellorship.[2] The improvement in his appearance, however has not kept pace with that of his strength,—and [any][3] person who should judge of him by his looks [could] not form a just

---

[1] See L. 197 above.

[2] This was C. W.'s second term as Vice-Chancellor. See L. 8 above.

[3] *MS. torn.*

estimate of his progress. His face is thin and wrinkled; and he says of himself "I can count all my bones," but his spirits are good, and, I think, his strength fully reestablished, and he takes great pains to convince himself and others that the state of thinness is favorable to health!!' I suppose you know that this good Brother of mine was dangerously ill in the summer.

My dear Friend you must forgive my scrawling penmanship. I hope to hear from you very soon—Remember your promise of the journal extract.[1] You will also have to tell us what you mean to do respecting Mr Kenyon: My sister, Miss H. Dora, and Willy send kind remembrances and good wishes.

Believe me ever your affectionate Friend, D Wordsworth.

Mrs Clarkson speaks of your poor Brother and his domestic arrangements.

271. W. W. to SAMUEL ROGERS

Address: Sam¹ Rogers Esqʳᵉ, St James' Place.
MS. Cornell. Hitherto unpublished.

[*In M. W.'s hand*]

Rydal Mount
Janʳʸ 12ᵗʰ 1827

My dear Rogers,

Mr Kenyon of Bath is desirous of being elected into the Athenaeum—he is a valued Friend of our's. Pray give him if not engaged, your vote and interest at the ballot which is to take place on the 5ᵗʰ of Febʳʸ.

Mr K. is much attached to literature and the arts—has travelled much, and is in powers of conversation surpassed by few—so that he would be a real acquisition to any Society.

There was some mistake about the brushes sent to Southey—so that I can only thank you for your kind intentions. I follow your System however so far, as to scrub with a rough towel for the present.

At last my Poems are in the Press with Longman—upon the terms you made with Murray.

Dora has had a long and languishing illness, but thank Heaven she is now much better—and would she stoop to take more care of

---

[1] About Goddard.

herself than young People generally do, we trust the Summer will restore her. Remember us all most kindly to your Sister and accept yourself our good wishes.

Ever your affec Friend
[*signed*] Wm Wordsworth

272. D. W. to MARY LAING

Address: To Miss Laing, at Wm Laing's Esqre, Lauriston Place, Edinburgh.
Postmark: 24 Jan. 1827. *Stamp*: Kendal Penny Post.
MS. Edinburgh University Library.
The Wordsworth–Laing Letters (—).

Rydal Mount near Kendal
January 23rd 1827

My dear Miss Laing,

My Brother would have written immediately to thank Mr David Laing for his valuable present,[1] had he not hoped in the course of a week or two to be able to give him his opinion on Dunbar's poems, which an unusual press of business, with other engagements, has hitherto prevented him from looking over. In a week or two, he expects to be at leisure, and will with the greatest pleasure read over, and, if needful, *study* the pages of the old Poet: however, as it may possibly be that his present occupations may detain him longer than he reckons upon, he is glad of the opportunity of first returning his best thanks to your Brother, through me. I received your pleasant letter in Herefordshire and have often reproached myself for not replying to it 'very soon' as you, with your accustomed kindness, expressed a wish that I would do so— and so I did intend to do, but—Nay I will not trouble you with a dull story of procrastination—but, beginning with an assurance that I have often thought of you and of Edinburgh, and your good Mother—and of the kindness of all your Family, I will tell you briefly how we have been going on. You know that I went into Herefordshire last February. There I remained till the beginning of September, staying a week at Worcester, another week at Leamington, above a Month at Sir George Beaumont's in Leicestershire, and a couple of days at Liverpool—on my homeward way. Here I arrived on the 4th of November—and, though I had had much satisfaction in the society of excellent Friends and much pleasure in seeing many interesting places, truly thankful I was

---

[1] Probably Laing's edition of *Early Metrical Tales*, 1826.

to be once again at Rydal Mount. The Country appeared to me more beautiful than ever. No disparagement to Herefordshire! for I was there delighted with the rich fields and woods and scattered hills and Orchards—but the contrast of rocks, mountains and un-cultivated pasturage—not to speak of the bright lakes—while it did not tempt me to detract from the other, rendered these a hundred times more interesting. I found all the Family in perfect health except my poor Niece, who in September had a severe attack of Diarrhoea, of which I, at a distance, knew nothing till all danger was supposed to be over; therefore I had been spared a great anxiety. You may judge how ill she was—for her Mother and Aunt were obliged to sit up with her eleven nights. At the time of my return she looked very delicate; and still continues so—being very subject to take cold on the Chest: but we hope that after a winter spent in perfect quietness at home, we shall see her in the Spring in better health than for two years past. Her spirits are excellent. She rides on horseback whenever the weather permits; but that has not been often lately, the state of the air has been so changeable. My Brother's eyes are become again useful. He holds the pen himself, and even reads aloud to us by candle-light. This happy change, through God's blessing, has been brought about by touching the eyelids with blue stone. A very few applications were sufficient. Your Mother, I know, suffered greatly from sore eyes; but in her case the cause did not, as I remember, like my Brothers', originate in the lids. I think when I last wrote to you, Miss Joanna Hutchinson was in Herefordshire. She remained there till June, when she accompanied one of her Brothers[1] to the Westmorland Election, and after spending seven or eight weeks at Rydal Mount, proceeded with him to the Isle of Man, where they settled them-selves for the Winter with great satisfaction. Every letter was filled with the comforts, the pleasures and the cheapness of the place; but alas! before Christmas she met with a frightful accident. While standing on the Quay at Douglas, she was thrown down by a rope, borne home by two men, and was supposed to have dis-located her hip. You know what a patient chearful Creature she is, and in a fortnight after the accident, when she could not stir one foot before the other without help of two [ ][2] she wrote in great spirits—thankful that it was no worse with her. You will, I am sure, rejoice to hear that the injury was not so great as was at first supposed, yet we are afraid she will never perfectly recover the free use of the limb; though, with help of a stick she now walks

---

[1] Henry Hutchinson.   [2] *MS. torn.*

from room to room, and even down stairs; and is herself hopeful that in the spring she may be able to go about as usual. I need not tell you how much her Sisters and all of us were distressed, at the idea of her being confined to her bed, without any female relative near her, or any Friend but the woman of the house where she lodges; yet she, good Creature! has never given way to lamentations: her letters only breathe the spirit of thankfulness for the kindness with which she has been nursed. She says there never was a better woman, or a more tender nurse than Mrs Bridstone of Douglas, at whose house you may direct to her if you should feel inclined at any time to indulge her with a letter.

What if you should take it into your head to have a trip in a Steam-packet from Glasgow to the Isle of Man! It is a spot well worth seeing—lodgings and provisions are cheap—the voyage not expensive—the distance short—and, best of all, the sight of you would delight our dear Friend. Many a pleasant Chat would you have together. Her rambles on foot, I fear, must henceforward be very short—but her Brother is a good walker.

Since I left Brinsop Court Mrs Hutchinson is become the happy Mother of a third Daughter[1] (she has two sons). Her youngest but one, my God-daughter,[2] is six years and a half old, and another Child was never expected nor wished-for a year ago—but it seems to be no less of a treasure than any one of its Brothers and Sisters; and the Mother's health, which was before very delicate, has been greatly improved ever since her pregnancy. She now writes that both she and her Baby thrive to admiration. I have told you we hope that my Niece, if we can guard against cold this winter, will be stronger than of late years. Our reason for this hope is, that she has regained a healthful appetite, and her digestion is much improved. *Your* Brother will be glad to hear that *my* Brother's poems in five volumes, including the Excursion with considerable additions,—are in the press. We hope they will be out in April at the furthest. He intends to desire Longman to forward a Copy to Mr David Laing as soon as the Work is published. Most likely the Concern in South Bridge Street has regular communication with the Longman's—but if not, pray inform us to what other Bookseller it may be sent in order that without a separate expence your Brother may have it as speedily as possible. I am desired to add that if your Father and Brother will spread the information of the new Edition being in the press they will oblige my Brother. Should you travel southward next summer, all who *have* seen you would rejoice—

[1] Sara (Sally) Hutchinson (1827–69).   [2] Elizabeth (Ebba).

and all who have *not* would be truly glad of the opportunity of becoming personally acquainted with you Adieu. Ever your affect^e Friend

Dorothy Wordsworth

I have not room for more than best regards to all your household.

273. W. W. to WILLIAM JACKSON

Address: Revd Wm Jackson, Queen's Coll., Oxon.
MS. Amherst College Library.
LY i. 262 (—).

26th Jan^{ry} [1827]

My dear Friend,

In consequence of your Letter just received we have thought it best that John[1] should set off for Oxon. this day.—

I shall be much obliged if you give him any advice and occasional attention that might tend to make his mind more firm and resolute in respect to the Profession which he is about to undertake; and to point out any thing respecting his course of study that would be useful.

I write in a great hurry—so you will excuse this abrupt scrawl. Should there be an opening in any corner, as at Magdalen, for him I should be well pleased; and I doubt not that you will be so kind as to keep your eye upon that point.

John will tell you every thing about us. Farewell and believe me very faithfully yours

W. Wordsworth

[*M. W. writes*]

Thank you my dear friend for your most kind letter—I should like to gossip a while with you, but I only have time to join my entreaties to the above suggestions for John's welfare—I crave such advice and support as you (from the great affection and respect he bears to you) are better able than any one else to afford him. I am necessarily very anxious about him.—Dora has you will be sorry to hear been thrown back by a very bad cold—she is mending but confined to her room—John will tell you all about her and

---

[1] John W. had taken his degree at Oxford in December, and was now preparing to take Orders. (He had applied the previous autumn to Blomfield, Bishop of Chester.) It looks from this letter as if W. W. had not entirely abandoned hope of his son obtaining preferment in Oxford.

others. Do let us hear from you soon—John is a bad correspondent I am sorry to say.

> God bless you and believe me ever most aff^ly yours
>> M. Wordsworth

Jan^ry 26.

274. W. W. and D. W. to H. C. R.

Address: To H. C. Robinson Esqre, 3 Kings Bench Walk, Temple, London. *Postmark*: 31 Jan. 1827. *Endorsed*: 29th Jany 1827. Wordsworth, business. *MS. Dr. Williams's Library.*
K (—). *Morley, i. 177.*

29th January [1827]

My dear Friend,

Thanks for the trouble you have taken in reporting this Conversation.[1] It has ocurred too late to be of use. My Poems have for this month past been printing with Mr Longman—upon the same terms as agreed upon with M.—With this latter my dealings have been as follows—Rogers, after waiting for half a year, came to the preliminaries of an arrangement, that M—should publish for one third of the profits, meeting one third of the expense and risk—upon this I wrote to know what the expense would be, and waited a long time, many months, without getting an answer—I then wrote to M. that, not hearing from him, I felt myself at liberty to enter into a treaty elsewhere accordingly I did so with Hurst etc. His failure last year stopped this—and something more than two months since I wrote to M—offering him the work upon the old terms, and begging an immediate answer, which, I told him, if I did not receive, I should regard his silence as evidence that the engagement did not suit him—I waited about a month, and receiving no answer wrote to Longman, and the work went to press with him immediately upon the terms mentioned—

You see, then, I can have little to say to M— It is remarkable that by the same Post as brought your Letter I had one from Col. Pasley, in which he had occasion to speak of M's inattention as a Publisher, and his displeasing manners, so that he broke with him —for my own part, upon the whole, I am as well pleased that the

---

[1] In a letter of 26 Jan. (Morley, i. 176) H. C. R. reported a conversation the day before with John Murray, in which the publisher had confessed himself 'shamefully inattentive' to W. W.'s recent proposals and 'happy to publish his works *on his own terms*'.

book should be where it is—for M and I, I am persuaded could never agree.—So that you will treat the matter with him as you think proper, only it is fit I should say I have no wish but to be civil,—and upon friendly terms with him. I have revised the poems carefully particularly the Excursion—and I trust with considerable improvement; but you will judge—

The deaths you mention among your friends, gave me much concern—Flaxman's[1] I had heard of through the public papers— A. Robinson's[2] not till you named it.—Thanks for your exertions on behalf of our amiable friend Kenyon, we have procured him several Votes, and I could have got many more but my parliamentary and fashionable friends are almost all out of Town—

We continue to be anxious about my dear Daughter—she is so susceptible of colds—the treatment of which defeats the strengthening system, and throws her back—

I shall not want your note about Goddard immediately—so you will have leisure to procure a frank.—I wish I could get one for this scrawl which is not worth postage.

[*unsigned*]

[*D. W. writes*]

My dear Friend

My Brother has given me this most elegant epistle of his to fold up and finish. I have little to say but to confirm his account of poor Dora. She is now confined to her room; but this is at present owing to the severe weather; for the cough which first drove her thither has been subdued by a Blister.

My Brother's heart would be as much fixed as ever upon Italy, were not anxiety kept almost constantly alive. It is our decided opinion that she ought not to pass the next winter here; and all schemes must give way to her benefit. If she be strong enough for so very long a journey, a winter in Italy might be the best.—But funds will, I am sure, be deficient; and it is probable that some warm nook on the southern shore of England may be fixed upon when summer comes, the time for deciding.

[1] John Flaxman, the sculptor, had died on 7 Dec.
[2] H. C. R.'s friend Anthony Robinson (1762–1827), formerly of Kirkland, nr. Wigton, had died on 21 Jan. See Sadler, i. 358; ii. 378. He was educated for the Dissenting ministry in Bristol, but changing his views, returned to Wigton where he resided in the 1780s before going into business as a sugar-refiner in London. He wrote on religious and economic questions for the reviews. H. C. R. wrote his obituary in the *Monthly Repository*, i. new series (Apr. 1827), 188–93.

My Brother wishes his Son John's name to be put down as a candidate for membership of the University Club. He has taken his Bachelor's Degree and is of *New College*. Perhaps you may have in Town some University Friend, a Member of the Club, whom you can oblige my Brother by asking to do this service.—My sister and I fancy that through your acquaintance with Murray, you may dispose him to help a little in pushing the Sale of the Poems. It would, in his fashionable quarter, be of no small use if he would expose them on his Counter etc among his Tribe of popular Authors.—If you can conciliate him I am sure you will.—It gives us great satisfaction to hear of Mr Clarkson's continued amendment—You do not mention Charles Lamb and his Sister; I trust they continue not worse than when he wrote to me a most pleasant letter. Miss Lamb was then quite well; but he sadly afflicted with the cramp. The detail of his sufferings was mixed with so much drollery that it was impossible not to laugh, though we were, and are heartily sorry that he should have such torments to endure. His connexion with the British Museum[1] is the best thing possible—supplying every need that his withdrawing from the India House caused him to feel. Pray return him, for all of us, a thousand thanks for his letter, with our Love to him and his Sister.

My Sister Miss Hutchinson Dora and Willy join with me in best wishes—

Ever your affectionate and much obliged Friend
D. Wordsworth.

Is Mrs Robinson[2] living? (My old schoolfellow) and, if so, in what state of mind and health?—You will tell us when you write, whether or not you know a Friend who can put Johns' name down in the U. Club

275. W. W. to FREDERIC MANSEL REYNOLDS

MS. British Museum.
LY i. 263.

Rydal Mount near Ambleside
[? Feb. 1827]

My dear Sir,

I drop you this Note by a Friend going to London to thank you once more for the service your application has done my eyes.

---

[1] Lamb had become a regular reader there since his retirement.

[2] Anthony Robinson's second wife, who survived her husband and lived on at Enfield, near Charles Lamb. She was formerly Miss Lucock of Cumberland.

They have been infinitely better than I ever expected they would
be; indeed all but quite well, and perhaps if I had more courage in
applying the remedy they would be entirely without inconvenience.
I can now read two or three hours by candlelight, a practice I had
been obliged to abandon all together previous to the use of your
remedy.—

I could not deny myself the gratification of once more thanking
you, and letting you know this. Be assured that if ever I go to
London one of my first calls shall be to you, to repeat my acknowledgements, and for the pleasure of renewing my acquaintance with
one to whom I consider myself so much indebted.

Mrs W. and all my family join in kind remembrances and believe
me my dear Sir

Very faithfully
yours
Wᵐ Wordsworth

276. W. W. and D. W. to MARY LAING

Address: To Miss Laing, Lauriston, Edinburgh.
Postmark: 7 Feb. 1827. *Stamp*: Kendal Penny Post.
MS. Edinburgh University Library. Hitherto unpublishea.

> The Curfew tolls the knell of parting day;
> The lowing herd winds slowly o'er the lea;
> The ploughman homeward plods his weary way
> And leaves the world to darkness and to me.

Wᵐ Wordsworth
Febʳʸ 1827.

Rydal Mount.

[*D. W. writes*]

Tuesday 6ᵗʰ Febʳʸ. [1827]

My dear Miss Laing,

I have just enclosed with the picture[1] two scrawly Autographs,
with which I was so little satisfied that I have desired my Brother
to give me another on this paper, as you see, above. I am sorry

---

[1] Sir George Beaumont's picture (1811) suggested by W. W.'s poem
The Thorn, which he had presented to the poet. See I. F. note, *PW* ii. 511–12.
The painting was going on loan to the Scottish Academy Exhibition in Water-
loo Place, Edinburgh, in March.

I have not time but for a short letter, as the messenger is going to the post-office in a quarter of an hour.

My brother is happy to lend the picture but could not do so till he had Sir G. Beaumont's consent. I wrote on the receipt of yours and his answer is this day arrived. No time to be lost. We have got the picture packed and it will go by this Night's Coach to Kendal and thence by coach to Edinburgh, as directed.

In our hurry I believe the name is not put on the back of the picture. Be so good as to write upon a piece of paper and paste it on the back—

William Wordsworth Esqre
Rydal Mount
Westmorland—

Let us hear from you of the safe arrival of the picture; but pray do not pay postage. You ought to have it on the same day as this letter.

Inquire if it be not duly delivered. I need not say we highly value the picture, and shall be anxious to know of its safety.

Dora is a little better—but still confined to her Room.

Have you heard any thing of your lost watch and the Thieves? God bless you—

Not a Moment more
Yours ever
D W.

Address Rydal M^t near Kendal, because it is better known than Ambleside. We are at the same Rydal Mount—and hope to remain here for years to come.

Do not fail to put the name on the back of the picture.

277. W. W. to CHARLES WILLIAM PASLEY

MS. British Museum. Hitherto unpublished.

Rydal Mount Ambleside.
Feb^{ry} 6th 1827

My dear Sir,

Thanks for your obliging Letter. I cannot ascertain where the blame lies, or what has occasioned my not receiving your Book.[1] Mr Southey's came to hand in due time, and he thinks that he

---

[1] See L. 205 above.

might have forwarded a Copy for me; sure I am we never received it; and I am not aware that a parcel of ours has ever been lost between Keswick and Ambleside. Our things of that kind, I mean our lighter parcels, all come by the Coach which is carefully managed.

I think it would avail nothing to inquire after the Copy at Murrays; so I shall be glad to receive the Vol: (as you kindly renew the offer) through the hands of Messrs Longman; to be forwarded in Mr Southeys first Parcel.

I was upon the point of connecting myself with Murray as a Publisher, but he was so very inattentive to my Letters that I broke with him.

With kindest regards in which Mrs W and my Sister unite, I remain dear Sir

faithfully yours
Wᵐ Wordsworth

278. W. W. to WILLIAM SOTHEBY[1]

MS. Henry E. Huntington Library. Hitherto unpublished.

Rydal Mount
near Ambleside
Febʳʸ 6ᵗʰ 1827

My dear Sir,

I duly received both your Letters, for which and your obliging attention to my request in favor of my Friend Mr Kenyon[2] (who by the bye is also an intimate Friend of Mr Southey) I sincerely thank you.—

It gave me pleasure to learn from the Advertisement under cover with your former Letter, that you are about to favor the world with so splendid a publication as is there announced.—[3]

I was gratified the other day by meeting in Mr Alaric Watts' Souvenir with a very old acquaintance, a Sonnet of yours, which I had read with no little pleasure more than 30 years ago. 'I knew a gentle Maid'.[4]

---

[1] The poet and translator of Virgil. See *EY*, pp. 455–6.
[2] To support his candidature for the Athenaeum, which was successful (see Morley, i. 180).
[3] Sotheby's handsome folio *Georgica Publii Virgilii Maronis Hexaglotta*, 1827. Besides Sotheby's English version, it included translations in Spanish, German, Italian, and French. (See *R.M. Cat.*, no. 680.)
[4] Sonnet VIII, *A Fancy Sketch* (*Poems*, 1790, p. 53).

Mrs W. and my Sister unite with me in best regards, to your-self and Mrs and Miss Sotheby

> and believe me my dear Sir
> faithfully your obliged
> Wᵐ Wordsworth

279. D. W. to H. C. R.

Address: To H. C. Robinson Esqʳᵉ, 3, Kings Bench Walk, Temple.
Endorsed: 18 Feb: 1827, Miss Wordsworth (Sir Geo: Beaumont)
MS. Dr. Williams's Library.
K (—). *Morley, i. 181.*

18th Febʳʸ [1827]

My dear Friend,

A Frank tempts me to slip in our united thanks for your zeal in the cause of our Friend, Mr Kenyon—I assure you, as the French say it has not been bestowed upon an Ingrate—as you will yourself perceive if ever you meet him at the Club. He will then, I am sure be glad to hold discourse with you, and to tell you how much he has been pleased by your kindness and that of others of our Friends. It does indeed appear that he came in with a 'high hand'.

My Brother is much obliged to you and to your Friend Mr Rolfe[1] and for getting John's name put on the University Club's Boards and will be further obliged if you will place him on those of the Athenæum. It *may* be useful; and can do no harm.

He is now at Oxford studying Divinity, and we hope the result will be a steady determination to apply himself to the Duties of a Minister of our Church.

The printing of the poems goes on rapidly. My Brother inserts your note[2] (I believe with [out?] any alteration)—only perhaps something may be added to it; and, besides, one or two extracts will, I think, be inserted from our journals as notes to some other poems.

My Niece is much the same—not worse—but very delicate, and we are unceasingly anxious during this cold weather to keep her from injury. The present moon has brought that kind of fine weather which is delightful to the Strong for exercise; but very trying to invalids, though confined wholly to the house as she is.

[1] Robert Monsey Rolfe, 1st Baron Cranworth (1790–1868), an old friend of H. C. R.: M.P. for Penryn and Falmouth (1832), Solicitor-General (1834–9) a Judge (1839), and Lord Chancellor in Lord Aberdeen's cabinet from 1852.
[2] About Goddard. See L. 274.

A heavy snow is now on the ground, and still falling;—We hope a thaw will follow—Nothing can exceed the purity of the scene now before my eyes—How different to you in London if the same snow is falling on streets and houses!

The death of Sir George Beaumont[1] is a great affliction to us, and was also a severe shock: for when he was at Ry[d]al in the summer, and when I parted from him at Coleorton at the end of October, he was in as good health and spirits as he has ever been since we first knew him 23 years ago, and appeared as likely for life for eight years to come as any of our younger Friends, though his 73rd birthday was on the 6th of November.—Dear Lady Beaumont has been wonderfully supported hitherto; but I fear the worst *for her* is yet to come; and that strength and spirits may wholly fail; for she is of a weak bodily constitution, and after having lived with a Husband 50 years in perfect harmony, sharing in all his pursuits, the change must be dreadful—and *such* a husband!

Sir George Beaumont was buried on Wednesday—just a week after his Death—His illness was short—I believe not more than ten days. Charles and Mary Lamb will I know sympathize with us. They knew and highly valued our inestimable Friend. Give our love to them.

In haste ever your affec^{te}
D Wordsworth

280. W. W. to ROBERT SOUTHEY

MS. untraced.
Mem. K. LY i. 264.

[late Feb. *or* early Mar. 1827]

My dear Sir,

Edith thanked you, in my name, for your valuable present of the 'Peninsular War'.[2] I have read it with great delight: it is beautifully written, and a most interesting story. I did not notice a single sentiment or opinion that I could have wished away but one—where you support the notion that, if the Duke of Wellington had not lived and commanded, Buonaparte must have continued the the master of Europe. I do not object to this from any dislike I have

---

[1] On 7 Feb. See L. 282 below. He left £100 to Mrs. Coleridge and to Southey, and £100 together with a life annuity of a similar amount to W. W. The title now passed to his cousin (see L. 175 above).
[2] The second volume had just appeared.

to the Duke, but from a conviction—I trust, a philosophic one—that Providence would not allow the upsetting of so diabolical a system as Buonaparte's to depend upon the existence of any individual. Justly was it observed by Lord Wellesley, that Buonaparte was of an order of minds that created for themselves great reverses. He might have gone further, and said that it is of the nature of tyranny to work to its own destruction.

The sentence of yours which occasioned these loose remarks is, as I said, the only one I objected to, while I met with a thousand things to admire. Your sympathy with the great cause is every where energetically and feelingly expressed. What fine fellows were Alvarez[1] and Albuquerque;[2] and how deeply interesting the siege of Gerona![3]

I have not yet mentioned dear Sir George Beaumont.[4] His illness was not long; and he was prepared by habitually thinking on his latter end. But it is impossible not to grieve for ourselves, for his loss cannot be supplied. Let dear Edith stay as long as you can; and when she must go, pray come for her, and stay a few days with us. Farewell.

Ever most affectionately yours,
W. W.

281. W. W. to SAMUEL ROGERS

Address: S. Rogers Esq[re], St James Place.
Postmark: 12 Mar. 1827.
MS. Sharpe Collection, University College, London.
Rogers. LY i. 265.

Rydal Mount
10th March 1827

My dear Rogers,

I am going to address you in character of Churchwarden of little St Clement's East Cheap: how came *you* by this odd distinction?

My friend Mr Johnson[5] is Minister of that Church, and having heard that certain pictures, and a fund for the purchase of pictures, exist at the disposal of the British Institution for the decoration of

---

[1] Mariano Alvarez de Castro (d. 1809), the heroic defender of Gerona.

[2] The Duke of Albuquerque (1775–1810), the Spanish general: in 1810 appointed Ambassador in London, where he died soon after.

[3] See Southey's *History*, ii. 520–61. Gerona in Catalonia was besieged by the French in 1809.

[4] See previous letter.   [5] The Revd. William Johnson.

Churches, he has got a notion that, through your influence, one might be procured for his own church, and has begged me to intercede with you for that purpose. I have therefore readily complied with his request, though I should fear he may be too sanguine in his expectations.—

And now my dear friend let me condole with you on the loss we have sustained in the death of Sir George Beaumont. He has left a gap in private society that will not be filled up, and the public is not without important reasons to honor his memory and lament his loss.[1] Nearly five and twenty years have I known him intimately, and neither myself nor my family ever received a cold or unkind look from him. With what tender interest do I think of the happy hours we three spent together last summer

> I prized every hour that went by
> Beyond all that had pleased me before,
> And now they are passed and I sigh
> And I grieve that I prized them no more.

The printing of my poems is going on pretty rapidly.
Ever, with kindest regards from all here,
most faithfully yours,
W W

Dora is improved in health, but the severe weather confines her to her room.

282. D. W. to MARY LAING

Address: To Miss Laing, Wm Laing's Esqre, Lauriston, Edinburgh.
Postmark: 11 Mar. 1827. *Stamp*: Kendal Penny Post.
MS. Edinburgh University Library.
The Wordsworth–Laing Letters (—).

[*c.* 10 Mar. 1827]

My dear Miss Laing,

We were glad that the picture[2] arrived safe—the more so as it was even more precious to us than before; the Painter our inestimable Friend, being at the time your acknowledgement arrived lost to us in this world. He died on the morning of the 7th of

---

[1] After the purchase by the nation in 1824 of the Angerstein pictures, which became the nucleus of the National Gallery, Sir George Beaumont added sixteen of his own two years later. He also presented his Michelangelo bas-relief to the Royal Academy.   [2] See L. 276 above.

February. When my letter asking permission to lend it reached Coleorton he was very ill; but Lady Beaumont herself wrote, to say that Sir George 'could have no objection' and added some directions respecting packing the picture. She informed us of his illness; and we were, as you may suppose, anxious concerning him when we sent it off—but far from hopeless of his recovery. Very soon after came the afflicting tidings. His illness was sudden, he having been perfectly well and in excellent spirits, and possessing the full vigour of his amiable and cultivated Mind, till the moment of his seizure. The first symptom was a fainting-fit, succeeded by a severe bilous attack to which he had at times, through life, been subject. The Erysiplas came on in a few days, and attacking the head and throat speedily brought on his Dissolution. He was not ill more than ten days. In such cases sudden Death is a Blessing for through life he had not been less distinguished for his *virtues* than his talents. He was a pious Christian and never losing sight of the uncertainty of life, he was in a constant state of preparation for the last awful change. As he told me when I was walking with him in his own Grounds at the end of last October he was 73 years of age—and 'if he lived till next August' should have been married 50 years. The most perfect harmony had subsisted between him and Lady B. during that long period. They had been constant companions in all pursuits; and never having had Children, you may judge what they were to each other; and what a bereavement and desolation she must now feel. Nevertheless we have had the happiness of hearing that she does not sink under it; but on the contrary bears her affliction with pious resignation to the divine Will, and is in a state of perfect composure. Forgive me for dwelling so long on a painful subject—yet not wholly painful. There is much to console the Friends of the Deceased; and in our Minds regrets will always be mingled with pleasure, in recalling the happy hours spent in his society. He was a faithful Friend to my Brother for upwards of twenty years.

It is time to give you the comfort of knowing that my Niece's health has been gradually, though slowly, improving since I wrote to you, and that our anxiety is therefore much abated. She gains strength and her looks are improved, though the fresh air never blows upon her, she being still confined to her bed-room. Several attempts have been made to get her back again to the Family-room; but she has always caught cold, and we are now determined that she shall stay where she is in the same equable though not very warm air till this winter weather gives place to Spring. Her spirits are good though on Monday she suffered a great loss in the departure of Miss Southey[1] after a visit to us of two Months. We expect her Sister Bertha shortly; and I hope that *their* companionship will not be confined to the fire-side and the bed-room but that they may be able to ride on horseback together. Your Friend William is quite well—nearly as tall as his Father—but very thin——and far from healthy *looking*. My Brother and Sister are well. The poems go on with tolerable speed; but cannot be out before May. I cannot have expressed myself clearly respecting my Brother's wishes. He only meant that, if your Brother could spread by conversation in his Shop or elsewhere the knowledge that there was in the press—and soon would come out—such an Edition in 5 Volumes, he thought it might be of service. He had no idea whatever of being at the expence of *advertising* in Magazines. This I am sure your Brother's friendly disposition will induce him to do, independant of the value he may set upon the Poems. My Brother is very sorry he has not yet had leisure to look over Dunbar with that attention he would wish to bestow upon the old Bard. I can, however, answer for him that he will so employ the first leisure he has, and I hope it will be ere long. I am truly sorr[y for]² the delicate state of your health. This has been a sad winter for invalids, though we have had much pleasant weather for the Strong and Vigorous. The Lake of Rydal has been frozen over. My Brother and his Son William greatly enjoyed skaiting upon it. I hope you have kept close to the house, and that when warm weather comes I shall have better news both of your health and strength. Miss Joanna Hutchinson writes in very good spirits. She is still lame, but hopes for a perfect recovery. She continues as much pleased as ever with the little Island.[3] I suppose they have little snow there. Yesterday our coaches were stopped—and a large party from Ambleside who had gone to dine with a family near Bowness were on their return stopped by a snow-drift, and obliged to house themselves at a cottage which was fortunately close by. The frost is now very keen—and the sun shines so bright that it is painful to look out of the windows. I now sit in my own Room to write, without a fire—and have no need of one, the sun-shine is so hot. Pray remember me very kindly to your Father, Mother, and Brothers.

My Brother begs his kind regards to Mʳ David Laing. Believe me ever your affectionate Friend

D Wordsworth

[1] Edith Southey.   [2] *MS. torn.*   [3] i.e. the Isle of Man.

What do you think of the scene when the great Unknown[1] was revealed to all eyes? I like Sir Walter Scott very much—and could not but grieve at such display.

283. W. W. to BASIL MONTAGU

MS. untraced.
K. LY i. 266.

[*c.* 20 Mar. 1827][2]

My dear Montagu,

First I received four volumes of your Lord Bacon,[3] and then separately, through the hands of Mr Strickland Cookson, I believe, the fifth. No more have reached me; if the sixth has been sent through the same channel as the fifth it ought to be inquired after; otherwise a set may be broken. I had a letter from Mr S. Cookson about a fortnight ago and he made no mention of another volume having reached him.

I have nothing important to observe on your preface. It is judicious and written with spirit. The head of 'Ignorance' as an objection to change is not, I think, so well treated as the rest. 'Habit' ought to have been distinctly stated as giving an undue weight to the reasons which may exist for continuing practices for which better might be substituted. Weighty must habit be when it has anything of reason to aid it, if the poor Italian[4] can through its influence alone be so absurd as your story represents. Are you aware that the horrid practice of wife-sacrifice in India is the result of the policy of the polygamist husband to guard his own life from the attacks of the malcontents among his numerous wives, by making it a point of honour that such sacrifice should take place upon his decease? The natural dread of death gives the whole band an interest in prolonging his existence.

Ever sincerely yours,
W. W.

[1] This refers to the public dinner held on 23 Feb. 1827 when Scott's authorship of the Waverley Novels was revealed. See Lockhart's *Life of Scott*, vii. 17–20.

[2] Dated from postmark recorded by *K*.

[3] See L. 242 above.

[4] The preface referred to is in vol. v, 1826. Under the head of 'Ignorance' Montagu refers to the practice of some Italian peasants who load the panniers with vegetables on one side and stones on the other, because their forefathers had done the like. (De Selincourt's note.)

284. W. W. to JACOB FLETCHER

Address: J. Fletcher Esqr, Allerton, near Liverpool. [*In Dora W.'s hand*]
MS. Cornell.
K. LY i. 266.

Rydal Mount near Ambleside
12th April 1827

Dear Sir,

It was gratifying to be remembered after your long and interesting wandering—I shall take care of your obliging Letter,[1] and if my fortune should ever prove favorable to my wishes by allowing me to revisit the Alps I trust I shall profit by some of your notices. —I wish you had been a little more particular upon the scenery of the Appennines about which there is much disagreement of opinion.—

In alpine Switzerland I think there is a good deal of sameness—Switzerland must be taken altogether—the Jura, its vallies and the views of the Alps and the intermediate plain from its eminences never can be forgotten—and in thinking of the Alps one should always bear in mind both their Helvetian and Italian features, otherwise great injustice is done to this region which is the pride not of Europe only but of the globe—Fine scenery is more widely spread perhaps than you are willing to allow—though not in Europe—yet think of the Pyrenees, and many parts of Portugal and Spain—never scarcely was any region so overpraised as La *Belle* France—its climate is good but all the interior is tame—it has been well compared to a Shawl of which the beauties are all in the border. —I have heard indeed the bold coast, and deep inlets of Norway praised as the finest things in Europe—Sir Humphrey Davy was particularly lavish in extolling them—I write in haste. Let me beg that if you should be drawn this way you would favor me with your company, when we may talk over these things—with warm thanks I remain dear Sir

very sincerely your obliged
W Wordsworth

[1] Of 9 Apr., describing his continental travels (*WL MSS.*).

285. W. W. to SAMUEL CARTER HALL[1]

Address: S. C. Hall Esqr, *No. 24* Paternoster Row, London. [*In Dora W.'s hand*]
Postmark: 14 Apr. 1827.
MS. Cornell.
Broughton, p. 65.

Rydal Mount
Near Ambleside Kendal
12th April 1827

Sir,

I hasten to thank you for a Note and your valuable Present of the Amulet 1 and 2 Numbers, which though your obliging Note is dated Dec^br last only reached me yesterday—This delay may perhaps have been caused by the misdirection of the Parcel, Hambleside Rigdale Route instead of my right address as above. I am truly sorry for the delay whatever may have been the cause, as it has both subjected me to a possible charge of incivility or worse, in not acknowledging such a mark of attention, and prevented me enjoying sooner the contents of your interesting work. The Embellishments are elegant, and the literary part is conducted upon a principle that cannot but be highly approved, that of uniting *instruction* with amusement. Without any disparagement of other Articles I will name two or three of those which I have read with particular pleasure—The account of the Armenian Christians—The Pastor of the Lac de Joux, The Chaldean Christians—The Albigenses, A Tale of the French Revolution.—In naming them it is proper to add that I have not as yet had time to do more than dip into the Vols. Of the Poetry I have scarcely read any thing but many of the Authors' names are of good promise[2]—Wishing your work the success it deserves I remain Sir

sincerely your obliged servant
Wm Wordsworth

[1] Samuel Carter Hall (1800–89) edited *The Amulet, A Christian and Literary Remembrancer*, 1826–36; the *New Monthly Magazine*, 1832–6; and the *Art Union Monthly Journal* from 1839. His *Book of Memories of Great Men and Women of the Age*, 1871, is a mine of literary anecdote for the period.

[2] Contributors included John Clare, Bernard Barton, W. L. Bowles, James Montgomery, and Mrs. Hemans.

286. W. W. to JACOB FLETCHER

MS. untraced.
LY i. 267.

Rydal Mount
April 30th [1827]

My dear Sir,

With many thanks for the pleasure your Journals have afforded me, I avail myself of what I deem a safe opportunity of forwarding them to you, and shall be glad to find the packet reaches you.

ever sincerely
Your obliged Servt.
Wm Wordsworth

287. W. W. to SAMUEL CARTER HALL

Address: S. C. Hall Esqre, 2 East Place, Kennington Road, Lambeth, London
[*In M. W.'s hand*]
Postmark: 4 May 1827. *Stamp*: Kendal Penny Post.
MS. Broadley Collection, Archives Department of the Westminster Public Libraries.
Hitherto unpublished.

Rydal Mount
near Ambleside.
May 2nd [1827]

Dear Sir,

I regret that it is out of my power to meet the wish you have expressed in a manner so flattering to me. The Editors or proprietors of every annual Publication on the plan of yours have applied to me for contributions, and to all I have returned the same answer, that I never had been connected with any periodical publication, except once or twice, when I had sent articles to a newspaper, and that I had no intention to change the resolution I had made, to keep apart from that field.—It cost me a good deal to hold to this Resolve in the case of Mr Alaric Watts, who, though personally unknown to me, had taken a great deal of trouble in making arrangements respecting the new Edition of my Poems now on the point of appearing—If I could possibly have made an exception to my general Rule, it must have been in his behalf.

Mr Watts's Book[1] confines itself to amusement merely, and for

---

[1] *The Literary Souvenir.*

525

this reason the plan of it is less agreeable to my taste than your's.[1] For myself, amusement is never so sure to be attained in a miscellany publication as when information and instruction go along with it, or when it is sought through those channels.—

Being really interested in the success of your work, I am happy to learn that so many leading names are to be added to the stock of your Contributors, and with best wishes

I remain
dear Sir
respectfully
your obliged
Wm Wordsworth[2]

288. W. W. to MESSRS. LONGMAN AND CO.

MS. Amherst College Library. Hitherto unpublished.

Rydal Mount
May 10th [1827]

Dear Sirs,

This day I have received six copies of the poems, the parcel must have been sent off previous to your receipt of a letter of mine, begging that five or six copies of the Excursion might be added, with a copy of the third vol. of Kirby and Spence's Entomology;[3] as these have not arrived, and are not immediately wanted, let them be made up into a parcel, together with the sheets which are wanting to complete the copy of the poems, great part of which were sent down from Mr Shaw[4] by my son; Mr Shaw has been informed what they are, and I have no Doubt has taken care of them. This parcel need not be sent off but may remain under your care till an opportunity occurs of having it sent by a private hand.

I am pleased with the appearance of the books except an error in

---

[1] *The Amulet* aimed at uniting instruction with amusement, as W. W. noted in L. 285 above.

[2] Hall adds the following note, dated 1 Nov. 1842: 'Although I cannot go the length of some others in admiration of the poetry of Wordsworth, I am still very glad to learn from the public papers that Government has just awarded to him a pension of three hundred a year. My impression was that he had been so complimented some time ago . . .'

[3] William Kirby and William Spence, *An Introduction to Entomology*, 4 vols., 1815–26. Kirby (1759–1850) was rector of Barham, Suffolk.

[4] The printer.

apportioning the matter in the third vol. which is too large, the miscalculation was my own fault.

I remain Gentlemen your Obed^t S^t

Wm Wordsworth

PS I am anxious for the odd sheets above spoken of as without them the rest of the copy which I have got will be useless.

289. W. W. to ALARIC WATTS

MS. untraced.
Alaric Watts, i. 262.

May 21, 1827

My dear Sir,

Along with a copy of my new edition I directed that two should be enclosed to you to be forwarded, the one to Miss Jewsbury, the other to Mrs Hemans, believing that you are in communication with those ladies. Certainly any paper has my good wishes that promises to be judiciously conducted with a view to support the Protestant cause. I am not a friend to further concessions to the Catholics, being convinced that, as those restrictions are not the cause of the misery and discontent of Ireland, so the removal of them neither will, nor can, tranquilize that unhappy country. The present aspect of public affairs is to me anything but encouraging. You will not, however, be surprised when I say that I participate in little of the heat which the late changes[1] appear to have called forth in London.

With respect to the seceders, my opinion is that they have acted most injudiciously. It must have been galling, I own, to act under Mr Canning, or any other concessionist Minister; but surely it would have been much wiser to stomach that, and make the best of a bad state of things, than to leave their places empty to their

---

[1] Lord Liverpool had united his ministers behind him by declining to make Catholic emancipation a cabinet issue; but after he was permanently incapacitated by a stroke on 17 Feb., the Tory administration became openly divided on this matter, and it seemed inevitable that when the King sent for Liverpool's successor, the choice was bound to involve the defection of others. Canning, the Foreign Secretary, would not consent to serve under an anti-Catholic premier and although he made it clear when finally asked to form a ministry on 10 Apr. that emancipation would still not be a cabinet measure, this did not prevent Peel, Wellington, Eldon, and some others from resigning. Canning was consequently forced, in the few months of life left to him, to look increasingly to the Whigs for support, and Tory solidarity was seriously weakened.

adversaries. I have no doubt that numbers of the party are heartily sorry for having decided so hastily; and this brings me to a part of the case which bears upon your engagements with the *St. James's Chronicle* and the *Standard*.[1] Undoubtedly there exists at present a strong feeling to support the principles which those papers undertake to defend, but I am inclined to think that it will not be long before much of that feeling abates. If it be true that many seceders regret the course they have taken, it is to be expected that they will fall back into the ranks as soon as they decently and conveniently can; but in what a sad condition will they find the cause which they have conscientiously supported, compared with the state it would have been in, however far short of their and our wishes, provided they had never retired. It grieves me to speak in this manner of men to whom the country has such reason to be grateful for their public services; and who, in the steps they have taken, have, I sincerely believe, been as much guided by a sense of duty as we have a right to expect any party of men to be. I am sorry on their account; and when I look on the other side, what consolation can be found? If I grieve for Mr Canning's position, it is not more so than he must grieve for it himself. He can have no comfort, knowing what the opinions of the King are on the Catholic question; and feeling what compromises and sacrifices must be reciprocally made to keep him and his new friends together for an hour.

Mr Canning is a man to whom I am personally attached. His attentions to me have been beyond what I had the least right to expect. I had occasion to ask a favour of him, not as a member of Parliament, some time ago,[2] and he met my wishes with the most obliging readiness. It is far less on this account that I regret Mr Canning's present embarrassment than because I shall ever feel grateful to him for the services he rendered the country and the world during the long protracted struggle against the domination of Bonaparte. He was no doubt one of the principal agents in keeping the British army in the Peninsula, at a time when his new friends were clamouring for its recall, and doing all in their power to discourage our noble exertions, and animate our deadly enemy. For this I never can forgive the Whigs, or cease to deplore that a man like Canning should have been brought to unite with such

---

[1] Watts was invited this year by Messrs. Baldwin, proprietors of the *St. James's Chronicle*, to write also for their new paper, the *Standard*, which was committed to opposing the Catholic claims.

[2] In connection with the Merton Fellowship in 1825. See L. 206 above.

heartless politicians, Englishmen so unworthy of their name and their country.

Ever sincerely, your obliged friend
W. Wordsworth

290. D. W. to JOHN WORDSWORTH

Address: John Wordsworth, Esqre, Trinity College, Cambridge.
MS. British Museum. Hitherto unpublished.

Wednesday 6th June [1827]

My dear John,

On Monday evening at ten o'clock, Owen Lloyd,[1] who is at present staying with us, came in, brim-full of joy. He had heard, at Calgarth, of the honours[2] showered upon the three Brothers, and was the Bearer to our fire-side of the first tidings, of all except Charles's—which had given us infinite delight—in so much that his Uncle, and Cousin Dora, who were both then at home, determined instantly to write to him their congratulations—which was never done—owing to the bustle and preparations for their long journey to Harrowgate. On Monday Evening, Owen, in the eagerness of his joy decreed that a joint letter was to be written to congratulate the three together. *He* was to begin,—put it off till next morning—went off with John to Windermere—was detained all night at a Friend's house by rain,—and is not yet returned—and half an hour ago arrives your letter to Dora (which her mother and I have taken the liberty of opening) and I can wait no longer, so for the present you must be satisfied with this poor substitute for the gay Fancies with which no doubt your Cousin Owen would have entertained you.

John, William, Owen and your two Aunts sate round the fire for two hours talking about you; and it is hard to say which of us was most glad. We shall forward your letter today, to Harrowgate, whence I doubt not you will hear from Dora—and perhaps her

[1] Charles Lloyd's son who succeeded Daniel Green as curate of Langdale. See L. 152 above.
[2] D. W.'s nephews John and Christopher (both at Trinity College, Cambridge) and Charles (at Christ Church, Oxford) had all carried off notable University distinctions recently. John had gained the Porson prize and his college Reading prize; Christopher had won University and college prizes in Latin verse, and the much coveted English verse prize (with his poem *The Druids*); and Charles had added a Fell Exhibition to college and University prizes for Latin verse.

Father; for he is there. The Southeys and Miss Hutchinson first set forward, making a tour to the Caves. Your Uncle followed in a little pony-chaise with D. last Wednesday, and they reached Harrowgate in safety on Saturday evening after a most prosperous journey. The Invalid gained strength daily, and her cough yielded to change of air, therefore, we have the best hopes, as the waters and air of Harrowgate formerly agreed with her, that she may return home in much improved, if not in perfect health. I come now to a disappointment and a cross arrangement—We are indeed much disappointed that *you* are not to be of the Bowness Party. Your Father said 'My Youths', from which expression we gathered that you were all coming—(*if any*, for he did not speak decidedly). I still hope however, that at the end of summer you may run down for a few weeks, and *I* may then have the pleasure of seeing all of *you* that is to be seen in these parts. As to Charles and Christ I shall miss a great deal of *them*, for I am going to Halifax on the 26th of this month to stay six weeks. This grieves me very much but it could not be avoided. Having declined my aged Friend Mrs Rawson's[1] invitation last summer, I felt myself bound to her now when another invitation came—indeed I had promised before we heard of the probability of your coming; but had it been otherwise, I could not have put off; for if I had done so, I might hereafter have had regrets from being deprived of the power of ever seeing her again. She is eighty three years of age.

Owen and John will, I doubt not, go to Bowness tomorrow to inquire about lodgings,[2] and they will make report of their success. I know not what lodgings are disengaged there at present; but should think, unless some of your party would be satisfied with apartments at one of the Inns, it would be better to *engage* the lodgings beforehand; but, after inquiries are made, Owen and John must advise you on this point: and in your answer pray specify the time of coming—and it would be well to add also the probable time of Departure.—Our Harrowgate Friends will remain there till the 22nd and perhaps longer. Should Charles and Chrisr come before that time, and should it suit them to turn aside on their way, what pleasure would it give to Dora! and I may add the whole party; for the Southeys are all interested about our Cambridge Nephews, and would welcome them as Friends. I

[1] Mrs. Rawson (*née* Threlkeld) with whom D. W. lived at Halifax as a child.

[2] The three nephews, with a group of friends from Trinity, made up a reading party at Bowness during the summer vacation of 1827. See Charles Wordsworth, *Annals of my Early Life*, p. 44.

think my Brother will not perhaps stay more than a week at Harrow-gate. He leaves the pony-chaise for Dora's benefit.

If the Bowness Party are later than I suppose, they perhaps might come round by Halifax. Your Father can testify that Mr and Mrs Rawson would give them a hospitable reception, and I know that they as well as several other worthy relatives of ours would be very glad to become acquainted with his Sons—I need not add that it would be a great happiness to me to see them at Halifax; especially as I might otherwise (unless they come before the 26th) have a long time to wait for that pleasure.

The weather with us is now very rainy, after a changeable and cold Spring. I hope we may have a dry summer and autumn; otherwise what will the Boys (Boys I must still call them) say to our climate?

We are very thankful for the good reports of your Father's health—and after so much business and bustle attended with so many cares!—How I wish he could have come to Rydal for a few week's quiet in August or September!—I conclude that Tindal[1] will oppose the Emancipation of the Roman Catholics or otherwise my Brother would not have voted for him: We have heard nothing of Lord Lonsdale's joining the Ministry. I do not think it at all likely that he has.

You do not mention Mrs Hoare. I was very sorry to hear from John that she had been utterly unable to overcome her deep dejection for the loss of her husband, even up to the time when he was at Cambridge. Is it really so? And how is her bodily health? Lady Beaumont has been wonderfully supported under her affliction. She is at Worcester, on her road from London to Coleorton, whither she goes without any companion. Mrs Merewether will I doubt not be a great comfort to her, as she was at the time of Sir George's death.

Do, dear John, contrive to come if but for two or three weeks at the end of summer. I am never quite satisfied unless I see you all three together.

Give our kindest Love to your Father, and hearty congratulations—and joining in the same to yourselves—Believe me

dear John, your affectionate Aunt

D Wordsworth

[1] Sir Nicholas Tindal (1776–1846), Lord Chief Justice from 1829, entered Parliament in 1824, becoming Solicitor-General two years later when Copley was appointed Master of the Rolls. In 1827, when Copley became Lord Chancellor, there was a vacancy in the representation of Cambridge University, and Tindal was elected in place of W. J. Bankes. He visited Rydal Mount in 1838 (*RMVB*).

Your Aunt Wordsworth and Dora will, after D's return from Harrowgate, be at home till towards the end of September, at which time they purpose going into Herefordshire, as Dora is not to winter among the mountains. Owen is pretty well—He was not so when he came to us on Sunday; but seems now to have cast off his head-aches. He is a pleasant creature, and quite at home and happy with us.

291. D. W. to MARY LAING

Address: Miss Laing, Wm Laing's Esqre, South Bridge S^t, Edinburgh.
Postmark: 11 June 1827. *Stamp*: Kendal Penny Post.
MS. Edinburgh University Library.
The Wordsworth–Laing Letters (—).

Rydal Mount—near Kendal
June 10th 1827

My dear Miss Laing,

The picture[1] arrived some days ago but was not unpacked till yesterday we being fearful to trust the unpacking to any one but the Carpenter employed when it was sent off, and all workmen are so busy at this season we could not at once get him to come. You will, I am sure, be sorry to hear that the frame is injured in two or three places. A nail (a skrew I suppose) has been *driven in*, in *one* place, and a part of the ornament at one of the corners knocked off. This we found in the Box and the Carpenter will bring glue to fix it again; but the hole made by the nail cannot be repaired. We were very anxious when the Box was opened to find the picture uninjured, more especially as the dear Friend who painted and gave it to my Brother is no more. I am happy to say that the Painting is uninjured—at least so we think. There are one or two small cracks; but it is probable they were there before it left Rydal Mount, as it does not seem likely they could be caused by the motion in removal from place to place. My Nephew William, the only one who has had time for reading since the box was opened, is very much interested by your Brother's volume.[2] You know reading is not his passion, but he has been nailed to the Book for some hours. As my Brother is not at home I cannot at present be commissioned with his thanks. He is at Harrowgate with his

---

[1] See L. 276 above.
[2] Perhaps the 1827 edition of the *Bannatyne Miscellany*, edited by Sir Walter Scott, Laing, and others.

Daughter, who was much benefited by her journey thither in an open Carriage, and finds the air and waters of Harrowgate very salutary, so that we hope she will return home much improved in health and strength. Miss Joanna Hutchinson told me she had heard from you, and desired me to thank you for your letter. She continues to like the Isle of Man, and is in very good health; but still her lameness continues, and I fear she will never be able to walk again without limping.

M^r and Mrs Southey are at Harrowgate with all their Family. Dora will return with them in about a fortnight. We expect my Brother before the end of this week.

The weather has been ungenial the whole of this spring except at the beginning of April; and after having faced rain, frost and snow in the winter I caught a severe cold and have walked much less than usual; but I am so ignorant of all that lies beneath the surface of this earth of ours that I think there is little chance of my bringing home any thing that the geologist would care about. Whenever I find a very pretty portable stone I shall think of you and pick it up.

The weather is now very delightful—and I heartily wish it may so continue for a fortnight to come, that I may have a full enjoyment of this beautiful country before I leave it, which I shall do, for six weeks, on the 26th of this Month.[1]

Do excuse this scrawl. I have hardly time to save the post.

My kind regards to your Father, Mother and Brothers. Believe me, dear Miss Laing

every your affect^e Friend
D Wordsworth

Pray admonish the Manager of the Exhibition to be especially careful in future to employ competent persons to pack the pictures when they are returned. I mention this, as if others are injured it may be prejudicial to the Exhibition—which I suppose will be hereafter continued, and I wish it all possible success.

---

[1] According to her MS. Journal, D. W. left for Halifax on 25 June.

292. W. W. to GEORGE HUSBAND BAIRD[1]

Address: The Rev[d] G. H. Baird D.D., University of Edinburgh.
Postmark: 18 June 1827. *Stamp*: Kendal [Penny] Post. *Endorsed*: W. Words-
    worth June 15. 1827—
MS. National Library of Scotland.
LY i. 268.

Rydal Mount
June 15th 1827

Sir,

Your Letter of the 6th Inst[nt] I did not receive till yesterday on my return home from an absence during which I was moving about, so that it could not be sent after me.—

The interest I take in all that concerns the welfare of the Church of Scotland would have induced me to make an attempt at producing some thing which might have suited the plan you have explained in a manner and with a care that proves the importance you attach to it, if I could have entertained the least hope of success. But I assure you Sir with frankness and sincerity, that I am unequal to the task. My own devotional feelings have never taken in verse a Shape that has connected them with scripture in a degree that would encourage me to an effort of this kind. The sacred writings have a majesty, a beauty, a simplicity, an ardour, a sublimity, that awes and overpowers the spirit of Poetry in uninspired men, at least this is my feeling; and if it has deterred me in respect to compositions that might have been entered upon without any view of their seeing the light, how much more probable is it that I should be restrained, were I to make the endeavour under a consciousness that I was writing with a national purpose! Indeed, Sir, I dare not attempt it.—

Trusting that I shall stand excused after this explicit avowal, and wishing that your application may be successful in quarters where there is less apprehension and more ability,

I remain Sir
very respectfully
Your obedient Ser[nt]
Wm Wordsworth

[1] George Husband Baird, D.D. (1761–1840), Principal of the University of Edinburgh, and convener of a committee of the General Assembly of the Church of Scotland appointed 'for enlarging the collection of Translations and Paraphrases from sacred scripture, and otherwise improving the Psalmody', had applied to W. W. for assistance. He also approached Campbell, Southey, and Scott, none of whom contributed. The scheme was afterwards abandoned.

293. W. W. to WILLIAM HOWITT[1]

Address: W. Howitt, Esq., Nottingham.
Stamp: Kendal Penny Post.
MS. Osborn Collection, Yale University Library.
Hitherto unpublished.

Rydal Mount
June 17th 1827

Sir,

On returning home yesterday after an absence in which I was moving about so that my Letters could not well be sent after me, I had the pleasure of receiving your elegant Volume with the obliging Letter accompanying it. I have not yet had time to do more than cast my eyes over it, but as I notice several compositions with which I had been not a little gratified when I read them before in periodical publications, I have no doubt that much pleasure is in store for me when I can give the rest a perusal at leisure. But as it is nearly three weeks since the day of your Letter, I have thought it best to lose no time in making my acknowledgements lest I should seem to be neglectful of an attention which could not but be acceptable. Thankful for your good wishes which I return both to yourself and the partner of your life and studies I remain Sir

respectfully your obliged friend
Wm Wordsworth

293a. D. W. to C. W. JNR.

Address: To Chris^r Wordsworth Esqre, Trinity College, *Cambridge*.
Stamp: Kendal Penny Post
MS. WL. Hitherto unpublished.

Saturday—June 23rd [1827]

My dear Chris,

I received your letter yesterday, and not being able to go to Bowness myself,[2] John did the business for me. We all thought

---

[1] William Howitt (1792–1879), Quaker author. He and his wife Mary (1799–1888) had settled in Nottingham in 1823, and had just published their joint volume, *The Desolation of Eyam and Other Poems*. William Howitt was active in radical politics during the Reform Bill agitations, and published a *Popular History of Priestcraft in All Ages and Nations* (1833). He subsequently moved into journalism, founding *Howitt's Journal* (1847); published *Homes and Haunts of the most eminent British Poets* the same year; travelled in Australia; published a *Popular History of England* (1856–62) on his return; and devoted his last years principally to spiritualism. Mary Howitt, a popular author of novels and children's books, ended her days in the Church of Rome. See her *Autobiography*, 2 vols., 1889. Their eldest child married Alaric Watts's son

[2] To arrange accommodation for her nephews. See L. 290 above.

that it would be best for the three Brothers to be under one Roof, therefore decided that if George Robinson's[1] house should prove pretty well situated it was best to take the *three* Bed-rooms and the one sitting room, it being the only house where three could be accommodated. John found the house clean and neat, and not unpleasantly, or inconveniently situated, and though the rooms are small it is probable that at the other houses they are in general not much larger if at all: therefore he took the 5 Rooms for 30/ per week. The Hostess provides linen, and will wash the same without additional charge. A Trifle is to be paid weekly for Fuel in the Kitchen, and if you have fires in the sitting-room, they also must be paid for.

John told G. Robinson that it was probable you might stay all the summer if you liked the lodgings; but he engaged them only for one month from the 10th of July.

A small sum weekly for cooking and attendance, or a present at the end of Term for the servant. They would not make a charge.

I am engaged with preparations for my departure, packing etc.—therefore you must excuse a hurried letter. On Monday morning at 4 o'clock I shall leave Rydal, and on Wednesday shall leave Kendal by the Leeds Coach for Halifax, where I shall remain six weeks. It grieves me that I shall not be here on your arrival, or for three weeks afterwards, but I trust you will all be so well pleased with your residence among the Lakes that you will not go away till summoned by College Duties, in which case I hope for opportunities of seeing you very often. John W.[2] of Sockbridge will be at Rydal for *his* holidays, and it pleases me to think that I shall see all my six nephews together.

You take no notice of my proposal of introducing you to your Relations at Halifax, therefore I do not suppose you like the whim —or perhaps it may be inconvenient. I will, however, repeat that it would give me great pleasure to gain a [   ][3] you there and that I know you would be most welcome to Mr and Mrs Rawson.

We have again had good tidings from Dora. She says she is very much stronger. It is unlucky that I shall be travelling Southward on the very day that she and her Party will reach Rydal—and, as our Roads are different we shall not [have] even a sight of each other in passing.

I have not heard whether Mr and Mrs Thompson[4] are yet arrived. Wm expected them today.

---

[1] A joiner who also let lodgings.   [2] R. W.'s son.
[3] *MS. torn.*   [4] Presumably Cambridge acquaintances.

With Kind Love for every one, believe me ever your affectionate
Aunt

D Wordsworth

Your Cousin John was exceedingly delighted with the account of
your various successes at Cambridge and Oxford. He has often
asked me whether I delivered his congratulations, and what I said—
all which I have forgotten—and really I am afraid I did not even
mention his name but included him in the 'all.'

294. W. W. to MESSRS. TAYLOR AND HESSEY[1]

Address: Messrs Taylor and Hessey, Booksellers, London.
Franked: Penrith Aug. twenty four 1827. Lowther. *Postmark*: (1) 24 Aug.
1827. (2) 27 Aug. 1827. *Stamp*: Penrith.
MS. Cornell.
LY i. 269.

Lowther Castle
August 24th, 1827.

Messrs Taylor and Hessey
Gentlemen,
Would you have the kindness to direct and forward the Enclosed
to the Authors of Guesses at Truth,[2] which I received from your
care some little time ago.

Accept my thanks, and believe me
Gentlemen
Sincerely yours
Wm Wordsworth

[1] The well-known firm, publishers of the *London Magazine*, Keats's
Endymion and *Poems* of 1820, etc. (De Selincourt's note.)
[2] i.e. Augustus and Julius Hare (see Ls. 94 and 123 above). *Guesses at Truth*,
by Two Brothers, had just been published.

295. M. W. to JOHN KENYON

Address: John Kenyon Esqre, Dover.
Franked: Kendal Augt. twenty eight 1827. C. J. Chester.[1] *Endorsed*: Mrs
  Wordsworth, August 31.
MS. untraced.
Transactions of the Wordsworth Society, no. 6, p. 98. K. LY i. 269.

August 28, 1827.

My dear Friend,

Having lost sight of you for so long a time, we had concluded
that you and yours were in progress towards the immortal City,
until the letter, received on Sunday, proved to us that you are still
on this side the channel—yet so near that I should not be surprized
to hear, at any moment, that you had taken flight across. Dover
must be a tantalizing situation to those whose desires have so long
dwelt upon foreign travel—to see those *Steamers* daily fuming
backwards and forwards! How can you resist them? otherwise those
ever varying scenes must be a constant source of amusement and
interest, and we think you could not have made a better choice,
unless indeed you had pitched your tent, for a time, among the
Lakes and Mountains. But we think you have some prudential
considerations for delaying to introduce Mrs K. to people of our
stamp. As far as we are concerned the dreams of Italy are passed
away, but they may, and I hope will, revive again for you; I hope
that no untoward event may stand in the way of the accomplishment of your wishes next year.

From Idle Mount, which just now well supports that title, I
have nothing but good to communicate—and to begin with the
best of good things, let me tell you, which I do with a thankful
heart, that W.'s eyes are quite well—how this good work was
wrought you shall hear when we meet.

Dora, whom you so kindly inquire after, is no longer an invalid
—she is become as strong as I ever remember her to have been,
but this happy state is only to be depended upon so long as the
beautiful weather lasts; she is a complete *air* gage; as soon as damp
is felt the trouble in her throat returns—something connected with
the trachea, that causes a cough and other inconveniences.

---

[1] The Bishop of Chester, C. J. Blomfield, was on holiday at the Ivy Cottage,
lent him by Tillbrooke. According to his letter to W. W. of 21 Apr., he had
originally planned to take a larger house at Brathay: 'We propose taking with
us our four children, four maid servants at least, and 4 men-servants. I thank
you much for your offer of *stalls*, an offer more commonly made *by* than *to* a
Bishop; and should I go to Rydal, I shall gladly avail myself of it.' (*WL MSS.*)

To keep this enemy aloof, she is not to winter in our weeping climate; therefore before the next rainy season sets in, perhaps in a very few weeks, she, with myself for her attendant, are to quit our pleasant home and friends—but we mean to go to others, and make ourselves as joyous as we can. Our first and longest sojourn will be with my brother at Brinsop Court, near Hereford (had we met you in the Cathedral, or wandering upon the Wye, how lucky we should have thought ourselves).

We shall visit Mrs Gee near Bristol, and, had you not so rashly given up your home at Bath, we should not have been so near without partaking for a few days of your and Mrs Kenyon's hospitality. You will say, what is to become of Mr W. all this time? this thought I do not encourage, except when we plan a scheme for meeting at Coleorton, or for his joining us in Herefordshire.

We are looking for Miss Wordsworth's return home, after a two months' absence, towards the end of the week. She will be stationed throughout the winter at R. M., as will also, I believe, my sister Sarah, John, and Willy—Willy grown, as you suspect, amazingly, though he has not yet reached his Father's height. John intends to take Orders as soon as he can meet with a Curacy— should you hear of any vacancy in a good neighbourhood, where the duty is not too heavy for a novice to undertake, you perhaps will be kind enough to let him know, and you might also say a good word for him.

My sister Sarah, Dora, and Mr Quillinan,[1] who has been our guest for the last few days, have ridden over to Keswick this morning. Southey's family are all well. I, together with Dora, spent a week very pleasantly with them since the commencement of the present month, and we also had a picnic meeting under Raven Crag by the margin of Wytheburn—the families of Greta Hall and Rydal Mount, with other vagrants, making a party of about 30— a merry group we formed, round a gypsey fire upon the rocky point that juts from the shore, on the opposite side of the lake from the high road.

Dr Wordsworth's three *distinguished* sons are now at Bowness, reading with several other Students and their Tutor. Except after the business of the week is over, on the Saturdays and Sundays, we see nothing of them. They are delightful youths, and have learnt, or rather time has taught them, to enjoy this country, which they thought little of when they were last in it, the summer you were

---

[1] E. Q. had returned in the spring from a visit to Portugal to take up residence in his new London home, 12 Bryanston St.

here, I think. Tillbrook made but a short stay, and was very unlucky, having imprudently taken too long a walk, to show the view *into* Langdale to a young friend, and fatigued himself so much as obliged him almost to keep to his sofa during the remainder of his stay; he was but twice up the hill.

The Bishop of Chester and his Lady took possession of Ivy Cot about 3 weeks since, and mean to make it their headquarters until October. The bishop is a delightful companion, and is indefatigable in the duties of his high Office; he preaches every Sunday, often twice, in some or other of the neighbouring churches,—a grand feast for us, who are so often doomed to feed on such a slender meal as our Westmorland divines lay before us. Mrs Blomfield, too, is a pleasant agreeable Person, but they are so much engaged among the grandees of the neighbourhood that we do not see much of them; besides, she is delicate, and the 'Hall bank' is too much for her.

The House at the foot of the hill is at present empty, but Fox Ghyll beautified by Mrs Luff is a delightful residence. Spring Cottage, the second house under Loughrigg upon the river, is occupied by two Maiden Ladies, who are admirers of *Scenery*, and understand the *ologies* (in the latter *we* do not participate, the sciences do not flourish at Idle M^t); thus you see that if the Travellers did not steal our industrious propensities from us, our neighbours would.

Here you must refer to the numerals for directions how to proceed, for, till I had written to the end of the third page, I did not discover I had turned over two sheets, after reaching the bottom of the first; and to this blunder you owe this long letter, for I should not have ventured beyond a single sheet, although I can command a frank.

With best regards to Mrs K. and kindest remembrances from all, believe me to be, very sincerely yours,

M. Wordsworth

296. W. W. to HARRIET DOUGLAS[1]

MS. untraced.
Angus Davidson, Miss Douglas of New York, 1952, p. 12.

[early Sept. 1827]

My dear Miss Douglas,

I volunteered to recapitulate what I said to you and now it seems to me that, were I to attempt it, the end would only be weakened. I have therefore taken up the pen with this view, to touch a point on which I have felt some anxiety since we parted, because I was silent upon it. When I expressed myself in such strong terms on the support which you might derive from the state of marriage, I ought by no means to have omitted cautioning you against any hasty choice of an individual. Your fortune would make you an object to too many in these Kingdoms, especially at this time, when such multitudes of young men are educated above the opportunities afforded them to turn their attainments to account, and so many others are checkered in their career whether of war or commerce. Be therefore very careful and wait till occasion be given of knowing the man to whom you commit your happiness. I have now eased my mind—what I have said may not be necessary for you to hear, but I felt it incumbent on me to utter it, and I am sure you will ascribe the caution to what is the source of all I have said to you; an anxiety to strengthen and improve your character, and to promote your welfare.

Instead of retreading the ground we travelled in conversation, I will rather enter on a few untraced paths which naturally diverge from it. I was anxious that your mind should be composed.—Let me recommend to you to observe and to read more—and to talk less —not that you do not talk well, but by silence your nerves will be enabled to recover their tone, and your discourse being then more under the guidance of voluntary power, will be sure of being profitable for those to whom it is addressed and will be more enjoyed by them. But I am mainly interested in pressing this upon you for your own sake. If you control yourself in small matters you will

---

[1] Harriet Douglas (1790–1872), of New York, an American heiress of Scottish extraction, visited Britain in 1812 and again in 1827, and lionized many of the leading writers of the day, including Scott, Wordsworth, Southey, and Rogers. In August of this year she visited the Lakes, carrying an introduction to W. W. from Mrs. Grant of Laggan, and joined the Wordsworths, Southeys, and Bishop Blomfield in an expedition up Saddleback (*SH*, pp. 350–1). She made no secret of her problems with suitors, and after her departure for Ireland the poet offered this letter of advice. They met again in London the following May.

find it much more easy to do so on great occasions; and you will
have less cause to lament this indecision which makes you so
unhappy. I have urged you to read more and pray do not (like the
multitude) read books to talk and prattle about them, but to feed
upon their contents in stillness. Need I add then, read the best,
above all the Bible. Are you acquainted with Bishop Taylor's
'Holy Living and Dying'[1]—whether you are or not, make it one
of your constant companions.

You have been brought to a point where you expect too much
from others, I mean more than they can do for you, and are in
doubt far too much to seek external support. We were agreed in
opinion that this had arisen, in a great degree, from others having
submitted to lean too much upon you. At all events, the coil has
been produced and a great coil it is. Would you diminish it—seek
comparative solitude, till your nerves are braced. In the words of
Scripture, commune with your own heart and be still—cheerfulness
will then come back to you, and regaining sustained contentment
will be your reward.

But I have no intention of writing at length, nor do I request
you to do so in reply, as very few words will suffice. Tell me of
what you have resolved upon and where you are.—

With kindest regards from all here believe me—dear Miss
Douglas

Your faithful Friend
W. Wordsworth

297. W. W. to ROBERT SOUTHEY

MS. Cornell. Hitherto unpublished.

[15 Sept. 1827]

My dear S—

The Bearers are Gentlemen of whom I cannot say half so much
as they deserve. Mr. Hamilton[2] is Professor Astronomer in The

---

[1] Jeremy Taylor (1613–67), Bishop of Down and Connor: author of *The
Rule and Exercises of Holy Living*, 1650, and *The Rule and Exercises of Holy
Dying*, 1651.
[2] William Rowan Hamilton (1805–65), mathematician and Professor of
Astronomy at Trinity College, Dublin, a post to which he was appointed while
still an undergraduate (1827). He was knighted in 1835, and was President of
the Royal Irish Academy in 1837. He was an enthusiastic lover of poetry and
throughout his life wrote much verse. His visit to Rydal in 1827 was the
beginning of an intimate friendship with W. W., who affirmed that Coleridge

University of Dublin, at 22 years of age. Mr Nimmo[1] is a civil engineer of distinction; Mr Otway[2] is a clergyman of the Irish Church and is acquainted with every corner of Ireland. You will find them all interesting. They did not ask for this Introduction but I know they wished for it.

ever yours W. W.

in extreme haste—

298. W. W. to SAMUEL ROGERS

Address: Saml Rogers, Esqre, St. James's Place, London.
Postmark: 22 Sept. 1827. *Endorsed*: not to be Published S. R.
MS. Sharpe Collection, University College, London.
Rogers. LY i. 272.

Rydal Mount 20th Sept^r [1827]

My dear Rogers,

Some time ago I heard from you in acknowledgement of the Receipt of my last Edition. Its contents you appear to esteem in a way which cannot but be highly flattering to me.[3] I am now writing to consult you about a small matter of Virtù, in which I am inclined to incur a little expense.

An advertisement has been forwarded to me, of the Prints of the Stafford Gallery at one third of the original price.—Are they well executed—and are they likely to be good or at least fair impressions, and not refuse? The advertisement says that the public is secured against inferior impressions, by the limited number. Do you know if this be true, or would you procure me a copy fairly

and Hamilton were 'the two most wonderful men, taking all their endowments together', that he had ever met. (De Selincourt's note.) Hamilton wrote to his sister Eliza on 16 Sept.: '. . . I must shut up this letter to go and present to Southey an introduction which I have received from Wordsworth, with whom I spent the evening—I might almost say the *night*—of yesterday, for he and I were taking a *midnight walk* together for a long, long time, *without any companion* except the stars and our own burning thoughts and words' (*Hamilton*, i. 262).

[1] Alexander Nimmo (1783–1832), first a schoolmaster at Inverness, later took up civil engineering and was employed surveying the harbours of Ireland. He designed the docks at Limerick, and towards the end of his life worked on several railway projects in England.

[2] The Revd. Caesar Otway (1780–1842), originally of Tipperary, was a notable preacher in Dublin, who in 1825 had helped to start the *Christian Examiner* in support of the Church Establishment in Ireland. He wrote topographical works about Ireland.

[3] Rogers had written on 14 July: 'They are full of Virtue, full of Piety, full of Wisdom, the Wisdom of the heart, and must console you under any circumstances whenever you lay your head upon your pillow.' (*WL MSS.*)

culled? Or lastly would it be at all an eligible purchase for one of my slender means, who is a passionate lover of the Art? If you think so have the goodness to select me one; we have no works of art near us, and must therefore be content with shadows.—

My Wife and Daughter are flown into Herefordshire where they will remain till the first Swallow returns, for the sake of a drier climate, which my Daughter's health requires.—I hope your journey to Italy will be deferred for one year—it would admit the *possibility* at least of my meeting you there. What a treat! How goes on your Poem?[1] The Papers spoke of a new edition being intended with numerous engravings, which, if executed under your presiding taste cannot but be invaluable.

I was at Lowther a week lately—I *missed* you and dear Sir George by the side of that beautiful Stream. The weather was exquisite;—and one solitary ramble through the Elysian fields and onwards I shall never forget. Could you believe that a flock of Geese, tame geese, could on land make an interesting Appearance. Yet that day so they did, reposing themselves under an umbrageous oak,—thirty at least all carefully shaded from the bright and over warm sunshine, and forming groups Reubens would have delighted in—with attitudes as various and actions still more so, than Cattle enjoying like comfort.

My Sister, Sons, and Miss Hutchinson are here—all unite in kindest regards—I wish you would join us for a week or two— ever faithfully yours

W Wordsworth

[*D. W. adds*]
Turn over

The Stafford Gallery complete in 4 volumes Folio, half bound, uncut, 12 £-12s. Published at 35 £-14. Sold by Sam¹ Leigh, 18, Strand.

My Brother has desired me to copy the above from the advertisement, and with pen in hand and the blank page before me I cannot help saying a word of friendly and affectionate remembrance to yourself and Sister. The season is so far advanced that I fear there is no chance of your being moved hither by my Brother's hint of the pleasure it would give us to see you, yet I will add, if you do come, you must bring Miss Rogers along with you, or I should not be half satisfied. My Brother, I see, says nothing of his intention of meeting Mrs W. at Coleorton—nor of a still

[1] The second part of *Italy* was published the following year.

larger scheme that he has of visiting London. I was very sorry not
to see you at Coleorton—the last week of my enjoyment of dear
Sir George Beaumont's society.—Adieu, dear Sir,

Believe me yours truly
D Wordsworth

299. W. W. to WILLIAM ROWAN HAMILTON

Address: W. R. Hamilton Esqr, Observatory, near Dublin.
MS. Cornell.
Mem. (—). *Grosart. Hamilton. K* (—). *LY i. 274.*

Rydal Mount, near Kendal,
Septr 24th 1827

My dear Sir,

You will have no pain to suffer from my sincerity. With a safe
conscience I can assure you that in my judgment your verses[1] are
animated with true poetic spirit, as they are evidently the product
of strong feeling. The 6th and 7th stanzas affected me much, even
to the dimming of my eye, and faltering of my voice while I was
reading them aloud. Having said this, I have said enough; now for
the *per Contra*. You will not, I am sure, be hurt, when I tell you
that the Workmanship (what else could be expected from so
young a writer?) is not what it ought to be—even in those two
affecting stanzas it is not perfect:

> Some *touch* of human sympathy find way,
> And whisper that while Truth's and Science' *ray*
> With such serene effulgence o'er thee shone—

Sympathy might whisper, but a '*touch* of sympathy' could not.
'Truth's and Science' ray', for the ray of truth and Science, is not
only extremely harsh, but a 'ray *shone*' is, if not absolutely a
pleonasm, a great awkwardness—A 'ray fell' or 'shot' may be said;
and a *sun*, or a *moon*, or a *candle* shine, but not a ray. I much regret
that I did not receive these verses, while you were here, that I
might have given you viva voce a comment upon them which would
be tedious by letter, and, after all, very imperfect. If I have the
pleasure of see[ing] you [again][2] I will beg permission to dissect
these verses, or any other you may be inclined to show me—but I am
certain that, without conference with me or any benefit drawn from

---

[1] Hamilton's poem *It haunts me yet* (*Hamilton*, i. 264).
[2] *MS. torn.*

my practice in metrical composition your own high powers of mind will lead you to the main conclusions—You will be brought to acknowledge that the logical faculty has infinitely more to do with Poetry than the Young and the inexperienced, whether writer or critic, ever dreams of. Indeed, as the materials upon which that faculty is exercised in Poetry are so subtle, so plastic, so complex, the application of it requires an adroitness which can proceed from nothing but practice, a discernment, which emotion is so far from bestowing that at first it is ever in the way of it.—Here I must stop; only let me advert to two lines:

> But shall despondence therefore *blench* my *brow*,
> Or pining sorrow sickly ardor o'er.

These are two of the worst verses in mere expression. 'Blench' is perhaps miswritten for 'blanch', if not, I don't understand the word. *Blench* signifies to flinch. If 'blanch' be the word, the next ought to be '*hair*'. You cannot here use *brow* for the *hair* upon it, because a white brow or forehead is a beautiful characteristic of Youth. 'Sickly ardor o'er' was at first reading to me unintelligible. I took 'sickly' to be an adjective joined with 'ardor', whereas you mean it as a portion of a verb, from Shakespeare, 'Sicklied o'er with the pale cast of thought'—but the separation of the parts, or decomposition of the word, as here done, is not to be endured.—

Let me now come to your Sister's verses,[1]—for which I thank you. They are surprizingly vigorous for a female pen but occasionally too rugged, and especially for such a subject—they have also the same faults in expression as your own; but not I think in quite an equal degree. Much is to be hoped from feelings so strong, and a mind thus disposed. I should have entered into particulars with these also, had I seen you after they came into my hands.—Your sister is, no doubt, aware that in her poem she has trodden the same ground as Gray, in his Ode upon a distant prospect of Eton Coll; what he has been contented to treat [in] the abstract she has represented in particular, and with admirable Spirit. But again, my dear sir, let me exhort you (and do you exhort your Sister) to deal little with modern writers; but fix your attention almost exclusively upon those who have stood the test of time.—*You* especially have not leisure to allow of your being tempted to turn aside from the right course by deceitful lights. My Household desire to be remembered to you in no formal way. Seldom have I parted—never I was going to say with one whom after so short

---

[1] *The Boys' School* (*Hamilton*, i. 682–5).

an acquaintance, I lost sight of with more regret. I trust we shall meet again, if not [   ]¹

[*Signature cut away*]

Pray do not forget to remember me to Mr Otway. I was much pleased with him and with your fellow-traveller Mr Nimmo,² as I should have been, no doubt, with the young Irishman,³ had not our conversation taken so serious a turn—The passage in Tacitus, which Milton's line so strongly resembles is not in the Agricola, nor can I find it—but it exists somewhere.

300. W. W. to THOMAS NORTON LONGMAN

Address: Messʳˢ L. and Co., A. Spottiswode Esqʳ,⁴ London.
Postmark: 15 Oct. 1827.
MS. Harvard University Library.
LY i. 276.

[*In M. W.'s hand*]

[15 Oct. 1827]

To Mʳ Longman

Dʳ Sir

I fear you may have thought me inattentive to these papers but I did not like to return them till they had been revised by a friend, whom I could not see till to-day—

I am very truly
Yours
[*signed*] Wᵐ Wordsworth

301. W. W. to DORA W.

Address: Miss Wordsworth, Brinsop Court, Hereford.
Franked: Penrith twenty seventh October 1827 Lonsdale.
MS. WL.
LY i. 276.

[Lowther Castle]
Friday afternoon [26 Oct. 1827]

My dearest Dora,

Never was this House so poor in franks. I have I know not how many Letters to forward to your Mother and to you—and I know

---

¹ A line has been cut away here, probably for the autograph.
² See L. 297 above.   ³ Nimmo's apprentice, named Jones.
⁴ Of New Street Square: printer of the new edition of W. W.'s poems.

not how to ask Lord Lonsdale. I promised you a letter and meant to write at length but have been deterred, partly by the little prospect of a frank and partly by engagement, as the mornings I have been here have been spent with Dr Satterthwaite and the after luncheons in going out with parties. We left Rydal on Wednesday morning—Aunt Wordsworth accompanying us two thirds up Kirkstone, but we did not get to Penrith till six in the evening, the roads were so bad and heavy. Ulswater was beautiful. Poor Aunt S. had a bad headache, and we have just seen her off from Ulswater on her way. I never had so tiresome a journey in my life. I found here Mr and Miss Senhouse[1] and Miss Wood,[2] and the two Misses Hasell,[3] and your old partner O'Callaghan[4].—Observe, dearest Dora, I do not call this a Letter, if possible I will write to-morrow—if not I will write from home whither I hope to return on [?]day, and my present intention, tell your dear Mother, is to leave Ambleside Monday week for Coleorton,—if I go by Liverpool I should be there on Wednesday Evening, if by Nottingham not till Thursday Morning, so that your dear Mother will be there on Wednesday Evening if possible. I know not what has been written to you so that when I sit down to write I shall scarcely know what topics to select. Do tell your Mother I have paid Dr Harrison's Bill. Mrs Ellwood expects me at Penrith to-morrow but I fear I must return without seeing her. How sorry I shall be to be so near you in Leicestershire and have to set my face Northward without seeing you, and part with your Mother into the bargain. I am quite sad about it. I have strange clouds hanging over me. Do take care to get well that nothing of this sort may occur again. Poor Mr Gee![5] I was sadly shocked at his death. Farewell again and again. Love to your dear Mother and your Aunts etc.

W. W.

[1] Elizabeth (1805–90), Humphrey Senhouse's eldest daughter, through whom the family property descended on the death of his only son in 1834.

[2] Humphrey Senhouse's aunt, and a member of the Senhouse–Southey–Calvert circle.

[3] The sisters of Edward W. Hasell of Dalemain (see *MY* ii. 537).

[4] George O'Callaghan. See L. 115 above.

[5] Capt. Gee had died on 13 Oct. at Wraxall, Somerset, of which county he had been Deputy Lieutenant.

302. W. W. to DORA W.

Address: Miss Wordsworth, Brinsop Court, Hereford.
Franked: Penrith twenty seventh October 1827 Lonsdale.
MS. WL.
LY i. 277.

Lowther Castle
Sat: Morn: [27 Oct. 1827]

My dearest Dora,

This scrawl may perhaps reach you as soon as one written last night—I am a good deal disappointed having hoped I might have written you a tolerably entertaining letter from this place —but I have wasted both franks and time—I expected to have returned by the Pony chaise to-morrow—but Aunt Sara has taken it to Appleby—and means to keep it there. I have this moment heard from her of the date of yesterday, she has got rid of her headache by medicine, and tells me Mrs Ellwood will be sadly disappointed if I don't go over to Penrith to see her—which must be this morning. I think I have at least 10 Letters which I want to get franked, several that we have received since you went, and three that your Aunt has sent me this morning which I must take back.

I hope to return to-morrow either by Patterdale or in some conveyance of Lord Lonsdale's, or what I should like better accompanying the Lowthers as far as Keswick, where I might see Southey, from whom I have had a note this morning; he says that his health is greatly improved, but does not write in good spirits, concluding with this remarkable expression—having said that his Uncle[1] could not be expected to live through the winter he adds 'and I have thorns in my side not of my own planting'—what this alludes to I cannot guess.

He and the family are going to Nether Hall and Tallentire,[2] for ten days. I have met here Mr Ingram[3] Receiver General for Cumberland. He tells me with no little indignation that his situation is far from a bed of roses—take for instance this fact,—he is obliged to send to his board an account of every Letter he receives on his business, from whom and whence it is, what is the subject of it, and what the Postage,—and all this from apprehension that he

---

[1] The Revd. Herbert Hill, who died in Sept. 1828. Southey paid tribute to him in the dedicatory poem to the *Colloquies* of 1829.
[2] Tallentire Hall, 4 miles NW. of Cockermouth: the residence of William Browne (d. 1861), a cousin of William George Browne (1768–1813) the oriental traveller. [3] A. R. Ingram of Penrith.

may charge letters he has no right to charge.[1] What then can we expect from the new Inspectors, one of whom by the bye is Ingram' nephew.

Mr I., when he was with the Board in Town remonstrate against this want of confidence and received for answer 'Wha could they do?' Mr Hume[2] was in Parliament and all those thing were dragged thither; What does your Mother think of such proceedings? Now for something less disagreeable.—The morning I left home we received a Letter from Mrs Cookson, saying she had just had a word from Mr Anthony Yates[3] who had been at Leven that Mrs Howard[4] of L. had been so charmed with my works that she was anxious to see me there, and begged that Mr Yates would conduct me—Mr Yates had described himself as knowing me most intimately, and yesterday I received a Letter in Form from her to the same effect. I do not like these things and I have answered, that I quit home so soon after my return from this place that I mus decline the honour of being presented to Mrs Howard, which would give me much pleasure at a more favourable opportunity— My note, be assured, was not wanting in respect to Mrs H. I do not know if I shall be able to add any more scrawl.

[*unsigned*]

303. D. W. to EDWARD QUILLINAN

Address: Edward Quillinan Esqre, 12 Bryanston Street, London.
Postmark: 5 Nov. 1827. *Stamp*: Kendal.
MS. WL.
LY i. 279.

Friday Nov^br 2nd [1827]

My dear Friend,

This morning's post brought us a letter from Mrs Wordsworth which informs us that you are likely to be in Herefordshire the 1st

---

[1] Cf. Southey's remarks to John Rickman: 'Wordsworth, in his capacity of Stamp Distributor, received a circular lately requiring him to employ person to purchase soda powders when sold without a stamp, and then lay an information against the vendors. It seems as if they were resolved so to reduce the emolument in the public services, and connect such services with them, that no one with the habits and feelings of a gentleman shall enter or continue in it.' (Southey, v. 312.)   [2] For Joseph Hume, see L. 27 above

[3] Anthony Yeates of Collinfield, an ancient house in Kirkland, Kendal, once the property of the celebrated Countess of Pembroke.

[4] Mary Howard (1785–1877) of Levens Hall, Westmorland, who inherited the estates of the 12th Earl of Suffolk and Berkshire. For her husband, the Hon. Fulke Greville Howard, Southey's schoolfriend, see L. 203 above.

or 2nd week of this month, and that therefore, if my Brother do not change the plan of his journey to Coleorton she will be disappointed of the pleasure of seeing you. He has therefore determined not to leave home until Monday the 13th, and will not reach Coleorton until the Thursday Evening or Friday Morning, which he hopes will give you and her the pleasure of each other's company; and he is truly sorry that he cannot also be of the party: but reconciles himself the more easily as he hopes to see you in London in the Spring. It is his present intention when Mrs W. returns to Brinsop to accompany her thither from Coleorton, and stay about a fortnight—whereas, if he had adopted Dora's plan of going to fetch her Mother he could not have stayed so long on account of his engagement with Lady B.

My object in troubling you with this hurried scrawl is to transmit a request from my Brother that you will hasten your journey to Brinsop as much as possible. I have just written to Lady Beaumont to inform her of the week's delay.

We are all well—Miss Hutchinson gone to Appleby. The weather is delightful—clear, cool and sunny. I had a charming walk this morning with my Brother on Loughrigg Fell. We looked down upon Ivy Cottage, but it is transformed into a *green Box*, being absolutely *cased* in ivy—and did not even look pretty, though burnished with sunshine. The rest of the Village—Rydal Mount especially—was enchanting—when we could get rid of the full staring view of the Hall.

I was very glad of Mr E. Brydges's establishment at Denton. Can you hear of a Curacy for 'our John'? William is quite well. His thoughts turn (I fear constantly) on the Army. What have you to say for and against the profession? Not I expect much for it.— And he seems little inclined to listen to the contra side. His health is now excellent—growth wonderful—and looks much improved.

If you could favour me with one of your pleasant letters from Brinsop I should be very grateful—and with details respecting your dear little Girls. When am I to have the good fortune to meet you again? I was sadly grieved at missing you last summer.

Miss Hutchinson will not return in less than five or six weeks. adieu. In greatest haste, ever your affecte Friend

D. Wordsworth.

Give my respectful and affecte remembrances to Captn Barrett.

304. W. W. to THOMAS CROFTON CROKER[1]

MS. untraced.
The Autographic Mirror, [1864], ii. 215. *W. T. Bandy, 'An Uncollected Letter from Wordsworth to Crofton Croker', MLR xliii (Apr. 1948), 242.*

Rydal Mount
Nov. 11th [1827]

Sir,

It would have given me pleasure to write with the distinguished authors you mention, for such a purpose, if your Publication had not been periodical. But it has not suited me to be connected with that class of works, and accordingly I have refused to all that have thought it worth while to apply to me, on the same general ground. With this answer to the request with which you have honored me, I cannot doubt but you will be satisfied. Wishing for the success of your undertaking

I am Sir
Your obedient servant
W. Wordsworth

305. W. W. to WILLIAM JACKSON

Address: The Revd Wm Jackson, Queen's Coll, Oxford [*In M. W.'s hand*]
Stamp: Ashby de la Zouch.
MS. Berg Collection, New York Public Library.
Hitherto unpublished.

Coleorton Hall
Nov 26th—1827

My dear Friend,

A Copy of your Letter has been forwarded to me at this place, where I arrived better than [a] week ago and met Mrs W from Herefordshire, well, and bringing pretty good accounts of Dora though she had been labouring under a severe cold. Her appetite however is good, and her strength improved accordingly—

I congratulate you on the improvement of your own health and can enter into your feelings respecting a College Life. But let me

---

[1] Thomas Crofton Croker (1798–1854), Irish antiquary and writer, employed as a clerk at the Admiralty. In 1825 he published *Fairy Legends and Traditions of the South of Ireland* (2nd series, 1827); and he was now editing for Ainsworth the 1828 volume of *The Christmas Box, An annual present for children*, for which he obtained contributions from Scott, Lamb (his lines for Lucy Barton's album), Hook, and Maria Edgeworth.

552

beg of you to be slow to return to Whitehaven—it is too burthen-
some a duty for your bodily strength—Now for the point on which
you do me the honor of referring to my Judgement—It should seem
that in *ordinary* circumstances, one would vote for the Person most
likely to *serve* the University,[1] or if not much is to be expected in
this way, for him who would do it most honor, while he was
obviously himself raised by the distinction; and this I think would
be a feather in any man's Cap, except like the Duke of Gloucester,[2]
he were of the royal Family; on him the distinction struck me as
thrown away; nor was his personal character such as could reflect
honor on a learned Body—But these are *not* ordinary circumstances,
and the election is likely to be made a party test; and upon that view
of the case I will say a few words, premising that to the personal
character of the Individual named, there appears to be no objection.
Of that of the Duke of Buckingham,[3] however, you probably know
much more than I. Lord Dudley[4] is a Bachelor, and immensely rich,
with more money perhaps at command than any one in England;
were he inclined to be munificent he might do great things for the
University—but this is neither the taste of the Age nor likely to be
his humour, for he is said to be *mean* if not avaricious. He is vain,
I think, but obviously not wanting talents. Lord Colchester's[5]
fortune, I would suppose, is very small for his rank, but as a
Scholar he is distinguished, and as a constitutional enlightened
Patriot, he appears to have decidedly the advantage over the others.
And on this point I should be inclined mainly to rest. As to mere
party, there is little satisfaction to be had by looking at any side.
[? Indeed] the old Tories are so anxious to get back into power
that they would make great sacrifices for the purpose, and we see
what the other side have done to get into, and to keep their places.[6]
But omitting all consideration of the patriotism or *moral* worth of
the several parties, I think you are agreed with me that the political
opinions, principles if you will, of the *Outs*, are better, that is safer

[1] i.e. the University of Oxford, as Chancellor, in succession to Lord Grenville.
[2] Chancellor of Cambridge. See *MY* ii. 648.
[3] Richard Brydges Chandos Grenville, 1st Duke of Buckingham and Chandos
(1776–1839), of Stowe, Bucks.: nephew of Lord Grenville.
[4] John William Ward, 4th Viscount Dudley (see L. 158 above), had been
Foreign Secretary in Canning's recent administration, and was created Earl of
Dudley on 24 Sept.
[5] Charles Abbot, 1st Baron Colchester (1757–1829), Chief Secretary of
Ireland (1801), Speaker of the House of Commons (1802–17), and M.P. for
Oxford University (1806): acknowledged to be one of the great Speakers.
[6] After Canning's death on 8 Aug., Lord Goderich (see L. 330 below)
presided over a short-lived coalition of Canningites and Whigs until the
following 9 Jan., when Wellington was commissioned to form a ministry.

and sounder, than those of the *Ins*. Now if the election for Chancellor is to be a test of the Opinion of the University of Oxford upon this question, I should like to see proof of its coincidence with what I take to be yours, and know to be my own, and on this account also, unless I see reason for change, I should vote for Lord Colchester; if I am not mistaken in supposing that he is averse to concession to the Romanists, to rash or hasty reform in parliament or of any kind, and to schemes of education pursued without due regard to religion, and respect for the Constitution—The question of education, and the dissemination of knowledge as now patronized by those who have most influence is of infinite moment, and much do I wish to see it taken up by some one capable of treating it like a Statesman and a Philosopher—I have now said all that strikes me on the subject, I wish it were more worthy of your regard.

Lady Beaumont bears her loss with admirable resignation; her resources are employment in improving this place, and religious meditation, doing what good she can in the neighbourhood. Mrs W is quite well, and begs her affectionate remembrances. Believe me ever

faithfully your friend
W Wordsworth

We hope to see Dr Wordsworth soon, in a few days—You will I think have no objection to my asking his opinion on the Chancellorship. If any thing important arises out of my consulting him I shall write again. Pray let me hear from you.—

WW

We shall stay here about a fortnight longer, and then I accompany Mrs W into Herefordshire—

Thank you for thinking about John. As to Willy I am sadly at a loss.

306. W. W. to SAMUEL ROGERS

Address: Samuel Rogers Esq, St James Place, London.
Postmark: 1 Dec. 1827. *Stamp*: Ashby de [La Zouche].
MS. Sharpe Collection, University College, London.
Rogers. LY i. 280.

Coleorton Hall [c. 30 Nov. 1827]

My dear Rogers,

Ten days ago Mrs W. (she from the neighbourhood of Hereford, and I from the North) met at this place, which we quit Saturday,

8th of next month, going together into Herefordshire, where Mrs W. will remain with her Daughter till the warm and dry weather of Spring returns. Thus is our little family broken up by the troublesome indisposition of my daughter, an affection of the throat, which returns along with a cough on rainy and damp days.—

Lady Beaumont was not well a few days after our arrival here, but she is now in good health and as little altered in appearance as could have been expected. She employs herself much in the concerns of this place, and has great resources in reading and religious meditation. You will be aware how much Mrs W. and I miss Sir George in this house and in the grounds about. There is a little picture on the Easel in his painting Room as it was left on his seizure there with a fainting fit, the commencement of his fatal illness, which lasted no more than eight days.—Lady B. begs that you will be quite easy on the subject of your not answering her Letter, as she did not look for a reply, being in general as averse to Letter-writing as you are. It seems that it was a consolation to her under her suffering to write to Sir George's Friends. I sincerely believe that she did so without wishing for, or thinking about, any notice of her effusion. She took up the pen from impulse, and it was a relief to her.

I am pleased to hear that the Stafford Gallery[1] is thought a bargain, but I will not trouble you any more on the subject. Before I had heard from you I mentioned to Mr Page,[2] whom I think you saw at Lowther, that I had named this subject to you, and he engaged to knock at your door to learn whether you were at home or in England. I thought you might be gone to Italy. Whether he found you or not, he obligingly offered to inspect the Prints himself, and report to me accordingly. I have not yet heard from him; at all events let the purchase be suspended at present. I know, and have often admired, the Rubens Lord Stafford[3] has given to the British Gallery; it would be worthy of you to follow his example and enrich the same Repository, either during your lifetime or by bequest, with some choice work of art, for the public benefit, and thus to connect your name, already distinguished in one of the fine arts, with another of the Sisterhood. Think of this, and by so doing, and in fulfilling the prophecy I often made to Sir George when he was talking of giving his Pictures to the Nation,

---

[1] i.e. the series of prints mentioned in L. 298 above.

[2] Unidentified.

[3] George Granville Leveson-Gower, 2nd Marquess of Stafford (1758–1833), created 1st Duke of Sutherland a few months before his death, had just presented 'Peace and War' by Rubens to the national collection.

that his example would be followed by many others, and that thus, in course of time, a noble Gallery would be produced.

Italy, alas! is to me an ignis fatuus[1]—every year the hope dances before me only to obstruct my sight of something else that I might attain. Were there no other obstacle, I could not think of leaving England for so long a time till I had disposed of my younger Son, who, as I have just learned from him, is bent upon being a beggar either in the honourable character and profession of a Soldier or of a Farmer. Could you suggest to me anything better for this infatuated youth—any situation in a Counting-House or a public office? He dislikes the thought of the University because he sees nothing afterwards open to him but the Church; which he does not think himself fit for, or that he ever can be made so. Excuse this weary Epistle, and believe me ever, with true affection,

Yours,

W. Wordsworth

307. W. W. to C. W. and C. W. JNR.

Address: The Revd Dr Wordsworth, Trinity Coll. Cambridge.
MS. British Museum.
K (—). *LT i. 282* (—).

[Coleorton]
[c. 30 Nov. 1827]

My dear Brother,

We are truly sorry that our meeting at Coleorton cannot be accomplished; you will not be at liberty till too late. We arrived here it will be a fortnight on Saturday since, with the intention of staying three weeks, but that would stretch our residence here to five weeks, which cannot be done,—consistent with Lady B's arrangements, or our's. Now I have a proposal to make. We quit this place Saturday week, meaning to stop two days at Birmingham, two at Worcester with Miss Willes, Lady B's Cousin, and one at Malvern if the snow be not on the ground. Our earnest wish is, that you should join us at Brinsop Court, Mr Hutchinson's, about 6 miles from Hereford where I will meet you with a Gig. My stay will be prolonged in that County sufficiently to allow of our passing

---

[1] In a letter of 5 Nov. Rogers had proposed that the Wordsworths should accompany him to the Continent: 'So pray prepare, one and all, and let us swim together in a Gondola and muse in the temples of Paestum and in the streets of Pompeii together . . .' (*WL MSS.*)

a week together—divided between Mr Hutchinson and Mr Monkhouse who lives at no distance from him on the banks of the Wye. You would have a saddle horse or a Gig at command while in that part of the Country. On the other side of this Sheet I shall beg of Christopher to hunt out the best conveyance from Cambridge to Worcester, which is four hours and a half from Hereford. I have looked at the Map and find that the distance from Cambridge to Worcester is not formidable, but the Conveyances may be cross. Mary gives you this invitation on behalf of her Brother and Cousin who would both be proud and happy to see you; and Dora would be overjoyed, as would Mary and I. So I leave the consideration of the journey to your kindness. Mr and Mrs Merewether were greatly disappointed that you cannot come. They look forward to a happier opportunity. Lady B. begged me also to express her regret. A Proposal was sent me from Oxford for a bronze Statue of Wickliff, to be erected in the Town of Lutterworth,[1] by subscription. I have been able to set it agoing in this County through Mr Merewether with a good prospect of success. We had a hope that John might have got a Curacy not far from Manchester, the situation apparently very desirable, but we are disappointed. Nothing better offers than Whitwick[2] near this place, which he declined some time ago; it has indeed few attractions, but John is anxious to be employed. We have written to him about it from this place. I have no more news so farewell with earnest hopes that you will be able to meet *our* wishes.

Most affectionately yours,
W. W.

My dear Chris,

Find out for me how your dear Father can most conveniently get from Cambridge to Hereford. The shortest road from the Map, appears to be through Warwick. Is there any coach from Cambridge to this place, or to Worcester? On looking again at the Map I find Warwick is a little to the North and the direct line across the Country is Cambridge, Northampton, Worcester, Hereford. If you have any acquaintance from these parts of the Country, pray learn which is the best road, for your Aunt and I are most anxious to tempt your Father to join us for a week or more, at Mr Hutchinson's, near Hereford, and Mr Monkhouse's on the Wye; both of

---

[1] John Wycliffe (*c.* 1329–84), the celebrated reformer, was vicar of Lutterworth from 1374 until his death.

[2] The following April John W. accepted a curacy under Mr. Merewether at Whitwick. See L. 331 below.

whom would be most happy to see *you* (I say nothing of John engaged as he must be), now or at any time. If a few days later than the time your Father mentions of his being at liberty would suit him better, pray tell him that it would equally suit [? you].[1] Now my dear Chris., I depend upon your zeal in this scheme, which we have much at heart on our own accounts and dear Dora's, as well as the Good friends we have in Herefordshire.

Should your father be afraid of the Journey, pray unite your eloquence with ours to give him the necessary courage. I have scarcely Space to advert to your Letter. Thank you for it. Your account of St Johns[2] is deplorable. As to the Virgil,[3] I have no objection to its being printed if two or three good judges would previously take the trouble of looking it over, and they should think it worth while. Could Mr Hare[4] find time for that purpose, he or any others. On the other side I have given you a few corrections, and shall be glad of any of yours, or those of anybody else. Adieu. Your aunt sends her best love.

Most affectionately your Uncle,
W. Wordsworth

I find here Rose[5] on the State of the Protestant Religion in Germany, which I never saw before. I have been very much interested in it. Did you learn whether Mr Rose as Editor of the *Museum Crit:*[6] could afford me any pecuniary remuneration for the Virgil?

dear Chris: pray thank Mr Skinner[7] of Jesus for his obliging intentions.

[1] *MS. torn.*

[2] i.e. the opposition of St. John's to the election of C. W. as Professor of Divinity. When John Kaye resigned the Professorship, C. W. offered himself as a candidate, though he was technically in breach of the Statutes, as it could not be held with the Mastership of Trinity or the Vice-Chancellorship. See Winstanley, *Early Victorian Cambridge*, pp. 296–7.

[3] i.e. W. W.'s versions from the *Aeneid* (see L. 115 above).

[4] Julius Hare.

[5] Hugh James Rose (1795–1838) of Trinity College, Cambridge: a native of Buxted, and C. W.'s curate in 1819. In 1824–5 he travelled in Germany, becoming acquainted with German rationalism at first hand, and on his return published *The State of the Protestant Religion in Germany* (see L. 384 below). He was frequently Select Preacher at Cambridge. A prominent but moderate high-churchman, his editorial work for the *British Magazine* and the *Theological Library* brought him into touch with Newman, Hurrell Froude, and Keble, and the conference at his rectory of Hadleigh in Suffolk in July 1833 has always been regarded as an important landmark in the early history of the Tractarian Movement.

[6] *Museum Criticum, or Cambridge Classical Researches*, 2 vols., 1814–26.

[7] George Skinner (*c.* 1796–1871), Fellow of Jesus College, Cambridge, 1818–42.

[The following is written crossed over the page]

> This way and that the vulgar are inclined,
> Split into parties by the fickle mind.
> Where hast thou tarried, Hector? From what coast
> Coms't thou long-wished for? After thousands lost,
> Thy kindred and thy friends such travail borne
> By all that breathe in Troy, how tired and worn
> We who behold thee! But why *thus* return?
> These gashes whence? This undeserved disgrace!
> Who first defiled that calm majestic face?
> My heart misgave me not, nor did mine eye
> Look back till we had reached the boundary
> Of ancient Ares.—[1]

Have the goodness to insert the above correction in your copy,
if not for preference at least for choice.

W. W.

308. W. W. to LORD LONSDALE

MS. Lonsdale MSS. Hitherto unpublished.

[Coleorton]
[early Dec. 1827]

My Lord,
   Yesterday I had the honor of your Lordship's obliging Letter;
and today I am called upon to condole with you upon the death of
Dr Satterthwaite;[2] the tidings of which have just reached me from
West[nd]. For himself, poor Man! it is a happy deliverance; but he
will not the less be regretted by many Friends who were much
attached to him. Of the particulars of his death I have learnt
nothing. It has struck me that Mr Head,[3] in consequence of the
fortune that will come to him upon the death of his Uncle, may
vacate his Curacy, in which case a word from your Lordship with
the succeeding Incumbent in favor of my Son, might introduce him
to that situation, or any other of the kind which the necessary
changes may create. My Son has been waiting nearly a year for an
eligible place to be ordained to. There is one now open in this
neighbourhood, the Curacy of Whitwick under Mr Merewether,

---

[1] See *Aeneid*, ii. 281 ff. and *PW* iv. 319.
[2] At Lowther Rectory on 28 Nov.
[3] Probably James Pearson Head, son of John Head, M.D., of Loweswater,
who had taken his degree at Pembroke College, Cambridge, in 1822.

but it is in many important points, undesirable. He is however, in the absence of a better thing, prepared to accept it. All I wish for in his behalf is some liberty of choice.

I thank you for your brief notice of the state of public affairs. If we are embroiled with foreign powers[1] this feeble administration cannot exist; how long it may keep together, if we are suffered to be at peace, I am afraid neither your Lordship nor your friends can foresee.

Lord Grenville's health lately was in so bad a state (he is now much better) that there was much talk in the University of Oxford about his Successor in the Chancellorship.[2] It is now blown over, but the persons named were the Duke of Buckingham, Lord Dudley and Lord Colchester. Many members of the University are anxious, should a vacancy occur, to avail themselves of the occasion of declaring their attachment to sound principles by voting for some one who has taken a decided part in opposition to the Catholics, to innovations in the representative system, on education, etc.: It would become the University to do so; and having had the honor of being consulted upon the point, I have strongly recommended to my Friends, to stick to their resolution, which advice I trust would have your Lordship's sanction.

Dr Wordsworth lost the Divinity professorship of Cambridge through the jealousy St John's has of Trinity.

Have you heard of the proposal for erecting a bronze Statue of Wicliff in the town of Lutterworth? It is likely to be taken up in this County with spirit. Lord Howe[3] as a Leicestershire Protestant (so he says) will support it.

Lady Beaumont, I am happy to say, continues well and active; we quit their place on Saturday for the neighbourhood of Hereford, stopping two days at Birmingham, and two with Mrs Francis Wills at Worcester; after that time my address for two or three weeks, will be Brinsop Court near Hereford.

I am truly concerned that the accounts of Lord Frederic are unfavorable. With respectful regards to Lady Lonsdale in which Mrs W. begs to join

I have the honor to be
your Lordship's
much obliged
W. Wordsworth

[1] Particularly over Greece. In July, Britain, France, and Russia had intervened to bring to an end the Greek war: on 20 Oct. the Turkish fleet was destroyed at Navarino. [2] See L. 305 above.

[3] Richard William Howe, Earl Howe (1796–1870), grandson of the celebrated admiral.

309. W. W. to ALEXANDER BLAIR[1]

Address: Alexander Blair Esqre., Church Lane, Fulham, London. [*In M. W.'s hand*]
Endorsed: From Wordsworth the Poet.
MS. Harvard University Library.
LY i. 283.

Birmingham
11th Dec. 1827

My dear Sir

Being in Birmingham for a couple of days, I have of course called on your excellent Friend Dr Delys,[2] from whom I learned that you intend offering yourself as a Candidate for the Professorship of English Literature in the London University. This information gave me much pleasure, and I heartily wish you success, persuaded as I am that this employment will be gratifying to yourself, and convinced that you are eminently qualified by your talents and attainments to do credit to it. I am lately come down from a neighbourhood[3] which reminded me of the pleasure which many years ago I enjoyed in your society, talking over with you the principles of taste, and discussing the merits of different Authors, during our pleasant ramble on the banks of the Trent.

We were agreed I think upon everything of importance, and I do not think it likely that your subsequent studies will have made any very important change in your notions, so that if you are elected to this important office, I am persuaded you will deal with our Mother tongue feelingly and reverently. Excuse this short Letter penned in great haste; in an hour or two I quit this place for Worcester and then I am going to Brinsop Court near Hereford to see my Daughter, who went there I am sorry to say on account of deranged health; but she is now, I may say, well.— With kind regards from Mrs W. who is with me I remain my dear Sir, faithfully yours

Wm Wordsworth

[1] For W. W.'s previous contact with Alexander Blair at Coleorton in 1810, see *MY* i. 431–2. Details of his career are scanty. He graduated at the University of Glasgow in Languages and Philosophy, *c.* 1800. Much later, in the early 1820s, he helped his boyhood friend John Wilson to prepare his philosophy lectures at Edinburgh, and was looking for work with *Blackwood's* in return. He was awarded an LL.D. in 1827 in preparation for his candidature for the newly established Chair of English Language and Literature at London University, which, however, he failed to get. He was successful two years later, in 1830, when the Chair became vacant again, but he brought no distinction to it and resigned through ill health in 1836.

[2] Gabriel Jean Marie De Lys graduated M.D. at Glasgow in 1808, and subsequently practised medicine in Birmingham until his death, *c.* 1831.

[3] Coleorton.

310. D. W. to JOHN MARSHALL JNR.[1]

Address: John Marshall, Jun[r], Esq[re], Headingley, Leeds.
MS. WL.
LY i. 284.

Rydal Mount, near Kendal
December 23rd [1827]

My dear Sir,

You will, I hope, before this reaches you, have received a parcel *for your Mother* and directed *to your care*, which a Friend of mine, going to Leeds, was so kind as to take charge of. That parcel consists of two school-books, specimens of the hand-writing etc. of George Green, a Son of the late Mr Green[2] of Ambleside, and, if Mrs Marshall be not yet arrived at Headingley, I beg you will be so kind as to open it, and look over the Books. I am aware that you are much more concerned in the matter, which I am going to lay before you, than your Mother, yet I should not have troubled you with it, except through her, had it not been of importance not to lose time.

A few weeks ago I wrote to inform your Mother and Aunts of the Death of Mr Green's eldest unmarried Daughter, who was the main prop of the Family, and of a plan which had been set on foot for their relief by raising a Subscription, to which I received a most kind and satisfactory reply. But it is not on that subject that I address you.

Some years ago you kindly offered to take Hartley Green, an elder Brother of George into your Factory, which he declined, having other views. This circumstance encourages me to hope that you may, if you have any opening for such a youth, be willing to take *George*, who is exceedingly desirous of obtaining the situation —or indeed *any* situation which through industry and a desire of improvement may hereafter insure a creditable independence; but, above all things he seems to wish that it may be possible for you to take him into a situation similar to that which was offered to his Brother.

George Green will be sixteen years of age next March. From the Books which I have sent, you will be able to judge of his hand-writing and perhaps also of his progress in arithmetic. To this I will add that he is a Boy of modest and pleasing manners, and is in all respects very well thought of in Ambleside and the neighbourhood.

---

[1] Son of John Marshall of Hallsteads. See L. 70 above.
[2] The artist (see *MT* i. 195).

He is a dutiful Son and of very industrious habits. His Mother tells me that he is of a mechanical turn, and I know that he has made some progress in mathematics. He has, besides, always been reckoned a 'good Scholar' among the Schoolboys at the Grammar School at Ambleside: and has the appearance of being quick and clever. In short, there is something very prepossessing in this youth, with a pleasing modesty in his address.

Many kind Friends interest themselves in George Green's behalf, and I find that by this day's post an application has been made for a specimen of his hand-writing etc. and a hope held out of a situation (in a Counting house, I believe), but if you were willing to take him, and if it could be arranged in other points, he would greatly prefer being in your establishment to any thing else.

Hartley Green, the elder, is about to establish an academy at Manchester, and might find employment for his Brother, but he wishes rather to make his own way.

And now, my dear Sir, having said this much on behalf of this deserving Youth, I must beg to assure you, that, however zealous my wish to be the means of serving him and his poor Mother, I do not wish, *on that account*, to influence you—Quite the contrary— I know that in similar cases, your benevolent views have been disappointed, and, perhaps, you have consequently made arrangements for the Future which may render it ineligible to take any youth in the same way as proposed to his Brother—even if you have at present—or are likely in course of a year or two—to have a vacancy. At all events, I shall be much obliged to you if you will write to me as soon as possible—in order that, if you do not hold out any hope, he may not lose time, and if you do, that you may receive further information; and he be put into the way of preparing himself, according to your wishes, for the situation. I *ought* to have said, that though not a *stout* young man, he has always been very healthy, and has no dread of confinement.

Excuse this long letter and believe me, dear Sir, your affectionate Friend,

Dorothy Wordsworth.

311. W. W. to JOHN BOWRING[1]

Address: John Bowring Esqre, No. 2 Queens Square Place, Westminster. [*In Dora W.'s hand*]
Postmark: 31 Dec. 1827. *Stamp*: Here[ford]. *Endorsed*: Hereford. Decr 29. 1827. Wm Wordsworth.
MS. Harvard University Library.
LY i. 286.

Brinsop Court, near Hereford
Dec^{br} 29th 1827

Dear Sir,

A protracted absence from home is the cause of my not having earlier received your obliging Letter of the 4th Ins^{tnt}, containing Professor Schwarts'[2] translations of two little pieces of mine. Of one, 'We are seven', it is mortifying to me to say that I can form no opinion, not being able to read the German Handwriting. I once knew something of it, but through long disuse have forgotten it; the other Translation seems very happily executed.—As I have Friends who are acquainted with German character, I shall avail myself of the first opportunity to read the other with their assistance. You will be kind enough to say to Professor Schwarts for me whatever is becoming under these circumstances. As the German People are such discerning judges, I cannot be indifferent to anything that introduces my attempts to their notice—

It gives me pleasure to see that you continue transplanting the flowers of foreign Poetry into our tongue.

I remain dear Sir
very sincerely yours
Wm Wordsworth

---

[1] John Bowring (1792–1872), traveller and linguist. His chief literary work was the translation of the folk-songs of many European nations. In 1824 he was appointed editor of the *Westminster Review*; later, he edited the works of his friend Jeremy Bentham. He was elected M.P. for Bolton in 1841 to oppose the Corn Laws; in 1847 he returned to the East as consul at Canton. He was knighted in 1854.

[2] Unidentified. The translations were not apparently published.

312. W. W. to ELIZABETH PALMER PEABODY[1]

MS. WL transcript. Hitherto unpublished.

[late 1827][2]

. . . If I am to serve the very young by my writings, it must be by benefiting at the same time, those who are old enough to be their parents . . .

[1] This fragment is apparently all that has survived of W. W.'s first letter to Elizabeth Peabody (1804–94), the American educationist and pioneer of the kindergarten movement, and is quoted in her reply. She had written from Brooklyn on 9 Dec. 1825 suggesting that W. W. should write a volume of poetry for children—which would give 'a new and deeper tone' to the art of education: 'I am an American girl of twenty five, and have read your Poetical Works. Need I tell you that I have found in them, "all that I myself have felt", and lived over again sensations and emotions and sentiments, which were strongly in my soul when "Life shook its rainbow wing", but might never have received again had not your spirit . . . called me forth from the *dissecting room* into "the light of things". For this I am indeed grateful, but like a thousand others who bless you as the High Priest of Nature, I should have cherished my admiration and gratitude in silence, were I not impressed with a feeling almost as strong as Duty, impelling me to direct your thoughts into a channel where it seems to me your genius would flow with mighty power and most important effect. . . . When very young, and during the whole period of youth, I was dissatisfied with the manner in which the old communicated with the young—feeling especially that the system pursued in schools, the whole theory of education, was essentially defective, holding converse only with that part of human nature which may perhaps be denominated mechanical—and that the soul was neglected. . . . The education I received was wanting in power to connect together the heart and the intellect, so as to produce that intelligent feeling or moral power, by which heaven is first gained and then enjoyed. . . . A strong impression was early made upon me, therefore, that the best system of education was defective. I found old people hardly ever knew how young people felt,—or it seemed to me they had *forgotten*, and a determination was elicited within me to keep a remembrance how *I* felt, and when I grew up to inform the world . . . I have arrived to the conclusion that genius can alone fully rise to the appreciation of children's innocence and therefore can most effectively address their minds—that *poetry* is the best means by which to develop the noble part of their nature, and this conviction has been growing, although except *yours*, I have never found any that would at all answer my purpose. . . .' Miss Peabody's eight letters to W. W. (among the *WL MSS.*) reveal his profound influence on Transcendental circles in New England. See also letter of 7 Apr. 1836 (in later volume).

[2] According to a P.S. added to her letter, Miss Peabody had not had the courage to send it off until 17 June 1827—hence the approximate dating for W. W.'s reply.

313. D. W. to JOHN MARSHALL JNR.

Address: John Marshall Esqre Junr, Headingley, Leeds.
MS. WL.
LY i. 287.

Rydal Mount January 8th, 1828.

My dear Sir,

I have delayed replying to your kind letter, wishing to give Mrs Green and her Son[1] time for deliberation, and for that reason, and because I wished to leave them to an unbiassed choice I have not seen them since the receipt of it until yesterday. They beg to return their sincerest thanks for your friendly disposition towards them, in which I heartily join.

George Green is exceedingly desirous to enter into your service, and, if we can have your answer in time, he would depart at the beginning of next week with his Brother-in-law, Mr Fenton,[2] (I believe of Thorpearch) who is now here. But there are one or two queries, put to me by Mr Benson Harrison[3] and Mr Carr, the managers of the subscription lately raised, the answers to which will probably decide whether the thing can be accomplished or not. i.e. What is the *probable* expence of board and lodging?

For what period would he be likely to have to serve at the rate of seven or eight shillings per week? What the progressive rate of wages afterwards? Mr Harrison is aware that the latter questions cannot be answered precisely, as much must necessarily depend on the Youth's ability, good conduct, and the degree of his usefulness: but perhaps you may be able to give us a notion of probabilities, both in this respect, and as to future permanent establishment. I fear, unless he can be boarded for less than 15/- per week (the price paid by Thomas Cookson) (the additional expence of cloaths being considered)—it may be more than can be managed— yet the Friends of Mrs Green would, I know, strain the point as far as could be done, for the sake of putting the Boy in the way of an honourable maintenance, with the chance of establishing himself permanently through industry, diligence, and integrity.

He has been very healthy all his life, but is not *strong-bodied*, or muscular. I should, however, imagine that great strength is not needful for the actual bodily labour, and therefore, if confinement and the entire change of air have not an injurious effect, I should not

---

[1] See L. 310 above.
[2] Schoolmaster at Thorpe Arch, nr. Wetherby.
[3] See *MY* ii. 112. He had recently married D. W.'s cousin, Dorothy Wordsworth of Whitehaven (1801–90).

be fearful on that score. Neither the dust of the Mill, nor the noise, nor the confinement, seem to daunt him in the least, in short, I never saw a more spirited Boy, and he is most desirous of obtaining the situation, and very anxious that there may be no unsurmountable difficulties. Will you *therefore*, and also on account of the opportunity of accompanying his Brother-in-law, who would be useful in fixing him in lodgings—be so good as to reply as soon as possible?

You kindly say you would take him for three months' trial, but Mr Harrison would by no means hold this out to the Boy. He says there is nothing like plunging into certainty at once. At the same time, should the situation not suit *him*, or *he* the situation, he would be glad to give it up, and *you* to part with him at the end of three months.

I think I have no more to say on this subject, and shall expect your answer with some anxiety. I cannot, however, help again thanking you for your zeal in a cause so interesting to myself.

It has grieved me much not to see any of your family during the last twelve months. I was in Yorkshire when you and your Brothers were at Hallsteads, but my Brother and Sister were disappointed that none of you made your way over Kirkstone. I believe they were indebted to you for a large Cargo of Game from the Scottish Mountains. Your [   ]¹ late reports of the state of Mr Marshall's health have been very satisfactory, and I trust we shall see him next summer on the banks of Ulswater at the head of his happy Family. My Brother is still in Herefordshire: but we shall look for him at home by the end of next week, or the beginning of the week following. He purposes to rejoin his Wife and Daughter in April at Cambridge, whence they will probably go to London, and I should hope will find your Father, Mother, Sisters, and probably your Aunts there. This winter has been peculiarly favourable to the beauty of our mountains. Their colouring has been richer than that of summer—for we have had no frost either to blight their greenness or to impoverish the orange-coloured Fern. Often, I doubt not, do you and your Brothers wish for a Christmas fire-side at Hallsteads and a view from the windows of Helvellyn.

Perhaps I might have ventured to direct to Mr Marshall—at Headingley—but do not venture on this expedient to save postage, fearful of delay. Believe me (not forgetful of your boyish days, when you first learned to *mow* on the grass-plot at Watermillock) your very faithful and affectionate Friend

Dorothy Wordsworth.

¹ *MS. torn.*

Mr Benson Harrison, whom I have so often mentioned, is an excellent amiable man—not long ago married to a Dorothy Wordsworth, our cousin. They reside in the house formerly occupied by Miss Knott, very near Ambleside.

314. W. W. to ALLAN CUNNINGHAM

MS. Mr. W. Hugh Peal.
K (—). LY i. 289 (—).

Brinsop Court
near Hereford
Jan^ry 9th 1828

My dear Sir,

Has my friend Mr Quillinan lately ordered a Copy of my Bust from you? If not, be so good as to have one cast for him, which I will pay for; he having left the one he possessed in Westmoreland for a connection of mine. I shall also want a Bust for one of my Nephews, who has lately distinguished himself at Oxford, and has just been elected a Student of Christ Church—where he has rooms as long as he chooses to remain unmarried. When my other two nephews who are now of Cambridge are likely to be as far settled as their Brother, I shall want a Bust for each of them. In the meanwhile be so kind as to have one executed as carefully as you can for Mr Quillinan, who will be directed to call upon you, and let the other be sent to Charles Wordsworth, Esq, Christ church Oxford. I shall be in Town in spring when I will take care to discharge my debt for these Busts; and will also take such steps as may ensure the payment of the one which at Mr Coleridge's request, I mean Mr Edward Coleridge of Eaton,[1] I begged might be cast for him, and which was accordingly sent to him at that place by you; but perhaps he has himself discharged the debt.

In the letter I had the pleasure of receiving from you some time ago you recur to the scheme of a selection from my Poems for circulation among the Scotch Peasantry.[2] When we meet I will talk this over with you, and we will discuss its practicability. I should myself be wholly at a loss what pieces to fix upon for such a Person. I am happy to see that your pen continues busy, but scarcely any new books find their way to me in Westmoreland. I am at present on a visit to a Brother in law, with whom my Wife

[1] See L. 126 above.   [2] See also L. 338 below.

and Daughter are residing for the winter, the Mother as companion to her child, whose health was so much decayed last winter that it was thought adviseable to try the effects of a drier climate. The season has thus far been very unfavorable but she is much better—indeed almost well, though far from being as strong as she needs to be——

Pray give my kind regards to Mr Chantry, nor let Mrs Cunningham or your young folks forget me——

I return to West^nd in about a fortnight.

believe me my dear Sir
faithfully yours
Wm Wordsworth

Be so good as send the Enclosed to the two penny post.——

315. W. W. to EDWARD QUILLINAN

Address: Edward Quillinan Esq, 12 Brianston Street, Portman Square.
Postmark: 12 Jan. 1828.
MS. Cornell. Hitherto unpublished.

Brinsop Court
9th Jan^ry 1828

My dear Mr Quillinan,

This is enclosed to Allan Cunningham with an Order for a bust for you—therefore be so kind as call about it.—Do not omit to thank your Brother for his obliging present from Paris. It shall be recorded on a blank leaf.—By the bye, don't get your Copy of my Poems bound without a few blank leaves in each Volume—to receive any future short pieces that I may write. Your Daughters will not grudge the trouble of transcribing them for you. Say the same to Barrett, for so I take the liberty of calling [him],[1] from affection, and if that be not a sufficient excuse, from ignorance of his present title. I wished you had named him and Sir Egerton in your last to Dora for which she thanks you. Her cold is almost gone—but her throat still seems to trouble her, as she hems too often for my paternal ears—

You will hear from Rydal how the wine is to be sent—Mr Cookson[2] is to be consulted—

We have had a pleasant Christmas here and at the House,

---

[1] *Word dropped out.*   [2] Thomas Cookson of Kendal.

Dr Wor[dsworth][1] and Miss Southey of the party.—To day I am going to Foxley[2] to pass a couple of days there—By this fortnight I must be in Westmorland—In spring I hope some of us will see you in London—

ever very faithfully yours
Wm Wordsworth

316. D. W. to JOHN MARSHALL JNR.

MS. WL.
LY i. 291.

Rydal Mount, 13th Janry 1828.

My dear Sir,

The Bearer of this is Mr Fenton, the Son-in-law of Mrs Green, who keeps a School, (I believe at Thorpe Arch). He has requested a letter of introduction from me (indeed I was the first *to offer it*) thinking it better that before George Green's coming, he, (Mr Fenton) should have a personal interview with you, by which means the Youth will be better able to understand what will be required of him than he possibly would through the letters which have passed between us.

I need say nothing further on the subject as Mr Fenton will give you whatever further information may be needful: but I will just mention that Mr Fenton was educated in this neighbourhood (I think at Hawkshead) and afterwards resided some time at Ambleside, where he was much respected.

With many thanks for your kind and speedy reply to my last letter, I remain, dear Sir,

your affectionate and obliged Friend,
D. Wordsworth.

---

[1] *MS. torn.*   [2] Sir Uvedale Price's estate.

317. D. W. to MARY LAING

Address: Messᵣˢ W. and D. Laing, South-bridge Street, Edinburgh. *For Miss Laing*.
MS. Edinburgh University Library.
The Wordsworth–Laing Letters (—).

Rydal Mount, near Kendal
Janʳʸ 21ˢᵗ 1828

My dear Miss Laing,

I should have answered your kind letter immediately; but having the prospect of an opportunity by a Friend going to Edinburgh I delayed. That opportunity did not arise; and having once delayed, it was quite in my character to go on delaying until a fresh one should spring up—which is at present the case. Mᵣ Allan Harden, (lately returned from India), is going to visit his Friends at Edinburgh, and he has not only kindly offered to convey a packet thither for me; but also, in the course of three or four weeks, to bring back any thing you may have to send. I think you know something of the Hardens. Mᵣˢ H. is the Daughter of the late Mᵣ Allan[1] of Edinburgh; Mᵣ Allan Harden[2] is her eldest Son, and she has a Brother[3] resident at E. who is, I *believe*, in the Law; but of his profession I am not certain; only I know that he is a Widower with three or four Children. His Wife was a Sister of the learned and accomplished Miss Elizabeth Smith,[4] who died young at Coniston, and was buried at Hawkshead. I think you must have heard and read of Miss Smith. Mᵣˢ Bowdler[5] published a short account of her life, and early and lamented death, with some of her letters and translations from the German—and a few other compositions. Thank you, my dear Miss Laing, for your kind recollection of my taste in caps!—I laughed heartily at reading of any thing to be put on my head so fantastic as a *black* Cap edged with blue—and said to myself—'Well, Miss Laing is very good but I cannot accept of her kindness'. However in mentioning it to a

---

[1] Robert Allan (1745–1818), Edinburgh banker and proprietor of the *Caledonian Mercury*. He moved to Bowness towards the end of his life, and is buried in the parish church of Windermere.

[2] Robert Allan Harden (1803–75), b. in Edinburgh and educated at Mr. Dawes's school, Ambleside. See also *MY* ii. 446.

[3] Thomas Allan, F.R.S. (1777–1834), the mineralogist, who married Christian (Kitty) Smith in 1805. They had two sons and three daughters.

[4] Elizabeth Smith (1776–1806), Oriental scholar, eldest daughter of Col and Mrs. Smith of Tent Lodge, Coniston. See De Quincey's *Works* (ed. Masson), ii. 404 ff. Her translation of the *Memoir of Frederick and Margaret Klopstock* was published in 1808 (see *MY* i. 316).

[5] Henrietta Maria Bowdler (1754–1830), religious writer, published *Fragments in Prose and Verse* by Elizabeth Smith in 1808.

Friend—about my own age, but certainly a little more of a fashion-ist than myself—she said: 'Pray refuse not such an offer. You will like it better than any cap you ever wore in your life—and as to unsuitableness to your age and style of dress *that* is all nonsense. You will look as well as another in it'. Such arguments how could a female heart resist? I therefore will thankfully accept your prof-fered gift—but only on the following conditions—

First that the cost be very small

Secondly that the cap can be packed in such small compass that Mr Harden may put it into his carpet-bag. Otherwise, I should beg that he may by no means be troubled with it.

and Thirdly—that *your* trouble in procuring it be not much. At the time you wrote, the thing might be easy—yet not so at present. You might then be in the way of making the like—and *now* there may be a hundred reasons for its being inconvenient.

Leaving then this important matter entirely to your discretion (the three conditions being understood as irrevocable) I turn to other matters. My Brother has been eight weeks absent. He met his Wife at Lady Beaumont's in Leicestershire, and after three weeks' stay, proceeded with her into Herefordshire, where they joined their Daughter, who, you will be glad to hear, is greatly improved in health, though yet far from strong. She is not to return to our variable and moist climate until May or June, and her Mother will remain with her. We expect my Brother at Rydal at the end of this week; but (God willing!) he intends to meet his Wife and Daughter at Cambridge in the Month of April; and he will remain with them till their return into Westmorland, when I trust poor Dora's health may be quite re-established. Her spirits are excellent—and the tone of her stomach seems to be restored. It is solely her liability to coughs and colds which now keeps us anxious. She caught cold towards the end of October, and until the beginning of this month, the cough, with frequent sore throat, continued very troublesome. These symptoms of weakness were, however, happily removed by change of air, at the expence only of a journey of twelve miles. They have been a large and happy party of Cumber-land and Westmorland Folks gathered together under one Roof—M^r and Mrs Hutchinson and their five Children (but the *Five* are natives of Radnorshire and Herefordshire)—Mr Monkhouse, the Brother of Mrs Hutchinson (of whom I am sure you must have heard before from me)—Dr Wordsworth, the Master of Trinity College—Miss Southey—the Laureate's eldest Daughter—my

Brother William, his Wife and Daughter—and, last of all, good old Mrs Monkhouse,[1] with whom Miss Joanna Hutchinson and I must surely have made you acquainted. She has resided many years with her Nephew and Nieces; and is now drawing near to the close of her life. But, though quite sensible of this, and suffering from a wasting malady, she never damps the cheerfulness of the Young—and is at times as merry as her *great-nieces*. As to Dora, if I may judge from her letters, she was never happier in the days of happy Childhood—it has been a treat so unexpected, that while both Father and Mother were with her, she should also have the company of the dearest of her Uncles—her God-father Uncle— and the dearest of her young Friends—Edith Southey.

We, at home, have been very snug and comfortable in a quiet way. Both my Nephews are at home; but John expects in the course of a few weeks to be called to employment elsewhere. He is in good health and spirits. So are we all. You would be astonished with William's strength—and his growth within the last year and a half surprizes every one. His various tedious illnesses in childhood so checked his growth, that at the time you saw him he might almost be said to be *dwarfish*—especially having such large features, and such hollow cheeks. He does not now, it is true, look hardy in the face; but has lost all sickliness of appearance, and is nearly as tall as his Brother.

I felt greatly obliged to Mr Laing for his kindness to my Nephew John Wordsworth (of Trinity College Cambridge) who accidentally called at his Shop in South Bridge Street—and, equally accidentally became known to him as a Wordsworth. At John's return, I was exceedingly sorry I had not *forced* upon him a letter of introduction to your Family—but his time was so short that he thought it would hardly serve for what was to be seen out of doors, and he therefore wished for no introductions whatever—and indeed *I* thought also that they would be useless on that account. He did but spend twelve hours with us, and proceeded straightway to Cambridge—exceedingly delighted with Westmorland and Scotland.

It is time I should speak of your Friend Miss Joanna Hutchinson, who never forgets you and your good Mother. She has no thought of quitting the Isle of Man, where, notwithstanding her unfortunate accident, which disables her from walking, she enjoys better health than for many years past. She has been spending a few weeks at Ramsay; but considers Douglas as head-quarters and is about to

---

[1] i.e. *Miss* Elizabeth Monkhouse, who died about three weeks after this.

return thither. Fortunately the Island agrees equally well with her Brother's[1] constitution, and the vicinity of the Sea to a disabled or superannuated Sailor is always pleasant.

I wish I may get over to see them next summer—but probabilities and possibilities are all at present wrapt up in darkness. Should I go, it would be no small addition to my pleasure to find or meet *you* there; and I need not assure you that if ever Joanna and you come together again it will be a real joy to her. You will have gathered from what I have said that her lameness continues. So, I fear, it will during life; but it is much better—and in time she may, I trust, walk without pain; and, meanwhile, if health do not fail she will be patient and contented.

I was very glad to hear so good an account of your Father and Mother and Brothers; but sorry that your health is delicate, and strength for walking diminished. Perhaps you may change your mind and accept your Friends' invitation to London, in which case I hope you may peep in upon us at Rydal.

My Nephews beg to be kindly remembered to you. William often talks of Miss Laing.

The Southeys are well. Miss Coleridge is returned from London —her Brother Derwent is married,[2] and has a Curacy and School in Cornwall. Hartley lives at present at Grasmere.

Adieu, my dear Friend, believe me your obliged and ever affectionate

D Wordsworth

My best regards to M[r] and M[rs] Laing and your Brothers. Pray let us hear from you by M[r] Harden.

I am glad to find you have so many rational and agreeable amusements. For my part I am neither mineralogist nor geologist, so you must expect no help from me. Were I to pick up hundreds of stones, it would only be for their pretty surfaces—and a cart-load of them might to you be wholly worthless.

I cannot look over this tedious long scrawl so pray excuse all mistakes etc etc etc—

I should think one of those very small Band-boxes such as hairdressers use for Ladies' Fronts might hold the Cap—but one a *little* larger, either of wood or paper, might be put in a carpet-bag.

[1] Henry Hutchinson.

[2] Derwent Coleridge had married Mary Pridham on 6 Dec. 1827.

318. W. W. to LORD LONSDALE

MS. Lonsdale MSS.
K (—). LT i. 290 (—).

Liverpool Jan^ry 25th
1828

My Lord,

I sit down to write from Mr Bolton's House Liverpool, where I am on my way to the North from Herefordshire, and my first word must be one in which Mr B. sincerely joins,—a hearty congratulation on the turn public affairs have lately taken, which it is to be hoped will bring back things to their right course.[1] I am sorry not to see Lord Lowther's name connected with Office[2] in the arrangements spoken of in the public papers, but I hope that this is no indication that your Lordship is dissatisfied with what is going on or that Lord Lowther disapproves.

I will now advert to a concern of my own, which I took the liberty of naming to your Lordship in my last; I mean my Son's Curacy. He is so anxious to be employed that he has written to the Bishop of Lincoln[3] that he means to offer himself at the next ordination his Lordship holds, which will be in March, for Mr Merrywether's Curacy at Whitwick. The objections to this are, that he must furnish part of the Rectory and keep House there, which both on account of the expense and every other consideration is unadvisable. Dr Wordsworth hoped that there would be an opening in one of his Curacies, but he has been disappointed. The Bishop of Chester, whom I saw two days ago at Chester, seemed to think he had better wait till his own summer Ordination, in the probability of something occurring in which he (the B^p) might be

[1] The Duke of Wellington was now forming his ministry, with Peel as Home Secretary and four Canningites, including Huskisson and Palmerston, in the cabinet. Lord Lonsdale wrote at length on 29 Jan. about the political manœuvres following the break-up of Goderich's administration: '. . . The Duke has had difficulties to contend with in all Quarters, and I fear these Difficulties are not overcome. I expect everything from his firm and decisive character, and I shall regret nothing more than that he should fail in providing a ministry adequate to the Exigencies of the moment.' (*WL MSS.*)
[2] Lord Lowther had turned down the Vice-Presidency of the Board of Trade. According to Lord Lonsdale, he would have accepted the office of Commissioner of Woods from the Duke, but it was at that stage already disposed of, '. . . and I am afraid into less efficient Hands. I am sorry for this, as it is a disappointment for him, and a loss to the public . . .' In the event, the office of First Commissioner of Woods and Forests and Land Revenue was later offered to Lord Lowther and accepted by him. As it was an office of profit under the Crown (it carried a salary of £4,000 a year), he had to submit to re-election for Westmorland (see *Carlisle Patriot* for 21 June 1828), but Brougham did not oppose him again.   [3] For Dr. John Kaye, see *MY* ii. 648.

of use to him; but the thing having gone so far with the Bᵖ of Lincoln, I think my Son will be for proceeding. Your Lordship will have the goodness to excuse my troubling you with these particulars, and I am sure will give me credit for due consideration of the delicacy of a Patron interfering with the Incumbent in the nomination of a Curate.[1] Your Lordship's interposition I could not in the slightest degree expect, except under circumstances altogether disagreeable to your feelings; and under these impressions I first named the subject.

This winter has been unusually wet in Herefordshire, so that the change of Climate has not been so beneficial to my Daughter as we had expected. She is however though not strong in good general health. Have you better accounts from Italy? and in what spirits does Lady Frederick write? I have had several Letters from Lady Beaumont who is going to Town at the end of the month to leave it early in May. Mr Bolton is threatened with an attack of Gout; Mrs B. is pretty well, both, with Miss Dixon[2] who is here, present their respectful regards to your Lordship and Lady Lonsdale.

I accidentally met with my old Friend Archdeacon Wrangham at Chester, who tells me he was to have had the Deanʳʸ of Chester,[3] if the late administration had continued. He says that the Bᵖ of Lincoln is preparing, with assistance from many quarters, a work of Biography for the University of Cambridge on the plan of Wood's Athenae[4] for Oxford; and that his own memoir of Dr Zooch[5] would make a part of it; perhaps the Archdeacon may himself name this to your Lordship. It is a pity that the Work should not include distinguished persons of whatever pursuit or profession, instead of being confined, as I understand is intended, to Men of Letters.

When in Herefordshire I passed a few days with Sir Uvedale Price, one of the late batch of Baronets. He is in his 81st year, and active in ranging about his woods as a Setter-dog. We talked much of Sir George to whom he was strongly attached. He has just writ-

---

[1] See L. 308 above.
[2] A local acquaintance, and probably a connection of the Boltons.
[3] Wrangham had been a Prebendary of Chester since 1827 and had recently succeeded to the rectory of Dodleston, Cheshire. He wrote to W. W. on 20 Sept. 1827: 'I enjoy, thank God, very good health in general. My hair to be sure is gone—but there is always, at the worst, or best, the resource of a wig. The Episcopal one, of course, is out of the question.' (*WL MSS.*) He was, however, appointed Archdeacon of the East Riding this year.
[4] *Athenae Oxonienses* by Anthony Wood (1632–95), the antiquarian. Dr. Kaye's projected work was never completed.
[5] For Wrangham's edition of Zouch, see *MY* ii. 523.

ten a most ingenious Work[1] on antient Metres, and the proper mode of writing Greek and Latin Verses; if he is right we have all been wrong; and I think he is. It is a strange subject to interest a man at his age; but he is all life and spirits.

Pray let me know if upon the whole you like the late changes, and are pleased with the aspect of things. Excuse this long Letter, and believe me my Lord

with faithful attachment
your Lordship's obliged Serv[vnt]
Wm Wordsworth

319. W. W. to JOHN TAYLOR

Address: John Taylor Esq[re], 92, Norton Street, Portland Place, London. [*In M. W.'s hand*]
Postmark: 1 Feb. 1828.
MS. Cornell.
K (—). *LY i. 291* (—).

Rydal Mount near Kendal
Jan[ry] 30th 1828[2]

My dear Sir,

You will wonder what had become of me,—I have been from home for several weeks and only returned yesterday; otherwise, believe me, I should not have left the valuable present of your two elegant Volumes[3] so long unacknowledged. I have also to thank you for an exhortation, urging me to pay a tribute to the memory of our departed Friend, Sir G. Beaumont. Be assured I feel strongly on the subject; but even from that very cause one often shrinks from what might prove an unworthy attempt.[4]—

I was not aware that you had written so much verse—the greater is the pleasure I have to look forward to—I have thought it best however after so long a delay to write immediately on my arrival. The Title, To myself, tempted me to glance my eye over one Sonnet, and either I have been singularly lucky, or I shall be sure to

---

[1] *An Essay on the modern pronunciation of the Greek and Latin Languages*, Oxford, 1827, in which he contended that 'our system of pronouncing the ancient languages is at variance with the principles and established rules of ancient prosody and the practice of the best poets'.

[2] 31 Jan., according to W. W.'s dating at the bottom of the letter.

[3] John Taylor's *Poems* of 1827. See L. 261 above.

[4] The memorial verses were not written till 1830 (see *PW* iv. 270).

find your Vols rich in good Verse. That Sonnet is of no common merit.—Farewell—believe me sincerely your

> obliged friend and Ser^vnt
> Wm Wordsworth

I am sorry I cannot send this Scrawl under Cover.

320. W. W. to UNKNOWN CORRESPONDENT

MS. Historical Society of Pennsylvania.
David Bonnell Green, 'Two Wordsworth Letters', NQ cc (Nov. 1955), 489–90.

> Rydal Mount, near Kendal,
> Westmorland
> Jan^ry 30th. 1828

Sir

Your Letter was not put into my hands till yesterday, on my return home after an absence of a few weeks.—A proposal, of the same kind has been repeatedly urged upon me by Mr. Allan Cunningham, viz—that I would make a selection of my own Poetry to be circulated among the Scottish Peasantry, in a cheap Form; to which I have replied that I should be utterly at a loss what portions to select; and I may add that at present nothing of the sort could be done without permission of my Publishers, who have an interest in the Edition of my Works collected last year.—My present intention is to forward your Letter to Messrs Longman; if they object, there is of course an end to the matter—till this Edition shall be disposed of; if they do not; it will then be for me to consider, whether it is prudent to consent to the choice pieces or passages of my Poetry being presented to the public in this manner; in homelier language, to the plumbs being picked out of five expensive Volumes, the whole of which have probably not yet brought to their Author a return equal to what one of the slightest novels of the season may produce.—You will excuse this narrow, though not narrow-*minded* view of the case; for I take it without scruple, having never *composed* a line for the sake of pelf—though I *some*times *published* from that immediate motive; and in so doing, as if the Muses resented even that indignity I have, through the intermeddling agency of the periodical critics, been disappointed.

[*cetera desunt*]

321. W. W. to FRANCIS FREELING[1]

Address: Francis Freeling Esq[r], Post Off., London.
Endorsed: 2 Feb. 1828 Rydal Mount Ambleside W. Wordsworth Esq.
MS. Pierpont Morgan Library.
LY i. 292.

Rydal Mount Ambleside
Feb[ry] 2nd 1828

Dear Sir,

The enclosed Cover contained four copies of an American Newspaper, Canfields Lottery Argus,[2] sent by some person unknown to me, and without any order of mine. It came during my absence, about a week ago, and I take the earliest opportunity of forwarding it to you, trusting that it is in your power to order the Postage l. 2. 8[d] to be returned to me by the Kendal or Ambleside Post Master.—To you I need not observe that it would be a great hardship on literary Men to be subject to demands of this kind; though no doubt in this case a civility was intended, the Party being ignorant that foreign Newspapers are not free of our Postage.

Excuse me if I say that I am glad of being recalled to your mind upon this occasion, and believe me with great respect

Sincerely your's
W[m] Wordsworth

[1] Francis Freeling (1764–1836), Secretary of the General Post Office in Lombard Street. He was given a baronetcy in March of this year.

[2] *The Lottery Argus, Commercial and Exchange Telegraph,* a fortnightly newsheet published from 1826 by Palmer Canfield, a journalist and dealer in lottery tickets with offices on Broadway, New York, and in Philadelphia and Baltimore: author of *An Explanation of a Lottery, on Mathematical Principles,* 1822. In 1829 he launched a weekly, *Canfield's American Argus.* Lotteries had been widely used in the United States since the beginning of the century to raise funds for a variety of public and educational purposes; but frequent abuses (to which Canfield himself drew attention in petitions to the New York Legislature) led to their gradual abolition soon after this. W. W.'s aversion to lotteries was noted by the Revd. J. Pering (see *MY* i. 271) during his visit to the poet in 1808, and recorded in his Journal (*WL MSS.*).

322. W. W. to FREDERIC MANSEL REYNOLDS

Address: Frederick Reynolds Esqre, Ambleside.
MS. Rice University Library. Hitherto unpublished.

[*c.* 8 Feb. 1828]

My dear Sir,

Enclosed is a Letter to Mr Coleridge. I have not said that I am about to be a Contributor.[1]

I am sorry we have no little parcel to send—every body's regards —in particular my Sister's—As pleasant a journey to you as your weak health and the Season will allow.

ever most faithfully yours
W. W.

323. D. W. to WILLIAM JACKSON

Address: To The Revd William Jackson, Queen's College, Oxford.
Stamp: Kendal Penny Post. *Endorsed*: Miss Wordsworth. 14 Feb.
MS. Cornell. Hitherto unpublished.

Rydal Mount 12th Febry.
[1828]

My dear Friend,

Your letter though especially intended for John, is addressed to all of us, and therefore in the name of all I thank you for it; which John would have done himself; but having a bad head-ache, and being withal rather busy, I thought he would only just confine himself to what is absolutely *necessary* and you would be left in the dark respecting our past goings-on and future plans. I shall leave the business for him, to be added to the end of my Letter. We are very much grieved that you have again been ill; and after a respite which had given *us* hopes as well as yourself, that you were about to become a strong man.—A college life is indeed doleful when you

---

[1] Reynolds, accompanied by Charles Heath, proprietor of *The Keepsake*, (see L. 329 below), called on W. W. early in February and offered him a hundred guineas for twelve pages of verse—just at the time when John W.'s Oxford debts had to be settled and money found for his move to Whitwick. As Dora W. wrote to Miss Jewsbury: 'Father could not feel himself justified in refusing so advantageous an offer—degrading enough I confess but necessity has no law, and galling enough but we must pocket our pride sometimes and it is good for us' (*Letters of Dora Wordsworth*, p. 39). For W. W.'s contributions see L. 327 below. Reynolds went on to visit Southey in search of contributions (see Southey, v. 321–3); he also approached Scott (see Lockhart's *Life of Scott*, vii. 107–8) and, later in the year, S. T. C. (see Griggs, vi. 749).

are employed in bleeding and blistering; and much do I wish that you were snugly out of it. But the thing wanted seems always to come slowly, which at present is almost marvellous, there have been of late so many removals by death among the Clergy.

I am glad, however, that you are better, and hope that as your illness has been of shorter duration than usual it may be taking a resolution to leave you altogether.—If so, a college life, or any life will be better than endurable; for it is a compensation for most of the evils we are subject to, if we can but feel ourselves useful to others—and I am sure you are eminently so.

My Brother came home in good spirits, and looking remarkably well. Miss Hutchinson stops me in my *song*—with telling me she has written to you since he came home—so, more is not needed than to assure you that he continues so, and we have good accounts from Brinsop. I think my Sister and Dora will commence their wanderings about the middle of March—first by visiting poor Mrs Gee, who intends to remain at least half a year in the house, so lately set up and improved by Mr Gee. Her plans for the future are not decided; but I think she will most likely live with her Sisters. Jannetta, you will be sorry to hear, has been even dangerously ill— a severe bilious attack. My Brother will meet his Wife and Daughter at Cambridge in April where they will remain till about the 11th of May; and then, probably, all proceed to London—and if once there, no doubt you will see them at Oxford; for Dora's heart will be set upon a visit to that renowned Spot, and to you and her Cousin Charles.

My Brother desires me to say that he hopes you will not look coolly upon our Nephew Charles—for it was no disrespect to you which prevented his calling—but a bad habit grafted upon a naturally shy disposition. At present his Uncle thinks him rather entitled to favour—as, in addition to the pain of calling at all where he was not very intimate, he had to encounter the sense of having done wrong, or rather having neglected what was right— and therefore, in calling at last he shewed at least a disposition to get the better of his faults. I can only add that Charles is a good Lad—so pray forgive him and trust to him as a true Wordsworth— with all his faults whatever they may be.

As you have probably heard, my Brother spent a few days at Liverpool. I only regretted that it was not in his power to see so much of old Friends as he or as [they][1] could have wished—and I was really *grieved* that he did not see my kind Friend and favourite

[1] *Word dropped out.*

12 February 1828

Mr Wardell[1]— As to news, we have little or none hereabouts.
Poor Owen Lloyd has awakened various anxieties, by having once
been unable to get through his Sermon, and various times so uncomfortable that his pain and misery were evident to every one.
Still, however, he is resolved to go on,—and for a few Sundays has
done so to his own and every body's satisfaction. I cannot but think,
however, that it would have been better to leave this place *for a while*
and *give up*; as it must disturb the legitimate object of preaching
when the Hearers' thoughts are occupied only, or chiefly, in noting
the state of the preacher's mind.

Mrs Luff's kindness to him is beyond all praise—and most
grateful he is for it; and so happy at Fox Ghyll that he never
wishes to leave that his pleasant home, except to take long walks,
which he does daily, and also never fails his Pupil, Kelly, who
profits much by his instructions. Kelly and William are great
friends; but not in study, only in bodily exercise—and all their
talk—though not of 'bullocks'—is of shooting, skating, etc., etc.,
etc. I think he will not be sent to College at all—for he declares
against the Church—and what the use of it for one not given to
Books? He is very amiable in temper—and disposition—his
manners much improved—and he is lively and pleasant—and (best
of all) is now very strong in body. But, of this I am sure,—hanging
over a Desk would kill him. What then is he to do? Grievous it is
that his heart is set on the Army—a profession no one can approve
of for him—and both his parents are against it—his mother irrecon-
cileably so. I *fear* he will not be turned from it—Take no notice of
this when you write, nor mention it to anyone; but you are so kindly
interested for him and for all of us I could not help telling you. John
has not been quite well for two days; but I hope it is going off. He
will prob[ably][2] go to Cambridge next week. Miss Hutchinson and
[M^{rs}] Ellwood are both well, and beg their kind regards. So do my
Brother and Willy—John is gone out, so after all, I had best add
his business part of our correspondence. Namely especial thanks for
your trouble about the Testimonials, and a request that you will be
so kind as to pay the Steward of the Junr Common Room at New
College, £23.3.3½, the Amount of an account which has just been
sent in to John. My Brother will pay the Sum into Wakefield's Bank
for your use. My Brother is writing verses[3]—but has not yet turned
to the Recluse—and we shall lose him again so soon that I fear this
winter will produce nothing—and how years roll away!

[1] William Wardell the banker, who married Elizabeth Crump.
[2] *MS. torn.*   [3] See L. 327 below.

I am now 56—and he two years older.—Thank God all we elders are stronger than usual at our years except Miss Hutchinson, and she is fairly well. I can walk 15 miles as briskly as ever I did in my life. We have now frost—and three inches of snow on the ground. Last week we had the warmth of June. Much Rain, but no winter till now except these three days—God bless you in haste ever your affect^e

D Wordsworth

If you see Charles give my Love to him and ask him to write to me—John has desired me to open my letter to say he believes he has a trifling Bill for Battles, not included in the Steward's account. Be so good as ask, and pay it—and when we know my Brother will send the whole to the Bank.

324. W. W. to ALLAN CUNNINGHAM

Address: Allan Cunningham Esqre, F. Chantrey's Esqre, Pimlico, London.
    [*In M. W.'s hand*]
Postmark: 28 Feb. 1828. *Stamp*: Kendal Penny Post.
MS. Mr. Robert H. Taylor.
K (—). *LY i.* 292.

Rydal Mount
Feb^{ry} 26th 1828

My dear Sir,
    You are too late in your application.[1]—I have been disagreeably circumstanced—in respect to these Publications. One of my friends, the conductor of a Public Journal,[2] applied to me some time [ago] for Contributions.—I refused on the ground that I had never been engaged in any periodical nor meant to be. A Gentleman whom I have not the honor of knowing, but to whom I am under considerable obligations,[3] is Editor of one of these Annuals, and had a claim upon me, though he did not ask for a Contribution, nor did I contribute, for the same general reason—I have since had applications, I believe, from nearly every Editor, but complied with none. I have, however, been smuggled into the 'Winter's Wreath' to which I contributed three years ago; it being then intended as a solitary Publication for charitable purposes. (The two pieces of mine[4] which

---

[1] For a contribution to *The Anniversary* for 1829, which Cunningham was editing.
[2] Probably S. C. Hall (see L. 285 above).   [3] Alaric Watts.
[4] *To a Skylark* (*PW* ii. 266), and *Memory* (*PW* iv. 101), composed in 1825 and 1823 respectively, and published in the *Winter's Wreath* for 1828.

appeared there had some months before been published by myself in the last Edition of the Poems.) This having broken the ice, I had less reluctance to close with a proposal the other day made me by Mr Reynolds,[1] the terms of which were too liberal to be easily resisted, especially as coming from a Gentleman who had put me on the use of an application to my eyes, from which, I believe, I derived very great benefit. Indeed they have ailed little since I used it. I need not say how much pleasure it would have given me to accede to your wishes, but I should think it unfair to assist in a work of this kind, upon other terms, nor would it be fair to give away what he pays so largely for.—At present therefore I cannot hold out a hope of being of service to you; if when I have the pleasure of seeing you in Town, which I hope will be in April or May, we may advert to this matter—but do not speak of it publicly; and I ought to add, that for the present year I do not see that I can do any thing.

Many thanks for your attention to the Busts—I am afraid the Bronze would be above my price, otherwise on account of its durability I should like it for the sake of my family—It pleases me much to be so feelingly remembered in your family. Give my best regards to Mrs Cunningham, and to the young people.—Mr Sharp[2] is entitled to the gratitude of the Poets of England for the elegant, and above all for what I am told is the case the very correct Editions published by him—Believe me my dear Sir

Very faithfully your much obliged friend
Wm Wordsworth

325. W. W. and D. W. to HARRIET DOUGLAS

Address: Miss Harriet Douglas, Greshams Hotel, Dublin.
MS. untraced.
Miss Douglas of New York, p. 266.

Rydal Mount,
February 29, 1828.

My dear Miss Douglas,

I should have written to you on my return when I found your interesting letter about six weeks ago, but I was immediately

---

[1] F. Mansel Reynolds, editor of *The Keepsake*. See L. 322 above.

[2] John Sharpe (1777–1860), bookseller of Duke St., Piccadilly, and publisher of *The Anniversary*. One of his most successful ventures was the 'British Classics' series, 24 vols., 1803–10, embellished with engravings by some of the best artists of the day. In 1829 he began *Sharpe's London Magazine*, to which Coleridge and Southey contributed, but it lasted only three issues.

apprized by my son William of the step he had taken[1] and he showed
me a copy of his letter to you and also your most friendly answer.
Under these circumstances we all have thought it best to await the
result of your application which was received yesterday. After
expressing my sense of your good will and ready kindness let me
say the result as conveyed in Lady Wellesley's letter to yourself is
to us no disappointment—quite the contrary.—Had the commission
been obtained I should have been greatly embarrassed, for everything would have been done on my part to prevent my son's
accepting it. The application to you was made entirely of his own
accord without the knowledge of any member of this family,
probably of anyone else. And upon its coming to my knowledge
I should have immediately written to you to beg you would not act
upon it any further but if possible undo what had been done, had I
not wished to let my son learn by experience in this case, as I was
certain he would, to what extent the avenues to the army were
blocked up; and had I not further deemed it both ungracious and
impolitic to endeavour to obstruct what he deemed his interest. In
that part of his letter to you in which he observes that the procuring
of a Commission by favour would reconcile his Mother to the step—
he is utterly mistaken. The expense was the least of his Mother's
objections—they lay much deeper—the strongest of all a conviction
that the shock given to his health while at the Charterhouse unfitted
him for exposure in hot climates and that if exposed to their influence, as a Soldier must be, his malady would return, without any
hope of recovery. This was a peculiar objection that took the lead
of the general ones which she has to the Profession. Pray do not fail
to let the Marchioness know that my son's application was made
wholly unknown to me; and if you choose to, add the fact that I was
truly thankful it failed. I am happy to say that his eyes are beginning
to open—that he is persuaded that the times are against his scheme;
and I doubt not that he will now be reconciled to a mercantile life;
and here, my dear Miss Douglas, I should be truly glad of any
suggestions from you or any service you can render him in that
line.

I am almost at the end of my paper and all about my own concerns. Let me now congratulate you on your Brother Wm's improved health. Truly sorry were we all to hear of the distressing

[1] Against the wishes and without the knowledge of his parents, Willy W.
had written to Miss Douglas in Dublin about his wish for a commission in the
army, and asked her to approach Lady Wellesley, the Lord Lieutenant's
second wife, an American lady from Baltimore, on his behalf.

event. Accept our congratulations on his convalescence, and mine
more particularly as I have not before had an opportunity of alluding
to the subject. You did not mention your Br George—I hope therefore he is well and happy. As to yourself I am glad to think that
you have supported your exertions so well, and seen so much.
You will recollect that I thought tranquillity indispensable—the
course you have chosen seems to have been infinitely better and
I rejoice in your gain. I could say much to you but I have neither
time nor space, having much to-day to do and purposing to go
to-morrow to Mr. Southey's, whose family I have not seen this
age. I also long to see Miss Coleridge, now under his roof after a
protracted absence in the south. In April, I shall meet Mrs Wordsworth and my daughter at Cambridge and proceed thence with
them to London. What are your own plans? Pray let us see you
here—I have plenty of room in my house. Do you think of the
Continent? I must give it up for this year, difficulties connected with
my son, yet unsettled, and other causes compel me to relinquish
the hope; which it was incumbent on me to mention to you, as I
do with much regret. I have no more space—farewell my dear
Miss D.

> Your affectionate Friend,
> W. W.

[*D. W. writes*]

My dear Miss Douglas,

My brother has put this most illegible scrawl into my hands to
look over and fold up, and without the excuse of having to correct
a mistake of his I could not have helped adding a word of kind
remembrance to yourself and Brothers, my fellow travellers on the
Steeps of Saddleback. But I must tell you that my Brother is mistaken
in supposing that William's application was made without the
knowledge of anyone. I knew of it—but gave no advice whatever.
The letter was written wholly of himself—but I did not discourage
his writing, thinking that your answer would most likely settle his
mind at once by assuring him of the impossibility of obtaining a
commission. So it has proved, and I am truly thankful that I acted
as I did; for no arguments of mine, or even of his parents (for he
thought we were influenced by private and particular objections)
could shake his inclinations. Besides, he persuaded himself that we
were ignorant of the present state of the army; and therefore were
swayed by imaginary obstacles. Miss H[1] thanks you for your letter

[1] i.e. S. H.

and will write when we hear again from you and know where you are. William intends to write to thank you for your great kindness to him—and in the meantime begs his affectionate and respectful remembrances.

This is a sad letter—pray excuse it and let us hear from you again as soon as you can. I see my Brother tells you the Continental scheme is given up for this year. So I fear it must be—but a hope still clings to me that difficulties may pass away or be overcome. Adieu, my dear Miss Douglas. Believe me affectionately yours,

Dorothy Wordsworth.

326. W. W. to WILLIAM JACKSON

Address: The Revd William Jackson, Queen's College, Oxford. [*In S. H.'s hand*]
Stamp: Kendal Penny Post.
MS. Cornell. Hitherto unpublished.

[early Mar. 1828]

My dear Friend,

I must scrawl you a Congratulation. You have done well in accepting the living[1]—it is a great honor to be brought so near such a Man as Lord Lonsdale by his own choice. I cannot say how highly gratified I am in seeing two friends among the highest in my esteem thus behaving, thus disposed, and thus circumstanced, towards each other. It will not escape the notice of the Lowther family that you have made a great sacrifice of income, and that will no doubt be considered upon a future occasion. Your place I fear will be but ill supplied in Queens—tell me about this, for the apprehension is almost the only drawback upon the event. There are certain points which I shall not allude to till I have the pleasure of conversing with you, merely hinting at present that they belong to the situation of the Rectory with regard to the Castle.

It concerns us much to hear that you have not been well. The professional duty of Lowther cannot be injurious to you, it is so light—but the contrary. We are pleased that you like Charles W.—you perhaps saw the Notice of his Brother C. in the Papers how near *he* was to the University Scholarship—I wish Charles may be more fortunate—but I fear his passion for Cricket tennis etc.

I am just upon the point of making up my Stamp Off. Quarterly

---

[1] Of Lowther.

Account so that I cannot request you to pay for the Battles[1] till I know how it stands; the Office very recently called upon us for payments not required till this quarter—such appears to be the want of money in the exchequer.

Your Brother[2] never approaches these Doors—so we had heard nothing from him about Lowther.

I have the pleasure to tell you that Mrs Benson Harrison was last night brought to bed of a stout and ponderous Boy. My Sister is with her. She had I believe a favorable time. Her Husband by medical advice has kept the house all Winter—for my own part I cannot but think him in a ticklish way—his malady is slight inflammation in the Trachea which nothing but care, in the opinion of his Physician D[r] Ainslie[3] and of Mr Carr, can prevent terminating in consumption. Farewell—God bless you. I give up the Pen to Miss Hutchinson—Lord Grenville I have heard is dying; [?][4] about his Successor as Chancellor—[5]

ever faithfully yours W. W.

[S. H. writes]

M[r] W. ought to have left me the only piece of *news* which the neighbourhood affords as he has ordered me to fill up the paper for you—I need not do it with congratulations for you know full well we shall all be *right glad* to have you in Westmorland again. Our Travellers send us upon the whole very favorable accounts of themselves—tho' poor Dora has had many attacks of cold during the winter—and was when we last heard suffering a little from indigestion—but she is in excellent spirits and her Mother thinks her health notwithstanding greatly improved. They leave Herefordshire next Monday—will visit poor Mrs Gee and in April, perhaps about the middle of that month, go to Cambridge. It is their intention to stop at Oxford on their way—and if you are not there the disappointment will be great—but no doubt they will acquaint you or Charles with their movements. M[r] W. will meet them at C. and intends being in Town in May—not sooner than the 11th.

John was ordained on the 2nd and is still at Cambridge. The examination was very easy and he got well through it. I wish he had had a *'tidier'* curacy than Whitwick. He will be quite *lost* among the Stocking weavers—especially as he is obliged to live alone— Our neighbours are all well—Mrs Luff as busy as ever making im-

---

[1] See next letter.   [2] Thomas Jackson of Waterhead.
[3] Dr. Henry Ainslie (1760–1834) of Kendal, and Dover St., London, Physician to St. Thomas's Hospital, and a landowner in Grizedale.
[4] *MS. torn.*   [5] Of Oxford University. See L. 305 above.

provements. So is Barber—building himself a bed-room 30 feet long—perhaps I told you this before for I recollect writing it to some one and I know no other of my correspondents that it was likely to amuse except yourself, or Quillinan.

Take care you do not use us as shabbily the next vacation as you did the last! God bless you! truly your Friend, S. H.

Mr W. will thank you if you can learn the expense of keeping John's name on the Books at New Col. John is this moment returned

7 oClock

I have tried in vain to *mend* W's letter—so you must make it out yourself—*if you can*

327. W. W. to M. W. and DORA W.

MS. British Museum.
'*Some Unpublished Letters of William Wordsworth*', *Cornhill Magazine, xx* (*1893*), *257–76. K* (—). *LY i. 294.*

Thursday [early Mar. 1828]

Dearest M. and D.,

From what I learn Mrs Gee[1] is left in such narrow circumstances that on that account alone, it would be better not to stay more than three weeks with her at the utmost. I could wish to assist Mrs Gee (tell her) in disposing of her portion of the Langdale Estate, but you are aware that no complete title can be made to it till little Mary M. is of age, so that I fear it will be almost an insurmountable objection. I will try. I shall be hurt if you do not so contrive as to spend at least a month at Cambridge with Dr W. It is not necessary that I should be there to *meet* you; I will follow as soon as I can. The day before yesterday Mrs B. Harrison[2] was brought to bed of a stout ponderous Boy—she is doing well. Mr W. Jackson has been presented by Lord L. to the living of Lowther[3] which he has accepted—write to him to ascertain whether he will be in Oxford when you pass—he could ask Charles W. also for you, which would spare the expense of two Letters. John arrived the day before yesterday, looking well and apparently in good spirits. Bills to the

---

[1] Mrs. Gee was moving to Hendon, where she opened a school, and she was now anxious to settle her affairs. Her late husband had been one of the partners in the Ivy How estate (see *MY* ii. 509); another share had been held by the late Thomas Monkhouse whose daughter and heir was a minor.
[2] Mrs. Benson Harrison.   [3] See previous letter.

amount of upwards of 60 pounds including the one paid by Mr Jackson, have been sent for Battles, the Taylor's bill not included, 7 pounds for a new suit, one also left at Cambridge, so that with Whitwick furniture, and John's journey and settling etc the expenses on John's account will be very formidable.

This was my main inducement for closing with Mr. Reynolds's offer for the Keepsake.[1] I have already written all that will be necessary to fulfill my engagement, but I wish to write a small narrative Poem by way of variety, in which case I should defer something of what is already written till another year, if we agree. I have written one little piece, 34 lines, on the Picture of a beautiful Peasant Girl bearing a Sheaf of Corn. The Person I had in my mind lives near the Blue Bell, Tillington—a sweet Creature, we saw her when going to Hereford. Another Piece, 82 lines, same stanza as Ruth, is entitled The Wishing-Gate at Grasmere. Both have, I think, merit. Mrs Ellwood and Dorothy dont go till Saturday—this evening, I am told they go tomorrow. W^m continues in good spirits and sufficiently industrious. Say to Mr Monkhouse, C. Wilson's behaviour shews the good sense of Dr Venables' advice, have nothing to do with Gentlemen.[2] I am sorry for his disappointment. I hope dear Dora's looks are better and that she will collect some flesh as Edith[3] did. I will add for D. a few additional lines for the *Promise*, that is the title of the poem.[4] After—'Where grandeur is unknown,' add

> What living Man would fear
> The worst of Fortune's malice, wert thou near,
> Humbling that lilly-branch, thy sceptre meek.
> To brush from off his cheek
> The too, too happy tear?
> Queen and handmaid lowly! etc.

[1] W. W.'s contributions to *The Keepsake* for 1829 consisted of *The Country Girl*, later entitled *The Gleaner* (*PW* iv. 159); *The Triad* (*PW* ii. 292); *The Wishing-Gate* (*PW* ii. 299); and two sonnets, *A Gravestone upon the Floor in the Cloisters of Worcester Cathedral*, and *A Tradition of Darley Dale, Derbyshire* (*PW* iii. 48–9).

[2] De Selincourt misread this word as a reference to 'Quillinan' (*LY* i. 295 n.). The sentence seems rather to refer to some local dispute in which John Monkhouse was engaged, which W. W. had heard about while at Brinsop the previous autumn. The Revd. Richard Venables, D.D. (1775–1858), of Llysdinam Hall, Brecon, had been a Fellow of Clare College, Cambridge, 1795–1808, and held a succession of livings in Radnor, as well as being Archdeacon of Carmarthen, 1832–58. He was a friend of the diarist Kilvert.

[3] Edith Southey.

[4] i.e. *The Triad*. The following lines differ in important respects from the published text.

Early March 1828

Before 'Next to these shades a Nymph,' etc., read thus

> Like notes of Birds that, after showers,
> In April concert try their powers,
> And with a tumult and a rout
> Of warbling force coy Phoebus out,
> Or bid some dark cloud's bosom show
> That Form divine, the many-coloured Bow,
> E'en so the thrillings of the Lyre
> Prevail to further our desire,
> While to these shades a Nymph I call,
> The youngest of the lovely Three:—
> With glowing cheek, from pastimes virginal
> Behold her hastening to the tents
> Of Nature, and the lonely elements!
> And as if wishful to disarm
> Or to repay the tuneful Charm,
> She bears the stringed lute of old Romance, etc.

for 'With the *happy* Rose enwreathed', on account of the 'happy tear' above, read 'with *Idalian* rose'.

read thus:

> Only ministers to quicken
> Sallies of instinctive wit;
> Unchecked in laughter-loving gaiety,
> In all the motions of her spirit, free.

After that lively line

> How light her air how delicate [her] glee!

the word 'glee' ought not to occur again.

Farewell, dearest Loves. I have shewn the above additions to Nobody, even in this House; so I shall shut up my Letter that neither it nor they may be read. Love to all at both Houses. Again farewell.

Your affectionate husband and father,
W. W.

328. W. W. to THOMAS JEWSBURY[1]

Address: Mr Jewsbury. [*Delivered by hand*]
MS. Cornell. Hitherto unpublished.

[*c. 6 Mar. 1828*]

My dear Sir,

I have just seen a Letter from Mr Reynolds to Mr S——[2] in which he says that the Contributors to the Keepsake for the year are fixed—so that there will be no further room.[3] Therefore you need not trouble yourself to mention the subject.

ever sincerely yours,

W Wordsworth

329. W. W. to ALLAN CUNNINGHAM

Address: To Allan Cunningham Esqre, Chantry's Esqre, Pimlico, London
[*In M. W.'s hand*]
Postmark: 10 Mar. 1828. *Stamp*: Kendal Penny Post.
MS. Mr. W. Hugh Peal.
K (—). *LY i. 293* (—).

Rydal Mount, March 7th 1828

My dear Friend,

I am sorry to find you rate my assistance so high—it would give me great pleasure to meet your wishes,[4] but I see little hope of it at present—even if the terms on which alone I should feel myself at liberty to contribute could be acceded to by you. Much as I should value the bronze Bust it is a mode of remuneration too indefinite for my present engagements. Considering the sums offered by Mr Heath[5] to literary men, I think it might be imprudent to enter into competition with him as far as Authorship goes, unless the Proprietor (or proprietors) of your work be prepared to enter upon it with a Capital that would allow a heavy expenditure for

---

[1] Miss Jewsbury's father was now employed as a dealer in worsted and insurance agent in Manchester.
[2] Southey. [3] i.e. for a contribution from Miss Jewsbury.
[4] See L. 324 above. Writing again on 3 Mar., Allan Cunningham had offered the bronze bust in return for a contribution to *The Anniversary*: 'Pay me in such coin as your heart and imagination stamp and I shall be enriched. Take up your pen and pay me with verse—a far better coin than minted gold. Then behold a miracle! a *Scotchman* prefers true poetry to current cash . . .' (*WL MSS.*)
[5] Charles Heath (1785–1848), the engraver, and proprietor of *The Keepsake* (see also L. 322 above). He worked extensively for the annuals, and illustrated *The Shakespeare Gallery*, 1836–7.

this branch only, though comparatively with the Embellishment insignificant.

I speak to you as *Editor* alone. The proprietors of some of these works have made large sums by them, and it is reasonable that the writers should be paid in some proportion.

For my own part I acknowledge that a wish to gratify you, and I feel it very strongly, comes and must come second upon an occasion like this. It is a matter of trade. All my natural feelings are against appearing before the Public in *this* way.—Having spoken thus frankly, I dismiss the subject.

My Sister remembers you with great interest and begs her kind regards—

Ever faithfully yours
Wᵐ Wordsworth

Steel engraving has given birth to these Publications, and the immense number of impressions of the Plates which it allows must be the support of those that succeed. It is therefore politic not to [?][1] the Authorship which after all forms but a small part of the expence.

330. W. W. to LORD LONSDALE

MS. Lonsdale MSS. Hitherto unpublished.

Rydal Mount
7th March 1828.

I have just learned from the Newspapers the death of Lord Frederick[2] and I sincerely condole with your Lordship and Lady Lonsdale on this melancholy occasion. Lady Frederick will not doubt of my sympathy with her distress; as it must have been long anticipated I hope she suffers less from the sad event.

I have to thank your Lordship for a long and interesting Letter[3] upon the state of public affairs. At that time I was much in the dark, and your account was most acceptable. Notwithstanding the explanations given in the two Houses many points are as dark as ever; Mr Herries,[4] as probably your Lordship is aware, complains of

---

[1] *MS. illegible.*

[2] Lord Frederick Bentinck, Lord Lonsdale's son-in-law, had recently died in Rome.   [3] Of 29 Jan. See L. 318 above.

[4] John Charles Herries (1778–1855), financial secretary to the Treasury under Lord Liverpool and Canning, had been appointed Chancellor of the Exchequer under Goderich at the express desire of the King. But thereafter he quarrelled with Huskisson, Colonial Secretary, over the appointment of a chairman of the finance committee; and Huskisson agreed to join Wellington's administration only on condition that Herries ceased to hold the office of Chancellor.

having been ill used by Lord Goodrich,[1] and declares to his private friends that the truth will, at a proper time, come out. He is not in good health. Mr Brougham, I understand, has not raised himself in the opinion of the Professions by his speech upon the abuses of the Law.[2]

As far as I could collect of opinions during my late absence from home, it seemed pretty generally agreed that a recurrence to a property tax, as equitably adjusted as possible, would be the best relief for our financial embarassments.

What will be the fate of Lord John Russell's motion,[3] in the House of Lords? A spirit is gaining ground which one cannot but be somewhat afraid of, because it seems rather to arise out of a want of reflection, than a due consideration of the bearing of things upon each other.

Mr Bolton has been very ill—his exertions in favor of Mr Huskisson[4] at the time of the election were too much for him.

I saw Mr Southey two days ago at Keswick; he is as busy as usual and quite well—he purposes being in London next May— and I shall probably be there myself about the same time.

With respectful regards to Lady Lonsdale I have

the honor to be
faithfully your Lordship's
Wm Wordsworth

[1] Frederick John Robinson, Viscount Goderich, later 1st Earl of Ripon (1782–1859), had been Chancellor of the Exchequer under Lord Liverpool, and Secretary for War and the Colonies under Canning, and on the latter's death in Aug. 1827 he was chosen by the King to form an administration. But his unfitness for office quickly became apparent, and the quarrel between Herries and Huskisson, coupled with the proposal to bring Lord Holland into the cabinet, led ultimately to his resignation in January. Goderich accepted office again under Lord Grey in 1830 and in Peel's second administration, 1841.

[2] On 7 Feb. Brougham had inaugurated a new era in law reform in a six-hour speech in the House of Commons (*Speeches*, ii. 319 ff.) on the anomalies and defects of the law of real property and in proceedings at common law: 'the most learned and thorough criticism', according to Sir William Holdsworth, 'of the many defects of the common law that has ever been made since the Commonwealth period'. See New, *Life of Lord Brougham to 1830*, pp. 390 ff.

[3] Lord John Russell, 1st Earl Russell (1792–1878), the celebrated Whig statesman: in these years devoted to the cause of Parliamentary reform. On 26 Feb. he had moved for the repeal of the Test and Corporation Acts, and though opposed by Peel, Huskisson, and Palmerston, his motion was carried by an unexpectedly large majority of 44. The resulting Bill passed the Commons, went through the Lords with the support of Lord Holland, and became law on 28 Apr.

[4] William Huskisson (1770–1830) had represented Liverpool in place of Canning since 1823 as the only Tory likely to conciliate the Liverpool merchants.

331. W. W. to LORD LONSDALE

MS. Lonsdale MSS. Hitherto unpublished.

Rydal Mount
Saturday
[mid-Mar. 1828]

My Lord,

My Son, being anxious to be employed has been ordained by the Bishop of Lincoln to the Curacy of Whitwick which I mentioned to your Lordship. He is just returned from Cambridge where the ordination took place, but it strikes me that I ought to have informed your Lordship *instantly* upon the Event, and I beg your excuses for not doing so, as you may have had some trouble in furtherance of your kind wish to benefit him. He is disposed to enter upon his duty chearfully and resolutely, but it is certain that there are not many places with fewer attractions or recommendations than Whitwick.

I could much wish to know how Lady Frederick is, and where she is—but I was unwilling to tax your Lordship on this occasion—particularly as you had been good enough to write me so long a Letter before. Perhaps Lady Lonsdale would give me a line upon this subject, but I knew how many enquiries she will have to answer upon this melancholy occasion.[1]

It is a long time since I heard from Lord Lowther—it mistified me much that an office[2] for which he was so eminently qualified as that you name should have been conferred on another.

Mr Wm Jackson (with a charge of secrecy) has informed me that he has been presented to the Living of Lowther. I was glad to hear this on every account; he writes most feelingly on the occasion; I have known him long and intimately, and with encreasing respect and esteem, so that I am persuaded your Lordship has every prospect of satisfaction from the honor you have done him by placing him so near you.

I remain
ever most sincerely and faithfully
Your Lordship's obliged
friend and servant
W Wordsworth

[1] The death of Lord Frederick Bentinck.
[2] The Commissionership for Woods. See L. 318 above.

Address: The Revd William Jackson, J. J. Crump's Esqre, 7, Queen Anne St.,
Liverpool [*In M. W.'s hand*]
Stamp: Kendal Penny Post.
MS. Berg Collection, New York Public Library, Hitherto unpublished.

[late Mar. 1828]

My dear Friend,

First let me mention what I forgot in my last and may forget again, that I do not mean to pay into the Kendal Bank the sum you advanced on John's account at Oxford, till after the present quarter is expired, which will be in two or three weeks. My reasons for taking this Liberty you will remember, are included in my last.[1]

Now to come to the important subject of your last.—

Lord L.'s inducement[s] for offering you Bolton[2] were twofold—he thought it better in point of income, and tenable with a fellowship.—It is not so, it therefore comes to a consideration whether the additional income is of sufficient importance to you to outweigh the reasons for accepting Lowther in preference.—These are first, the gratification of Lord L.'s mind if he wishes you to accept Lowther; as far, I mean, as he himself is concerned. His wish would have I know, as it ought to have, great influence with you.

Next look at yourself—you have already stated to Lord L. your notions of the advantages of being so near his residence. Could these be given up upon a mere money consideration unless the difference was so great as almost, in common prudence, to inforce it; I think not, and you seem to have thought so too.—

It follows therefore that you have only to consider how far your plans of happiness and usefulness in this life, are dependant on this difference. Without any thing discreditable to you they may be so to a degree, that would make it proper to accept Bolton; if so—do it; if not—do not—

For my own part I am fond of the generous impulse in life—I like to trust to it—You acted under it when you made up your mind to accept Lowther (with great sacrifice of income) before Bolton came in between—I am inclined strongly to say, but without losing sight of the suggestion above of which you alone can be an adequate judge, stick to the first resolution.—Lord L. cannot be ignorant, sooner or later, of the loss of income in giving up your

---

[1] See L. 326 above.
[2] A parish between Lowther and Appleby. Lord Lonsdale was patron of the living.

Fellowship etc, and a further sacrifice of the kind he has delicacy to appreciate. So I am sure Lord Lowther would have, one of the kindest men breathing. So that in the end the generous course may be proved to have been the prudent one—Farewell I wish I could have seen you—before I spoke thus confidently. Best regards to all the family you are with—

ever most affectionately
your W W.

My pen not worth a straw, and I have neither time nor ability to mend it—

John read prayers at Grasmere last Sunday and at Rydal today—He has a good voice, not ill managed, which is of great importance in a Northerner, an excellent and easy pronunciation.

332. W. W. to JAMES DYER[1]

Address: Ja[s] Dyer Esq[re], English Academy, Edinburgh.
Postmark: 4 [Apr.] 1828.
MS. Messrs. Oliver and Boyd.
English Language Notes, vol. vi, no. 1 (Sept. 1968).

Rydal Mount April 3rd
1828

Dear Sir,

Mess[rs] Oliver and Boyd[2] (as perhaps you may have learned from themselves) decline the proposed Publication, because I cannot accede to their proposition; that all future editions of the work, if any be called for, should be theirs upon the same terms. I told them that I should regard them as having a prior claim to consideration, but that I would not *bind* myself to them, as to any future Edition, having not done so with any publication whatsoever in which I have been engaged. They ground this proposition of theirs upon the trouble and difficulty of getting a School-book introduced, and therefore, say they, a Publisher would never be remunerated or stimulated to exertion upon one Edition unless he retained a permanent interest in every succeeding one!! It is obvious that a claim grounded upon this view of the Case, would not only prevent

---

[1] English master at Edinburgh Academy, 1825–32.
[2] The Edinburgh publishing house which had been planning, probably at Dyer's suggestion, a selection of W. W.'s poetry for schools.

me from transferring the Publication to another if I were dissatisfied, but might also be urged to prevent me withholding even my *Refusal* to the Printing a second Edition. They might plead that they had incurred trouble and expense, etc, and that it was dealing hardly with them if having granted them the liberty to print all future Editions I came to a resolution that none should be printed, though there was a demand for a second—a demand, as they might say, in no small degree created by the pains they had taken.—They overlook the fact that though they be intended principally for a School-boo[k] it would have a wider sale. We differed also upon another Point of Minor importance—they require a discount or Commission of ten per Cent etc, to this I objected as unreasonable, though I am aware that authors either from necessity or carelessness, too frequently submit to this demand; the consequence of which is, that instead of having one half of the proceeds of the Sale, after printing, paper, advertising, etc, are found, they have only two shares out of five—

I am truly sorry that you should have had so much trouble upon this occasion—to no purpose—as other Publishers would probably take the same view of their interests Messers O. and B. have done; and to such an arrangement I must give a positive refusal.—

I cannot conclude without expressing my pleasure on finding that you have taken such an interest in these volumes, and my thanks for the trouble you have had upon the occasion. If the beauty of this Country should attract you hither I hope you will favor me with a call—

I remain dear Sir
yours respectfully
W. Wordsworth

(turn over)

PS. It has just struck me—that if you might be disposed to venture upon striking off as many copies as might answer the demand of your own Academy or a few friends; and so manage the thing as not to be out of pocket by it; if you should be of that opinion, and have the inclination, I give my consent with great pleasure to the attempt; not looking for any pecuniary emolument for an Edition upon such a Scale.

MS. WL.
LY i. 297.

Rydal Mount, April 3rd 1828

My dear Sir,

The Bearer of this is Mr George Green, the Youth about whom you have so kindly interested yourself. He is on his road to Howdon, where he has obtained a situation, which I hope may suit his bodily constitution better than the labour of a Mill, and also, (provided his future conduct corresponds with the wishes and hopes of his Friends) may lead to a comfortable maintenance hereafter.

I wish much that George Green may be so fortunate as to find you at home, as I should like you to see him; but the reason why he ventured to ask me for a letter to you was, that he might have an opportunity of getting his copy-books, which I sent as a specimen of his hand-writing etc, and which you will be so kind as to restore to him I think you will be pleased with the countenance and demeanour of the youth, and will, I am sure, heartily join with me in wishes for his health and prosperity.

I hope your Father and Mother and Sister are now at, or on their road to, Headingley: for I was told on Thursday by a Gentleman (in the Coach between Carlisle and Penrith) who seemed well acquainted with your Family and their movements, that you were all to be at Headingley during the Easter Vacation.

On the strength of this, I ventured yesterday to send two letters to your Mother, requesting her to beg Mr Marshall to be so good as to forward them to Mrs Wordsworth.

My Brother is at home, and begs his kind regards. On the 20th he will set off for Cambridge to meet his Wife and Daughter there, and the three, probably, (with Dr Wordsworth) will proceed to London. At least, this is what they talk of. But at all events, my two Brothers, at least, will be there about the 12th of May. My Nephew John will finally leave home about the 25th to enter upon the Curacy of Whitwick, near Coleorton, in Leicestershire

With kind regards to all around you,
I remain, dear Sir,
Your sincere Friend,
D. Wordsworth.

334. W. W. to BARRON FIELD[1]

Address: Barron Field Esq[r], 8 Great George's Square, Liverpool.
MS. John Rylands Library. Hitherto unpublished.

Rydal Mount
16th April 1828

My dear Sir,
The enclosed was written on the morning I received yours. I
kept it with a hope of sending it with some trifling additions,
through a Frank. But on Friday next, I expect to be at Liverpool;
and I much regret without a chance of seeing you, as I purpose to
arrive on Friday Evening by the Kendal Coach, to depart early
next morning for Ashby de la Zouche; my object is Cambridge—
but I go that way to accompany my Son, who has undertaken a
Curacy in that neighbourhood. I shall stop with him a Couple of
days and then proceed to Cambridge where I shall stay till the tenth
of next month and then go for a short time to London where I have
business. During the summer I hope to be here, where I shall be
very glad to see you and Mrs Field, as will my family—
I will now add a few things upon the subject of your interesting
Letter.[2] On referring to my corrected Copy, I find the Cuckoo
stanza thus,

---

[1] Barron Field (1786–1846), lawyer and miscellaneous writer: friend of
Lamb, Coleridge, Wordsworth, Hazlitt, and Leigh Hunt: Judge of the Supreme
Court of New South Wales, 1817–24, Chief Justice of Gibraltar, 1829. In 1840
he completed his 'Memoirs of the Life and Poetry of William Wordsworth,
with Extracts from his Letters to the Author', which, however, W. W.
persuaded him not to publish. (His objections are contained in a number of
MS. notes added to Field's text.) Field was a keen student of W. W.'s textual
alterations, maintaining his own elaborate variorum edition of the poems.
'When Mr Wordsworth first collected his whole works in 1827,' Field wrote in
the MS. Memoirs, 'he made sundry alterations in them, in deference to Mr
Jeffrey's Edinburgh Review, which appeared to me to injure their simplicity;
and I took the freedom of expostulating with the great poet upon these
refinements.' (*British Museum MSS.*)
[2] Barron Field had written from Liverpool on 10 Apr.: 'Since you were kind
enough to visit me here, I have been thinking of what you said concerning the
several alterations of your Poems, which you made upon collecting them into
5 volumes; and I have gone through the long and instructive lesson of collating
them all with the previous editions, correcting those editions with my pen, so
as to shew the eye hereafter the various readings at a glance; and in performing
this task, I have been amply repaid by both a deeper insight into the poet's
meaning and a better lesson in the art of poetry, than I could have derived from
any other sources. . . . I am he who formerly completed in MS. interleaved in
my copy of your 2 octavos, your Epistles from the Lakes and from the Alps
and your Female Vagrant, which you may remember to have seen at our friend
Charles Lamb's, 13 years ago—such has always been my love for your poetry!'
And Field then went on with a detailed criticism of many of W. W.'s alterations: 'And first I think I have detected a little disposition in your alterations

16 April 1828

Often as thy inward ear
Catches such rebounds, beware—[1]

Listen, ponder etc—. I cannot correct The Beggars more to my
own liking than thus. I mean keeping up to the higher tone of
diction assumed in it for the reasons in the former sheet: if you can
do better I shall be obliged.

> She had a tall man's height or more;
> No bonnet screen'd her from the heat;
> A long drab-coloured cloke she wore,
> A mantle reaching to her feet;
> Luxuriant curls half-veil'd her ample brow,
> Shed from beneath a cap white as the new-falln snow.[2]

Next stanza unaltered, Then—

> She begg'd an alms—no scruples check'd
> The current of her doleful plea,
> Words that could challenge no respect
> But etc—[3]

Page 168 2nd vol. for

> To take an image which was felt no doubt

Read

> As at some moments might not be unfelt,[4]

Simon Lee page 215–vol: 4th.[5] If the stanza now standing 2nd

to mitigate that simplicity of speech, which you taught us was the true language
of the heart, and to make some tardy sacrifice at the shrine of poetic diction; and
thus, after having "created the taste by which you have been enjoyed", in a
small degree deserting your disciples, Why should Alice Fell and Andrew
Jones have been omitted, or the Beggars and the Blind Highland Boy and the
Gipsies altered, whether or not in deference to the utter want of sympathy of
Mr Jeffrey or the conceit of Mr Hazlitt?' W. W. takes up a few of Field's
criticisms in his reply; many more are discussed in a later letter of 24 Oct.
(L. 366 below).

[1] *Yes, it was the mountain Echo* (*PW* ii. 265), ll. 17–18 (1832 edn.).
[2] See *PW* ii. 222 and *app. crit.* The version of the opening of the poem quoted
here differs at ll. 5–6 from the 1827 edn. and the earlier and later readings cited
by de Selincourt.
[3] ll. 14–16 (1832–43), but 'doleful' substituted for 'ready'.
[4] *French Revolution As it Appeared to Enthusiasts at its Commencement* (*PW*
ii. 264), l. 15. See also *Prel.*, pp. 406–7.
[5] See *PW* iv. 60, 413. *Simon Lee* was the most revised of all W. W.'s
shorter pieces.

followed as the 4th after 'he dearly loves their voices;' altering it at the beginning thus

> But oh the heavy change—bereft[1]
> Of strength, of friends, and kindred, see

And he is lean, for 'but'. This position would let the reader hear of Simon in his luckier days first, which I cannot but think is better than jumbling about, as is now done, the melancholy and chearful part. Pages 258–9 of the same vol: let the Stanza, now the 4th,[2] beginning 'Ever Strangers slackening here their pace' be the third, thus altered.

> How fondly will the woods embrace
> This Daughter of thy pious care
> Lifting her front with modest grace etc

Then comes the Stanza
Well may the Villagers rejoice etc as 4th.
And the 5th to be thus altered—

> Nor deem the Poet's hope misplaced
> His fancy cheated that can see
> A Shade upon the Structure cast
> Of Time's pathetic sanctity;
> Can hear the monitory clock
> Sound oer the Lake with gentle shock
> at Evening etc.—[3]

It is now high time to release you. Liverpool did not inspire me, I composed one Sonnet,[4] on the roof of the Coach upon the first sight of my native mountains, but it is not worth sending you. I have since written some thing above 300 verses which will be printed next November in the Keepsake; the Proprietor having paid me very handsomely for them.

Did you see the notice of my writings, in the Athenaeum—[5] it fell into my hands by accident—having been transferred to the Cumberland Pacquet. I have not a guess who is the Author.

---

[1] heavy *written in above* wintry.
[2] Of *To the Lady Fleming* (*PW* iv. 165).
[3] The final version of the stanza reads 'future' for 'Structure' in l. 43.
[4] Probably *Filial Piety* (*PW* iii. 50). See also L. 394 below.
[5] 'Sketches of Contemporary Authors. No. V.—Mr Wordsworth', *Athenaeum*, 19 Feb. 1828: a notable appreciation of W. W. that attempts to answer the contemporary objections to his poetic methods.

16 April 1828

Thank you for your Comment on The Force of Prayer,[1] it ramifies a little more than I intended.

ever faithfully your [? sincere Friend][2]
W. W.

335. W. W. to SAMUEL ROGERS

Address: Samuel Rogers Esq. St James' place, London.
Postmark: 19 Apr. 1828. *Stamp*: Kendal Penny Post. *Endorsed*: not to be published   S. R.
MS. Sharpe Collection, University College, London.
Rogers. LY i. 298.

[17 Apr. 1828][3]

My dear R—

To-night I set off for Cambridge, passing by Coleorton, where I shall stay a couple of days with the Rector.[4] My Son accompanies me; being about to undertake a Curacy in a Parish adjoining that of Coleorton, near Grace-Dieu, the birth-place of Beaumont[5] the Dramatist. At Cambridge I purpose to stay till the 10th or 11th May, and then for a short, very short, visit to London, where I shall be sadly disappointed if I do not meet you. My main object is to look out for some situation, mercantile if it could be found, for my younger son. If you can serve me, pray do.

I have troubled you with this note to beg you would send any further sheets of your Poem,[6] up to the 8th or so of next month, to me at Trin: Lodge, Cambridge. Farewell. My Wife and Daughter are, I trust, already at Cambridge. My sister begs her kindest regards. Miss Hutchinson is here, who has also been much gratified by your Poem, and begs to be remembered to you.

Ever faithfully yours
Wm Wordsworth

[1] *PW* iv. 88.
[2] *Scrawled over edge of paper.*
[3] Date established from *SH*, p. 362 and D. W.'s MS. Journal recording W. W.'s departure for Coleorton with John W.
[4] Francis Merewether.
[5] See *EY*, p. 588.
[6] The Second Part of *Italy*. W. W. was apparently receiving proofs, but no record remains of his criticisms or other observations, if any were made.

336. W. W. to FRANCIS MEREWETHER

Address: The Revd F. Merewether, Rectory, Coleorton, Ashby de la Zouch.
[*In M. W.'s hand*]
Postmark: 5 May. *Stamp*: Cambridge.
MS. Cornell.
LY i. 299 (—).

[Cambridge]
May 5th [1828]

My dear Sir,

My Brother who is now closeted with the Proctor, has begged of me to answer a Letter of yours, received this morning. Be assured I should undertake this office with great[1] reluctance (knowing how much more satisfactory a reply from himself would and ought to be) could I not honestly affirm that his time is occupied from morning to Night.—In fact since my coming here I have never seen him scarcely but at meals, and not a moment has his mind been[2] at liberty. He has had his Accounts to make up as Vice chancellor, the University has been disorderly, three men having been recently expelled, and his Icon. is going rapidly through the Press.[3]—You will excuse me then, for not scrupling to comply with his request.—He says, that as a prudential measure, the Letter[4] had better not be published, with your name, at least. Your Diocesan[5] is obviously committed upon the question, *prominently* so indeed, and in consequence he might be less disposed to serve you.—This you would disregard and it would be right, he says, to do so, if you have it as a burthen upon your conscience, but it is his opinion that you alone can decide this point; and he repeats upon this occasion the same judgement that he gave before. Personal prudence is against it; and the rest must be determined by your own mind——

I hope you will not consider it impertin[ence] *in me*; if upon the supposition that you cannot be at ease without communic[ating] your thoughts upon this important subject, you take a middle course; and publish them anonymously through the best channel for spread-

---

[1] *Written* greatly.

[2] *Written* being.

[3] i.e. C. W.'s answer to the various objections put forward to his original pamphlet. See L. 151 above.

[4] Merewether was apparently proposing to publish a pamphlet against the recent repeal of the Test and Corporation Acts: in the end he seems to have abandoned the plan, probably as a result of W. W.'s advice in this letter.

[5] i.e. Dr. John Kaye, the Bishop of Lincoln, who had supported the repeal in a speech on the Report stage of the Bill in the House of Lords on 25 Apr., on the ground that it threatened none of the spiritual doctrines or prerogatives of the Church of England, and who finally voted in favour of it.

ing them that you have access to—. I have said 'if your mind cannot be at ease', because it is obvious the measure is not to be prevented by any thing you or any body else can write or do—Upon the importance of the question, in the abstract, there can be but one opinion, but as the course of things cannot be stopped, nor what is done recalled, does not this diminish the urgency for its being treated at the present moment; and would not a more dispassionate hearing be given to sound argument hereafter?——

When you see John tell him we go on the 10th to London, proposing to stay till the end of month; when, or *before*, his Mother will certainly join him.

Be so good as to say also, that I can not see any necessity for his Aunt taking the journey at present; and I have endeavoured to dissuade her from it; thinking it better that she should defer her journey to the Autumn, as his Mother will be with [?],[1] as will probably his Sister and myself, who will follow if we do not accompany his Mother to Whitwick—I remain, my dear Sir, with kindest remembrances, from all here, to Mrs Merewether and yourself—very faithfully yours

W. Wordsworth

Pray give my regards to Mr Drummond.[2]

[*M. W. writes*]

My dear *Mrs* M,

I am tempted to appropriate this blank space of your husband's letter to thank you for your kindness to John, and to express the pleasure I promise to myself in the prospect of seeing you so soon—which (whether my Sister goes to Whitwick, or, according to her Brother's recommendation defers her visit till the autumn) I trust will not be later than the end of the month. I pray that we may find Mr M. better than late letters have reported of him, and that you and the young ones are well. If the coach from Leicester does not pass you *every day* pray desire John to mention it, and unless he writes in time for his letter to reach Cambridge on or before Saturday tell him to direct to us 12 Bryanston St. Portman Sq.[3] We have had much pleasure in finding Dr W. greatly improved in health, tho' harrassed by business. The young men are every thing their Father could wish, and so affectionate to us as to render our

---

[1] *MS. obscure.*
[2] Mr. Merewether's new curate, the Revd. Robert Drummond (1804–83), a grandson of the 4th Duke of Atholl, who until recently had been at Trinity College, Cambridge. He was vicar of Feering, Essex, 1829–66.
[3] E.Q.'s London residence.

stay at Cambridge quite delightful. If Lady B. and Mrs Willes
have arrived at the Hall pray give my best remembrances to them.
Very sincerely yours,

M. Wordsworth

337. D. W. to MARIA JANE JEWSBURY

MS. Historical Society of Pennsylvania.
Letters of Dora Wordsworth, pp. 40–2.

21st May. [1828]

My dear Friend,

I had been thinking of writing to inquire after you when your
welcome letter arrived. You wish to hear of our goings on, and
though I have little leisure just at present I will not delay—nor
will take up either your time or my own with telling truths that
you can well divine—of forgiveness—or rather of offences having
never come—of conjectures about you—of hopes and fears etc.,
etc.,—and last of all—of my own resolves to write—resolves made
and broken. Happy am I that your state of health is so tolerable,
and that you have no bad tidings for us of your Father or any other
member of the Family: and am very glad that you have found so
nice a plan for retirement and pleasure during the summer. Mrs
Hemans must be a sweet-minded woman, and I have no fears of
disappointment on either side when you do actually see one another,
and live together under one Roof. With my thanks to Mrs Hemans
for her care in transmitting good Dr Channing's[1] message, pray
tell her that I should have been happy indeed had our plans for the
present summer led us into Wales. In that case, nothing should
have prevented us from seeking out you and her. I distinctly

[1] William Ellery Channing (1780–1842), the American Unitarian theolo-
gian, minister of the Federal Street Church in Boston for nearly forty years,
and author of *The Evidences of Revealed Religion*, 1821, etc.: an admirer of
S. T. C. and W. W., to whom *The Excursion* 'came like a revelation'. He had
visited Rydal Mount in mid-July 1822, on his first arrival in England, and
spent one Sunday afternoon with W. W. 'Mr Wordsworth's conversation was
free, various, animated. We talked so eagerly as often to interrupt one another.'
(*Memoir of William Ellery Channing*, 3 vols., 1848, ii. 220.) Some years later,
on 4 Mar. 1835, in sending a sermon on the evils of war which embodied some
of W. W.'s remarks during their talk together, Channing paid tribute to
W. W.'s influence: 'My principal object in writing is to discharge a pleasant
duty. I wish you to know, how much I am indebted to you for the pure and
quickening influences of your writings on my mind and heart. I think myself a
wiser and better man for your poetry. It has been for me for years a familiar
friend, and I hope I may say, a fountain of spiritual life.' (*WL MSS.*)

remember Dr Channing, who was in bad health when at Rydal. My Brother was very much interested by him, and thinks highly of [his] Talents, and will, I am sure, be glad to hear that he is remembered with such pleasurable feelings by him on the other side of the Atlantic. I have not read any one of the new works you mention—nor indeed any thing that is new—and far too little of what is old; for I have been more than usually engaged by domestic duties during the winter and spring; and am now, at this very time, with Miss Hutchinson, engaged in the same way as when you first set foot at Rydal Mount, finding us on the grand-platform in the midst of old carpets and dusty Books: and, what is worse, we are new-papering—and making *new* carpets and about to have a new servant—

But the week after next, we hope, will finish all—and we shall be quite ready for our dear long-absent Friends—not that we expect them *before* the third week in June—and hardly till the end of it. My Sister talks of leaving her Husband and Daughter in London on the first of June—but I should not be surprized if she were detained a few days longer—for they are overwhelmed with engagements. On the 11th they all went thither. Pray write to Dora. Their address is, 12, Bryanston Street, Portman Square. There seems to be no chance whatever, of their passing through Manchester before the 17th nor do I even think they will take that road from Ashby, as you will not be at M. My Brother and Dora are to join Mrs W. at Whitwick (John's Curacy) adjoining Coleorton Parish—and no doubt they will stay at least a week to see how John gets on in his new and important Station. Poor Fellow! he wanted me sadly to go with him; fearing that his Mother's anxiety to be at home after her long absence would hurry her away; but, now that he is a little settled, and his Mother is likely to stay not less than three weeks with him, he thinks it much better that I should enjoy the summer at home, and go to him, according to my promise, in the Autumn. Do you remember our homely Westmorland housemaid, Mary? She is an honest good creature, much attached to her Family, and is elevated to the rank of John's housekeeper. Anne, who was at Kent's Bank, still lives with us at Rydal Mount. You will be glad to hear that John gave us much satisfaction in the pulpit and reading-desk of our little Chapel. His voice is very good—and his manner of reading agreeable. He now writes in excellent spirits, and aims to be satisfied with the nature of his employments—and even to like the *situation* of his parish—which, though populous, is somewhat lonely as to society; but he says there is plenty within three or four miles, and he much prefers being out of the way of—Tea visits—and Gossiping with the Ladies. His parsonage-house and garden are much to his mind, and as he is one of the best-tempered Men in the world I doubt not honest Mary and he will get on nicely through the summer.— She will be a right frugal house-keeper and he an easy Master. Dora's health *must* be greatly improved, but she cannot walk—at least cannot do what her old Aunt calls *walking*—She is delighted with plays and operas—but I doubt not will return without the loss of one shade of her simplicity of character to Rydal Mount and her Doves, and the pony and Neptune.[1] Yet alas! her poor head has been submitted to a French Hairdresser!—This *does* vex me—I cannot condone the notion of seeing her decked (nay not decked— depressed) by big curls—and Bows and Giraffe Wires. Sir Walter Scott is in Town. They live near him, and many others—of whom the newspapers mention. It was a very great disappointment to Dora, when she went the day after her arrival in London to see Elizabeth Cookson—and find her gone. Her Father had arrived unexpectedly, and taken away dear Elizabeth—who is now at Liverpool—able to walk three or four miles as well as anybody. She is expected at Kendal tomorrow, and will probably the same night go on to Stourby, where Mrs Cookson and the whole Family are settled for the summer. Our dear William is still at [? home] but will probably leave us ere long—and if he passes through Manchester, and if you are there, he will see you. He has long resolved not to go into the Church. And what is he to do?—Here is his great difficulty—and his Father and Mother hope some prospect may open to him while in London. He is very tall and very strong— and of just the same loving disposition as when you knew him *little* Willy. Probably he may even go to France for a short time to hear the language. I am [?] is not the time to enter on such a subject. No doubt you have heard of his inclinations to the Army. These perforce have been given up. You do not mention Miss Kelsall[2]— I want to hear of her marriage. My love to her. Pray write from Wales—Nor do you mention Miss Bosley[3]—I grieved for her Father's misfortunes. God bless you my dear Friend—Ever yours

D Wordsworth

My kind regards to your Father—Excuse this hurried scrawl—

[1] Dora W.'s Newfoundland dog.

[2] One of Miss Jewsbury's Manchester friends: probably the daughter of John Kelsall, a cotton merchant.

[3] Another Manchester friend, whose father was probably James Bosley, a silk manufacturer, who seems to have fallen on bad times.

no time to look it over—so correct yourself, in the reading, all mistakes—God bless you! and again

338. W. W. to ALLAN CUNNINGHAM

MS. Mr. W. Hugh Peal. Hitherto unpublished.

12 Bryanston Street
[late May *or* early June 1828]

My dear Friend,

I sincerely condole with you and Mrs Cunningham on the loss of your dear Boy. Having suffered in this way twice myself I can truly sympathize with you—

Perpetual engagements[1] have prevented my visiting you again.— In the course of the next week I shall try my fortune, meaning to breakfast with Mr Chantrey. We will then discuss the Selection for which I thank you, and talk about the vol.[2]

most faithfully yours
W Wordsworth

339. W. W. to JULIUS CHARLES HARE

Address: Revd. Julius Hare, Ibbotson's Hotel.[3] The favour of an answer requested.
MS. Cornell. Hitherto unpublished.

12 Bryanston Street.
[?late May *or* early June 1828]

My dear Sir,

If not better engaged could you breakfast with me this morning— the sooner the better, and walk with me afterwards to see Mr Coleridge at High-gate as we mean to do—only I ought to mention that we are engaged to dine at High-gate.

faithfully yours
W Wordsworth

[1] W. W., M. W., and Dora W. had been living at E. Q.'s London home since about 10 May, caught up in a round of visits to theatres and galleries and social engagements with such old friends as H. C. R., the Lambs, Talfourd, Kenyon, Rogers, and Scott. W. W. also saw something of Thomas Clarkson, Basil Montagu, and Joshua Watson (see *HCR* i. 355–60). Dora W. gives a lively account of their activities in a letter, *c.* 14 May, to her cousin C. W. jnr. (*British Museum MSS.*), published almost in full in J. H. Overton and Elizabeth Wordsworth, *Christopher Wordsworth Bishop of Lincoln*, 1888, pp. 64–5 (with, however, the omission of an encounter with William Crackanthorpe). For the visit to Hampton Court with Sir Walter Scott, see L. 341 below.
[2] For Cunningham's proposed selection from Wordsworth, see L. 314 above and L. 369 below.   [3] Off Oxford Street.

340. D. W. to JOHN MARSHALL JNR.

Address: John Marshall Esqre Junior, Leeds.
MS. WL.
LY i. 300.

Rydal Mount June 2nd [1828]

My dear Sir,

I have this morning received a kind letter from your Mother stating that there is now a vacancy in your counting-house, which she thought much more likely to suit George Green than the one he applied for, and desiring me, if I thought fit, to acquaint his Mother in order that application might be made to you.

Accordingly I have just been with Mrs Green who is exceedingly grateful to Mrs Marshall for the interest she has so kindly taken in behalf of her Family, and would be happy indeed should it suit you to take George into your counting-house. He is at present with his Brother-in-law, Mr Fenton, who has been looking out for a place for him in a school, as Assistant and Learner; but such things are not easily met with, and I should think as he at first most wished to get into a counting-house, that he will be glad and thankful to go to you if it suit you to take him.

By this day's post the Mother writes to George, and desires him to wait upon you without delay, and as he is at no great distance from Leeds, most likely you will see him—and probably also Mr Fenton—the day after you receive this—at all events, in the course of two or three days, for the Post may possibly not be a direct one to the place where Mr Fenton lives.

I am very glad to hear of the expected marriage[1] in your Family, and hope for a happy meeting with all of you on the Banks of Ulswater before Summer is over. I need not say any thing concerning our absent Friends, as you have so lately seen them. Excuse haste—I write at Ambleside, having walked over purposely to see Mrs Green.

Believe me, dear Sir,
Yours truly,
D. Wordsworth

[1] i.e. John Marshall jnr.'s marriage to Mary Ballantine Dykes (see L. 70 above) on 18 Nov.

341. D. W. to MARY LAING

Address: To Miss Laing, Wm Laing's Esqre, South Bridge Street, Edinburgh.
Postmark: 9 June 1828.
MS. Edinburgh University Library.
The Wordsworth–Laing Letters (—).

Rydal Mount, near Kendal
June 3rd [1828]

My dear Miss Laing,

I am ashamed of my seeming ingratitude. Little did I think when I received your kind Letter and present that I should suffer you to remain without thanks or the least acknowledgement for so many weeks. The truth is that having little that was new to tell you I thought a letter hardly worth postage—and waited for some Friend going to Edinburgh, when matter for a packet, such as my last, might arise. No such opportunity has fallen out: and I can wait no longer. The Cap is a very pretty one indeed, and in shape perfectly becoming to me. But you were afraid it would make too much of the old Woman of me—yet would you believe it! the only fault the Cap has with me is that it is too youthful and too gay—too much of the Fashionable. I thank you heartily for thus remembering me—and no more on this subject.——I was sorry to hear but an indifferent report of your health and strength. For my part I have great reason to be thankful, having had but one cold (and that not a very bad one) through the whole winter, and I am just as well able to walk, and enjoy this beautiful Country as when I had the pleasure of seeing you here. I hope your good Father and Mother continue pretty well. My Nephew John report[s] of Mr Laing's kind greeting of him as a Wordsworth and, as John reported to me, especially for his Aunt's sake. Glad should I be to see you all again in Edinburgh or glad to meet you at the Isle of Man: but I shall hardly stir from home this summer, my Sister and Niece having been so long absent. Besides, I shall spend the best part of Winter with my Nephew John, at his Parsonage in Leicestershire. He keeps house, attended by an old and faithful Servant of ours, and writes that he is very comfortable, and that he has plenty of society within three or four miles, which he prefers to a very close neighbourhood: but, no doubt, in winter he will be glad of a fire-side companion; which is the reason why I fix on that time for visiting him. My Brother is in London, and his Daughter visiting Friends at Hampstead and elsewhere. This day Mrs Wordsworth appointed to leave them and I suppose she is now travelling towards her Son John at Whitwick, where she will remain till joined by her Husband and Daughter, and we hope to see them all

611

at home by the end of this, or the beginning of *next*, month. William is still at home, and undecided respecting his course of life, though very anxious to be doing something. He has no inclination for the Church—and is not fitted for the profession of the Law either in body or mind, therefore is not to go to the University; for, without following one of the learned professions, it would be an expensive education thrown away. Dora's health must be much improved, for she is able to go through a great deal in London in the way of sight-seeing and visiting—though not strong enough to walk much in the streets. She has heard all the famous singers, and seen many interesting people. As no doubt you know, Sir Walter Scott is in London. They spent a charming day with him at Hampton Court[1]—and have seen Mrs Lockhart,[2] with whom they are much pleased, as every body is, who knows her. My Sister writes that all their Friends are surprized with my Brother's good looks and good spirits, and I am happy to tell you this. She has been quite well during the whole of her long absence. You may guess how we long to have them all at home again. I have now, according to your desire, given a full account of our own Family and if it be tedious you must blame yourself.

Mr Southey is in London. I spent a few days at his house lately. He was then very well in health, and, as usual, a most delightful companion when he left his Study to come among us. Poor Mrs Southey has never got over the effects of her affliction at the death of Isabel; but was in pretty good spirits, and the rest of the Family quite well. Miss Southey is at Bath. Bertha is grown a very fine young Woman, and Kate is very pretty and very agreeable. Miss Coleridge, I think, looks a little faded; but no wonder. She has the an[xiety][3] upon her of a Marriage engagement, without certain prospect of the period at which it is to terminate. Probably you know that the young Man to whom she is engaged is her Cousin, Mr Henry Nelson Coleridge[4]—the author of a Book published two

---

[1] On 25 May. Scott's son, Major Walter Scott, who was stationed there, Tom Moore, and Rogers were also of the party. See *The Journal of Sir Walter Scott*, p. 481. Tom Moore noted in his diary: 'On our arrival at Hampton (where we found the Wordsworths) walked about . . . in the gay walk where the band plays, to the infinite delight of the Hampton *blues* who were all *eyes* after Scott, the other scribblers not coming in for a glance.' (*Memoirs*, v. 287–8.)

[2] Scott's daughter Sophia.

[3] *MS. torn.*

[4] Henry Nelson Coleridge (1798–1843), son of Col. James Coleridge (1759–1836), of Ottery St. Mary, was a Chancery lawyer. In 1825 he accompanied his cousin William Hart Coleridge, Bishop of Barbados (see *MY* ii. 597), to the West Indies, and published *Six Months in the West Indies in 1825* on his return. He took down S. T. C.'s *Table Talk* (1835), and edited his *Literary Remains* (1836–9), the *Aids to Reflection* (1839), and *The Confessions of an*

years ago concerning a few Months' Residence in the West Indies. He accompanied thither his Cousin the Bishop. If the English Newspapers reach you, you will have seen the name of my youngest Cambridge Nephew[1] again in the Papers, as being honored with the Chancellor's Medal for an English Poem on the Invasion of Russia by Buonaparte. He got the same prize last year, and two other University prizes for Greek and Latin compositions. I wish your travels may bring you our way this summer. Perhaps you may go to London—and if so, will surely pass among the Lakes. Give my kind regards to your Brother David whom it would give us pleasure to see again at Rydal Mount. Give my best regards to your Father and Mother, and believe me dear Miss Laing, Your affectionate and much obliged Friend,   D Wordsworth.

I hope ere long to hear from you again with full accounts of yourself and Family. Miss Joanna Hutchinson[2] is quite well except her lameness, and the lameness much better.

342. W. W. to H. C. R.

Address: H. C. Robinson Esqre, Temple—
Postmark: 16 June [ ] *Stamp*: Gt. Portland St. *Endorsed*: June 1828, Words-
   worth Autograph.
MS. Dr. Williams's Library.
Morley, i. 188.

Monday Morn [16 June 1828]
12 Bryanston [St.]

My dear Friend
   Pray meet me at Mr Aders[3] on Wednesday to Breakfast. I shall be obliged by the loan of your Carpet Bag—which you were kind enough to offer—
                                        Ever Yours
                                        W. Wordsworth

Enquiring Spirit (1840). His marriage to Sara finally took place on 3 Sept. 1829 at Crosthwaite Church, Keswick. The anguish and trials of their long engagement, and the opposition of his father, are only briefly alluded to in *Memoir and Letters of Sara Coleridge*, ed. her Daughter, 2 vols., 1873, but make up the poignant theme of many unpublished letters from these years. (*University of Texas MSS.*)   [1] i.e. C. W. jnr.
   [2] D. W. spent over three weeks with Joanna and Henry Hutchinson in the Isle of Man later this summer (26 June–19 July). Willy W. was also on holiday there. See *DWJ* ii. 401–19.
   [3] Charles Aders, a 'foreign merchant' in partnership with Jameson, both of whom were known to H. C. R. from the beginning of the century. Aders and his wife Elizabeth were art connoisseurs and Mrs. Aders a singer of consider-able ability. They lived in Euston Square, and were famous for their musical and artistic parties. (Morley's note.) Ultimately Aders lost his money, sold his collections, and he and Mrs. Aders settled in Italy where he died in 1846. Later, she returned to London and died there in 1857.

343. W. W. to SAMUEL TAYLOR COLERIDGE

MS. Berg Collection, New York Public Library. Hitherto unpublished.

Tuesday 17th [June 1828]

My dear Coleridge,

My Daughter is overjoyed at the thought of our proposed Tour.[1] Tomorrow I breakfast with Mr Aders, where every thing will be settled—if you could meet me there it would be well[2]—And more than that—I should have written sooner, but I had many things to bring to a close.—The earlier you can come to Mr Aders the better; at all events tell me how soon you can be ready. Dora and I only purpose to take each a Carpet bag—it being desireable to travel as light as possible—If you cannot come to Mr Aders write to me in Bryanstone Street.

Ever faithfully yours
Wm Wordsworth

Mr Aders will provide us all with passports and Lett[ers] of credit.[3]

[1] W. W., Dora W., and S. T. C. were now about to set off on a tour of Belgium, the Rhineland, and Holland. Exactly when the decision was made is not clear; but it was not apparently until after the Wordsworths arrived in London. Perhaps W. W.'s visits to Longman and Philip Courtenay, his man of business, together with the completion of his arrangement with F. Mansel Reynolds, finally removed his financial anxieties and made the journey possible. In the event, the tour cost just over £91, according to Dora W.'s unpublished 'Journal of a Tour to the Continent, 1828' (*WL MSS.*), and was therefore amply covered by W. W.'s earnings from *The Keepsake*.

[2] S. T. C. accepted the invitation. H. C. R., who was also present, noted: 'Coleridge was, as usual, very eloquent in his dreamy monologues, but he spoke intelligibly enough on some interesting subjects' (*HCR* i. 359).

[3] Aders sent these to W. W. on the Thursday after their breakfast together, along with a letter of advice about currency problems (*Cornell MSS.*). It may be that it was at his suggestion that W. W. and S. T. C. turned their steps towards the Rhineland, where Mrs. Aders was spending the summer at her villa at Godesberg. See L. 346 below.

344. W. W. to BARRON FIELD

Address: Barron Field, Esq., Barrister at Law, Liverpool—
Postmark: 20 June 1828.
MS. Cornell. Hitherto unpublished.

Bryanston Street
June 20th 1828

My dear Sir,

I am afraid you will think me very inattentive. Your kind Letter would have been answered long ago but I could not settle what would become of us.—I stayed ten days at Cambridge where I had the pleasure of seeing your Br[1] several times. To morrow I start for a Tour on the Rhine with my Daughter and Mr Coleridge. We shall return in five weeks at the latest—then Dora and I proceed to Leicestershire, where Mrs W. is with her Son—and so on to Rydal where we hope to arrive the 2nd week of August, not too late I trust to receive you and Mrs Field—[2]

Many thanks for your Criticism[3]—Excuse extreme haste—as I have a score of Notes and Letters to write this morning—with the bustle of packing etc etc besides.

> I remain my dear Sir
> faithfully your much
> obliged W Wordsworth

I am sorry we cannot profit by your kind invitation as we must return through Manchester—Should our plan be altered you shall hear of us again.

345. W. W. to FREDERIC MANSEL REYNOLDS

Address: F. Reynolds Esqre Jn^r, 48, Warren S^t. [*In Dora W.'s hand*]
Postmark: 21 June 1828.
MS. British Museum. Hitherto unpublished.

[21 June 1828]

My dear Sir

The enclosed I found was too late to be of use by the Post. My Messenger was not in the way—and Mr William [? Scott][4] is not in Town—so I trusted to a hope that you would call in which I have been disappointed.

---

[1] Frederick Field (1801–85), Biblical and Patristic scholar, was elected a Fellow of Trinity College, Cambridge, in 1824. He edited St. Chrysostom and Origen, and became rector of Reepham, Norfolk, in 1842.

[2] Field had written on 28 Apr. proposing to visit W. W. at Rydal Mount from Lancaster Assizes by way of the Duddon Sands as soon as the poet returned from the Continent (*WL MSS.*).

[3] See L. 366 below.   [4] Probably a business associate of Reynolds.

I am truly sorry that I could not procure a ticket for Mrs Heath[1]—
in fact I have been harried more than I can express these last two or
three days and am quite uncomfortable—

Tomorrow at half past four in the morning we are off for Ostend.
Do not let my Poems[2] be printed off till my return—

Mr Southey suffered much pain yesterday—he is better today—
Kind regards to Mrs Reynolds.

faithfully yours

Wm Wordsworth

346. W. W. to MRS. ELIZABETH ADERS

Address: Madame Aders, Godesberg.
Postmark: [? July 1828].
MS. Mr. Robert H. Taylor. Hitherto unpublished.

St Goar—4

oclock day after we left

Godesberg. [12 July 1828][3]

My dear Madam,

Pray don't let our Coachman be paid till we return. We left
Coblentz a little after ten this morning and he refuses to take us

---

[1] Wife of Charles Heath, the engraver (see L. 329 above).

[2] i.e. his contributions to *The Keepsake*.

[3] W. W., Dora W., and S. T. C. set out for the Continent on 22 June,
called on Major Pryse Gordon (see L. 351 below) at Brussels on the 25th, and
there met Thomas Colley Grattan (1792–1864), the novelist, who accompanied
them some way on their journey, and who left a lively account of their
appearance and conversation. 'Wordsworth was, if possible, more unlike what
he must appear in the fancy of those who have read his poetry and have never
seen the author. He was a perfect antithesis to Coleridge—tall, wiry, harsh in
features, coarse in figure, inelegant in looks. He was roughly dressed in a long
brown *surtout*, striped duck trousers, fustian gaiters, and thick shoes. He more
resembled a mountain farmer than a "lake poet". His whole air was unrefined
and unprepossessing. . . . But, on after observation and a little reflection, I
could not help considering that much that seemed unfavourable in Wordsworth
might be really placed to his advantage. There was a total absence of affectation, or egotism; not the least effort at display, or assumption of superiority
over any of those who were quite prepared to concede it to him. . . . I remarked
Wordsworth's very imperfect knowledge of French, and it was then that he
accounted for it by telling me that five and twenty years previously he understood and spoke it well, but that his abhorrence of the Revolutionary excesses
made him resolve if possible to forget the language altogether, and that for a
long time he had not read nor spoken a word of it.' (*Beaten Paths; and Those
Who Trod Them*, 2 vols., 1862, ii. 107–40.) According to Dora W.'s MS.
Journal, the travellers arrived at Mrs. Aders's villa at Godesberg on 3 July and
remained there until the 11th. On the 8th a 'party of Bonn lions', including
Niebuhr, Becker, and A. W. von Schlegel, were invited to meet them. Another
English visitor recorded his impressions of the gathering: 'Wordsworth was a
single-minded man, with less imagination than Coleridge, but with a more
harmonious judgment, and better balanced principles . . . Wordsworth chatted
naturally and fluently, out of the fullness of his heart, and not from a wish to
display his eloquence.' (Julius Charles Young, *A Memoir of Charles Mayne
Young, Tragedian, with Extracts from His Son's Journal*, 2 vols., 1871, 176–7.)

farther than this place St Goar, where we arrived about four—We have had a charming journey—as far as delight in the scenery goes but our Coachman has driven like a snail—and has turned restive. So adieu to him. We have hired a post chaise to the next stage— and probably shall reach Bingen this evening—whence if we meet difficulties we shall return to Godesberg—if not we will venture further[1]—excuse extreme haste.

affectionately yours

W. W.

347. D. W. to JOSEPH COTTLE

Address: To Joseph Cottle Esqre, Bristol.
Stamp: Kendal Penny Post. *Endorsed*: from Miss Wordsworth August 2^d 1828.
MS. Cornell. Hitherto unpublished.

Rydal Mount near Kendal

July 31st 1828

In the absence of my Brother I am empowered to open letters addressed to him;[2] and thus it falls upon me to reply to your kind and very interesting one, received yesterday. I assure you, my dear Friend—(for by that name I must call you, though distance and other circumstances have prevented all intercourse between us, personal or by letter, for more than thirty years) it gave me true pleasure on turning to the signature of a hand-writing which though I could not recognise it, reminded me of something that I *ought* to recognise, to find the name of Joseph Cottle—the hospit- able and good Friend in whose society many happy days of my youth were spent.

Mrs Wordsworth and my Niece gave us a full account of their visit to you[3] and of the pleasure they had had in becoming acquainted with your Sisters and the younger part of your Family. They left Bristol with most pleasing remembrances of you all, and Dora was indeed very sorry she could not see more of your Nieces, to whom

---

[1] They returned briefly to Godesberg on 21 July, when Schlegel dined with them. The following day he conducted the party round Bonn.

[2] Joseph Cottle (see *EY*, p. 163) had written from Bristol on 25 July regretting the cessation of all communications between W. W. and himself for thirty years: 'No individual has watched the progress of your reputation with more interest than I have done, or rejoiced more sincerely, than myself in beholding its extension and confirmation . . .' (*Bristol University Library MSS.*: see George Lamoine, 'Letters from Joseph Cottle to William Wordsworth: 1828–1850', *Ariel*, iii (Apr. 1972), 84–102).

[3] The previous March, when they visited Mrs. Gee near Bristol. (See *Letters of Dora Wordsworth*, p. 38.)

she took in an uncommon degree. I say this because she is slow to receive new Friends—and, though her opportunity of seeing them was but brief, she, I am sure, parted from them with affectionate regret.—Perhaps, ere this reaches you, you may have chanced to hear that after a three week's stay at Cambridge and a six week's stay in London, the Father and Daughter with our old Friend S. T. Coleridge took it into their heads to cross the Sea by steam to Ostend, thence up the Rhine—and homeward through Holland. We hope to hear of their safe arrival again in England before the end of next week: they will halt only one day in London, and will then join Mrs Wordsworth who parted from them in London, and has ever since been with her eldest Son who has a curacy in Leicestershire. Her Husband and Daughter will remain with her a short time at *Whitwick* (the name of the Village where John Wordsworth is Curate) and they will then all return to Rydal Mount; and if it please God that Dora's health be restored you may judge that after so long an absence the Meeting at home will be a happy one.

With respect to the request contained in your letter[1] I can only answer that if my Brother does not comply with it, the failure of a *wish* to do so will not be the cause. I am sure, indeed, that he will have the strongest inclination to do it: but his Muse is freakish as she ever was in the time of his youth—and will not always obey his Bidding. In fact he cannot write at all times or when he will and therefore it is impossible for me to promise for him; but of this I am sure, he will have the strongest desire to gratify you on a point to which you seem to attach so much importance: and further, that it would give him great pleasure to make a public Testimony of his respect for one who had such friendly dispositions towards him when life was beginning.

---

[1] Cottle was preparing the 4th edition (2 vols., 1829) of *Malvern Hills, and other Poems* and wished for a contribution from W. W. 'It was indeed a very remarkable coincidence that in the few years in which I was a bookseller in Bristol (for I quitted the profession at the age of twenty eight,) I should have been the means of introducing to the world, by publishing their First Volume of Poems, three such names as *Wordsworth, Coleridge* and *Southey*, and that with a liberality towards them which almost exceeded my ability. . . . My object in troubling you, at this time is, (and I am almost ashamed to name it,) to express the high gratification which I should experience, if you would address to me a few lines, (a sonnet, or any thing else, by *Octr next*) to be appended to the Volume, with those of Coleridge and Southey (which you doubtless recollect). However brief, it would be equally acceptable, and if your mind should retain, after so long an interruption, any remembrances of friendly acts, on my part, your compliance with this request, will be making me an ample return, and will leave on my mind a permanent sense of obligation.' W. W. found himself unable to meet this request: see letter of 27 Jan. 1829 (in next volume).

I beg to be kindly remembered to your Sisters; and believe me, it gives me true pleasure to hear of their happiness and prosperity.[1] How your good Mother's heart would have overflowed with thankfulness for the blessings which have been showered on them and you!—

I need not describe our situation and way of Life at Rydal Mount, as you will have heard all from my Sister and Niece. Miss Hutchinson (Sarah) whom you will recollect having seen at Sockburn,[2] lives with us. She desires her best regards to you.

I saw Mrs Coleridge and her Daughter at Keswick last week, and Mrs Southey and her Son and Daughters. All were well and very comfortable, except poor Mrs Lovel, whose health is very delicate. Hartley Coleridge is in lodgings at Grasmere, about two miles from us. He empl[oys] himself chiefly in writing for Magazines and other periodical publications;[3] but is at present talking of publishing a small volume of poems.[4] Derwent is happily married, and is much respected at the small town of Halston, in Cornwall, where he is school-master and Curate. I thank you for the pleasure I have had in the verses you have transcribed from your poem,[5] and entirely sympathize in your sentiments. You may expect to hear from my Brother soon after his return to Rydal Mount, and heartily do I wish that he may be able to satisfy himself in his attempts to comply with your request.

Believe me, my dear Sir

Your affectionate Friend

D. Wordsworth

P.S. I am almost tempted to pay the postage of my letter in revenge. Why did you do so? The business of the letter being all your own is no excuse in writing to an old Friend.

---

[1] Cottle's sister Anne had recently married John Hare of Firfield House, nr. Bristol: a manufacturer and prominent Nonconformist.

[2] In 1799. See *EY*, p. 271.

[3] At this time, with the help of Professor Wilson, he was contributing occasionally to *Blackwood's*.

[4] This volume did not in fact appear until 1833.

[5] A passage about Chatterton and the pursuit of Fame.

348. DORA W. and W. W. to EDWARD QUILLINAN

Address: Edward Quillinan Esqre, Bryanston S^t, Portman Sq^re, London,
Angleterre. [*Readdressed to*] Lee Priory, Wingham, Kent.
Postmark: (1) [?] 1828. (2) 4 Aug. 1828. *Endorsed*: From Wordsworth 1828.
MS. Bodleian Library. Hitherto unpublished.

Antwerp—Aug^st 1st—1828.
Thursday night.[1]

My dear Mr Quillinan,

This letter with the usual Wordsworthian coolness is to give
note that the two Poets and their amiable Daughter hope to steam it
from Ostend Tuesday [Monday evening *W. W. adds*] the 6th[2] and
further hope to reach London the same day—

My Mother has already told us your house is turned topsy turvy
and most probably cannot receive us—as our trunks are in Bryanston
S^t we had best drive there first—and if we cannot be taken in—
seek a rest in Baldwin Gardens or else where—for the three days at
most Father *must* remain in Town. Do contrive some important
business about that time to call you up to London—that we may
tell you all the pleasure we have had—what seen—what unseen—
how much I like some things in *your* Churches and how others
shock my protestant feelings—Father would have written to you
himself—but scarcely had we entered the Cathedral (which we did
before we sought out our Inn) when his Lover the Cambridge
Hare[3] rushed upon him. He is now at tea with him Lady (John)
Malcolm[4] and a large party—and requests me to inform you of his
intentions—

I trust Darling Minna and [? Rotha] are quite well love and
kisses to them—I shall be thankful to get home though not the
least 'we tramping'—I have made the best traveller of the trio—
The heat the first part of our journey overpower'd Mr Coleridge
and when at Godesbergh for two days was very ill—but since he has
been more than tolerable—and we get on delightfully—Father
perhaps may have time to add something tomorrow but a letter a
day or two before meeting is too dull for aught—so I will say farewell—and Believe me dear Mr Quillinan

Yours very affect^n
Dora Wordsworth

As I know not where you are I had best direct to B^ton St. M^r
Hare gives such reports of 'Chris'!! carried off *every thing his*

---

[1] Thursday was 31 July.   [2] The 6th was a Wednesday.
[3] Julius Hare.   [4] See *MY* ii. 216.

620

college had to give—and out of the 5 University prizes—4 awarded to him! may not I be proud of 'Chris'!

In spite of all our fears we have caught none of the diseases prevalent among the 'amphibious animals' yesterday a day of pouring rain at Rotterdam[1] gave Father time to half persuade himself into an Ague—but the symptoms have disappear'd—I am a saucy Child as you know full well.—he had a little cold from damp feet—was a little doleful and I was wicked enough to say it was Ague—heavy showers every day since last Monday week—and before we left Godesbergh—but nothing to keep us Prisoners till yesterday.

Friday morning—

[*W. W. writes*]

My dear M^r Q

I add a few words of greeting—I am truly sorry that we cannot include Lee in our return—We are much wanted at home—I also am due with my Masters at Somerset house[2]—Mr Coleridge is not in the best plight[3]—and last and least though not a trifle our scanty wardrobe—with six weeks service is not fit to appear in—especially among Strangers—give as many of these reassurances to Col^{nel} Barrett and to Mr Egerton as you think proper—expressing our regrets, which on my part are very sincere indeed, I may add on Dora's also—only you know she is shy of strange faces—

affectionately and faithfully yours

W Wordsworth

---

[1] Amsterdam *altered to* Rotterdam *by W. W.*

[2] i.e. the Commissioners of Stamps.

[3] S. T. C.'s brief notices of this tour in his MS. Notebooks in the British Museum record a period of illness around 29 June, when the travellers were at Liège, en route for Spa, Aachen and Cologne. The journal peters out in the middle of July, after they had reached Godesberg, but was resumed briefly at Antwerp on 1 Aug. 'The sweet prattle of the chimes—counsellors pleading in the court of Love—then the clock, the solemn sentence of the mighty Judge—long pause between each pregnant, unappellable word, too deeply weighed to be reversed in the High-Justice-Court of Time and Fate. A more richly solemn sound than this eleven oclock at Antwerp I never heard—dead enough to be opaque as central gold, yet clear enough to be the mountain air.'

349. W. W. to SAMUEL ROGERS

MS. Sharpe Collection, University College, London.
Rogers. LT i. 301.

Anvers (Antwerp, we call it)
2nd August [1828]

My dear Rogers,

A note will suffice to tell you that here we are after a long and pleasant ramble upon the Rhine and through Holland and the Netherlands—on Tuesday I hope to be in London—shall drive to my old quarters in Bryanstone Street, intending to stay not more than three days—should be happy to meet you again.

Farewell, with kind regards from my Daughter, who is [in] the room where I write,

ever yours
Wm W

350. W. W. to CHARLES ADERS

Address: Charles Aders, Esqre, 11, Euston Square.
Postmark: 7 Aug. 1828.
MS. Auckland Public Libraries. Hitherto unpublished.

12 Bryanston street
Portman Square
Thursday Morng—[7 Aug. 1828]

My dear Sir,

We arrived in good health yesterday—Pray let me know what time I may call upon you tomorrow—No doubt you have heard from Mrs Aders since we left her hospitable roof[1]—With a thousand thanks for her and your many kind attentions, I remain dear Sir

Your much obliged
W Wordsworth

[1] See Morley, i. 190: 'Mrs A. is delighted with Wordsworth but still claims our old affectionate friend Coleridge as "her" Poet.' Later in the year H. C. R. heard more from her about the visit. 'Wordsworth, I am not surprised to learn, was not liked in Germany; he was too haughty and reserved' (*HCR* i. 361).

351. W. W. to GEORGE HUNTLY GORDON[1]

Address: G. Huntly Gordon Esqre, Cannon Chambers, 16 Cannon Row Westminster. [*In Dora W.'s hand*]
Postmark: 7 Aug. 1828.
MS. WL. Hitherto unpublished.

Thursday morning [7 Aug. 1828]
12 Bryanston St
Portman Square.

Dear Sir,

I was charged with an open Letter from your Father,[2] which I should have had the honor of enclosing but it was demanded of me by the Custom house officer, who engaged to forward it by the twopenny post.—Your Father knowing how short would be my stay begged me to let you know my address, assuring me it would give you pleasure to call. I quit town on Sat. morn: if possible—could you breakfast with me tomorrow morning, I mean take a cup of tea, for I shall have nothing better to offer [about nine oclock. *Dora W. adds*].

When I left Major Gordon at Brussels, our intention was to go from Namur to Luxemburg, Treves etc. and descend down the Moselle to Coblentz. Had this been effected I was under engagement to give your Father some particulars of the Expedition; but we were obliged to give it up and to content ourselves with floating down the Meuse to Liege.—Pray have the kindness to mention this when you write to Brussels, or Major Gordon will have cause to complain of me.

I remain dear Sir
Sincerely yours
Wm Wordsworth

---

[1] George Huntly Gordon (1796–1868), for whom Sir Walter Scott had written the *Religious Discourses by a Layman*, published this year. (See Lockhart's *Life of Scott*, vii. 98 ff.) Huntly Gordon had been prevented by deafness from becoming a minister of the Church of Scotland, as he had wished; and he acted as Scott's amanuensis for a time, until in 1826 Scott procured him a post as assistant private secretary to Lushington, Secretary of the Treasury. He later held a post in the Stationery Office.

[2] Major Pryse Lockhart Gordon (b. 1762), who had shown Scott the field of Waterloo in 1815: 'though a bit of a roué . . . a clever fellow in his way' (*Journal of Sir Walter Scott*, p. 336). He had entertained W. W. and his companions at Brussels on 25 June (see L. 346 above). Two years later he published his *Personal Memoirs* of life on the Continent, and in 1834 *Belgium and Holland . . . in the year 1830* (see *R.M. Cat.*, no. 375).

352. W. W. to H. C. R.

Address: C. H. Robinson Esqre, 3 Kings Bench Walk, Temple.
Endorsed: Augt 1828, Wordsworth Autograph.
MS. Dr. Williams's Library.
Morley, i. 189.

Thursday morng
[7 Aug. 1828]

My dear Friend,

I write this Note in fear you may be gone. We arrived yesterday afternoon—I much regret I did not call in the Temple in passing. I thought you were on the circuit. We have had a pleasant ramble—Ever faithfully yours. Your Bag is yet at the Custom house with our other things. farewell. bon voyage—

Bryanston street—W. Wordsworth

[Underneath the address, which is not in his hand, W. W. adds]
how unlucky!
called just after your departure—

353. W. W. to CHARLES JAMES BLOMFIELD

MS. Pierpont Morgan Library. Hitherto unpublished.

August 9th [1828]
12 Bryanstone Street

My Lord,

The day after my return from an Excursion on the Continent I did myself the honor of calling in Bishopsgate Street,[1] to congratulate your Lordship on your Translation to the See of London.[2] Much as I rejoice in this event on many accounts, I may be allowed to say that the feeling is not unmixed with regret, know[ing] how much the extensive Diocese you have left stands in need of such a Superintendent, having witnessed the good [you] were doing there. Indeed my Lord, you will be much regretted.—

Mrs Blomfield I learn is at Chester; I hope in good health. On Monday I depart for Westmorland, calling on my way to take up Mrs Wordsworth who has been staying with her Son to initiate him in Housekeeping, a task which his Curacy imposes—

[1] Blomfield had been appointed rector of St. Botolph, Bishopsgate, in 1819 in succession to Richard Mant, and he continued to hold this valuable benefice after his appointment to the see of Chester.

[2] In place of Dr. William Howley, who now succeeded Dr. Charles Manners-Sutton as Archbishop of Canterbury.

We hear much of the liberality of the Continental Governments, Prussia especially, in respect to the two Religions—Heaven forbid *we* should have such liberality at the same price, which among the leading classes, is nothing less than indifference, utter indifference. This I can affirm from recent experience—

> With high respect
> I have the honor to be
> my Lord Bishop
> your faithful and obed^{nt} Ser^{vt}
> Wm Wordsworth

354. W. W. to WILLIAM JERDAN

Address: W. Jerdan Esq., Grove House, Brompton.
Postmark: 9 Aug. 1828.
MS. Henry E. Huntington Library. Hitherto unpublished.

> 12 Bryanstone Street
> 9th August [1828]

Dear Sir,

Your obliging Note of the 21st June I found on my return from the Continent on the 6th In^{stnt}. I have since been extremely hurried or should have replied to it earlier.—

You overate my powers of amusing and my opportunities in supposing any thing observed by me, could have interested your Readers—I am sensible, however, of your attention in making the proposal[1]—

I saw Mr Southey just before I left London, but he was then in a state of suffering from his recent operation.—I shall make a point

---

[1] Jerdan had proposed that W. W. should contribute a journal of his continental tour to the *Literary Gazette*. See L. 360 below, and the *Autobiography of William Jerdan*, 4 vols., 1852–3, iv. 238–40: 'Wordsworth in town was very different from Wordsworth in the country, or rather, perhaps, he was not the same person in mixed company as when *tête-à-tête*, or with a couple of friends. In the former case he was often very lively and entertaining. I recollect meeting him at breakfast after his being at the Italian Opera the preceding night, and his remarks on the singing and his limning of the limbs of the dancers, were as replete with shrewdness and pleasantry as anything I ever heard from the most witty and graphic lips. I was so charmed both with the matter and manner, that I wrote immediately to offer *carte blanche* for his correspondence, from the continent . . . Had he complied with my wish, and written letters in the tone and spirit of the criticisms on the opera, I am sure the public would have had a variation in the style of Wordsworth which would greatly have surprised it, little anticipating that the tender poet could also be the grotesque delineator of individual peculiarities, and humorous caricaturist of social anomalies.'

of communicating to him your notices on Mr Percival's death;[1] but perhaps you may have an opportunity of doing it yourself, since I had the pleasure of seeing you.

On Monday I leave town, and tomorrow go to Mr Lambe at Enf[ield][2] Chase—otherwise I might perhaps have had the pleasure of a call from you.

> I remain dear Sir
> faithfully yours
> Wm Wordsworth

355. D. W. to WILLIAM PEARSON

MS. untraced.
Pearson. K (—). *LY i. 301* (—).

Sunday, 10th August [1828]

My dear Sir,

I am exceedingly obliged to you for the book, and happy to say I was not the least the worse for our walk to the top of Fairfield,[3] which has left behind some pleasant remembrances. We will read Lockhart's Life of Burns,[4] before next Tuesday, when we shall be very happy to see you.

This morning we had a letter announcing my Brother and Dora's safe arrival in London, in good health.

William returns a thousand thanks for your kindness in sending over the Dog. He had intended despatching a boy for it, to-morrow morning.

> In haste, believe me, yours truly,
> D. Wordsworth.

I shall be very glad before the summer and autumn are gone by to have another mountain walk with you.

---

[1] Spencer Perceval (1762–1812), Prime Minister from 1809 until his assassination in the lobby of the House on 11 May 1812 by a crazed bankrupt named John Bellingham (see also *MY* ii. 21). Jerdan had been a witness of the incident, and described it in his *Autobiography*, i. 133–41.

[2] *MS. torn.*

[3] On 7 Aug., according to D. W.'s MS. Journals.

[4] Published this year in *Constable's Miscellany*.

356. W. W. to SIR WALTER SCOTT

MS. Harvard University Library.
LY i. 302.

[Rydal Mount]
28th August [1828]

My dear Sir Walter,

Professor Norton[1] of Cambridge University, America, is the Bearer of this. His request for a Letter of introduction, his *desire* rather to have one (for a request he did not make) was expressed with such diffidence that I had a real pleasure in telling him that I could venture to meet his wishes. He is highly respected in his own Country, and came to me with a Letter from Professor Ticknor[2] of Boston, whom probably you remember. He is travelling in search of health and Mrs Norton and a female Friend accompany him.—

Perhaps you may have heard that I have been rambling on the Continent with my Daughter and Mr Coleridge since we met in London: Our principal objects were the Rhine and Holland, and Flanders, which countries were not new to me, but were revisited with great interest in such pleasant Company. You would have enjoyed floating down the Meuse and the Rhine with us, and I heartily wish you could have made a fourth to the Party, had it only been for one day.—

Short as was my stay in London, on my return, I called at Mr Lockart's, but was not lucky enough to find either him, or Mr Charles,[3] your Son, at home; pray express my regret, especially to the latter who left a Card for me a short while before we started for the Continent: when I was so hurried that I could not return his visit.—

We only reached home last night—Mrs Wordsworth and my Daughter after a year's absence—so that all is new and strange to them; and myself after so long an interval that I cannot encourage the hope of getting to Abbotsford this Summer, or rather Autumn— for alas the Summer is fled, if indeed we have seen her face this

[1] Andrews Norton (1786–1853), Professor of Sacred Literature at Harvard, 1819–30, and a conservative Unitarian, published *The Evidences of the Genuineness of the Gospels*, 1837–44. His address *On the Latest Form of Infidelity* (1839) was commonly held to be a reply to R. W. Emerson's 'Divinity School Address' of the preceding year. He was the father of the distinguished scholar Charles Eliot Norton.

[2] George Ticknor (see *MY* ii. 504), Andrews Norton's brother-in-law: Professor of French and Spanish at Harvard, 1819–35.

[3] Charles Scott (1805–41), Scott's younger son, at present a clerk in the Foreign Office. He died at Teheran, where he was attaché to the British Embassy.

year.—This inability, for such it strikes me at present, is I assure you a great disappointment; another year I hope to be more fortunate.

Southey is wonderfully well—he had an operation performed when in Town, which has removed an infirmity he has suffered from for ten years. To-morrow he will be on the top of Saddleback with Sir Robert Inglis.[1] My Sister and I should have joined them if I had not been so freshly arrived—But I am tiring you—I could ask a hundred questions, about Mrs Lockart and her little Boy,[2] but I have heard he is not better. Do not let Major Scott or Mr Charles, or any body belonging to you, pass this way without calling here—farewell, a thousand kind wishes in which I am joined by Mrs W. my Sister and Daughter—ever most

faithfully yours
Wm Wordsworth

[For 356a, see Addendum, p. 730]

357. D. W. to WILLIAM PEARSON

MS. untraced.
Pearson. K. LY i. 303.

Rydal Mount,
Thursday, 25th Sept^r [1828]

My dear Sir,

I was very sorry to find you had not seen my Brother at Mr Tilbrook's when you were last here, and that you were gone when I inquired for you. It was indeed very unlucky that you should have come at a time when so many strangers were gathered together at Rydal Mount.

I now write for two reasons. In the first place, to say I hope to ascend Helvellyn with you before my departure to Whitwick—and in the second, to request that you will bring with you my Scotch Tour when you come; if you have not an opportunity of sending it before, by some individual whom you can depend upon for leaving it at Rydal Mount—one who will give it into the hands of one of our servants, or other person of the family, to be delivered to Miss Wordsworth, Senr.

We are at present in want of the Journal—but (it not being here) there is no need that you should trouble yourself to send it purposely. A week or two now will make no difference.

---

[1] The Tory politician and churchman. See L. 178 above.
[2] John Hugh (the Hugh Little John of Scott's *Tales of a Grandfather*), d. 1831.

Next week we expect company. But after that time my Brother and I will be at perfect liberty to climb Helvellyn with you any fine morning when you may happen to arrive. Come by half-past 8 o'clock, and if on a Keswick-*coach* day, so much the better, as we could go on the coach to Dunmail Rays.—Mondays, Wednesdays, and Fridays are the days on which the coach *goes* to Keswick.

I shall depart towards Leicestershire about the first week in Nov^r, therefore the sooner you come the better, *after* next week.

With kind respects from all the family, and my Brother especially, who much regretted he did not see you,

I remain,
Yours truly,
D. Wordsworth, Senr.

358. W. W. to WILLIAM JACKSON

Address: The Revd W. Jackson [*In M. W.'s hand*]
MS. Berg Collection, New York Public Library. Hitherto unpublished.

[early Oct. 1828]

My dear Friend,

I am truly sorry we are not to see you. Mrs W. has been unlucky in her expression 'of importance to us all'—which naturally led you to include yourself in the *business*.—In fact she meant of importance to this family, and ought to have mentioned that it referred to W^m whom we wanted to talk to you about, and to learn from you whether it would be impossible for you to take him for a certain number of months under your care. You will be startled, I fear, at this as a bold proposition—if so: regard it at least as another proof of the reliance we have upon your Friendship. We have been disappointed in every attempt, in every quarter (America included) to procure a situation in business for W^m which might give reasonable grounds to expect an opening in due time—and are at last impelled to return to our original track, the University. Is it indispensible that he should quit home, and be placed somewhere as preparatory to this.—It might seem that he could be put under his Brother John; but the objections will strike you at once. John could not have the necessary authority over him; they would be upon too familiar terms with each other; were it not for this, John is perfectly qualified to instruct him in Latin and Greek, and Euclid—the main things which he would want.—

Early October 1828

Finding all my attempts at an opening in business of no avail, I applied to Lord Lonsdale to get him a place under Government. His Lordship kindly undertook to write to Lord Lowther, whose answer was, that he had been two years looking out for a situation for a son of Mr [? Parkin][1] and till that engagement was satisfied he could do nothing. My views in sending W. to the University are these; He *must* go somewhere, and where could he be better; whether as qualifying him in a general way for the world, and for any office that might prove vacant; or in the end for the Church if he should become seriously disposed towards it, which I am inclined to think he may, finding his Brother so happy and so useful in that profession. There is yet another course which he might take ultimately; there are several Offices of not very severe duty, nor requiring first-rate talents, which are tenable by *Barristers only*— and when he has taken his degree at College he might keep terms with a view to be eligible to one of these.—I have thus laid before you the present state of our minds in respect to him; and may now return to the point—with due diligence he might go to College next October—and what we wished to talk to you about was whether he could read under you any considerable part of this time, for such remuneration as it would be in my power to make you. I am well aware of your general indisposition to take pupils at all, and equally so that the Son of an Individual in my circumstances is not exactly the Sort of connection that might prove most benificial to you—But to this it is sufficient to advert—I bear in mind also your personal connection with Lord de Tabley[2]—but I should think that might not interfere; and possibly in some things might prove advantageous to the young Peer, and a relief to you all to have another young person of good behaviour benefiting at the same time, in a certain degree by your instruction.—But in all this I expect you to deal with us, with entire frankness. Somewhere, as I said before he must go, whatever is done with him, or for whatever he may be designed.—Write at your leisure, and believe me my dear friend

very faithfully yours

Wm Wordsworth

[M. W. adds]

My dear Friend, I was half inclined to go over Kirkstone with my friend Miss Weir[3] (who is now at Rydal) next Wed: to meet

[1] Probably Hugh Parkin of Skirsgill, nr. Penrith. See L. 115 above.

[2] Sir George Leicester, 6th Bart., and 2nd Baron de Tabley (1811–87), of Tabley House, Cheshire: treasurer of H.M.'s household, 1868–72. He had succeeded his father, a munificent patron of the arts, the previous year.

[3] See *MT* i. 170, 233.

you at Penrith and have the satisfaction of talking with you—but
2ᵈ thoughts deterred me from making such an engagement—and
W. has said all that could have been said, at such meeting. M. W.

359. W. W. to GEORGE HUNTLY GORDON

MS. Cornell.
Broughton, p. 3.

Rydal Mount
Ambleside
October 7ᵗʰ—[1828]

My dear Sir,

I have been long in availing myself of your kind offer. In fact I am
scarcely yet settled in my home which we did not reach till some
weeks after we left London; having been agreeably detained in
Leicestershire upon a visit to my Son, officiating there as Curate in
a pretty large Vicarage which he has all to himself and his House-
Keeper.

Have you yet seen Mr Coleridge—if not pray let me know, and I
will enclose you a Letter of introduction to him. He is shy, I own,
of encreasing his acquaintance, being somewhat peculiarly circumstanced; but be not you afraid—I have seen enough of you to be
assured that he would be pleased to be known to you.

I hope you have good news from Brussels, at least as favorable as
your Fathers deranged health will allow.

I shall not see Sir Walter this autumn—but I think I *told* you so.—

Our neighbourhood is splendid with the hues of Autumn—but the
winds are whistling wildly on all sides of us—and black showers,
every five minutes scattering drops as thick, and as heavy as hail; so
that there is no riding out, and little walking except for the bold.—

One of these Letters (the one imperfectly directed) will occasion
you more trouble than I seem thoroughly justified in imposing. I
have no means of coming at the address, but will you have the
kindness to fill up to my Namesake from the Court Guide of 28—
where you will be sure to find it.

My Daughter begs her remembrance; and believe me my dear Sir

very faithfully yours
Wᵐ Wordsworth

[*In Dora W.'s hand*]

The four letters are all for the two penny Post—

360. W. W. to WILLIAM JERDAN

Address: W. Jerdan Esq, Grove House, Brompton.
MS. Cornell.
Autobiography of William Jerdan, iv. 239.

Rydal Mount,
near Ambleside
October 7th [1828]

Dear Sir,

Your Letter of the 23^d August, I did not receive till my arrival here several Weeks after it was written. My stay in London was only of a few days, or I should have been pleased to renew my acquaintance with you.

I really cannot change my opinion as to the little interest which would attach to such observations as my ability or opportunities enabled me to make during my ramble upon the Continent;[1] or it would have given me pleasure to meet your wishes. There is an obstacle in the way of my ever producing any thing of this kind, viz—idleness,—and yet another which is an affair of taste. Periodical writing, in order to strike, must be ambitious—and this style is, I think, in the record of Tours or Travels intolerable—or at any rate the worst that can be chosen. My model would be Gray's Letters and Journal[2] if I could muster courage to set seriously about any thing of the kind—but I suspect Gray himself would be found flat in these days.

I have named to Mr Southey your communications about Mr Percival's Death; he received them and wrote you a Letter of thanks, which by some mishap or other does not appear to have reached you.

If you happen to meet with Mr Reynolds, pray tell him that I received his prospectuses[3] (an ugly word!) and did as he wished with them.

I remain dear Sir
very sincerely yours
Wm Wordsworth

[1] See L. 354 above.
[2] *Journal in the Lakes*, 1769. See *EY*, p. 115.
[3] For *The Keepsake*, 1829.

361. D. W. to WILLIAM PEARSON

MS. untraced.
Pearson. K. LY i. 304.

Rydal Mount,
Tuesday, 9th October, [1828]

My dear Sir,
The weather seems now to be taking up; but I am sorry to say we cannot ascend Helvellyn this week, on account of engagements; and next week also, we are engaged for Thursday, Friday, and Saturday; but should Monday, Tuesday, or Wednesday prove fine, we should be glad to accompany you on any one of those days, for we give up the coach scheme, and intend to take the pony chaise as far as the Nag's Head.[1]

I am, dear Sir,
Yours respectfully,
D. Wordsworth.

362. W. W. to C. W.

Address: The Revd Dr Wordsworth, Trinity College, Cambridge.
Stamp: Kendal Penny Post. *Endorsed*: Tour in the Netherlands, Holland etc.
MS. British Museum.
K (—). *LY i. 323* (—).

Rydal Mount
Friday [mid-Oct.] 182[8]

My dear Brother,
The sight of your Letter was truly welcome—and the good account you give of your health, and every thing else except poor Charles,[2] (of whose indisposition we had heard through Hamilton the Brother of one of his companions) was all that could be wished. John and Chris: will I suppose return together, pray beg of either of them to create half an hour's leisure, for the purpose of sending us a little detail of what struck them most in Paris,[3] or in France.

---

[1] The inn at Wythburn, closed by the Manchester Waterworks in 1933. (De Selincourt's note.)

[2] Charles Wordsworth had been taken ill during a long vacation visit to Guernsey with Hamilton, a fellow Student of Christ Church. Walter Kerr Hamilton (1808–69), Fellow of Merton College, Oxford (1832), and vicar of St. Peter's-in-the-East (1837), became a Canon of Salisbury (1841) and eventually Bishop of Salisbury in 1854. For Edward Hamilton, his younger brother, see L. 365 below.

[3] C. W. jnr.'s unpublished 'Journal of a Visit to Paris, 1828', is in the British Museum. For a brief extract critical of Church and society in France, see *Christopher Wordsworth*, pp. 61–2. He was accompanied by two friends from Trinity, Francis Martin and James Brogden, and C. W. joined the party later.

Our expedition answered perfectly. Our route was by steam from London to Ostend, by barge to Ghent, by diligence to Brussels, by diligence to Namur, stopping 4 hours at the field of Waterloo, up the Meuse en voiture to Dinant, and back to Namur; thence by barge down the Meuse to Liege, in voiture to Spa, and by the same conveyance to Aix-la-chapelle and Cologne; thence to Godesberg, two leagues above Bonn on the Rhine. Here we halted a week, and thence up the Rhine, as far as it is confined between the rocks, viz. to Bingen, and down it by water to Godesberg again, having stopped a day or two wherever we were tempted. At Godesberg we remained nearly another week, and thence down the Rhine by Steam to Nimeguen;[1] thence en voiture to Arnheim and Utrecht, and by barge to Amsterdam, and so on through Haarlem, Leyden, The Hague, Delft, to Rotterdam; thence in Steam boat to Antwerp, in Diligence to Ghent, and by barge again to Ostend, where we embarked for London. Dora was delighted with this ramble which shewed her the most interesting parts of the Kingdom of the Netherlands—including Holland; and also all that is striking upon the Rhine. Her health or rather her strength, (for her health was good before), was much improved; and Coleridge enjoyed himself greatly. At Antwerp he fell in with Julius Hare, and passed nearly two days in his Company and that of Lady Malcolm. Praed[2] of your College was of the Party. Dora here unluckily was overpowered with the heat, having relied too much upon her strength; so that she saw little of that pleasant party. On our return to the North we stopped a fortnight with John, with whom his mother had resided during our absence of nearly seven weeks; and found John happy in the quiet and solitude of Whitwick, and in the discharge of his professional duties. He wants nothing but more quietness and regularly sustained energy. The latter I think he would possess did not his Body hinder it; close application forces the blood into his head and eyes, and otherwise disorders him.— I have been baffled in all my attempts to find a situation for William, so that after having taken him off from his Greek, and remitted his Latin reading in some degree, I am now obliged to turn my thoughts again to college. With this view he must quit home for a year's preparation. I have written to Mr Jackson to learn if he can take him; if he cannot, I must place him somewhere else, and should be

---

[1] i.e. Nijmegen.
[2] Winthrop Mackworth Praed (1802–39), barrister and poet: Fellow of Trinity College, Cambridge (1827), M.P., and secretary to the Board of Control under Peel, 1834. The first collection of his poems appeared in New York in 1844; the authorized edition was produced by Derwent Coleridge in 1864.

glad of a suggestion from you on the subject. His Brother would be quite equal to instruct him, but that would never answer, as he would have no authority over him. Our Nephew John[1] also must no longer be left to run wild at Keswick. A new Master, by name, Hicky,[2] is to succeed Mr Bowman[3] at Christmas, at Hawkshead; and if he brings a good Character if you approve we will send him there. Alas! There are no funds for the expense, and there is no prospect of the lands being so well let again; as land is gradually falling in value. I employed two mornings in going over the Sockbridge property, when I was at Lowther lately, in looking to the Plantations and necessary repairs; and I then learned that Land as good as most of ours is letting now at half the price, in that neighbourhood. John is to come over to Rydal in ten days, and I shall examine him in his books; in which I fear he is very backward— at all events he cannot remain where he is.

You do right to resolve on taking relaxation in the summer; it might seem, however, that Persons in Power hardly thought you had earned that privilege by the quantity or value of your past Labours. It is the fashion among these people to neglect you; and this, I own, grieves me; but it raises my indignation to learn how one person[4] late, perhaps still, of Lambeth has presumed to speak of the Heads of Cambridge yourself included. You will guess whom I mean. Love from all. Our Sister on the 6th of Nov^b goes to Whitwick to help John through the solitude of the winter.

I will learn whether Southey has received your Eikon.[5] What do you hear about it?

[*unsigned*]

[1] i.e. R. W.'s son.

[2] Daniel Bamfield Hickie, LL.D. (1784–1867), headmaster of Hawkshead Grammar School, 1829–62.

[3] The Revd. Thomas Bowman, headmaster, 1786–1829. See T. W. Thompson, *Wordsworth's Hawkshead*, ed. Robert Woof, 1970, pp. 342–5.

[4] The Revd. John Lonsdale. See L. 371 below.

[5] i.e. C. W.'s new pamphlet on the authorship of the *Icon Basilike*. See L. 151 above. Southey had commended C. W.'s original argument in his review of 'Hallam's *Constitutional History*', *Quarterly Review*, xxxvii (1828), 194–260; and he had written to him on 19 Dec. 1827, urging him to resume the subject. 'I have likewise called upon some person to write the history of that reign, and counteract the infamous misrepresentations which are now sent into the world. *You* were in my mind. No person is so competent to undertake that subject as you are.' (*MS. Jonathan Wordsworth*.) De Quincey also had an interest in C. W.'s original pamphlet; and according to C. W.'s letter to W. W. of 21 Dec. 1825, he was planning to write on the anti-Caroline side, but was completely won over by C. W.'s arguments. 'As you told me, that if there were flaws in my argument his logical head would find them out, you will easily believe me, that I reckon the Opium Eater's friendship at a much higher rate than the hostility of Mr Todd.' (*WL MSS.*)

363. W. W. to WILLIAM WOOD[1]

Address: Mr Wood, Cockermouth. *Post paid.* [*In M. W.'s hand*]
Stamp: Kendal Penny Post.
MS. Harvard University Library.
LY i. 305.

Rydal Mount
Oct[br]. 15th, 1828.

Dear Sir,

My Subdistributor at Workington Mr Mordey being dead, and Mrs Mordey declining business, it is necessary to appoint a Successor. Three Individuals have made application for the Employment. Now as I do not happen to know any Person living in Workington, I am at loss to whom to apply for information respecting their characters; and in this difficulty I have presumed upon your kindness, thinking it not unlikely that you may either possess or be able to put me in the way of obtaining the knowledge I stand in need of.—It is an office that cannot be intrusted with propriety to any but active, regular, and sober persons—The Individuals who have applied are 1st Wm Dixon, Bookseller and Stationer, who refers me to Mr Joseph Thompson, Sol[r], Curwen Street; 2nd Anne Collins of the Post Office: 3[d] Mr Kirkonnel of Mary Port, through Mrs Mordey who is treating with him for her deceased Husband's Stock.—

As Mr Wm Dixon was the first Applicant and has been a Resident ten years as a Bookseller in a central Part of Workington, if you could satisfy me that he is a proper Person to be entrusted with the Stamps, you need not give yourself any further trouble. But if you happen to know the other Applicants, I should be obliged if you would say a word or two on that subject, as in the event of Mr Dixon not having the appointment, such information might be useful to me.

I have so often experienced your obliging Services, that I have no doubt you will readily excuse my troubling you upon this occasion.—

An answer at your earliest convenience would be very acceptable——

I remain dear Sir
With Comp[ts] to Mrs Wood,
Very sincerely your
obliged Ser[nt]
Wm Wordsworth

[1] The Cockermouth attorney (see *MY* ii. 341).

364. W. W. to EDWARD QUILLINAN

Address: Edward Quillinan Esqre, no. 12 Bryanston S^t, Portman Square, London. [*Readdressed to*] C. Wake's,[1] Tapton Grove, Chesterfield, Derbyshire.
Postmark: (1) 20 Oct. 1828. (2) 27 Oct. 1828. *Stamp*: Kendal Penny Post.
MS. WL.
LY i. 306.

> Rydal Mount
> Oct 17th 1828.

My dear Sir,

Your letter confidently supposed to be Precursor of yourself arrived a Day or two ago. Judge of our disappointment[2]—but then we have no Pheasants in these beautiful woods; and so we must digest the disappointment, as is the duty of disinterested Friends to do: being persuaded, that notwithstanding your hint about mercantile disagreeables,[3] you have enjoyed yourself where you have been.

Our Tour went off à merveille—especially for Dora—to whom every thing was new. But, if I am not mistaken, I said something to this purpose, in my short note from Antwerp.—Mr Rogers undertook your Introduction, that is the introduction of your Name to the Athenaeum, but it may possibly have escaped his recollection; but a note from you reminding him of what passed between him and me on the subject would be all that is required. By the bye, I left in Bryanston Street a flesh-brush with a long handle, a present from him; be so good as to direct its being taken care of for some favorable opportunity of its getting to Rydal. It is the 2nd he has designed for me, and I should be sorry this also should be lost. I left, likewise, an Umbrella, old and much worse for wear; but as it is unfit for London, beg of your Housekeeper to put it

---

[1] E. Q.'s friend Charles (later Sir Charles) Wake, 10th Bart. (1791–1864), with whom he often stayed. Wake's first wife was a sister of Sir George Sitwell, 2nd Bart., of Renishaw Hall, nr. Sheffield: his second wife was Lady Sitwell's sister.

[2] According to his MS. Diary for 1828, E. Q. had been staying with Col. Holmes in Edinburgh in late September, and then went on a shooting expedition with him. Thereafter he accompanied Holmes to Newcastle, arriving at Charles Wake's on 24 Oct., and soon after that he went on to stay with Sir George Sitwell at Renishaw.

[3] In his letter of 13 Oct., E. Q. had promised W. W. a consignment of wine: 'Between you and me, I have so many reasons of disgust at this Wine-Concern, that, but for that *wicked Will*, which, by defrauding me of my just expectations in favor of another not more worthy, almost forced on me the necessity of business, I would gladly leave all the plague and profit of it to my Brother who was brought up to it; and is in every way more fit for it. But I may as well keep my spleen to myself . . .' (*WL MSS.*)

aside also; it would still keep off a mountain-storm.—I owe Mr Robinson £12 and a few shillings. I will include it in a Bill for the wine—pray tell him so—I have written to Whitehaven to have both Hogsheads ensured: I hope Southey will take one of them, if not, there can be no difficulty in disposing of it.

The weather is charming, and our woods most beautiful. Sorry we all are you had not come to look at them. John has taken out a license, and though we have neither Pheasants, nor Partridges, he could have put you in the way of a Snipe and an accidental Hare,—but this perhaps would be poaching, About the 6th of Novbr my sister (who is much disappointed in not seeing you) leaves us to assist her Nephew John in getting through the solitude of the Winter, under the Rocks of Charnwood. Miss H. quits us at the same time, for Herefordshire; she has had, you will be sorry to hear, a return of spitting of blood, and is put by Mr Carr upon abstinence from animal food and her glass of wine. With these precautions and a little medicine, he apprehends no further mischief. After all I fear it must end in Wm's going to College—Poor lad, his life thus far has been untoward. I give up the Pen to Dora,[1] who has a good scold to inflict upon you—Farewell my dear friend,[2] and believe me very faithfully yours Wm Wordsworth.

365. D. W. to C. W. JNR.

Address: Chrisr. Wordsworth Esqre, Trinity College, Cambridge. *By Favor of Mr Isaac Green.*
MS: WL. Hitherto unpublished.

Monday 21st October [1828]

My dear Christopher,

Mr Isaac Green[3] of Queens' College called for commands for Cambridge, and I *promised* to entrust him with a letter for you,

---

[1] 'Pray tell Dora', E. Q. had written, 'that I am not sure that the alarm of the rencontre she threatened me with had not had a good deal of influence in keeping me away from Rydal this year; but I hope to take my revenge the next year.'

[2] Dora W. adds: '*My Dear friend* indeed!! Father is far too good natured with you. He is very angry though, I can tell you, and if we Ladies were near, you would certainly be kill[ed] outright. Letting us expect and expect you . . . and then sending a long *rigmarole* letter about wine, and then cooly adding that you had stayed so long in Scotland you cannot come to Rydal . . . and pretending too that my threatened rencontre kept you away—when you know you are hastening southward on purpose to meet the dear Douglas [i.e. Harriet Douglas]. She play'd us the slip so you chose to do the like. . . .' There is also a brief PS. from S. H.

[3] The Revd. Isaac Green (1804–75), master of Ambleside School; second master at Sedbergh, 1831–69, and incumbent of Howgill, Yorks.

which I intended should be a long one filled with all sorts of Rydal chit-chat, but visitors, coming in unexpectedly, have filched away all my time, and but that I would not disappoint the young man of the notion that he is doing me a service I would not write at all today. He is to stop the Coach at the Foot of the Hill to take up my dispatches.

My dear Nephews, I hope I may congratulate you all on a safe and happy return to Trinity Lodge, for no doubt Charles would join you there (though but for a day or two) after so long an absence; but no doubt ere this reaches you he will have taken his place in Christ-Church. I was very much pleased with your Father's account of his excursion, and of the satisfaction and profit you had all shared. I will not say I envyed you, but should have had no objection to a Run through Paris with such good and Kind Friends, young and old.—I wish you would find time—you or John—about three weeks hence to give me a long letter with a full account of your travels, to cheer my solitude at Whitwick, whither I am going, as soon as I can after the 6th of next month, to spend five months with John in his lonely Parsonage.—I will promise you in return all my adventures per Coach—through Manchester, or Liverpool, for my route is uncertain—and a full account of Whitwick arrangements, and of our Congregations in the ancient Church, our warfare with the Methodists, and our attempts—'feeble and ineffectual I fear'—to 'ameliorate the condition' of the Poor.

I am anxious to hear of poor Charles, concerning whose health but indifferent reports reached us, through Mr Edward Hamilton,[1] who spent the summer at Bowness, and is soon to become a Member of your College. He is a pleasant young man, and I hope will be among your acquaintances, if only because he is so fond of Bowness and the Lakes.

Dora has written to you I believe, and no doubt told you how much she was delighted with *her* tour. I dare say she never once mentioned her health, therefore I must tell you that it is much improved. She can eat like other folks, and though still lamentably subject to cold-taking, is greatly improved in strength.

Your Uncle is just come in from a Drive. He says he hopes one or other of you will write him an account of your travels.

By the bye I must mention the Bearer of this, though I cannot

[1] Edward William Terrick Hamilton (1809–98), until recently at Eton: Fellow of Trinity College, Cambridge, 1834–42; Parliamentary Agent in England for New South Wales, 1863; and M.P. for Salisbury, 1865–9.

expect you to take much nay *any* trouble; but if you should be in
the way when he delivers this, pray be kind and civil to him. He is
a very deserving and industrious young man, and I believe a good
Scholar, the Son of our Butcher at Grasmere who has furnished
you with many a good slice out of a leg of mutton. Excuse extreme
haste and believe me dear Christopher, with Love to y[r] Father and
Brothers,

> ever your affectionate Aunt
> D. W.

I was much gratified by your note and present of Poems,—The
ercer I like very much.

366. W. W. to BARRON FIELD

MS. British Museum.[1]
K (—). *LY i. 307* (—).

> Rydal Mount
> 24th Oct., 1828.

My dear Sir,

I will not spend time in thanking you for your kindness,[2] but
will go at once to the point and to the strongest case, *The Beggars*.[3]
I will state the faults, real or supposed, which put me on the task
of altering it.

> What other dress she had I could not know,

you must allow is a villainous line, one of the very worst in my
whole writings.—I hope so at least.
'In all my walks,' I thought obtrusively personal.

> Her face was of Egyptian brown.

The style, or rather composition, of this whole stanza is what I call
bricklaying, formal accumulation of particulars.

> Pouring out sorrows like a sea,

I did not like; and *sea* clashes with 'was beautiful to *see*' below.

---

[1] Quoted in Field's MS. Memoirs: his draft of the letter differs in some small
details from his fair copy.
[2] Field had followed up his long letter of 16 Apr. (see L. 334 above) with
another on the 28th, in which he added to his previous criticisms of W. W.'s
alterations and revisions. W. W. had not had time to refer to these in detail in
his letter of 20 June (see L. 344 above), and only now did he address himself
to them.
[3] *PW* ii. 222. See *app. crit.* for a full textual history of this poem, including
W. W.'s revisions in the 1827 and subsequent editions.

'On English land' is the same rhyme as 'gayest of the land', in the stanza below. Such were the reasons for altering. Now for the success.

> Nor claimed she service from the hood,[1]

is (I own), an expression too pompous for the occasion; and if you could substitute a line for the villainous 'What other dress, etc.', I would willingly part with it. But there is still a difficulty.

> She had a tall man's height, or more,

would anticipate

> She tower'd, fit person etc.

The boys could well understand '*looking* reproof'. There is frowning, shaking the head, etc. 'Telling me a lie' might be restored without any objection on my part,[2] for 'Heaven hears that rash reply' is somewhat too refined; but as

> It was your mother, as I say,

is retained, the fact is implied of my knowledge of their having told an untruth. It is not to be denied that I have aimed at giving more elegance and dignity to this poem, partly on its own account, and partly that it might harmonise better with the one appended to it. I thought I had succeeded in my attempt better than, it seems, I have done. You will observe that in any meditated alteration of the first stanza, which I should be very thankful if you could do for me, the word *head* cannot be used, on account of '*head* those ancient Amazonian files', in the stanza below.[3]

The Blind Highland Boy[4]

The 'shell' was substituted for the 'washing-tub', on the suggestion of Coleridge; and, greatly as I respect your opinion and Lamb's, I cannot now bring myself to undo my work; though if I had been aware beforehand that such judges would have objected, I should not have troubled myself with making the alteration. I met the other day with a pretty picture of hazardous navigation like this. I think it is on the coast of Madras where people are described

[1] l. 3, rejected in 1832.   [2] l. 44, restored in the 1836 edn.
[3] l. 11, 'lead' substituted for 'head', 1836.
[4] *PW* iii. 88. For Coleridge's criticism see *Anima Poetae*, ed. E. H. Coleridge, 1895, pp. 207–8; for Lamb's, see *Lamb*, ii. 153.

as trusting themselves to the rough waves on small rafts, in such a way that the flat raft being hidden from view by the billows, the navigator appears to be sitting on the bare waters.

Rural Architecture[1]

From the meadows of Armath, etc.

My sister objected so strongly to this alteration at the time, that, her judgment being confirmed by yours, the old reading may be restored.

Pedestrian Tour among the Alps[2]

No more, along thy vales and viny groves,
Whole hamlets disappearing as he moves,
With cheeks o'erspread by smiles of baleful glow,
On his pale horse shall fell Consumption go.

I had utterly forgotten this passage: at all events, as a bold juvenile thing, it might be restored. I suppose I must have written it from its being applied here in my mind, not to an individual but to a people.

Ruth[3]

And there exulting in her wrongs,
Among the music of her songs,
She fearfully caroused.

This was altered, Lamb having observed that it was not English. I liked it better myself, but certainly to carouse cups—that is to empty them—is the genuine English.[4]

The Sailor's Mother[5]

And, thus continuing, she said,
'I had a son, who *many a day*
Sailed on the seas

[1] *PW* i. 244. l. 1 (1827 edn. only):
From the meadows of Armath, on Thirlmere's wild shore.
[2] *Descriptive Sketches* (1793), ll. 788–91 (*PW* i. 88).
[3] *PW* ii. 227.
[4] ll. 196–8 (1836 edn.):
And there, with many a doleful song,
Made of wild words, her cup of wrong
She fearfully caroused.
[5] *PW* ii. 54.

These words shall be restored. I suppose I had objected to the
first line, which, it must be allowed, is rather flat.[1]

> He to a fellow-lodger's care
> Had left it to be watch'd and fed
> Till he came back again.

Than this last line,

> And pipe its song in safety,

I own strikes me as better, because 'from the bodings of his mind'
he feared he should not come back again. He might dramatically
have said to his fellow-lodger, 'Take care of this bird till I come
back again', not liking to own to another, or to himself even, in
words, that he feared he should not return; but as he is not introduced here speaking, it is I think better, and brings in a pretty
image of the bird singing, when its master might be in peril, or
no more.

The Emigrant Mother[2]

> Smiles hast thou, bright ones of thy own;
> I cannot keep thee in my arms,
> For they confound me; as it is,
> I have forgot those smiles of his.

Coleridge objected to the last two lines, for which

> By those bewildering glances crost,
> In which the light of his is lost

is substituted. The alteration ought, in my judgement, to be
retained.[3]

The Idiot Boy[4]

'Across the saddle', is much better. So 'up towards', instead of
'up upon' in *Michael*.

The Green Linnet[5]

A brother of the leaves he seems

---

[1] ll. 19–21 (1820 and 1827 edns. only):
> I had a son—the waves might roar,
> He feared them not, a Sailor gay!
> But he will cross the waves no more.

[2] *PW* ii. 56.

[3] ll. 63–4 (1836 edn.):
> For they confound me;—where—where is
> That last, that sweetest smile of his?

[4] *PW* ii. 67. See ll. 10–11 and *app. crit.*   [5] *PW* ii. 139.

may be thus retained:—

> My sight he dazzles—nay deceives:
> He seems a brother of the leaves.[1]

The stanza, as you have been accustomed to quote it, is very faulty. 'Forth he *teems*' is a provincialism. Dr Johnson says, 'A low word, when used in this sense.' But my main motive for altering this stanza was the wholly unjustifiable use of the word *train* as applied to leaves *attached* to a tree.[2] A train of *withered* leaves, driven by the wind along the gravel, as I have often seen them, sparkling in April sunshine, might be said. '*Did* feign' is also an awkward expletive for an elegant poem, as this is generally allowed to be

To the Small Celandine[3]

'Old Magellan' shall be restored.

To the Daisy[4]

Thou wander'st the wide world about. Etc. etc.

I was loath to part with this stanza. It may either be restored, or printed at the end of a volume, among notes and variations, when you edit the fifteenth edition.[5]

To a Skylark[6]

After having succeeded in the second 'Skylark', and in the conclusion of the poem entitled *A Morning Exercise*,[7] in my notice of this bird, I became indifferent to this poem, which Coleridge used severely to condemn, and to treat contemptuously. I like, however, the beginning of it so well that, for the sake of that, I tacked to it the respectably-tame conclusion. I have no objection, as you have been pleased with it, to restore the whole piece. Could you improve it a little?

To the Cuckoo[8]

At once far off and near.

---

[1] This version of ll. 33–4 was never adopted.
[2] ll. 38–40 (1807 edn.):

> And mock the Form which he did feign,
> While he was dancing with the train
> Of Leaves among the bushes.

[3] *PW* ii. 144. See l. 51 and *app. crit.*
[4] *PW* iv. 67.　　　　　　　　　　[5] ll. 17–24 restored in 1836.
[6] *PW* ii. 266.　　　　[7] *PW* ii. 124.　　　　[8] *PW* ii. 207.

Restore this. The alteration was made in consequence of my noticing one day, that the voice of a cuckoo, which I had heard from a tree at a great distance, did not seem any louder when I approached the tree.[1]

Gipsies[2]

The concluding apology should be cancelled. 'Goings-on' is precisely the word wanted; but it makes a weak and apparently prosaic line, so near the end of a poem. I fear it cannot be altered, as the rhyme must be retained, on account of the concluding verse.

In the second *Cuckoo*,[3] I was displeased with the existing alterations; and in my copy have written in pencil thus:

> Such rebounds our inward ear
> Often catches from afar:
> Listen, ponder, etc.,

restoring 'listen, ponder'.[4] The word 'rebounds' I wish much to introduce here; for the imaginative warning turns upon the echo, which ought to be revived as near the conclusion as possible. This rule of art holds equally good as to the theme of a piece of music, as in a poem.

Prima dicte mihi, summa dicende Camæna.[5]

(Horatius)

Peele Castle in a Storm[6]

The light that never was on sea or land

shall be restored. I need not trouble you with the reasons that put me upon the alteration.[7]

[1] l. 8 (1827 edn.): As loud far off as near.

[2] *PW* ii. 226. 'The alteration was made in consequence of Coleridge's critique, in his *Biographia Literaria*, in which he charges Wordsworth with not reflecting that the poor tawny wanderers might probably have been tramping for weeks together, and consequently might have been right glad to rest themselves for one whole day. I believe that I replied to this objection that travelling industry was not the habit of gipsies, who are naturally loitering basking idlers, "taskless", in the strongest sense of the word, and that the poet's moral was truly drawn, though perhaps the contrasted images and thoughts might be too great for the subject.' (MS. *Memoirs.*)

[3] *Yes, it was the mountain Echo* (*PW* ii. 265).

[4] ll. 17–20 *thus* in 1836. [5] *Epistles*, i, i. 1. [6] *PW* iv. 258.

[7] ll. 14–16 (1827 edn.):
... and add the gleam,
The lustre, known to neither sea nor land,
But borrowed from the youthful Poet's dream.

Barron Field protested that the original lines 'have passed into a quotation: they are *feræ naturæ* now; and I don't see what right you have to reclaim and clip the wings of the words and tame them thus'. (*WL MSS.*)

The passages in *Peter Bell*[1] were altered out of deference to the
opinion of others. You say *little* is a word of endearment. I meant
'*little* mulish', as contemptuous.[2] *Spiteful*, I fear, would scarcely
be understood without your anecdote.

> Is it a party in a parlour?
> Cramm'd just as they on earth were cramm'd,
> Some sipping punch, some sipping tea,
> But as you by their faces see,
> All silent, and all damned.

This stanza I omitted, though one of the most imaginative in the
whole piece, not to offend the pious.[3]

The Excursion edition of 1827

And make the vessel of the big round year, p. 364

I know there is such a line as this somewhere; but, for the life of
me, I cannot tell where.[4]

> He yielded, though reluctant, for his mind
> Instinctively dispos'd him to retire
> To his own covert: as a billow heav'd
> Upon the beach rolls back into the sea. p. 192[5]

I cannot accede to your objection to the billow. The point simply
is, he was cast out of his element and falls back into it, as natually
and necessarily as a billow into the sea. There is imagination in
fastening solely upon that characteristic point of resemblance,
stopping there, thinking of nothing else.

> And there,
> Merrily seated in a ring partook
> The beverage drawn from China's fragrant herb. p. 380

---

[1] *PW* ii. 331. '. . . in *Peter Bell* . . . have you altered the homely beginning
of a home-loving tale, the opening of which should essentially be homely,
to contrast with the flights of the prologue?', Field had asked.

[2] See l. 458.

[3] Chiefly, it seems, on the advice of H. C. R. (see *HCR* i. 241). Later,
W. W. was planning to restore the passage, but never in fact did so. See letter
to Richard Howitt, 30 Aug. 1837 (in later volume).

[4]   And make the chalice [Vessel *1827*] of the big round year
     Run o'er with gladness . . .

(*Excursion*, ix. 134–5: *PW* v. 291.)

[5] *Exc.*, v. 73–6 (*PW* v. 155).

'Drank tea' is too familiar. My line is (I own) somewhat too pompous, as you say.[1]

Read p. *332* thus:

> Though apprehensions cross'd me that my zeal
> To his might well be liken'd, etc[2]

—shorter. Page *220*, for 'When night' read 'Till night' etc.[3]

I am much pleased that you think the alterations of *The Excursion* improvements. My sister thinks them so invariably.

I remain, very faithfully yours
W. Wordsworth.[4]

367. W. W. to ALEXANDER DYCE[5]

MS. Victoria and Albert Museum.
K (—). LY i. 313.

Rydal Mount Near Kendal
October 29th, 1828

Sir,

I have to thank you for your elegant Edition of Collins, an Author who from the melancholy circumstances of his life,

---

[1] *Exc.*, ix. 530–1 (*PW* v. 304), altered in 1837 to:

> A choice repast—served by our young companions
> With rival earnestness and kindred glee.

[2] *Exc.*, viii. 21–2 (*PW* v. 266).

[3] *Exc.*, v. 766 (*PW* v. 177). Field had praised the alterations in *The Excursion* as '. . . many and judicious—principally abridgments—always improvements in the rhythm, the harmony and variety of which you have studied carefully'. And he added a message from Horace Smith: 'I hope you told Mr Wordsworth that I was quite ashamed of the ridicule in the Rejected Addresses (not mine, by the by)—that I had read his Excursion under my own walnut-trees with infinite delight; and had now the honour of being enrolled among his warm admirers.'

[4] Barron Field reproduces the whole of this letter as a valuable lecture on the art of poetry. 'I think it proves that there was a considerable difference between the poet's theory and his practice . . .' (MS. Memoirs.) 'I reserve what I have to say upon this word *theory* till I have the pleasure of seeing you.' W. W. commented.

[5] The Revd. Alexander Dyce (1798–1869), scholar and editor. In his edition of *The Poetical Works of William Collins*, 1827, Dyce had followed John Bell's text of the *Ode on the Popular Superstitions of the Highlands of Scotland* (British Library, Strand, 1787). Hearing it said that W. W. regarded Bell's corrections and additions as spurious, he wrote to W. W. on 13 Oct. to inquire on what evidence this opinion was founded (*Dyce MSS., Victoria and Albert Museum*). This letter, which is W. W.'s reply, marks the beginning of a long and fruitful literary association. The two friends met frequently in London, either at Dyce's chambers in Gray's Inn Square, or at the houses of mutual friends; but Dyce never visited Rydal Mount. Dyce's *Reminiscences* (ed. R. J. Schrader, Ohio, 1972), are rich in literary anecdotes of the period.

particularly the latter part of it, has a peculiar claim upon such attention as you have bestowed upon him and his works.

I do not doubt that the lines in Bell's Edition of the Highland Ode are spurious; but on this opinion I am far less disposed to insist, than to maintain that the principle is decidedly bad of admitting anything as the genuine work of a deceased Author but upon substantial external evidence. There may be exceptions to this rule, but they are very rare; and in our Literature are almost confined to certain works of Shakespear (Pericles for example) which ought to be admitted from internal evidence alone.

In the case of this ode of Collins there is not a jot of *external* evidence entitled to consideration.—What are the facts? In 1779, according to Dr Anderson, or according to Boswell, 1781— Johnson's Lives of the Poets was published, and made known to the literary world that Collins had composed an Ode on the Popular Superstitions of the Highlands of Scotland, which the Wartons who had seen it thought the best of his works. In 1784 Dr Carlyle[1] read from a MS. in Collins's own hand-writing this Ode, of which a Stanza and a half were wanting, and in 1788 the Ode was first printed[2] from Dr Carlyle's copy, with Mr Mackenzie's supplemental lines—and was extensively circulated through the English newspapers, in which I remember to have read it with great pleasure upon its first appearance. Every thing thus far was open and explicit, but shortly after (in the same year) appears from the Press of Mr Bell—An Ode etc. *Never before printed*. Dedicated to the Wartons.[3] Surely it is not a little bold to affirm that this Ode was never before printed, when thousands had read it in the English newspapers, verbatim the same, except the parts wanting in Dr Carlyle's Copy and a few verbal differences. The preface by the *anonymous* Editor begins thus—'A Gentleman who *for the present* chuses not to publish his name'—Afterwards occur these sentences 'By the public prints we are informed that a Scottish Clergyman lately discovered the first rude draught of this Poem— it is however *said* to be very imperfect—the 5th Stanza and a half of the 6th, *say the Prints*, being deficient, *has* been supplied by Mr M—"It" (what grammar have we here?) has been published

[1] The Revd. Alexander Carlyle (1722–1805), minister of Inveresk: known as 'Jupiter Carlyle'.
[2] In *Transactions of the Royal Society of Edinburgh*, i (1788), 63. Henry Mackenzie (1745–1831), author of *The Man of Feeling*, supplied stanza v and part of vi, which were missing in the authentic copy.
[3] Joseph Warton (1722–1800), and his brother Thomas (1728–90), the celebrated critics.

in some of *these* diurnal papers'—why does this Anonymous Editor, of a MS handed to him from one without a name, first talk of Dr C's Edition as if he had never seen it—'it is said to be imperfect', and then deliver an opinion upon Mr Mackenzie's addition, from his own judgement in these words—'It', meaning the part added by Mr Mackenzie, 'is undoubtedly pretty but wants' etc. What probability is there of his having seen that part without having seen the whole, of which in the previous sentence he affects to have no knowledge but by hearsay? In the dedication to the Wartons, it is boldly asserted, that, as their mentioning the Poem to Dr Johnson was the means that led to the imperfect first draught, it likewise was the happy means of bringing this *perfect* copy to light. The *proximate* means certainly was the publication of Dr Carlyle's copy, of the authenticity of which no doubt can be entertained—and if it were a rude draught it certainly was not so compared with this Editor's Copy, for they appear to be the same with the exceptions only above mentioned—viz. the supplemental part, and a few alterations made as should seem for alteration's sake, and a hemisstich and word or two supplied—observe the declaration—'A Gentleman who *for the present.*' 40 years have since elapsed, and the Gentleman does not yet *chuse* to publish his name. The fair inference is that no such gentleman ever existed, and according to the plain rules of evidence the longer the name is concealed the less is the assertion entitled to credit, if it ever had a claim at all to be respected.

It is not to be doubted that the Copy which Collins himself read to the Wartons in 1754 of this ode, which was composed in 1749, had undergone a studious revisal. That Copy in all probability has perished in the wreck of Collins's papers—assuredly the stanzas supplied in Bell's Edition were not there, at least as printed by his Editor. Collins could at no period of his life have suffered so bad a line to stand as They mourned, in air, *fell fell* Rebellion *slain*, or such a one as *Pale red* Culloden where those hopes were *drowned.* Or is it likely that Collins, how far soever participating the popular Enthusiasm in favour of the Duke of Cumberland, would have pronounced him a person more glorious than one who had 'gained heroic fame' because he, the Duke, *Broke slavery's chain* to reign a *private* Man, that is, to be content with a station from which he could not have attempted to raise himself without being a Rebel and a Traitor?—I never saw the Edinburgh Transactions, in which Dr C.'s Copy was printed: if I had it before me, I should enter for your satisfaction into the minutiae of the internal evidence, but I will now merely ask—What is the meaning of 'some hundred miles astray' and what is the probability that Collins, as in Bell's Edition, wrote 'they drain the *scented* spray' when 'scented grave' occurs before: Is *sainted* a word supplied by Dr Carlyle? as wells were formerly dedicated to saints it is surely much preferable to *scented*, which besides its being used before is nonsense.

By the Bye, I am almost sure that that very agreeable line

> Nor ever vernal Bee was heard to murmur there

is from Martin's account of St Kilda, not from his volume on the Western Islands,[1] but a separate pamphlet which he published on St Kilda,[2] and which I once possessed, but have unfortunately mislaid.

Excuse this tedious scrawl, which I fear you will find illegible. I have been impatient in writing it, *as I always am*. I remain,

Sincerely, your obliged serv[nt],

Wm Wordsworth

P.S. How does the Quatrain 'There Shakespear's self' etc. stand in the Edinburgh Copy? as printed in Bell's edition which you follow it is downright nonsense.

> There Shakespear's self with every garland crown'd
> his wayward sisters found

is sense, but what do *you* make of the intermediate words

> Flew to those fairy climes his fancy *sheen*[3]
> In musing hour.

368. W. W. to GEORGE HUNTLY GORDON

Address: G. H. Gordon Esq[re] [*In Dora W.'s hand*]
MS. Cornell.
Broughton, p. 4.

Rydal Mount
Ambleside
Nov[br] 10th [1828]

My dear Sir,

Many thanks for the care you took of the last Pacquet, I venture to send you more—

[1] Martin Martin, Gent., *A Description of the Western Islands of Scotland*, 1703.
[2] Id., *A Late Voyage to St. Kilda, the Remotest of all the Hebrides or Western Islands of Scotland*, 1698.
[3] This line was an addition in Bell's copy; it is not in the Edinburgh copy. (De Selincourt's note.)

The Enclosed to Mr Coleridge may be presented at your leisure
—Mr C. is somewhat peculiarly circumstanced as to his domestic
situation at High-gate, and I know that he has, in consequence of
that and of illness, contracted the circle of his acquaintance—I
mention this that you may not be disappointed in case less comes
from this Introduction than either you or I might wish, or would,
I know, have been agreeable to Mr C. had he been more at
liberty—

Upon some future occasion, I hope to profit by your suggestions
upon the purchase of old Books—at present I scarcely can, having
given to Cornish[1] a considerable order, chiefly books of Divinity,
on my elder Son's account who is in orders. It would have been
fortunate if this subject had been named between us, in London.

I have now to request your attention and *assistance* in a point of
much more importance; it is to trouble you to give me information
respecting your notions of the advantages and disadvantages of a
situation in some government office for a Young Man, with some
talent, but which has not been adequately cultivated, his studies
having been interrupted by severe illness. The individual is my
Younger Son. The best way of explaining myself will be to give
briefly his history. He was 18 years of age last June. Before the
age of 10 he was sent to the Charterhouse where he was obliged to
quit after nearly three years trial; his health having been utterly
ruined by the confinement etc. In the Course of the summer after
he came down, for the last time, he was attacked with dropsy,
first in the abdomen and afterwards in the chest; by care and
medical skill, he was restored, but he was not permitted to read
except for the merest amusement for more than two years—during
which time, as it had been before, his growth was utterly stopped
—Afterwards I did not venture to send him to a public School,
for fear of a Relapse—but home is a bad place for progress in
study, though he had unusual advantages. The consequence was,
that a Mind not particularly disposed to Books by nature, was
rendered still less so—he dreaded the notion of College—and
could think of nothing but the Army, to which he is still strongly
inclined, but which we are decidedly averse to. The object which
took me to Town last Spring, was to procure him a situation
either in a Counting House, or a manufacturing concern—in this
I failed—And though he is decidedly averse to the scheme—I have
been obliged to think of a situation for him in some public office.
I have no hope of succeeding immediately, though my Friends of

[1] The bookseller in Lincoln's Inn Fields.

the Lowther family have the best disposition to serve me. But my Son as I said before has a prejudice against such a situation, grounded *mainly* I believe upon his humble sense of his own talents, by the bye another disadvantage of his private education, and upon an apprehension that he cannot bear the Confinement. Now, dear Sir, be so good as to enlighten us upon these two points—how much confinement and what sort of labour are required in the offices with which you are acquainted. I ought to add that W^m (he bears his Father's name), is now in excellent health, nearly six feet high, and for the exercise of walking equals perhaps to any man in Westmorland. Notwithstanding, I am afraid, that severe confinement, with hard *head*-labour, would revive his old complaint. —I have yet another question to ask—as I have no means of procuring him such a situation at present, how could he pass the intermediate time with most advantage—at an English University, or abroad? where he might learn French and German—In the Courier I saw the other day an advertisement which shall be transcribed—tell me whether you think there is any promise about it. —Pray excuse my vile penmanship—it is always bad—but today I have no command of my pen at all, for I am just come from 2 hours hard labour with the mattock and spade in my Garden, where we are making improvements, and a Labourer has disappointed me—

Advertisement.[1] 'A married Clergyman of the Church of England, M.A. of the University of Cambridge and resident in France, receives into his Family a few Pupils whom he prepares for the English Universities, and the different departments of his Majesty's Service. The French and German Languages are taught by Professors of eminence, living in the family, in which no conversation except through the medium of one of the above languages is permitted. Terms 100 Guineas per annum. In this sum, Board, Tuition, a separate room, and washing are included. Address, Mr Valpy,[2] Red Lion Court Fleet Street; to Mr Power,[3] 34 Strand; to Messrs Birchall and Co.,[4] 140 New Bond Street, London, or to Mr Galignani,[5] 16 Rue Vivienne, and Messrs Treuthel and Wurtz, 17, Rue de Bourbon Paris.'

Should enquires respecting this Advertizer prove satisfactory, would it, think you, be an eligible thing—If you cannot forward French Letters without charge of Postage—I shall send no more, and will take especial care that you shall be repaid what these now

---

[1] Copied in an unidentified hand.
[2] Abraham Valpy, printer and publisher.   [3] Francis Power, merchant.
[4] Music-sellers.   [5] The publisher.

sent may occasion. Farewell. My daughter to whom you are so kindly complimentary sends her kind regards, in which I cordially join.

> I remain my dear Sir
> Very sincerely yours,
> Wm Wordsworth

369. W. W. to ALLAN CUNNINGHAM

Address: William Wordsworth Esq, Rydal Mount, Kendal, Westmorland [*readdressed to*] Alan Cunningham Esq, F. Chantreys Esq, Pimlico, London.
Postmark: (1) 3 Nov. 1828 (2) 11 Nov. 1828. *Stamp*: [? Kendal Penny Post].
MS. Mr. Robert H. Taylor.
K (—). *LY i. 316.*

[11 Nov. 1828]

My dear Friend,

I send back your preface[1] with two or three verbal alterations: there is no need of Mr Southey's assistance—it will do as it is.—I wish the Selection may answer the purpose, for myself I can form no conjecture.[2]—I congratulate you on the success of your Annual[3] —I am engaged on the same terms for the Keepsake,[4] and am not quite easy under the engagement as I have not written a line, nor am in possession of one which would answer their purpose—so that I really could not promise a contribution to any other work of the kind, were the publishers prepared to pay me at the rate which I am at liberty to accept. I regret this both on your account and for Mr Alaric Watts whom I wished to serve.

I send you back your own Letter thinking it may save you some trouble of transcription—I see that 'Simon Lee' is down on your

---

[1] Cunningham had written on 3 Nov. about his proposed Selection of Wordsworth, enclosing a draft preface and table of contents (see Appendix II). 'From such a pen as mine this Preface ought not to come—our friend Southey is the man for *it* and I only rough-write mine to show you with what perfect willingness and honest feeling I contemplate the task.'

[2] Cunningham had written by the same post to Oliver and Boyd of Edinburgh offering them the volume: 'I have requested to know how much they will give the Poet for leave to Print 4,000 Copies.' W. W.'s somewhat non-committal reply now may have been due to his refusal the previous April to accept Oliver and Boyd's terms for a similar Selection (see L. 332 above), and he was in any case anxious that sales of the *Poetical Works* of 1827 should not suffer (see L. 201 above). The proposed Selection was in fact never published.

[3] Six thousand copies of *The Anniversary* had already been sold.

[4] i.e. for the following year.

list.—I could wish that Piece to be slightly altered thus. The 2nd Stanza to be transposed and to stand as the 4th thus altered

> But oh the heavy change! bereft
> Of strength, of Friends and kindred, see etc

The next Stanza to begin thus

> And he is lean etc

> [*unsigned*]

[*In Dora W.'s hand*]

Is the Bust sent off to Mr Charles Wordsworth Christ Church Oxon? Do you know the address of Mr James Wilson[1] of Edinburgh, Brother to the Professor. He wishes for one to be sent to him to Edinburgh by sea.

> [*At the bottom of the page containing the proposed Preface W. W. writes*]

Excuse this verbal alteration. I hope care will be taken that the Vol. is correctly printed.

> [*At the bottom of the page of Contents W. W. writes*]

Would not 'Repentance a pastoral Ballad' 'The Affliction of Margaret' 'The Childless Father' and 'Address to a Child during a boisterous Winter Evening' be suitable?—and if you want a long piece 'The Brothers' or the Tale of 'Ellen' in the Excursion. Would not also the two April mornings and The Fountain a Conversation suit?

---

[1] James Wilson (1795–1856), Scottish zoologist and entomologist, who referred to W. W. as his 'mind's father', first met the poet in the summer of 1824 when he was staying with his brother Professor Wilson at Elleray, and he subsequently visited the Lakes regularly, seeing much of the Wordsworths. See James Hamilton, *Memoirs of the Life of James Wilson Esq. . . . of Woodville*, 1859.

370. W. W. to EDWARD QUILLINAN

Address: Edward Quillinan Esqre. no. 12 Bryanston S^t, Portman Square.
[*In Dora W.'s hand*]
Postmark: 12 Nov. 1828. *Stamp*: Kendal Penny Post. *Endorsed*: Answered
Nov^br 13, 1828.
MS. WL.
LY i. 317.

[11 Nov. 1828]

Advertisement[1]

A married Clergyman, of the Church of England, M.A. of the
University of Cambridge, and resident in France, receives into his
family, a few Pupils, whom he prepares for the English Universities, and the different departments of His Majesty's Service. The
French and German Languages are taught by Professors of
eminence living with the family, in which no conversation except
through the medium of one of the above languages is permitted.
Terms 100 guineas per annum. In this sum, board, tuition, a
separate room, and washing are included: Address, with further
particulars, may be obtained by applying to Mr Valpy, Red Lion
Court, Fleet Street: to Mr Power, 34 Strand: to Messrs Birchall
and Co. 140 New Bond Street, London: or to Mr Galignani, 18
Rue Vivienne, and Messrs Treuthel and Wurtz, 17 Rue de Bourbon,
Paris.

My dear Quillinan,

I have received the draft £9 odd. The Whitehaven office, not
insuring for less than £100, it could not be done; but the vessel
is arrived. I wish you had kept the money either for yourself or
Mr Robinson. The wine, I believe, is now in Bond at Whitehaven,
as I wrote to a person there to take care of it. Mr Southey will
take his share—and I will remit the money, together with Mr
Robinson's and the little account Mary has with you shortly.

Would you be kind enough to inquire the particulars of the above
advertisement; the where, the who, and if as the A—expresses
every expense of Languages, in short all but books, clothes and
pocket money be included in the £100, but above all what pupils
the person has and who they are. These may be disagreeable
offices—but as it is not for yourself it may be more easily gotten
over. Wm must go somewhere, as he is doing nothing at home,—
but don't mention names—if this were a thorough good establishment I should incline strongly to send him.

---

[1] The Advertisement is in John Carter's hand.

Did you know the Flemings of Rayrigg? This moment Dora tells me that Mrs F. was twice at Church yesterday, quite well, and died in the night.[1] My son Wm is just gone out to look after woodcocks, 4 were seen together yesterday. I wish you were among them.

Miss Hutchinson left us this morning for Brinsop. Lady Farquhar takes her as far as Birmingham. I drove my Sister to Stavely, near Kendal, Friday last on her way to Whitwick, John's curacy. We shall not, alas! see her again for half a year—nor Miss H. probably for 18 months. Joanna is here[2] for the winter, an invalid —Dora is well—but suffers occasionally, indeed too often, from toothache, and the utmost care is needed for what she eats. She no longer encourages your trade, having taken to ginger tea instead. I ought to have mentioned before, that Miss H. has been put upon a low diet by Mr Carr, on account of a recurrence of spitting of blood. In consequence of this change of regimen she has lost much strength, and a walk to Ambleside fatigued her yesterday to a degree she never knew before; we are of course very thankful that she has so pleasant a companion and so easy a conveyance, so far.

Of the Keepsake I have neither seen nor heard anything. Besides the Triad it contained two short pieces of mine, and 4 or 5 sonnets.[3]

I have not written a verse these 9 months past—my vein I fear is run out. Galignani has printed my Poems in one Vol:[4] at Paris, so there is an end to the sale of the London Edition, his being to be had at a third or a 4th of the price.

We are glad to hear so good an account of the Children. Love to them both. Poor Sir Egerton! coelum non animum mutant qui trans mare currunt.[5] Tell Mr Robinson to write to us as soon as you see him. Farewell. Affectionate regards from Mary, Dora, Wm, in which I heartily join.

Faithfully yours,
W. W.

[1] Jane, wife of John Fleming of Rayrigg, had died on 10 Nov. at the age of 54.

[2] From the Isle of Man.

[3] In fact, Reynolds had printed only two of the sonnets submitted, as W. W. discovered the following January. See L. 388 below.

[4] The 'pirated' edition published by A. and W. Galignani in 1828.

[5] Sir Egerton Brydges had returned to the Continent in October after an eighteen-month visit to England, the only one he made after he had settled abroad in 1818.

371. W. W. to C. W.

Address: The Revd The Master, Trin: Coll:, Cambridge.
Endorsed: No. 24. My brother.
MS. British Museum. Hitherto unpublished.

[11 Nov. 1828]

[In unidentified hand]

Advertizement

A Married Clergyman, of the Church of England, M.A., of the University of Cambridge, and resident in France, receives into his Family a few Pupils, whom he prepares for the English Universities, and the different departments of his Majesty's Service. The French and German Languages are taught by Professors of eminence, living in the family, in which no conversation except through the medium of one of the above languages is permitted. Terms 100 Guineas per annum. In this Sum, Board, Tuition, a separate room, and washing, are included. Address, with further particulars, may be obtained by applying to Mr Valpy, Red Lion Court, Fleet Street; to Mr Power, 34 Strand; to Messrs Birchall and Co., 140 New Bond Street, London, or to Mr Galignani, 18, Rue Vivienne, and Messrs Treuttel and Wurtz, 17 Rue de Bourbon, Paris.

[W. W. writes]

My dear Brother,

Should enquires prove satisfactory, would there be any promise in this for W^m. Home he must quit; he is doing nothing here, and our lives are saddened and our hearts troubled by that consciousness. Mr W. Jackson would willingly have taken him, out of kindness; but he will be too much engaged, and too unsettled for the ensuing 12 months.

Chris's parcel arrived duly, pray thank him for it, and his interesting Letter, to which I will myself reply shortly. Perhaps he or John may know something of this Advertizer—

The person alluded [to] was Lonsdale,[1] I mention this in

---

[1] See L. 362 above. The Revd. John Lonsdale (1788–1867), formerly Fellow of King's College, Cambridge, had been elected chaplain to Archbishop Manners-Sutton *c.* 1816, and thereafter preferment came swiftly and in many forms. He had this year been made precentor of Lichfield and rector of St. George's, Bloomsbury, and a prebendal stall at St. Paul's came his way soon after. In 1843 he was made Bishop of Lichfield on the recommendation of Howley and Blomfield, and was a highly successful diocesan. In his reply of 19 Nov., C. W. explained that Lonsdale had been a rival candidate to himself for the Cambridge Divinity Professorship. (*WL MSS.*)

confidence, the conversation was related to me not with a charge of
secrecy but it is generally understood in things of this nature that
names are not to be repeated. It was observed that in the late
ecclesiastical Movements the Cambridge heads had been neglected
—which called forth the reply that they were not deserving of
promotion, as being all men unfit for the off:—Surely, it was said,
the Master of Trin: is an exception. No, he fails in every thing he
undertakes. Your Friend replied—grant that what he proposes is
not carried in the shape in which it is proposed by him, Does not
something come of his endeavours for the benefit of the University
and his College, better than if his aims had been lower pitched.—
I am not quite easy in reporting this to you, but it seemed right
that you should know it; and who your friends are. I suspect that
since the unfortunate affair of the [? S——][1] you have not been in
good odour at Lambeth.

The other day I saw Mr Stanley[2] of Ponsonby, who married a
niece of the Bp of Durham[3]—he had just left Bp Auckland; and
he told me that the Bp is in very bad heart with the late movements
on to the Bench. He says if things continue to be of the same kind
it is all over with high Church principles. The Bp of D. is exceedingly dissatisfied with Blomfield,—says he owes his election
to Howley, and that he can make Howley do what he likes. The Bp
of D. had a sharp altercation with Bp Blomfield in the robing room
of the House of Lords, B. having declared that he on the Catholic
Question would be satisfied with the minimum of securities. 'To be
consistent you must be so' replied the Bp of D., 'after the speech
you made on such an occasion'.

But all this you perhaps may think hardly worth repeating—Mr
De Quincey is, and has been long in Edinburgh—He shall have
your present when he returns.

I am afraid the Paris Edition of my Poems,[4] will greatly injure
the sale of the London one—

I like your Reply upon the Eikon[5] the more the oftener I read it.

[1] i.e. the Speaker, Charles Manners-Sutton, whose candidacy for the representation of Cambridge University (see L. 151 above) had stirred up controversy.
[2] Edward Stanley (see *MY* ii. 490), who in 1821 married Mary, daughter
of William Douglas, a Judge in the East Indies.
[3] William Van Mildert (1765–1836), Bishop of Durham since 1826, and the
last bishop with palatine rank. He had been Regius Professor of Divinity at
Oxford (1813), and Bishop of Llandaff (1819), and became Dean of St. Paul's
(in plurality) in 1820. He published an important edition of *The Works of
Daniel Waterland*, 11 vols., 1823–8, and was a leading high-churchman of the
old school.   [4] Galignani's 'pirated' edition in one volume.
[5] *King Charles the First the author of Icon Basilike*. See L. 151 above.

It is triumphant. Have you heard any thing of the work—I have been faulty in not asking the question you wish of Mr Southey—it shall be done in a day or two. We have seldom communicated with him lately. Dorothy left us for Whitwick two days ago, and Miss Hutchinson for Brinsop this morning—Dora is well, except for fits of tooth ache. She and Mary send their best love to you and yours, in which I cordially join. Have you heard any thing how your Reply has been received, especially by your antagonist?[1]

ever yours
W. W.

372. W. W. to LORD LONSDALE

Address: The Earl of Lonsdale, Cottesmore, Greatham, Grantham.
Stamp: Kendal Penny Post.
MS. Lonsdale MSS. Hitherto unpublished.

[mid-Nov. 1828]
My Lord,

I am sorry that I cannot call to mind the Person, named to your Lordship by Mr Bolton as one he wished to have placed in the Commission of the Peace. The Purchaser of Miss Pritchard's property is named Branker.[2] His Father and he, I understand, have made a considerable Fortune by sugar-refining, part of which he seems strongly inclined to throw away in improvement-making. I have barely seen his person, but by those who have dined at his Table, he is not reckoned likely to prove an acquisition. He has many Workmen about him whom he *swears* at, as we are told, in a disgusting manner to which they are wholly unaccustomed. I have heard also that *Gin* is distributed among them. I have heard from a Gentleman who dined with him a few days ago, that in his presence and Mr Hartley Coleridge's, Mr Southey's Nephew, he made a violent attack upon the sincerity of Mr Southey in his

[1] C. W.'s principal antagonist was the Revd. John Lingard (1771–1851), the Roman Catholic historian, of Hornby, nr. Lancaster.
[2] Miss Letitia Pritchard (1756–1827) had owned a small farmhouse on the slopes of Loughrigg overlooking Windermere since 1793. On her death, the property was bought by James Branker, a Liverpool sugar merchant, and much enlarged into the grander mansion Croft Lodge, which still survives today. Hartley Coleridge received much kindness from Branker, and several letters pays tribute to his generosity: 'In truth, he has all the generosity, all the hospitality, all the independence which should belong to a man who has made a princely fortune by his own skill and industry: and may well be forgiven, if he have not quite all the polish of a man bred up from infancy among those who had nothing to do but refine their manners . . .' (*Letters of Hartley Coleridge*, pp. 155–6).

Book of the Church, a charge which Mr Coleridge repelled with becoming indignation. Your Lordship will know that I state these facts with much reluctance—but they are the best answer to the question. With all this he may be a good-natured man as it is called—but the impression here is that he is purse-proud and coarse-minded; Mr Lutwidge[1] is a man of sound loyal principles, but his manners and conversation are without steadiness or gravity. He is disposed to be active, but his judgement is not equal to his good intentions. His name is Henry, if he bear any other I do not know but will learn before this letter is closed. Beyond all comparison, in my judgement, the most [suitable][2] person for the office of Magistrate for property, for temper, for knowledge of the manners and feelings of the people in this neighbourhood, in short as a practical man, is Mr Benson Harrison of Green Bank, Ambleside. I have occasionally mentioned the thing to him, but he wished first to act as Churchwarden, with a view to a further knowledge of business, and the neighbourhood. A Complaint in the Trachea has driven him for the winter to Hastings—but we learn that he is much better. Being upon the subject of the Magistracy let me mention to your Lordship—that I would rather my own name were removed from the Commission. When you did me the Honor of recommending it to be placed there,[3] I had landed Estate sufficient for a qualification but it has been sold several years ago—and it strikes me there is an indelicacy under these circumstances in my name continuing.

With much pleasure I avail myself of the present opportunity to return thanks for your application to Lord Lowther in behalf of my Son, and your most friendly assurance that you will bear my wishes in mind. I am looking about for an Establishment on the Continent, where proceeding with his classical studies he might learn also German and French for two years, either with a view to a public office, or, in the last necessity, to a degree at an English University. Allow me to say, that of my other Son, I have from his Rector, and other quarters, the most pleasing accounts. He is happy in his profession, of which he promises to be a zealous and *judicious* member. Your Lordship will excuse my mentioning this last quality—but in no profession is it of such importance, and especially at this time, when the foundations of the Church are shaken by her own ministers. Mr Fleming[4] I have not seen since

---

[1] For Henry Thomas Lutwidge, see L. 180 above.
[2] *Word dropped out.*
[3] In 1819. See *MY* ii. 521, 532. [4] John Fleming of Rayrigg.

his loss, he is to let me know when he would wish me to call. He must have suffered greatly being a man of strong feelings.

May I trouble you to present my kind respects to Lady Lonsdale, not forgetting Miss Thompson.[1]

> I have the honour to be
> Your Lordship's
> faithful and much
> obliged Ser^nt
> Wm Wordsworth

Mr Jackson tells me Mr Lutwidge's name is Henry Thomas— Mrs W. will be obliged to Lord Lonsdale to forward the enclosed at his Lordship's convenience.

373. W. W. to GEORGE HUNTLY GORDON

Address: G. Huntly Gordon Esqre.
MS. Cornell.
Broughton, p. 6.

> Rydal Mount
> Nov: 25th / 28

My dear Sir,

How am I to thank you for your long and interesting Letter, and the trouble you have taken on my account!—You will think, I know, that my words may be better employed, and I will act on that conviction and to business at once.—In the first place, you over[r]ate the Power of my Friends of the Lowther family. Lord Lonsdale has delegated his in a great measure to his Son Lord Lowther, to whom I named my wishes, when I was in Town— without very much pressing the subject, as I still had hopes that I might find an opening in trade—Failing in this, I wrote to Lord Lonsdale from this place; who, with his usual zeal and kindness, took up the matter, and wrote to Lord Lowther—his answer was, that he had been two years in search of a situation for the son of a gentleman whom he named, and till that claim was satisfied he could not pledge himself for any thing else. I must observe, by the bye, that I am upon as intimate terms of intercourse with Lord Lowther, as our very different pursuits will admit. So that I have no doubt of his exerting himself hereafter in my behalf. But then this hope, is very distant, as you see. Had Mr Canning been

---

[1] A member of Lady Lonsdale's household (d. 1844).

alive, with whom I was also personally acquainted, and who never came into this Country (which he did several times) without calling upon me, who was a good natured man and had a respect for Literature, I should openly though briefly have given him my Son's hitherto somewhat unfortunate history, and solicited his patronage—But this is idle talk.—Where is he to be placed at present is the question before us. My wish would be, to go forward with a course of tuition, which while it fitted him for one of these offices would also keep in view what disappointment might render necessary, the sending to one of our Universities in the course of two years at the latest. I do not look to his distinguishing himself a[s] a scholar at Oxford or Cambridge, it is out of the question —but by the time that he had gotten his degree, he might possibly be not indisposed to the Church. In this profession I do not wish to influence him in any respect—nor do I at all like to look upon it as a pis-aller, but his elder Brother is so happy and so useful in discharge of his pastoral duties—that it is possible he might be inspired by his example.—But it is time to go back—if he were two years abroad he would be sure of learning the French or German language or both; and were he well situated his classical studies ought to proceed chearfully at the same time.

We shall make further inquires immediately about Mr Lonsdale[1] —but I don't know any of the Referees, and shall be obliged to you by any information you can gain from Mr Duff.[2]—I agree with you that the terms are very high for the Continent, and in a house with so many pupils— But I would willingly go to that sum rather than miss a situation to my mind. Pray communicate with the Lady you mention. The Classics, German, and French are my objects—the two latter as much by conversation as may be.—I am sorry to say that Wm is backward for his age in Latin and Greek; I know not how it happened—but he never was bookish—and though I believe he would have done pretty well at a public school, home tuition, solitary as it is at best, was for one of his intellectual Constitution, particularly *unfavorable*—You name Brussels—I fear it is too gay a place—and therefore at present you need not write to your Father as you kindly offer to do—I have said nothing of

[1] The Revd. William Lonsdale (1796–1868), whose advertisement for pupils is quoted in earlier letters, was educated at Eton and St. John's College, Cambridge, and had just taken his M.A. He was later headmaster of the Commercial and Collegiate School, nr. Grosvenor Square, and chaplain of the Brentford Union, Middlesex.
[2] Richard Wharton Duff (1782–1862), of Orton, Fochabers, Moray: Comptroller of Excise for Scotland, 1804–34.

the continental morals—but of course one would wish as much safety upon this point as could be had—and above all—one would be anxious, for what it is so difficult to obtain: a fair an[d] open account of the use he was making of his time. I have now said all that can be necessary and trust the rest to your goodness—

North-Wales is a country worthy of your admiration—Mrs W. and my Daughter (whom you so kindly mention and who returns her kind regards,) went through and through that region under my guidance and that of my old pedestrian Companion[1] in the Alps, in the Autumn of 24—I had explored the whole twice before; and next summer hope to be my sister's guide through same scenes.—How happy should I be could you meet us there! but it so rarely happens that people are at liberty when they wish. Some time or other, in your way to Scotland we shall expect to see you here, and shew you what is lying about us. Mrs W. is anxious to know you, as well she may, after the kindness you have shown to hers—My Sister would be hardly less so—but she is now in Leicestershire with her Nephew— Our employments are odd enough here; my Daughter is at this moment at, in my sight, finishing the picture of a Dragon—and I have just concluded a kind of romance[2] with as much magic in it as would serve for half a Dozen—but I prefer poems to Dragons for my aerial journey. I hope you will be pleased with this poem of 360 verses when you see it—it rose from my brain, without let or hindrance, like a vapour—farewell with a thousand thanks

I remain faithfully yours

Wm Wordsworth

(turn over)

My Daughter, who was about to forward her Monster to her Cousin by Post, at my request, sends it unsealed through you— Pray honour it with a look, before forwarding it at your *perfect convenience*. She had sent her a *pen-wiper* of her construction. We quarreled with the name as inelegant which gave birth to a Pun and a Performance—Excuse this trifling with your precious time. I hope you have seen Mr Coleridge—

[1] Robert Jones.
[2] *The Egyptian Maid; or, The Romance of the Water Lily* (*PW* iii. 232), W. W.'s sole excursion into Arthurian romance.

374. W. W. to MESSRS. LONGMAN AND CO.

Address: Messrs Longman and Co, 39, Paternoster Row.
Postmark: 28 Nov. 1828. *Stamp*: Chas St. Westm^r.
MS. Harvard University Library.
LY i. 319.

[*In M. W.'s hand*]

Rydal Mount Novr 25th [1828]

Gen^tn,

The draft on account of the Book of the Lakes[1] did not reach me till within a very few days before I received your letter of enquiry —I, having left London previous to your sending it to Bryanston St—where it had lain during the long absence of my friend.[2] The bill is now afloat, and will no doubt soon find its way to you.

I was surprized to hear from a Gentleman yesterday, by letter, that he had sent to P. N.[3] Row for a copy of the *Companion to the Lakes* but was told it could not be had.—I presume it being asked for by that title has been the cause of the disappointment—not that the book is out of Print? Pray send a copy with the author's respects to G Huntly Gordon Esqre Cannon Row Chambers, Cannon Row.

> I am, dear Sirs
> very sincerely y^rs
> [*signed*] Wm Wordsworth

---

[1] *A Description of the Scenery of the Lakes in the North of England*, 4th edn., 1823.

[2] i.e. E. Q.

[3] Paternoster.

375. M. W. and W. W. to EDWARD QUILLINAN

Address: Edward Quillinan Esqre, 12 Bryanston St, Portman Square.
Postmark: 28 Nov. 1828. *Stamp*: Chas St Westm.
MS. WL and Miriam Lutcher Stark Library, University of Texas.
LY i. 322 (—). *MW, p. 127* (—).

[*c.* 25 Nov. 1828][1]

Wine	£42 – 0 – 0
Barber's Wig	2 – 4 – 10
Please to pay Mr H. Robinson	11 – 10 – 6
For 2 pairs of Nankeen Pantaloons which W. says you know about perhaps	2 – 0 – 0
	57 – 15 – 4
Deduct for Carriage paid for you to Mr Cookson	3 – 6 – 10
which leaves a balance in your favour of according to my arithmetic.	54 – 8 – 6

My dear Friend,

Having deferred some time to write to you expecting to be able to enclose a bill to discharge the above account, I at last am told by Mr Carter that it is best for you to receive the money in London—he will therefore this day give orders to Masterman's to pay to you on application £55, which will leave a small balance in your hands.

The Wine is safe in the Cellar and I look forward to no pleasant job in the bottling of it.

Many thanks for your prompt reply to Wm's enquires. We are yet in a painful sort of uncertainty what is best to be done for Willy. You shall hear when a decision is made, which ought to be shortly—meanwhile, he does not make much havoc among the Snipes and Woodcocks—but he has caught a bad cold in his search after them—wading up to the knees does not suit him.

Doro too, has a baddish cold, and my sister Joanna is an invalid and come for Mr Carr's aid, from the Isle of Man—I too have a face-ache, so that, were it not for Wm (who has within the last 8 days composed a Poem (for next Keepsake[2]) of above 300 lines

---

[1] This letter was written before W. W. received H. C. R.'s letter of 17 Nov. (Morley, i. 191) announcing his return from his tour to the Pyrenees.

[2] Not the volume for 1829 which appeared this month, but the next one. But because of W. W.'s disagreement with Reynolds (see L. 388 below), he made no further contributions to *The Keepsake*, and *The Egyptian Maid* finally appeared in the *Yarrow Revisited* volume of 1835.

without let or hinderance from one uneasy feeling either of head or stomach), we are but a sorry household just at present.

Therefore, to speak of distant friends—Sarah has arrived in safety at Brinsop, after a pleasant journey, unfatigued—found all well there. Miss W. I hope is also safely landed at Whitwick—but she lingered some days, beyond her intention, with Miss Jewsbury at Manchester[1]—so that we have not heard from her since she reached her journey's end: but I look with no little anxiety for a letter next Wednesday.

How delighted they will be to see you at Whitwick. W^m says it will be a Godsend to them and, scanty as the Curate's accommodations are, will do their best to lodge both you and the Darling Mima, should she be with you. The book perhaps you will take down with you—and if it were not out of your way, on your return home from the City (*at some leisure time*) to call at Cornish the Bookseller's shop, Princess St. New Turnstile, Lincolns Inn fields —He may have 2 or 3 more that it might not be inconvenient to you to take charge of also. He covenanted to procure several at a low rate, and if he has done so, will you be kind enough to pay him for such as you take—i.e., if they are books named in the list he must first shew you. *And*, at the same time say to him, that he need not give himself further trouble—For—we have since heard of a cheaper Old-book Man, than even Mr Cornish, when we know his name[2] you shall be made as wise as we. You know *my way* of making my friends useful when I can do so, without putting them to any *rational* inconvenience—and you know also that I do not care if you tell me you won't do my errand, and that I am impertinent to ask such a service—therefore I make no apologies.

Is H. Robinson returned? When you see him—say to him that Dora often hopes he will pay us a visit during the winter—when she means to profit by some lesson[s] in the German language from him. She has threatened to be a German student, but Colds and Poetry—for she is now her Father's amanuensis—if they go on at their present pace, will leave no time for aught else. We have not seen the Keep-sake yet—nor heard much about it.

[*W. W. writes*]

My dear Friend, Mrs W—has not only written the above, but

---

[1] D. W. spent a week at Manchester. Her MS. Journal records a busy round of engagements, including visits to a cotton factory and an infant school. '. . . She won all hearts before and around her,' Miss Jewsbury wrote to Dora W.: 'She is the very genius of Popularity—an embodied spell' (Gillett, p. xlv).
[2] From this point on the MS. is in the University of Texas.

read it to Dora and me—we both protest against the dark account of the Article, HEALTH in it; particularly as respects herself. She chose the other [day] to face on Horseback a fierce storm of rain from the Grasmere Quarter (you know what kind of assailants they are) and she caught an inevitable cold, but it seems passing away. Her spirits are excellent and were she but a little stronger with digestive powers less liable to disorder, we should have little to complain of on this score. Undoubtedly poor Wm is in wretched spirits as well he may be; losing his time as he is from want of aim or hope for his future course. Had Mr Canning now been living, I would have stated his situation, and given briefly and openly Wm's History to him; and I am simple enough to believe, for Canning had a respect for literature, and was a good natured man, that such a step would not have been without effect. As things are, his Mother and I are very anxious about him.—

The Nankeen Pantaloons were furnished by a Taylor of your recommendation. I promised to pay ready money for them—but I lost sight of him—he talked about 20 shillings, but I said 18/- was the price I should give—but as I have not paid him ready money, I do not mean you to be my representative in keeping him to those terms—therefore, pay what you think proper. The Poem Mrs W— mentions is a sort of Romance—with no more solid foundation than the word—Water lily but dont mention it —it rose out of my mind like an exhalation—no better, probably, you will say for that. Never fail to mention your Children. Give my love to them both, and a Godfather's blessing to my own.[1] I shall write to Rogers about the Athenaeum[2] in a day or two. We long to hear of Henry Robinson—tell him, now that he is a Gentleman at large, that we shall growl if he does not come to look at us and our mountains in Winter, farewell—a thousand good wishes

faithfully yours W. Wordsworth

[1] i.e. Rotha.   [2] i.e. about E. Q.'s candidature.

376. W. W. to C. W. JNR.

Address: Chris: Wordsworth Esqre, Trinity Coll: Cambridge. [*In M. W.'s hand*]
Stamp: Kendal Penny Post.
MS. British Museum.
Mem. (—). *Grosart* (—). *K* (—). *LY i. 320* (—).

Rydal Mount, Nov^br 27th [1828]

My dear Nephew,

Be not alarmed at the sight of this Folio—the other side—to save postage, is for your Father. It gave me much pleasure to learn that your residence in France has answered so well. As I had recommended the step, I felt more especially anxious to be informed of the Result. I have only to regret that you did not tell me whether the interests of a foreign Country and a brilliant metropolis had encroached more upon the time due to your academical studies than was proper. I ought to have asked this question through your Father.—There is little or no religion among the male portion of the French people except a few old men, and certain Priests who, I doubt not, are sincere. You are therefore probably not mistaken in imputing to that want most of the vices and defects of the French character.

As to the revolution which Mr Digby[1] calculates upon, I agree with him that a great change must take place, but not altogether, or even mainly, from the causes which he looks to; if I be right in conjecturing that he expects that the Religionists who have at present such influence over the King's mind will be predominan The extremes to which they wish to carry things are not sufficiently in the spirit of the Age to suit their purpose. The French monarchy must undergo a great change, or it will fall altogether. A Constitution of Government so disproportioned cannot endure. A monarchy without a powerful aristocracy or nobility graduating into a Gentry, and so downwards, cannot long subsist. This is wanting in France, and must continue to be wanting till the

---

[1] Kenelm Henry Digby (1796–1880), medievalist and pioneer of the Catholic revival, who had graduated at Trinity College, Cambridge, in 1819: author of *The Broad Stone of Honour: Or, Rules for the Gentlemen of England* [anon.], 1822 (2nd edn., 1823), enlarged—after Digby became a Roman Catholic in 1825—with new sub-title, *The True Sense and Practice of Chivalry*, 4 vols., 1826 and 1828–9. He spent much time on the Continent, corresponding with his friend William Whewell (see L. 382 below), but W. W. met him occasionally at Cambridge in these years. Digby's most influential works later on were *Mores Catholici: Or, Ages of Faith*, 11 vols., 1831–42, a monument to the glories of the medieval Church, and *Compitum: Or, The Meeting of the Ways at the Catholic Church*, 7 vols., 1848–54. See Alan G. Hill, 'A Medieval Victorian', *TLS*, 5 Sept. 1958.

restrictions imposed on the disposal of property by Will, through the Code Napoleon, are done away with; and it may be observed, by the bye, that there is a bareness, some would call it a simplicity, in that Code which unfits it for a complex state of society like that of France, so that evasions and stretchings of its provisions are already found necessary, to a degree which will ere long convince the French people of the necessity of disencumbering themselves of it. But to return.—My apprehension is, that for the cause assigned, the French monarchy may fall before an aristocracy can be raised to give it necessary support. The great monarchies of Russia, Prussia, and Austria, having not yet been subject to popular Revolutions, are still able to maintain themselves, through the old Feudal *Forms* and qualities, with something, not much, of the feudal *virtues*. This cannot be in France; popular inclinations are much too strong—thanks, I will say so far, to the Revolution. How is a government fit for her condition to be supported but by Religion, and a spirit of honour or refined Conscience? Now religion, in a widely extended Country plentifully peopled, cannot be preserved from abuse of priestly influence, and from Superstition and fanaticism, nor honor be an operating principle upon a large scale, except through *property*—that is, such accumulations of it, graduated, as I have mentioned above, through the community. Thus and thus only can be had exemption from temptation to low habits of mind, leisure for solid Education, and dislike to innovation, from a sense in the several classes how much they have to lose; for circumstances often make men wiser, or at least discreet, when their individual levity or presumption would dispose them to be much otherwise. To what extent that constitution of character which is produced by property makes up for the decay of chivalrous loyalty and strengthens governments, may be seen by comparing the officers of the English army with those of Prussia, etc. How far superior are ours as Gentlemen! so much so that British officers can scarcely associate with those of the Continent, not from pride, but instinctive aversion to their low propensities. But I cannot proceed, and ought, my dear Chris, to crave your indulgence for so long a prose. My mind is full of anxiety about Dear W^m—so is his mother's—so is Dora's, and poor Fellow he is bowed to the dust with fear of the future. He has many excellent qualities and no mean talents—but his private education has been much against him, as he is not naturally bookish.—It is probable that after some time, (heaven knows how long) I might succeed in getting [him][1]

[1] *Word dropped out.*

into a public office; but then I might fail in procuring a promising situation. Where then poor Fellow would he be. We talk of two strings to a bow, killing two birds with one stone etc—but after all twofold views are not apt to answer. Nevertheless I know not what other plan to follow. My wish would be to place him on the Continent for two years where he might learn either the French or German languages, or both, chiefly by conversation, and be advanced in his classics so far as to be ready for one of the Universities at that time if no opening in a public office should occur.—I cannot bear to think of the Church as 'pis aller' but his Brother is so happy and so [? extremely]¹ useful in his situation, that I have pleasure in the thought of the probability of Wᵐ taking a turn that way through his happy example. But my pen is rambling—to come to particulars. The name of the Conductor of the establishment is Wᵐ Lonsdale (of St. John's) M.A. The place St Omere. I think the terms very high for 20 pupils (such is the number he has) upon the Continent.—Nevertheless I should like to hear through you or any of your Friends, a report of his character as to conscientious discharge of his Duty, abilities and attainments. Since I wrote to your Father I have learned the above and had the following References. Geo Arbuthnot Esq,² 25 Upper Wimpole St. Wᵐ Polson Esq,³ 2 New Sq. Lincoln's Inn. John Wise Esq, Maidstone Kent. Adam Cumine Esq,⁴ Aberdeen. Rd W. Duff Esqʳᵉ⁵— Scotland.—I do not wish to restrict your inquires to this Individual. I should be glad of information relating to any other Establishment of the kind. I must conclude in a great hurry. Dora who is dutifully gone out to ride, charges me with a message about signing, sealing and delivering a pardon—in fact she wishes to put you off without a Letter—pleading to me her inability to write one that would interest you. I shall uge [? her] to try—but be patient—no difficult duty considering how much you are engaged. I congratulate you though late on your success in college prizes. I cannot fulfill my engagement to your father as announced at the commencement of this wretched Scrawl. Pray tell him instead, reading to him all of this letter that relates to Wᵐ, that I have written to Mr Wilkinson of Sedbergh and have had his answer as to terms there for your Cousin John.⁶ In the house he recommends they are formidably, I fear insuperably high—not less than 35 £ per ann—What with Books clothes etc [he] would require

¹ *MS. torn.* ² Of Elderslie, Surrey (1772–1859).
³ Conveyancer and barrister. ⁴ Of Rattray, nr. Peterhead, d. 1841.
⁵ See L. 373 above. ⁶ R. W.'s son.

670

50£ per ann. for his education, and I am not sure we have a farthing of his property available for that purpose. But I will make the exactest inquires and give the result in a future Letter. I shall have John with me the Christmas Vacation, and will make the same inquiries at Hawkshead.—

When you see Frere,[1] pray give him my kind regards, and say that he shall hear from me the first frank I can procure. Farewell, with kindest love from all,

Your very affectionate Uncle,
W. W.

Last week I threw off a Romance[2] of 360 verses or regular stanzas. I should like to read it to you, to know if it be good for any thing.

377. D. W. to C. W. JNR.

Address: To Christopher Wordsworth Esqre, Trinity College, Cambridge.
Stamp: Ashby de la Zouche.
MS: WL. Hitherto unpublished.

Thursday 27th Nov^r [1828]
Direct to me Whitwick near Ashby de la Zouche.

My dear Christopher,

It was a week on Tuesday since I reached Whitwick, when you may be sure I was welcome to John in his Loneliness. Not that he complained of any thing but the lengthened evenings, which must needs have been often dull and heavy; for his eyes will not allow of continuous candlelight reading. Many thanks for your letter and to my dear Brother for his kind wish to see me at Cambridge, to you also, and to John for the same, though he had not taken the opportunity of sending them to me. I should like on many accounts to accompany your Cousin J, who proposes presenting himself for Priests' Orders on the 22nd, and who desires me with his love to his uncle to inform him that he shall hope to spend the time needful, and perhaps a few days more under his Roof if not inconvenient.—I say that I should like to accompany him, but it does not seem worth while to take so long a journey at this time of the year without making a longer stay than would be in my power,

---

[1] The Revd. John Frere (1807–51), C. W. jnr.'s future brother-in-law, had been at Trinity College, Cambridge, since 1826. He later held curacies in Essex and Suffolk, and was rector of Cottenham, Cambs., from 1839.
[2] *The Egyptian Maid.*

for I am determined not to leave John to solitude while the short days continue. If it were not for the intervention of Christmas-day Mr Merewether, it is true, might spare him a little longer; but I doubt not that his presence will be required on that day, and therefore it seems better that I should defer my visit to you till a more favorable season.—You know my loco-motive propensities, therefore you will not be apprehensive of my making difficulties about a journey to Cambridge either alone or with a companion; and therefore you will probably agree with me it is better at this time to put it off; and depend upon it I shall not willingly turn my steps northward without seeing you all at Cambridge, which I look forward to with the greatest pleasure. It is one of the comforts of Whitwick that it is within a day's journey of Cambridge.—

Mr Merewether confirms your agreeable account of my Brother's health and spirits. I do indeed rejoice that he summoned the resolution to go abroad and hope he will not flinch from a repetition of the voyage. I long to talk with you of your adventures and observations. The little which you gave your uncle of the latter made me very desirous of more.—

You will be glad to hear that John is very contented at Whitwick, earnest in the discharge of his duty, and not hopeless of doing a little service, in spite of Conventicles, poverty, and all the bad habits attendant upon petty manufactories in a crowded village. He certainly draws together larger congregations than have been seen within the venerable walls of Whitwick Church for many years.—I cannot say that he yet *preaches* with boldness and full effect; but really he reads the prayers, to my ear, very pleasingly, having a fine voice, and a serious manner of delivery with on the whole a distinct utterance.—

Cannot you, or cannot John[1] rather who is not *confined* to his studies, in the spring run over to see us? We have many inducements besides the hearty welcome of our thatched cottage, the Merewethers, Coleorton Hall, etc etc.—But it is time enough to talk of this. I shall certainly remain with John till May. It may be longer for I foresee that I shall not find it an easy task to leave him *finally*, in a place where I feel myself of so much use to him. This being the case you will see that at any favorable and convenient Season there will be no difficulty on my part to prevent my accepting my Brother's kind invitation.

So poor Sophy[2] is married! I shall miss her very much [at]

[1] i.e. C. W.'s son, John, who had taken his final examinations the previous summer.   [2] Sophia Carter, an old family servant.

Trinity Lodge, and so, I am sure, will the [Master][1] and all of you. Mr M. tells me she is still there. Pray give my Respects to her with best wishes for her health and happiness.—

I write from Coleorton Hall. Lady B. sent her carriage for me yesterday, John came to dinner, walked home in the evening, and Lady B will send me back today to dinner. She begs to be most kindly remembered to Dr Wordsworth. I am glad to tell you she is in good health and spirits. She has a large Family around her, Sir George, and Lady B, the young heir,[2] and the two Misses Beaumont.[3]

Dear Christopher, you must plead with John to write to me now and then. I hope he is returned well and happy, and if he will send me the Versailles news[4] while it is fresh in his remembrance I shall be glad and thankful. I wish to hear of Mrs Lloyd, of the Girls, and of Owen, and also to know in what state Mr L. himself is, and whether any hopes are entertained of his recovery. I have had only one short note from Rydal. All was well at home, but in the course of ten days a great change has taken place, affecting nearly our Minister of the Chapel.[5] His mother attended Church twice on the Sunday, went to bed apparently as well as usual and was dead at four o'clock the next morning—Mrs Fleming of Rayrigg.

John has not fixed the day of his departure, but of course it will be in the course of the week preceding the 21st. With my kind Love to my Brother, to John, and to Charles, when you write to him. Believe me, dear Chris,

Your ever affectionate aunt,
D Wordsworth

You do not name Mrs Hoare.—Tell me about her and Miss H.

---

[1] *MS. torn.*

[2] George Howland Beaumont (1828–82), eventually the 9th Bart., was born on 12 Sept.

[3] Sisters of the new Sir George Beaumont.

[4] The Lloyds were now living at Versailles.

[5] For the Revd. Fletcher Fleming, see L. 153 above.

378. W. W. to H. C. R.

Address: H. C. Robinson Esqre, King's Bench Walk, Temple, London. *No 3*.
Postmark: 1 Dec. [   ]. *Endorsed*: 28 Nov. 1828. Wordsworth.
MS. Dr. Williams's Library.
K (—). *Morley, i. 191.*

Rydal Mount
28 Nov^r [1828].

My dear Friend,

Welcome to England—and thanks for your interesting Letter which will be carefully preserved with its predecessors of the same class—in my Sister's possessions. Your account of the Pyreneean Vallies falls in pretty much with my own expectation—I never heard but of one Person, Walter Savage Landor, who preferred the Pyrenees to the Alps.—Have you read Raymond's[1] account of the former—it is well worth looking over, more for the beauty of particular passages, than its general interest, or its merit as far as I am able to judge, as an acquisition to Geology—It is however on this account that the Author seems to pride himself—His translation of Coxe, I think, I recommended to you before—I am now about to consult you on my Son W^{m's} present destination. And to come to the point at once—I want to place [? him] in some establishment on the Continent, or rather some family arrangement with a protestant Clergyman who had two or three pupils, not less than 16 or 17 years of age—though perhaps that might not be of consequence, where he might continue his classical studies, as preparatory to one of our Universities, and at the same time learn German and French or both, with a little desk-diligence but mainly by conversation. It is possible that through my friends of the Lowther family, I may be able in course of time to get him into a Government Office. They have been spoken to on the subject, but should that hope fail—he must face one of our universities as his only resource. I will not tire you with further particulars, as I fancy you know a little of his history—his strong bent to the Army etc etc. He is turned 18—

Pray come and see us. I remember a Man who got a prize in the Lottery for which he was heartily sorry he was so pestered by distressed persons and their patrons with begging petitions. You are now rich in leisure,[2] and will be exposed to as many demands upon your time, as this Unfortunate was, upon his money. We of this Household are likely to be among the number of these appli-

---

[1] See L. 120 above and *EY*, p. 235.
[2] H. C. R. had quitted the Bar at the end of the summer circuit.

cants, and our first demand, a pretty lusty one is, that you would
put yourself upon the top of a Coach advanced as the season is,
and brighten our fire side. We are not dull however I assure you
and pretty busy in our little way, of which one proof is that last
week I threw off 360 verses at a heat.—I should like to tell you
something about our Rhine-trip though you do not ask—so I will
put it off—the more so because you will hear of it from Mr Ardres[1]
—to whom by the bye we are in debt for a thousand kindnesses
and for one small sum of money—he paid for our Passport and on
settling accounts I forgot to reimburse him. This I have mentioned
to Coleridge but it may slip his memory. Therefore if you do not
learn that C. has discharged the debt pray do it for me—with my
kindest regards, and tell us in your next how Mrs Ardres is.
Mr Quillinan has the power to[2] receive the amount of our debt
to you—therefore get of him[3] the deficit at your leisure—We had
not heard of my Sisters payment through Miss Barker—I am just
told this is wrong[ly] stated—no matter—you understand me. We
had yesterday a delightful Letter from my Sister who is with her
Nephew, at Whitwick, between Loughborough and Ashby de la
Zouche. She speaks with high delight of her journey from Buxton
down Darley-dale (i.e. through Matlock) to Derby and [Nottin]g-
ham.[4] I am sorry I cannot secure a frank; kindest remembrances
from all here, and to the Lambs when you see them. Have your
friends the Maskelynes[5] (do I spell right) returnd from their
continental Tour. Mrs Ardres told us that Mr M. had been very
unwell—I hope he is recovered. farewell.

Most faithfully yours
Wm Wordsworth

[1] i.e. Aders.
[2] has the power to *written above the line*: has received the amount *crossed out*.
[3] *Written* his.   [4] *MS. torn.*
[5] The Masqueriers? James Masquerier (1778–1855) was a portrait painter
with a considerable reputation in his day. He and H. C. R. were intimate for
many years, and Robinson frequently stayed with him at Brighton, whither he
retired in 1823. The friends also made a tour together in Germany in 1851.
Masquerier's name constantly recurs among H. C. R.'s papers, the readers of
which have no difficulty in understanding his popularity in contemporary,
literary, artistic, and social circles. (Morley's note.)

379. D. W. to H. C. R.

Address: To H.C. Robinson Esqre, 3. Kings Bench Walk, Temple, London.
Postmark: 2 Dec. 1828. *Endorsed*: 30 Novr 1828. Miss Wordsworth.
MS. Dr. Williams's Library.
K (—). *Morley, i. 193.*

Whitwick near Ashby de la Zouche
Novr 30th 1828

My dear Friend,

I will not say that I like a letter the worse for being franked;
but I should have been very angry with you (could I have known
of my loss) had you kept yours back, as you threatened to do in
case of not meeting with a Franker—so, once for all let me assure
you that the sight of your hand-writing is always welcome to me
at whatever cost; and at the same time I beg that whenever you
have the inclination to take the pen—whether you have anything
new to tell me or not, you will favour me with a letter—of Chit-
chat or whatever may come into your head. You are now a man
of leisure, therefore I make no scruple in asking this of you. You
can hardly form a notion of the pleasure it will be to me during
the coming lonely winter to receive tidings of distant Friends,—
lonely I mean in comparison with past years; for my nephew
John is my constant companion; and we are very comfortable and
happy together. To be sure I have only had a fortnight's trial;
but I think I have already seen enough of Whitwick fireside to be
justified in my belief that time will not hang heavy on our hands—
yet never was there a place, though it is a crowded village, more
barren of society, except at the distance of three miles, where our
Rector and his Family and Lady Beaumont are always glad to see
us—and a visit to them makes a pleasant termination of a walk not
longer than we take daily. You will, I am sure, be glad to hear
that John enters with zeal into the Duties of his profession—and
gives much satisfaction both to the Parish and his Rector. He has a
fine voice—reads agreeably (according to my notion at least)
and is much liked in the pulpit by his hearers, they having been
accustomed to a spiritless humdrum Curate. I, however do not
find John so much at home at preaching as in reading: but time
will give him more confidence—and he is so desirous of doing his
duty that I cannot doubt—if God grant him health and strength—
of his becoming an effective preacher.—I know not into what
quarter your English Travels may lead you this Winter or in the
Spring—but we are only a few miles out of the great North road
—13 miles from Leicester—8 from Loughborough—5 from Ashby

676

de la Zouche. By the bye in future direct to me at Whitwick near Ashby de la Zouche.—It is our regular post town and we only get letters from Leicester by chance—This evening's post has brought pleasant tidings from Rydal—All well, and my Brother busy with poetical labours—and (what nearly concerns John and me)—Mr Quillinan has thoughts of paying a visit in Derbyshire with his eldest Daughter, and if so will come to see us. This is what he tells my Sister, and I heartily wish he may put this scheme in execution.—Pray, if you see him, tell him so—indeed I must not trust to chance—If you do not see him, be so good as to write him a line by the Twopenny post to the above effect—and desire him if he comes to write a line if possible, to say when we may expect him and to direct near Ashby etc.

With respect to the £10, I find my Brother has provided for payment of his debt to you, therefore be so good as to keep that Sum a little while longer. John is ordering Books to about that amount and when he has received them I shall trouble you to pay it to the Bookseller.—Am I unreasonable in wishing to have your sketch of the Pyrannean Tour filled up with your actual adventures?—I fear I am—for I have no claim for such a favour, having not once written to thank you for the last addition to my little collection of your Tours. I will not trouble you with explanations—excuse I have none—But, believe me, I was not less interested by the last than heretofore, and that [I] do greatly prize—and always shall prize these proofs of your kindness—

Alas! for Rome—I never expect to set foot upon that sacred ground—nor do I ever visit it even in a day-dream—but once again, I do hope to see Switzerland, if we all live a few years longer—and perhaps the country of the Tyrolese—indeed, when my Brother talks of Rome—it always rather damps my hopes of even crossing the Channel again, so many circumstances must concur to make so large a scheme practicable—and years slip away—On the 25th of next Month (Xmas Day) I, the youngest of the three Elders of the house shall have completed my 56th year.— I intend to stay at Whitwick six months without stirring from the spot—i e till May—My plans, after that time, are not fixed; but certainly before I turn northward I shall visit my Brother C. at Cambridge—and perhaps a Friend at Worcester—and, if so, shall work on to Brinsop, where Miss Hutchinson now is, so that it is probable I shall not return to Rydal till July—but, as I said, nothing is fixed but six months at Whitwick—and feeling that I am so much of a comfort to John here—and being also myself

[ver]y[1] comfortable, I shall not find it easy to resist coming [to] him again next winter. This brings me to the wish that he had a good Living and a good Wife, both which Blessings I hope he will deserve.—I wish you had seen Charles and Mary Lamb when you wrote—Pray give my kindest remembrances to them—I ask them not for a letter; but trust that you will write ere long and tell me all about them—also the Clarksons. It is very long since I had any tidings of them—When you see Tom remember John and me to him and tell him if his Law concerns ever bring him this way we should be glad to see him.—When you write for me to Mr Quillinan pray add John's best regards and assurances that he will be most happy to see him in his little Parsonage.—Do excuse this long and dull, and ill-penned letter—and believe me, my dear Friend, Your much obliged

and affectionate D Wordsworth

380. W. W. to BENJAMIN DOCKRAY

Address: Benjn Dockray Esqre, Lancaster. [*In M. W.'s hand*]
Stamp: Kendal Penny Post.
MS. Harvard University Library.
LY i. 324.

Rydal Mount,
Decr 2^d / 28.

Dear Sir,

The Papers[2] to which you kindly direct my attention are written in that spirit which the question eminently requires; But as I have not seen the Article in the Q.R. which called them forth I am less able to judge how far they meet the arguments there advanced. I shall therefore not comment upon any particular passages in your Letter, though some things which you have said upon the Church of England, and the relation in which its members stand to it, do not seem to me to be borne out by the fact.—My own conclusions upon the general question differ from yours, because, without considering whether in religious matters, or matters so intimately connected with religion as this, the Romanists are bindable by oath or not; I

---

[1] *MS. torn.*

[2] Contributions by Benjamin Dockray (see L. 253 above) to the *Lancaster Gazette*, 22 and 29 Nov., under the signature B. D. The paper had printed an extract from an article by Southey, 'The Roman Catholic Question—Ireland', *Quarterly Review*, xxxviii (1828), 535–98 (repr. in *Essays Moral and Political*, ii. 331 ff.), reflecting on the Roman Catholics, and Dockray hastened to their defence with a plea for mutual tolerance and understanding. His comments were later expanded and published as *Remarks on Catholic Emancipation, and on the Former Ascendency and Present State of the Roman Catholic Religion*, 1829.

apprehend that they are not prepared to give securities at all; or to submit to such regulations as would leave an attached member of the Church of England at ease. The subject has great difficulties on every side. The strongest argument in my mind against concession is the danger not to say the absurdity of allowing Catholics to legislate for the property of a protestant Church. This property is most inadequately represented in Parliament, scarcely at all—the Clergy being excluded from the Lower House, and the Bps dependant in the degree they are, upon the Minister[s.] Now we all know that the Romanists consider this property as having formerly belonged to them; and many to my certain knowledge (however extravagant the expectation may seem as to the Church of England) look to the Recovery of it.

The legal maxim nullum tempus occurrit Regi has in the minds of the zealots of this body its parallel in respect to their Church.— Catholics have sate in Parliament we know well without directing a battery against the Property of the Protestant Church; they have I believe even been its Defenders, but that was at a time when Episcopacy and the rights and property of the Church were assailed by Fanatics, endeavouring to subvert every thing. No inference can be drawn from the Conduct of Papists when that hostility was going forward; in favor of their abstinence from attack in the present day. I point your attention to this part of the subject, from the interest I take in it not merely as a conscientious member of our church, but from a firm belief that in a secular view only it is eminently beneficial that so much property should be held by that kind of tenure—circulating from individual to individual and from family to family, without being locked up and confined to particular persons and families. This part of the argument deserves to be enlarged upon and is capable of being most forcibly put—but I have not time to do it.

I own I do not see much force in what is said of the oppressiveness and injustice of exclusion from Parliament—when we consider what large bodies of men are excluded—the whole of the Clergy from the lower House, and every man who has not £300 per ann. real estate, besides other large classes. Then again as to the Stigma, unless you are prepared to open the Throne itself to Catholics, and overturn the provision of the Revolution of 1688, that still must cleave to their name and faith.

But I must conclude, believe me, dear Sir, in haste,
very respectfully yours
Wm Wordsworth

381. W. W. to ALLAN CUNNINGHAM

Address: Allan Cunningham Esqre, No 27 Lower Belgrave Place, Pimlico. [*In Dora W.'s hand*]
MS. Mr. W. Hugh Peal.
K (—). LY i. 344 (—).

Rydal Mount
Monday [early Dec. 1828][1]

My dear Friend,

I have this moment received your urgent Letter: it brings me to the point. My engagement with the Keepsake was 100 Guineas for verses, not less than 12 pages, nor more than 15, and that I was to contribute to no other work at a lower rate, but if any editor would give me as much I was at liberty to take it.—

Now I think this engagement would be broken, and it must seem so to you, should I accept your offer—for 50£ for seven pages, could you or any one else afford to give it, would I think be an evasion, as they pay for my name fully as much as for my verses; and this would sink in value, according to the frequent use made of it.

Mr Watts has also a prior claim to you, and I could not accept one from you without giving him the refusal of the same terms. Though Mr Watts has done a good deal to cancel any claim upon him, by entertaining a notion, that I was not content with recommending the Keepsake, but that I depreciated other works of the same character. How he could suppose me capable of such indelicacy I cannot comprehend; I never wrote or said a word in depreciation of any particular Annual in my life, and all that I have done for the Keepsake was to say among my acquaintances that I was a Contributor, and that if high prices given to writers could secure good matter it would be found in the Keepsake, but I added frequently that it was far from certain that would be the case.

You see then exactly how the matter stands. I would most gladly meet your wishes as a Friend—be assured of this—but I must not break my word: and it is right that Poets should get what they can, as these Annuals cannot but greatly check the sale of their works, from the large sums the public pay for them, which allows little for other Poetry.

[*unsigned*]

I fear Oliver and Boyd will not be liberal in their terms—[2]

---

[1] Dated by reference to letter of Allan Cunningham to Professor Wilson of 12 Dec. 1828, quoted in David Hogg, *Life of Allan Cunningham*, 1875, p. 296.
[2] For the proposed Selection from W. W. poems. See L. 369 above.

[In Dora W.'s hand]

Pray do not speak publicly of the sum I receive from the Keepsake as others more deserving receive less—and I *promised secresy* except on[1] an occasion like this.

382. W. W. to WILLIAM WHEWELL[2]

MS. Trinity College, Cambridge. Hitherto unpublished.

Rydal Mount Ambleside,
4th Decbr 1828

My dear Sir,

Accompanying this are the Comments on Sir Uvedale Price's Book on Metre,[3] which you were so kind as to write at my request —They are returned along with a Letter of Sir U. addressed to myself, with a modest request that if I thought his observations worthy of your attention I would forward them to you. This I have much pleasure in doing (through a private hand). Pray (it is the request of Sir Uvedale) return your own remarks to him under Cover to Robert Price Esqr[4] M.P. Foxley, Hereford—and if you could find a few minutes leisure for a word or two on Sir Uvedale's reply it would gratify him I am sure, not a little. I cannot but think you will be pleased by the Paper now sent, as an indication of extraordinary activity of mind, and clearness also, in a Person now in his 81st or 82nd year. The Letter though addressed to me and in *law* mine, is in *equity* yours, and therefore I know not with what face I can put in a claim for its being returned—nevertheless, as Sir Uvedale is an old friend of the late Sir George Beaumont, and

---

[1] beyond *crossed out.*

[2] The Revd. William Whewell, D.D. (1794–1866), scientist and philosopher: C. W.'s successor as Master of Trinity. After a brilliant academic career at Heversham Grammar School and Cambridge, he was elected Fellow of Trinity (1817), tutor (1823), and Professor of Mineralogy (1828). He first met W. W. at Cambridge and again in Aug. 1821, during a visit to the Lakes, and they met occasionally thereafter at Cambridge.

[3] See L. 318 above. Whewell replied to W. W. on 26 Dec.: 'Your strong impression of the *dryness* of the subject somewhat reminds me of a tenet of Sedgwick's who maintains sometimes that a person may be too good a mineralogist for it to be possible for him to be a good geologist. In the same way I suppose a person may be too good a writer of verses to be a good critic of versification, or rather I should say a good anatomist of verse.' (*WL MSS.*)

[4] Robert Price (1786–1857) succeeded his father as 2nd and last baronet in Sept. 1829: he was M.P. for Herefordshire, 1818–41, and for the city of Hereford, 1845–56.

an acquaintance not to say Friend of my own, of many years standing, I will, on that ground, beg of you to send the Letter back at
your Convenience. My Son will be in Cambridge (for ordination)
about the 20th Inst[nt]—it might be given to his care, or if (this
being Term time) you should not have leisure to attend to it,
pray keep it till a time of perfect convenience, as I do wish Sir U.
should hear from you again on the subject, dry as it is—

We shall all be looking for great things from your last Summer's
doings in Cornwall.[1] Professor Airey,[2] Professor Sedgwick[3] and
Professor Whewell (for that honor I believe is yours) cannot have
been so long underground together for a slight purpose.—For my
part, as a little bit of a Poet, and still less of a Philosopher, I am
looking for a new Edition of Kircher's[4] Mundus Subterraneus with
Emendations and large additions to be printed at the University
press. No doubt you will be able to add largely to his enumeration
of subterraneous animals, a Subject eminently important to
naturalists, and not indifferent to Poets, who are much at a loss how
to do these things correctly. e.g. as one of the body I should like to
know whether the figure of the Dragon delineated page 117 Edit.
Amsterodami 1678 is to be depended upon, also, (and here
Mr Malthus[5] and the population men are mightily concerned)
whether any notices occurred tending to confirm the grave affirma-
tives of the next page, that a certain unfortunate who had fallen
into a den of these Monsters from which there was no escape, was
able to live comfortably for six winter months by licking the stony
sides of the Cavern after the Example of its hideous Occupants.—
On the return of Spring it appears that this Stone-licker (not
Stone-eater for that is a vulgar wonder) escaped by one of the said
Dragons having allowed him to lay hold of his tail, a degree of
good nature not to be expected I suppose but on the recurrance of
the genial season.—This hint ought not however to be forgotten

[1] In 1826 and 1828 Whewell and Airy had carried out experiments at the
bottom of Dolcoath copper mine, nr. Camborne, 1,200 feet below the surface,
with the aim of determining the density of the earth.
[2] George Airy (see L. 8 above), lately elected Plumian Professor of
Mathematics at Cambridge.
[3] The Revd. Adam Sedgwick (1785–1873), Fellow of Trinity College,
Cambridge, 1810: Woodwardian Professor of Geology from 1818. He was a
frequent visitor to the Lakes in the early 1820s, and first met W. W. in 1822.
[4] Athanasius Kircher (1602–80), German scholar and Jesuit: author of
Mundus Subterraneus (Amsterdam, 1665), a treatise on fabulous geography.
W. W. had several of his other works in his library (see *R.M. Cat.*, nos. 262
and 263).
[5] Thomas Robert Malthus (1766–1834), the political economist, and author
of the famous *Essay on Population*, 1798.

by Adventurers like yourself and friends—you have a resource in the last extremity.—After this Balderdash it is high time to release you. Believe me with kind regards to your B^r Adventurers and no indifference about the serious results of your Labours,

faithfully yours
Wm Wordsworth

383. W. W. to LORD LONSDALE

MS. Lonsdale MSS. Hitherto unpublished.

Rydal Mount
6th Dec^{br} 1828

My Lord,

I should not have let a day pass without returning my grateful thanks to your Lordship for the offer of the Living of Moresby[1] to my Son, if I had not wished to send the enclosed which was not in my possession yesterday. It is from Mr Merewether, and you will excuse me if I request you would take the trouble to read the former part in which Mr M. speaks of my Son. It gives strong ground for hope that he will not prove unworthy of the Patronage with which your Lordship has honoured him.

In ordinary course, A Curate ordained to a particular place is bound to remain there for at least two years. Mr Merewether when a Substitute is procured would I believe not insist upon this—with a prospect of his Curate being benefited. Nevertheless it seems to me on many accounts desirable, that my Son should remain where he is for some months—he has Mr Merewether's example, and the duty is of the best kind for a beginner, being chiefly, almost entirely, among the poor in a populous district. It is therefore expedient, in this stage of the business, to learn, which I hope may be done without troubling your Lordship, whether he could appoint a Curate or Representative at Moresby till the engagement with Mr M. has been fulfilled, or brought nearer to a close. My son entered upon his duties as Deacon last April and will offer himself for Priest's orders at Christmas. Thus far is written upon the supposition that my Son will prefer Moresby to Whitwick. I wrote to him yesterday to give him knowledge of your Lordship's offer—and I shall endeavour to procure such information as is

---

[1] A small village on the cliffs two miles NE. of Whitehaven, on the high road to Workington. Lord Lonsdale was about to open up a new coalfield there. A new church had been built in 1822.

reasonable to have before he can determine; and may I beg to know how soon the Living must necessarily be filled up.

At the close of Mr M's Letter is an observation upon the political opinions of a large Body of Religionists that may be worth your Lordship's notice; it is marked in the margin.

I have the honor to be
very gratefully your Lordship's
much obliged Ser^t
Wm Wordsworth

384. W. W. to HUGH JAMES ROSE

MS. untraced.
Mem. K. LT i. 326.

Rydal Mount,
Dec. 11, 1828.

My dear Sir,

I have read your excellent sermons delivered before the University[1] several times. In nothing were my notions different from yours as there expressed. It happened that I had been reading just before Bishop Bull's sermon,[2] of which you speak so highly; it had struck me just in the same way as an inestimable production. I was highly gratified by your discourses, and cannot but think that they must have been beneficial to the hearers, there abounds in them so pure a fervour. I have as yet bestowed less attention upon your German controversy[3] than so important a subject deserves.

[1] *The Commission and Consequent Duties of the Clergy: In a Series of Discourses Preached Before the University of Cambridge in April 1826*, 1828.

[2] *The Great Difficulty and Danger of the Priestly Office*, published posthumously in 1714 along with his episcopal charge as *A Companion for the Candidates of Holy Orders* (see *Works of George Bull*, ed. Edward Burton, 7 vols., 1827, i. 137–67). George Bull (1634–1710), a staunch high-churchman, became Bishop of St. Davids in 1705. His best-known work is the *Defensio Fidei Nicaenae*, 1685, which earned the commendation of Bossuet.

[3] The controversy arising out of the publication of Rose's *State of the Protestant Religion in Germany* in 1825. The work was translated into German the following year and provoked much comment, notably by K. G. Bretschneider, the liberal Lutheran scholar, in his *Apologie der neuern Theologie des evangelischen Deutschlands* (English version, 1827). Rose went on to publish a Reply to his German critics in 1828; but meanwhile Edward Bouverie Pusey (1800–82), the new Regius Professor of Hebrew at Oxford, brought out his *Historical Enquiry into the Probable Causes of the Rationalist Character lately Predominant in the Theology of Germany* in which he put Rose's strictures in a somewhat different light, based on his own studies in Germany in 1825. W. W. had already written to Rose about his controversial book earlier this year in a letter that has

11 December 1828

Since our conversation upon the subject of Education, I have found no reason to alter the opinions I then expressed. Of those who seem to me to be in error, two parties are especially prominent; they, the most conspicuous head of whom is Mr Brougham, who think that sharpening of intellect and attainment of knowledge are things good in themselves, without reference to the circumstances under which the intellect *is* sharpened, or to the quality of the knowledge acquired. 'Knowledge', says Lord Bacon, 'is power', but surely not less for evil than for good. Lord Bacon spoke like a philosopher; but they who have that maxim in their mouths the oftenest have the least understanding of it.

The other class consists of persons who are aware of the importance of religion and morality above everything; but, from not understanding the constitution of our nature and the composition of society, they are misled and hurried on by zeal in a course which cannot but lead to disappointment. One instance of this fell under my own eyes the other day in the little town of Ambleside, where a party, the leaders of which are young ladies, are determined to set up a school for girls on the Madras system,[1] confidently expecting that these girls will in consequence be less likely to go astray when they grow up to be women. Alas, alas! they may be taught, I own, more quickly to read and write under the Madras system, and to answer more readily, and perhaps with more intelligence, questions put to them than they could have done under dame-teaching. But poetry may, with deference to the philosopher and the religionist, be consulted in these matters; and I will back Shenstone's schoolmistress,[2] by her winter fire and in her summer garden-seat, against all Dr Bell's sour-looking teachers in petticoats that I have ever seen.

What is the use of pushing on the education of girls so fast, and mainly by the stimulus of Emulation, who, to say nothing worse of her, is cousin-german to Envy? What are you to do with these girls? What demand is there for the ability that they may have

not survived; for Rose replied on 8 May: 'It is a source of great gratification to me to find that my little work on the Germans has fallen under your notice. And I deeply lament that I had not an opportunity of benefiting by your strictures on any part of it. I say with the most perfect and entire sincerity and under the remembrance of the inestimable advantages which I have derived from your works, that I know few things which I should value so highly as the opportunity of hearing your opinions and benefiting by your advice on the many great and interesting moral questions which you have touched on in the *Excursion*.' (*WL MSS.*)

[1] W. W.'s comments here on the Madras system show that his original enthusiasm for it had considerably cooled. See *MY* i. 269, 514; ii. 210.

[2] One of W. W.'s favourite poems. See *EY*, p. 255; *MY* i. 419.

prematurely acquired? Will they not be indisposed to bend to any kind of hard labour or drudgery? And yet many of them must submit to it, or do wrong. The mechanism of the Bell system is not required in small places; praying after the *fugleman*[1] is not like praying at a mother's knee. The Bellites overlook the difference; they talk about moral discipline; but wherein does it encourage the imaginative feelings, without which the practical understanding is of little avail, and too apt to become the cunning slave of the bad passions? I dislike *display* in everything; above all in education. . . . The old dame did not affect to make theologians or logicians; but she taught to read; and she practised the memory, often, no doubt, by rote; but still the faculty was improved; something, perhaps, she explained, and trusted the rest to parents, to masters, and to the pastor of the parish. I am sure as good daughters, as good servants, as good mothers and wives, were brought up at that time as now, when the world is so much less humble-minded. A hand full of employment, and a head not above it, with such principles and habits as may be acquired without the Madras machinery, are the best security for the chastity of wives of the lower rank. Farewell. I have exhausted my paper.

> Your affectionate
> W. Wordsworth

385. W. W. to ROBERT SOUTHEY

MS. untraced.
Mem. Grosart. LY i. 343.

[mid-Dec. 1828]

My dear S.,

I am ashamed not to have given your message about the *Icôn* to my brother. I have no excuse, but that at that time both my body and my memory were run off their legs. I am very glad you thought the answer[2] appeared to you triumphant, for it had struck me as, in the main points, knowledge of the subject, and spirit in the writing, and accuracy in the logic, one of the best controversial tracts I ever read.

I am glad you have been so busy; I wish I could say so much of

---

[1] *fugleman*: 'a soldier especially expert and well drilled, formerly placed in front of a regiment as a model to the others in their exercises.' (*O.E.D.*)
[2] C. W.'s *King Charles the First the author of Icon Basilike.*

myself. I have written this last month, however, about 600 verses, with tolerable success.

Many thanks for the Review: your article[1] is excellent. I only wish that you had said more of the deserts of government in respect to Ireland; since I do sincerely believe that no government in Europe has shown better dispositions to its subjects than the English have done to the Irish, and that no country has improved so much during the same period. You have adverted to this part of the subject, but not spoken so forcibly as I could have wished. There is another point that might be insisted upon more expressly than you have done—the danger, not to say the absurdity, of Roman Catholic legislation for the property of a *Protestant* church so inadequately *represented in Parliament* as ours is. The Convocation is gone;[2] clergymen are excluded from the House of Commons; and the Bishops are at the beck of Ministers. I boldly ask what real property of the country is so inadequately represented: it is a mere mockery.

Most affectionately yours,
W. W.

386. W. W. to GEORGE HUNTLY GORDON

MS. Cornell.
K (—). LY i. 335 (—). Broughton, p. 9.

Rydal Mount
15th Dec 1828

My dear Sir,

A thousand thanks—pray give yourself no more trouble about Mr Lonsdale's Establishment[3]—nothing can be more promising than the thing you name; and happy shall I be to entrust the Engagement to you; provided you can obtain sufficient conviction that the Gentleman[4] will have leisure and inclination to keep my Son pretty close to his classical studies, with such reasonable assistance on his part as the Pupil may require.

---

[1] On 'The Roman Catholic Question—Ireland', in the *Quarterly*: see L. 380 above.

[2] Both Houses of Convocation were suppressed for all practical purposes in the early eighteenth century after growing tension between the high-church clergy and the Whiggish bench of Bishops came to a head in the Bangorian Controversy of 1717; and thereafter their meetings were purely formal. The Convocation of Canterbury claimed the right to discuss business again in 1852 after the Gorham Judgement. York followed the example of Canterbury in 1861. [3] See L. 373 above.

[4] G. E. Papendick (d. 1835), of Bremen. See also next letter.

My Friends of the Lowther Family have the best disposition towards me, as manifested only the other day, by Lord Lonsdale having presented my Son to a benefice,[1] under his Patronage; but still there are so many claimants upon Government that even their influence may not avail to introduce my Son to an eligible situation —one cannot but fear this, bearing in mind that Lord Lowther has been two years looking about for a young Person whom he was engaged to serve.—So that after all, my Son may be forced into an English University—if you are at ease on this point I earnestly beg that no time may be lost in securing the vacancy—I should much prefer the *sole* tuition of Mr Papendick—if he will undertake it. You will excuse my recapitulating the above—some part of it might have slipped your memory. I have made enquiries through other quarters—which shall instantly be put a stop to.

I knew some thing of the toothache thirty years ago—and see at present too much of the sad effects of it in my Daughter—who has recently suffered much from it—which she can little afford to do—it is at present gone.—By the bye—a Friend and Neighbour of mine, now a goodly Bachelor, of 54, suffered from toothache long ago— but he has now the soundest teeth of any man of his age I ever saw, which he ascribes to having used Sabilla snuff as a Powder. His Sister he tells me has had from it the same benefit. My Daughter tried it about a week. I wished she could have persevered—but it made her reeling tipsy—that would have gone off—my Neighbor is confident of its powers—as a preservative—but then I must add, that he makes brushing an exercise and amusement—he says, reading at the same time—but would you believe it, he employs two hours every day in this duty—but pray try it—a few minutes I imagine would do as well—

I know not what to say about Mr Coleridge, he has not yet noticed my Letter[2]—nor one from my daughter accompanying it. I therefore infer that he is either not well, or much engaged—or in bad spirits or it may be nothing but procrastination—My Daughter thinks this last Power is with him strong enough to account for a great deal, judging I suppose from what it does with her Father— At all events I think we had best wait awhile—The delicacy due to you will require it for the present—Perhaps I may hear from him —at all events I will keep your wishes in mind.—

You do not notice my suggestion about Wales—no wonder, having so much to think about.

[1] Moresby.
[2] Presumably a letter of introduction (which has not survived). Huntly Gordon had written on 13 Dec. that he had not yet seen S. T. C. (*WL MSS.*)

15 December 1828

How strange that any one should be puzzled with the name, Triad, *after* reading the Poem. I have turned to Dr Johnson, and there find, "*Triad, three united;*" and not one word more, as nothing more was needed. I should have been rather mortified, if *you* had not liked this Piece, as I think it contains some of the happiest verses I ever wrote. It had been promised several years to two of the Party[1]—before a fancy fit for the performance struck me—it was then thrown off rapidly—and afterwards revised with care.—

The remainder of this Page shall receive a few stanzas[2] to which you must be indulgent as they were *strictly* extempore—and no older than yesterday evening. I scarcely seem to have a right to send them to you—because as I des[i]gn them for the Keepsake of next year,—they are not strictly my own—therefore be so good as to destroy the Copy as soon as you have read them. I forgot that I am writing with the advantage of a frank; the verses shall be sent on a slip of Paper—read, and throw it into the fire—My little Romance[3] is an odd thing and I can scarcely guess how any one could relish it—I do not consider *that* my own nor any detached Poem which I am now writing—During the last week I wrote some stanzas on the Power of Sound[4] which ought to find a place in my larger work—if aught should ever come of that.—

In the Book of the Lakes, which I have not at hand—is a passage rather too vaguely expressed where I content myself with saying— that after a certain point of elevation—the effect of Mountains depends much more upon their form than their absolute Height— This point which ought to have been defined, is the one to which fleecy clouds (not thin and watery vapours) are accustomed to descend.—I am glad you are so much interested with this little tract—it could not have been written without long experience. We have seen Butterfly pen wipers which are as useful as they are pretty—but the Pun is wanting.

I will conclude with a short recurrence to W^m—he is ready to start at any time—and I hope could be admitted before April—for he has nothing now to lose—being very backward—indeed I grudge every moment—his time here, from suspense and other causes is turned to little account—If I were sure, he could be

---

[1] The three daughters of the poets, Edith Southey, Dora Wordsworth, and Sara Coleridge, form the subject of the poem.

[2] Probably *A Jewish Family* (*PW* ii. 321, 525), written apparently the previous July during a visit to St. Goar, but not published till 1835.

[3] *The Egyptian Maid.*

[4] The first draft of the poem. See *PW* ii. 323, 526. It was considerably expanded *c.* Nov. 1829, and published 1835. See W. W. to Samuel Rogers, 30 July 1830 (in next volume).

received, you being satisfied on the points mentioned—he should be sent in a few days to his Brother—in Leicestershire as so far on his way toward London—or would it be better that he should embark at Hull—on this I should be happy as in every thing else to go by your advice—

Mrs Wordsworth begs me to thank you for your kind notice of her—You will bear in mind that whether on your way to Scotland or not we shall be equally glad to see you here—

Farewell I shal[l] trouble you with a two penny Postage or perhaps more—I remain

most faithfully your
much obliged
Wm Wordsworth

387. W. W. to H. C. R.

Address: H. C. Robinson Esqre, King's Bench Walk, Temple
Endorsed: Decr 18–1828.
MS. Henry E. Huntington Library.
Morley, i. 196 (—). LY i. 336.

[15 Dec. 1828]

My dear Friend,

I wrote to you some time ago about my Son Wm, if you have received the Letter I doubt not you are prosecuting enquiries. I now write to say that I have heard, through Mr Gordon—private Secretary to Mr Planta,[1] of a very promising situation under Mr Papendich of Bremen—Perhaps you may know the Gentleman, Mr Planta and others speak highly of him—if you do, pray tell me about him—at all events I am so satisfied with this prospect—that I cannot feel justified in leaving you to continue your inquiries.

I have this morning written to Mr Gordon to tell him so. I forgot to notice Gagliani[2] in my last—he has sent me a Royal Vellum Copy—a poor Compensation for his Piracy—one thing however is laudable, the book is printed with admirable accuracy, I have not noticed a single error that I am not myself answerable for—I agree with you that the honour is worse than nothing, and I cannot but think the Paris Edition will much hurt a Sale sufficiently

---

[1] Joseph Planta (1787–1847), diplomatist, son of the Librarian of the British Museum. He served as private secretary in turn to Canning and Lord Castlereagh. In 1813 he had toured the English Lakes, and perhaps became acquainted with W. W. at that time. (De Selincourt's note.)

[2] i.e. Galignani.

languid. But how can we expect that foreign Nations will respect our literary property when our laws of copy right are so shamefully unjust.—Hereafter—a remedy must be applied to this grievance— the law as it now stands, as to the point of duration of copy right is a premium upon bookmaking and mediocrity. My own Poems have been thirty years struggling up hill, and are yet crossed in their way by [? Blockheads] see an instance in the last Quarterly, the article Sotheby's Georgics[1]—Were I to die tomorrow, my Mss—whatever might be their advantage to Booksellers, would in 28 years time be of no value to my Children or their descendants. You are a Lawyer, a Man of Letters, and now have leisure, pray reflect upon this subject; and do more, write upon it through the Quarterly or any other leading Publication.

Let us see you.

Lord Lonsdale has just pres[ented][2] my eldest Son to a small Li[ving] adieu—most affectionately yours

Wm Wordsworth

I hope you liked the Triad,[3] as to the other things—some of them particularly the Wishing-gate have given pleasure—but the Triad is my *own* favorite.

388. W. W. to FREDERIC MANSEL REYNOLDS

Address: F. Mansel Reynolds Esqre, 48 Warren S^t, Fitzroy Sq^re, London. [*In Dora W.'s hand*]
Postmark: 23 Dec. 1828.
MS. Harvard University Library.
K (—). *LY i. 337.*

Rydal Mount
Decr 19th 1828.

My dear Sir,

The best way of thanking you for your obliging Letter is by replying to it immediately, which I shall do *snappishly*—not in temper, but for the sake of conciseness in style.—You would have heard from me sooner, but I was looking for the Keepsake—which I thought would probably find its way to me through one of Mr Southey's Longman or Murray parcels which he is so frequently

---

[1] 'Hexaglot Georgics', *Quarterly Review*, xxxviii (1828), 358–77. The author was Thomas Mitchell (1783–1845), the Classical scholar.
[2] *MS. torn.*
[3] In his reply of 31 Dec. (Morley, i. 197), H. C. R. wrote that he was 'delighted' with the *Triad*. 'There are an elevation and a purity in the groupe quite etherial—'

receiving. You probably were not aware of this; or your very commendable wish to spare my Purse might have been gratified through this channel.—The Keepsake must be better stitched or its sale will suffer in the Country. A neighbour of mine had to send his 1829 Copy 20 miles—to have the leaves refastened. The Copy Mr Heath gave me had several leaves started. In London you may not so much mind this—but in many places it would be fatal to the work. I have not seen it—and in winter we live so much to ourselves that I have scarcely heard of *it* or any of its Brethren. You do well to point out to me what would suit you best—but some of the pieces you mention are among the happinesses of a life.—Such articles cannot be bespoken with the probability of the Contract being fulfilled.—You must take what comes and be content. I hope you did not patronize Gagliani's[1] piracy by yourself purchasing the work. My Friend Mr Robinson laudably declined doing so when at Paris—because he would not encourage so unfair a proceeding.—My last Edition is yet a few pounds in my debt—and I am certain that the sale will be much impeded by the Paris Edition at less than half the price of the London one. Everybody goes to Paris nowadays.—I see you are a conscientious Reckoner— I feared my Quota would prove short of my engagement—but not as you say *'very short'* of our stipulated Mark. The strict letter was 12 pages at the least and 15 at the most.[2] Depend upon it one year with another you shall have no right to complain—And this year the account shall be set straight. I am rather rich, having produced 730[3] verses during the last month—after a long fallow—In the list are two stories—and three incidents—so that your wish may be gratified, by some one or more of these Pieces. But I will tell you frankly—I can write nothing better than a great part of *The Triad* —whether it be for your purpose or no.—I cannot yet dismiss the 'Keepsake'—it has got me into a scrape with Alaric Watts—he sent me a message through Mrs Coleridge (I hope not accurately delivered) that I had not only puffed everywhere the Keepsake, but *depreciated* the other works of the kind—his own of course included.

---

[1] i.e. Galignani's.

[2] See L. 322 above. W. W. was at this stage willing to make up the alleged deficiency out of his most recent compositions. It was not until the following month, when he received his copy of *The Keepsake*, that he discovered that four sonnets which he had submitted as part of his agreed quota had not been inserted. See his letter to Reynolds, *c*. 27 Jan. 1829 (in next volume).

[3] Including, presumably, in addition to *The Egyptian Maid, A Jewish Family*, and the first draft of *On the Power of Sound*, the following: *Incident at Bruges* (*PW* iii. 166), *The Wishing-Gate Destroyed* (*PW* ii. 301), and *A Morning Exercise* (*PW* ii. 124).

How he could think me capable of anything so presumptuous, so ungentlemanly, and so *ungenerous*, I cannot conceive. I was offended —and did not reply—though he offered through the same channel to give me as much as you had done.—It is true that I have frequently mentioned the Keepsake among my friends and acquaintance recommending it so far as to say that if high prices could procure good writing it could be found there—but I sometimes added that such a result was by no means sure—But as to any disparaging comparison between it and other works, especially of those Editors with whom I am acquainted—had I even known the Contents of the Keepsake, I *could* not have done such a thing.—And here let me remind you that I consider myself quite at liberty to contribute to any of these works that will pay me as you have done, and have engaged to do so. I care not a straw whether they will or no, but that liberty I reserve, also the right of reprinting the Pieces in any New Edition of my Works that may be called for.—Pray confirm this by Letter—

We have only one Letter from Mr Coleridge, since we left London—I doubt even that as I believe the short note was received while we were in Town. So that we know nothing of his proceedings, his jollifications with you included.

Allan Cunningham has been very urgent with me to write for him—we are on terms of intimacy, but my answer was as above. He offered me 50 Guineas—without mentioning quantity, before he knew the particulars of my Engagement with you—but I told him Alaric Watts had a prior claim.—

I am sorry I have not the command of a Frank for this Letter— put it down to the Keepsake account. Your prospectuses came to me at Lowther Castle—where was a large party of people of rank—so that it was rather fortunate. Mr Alaric Watts, I hope, would not think my circulating these Prospectuses unfair—I should as readily have done as much for him.—Shortly I shall have occasion to write to Messrs Longman and as they have an interest in the Souvenir I shall advert to Mr Alaric Watts proposal and message through Mrs Coleridge—With kind compts [from] Mrs W. and my Daughter—I remain my dear Sir very faithfully yours

Wm Wordsworth

Pray send *without delay* the Keepsakes directed to me to the care of Mrs Carr, Mr Dowling's,[1] 4 Norfolk Street, Strand. I find I can send this free of Postage by detaining it a couple of Days.—

---

[1] Vincent Dowling, the journalist (see L. 103 above), whose daughter Ann had married Thomas Carr, the Ambleside surgeon.

389. W. W. to ALLAN CUNNINGHAM

Address: A Cunningham Esqre, F. Chantrey's Esqre, Pimlico [*In M. W.'s hand*]
Postmark: 26 Dec. 1828.
MS. Mr. W. Hugh Peal.
K (—). *LY i. 341* (—).

Rydal Mount
20th Dec^br [1828]

My dear Friend,

Pray prepare one of my Busts for Mr Barron Field, who will be in Town in Spring—and will receive and pay you for it. He is going out to Ceylon as Advocate Fiscal, and wishes to take it along with him, being one of my most ardent admirers. He is also a particular Friend of Mr Charles Lamb. I hope my Nephew has received his at Oxford.—

As I have an opportunity of sending this to London without putting you to the expense of Postage I may without scruple conclude with best wishes for you and yours at the coming Christmas—

Does the Scotch selection go on?

ever faithfully your Friend
Wm Wordsworth

[*In M. W.'s hand*]

turn over

I have received directions for the Bust, which I mentioned to you some time since to be sent to Edinburgh, 'to be addressed to R. S. Wilson Esq, Royal Bank, Edin. It should be sent by Sea to Leith in the first place, and the sooner the better.'

Mrs W. begs to join her own good wishes to those of her husband, for the health and happiness of Mr A. C. and his family.

390. W. W. to BARRON FIELD

Address: Barron Field Esqre, Liverpool. [*In M. W.'s hand*]
Stamp: Kendal Penny Post.
MS. Harvard University Library.
K (—). *LY i. 340.*

Rydal Mount
20th Dec^br 1828

My dear Sir,

I have just received your Letter, announcing that your destination is Ceylon—it is a weary distance—but you say that the

Climate is good. How long are you to be absent? Mrs Field you say goes along with you—Take with you our best wishes for your joint health and prosperity—and *safe return.*—We may meet again—but I am growing old—and all is dark. God bless you.

Mr Allan Cunningham, the Manager of Mr Chantrey's Busts, used to charge 5 pounds for them to Strangers—but to my Friends only 3 pounds or guineas I forget which.—Call upon him with this Letter and one will be yours at that price—But I must add that it will be well to do this as soon as you go to London—for he has been very slow in getting them executed lately.—One for my Nephew at Oxford was ordered by me long ago—and I fear he has not yet received it—But I will write to him today to prepare one for you—I am truly glad you liked the Triad—I think [a] great part of it is as elegant and spirited as any thing I have written—but I was afraid to trust my judgement—as the aery Figures are all sketched from living originals that are dear to me.

I have had a Worcester paper sent me that gives, what it calls the *real* History of Miserrimus[1]—spoiling, as *real* Histories generally do, the Poem altogether—I doubt whether I ought to tell it you—yet I may for I had heard before, though since I wrote the Sonnet, another History of the same Tombstone. The first was that it was placed over an impious wretch who in popish times, had profaned the Pix. The Newspaper tale is, that it was placed over the grave of a Nonjuring Clergyman at his own request—one who refused to take the oath to King Wm—was ejected in consequence, and lived upon the Charity of the Jacobites.—He died at 88 years of age—so that at any rate he could not have been ill fed—yet the Story says, that the word alluded to his own sufferings on this account, i.e. his ejection only—He must have been made of poor stuff—and an act of duty of which the consequences were borne so ill has little to recommend him to posterity.—I can scarcely think that such a feeling would have produced so emphatic and startling an Epitaph—and in such a place—just at the last of the Steps falling from the Cathedral to the Cloister—The Pix story is not probable, the stone is too recent.—

I should like to write a *short* India Piece,[2] if you would furnish me with a story—Southey mentioned one to me in Forbes's

[1] See *A Gravestone upon the floor in the Cloisters of Worcester Cathedral* (*PW* iii. 48) and I. F. note p. 434.
[2] 'By the bye', Field had written in his letter of 19 Dec., 'all your travellers "step westward". You have no oriental poem. I wish you would write me one, as unlike "Lalla Rookh" as possible.' (*WL MSS.*)

travels in India[1]—have you access to the Book at Liverpool, and leisure to consult it. He has it not—it is of a Hindoo Girl—who applied to a Bramin to recover a faithless Lover, an Englishman.— The Bramin furnished her with an Unguent with which she was to anoint his Chest while sleeping—and the Deserter would be won back—If you can find the passage and as I said before, have leisure, pray be so kind as to transcribe it for me and let me know whether you think any thing can be made of it. Adieu—and believe me affectionately and faithfully yours

Wm Wordsworth.

Kindest regards to Mrs Field
I am not likely to be in London in Spring.—
My Sister is in Leicestershire—at my Son's Curacy.

391. W. W. to LORD LONSDALE

MS. Lonsdale MSS. Hitherto unpublished.

23rd Dec^r [1828]
Rydal Mount.

My Lord,
    This day's Post enables me to thank your Lordship for your last letter, which I deferred to do till I had heard from my Son who writes from Cambridge where he has just been admitted to Priests Orders. Having consulted his Uncle he is at liberty to follow his strong inclination to accept the living of Moresby with grateful thanks to your Lordship in which I most cordially join.

    I have not yet seen Mr Fleming[2]—he has been at Bootle—but your Lordship's message was communicated to him some time ago through his Son.

    I have been introduced to Mr Branker,[3] he has a most good-natured Countenance but his head is a little turned by the quantity of money he has got so easily, and which he is lavishly spending. On the opening of the Westmorland Contest, such a Person might have given us a great deal of trouble in this neighbourhood, had he taken an adverse turn, which is probable enough from his Politics —which are, like these of new-made men, I understand, not a

---

[1] James Forbes (1749–1819), traveller. His *Oriental Memoirs: Selected and Abridged from a Series of Familiar Letters, Written during Seventeen Years Residence in India* . . . appeared in 4 vols., 1813.
[2] John Fleming of Rayrigg. He had been rector of Bootle, nr. Millom, since 1814.   [3] For James Branker, see L. 372 above.

little tinctured with aversion to the Aristocracy. At present, I trust, it is of little consequence what course he may chuse.

Mr Curwen is departed[1]—his life is unpleasing to look back upon, and his end is somewhat painful to think of.

Gagliani[2] of Paris has just added my works to the English Authors whom he has published. These piracies are very injurious, and in addition to the so short duration of English Copy-right, must materially hurt the fortunes of the families of literary men who look beyond the day. I cannot but think that sometime or other this injustice will attract the notice of Parliament.

We have been deluged with Rain; a month almost without inter-mission. We have had no Winter's cold, except two days long since.

I have the honor to be my Lord
most gratefully
your Lordship's
much obliged Friend and Ser[nt]
Wm Wordsworth

392. D. W. to JANE MARSHALL

MS. untraced.
K (—). *LY i. 342.*

[Whitwick]
26 Dec., [1828]

. . . The small living of Moresby, vacated by Mr Huddlestone[3] of Whitehaven, has been offered to John by Lord Lonsdale, and he thankfully accepts it. The manner in which Lord L. has done this favour is not less gratifying than the favour itself.

Our rector, Mr Merewether, is truly sorry to lose John, yet disinterested enough to be glad of his advancement. . . . He will remain here six months longer, and I of course shall remain with him. In fact, if he had continued here another winter, I should have done so also; as, in the first place, I am more useful than I could be anywhere else, and, in the second, am very comfortable. The walk to the rectory and the hall at Coleorton is not too long for a winter's

---

[1] John Christian Curwen had died at Workington Hall on 10 Dec. He had alienated many of his supporters by the way in which he had chopped and changed between the Carlisle and the Cumberland County representation; and more recently, by his attitude to Protection.   [2] i.e. Galignani.

[3] The Revd. Andrew Hudleston, D.D. (1777–1851), educated at Hawks-head School and Trinity College, Cambridge, was perpetual curate of St. Nicholas, Whitehaven, 1811–51. He had just vacated the living of Moresby on his appointment as rector of Bowness-on-Solway.

morning call. Therefore we have no want of society, and our fireside at home has never been dull, or the evenings tediously long. It gives me great satisfaction also to see that John does the duties of his profession with zeal and cheerfulness, and is much liked and respected by the parishioners. His congregations, notwithstanding the numerous dissenting meeting-houses, are much increased.

Perhaps you know that we are on the borders of Charnwood Forest. There is much fine rocky ground, but no trees; the road dry in general, so it may be called a good country for walkers. There is one hill from which we have a most extensive prospect, twenty-one miles distant from us. The air is dry though cold (for we are at a great height above the sea). . . . John was at Cambridge last week, to be ordained priest; my brother Christopher and my nephews are well, and in good spirits. . . . Five weeks have I been here, and not a single rainy day. . . .

[*cetera desunt*]

393. W. W. to WILLIAM JACKSON

MS. Berg Collection, New York Public Library. Hitherto unpublished.

My dear Friend,   Wednesday—[late Dec. 1828]

I have this moment a Letter from Lord Lonsdale, his Lordship says—'If your Son will direct a presentation of Moresby to be sent to me, I will execute and return it to him.'—I presume a Stamp will be necessary on this occasion, the amount of which cannot be known without knowing the exact value of the Living—knowing how busy you are I am loth to trouble you—but I know not whom else to apply to—Would you then either write to John or answer to *me* the following particulars, adding any thing else needful—

What is the Value of the Living?—

What the Curate's[1] Salary?

Is he willing to remain at the same Salary, till John can free himself from Whitwick, and, what time has John for this purpose—

Can all that is needful be effected as to presentation, Induction etc without John coming into the north previously—

In short tell him or me, which ever you prefer, any thing it may be expedient for him to know——

---

[1] The Revd. George Wilkinson (1787–1865), curate of Moresby (1815–29), perpetual curate of Arlecdon (1829–47), and rector of Whicham (1847–65): a noted local antiquary, who excavated the Roman fort at Moresby.

I earnestly wish that your fatiguing Duties at this period may not have been too much for your health and strength—Miss Joanna H. is a good deal better, Dora does not get rid of her Cough. I am obliged to write in a great hurry—

ever most faithfully yours
Wᵐ Wordsworth

394. W. W. to UNKNOWN CORRESPONDENT

MS. Pennsylvania State University Library. Hitherto unpublished.

[1828–1829]

. . . I am happy to say that my Son[1] yields to necessity with some chearfulness, and is now engaged in preparing himself for merchantile life.—I have no connections in that line, but I trust to Providence for an opening—I shall look out in every direction, and should be most thankful for the assistance of any of my Friends.

The Coach Sonnet[2] is too personal for general interest—it seems to have pleased you full as much as I had reason to expect. With kindest wishes for your recovery, which I should be glad . . .

[cetera desunt]

395. W. W. to SARA COLERIDGE

Address: Miss Coleridge.
MS. Victoria University Library, Toronto. Hitherto unpublished.

[before 1829][3]

My dear Sara,

Why are my weak points to be exposed? Penmanship you well know is one of them. Take this as a favorable specimen, thanks to a good pen furnished by your kind Friend Miss Hutchinson.

When are we to see you again in the North?

With a thousand good wishes I remain

affectionately yours
Wᵐ Wordsworth

[1] i.e. W. W. jnr.
[2] Either *A Tradition of Oker Hill*, published in *The Keepsake* for 1829; or *Filial Piety*, published as *The Peat Stack* in *The Casket*, 1829, p. 259, at the request of H. C. R. (see Morley, i. 187–8). See *PW* iii. 49–50, 435. As de Selincourt notes, these sonnets are headed in the MS. 'Stage Coach Inspirations by an Outside Passenger'.
[3] This note was written before, perhaps some years before, Sara Coleridge's marriage in Sept. 1829.

APPENDIX I

Edward Quillinan's Recollections of his First Meeting with Wordsworth

(see L. 37)

From E. Q.'s MS. Diary for 1821:

[Tues. 1st May, Rydal] 'Saw Mr Wordsworth come out of his Cottage with a party of visitors among whom were some lovely young ladies. He accompanied them to a carriage with 4 horses that waited at the bottom of the hill. Was pleased with finding the retirement of the Poet so respectably invaded. It seemed to be the homage paid to Genius by wealth and Beauty. Had a full and close view of him again on his return; but did not present the letter of introduction to him which I had in my pocket from Mr Gillies.— Mr Wordsworth is very like his portrait in Haydon's grand picture of Christ entering Jerusalem; he struck me also as like that profile of Milton prefixed to Fenton's pocket edition of Milton's Poems. . . .

Mr G. of Edinburgh had given me a letter of introduction to Mr Wordsworth the Poet. It was unsealed, for my inspection; and I found it so flattering to me that I was unwilling to present it, though most anxious for the acquaintance of so admirable a Genius. —I rode over twice from Penrith and back again (50 miles, over Kirkstone, that is 25 and back) yet when I approached his dwelling, I lost heart; at last I went over a third time, and having made up my mind to quit the army, and settle in this delightful country, I screwed up my courage to the mark, and walked up the steep hill, and passed his gate, and rang at his door-bell, resolved to introduce myself. It so happened that Mr Marshall of Ullswater had heard me say at his house that I had a letter for Mr W., and he had reported to him this fact. Several weeks elapsing without the delivery of the letter, Mr W., little aware of the cause of its detention, was prepared to be offended at my supposed neglect. I was ushered into the library at Rydal. He received me very stiffly, but asked me for the letter. I told him, and it was true, that I had not brought it with me, but that it was an open letter of introduction, but that it spoke of me in a manner so extravagantly laudatory that I had not the face to present it. He seemed quite angry: whirled a chair about, and made short and stiff remarks. I was getting indignant and thought him most disagreeable.—Suddenly the door opened, and a young lady, rather tall of good features perhaps, not handsome—but of most engaging innocence and ingenuousness of aspect, stood at the door, seemed impressed at seeing a stranger, and half drew back. Then it was that I saw the Poet's countenance to advantage. All the father's heart was thrown into his eyes and voice as he encouraged her to come in. She did so; but only staid a few moments. It was a most timely interruption. I have loved that sweet girl ever since. Here however the patriarchal expression vanished, and the poet resumed his frigidity of tone and his twirl of the chair. I was about to retire much disappointed, when in came Miss Hutchinson, who saw at once that there was some awkwardness between us. She relieved me in a moment, with that fine tact and benign politeness thoroughly understood only by women. She civilly accosted me, rallied the Poet for twirling the chair, took it from him and appropriated it to her own use; made herself mistress of the causes of our restraint, laughed him into good humour, and sent him out to shew me the garden and the terrace. We rambled together for hours; talked of poetry, his taking the lion's share of the conversation, to which he was entitled, and in triumph I returned with him to dinner. That day was the precursor to many and many a happy one under the same roof.—When I returned to Penrith I sent him the letter under cover by post. Soon afterwards I was settled with poor Jemima and her little baby name-sake at Spring Cottage, Loughrigg . . . Never did I pass so happy and satisfactory a summer. De Quincey, the Opium Eater, was my nearest neighbour, and let me his coach house and stables; but I saw very little of him; for he remained in bed, I understood, all day, and only took the air at night, and then was more shy than an owl.

APPENDIX II

Preface and Table of Contents from Allan Cunningham's Proposed Selection of Wordsworth

(see L. 369)

Preface.

This little volume was suggested by several of the admirers of the genius of Mr Wordsworth and though the Poet permitted the undertaking he is neither accountable for the selection nor for the arrangement. It was felt that his poetry had been too long withheld from the lower classes of the community whose feelings and sympathies it appeared so well calculated to awaken. The original power of thought: the deep sympathy with nature: the philosophical grandeur and the supremacy claimed for genius and nature over the artificial dignitaries of the earth which distinguish all his works seemed calculated to secure popular affection had not the progress of his fame been materially retarded by the price of his works and by the captiousness of Criticism. It is the object of this selection to place his poetry within the reach of the more simple and unsophisticated classes of the People—to lay before them a series of verses full of social and philosophical feeling—exhibiting manifold images of domestic love and home-bred enjoyment and counting nothing too humble in which the hand of God is seen and poetic emotions called forth. Some little has been conceded to popular taste in making these Selections—much has been omitted that was lofty and profound and much that spoke to the universal sympathies of human nature: but there is enough given to enable the people at large to taste the spirit of one of their most exquisite Poets.

Appendix II

Contents

1. Lucy Gray ————
2. Louisa ————
3. She dwelt among etc. ———
4. Complaint of an Indian Wᵐ
5. Seven Sisters of Binnorie ——
6. Last of the Flock ————
7. The Cuckoo ————
8. The Thorn ————
9. Her eyes are wild ————
10. Female Vagrant ————
11. The Columbine ————
12. Binnorie ————
13. Rob Roy's Grave ————
14. Yarrow Unvisited ————
15. Yarrow Visited ————
16. Three Cottage Girls ———
17. Poet's Epitaph ————
18. Simon Lee ————
19. Cumberland Beggar ———

20. We are Seven ————
21. Mary Queen of Scots ———
22. Idiot Boy ————
23. Oak and Broom ————
24. The Danish Boy ————
25. Sailor's Mother ————
26. A spirit yet a woman still —
27. Ruth ————
28. Hart Leap Well ————
29. The Highland Girl ———
30. Glen Almain ————
31. Solitary Reaper ————
32. Killiecrankie ————
33. Matron of Jedburgh ———
34. Blind Highland Boy ———
35. Expostulation and Reply —
36. Tables Turned ————
37. To the Sons of Burns ———
38. Three first Pages of the White Doe ————

P.S. Should these Poems fall short of completing such a volume as the Bookseller may think most suitable in size for circulation—a few Passages from the Excursion and a few of the Sonnets would do all that was proper and these are selected in a moment.

704

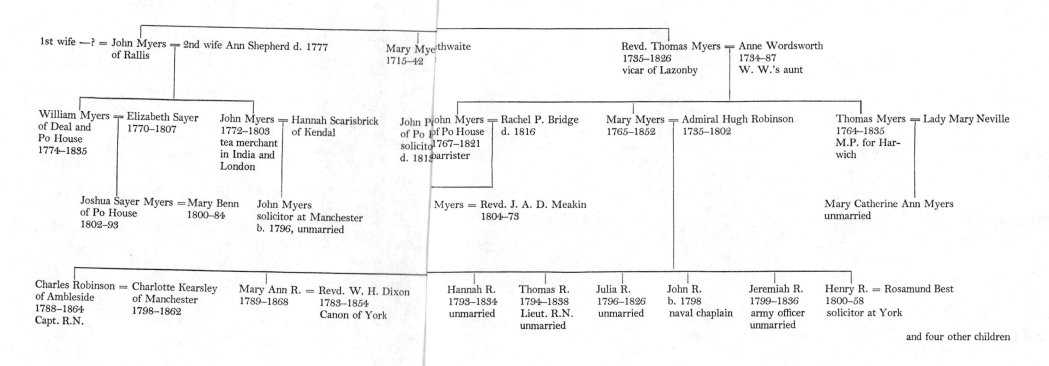

INDEX

Abbot, Charles, 1st Baron Colchester, 553 and n., 554, 560.
Abbotsford, 368–9, 627.
Adamthwaite, Revd. John, 466 and n.
Addington, Haviland John, 399 and n., 408.
— Henry, 1st Viscount Sidmouth, 408 and n.
Addison, Jane (née Hindson), 331 and n.
— Lancelot (Dean of Lichfield), 403 and n.
— Richard (of Staple Inn), 94, 109, 155, 331 and n., 356.
Aders, Charles, Letter to: 622; 613 and n., 614, 675.
— Mrs. Elizabeth, Letter to: 616; 622, 675.
Aeschylus, 335.
Ainslie, Dr. Henry, 588 and n.
Airy, George Biddell, 17 and n., 34 and n., 53, 105, 682.
Albuquerque, Duke of, 518 and n.
Alderson, Edward Hall, 464 and n., 465.
Allan, Robert (of Edinburgh), 571 and n.
— Thomas, F.R.S., 571 and n.
Allan Bank, 168.
Alvarez de Castro, Mariano, 518 and n.
Ambleside, ball at, 83, 85; want of magistracy at, 370; party divisions in, 446–7.
Amsterdam, 634.
Anderson, Dr. Robert, 648.
Anniversary, The, 653 and n.
Anstie, Mrs., 259.
Antwerp, 620, 622, 634, 637.
Appleby, 549, 551.
Arbuthnot, George, 670.
Ariosto, 79, 185.
Armstrong, John (poet), 402 and n.
Arnhem, 634.
Ashburner, Peggy, 50 and n.

Askham, 136.
Athenaeum (Club), 503 and n., 505, 516, 637, 667.
Athenaeum, The, 602 and n.
Atkinson, Matthew (of Temple Sowerby), 465 and n.
Austria, 669.

Backhouse, Mr., Mrs., and Miss, 131.
Bacon, Francis Lord, 475; quoted, 685.
Baird, George Husband, Letter to: 534.
Ballingham Seminary (Hereford), 479 and n.
Bamford, Robert W. (schoolmaster), Letter to: 349.
Bankes, William John, M.P., 158 n., 421 and n., 448 n., 454.
Barbauld, Mrs. Anna Letitia, stanzas To Life, 429 and n.
Barber, Samuel (of Gell's Cottage), 32 and n., 33, 63, 100, 149, 168, 200, 205, 219, 323, 352, 388, 589.
Barker, Mary, 318 and n., 433, 675.
Barlow, Mrs. Fanny, 378 and n., 480.
Barmouth, 278, 303.
Barret, Mr. (gardener at Coleorton), 324 and n.
Barrett, Capt. Thomas Brydges, Letter to: 285; 141 and n., 150, 166, 257–8, 261, 264, 569.
Barton, Bernard, 33 and n.
— Revd. William (of Windermere), 121 and n.
Basset, Francis, Lord de Dunstanville, 408 and n.
Bateman, Richard (stationer), 14, 25 and n., 26, 77.
Bath, 287, 472, 539.
Bathurst, Henry 3rd Earl, 488 and n.
Baudouins, the, 94 n.
Bayley, Miss, 480.
Beaumont, Francis, 603 and n.

Beaumont, Sir George, 7th Bart., *Letters to*: 3, 275, 349; gift of painting, 6 n.; on Chantrey's bust, 69 and n., 86; 242, 273, 275, 342; his *Mont-Blanc*, 350; 357, 386, 395; at Rydal, 485; 494–5, 503, 506; his picture *The Thorn*, 513–14, 519, 532; his death, 517–19, 520; 544, 555, 576–7, 681.

— Sir George and Lady, 189, 240, 254, 256, 258, 261–2, 282, 297–8, 301, 305, 332, 392.

— Lady, *Letters to*: 186, 272, 323, 411; 100, 350, 354, 517, 531, 551, 554–5, 557, 570, 572, 576, 673, 676.

— George (later 8th Bart.), 349 and n., 354, 673.

— Lady, 673.

— George (later 9th Bart.), 673 and n.

— the Misses, 673.

Beckett, John (later Sir John), 39 and n., 69, 108, 246, 254, 460.

Beddgelert (Caern.), 278, 477–8.

Bell, Dr. Andrew, 349 and n.; his Madras system, 685 and n.

Bell, John, his text of Collins's *Ode*, 648–50.

— Bros. and Co., *Letter to*: 309.

Belzoni, Giovanni Battista, 488 and n.

Benson, Miss (governess), 111 and n.

Bentinck, Maj.-Gen. Lord Frederick Cavendish, 85 n., 226, 560; his death, 593.

— Lady Frederick (Lady Mary Lowther), 85, 153, 407, 419, 576, 593, 595.

Bergami, Bartolomeo, 38 and n.

Bewley (river), 69, 144, 334.

Biddell, Arthur, 34, 88.

— Mr. and Mrs. Arthur, 17 and n.

Bingen, 617, 634.

Birchall and Co., 652 and n., 655, 657.

Birkett, Revd. William, 264 and n., 291 n.

Birmingham, 255, 299, 339, 353, 556, 560–1, 656.

Blackwood's Magazine, 94 and n.

Blair, Alexander, *Letter to*: 561; seeks professorship in London University, 561.

Blakeney, Robert (of Fox Ghyll), *Letter to*: 117; his death, 168; affairs, 171, 213, 218.

— Mrs., 168, 210, 282–3, 318.

Blomfield, Dr. Charles James, Bishop of Chester, *Letter to*: 624; 354 and n., 413, 540, 575, 658; translated to London, 624.

— Mrs., 540, 624.

Bolton, John (of Storrs), 381 n., 464, 575–6, 594, 659.

— Mrs., 576.

Bolton (nr. Appleby), 596.

— Priory, Yorks., 69.

Bonaparte, Napoleon, 97, 225, 245, 361, 517–18, 528.

Bonn, 634.

Borrowdale, 82, 148, 274.

Bosley, Miss, 608 and n.

Boswell, James, 648.

Bourne, Vincent, 80 and n.

Bouverie, Revd. William Arundell, 399 and n., 409.

Bowdler, Henrietta Maria, 571 and n.

Bowman, Revd. Thomas (of Hawkshead), 635 and n.

Bowring, John (later Sir John), *Letter to*: 564.

Boyer, Jean Pierre (President of Haiti), 30 and n.

Braithwaite, Miss (of Kendal), 317.

Bramah, Mr., 95 and n.

Branker, James (of Croft Lodge), 659 and n., 696.

Brathay, Old, 167, 170.

Brewster, Revd. John, *Letter to*: 384.

Bridges, Brook-Henry, 399 and n., 409.

Brinsop Court, 319 and n., 339, 351, 353, 389, 426–7, 435, 508, 539, 551, 556, 560–1, 581, 659, 666, 677.

British (National) Gallery, 555–6.

Brockbank, Mr., 220.

Brougham, Henry (later Lord), 38, 122, 311, 371, 420, 446–8, 451–2, 456–65; defends his political conduct, 465–7; 469–70, 594, 685.

— James, M.P., 82, 464 and n.

Brown, Dr. John, 402 and n.

Brussels, 631, 634, 662.

Brydges, Sir Egerton, 77 and n., 125, 286, 569, 656 and n.; *Polyanthea*, 286 and n.; *Cimelia*, 286 and n.
— John William Egerton, 141 and n., 269, 551.
Buck, William (C.C.'s father), 49 and n.
Buckingham, Duke of, *see* Grenville, Richard Chandos.
Buckley, Revd. Henry William, 399 and n., 409.
Bull, George (Bishop of St. Davids), his sermon, 684 and n.
Bullock-Marsham, Robert, 399 and n., 408.
Burns, Robert, 144.
Burrard, Admiral Sir Harry, Bart., 409 and n.
Bury St. Edmunds, 9, 270, 426.
Butler, Lady Eleanor, 274 n., 277.
— Revd. Samuel, *Letter to*: 730; 371 and n.
Buttermere, 148, 485.
Buxton, 675.
Byron, Lord, quarrel with Southey, 101 and n., 123, 212; joins in starting *The Liberal*, 124 and n.; *Lara*, 237; *Childe Harolde*, 237; *Siege of Corinth*, 237; his death, 308.

Cader Idris (Merion.), 278, 279, 303, 322, 477.
Caernarvon, 275.
Calvert, Mary, 219 and n.
— William, 82 and n., 232.
Cambridge, 255; floods at, 272; 582, 588.
— University Representation, 158 and n., 169, 298–9, 301, 421 and n., 422, 448, 453, 457.
Campbell, Col. and Mrs., 168 and n., 225, 239.
— Thomas, 450 and n.
— William (Comptroller), *Letter to*: 236.
Canfield, Palmer, *Lottery Argus*, 579 and n.
Canning, George, 42 and n., 55 and n., 145 n., 192 and n., 285, 310–12, 359 and n.; at Rydal Mount, 387; 412, 527–9, 661, 667.
Capel Curig (Caern.), 276, 278, 477–8.

Capell, Maj.-Gen. the Hon. Thomas Edward, 399 and n., 408, 412.
Carlisle, 468.
Carlisle Patriot, 459, 460, 469.
Carlyle, Revd. Alexander, 648 and n., 649.
Caroline, Queen, 33 and n., 53.
Carr, Thomas (surgeon), 133 and n., 134, 135, 145–6, 169, 240, 566, 588, 638, 656, 665.
— Mrs., 352, 693; *see also* Dowling, Ann.
Carruthers, Richard, 87 and n.
Carter, John, 168, 196, 282, 346, 413, 501–2, 665.
— Sophy (servant at Trinity Lodge), 34 and n., 672.
Catholic Association, The, 310 and n., 311.
— Question, 20, 42 and n., 55 and n., 58, 310–15, 347–8, 354 and n., 358–65, 447, 452, 461, 527–9, 531, 658, 678–9, 687.
— Relief Bill, 312 n., 369.
Cato, the Elder, *De Re Rustica*, 244.
Catullus, 125.
Channing, William Ellery, 606 and n., 607.
Chantrey, Francis Legatt, *Letters to*: 69, 86; bust of Wordsworth, 69 and n., 86, 137–8, 249, 400, 694; bust of Scott, 400, 422; 261, 401, 403, 609, 695.
Chantreys, the, 192, 249, 403.
Charnwood Forest, 698.
Charterhouse School, 46, 54, 67, 81, 82 and n., 115, 368, 585, 651.
Chaucer, Geoffrey, 284, 402.
Chester, 575.
— Bishop of, *see* Blomfield, Dr. Charles.
Christophe, Henry (King of Haiti), 30 n., 88, 103.
— Madame, 30 and n., 87 and n., 88, 93, 103, 114.
Cicero, 228.
Clappersgate, 484.
Clapperton, Capt. Hugh, 488 and n.
Clark, Robin (farmer), 209.
Clarkson, Catherine (Mrs. Thomas), *Letters to*: 7, 15, 30, 47, 60, 72, 87,

Clarkson, Catherine (*cont.*):
103, 229, 324, 344, 391, 434; 1, 2,
255, 268, 281, 290, 337, 374, 407,
428, 499, 504.
— Mary (C. C.'s niece), 393 and n.
— Thomas, interest in Haiti, 17;
letter to Lord Castlereagh, 51 and
n., 64; learning French, 52; his
portrait, 256 and n., 271; *Cries of
Africa*, 72 and n., translated into
French, 52, 65, 73 and n.; *Memoirs
of Penn*, 48 and n.; 35, 49, 72, 88,
229, 337, 344–5, 504, 512.
— Tom (C. C.'s son), 10 and n., 49,
73, 233, 325, 337, 391, 393, 428,
434, 440, 504, 678.
Clarksons, the, 136; visit Rydal, 141;
678.
Clifton, 318, 321, 325, 332, 336, 352,
398.
Clwydd, Vale of, 274, 275, 277, 448.
Coblenz, 616.
Cockerell, Samuel Pepys, 399 and n.,
409.
Colburn, Henry (publisher), 450 and
n.
Colchester, Lord, *see* Abbot, Charles.
Coleorton, 253, 273, 282, 301, 324,
349–50, 357, 388–9, 392, 404,
413, 531, 539, 544–5, 548, 551,
556, 599, 603, 672–3, 697; Church,
4 and n.; Winter Garden, 5 and n.
See also W. W., Visits and journeys.
Coleridge, Derwent, at Cambridge,
8 and n., 14; ill with typhus, 150;
at Plymouth, 288; marriage, 574;
at Helston, 500, 574, 619.
— Edward (S. T. C.'s nephew), 249
and n., 400, 568.
— Hartley, on mythology in poetry,
114; D. W.'s description of, 169;
teaching in Ambleside, 168 and n.,
173, 187, 188, 218, 223, 239, 256,
281, 288, 340–1, 433–4; begins
to write for magazines, 394 and n.,
395, 455, 619; 191, 203–5, 207–9,
213, 473, 500, 574, 659.
— Henry Nelson, 612 and n.
— Samuel Taylor, *Letter to*: 614;
article in *Blackwood's*, 94–5
and n.; 96, 107; advertises for

pupils, 114 and n.; 127, 187;
plagiarized by Byron, 237; 258,
288, 344–5, 401, 423, 580, 609;
Continental tour (1828) with
W. W. and Dora W., 614–22, 627,
itinerary, 623, 634; 615, 620; at
Antwerp, 621 and n.; 631, 641,
644, 651, 663, 688, 693.
— Mrs. S. T., 169, 173, 180, 187,
200, 214, 274, 281, 346, 423, 500,
619, 692–3.
— Sara, *Letter to*: 699; D. W.'s
description of, 274; *Account of the
Abipones*, 90 and n.; translation of
the *History of the Chevalier Bayard*,
292 and n., 346; 102, 110, 150,
169, 173, 180, 187, 200, 232, 287,
346, 393, 395, 398, 433, 473, 500,
574, 586, 612.
— William Hart, Bishop of Barbados,
612 n., 613.
Collier, Mrs. Jane, 426 and n., 429.
Collins, Anne (of Workington), 636.
— William, *Ode on the Popular Super-
stitions of the Highlands of Scotland*,
648–50.
Cologne, 634.
Columbian Bonds, failure of, 428,
436, 482.
Comet, The (steamboat), 395 and n.
Commissioners of Stamps, the, *Letters
to*: 14, 23, 26, 29, 59, 116, 131,
132, 151, 220, 295, 430.
Como, 124.
Compton, John Combe, 400 and n.,
409.
Coniston Water, 205, 208.
Constitutional Association, 11 and n.
Convention of Cintra, 97, 225–6.
Conway Bridge, 274; Castle, 274,
478; river falls, 276.
Cookson, Edwin, 316.
— Mrs. Elizabeth (of Kendal), *Letter
to*: 109; 91, 194, 215, 315–16, 317,
372, 550, 608.
— Elizabeth, 219, 315–16, 319, 372,
434, 482, 608.
— James, 317.
— John, 316, 317.
— Mary, 316.
— Richard, 317.

— Sarah, 315, 316.
— Strickland, *Letter to*: 500; 91 and n., 94, 109, 155–6, 160, 210, 218, 219, 316, 384, 475, 487, 522.
— Thomas (of Kendal), 315–17, 322, 569, 608.
— Thomas (jnr.), 316, 417, 566.
— Mrs. William (W. W.'s aunt), 17.
Copley, Sir John, Lord Lyndhurst, 67 and n., 421 and n., 448 n., 453–4.
Corn Bill (1815), 121.
Cornish, Mr. (bookseller), 651 and n.
Corporation Act, 312, 594 and n., 604–5 and n.
Corsbie, John (C. C.'s brother-in-law), 49 and n.
— Mrs. John (C. C.'s sister), 7.
Cottle, Joseph, *Letter to*: 617.
Courier, The, 33, 55, 652.
Courtenay, Philip, 121 and n., 261, 309, 380, 730 and n.
Coward, Fleming, 445 and n.
Coxe, William, *Lettres* (trans. Raymond), 237, 674.
Crabbe, George, 285 and n.
Crackanthorpe, William (W. W.'s cousin), 416 and n., 456–7, 467.
Crackanthorpes, the, 416.
Croker, Thomas Crofton, *Letter to*: 552.
Crump, Elizabeth, *Letters to*: 172, 204, 216, 221, 338; at Rydal, 197, 203; 240.
— John G. (of Allan Bank), *Letter to*: 484; 239.
— John (jnr.), 173, 221, 338.
— Julia, 172 n.
— Louisa, 172, 340.
Crumps, the, 33, 172 and n., 241.
Cumberland, Duke of, 649.
Cumberland Pacquet, 602.
Cumine, Adam, 670 and n.
Cunningham, Allan, *Letters to*: 137, 192, 249, 400, 568, 583, 592, 609, 653, 680, 694; sends book and medallion, 193; *Songs of Scotland*, 401 and n.; his proposed selection of W. W.'s poems, 568, 578, 653–4, 703–4; 422, 503, 569, 693, 695.

— Mrs., 609.
Curwen, John Christian, M.P., 27 and n., 33, 85–6, 458; his death, 697 and n.

Dance, George, R.A., 324.
Dante, 79 and n., 244, 245–6.
Davy, Sir Humphry, 368, 523.
Dawes, Revd. John, 142, 168, 173, 187.
Deighton's Bookshop (Cambridge), 9 and n.
Delille, Abbé Jacques, 290 and n.
De Lys, Gabriel Jean, 561 and n.
Demerara, insurrections in, 229 and n.
Demosthenes, 228.
Dent, Mrs. (of Appleby), 465.
Devil's Bridge (Card.), 273, 278; sonnet composed at, 279, 297, 299; 477.
Dibdin, Revd. Thomas Frognall, 259 and n.
Digby, Kenelm Henry, 668 and n.
Dixon, Miss, 576 and n.
— William (bookseller), 636.
Dockray, Benjamin, *Letters to*: 485, 678.
Donaldson, Mrs., 263 and n., 479.
Douglas, George, 586.
— Harriet, *Letters to*: 541, 584.
— William, 585.
— Mr. (tenant at Brathay), 340.
Douglas, I.O.M., 507, 573.
Dover, 538.
Dowling, Ann (schoolmistress), 31, 34; holds ball, 100–1; 195, 197, 214, 221, 223, 239; marriage, 240; 273. *See also* Mrs. Carr.
— Eliza, 221, 223, 240.
— Jane, 239.
— Mary, 219, 223, 352.
— Vincent George, 203 and n., 693.
— Mrs., 203 and n.
Dowlings, the Miss, 169.
Drake, Sir Thomas Fuller Eliott, Bart., 218 and n.
Drewry, Joseph, 501 and n.
Drummond, Revd. Robert, 605 and n.
Dryden, John, *Aeneid*, 247, 253, quoted 251–2, 254; 228.
Dublin, 366.

Index

Duddon (river), 4, 486.

Dudley, Lord, see Ward, John William.

Duff, Richard Wharton, 662 and n., 670.

Dunbar, William, 506, 521.

Dungeon Gill, 110.

Durham, Bishop of, see Mildert, William Van.

Dyce, Revd. Alexander, Letter to: 647; his edition of Collins, 647–50.

Dyer, George, 112 and n.

— James (schoolmaster), Letter to: 597.

Eden (river), 4, 5.

Edinburgh, Arthur's Seat, 154, 223; Holyrood House, 154; 168, 206, 213, 222, 238–9, 431, 433, 493, 498, 506, 514, 611. See also D. W., Visits and journeys.

Edinburgh, Transactions of the Royal Society of, 648 n., 649.

Edinburgh Review, hostile review of W. W., 183; 459.

Edmonds, John (attorney), 471 and n.

— Mrs., 85 and n.

Eldon, 1st Earl of (Lord Chancellor), 28 and n.

Elizabeth (C. C.'s maid), 8, 18, 35.

Elliot, Mr. (tenant of Ivy Cottage), 146 and n., 168, 196, 218, 243, 352.

— Mrs., 218, 223, 417.

Elliots, the, 164, 293.

Ellwood, Mrs. Jane, 20 and n., 148, 548, 549, 582, 590.

Emont (river), 4.

Eusemere, 392.

Evening Mail, 382.

Exeter, 318.

Fairfield, 62, 626.

Faraday and Grime (drapers), 77, 132.

Farquhar, Sir Robert, 1st Bart., 258 and n.

— Lady, 388, 392, 656.

— Walter Minto (later 2nd Bart.), 262 and n., 482.

Farquhars, the, 346, 393, 482.

Fenton, Mr., 566 and n., 570, 610.

Fermor, Mrs. Frances, 297 and n., 301.

Ffestiniog (Merion.), 278.

Field, Mr. (Brinsop acquaintance), 482–3.

Field, Barron, Letters to: 600, 615, 640, 694; his bust of W. W., 694.

— Mrs., 695.

Fields, the, 293.

Fisher, Elizabeth, 59.

— Mary (née Cookson), 17 and n.

Flaxman, John, R.A., 192 n., 338 and n.; death of, 511.

Fleming, Revd. Fletcher, 301 and n.

— Revd. John (of Rayrigg), 656, 660, 696.

— Mrs., her death, 656, 673.

— John (farmer), 168 and n., 218.

— Leonard, 451 and n.

— Thomas (owner of Spring Cottage), 211 and n.

— Mrs., 232.

Fleming, Lady Ann le, Letters to: 129, 185; 213, 214, 301, 355, 370, 416, 417, 471, 477.

— Lady Diana le, 370.

— Sir Richard le, 142 and n., 149, 370, 469.

Fletcher, Miss (schoolmistress), 111 and n.

— Jacob, Letters to: 302, 321, 333, 523, 525; his tragedies, 322, 333–4.

Fonthill, 157 and n.

Forbes, James, Oriental Memoirs, 696 and n.

Forshall, Revd. Josiah, 190 and n., 191.

Fox, Charles James, 97.

Fox Ghyll, description of estate, 210–11; 168, 282–3, 318, 326, 340, 356, 482, 540, 582.

Foxley (Herefordshire), 279, 570.

Foyers, Fall of, 144, 334.

France, political situation, 121, 122 and n., 300, 668–9; intervention in Spain (1823), 179 and n., 180, 499; Code Napoléon, 669.

Freeling, Francis, Letter to: 579.

French Funds, 159, 160.

Frere, Revd. John, 671 and n.

Furness Abbey, 83.

710

Index

Galignani, A. and W., 652, 655, 657; 'pirated' edition of W. W., 656, 658, 690, 697.

Garnet, Thomas (postmaster), 215.

Gauden, John (Bishop of Exeter), 296 and n.

Gee, George (tenant of Ivy Cottage), 26 and n., 34, 47, 84, 110, 135, 138, 158, 171, 194, 195, 196–7, 211, 390, 470, 472, 473, 474, 482, 581; his death, 548 and n.

— Mrs., 64, 92, 196, 539, 581, 588, 589 and n.

Gees, the, 76, 114, 167, 318, 336.

Genlis, Mme de, *Mémoires*, 375 and n.

Gerona, Siege of, 518 and n.

Ghent, 634.

Giant's Causeway, 68, 478, 498.

Gibbon, Edward, quoted, 118.

Gifford, Sir Robert (Attorney-General), 28 and n.

Gillman, James, 344 and n., 345.

Glasgow, 159, 177, 366, 373, 478, 508.

Glencoe, 69, 144, 334.

Gloucester, William Frederick, Duke of, 553 and n.

Goddard, Frederick Warren, 94 and n., 500, 511.

Goderich, Lord (Prime Minister), 594 and n.

Godesberg, 616–17, 620, 621, 634.

Goodenough, Revd. Edmund, 407 and n.

— Samuel, Bishop of Carlisle, 408 and n.

Gordale, 69.

Gordon, George Huntly, *Letters to*: 623, 631, 650, 661, 687; 664, 690.

— Major Pryse Lockhart, 623 and n.

Goulburn, Henry, M.P., 298 n., 421 and n., 448 n., 454.

Graham, Sir James, M.P. (of Netherby), 452 and n.

— William G., 429 and n.

Grande Chartreuse, the, 176.

Grant, Mrs. Ann, 84 and n.

Grasmere, Lake, 76; Church, 219; enclosure at, 304–5; petition, 348 and n.; day in the fields of, 351; 469.

Gray, Thomas, *Ode on the Spring* quoted, 44 and n.; *Elegy* quoted, 513; *De Principiis Cogitandi*, 80 and n.; *On the Death of Richard West*, 80 and n.; *Ode on a Distant Prospect of Eton College*, 546; *Letters*, 632; *Journal in the Lakes*, 632; on Nature poetry, 118–19; plagiarized, 238.

Green, Revd. Daniel, 218 and n.

— George, 562–3, 566, 570, 599, 610.

— Hartley, 562–3.

— Revd. Isaac (brother of Daniel), 638 and n.

— William (artist), 562 and n.

— Mrs. William, 566, 570, 610.

Gregg, Christopher, 41, 57 and n.

Grenville, Richard Chandos, Duke of Buckingham, 553 and n., 560.

— William Wyndham, Lord Grenville, 457 n., 560, 588.

Grey, Charles, 2nd Earl, 26.

— Matthew Robert, 399 and n., 409.

Griffith, Revd. Henry Moses, 399 and n., 408.

Guillemard, Mr. and Mrs. Lewis, 280 and n., 281, 287 and n.

Gwerndovenant (nr. Hindwell), 481 and n.

Haiti, unrest in, 17 and n., 30 and n.

Halhead, John, 150 and n., 194, 196.

Halifax, Yorks., 417, 536.

Hall, Samuel Carter, *Letters to*: 524, 525; his *Amulet*, 524.

Hallsteads, 230, 567.

Hamilton, Edward William Terrick, 633, 639 and n.

— Eliza, her verses, 546.

— Walter Kerr, 633 n.

— William Rowan (later Sir William), *Letter to*: 545; his verses, 545–6; 542 and n.

Hammond, George, 399 and n., 409.

Hampton Court, 612.

Hanover, 311, 457.

Harden, Mrs. Jane, 172, 206, 222, 223, 340, 571.

— Jane Sophia, 101 and n., 203, 338.

— John, 101 and n., 168, 340.

711

Harden, Robert Allan, 571 and n., 574.
Hardens, the, 220.
Hare, Revd. Augustus William, 188
and n., 190, 191, 246, 249, 278;
Guesses at Truth, 537 and n.
— Revd. Julius Charles, *Letter to*:
609; 246 and n., 290, 558, 620,
634.
Harrison, Anne, 219 and n.
— Anthony (attorney), 304 and n.,
502.
— Mrs. Anthony, 7 and n.
— Benson, 566 and n., 567, 568, 660.
— Mrs. Benson (*née* Dorothy Words-
worth), 568, 588, 589.
— George (auditor), 411 and n.
— — (of Highgate), 344 and n., 345.
— Revd. John (of Kendal), 317 n.
Harrisons, the (children), 317.
Harrison, Thomas (surgeon), 139,
142, 548.
Harrogate, 50, 68, 240, 288, 374–5,
529–32.
Hasell, the Misses (of Dalemain),
548 and n.
Haweswater, 228, 231.
Hawkshead, 208, 571.
Haydon, Benjamin Robert, *Letter to*:
70; *Raising of Lazarus*, 70 and n.;
350.
Hayley, William, *Memoirs*, 338 and n.
Hazlitt, William, criticisms of Words-
worth, 106 and n., 107.
Head, Revd. James Pearson, 559 and
n.
Headingley, Yorks., 599.
Heath, Charles (engraver), 592 and
n., 692.
— Mrs., 616.
Heber, Richard, M.P., *Letter to*:
398.
Helston, 619.
Helvellyn, 368, 567, 628, 629, 633.
Hemans, Felicia Dorothea, 480 and
n., 527, 606.
Hendon, 230, 239, 240, 258.
Herbert, Algernon, 400 and n., 409.
— George Augustus, 11th Earl of
Pembroke, 409 and n.
Hereford, 436, 539, 556, 557, 560,
561.

Herries, John Charles, M.P., 593
and n.
Hervey, Thomas Kibble, *Letter to*:
419; *Australia*, 419 and n.; 476
and n.
Hesketh, Henry, 220 and n.
Heylyn, Peter, *Cyprianus Anglicus*,
55 and n.
Heywood, John Pemberton (Asses-
sor), 458 n.
Hickie, Daniel Bamfield, 635 and
n.
Hill, Revd. Herbert (Southey's uncle),
549 and n.
Hindson, Miss, 331 and n.
Hindwell (Radnorshire), 229, 263,
267, 273, 275, 318, 331.
Hoare, Mrs. Hannah, 1 and n., 14, 17,
260, 531, 673.
— Samuel (banker), 14, 17, 531.
— Miss, 673.
Hoares, the, 344.
Hobart, John Henry, Bishop of New
York, 276 and n.
Hodgson, Mrs. Frances, 132.
— Peter (attorney), 12, 29.
Hogarth, Richard, 403 and n.
Holland, Sir Henry, Bart., 83 and n.,
258.
— Lord, 183.
Holland House, 153.
Holmes, Col. George, 83 and n.
— Col. and Mrs., 202.
— William, M.P., 471 and n.
Holt, Francis Ludlow, 463 and n.,
469.
Homer, 335.
Honeyman, Miss, 392 and n., 393.
Horace, 125.
Horrocks, Alice, 292 and n., 332,
336; marriage, 352.
— Ann Eliza, 217, 292 and n., 398.
— Mary (Mrs. Birkett), 291 and n.
— Samuel, M.P., 113 and n., 241.
— — (jnr.), 142 and n.
— Sarah (Mrs. St. Clare), 1 and n.,
7, 46, 134, 257, 262, 291, 325,
332, 336, 339, 352, 355, 427;
marriage, 397–8, 407.
— Susannah (Mrs. Raven), 291 and n.
Houtson, James, 488.

— John, 488 and n.

Howard, Col. the Hon. Fulke Greville, 408 and n.

— Henry (of Corby), 462 and n., 463.

— Mrs. Mary (of Levens Hall), 550 and n.

Howe, Richard William, Earl, 560 and n.

Howitt, William, *Letter to*: 535; *Desolation of Eyam*, 535.

Howley, Mary Anne, 349 n., 354.

— Dr. William, Bishop of London (later Archbishop of Canterbury), 410, 412, 658.

Huddles, David, 410.

Huddlestone, Revd. Andrew, 697 and n.

— Mrs. Elizabeth, 412 n., 416–17.

Huddlestones, Castle of, 3 and n.

Hume, Joseph, M.P., 54 and n., 55, 58, 66, 550.

Hunt, Leigh, starts *The Liberal*, 124 and n.

Hurst and Robinson, 381, 383, 397, 418; failure of, 424–5, 428, 433; their terms, 443; 439, 450, 455, 487, 496.

Huskisson, William, M.P., 594 and n.

Hutchinson, Elizabeth ('Ebba', niece of M. W.), 354, 508.

— George (brother of M. W.), 33 and n., 64.

— — (of Sockburn, uncle of M. W.), 120.

— — (nephew of M. W.), 326 and n., 479.

— Henry (brother of M. W.), 50 and n., 389, 482, 507–8, 574.

— Joanna (sister of M. W.), *Letter to*: 315; with D. W. in Edinburgh, 154, 157, sickness there, 159, 169, 173, 177; at Stockton with Dora W., 159, 167; failure of her Columbian Bonds, 428, 436; removes to I.O.M., 482, 507, 521, 533; her accident there, 507–8; at Rydal, 656, 665, 699; 50 and n., 64, 148, 160, 162, 170, 212, 215, 223, 234, 282, 325, 395, 431, 433–4, 435, 479, 483, 573, 574, 613.

— John (of Stockton-on-Tees, M. W.'s brother), bankruptcy, 428, 450.

— Mary (*née* Monkhouse), *Letter to*: 351; 1, 64, 89, 148, 318, 326–7, 339, 352, 354; at Harrogate, 374–5, 392; 378, 427, 432, 435–6, 437, 479, 482, 483, 572; birth of Sally, 508.

— Sara (sister of M. W.), *Letter to*: 454; learning French, 128; at Stockton-on-Tees, 32, 50, with Dora W., 173, 177; in London, 189; at Lee Priory, 197, 211; at Boulogne, 215, 217; at Hendon, 230; in Wales, 259; at Torquay, 287, 288, 291, 297, 318; at Clifton, 325, 326, 336; at Harrogate, 140, 375, 392, 530; at Coleorton, 392; at Brinsop, 656, 659, 666, 677; 61, 68, 77, 89, 150, 179, 223, 240, 242, 243, 261, 263, 268, 330, 339, 353, 355, 374, 386, 388–9, 428, 429, 441, 450, 479, 482, 499, 501, 539, 548, 549, 551, 607, 619, 699.

— Sara (Sally), born, 508.

— Thomas (of Hindwell and Brinsop, brother of M. W.), 49, 120–1, 273, 282, 297, 317; at Coleorton, 392; 431–2, 436–7, 481–3, 557, 572.

— — (son), 121, 356.

— Mrs. (of Harrogate, S. H.'s cousin), 50, 62, 200.

Hutton, Thomas (solicitor), 40 and n.

Inglis, Sir Robert, *Letter to*: 358; 628.

Ingram, A. R. (Receiver General), 549–50.

Ireland, 445, 448, 451, 478.

Irish Question, 98, 358–65, 527, 687.

Irving, Edward, *Orations*, 212 and n.; his preaching, 262; 264, 402.

— Washington, 401 and n.

Isle of Man, 507–8, 533, 573, 611, 665.

Italy, 177, 350, 445, 495, 511, 538, 544, 555, 556.

Ivy Cottage, 110, 140, 148, 150, 166, 203, 232, 293, 352, 540, 551.

Ivy How estate (Little Langdale), 211, 589 and n.

Index

Jackson, Revd. Thomas (rector of Grasmere), 19, death of, 100; agent for Lady le Fleming, 129 and n.
— Thomas (of Waterhead), 129 n., 588 and n.
— Revd. William, *Letters to*: 509, 552, 580, 587, 596, 629, 698; accepts living at Lowther, 587, 589, 595; offered living at Bolton, 596–7; 19 and n., 147, 149, 188, 219, 221, 274, 282, 298, 338, 340, 451, 634, 657, 661.
Jameson, Anna Brownell, *Diary of an Ennuyée*, 480 and n.
Jedburgh, 356.
Jeffrey, Francis, 459.
Jenkinson, Hon. Charles Cecil Cope (later 3rd Earl of Liverpool), 152 and n.
Jerdan, William, *Letters to*: 625, 632.
Jerningham, Sir George William Stafford, Bart., 348 and n.
Jewsbury, Geraldine, 378 and n.
— Maria Jane, *Letters to*: 342, 377, 480, 606; *Phantasmagoria*, 342–4; 376, 405, 435; 389, 418, 425, 427, 434–5, 455, 527, 666.
— Thomas, *Letter to*: 592; 434 and n.
John Bull, 47 and n., 350 and n.
Johnson, James (attorney), 304.
— Mrs. James, 317 and n.
— Dr. Samuel, quoted, 253, 327, 644, 689; *Lives of the Poets*, 648; 649.
— Revd. William, 1 and n., 32, 35, 36, 54, 261, 518.
— Mrs., 259, 265.
Jones, Revd. Robert, *Letters to*: 226, 386, 420, 448; his character, 297; his weight, 277; 149, 176, 273, 275, 354.
Jonson, Ben, parodied, 88, 90.

Kaye, Dr. John, Bishop of Lincoln, 575 and n., 576, 595, 604 and n.
Keble, John, *Letters to*: 174, 187, 190, 191.
Keepsake, The, 590 and n., 592, 602, 616 and n., 653, 656, 665, 680–1, 691, 692.
Kelly, Fanny, 262 and n.

Kelsall, Miss (of Manchester), 608 and n.
Kendal Chronicle, 25 and n., 37.
Kentmere, 231.
Kent's Bank, 376, 378, 392 n., 607.
Kenyon, Edward, 68, 256.
— John, *Letters to*: 24, 68, 82, 99, 198, 256, 280, 287, 472, 490, 491, 538; sends eyeshades, 24; second marriage, 99 and n., 124; 78, 170, 244, 503–4, 505, 515–16.
— Mrs., 256, 490, 538.
Kilchurn Castle, 143.
Killarney, 68, 478, 498.
Killiecrankie, 144.
King, Mrs., 172, 173.
Kinnaird, Maria (later Mrs. Thomas Drummond), 157 and n.
Kirby, William, *Introduction to Entomology*, 526 and n.
Kircher, Athanasius, *Mundus Subterraneus*, 682 and n.
Kirkbank, Isaac, 12.
— John, 12, 29.
Kirkonnel, Mr. (of Maryport), 636.
Kirkstone, 135, 139, 230, 548, 567.
Kitchener, Mrs. (C. C.'s housekeeper), 7 and n., 270.
Knott, Miss, 502 and n., 568.

Laing, David, *Letters to*: 154, 160; at Rydal, 209; 506, 508, 573, 611.
— Mary, *Letters to*: 160, 207, 213, 222, 233, 238, 394, 431, 506, 513, 519, 532, 571, 611; at Rydal, 205–6; 154 n., 177, 217.
Lamb, Charles, 'superannuated', 331, 336, 374; essays by 'Elia' in *London Magazine*, 1 and n., 93 and n., 114 and n.; *Essays of Elia*, 179; 7 and n., 95, 128, 257, 293, 294, 337, 338, 375, 396–7, 404–5, 440 and n., 444, 499, 503, 512, 517, 626, 641, 678, 694.
— John, death of, 93 and n., 95, 112.
— Mary, 7, 95, 290, 293, 338, 396–7, 404, 517, 678.
Lambs, the, 262.
Lambert, Anne (of Kendal), 317 and n.

714

Index

Landor, Walter Savage, *Letters to*: 78, 122, 243, 289; *De Cultu atque Usu Latini Sermonis*, 79 n., 80; *Gebir*, 79; *Idyllia heroica*, 79, 246; *Imaginary Conversations*, 123 and n., 243–4, 289–90; *Simonidea*, 125; *Sponsalia Polyxenae*, 125 and n.; *Washington and Franklin*, 289 and n.; 78 n., 674.

Langdale, 491.

Langhorne, John, 402 and n.

Laroche, Benjamin, 61 and n., 72 and n., 73 and n., 87, 105.

Lasswade, 356, 366.

Leach, Sir John, 28 n., 409 and n.

— Revd. John (of Askham), 462–3, 469.

Leamington, 506.

Leeds Intelligencer, article on W. W., 284 and n.

Lee Priory, 141 n., 150, 166, 194–5, 199, 203, 261, 265, 270. *See also* W. W., Visits and journeys.

Legge, the Hon. Edward, Bishop of Oxford, 408 and n.

Leicester, Sir George, Bart., Lord de Tabley, 630 and n.

Leslie, Charles Robert, R.A., *Sancho and the Duchess*, 271; 350.

Leveson-Gower, George Granville, 2nd Marquess of Stafford, 555 and n.

Lewis, Sir Thomas Frankland, Bart., 89 and n., 121.

— Mrs., 352 and n.

— Miss, 352.

Leyden, John, 402 and n.

Liberal, The, started by Hunt and Byron, 124 and n.

Lichfield, 357, 368.

— Cathedral, 367–8.

Liège, 623, 634.

Lincoln, Bishop of, *see* Kaye, Dr. John.

Linnhe, Loch, 143, 334.

Literary Gazette, 127, 625 n.

Literary Souvenir, The, 455.

Littledale, Sir Joseph, 420 and n.

Liverpool, Lord (Prime Minister), 312.

Liverpool, 216, 221, 241, 275, 338, 366, 370, 461, 478, 506, 548, 575, 581, 600, 602, 639.

Llanberis (Caern.), 275, 478.

— Lake, 276.

— Pass, 276.

Llangollen, ladies of, 274, 277; 478.

Lloyd, Charles, *Letter to*: 299.

— Mrs. Charles (Mary), her death, 106 and n.

— Charles (jnr.), *Letter to*: 106; 673.

— Mrs. Charles, 107, 232, 673.

— Revd. Owen, 108, 300 and n., 529 and n., 532, 582, 673.

Loch Lomond, 143.

Loch Ness, 69.

Lockhart, John Gibson, *Life of Burns*, 626 and n.; 627.

— Mrs. Sophia (*née* Scott), 369, 612, 628.

— John Hugh, 628 and n.

Lockier, Charlotte (of Hendon), 37 and n., 64, 260.

Lockiers, the Miss, 259, 260.

London College Committee, 371 and n.

London Magazine, 237, 244 and n.

Longinus, 335.

Longman and Co., *Letters to*: 108, 384, 495, 502, 526, 664; 73, 127, 128, 145, 306, 307, 319–20, 328, 372–3, 390, 411, 443, 495, 504, 505, 508, 510, 515, 578, 693.

— Thomas Norton, *Letter to*: 547; 383, 397.

Long Meg and her Daughters (stone circle), 4–5.

Longsleddale, 231.

Lonsdale, Revd. John, 635 n., 657 and n.

— William, Earl of, *Letters to*: 10, 19, 27, 84, 85, 142, 157, 171, 182, 184, 227, 235, 246, 250, 253, 304, 347, 369, 407, 410, 418, 445, 451, 455, 459, 460, 461, 463, 465, 468, 470, 559, 575, 593, 595, 659, 683, 696; fall from horse, 137, 142; 227, 231, 412, 420, 531, 548, 587, 589, 596, 630, 661, 688, 691, 697, 698.

— Lady, 85, 447.

— Revd. William, 662 and n., 670, 687.

715

Losh, James, *Letter to*: 96.

Loughrigg, 305, 491, 551.

Louis XVIII, 156 and n.

Lovell, Mrs. Robert (Southey's sister-in-law), 275 and n., 619.

Lowther, Revd. Henry (of Distington), 453 and n.

— Col. the Hon. Henry Cecil, M.P., 148 and n., 172, 183, 456, 460, 461, 462, 464, 465, 469 and n.

— Sir John, Bart. (of Swillington), 462 and n.

— Viscount, M.P., *Letters to*: 25, 37, 38, 41, 54, 57, 66, 77, 81, 82, 120, 309; at Rydal Mount, 471; 171, 320, 421, 445, 456–7, 461, 463, 465, 467, 468, 469, 575, 595, 597, 661, 688.

Lowther, 140, 231, 490, 544, 635. *See also* W. W., Visits and journeys.

Low Wood, regatta at, 150; 231.

Lucas, Mrs. (nanny), 266, 270.

Lucretius, 125.

Luff, Mrs. Letitia, *Letter to*: 254; her singing birds, 270; her character, 393; 230, 262–3, 268, 269, 272, 274, 282–3, 317–18, 326, 340, 346, 356, 388, 392, 428, 438, 540, 582, 588.

Lugano, Lake of, 429.

Lutterworth, statue of Wycliffe in, 557 and n., 560.

Lutwidge, Cdr. Henry Thomas, R.N., 369 and n., 660, 661.

Machell, Col. Christopher, 272 and n., 273.

— Matilda, 273.

Mackenzie, Henry, 648 and n., 649.

Mackintosh, Sir James, 388 and n.; at Rydal Mount, 393.

— Miss, 388, 393.

Macpherson, James, 402 and n.

Malcolm, Lady (John), 620 and n., 634.

Malham Cove, 69.

Malthus, Thomas Robert, 682 and n.

Malvern, 482, 556.

— Hills, 427, 435.

Manchester, 378, 383, 389, 392, 405, 425, 427, 435, 461, 557, 607, 608, 615, 639, 666.

— Cause, 122 and n.

Manners-Sutton, Charles, M.P. (later 1st Viscount Canterbury), 298 and n., 658.

Marshall, Cordelia, 139, 417.

— Mrs. Jane, *Letters to*: 138, 289, 415, 484, 697; 562, 610.

— John, 371, 392, 416, 417, 485, 490, 567, 599.

— — (jnr.), *Letters to*: 562, 566, 570, 599, 610; 139.

— Julia Anne, 141.

— Mary Anne, 416 and n.

Marsham, Charles, 1st Earl of Romney, 408 and n.

— Revd. Jacob, 408 and n.

Martin, Martin, Gent., *Description of the Western Islands of Scotland*, 650 and n.; *A Late Voyage to St. Kilda*, 650 and n.

Masqueriers, the, 675 and n.

Master, Revd. James Streynsham, 292 n.

Masterman and Co. (bankers), 309 and n., 386, 665.

Mathews, Charles, 262 and n.

Matlock, 140, 166, 675.

Medwin, Thomas, *Conversations of Lord Byron*, 307 and n.; 307–8.

Menai Straits, 275.

Merewether, Revd. Francis, *Letters to*: 300, 604; his pamphlet, 302 and n.; 557, 559, 575, 672, 683, 697.

— Mrs., 531, 557.

Methodists, the 639.

Meuse (river), 623, 627, 634.

Mickle, William Julius, 402 and n.

Milan, 124.

— Cathedral, 124.

Mildert, William Van, Bishop of Durham, 658 and n.

Mildmay, Revd. Charles William St. John-, 399 and n., 409.

Millom, appointment of coroner, 12 and n., 29.

— Church, 3.

Mills, Francis, 400 and n., 409.

Milton, John, 79, 250, 284, 402, 547; *Sonnets*, 125–6; first edition of his minor poems, 163.

Monkhouse, Elizabeth (M. W.'s aunt), 148, 211, 227, 233, 435, 483, 573.
— Mrs. Jane (*née* Horrocks), 7, 15, 35, 46, 75, 89, 127, 134, 179, 217, 257, 259, 261, 266, 268, 291, 325–6, 332, 336, 339, 352, 355, 398, 407, 427, 451.
— John (M. W.'s cousin), *Letters to*: 258, 330, 479, 481, 482; 211, 212, 297, 318, 325, 326, 336, 339, 352, 356, 375, 433, 437, 451, 557, 572, 590.
— Joseph (M. W.'s cousin), death of, 167 n.; 326.
— Mary, 100 and n., 166, 262–3, 336, 352, 355, 398, 407, 427, 589; W. W.'s verses to, 287, 292, 294.
— Thomas (M. W.'s cousin), *Letters to*: 1, 13, 20, 35, 46, 209, 267; at Rydal, 133; interest in Fox Ghyll, 209–11, 218; seriously ill, 279, 281, 286–8, 290–1, 297, 305, 308; at Torquay, 288; at Clifton, 318, 321; death of, 325–6, 329, 335–6, 337, 339; funeral, 325; his affairs, 326, 336–7, 451; 68, 93, 113, 126, 135–6, 142, 167–8, 179, 189, 199, 222, 254–5, 257–8, 261, 269, 270, 272, 293, 374, 427, 432, 503.
Montagu, Basil, *Letters to*: 475, 522; his edition of Bacon's works, 475 and n., 522.
— Mrs., 111 and n.
Montagus, the, 128.
Montgomery, James, *Letter to*: 248; 476 and n.
Moore, Thomas, 124.
Mordey, Mr. (sub-distributor), 636.
— Mrs., 636.
Morgan, Charles Gould, M.P., 479 and n., 483.
Morning Chronicle, 1, 33, 55, 455.
Morris, Wilson (of Rydal), 135, 168.
Moselle (river), 623.
Moultrie, John, 45 and n.
Moxon, Edward, *Letter to*: 497; *The Prospect and other Poems*, 497.
Mulock, Thomas Samuel, 45 and n.

Murray, John (publisher), *Letters to*: 379, 496; 327 and n., 328, 329, 341, 376, 378, 381, 397, 439, 443, 505, 510–11, 512, 515.
Museum Criticum, 558 and n.
Myers, John (W. W.'s cousin), death of, 2, 3, 12, 17; funeral of, 4; 26, 33–4, 40, 47, 75, 182.
— John (of Manchester), 40 and n.
— Julia, 3, 34, 76, 169, 202, 352.
— Mary Catherine Ann, 75 and n.
— Thomas (W. W.'s cousin), *Letter to*: 2; 34, 75–6.
— Revd. Thomas (of Lazonby), 34 and n., 228.
— William (of Deal), *Letter to*: 40.

Nab, the, 388.
Namur, 623, 634.
National Gallery, *see* British Gallery.
Natland Beck (Kendal), 315.
New Lanark, 143 and n.
Newton, William (of Ambleside), 38 and n.
Nichols, John, *History and Antiquities of Leicester*, 6 and n.
Nicholson, William (land agent), 304 and n., 305.
Nijmegen, 634.
Nimmo, Alexander, 543 and n., 547.
Nith, Vale of, 143.
Norman Conquest, the, 362.
North, Ford (of Ambleside), 41 and n., 235.
Norton, Andrews, 627 and n.
Nunnery (residence of Francis Aglionby), 5 and n.

O'Callaghan, Hon. George, 228 and n., 548.
O'Connell, Daniel, M.P., 498 and n.
Oglander, John, 399 and n., 408.
Oldham, John, *Satyr against Value* referred to, 189.
Oliver and Boyd, 597 and n., 680.
Ostend, 620, 634.
Otway, Revd. Caesar, 543 and n., 547.
Oxford, John W.'s admission to, 174–5, 187–8, 190–1, 199, 222,

Index

Oxford, John W.'s admission to (*cont.*):
227, 256, 282; typhus at, 318; election of Chancellor, 553–4, 560; 240, 255, 287, 292, 339, 346, 499, 557, 588.
— Merton College, Fellows of, 399–400; their connections, 408–9.
— New College, 190, 191, 199, 227, 256, 353, 582, 589.

Palmerston, Lord, 158 n., 422, 453–4, 457.
Papendick, G. E. (of Bremen), 687 n., 690.
Paris, 401.
Parkin, Hugh (of Skirsgill), 228 and n., 630.
Parry, Hugh, 259 n.
— Mrs., 259, 260.
— Sir William Edward, *Journal of a Voyage for the Discovery of a North-West Passage*, 165 and n.
Pasley, Col. Charles William, *Letters to*: 411, 514; his *Inquiry*, 411 and n., 514–15; 510.
Patmore, Peter George, 44 and n., 47.
Peabody, Elizabeth Palmer, *Letter to*: 565.
Pearson, Allan (of Bridekirk), 247.
— William, *Letters to*: 143, 385, 430, 626, 628, 633.
Peile, Revd. Thomas Williamson, 370 and n.
Penn, William, 47, 48 n.
Penrith, 206, 207, 393, 548, 549, 631.
— Balls, 222, 234.
— Races, 217, 230, 232, 234.
Perceval, Spencer (Prime Minister), 626 and n., 632.
Percy, Lady Susan, 413 and n.
— Thomas (Bishop of Dromore), 402 and n.
Perrin, Robert, 450, 469.
Petrarch, 79.
Petre, Henry William, 463 and n.
Philips, George Richard, M.P., 261 and n.
— Mrs., 261.
Pigou, Robert Richard, 400 and n., 409.

Pitt, Christopher, 228.
— William (the Younger), 457.
Planta, Joseph, 690 and n.
Playford Hall (home of the Clarksons), 1, 51, 65, 77, 87–8, 93, 104, 180, 230, 255, 262–3, 268, 269–70, 325.
Pleydell-Bouverie, William, Lord Folkestone, 408 and n., 409 and n.
Po House (residence of John Myers), 2 and n., 17, 33.
Pollard, Anne, 417.
Polson, William (barrister), 670 and n.
Ponsonby, Hon. Miss, 274 n., 277.
Poole, Thomas, 288 and n.; at Rydal, 491 and n.
Poor Rates, 39 and n.
Pope, Alexander, his Homer, 247, 402.
Portuguese, the, 226.
Power, Francis (merchant), 652 and n., 655, 657.
Praed, Winthrop Mackworth, 634 and n.
Pratt, John Jeffreys, Lord Camden, 85 and n.
Preston, 325, 336, 352, 355, 398, 407, 427.
— Guild, 148 and n.
Price, Lady Caroline, 324 and n.
— Robert, M.P., 681 and n.
— Uvedale (later Sir Uvedale), 279 and n., 308, 324, 576; *Essay on the modern pronunciation of the Greek and Latin Languages*, 577 and n., 681.
Prince, Mr. (bookseller), 37, 47.
Pringle, Thomas, 284 n., 285.
Pritchard, Miss Letitia (of Lough-rigg), 659 and n.
Procter, Bryan Waller ('Barry Cornwall'), production of *Mirandola*, 23 n.; W. W.'s opinion of, 44; 128.
Prussia, 56 and n., 625, 669.
Pyrenees, 674.

Quarterly Review, 237, 337, 678, 687, 691.

Index

Quillinan, Edward, *Letters to*: 132, 134, 145, 164, 193, 195, 200, 201, 241, 257, 264, 265, 266, 269, 388, 550, 569, 620, 637, 655, 665; leaves Rydal, 141; affairs managed by D. W., 145–7, 193–4, 195–6, 241, 243; verses in wife's memory, 149 and n., 169; at Geneva, 150 and n.; *The Nightingale*, 242, 266; first meeting with W. W., 701–2; 68, 76 and n., 83, 124–5, 138, 140, 173, 193, 199, 232, 249, 261, 353, 354, 383, 539, 568, 589, 675, 677, 678.

— Mrs. Jemima, 92 and n., 100, 113; her accident, 132 and n., 134–5, 139; her death, 140, 294; funeral, 141; funeral expenses, 145–7; memorial tablet, 149 and n., 193, 249.

— Jemima, 92, 195, 196, 242, 265, 267, 666, 677.

— Rotha, 83, 100, 134, 195, 265, 267, 269; W. W.'s verses to, 286–7, 292, 294.

Quincey, Thomas De, *Letter to*: 492; at Fox Ghyll, 168, 210, 218, 283; in London, 318; at the Nab, 388, 415; at Edinburgh, 492, 658; 375, 455.

— Mrs. De, 283, 492–3, 494.

— Horace, 492.

— Margaret, 492.

— William, 492.

Raincock, Fletcher, 49 and n.
Ramsgate, 259, 268, 270, 272.
Raven, Revd. Thomas, 291 n.
Rawson, Mrs. Elizabeth (*née* Threlkeld), 230 and n., 231, 415, 530 and n., 536.

— William, 230, 536.
Reding, Aloys, 189 and n.
Relfe, Lupton, *Letter to*: 476; 419 and n.; *Friendship's Offering*, 476.
Retrospective Review, 419 and n.
Reynolds, Frederic Mansel, *Letters to*: 489, 512, 580, 615, 691; 584, 590, 592, 632.
Rhaidr Gwy (falls on R. Wye), 477.
Rhine, the, 279, 627, 634.

Ricardo, Osman, 437, 483 and n.
— Mrs., 483.
Richardson, Edward (tobacconist), 25, 26, 29.
Richmond (Yorks.), 479.
Robertson, Capt. James, 304 and n.
Robinson, Anthony (H. C. R.'s friend), 511 and n.
— Mrs. (*née* Lucock), 512 and n.
— Capt. Charles, R.N. (of Ambleside), 42 n.
— Mrs. Charles, 196, 218.
— George (joiner), 536 and n.
— Henry Crabb, *Letters to*: 22, 43, 91, 95, 110, 126, 176, 270, 282, 290, 335, 372, 396, 403, 426, 438, 442, 450, 477, 498, 503, 510, 516, 613, 624, 674, 676, 690; visits O'Connell, 498; article in *Quarterly Review*, 337; his note on Goddard, 94 n., 500, 511, 516; 10 and n., 52, 71, 86, 89, 109, 232, 260, 261, 264, 320, 324–5, 487, 638, 655, 666, 667, 692.
— Admiral Hugh, 75.
— Jeremiah, 75 n., 218.
— Revd. John (of Newbiggin), 466 and n.
— Mrs. Mary (W. W.'s cousin), 75 and n., 76.
— Mary Ann, 75 and n.
— Mary (H. C. R.'s sister), 374 and n., 428.
— Mr. and Mrs. Thomas (H. C. R.'s brother and sister-in-law), 7 and n., 270.
— Lieut. Thomas, R.N., *Letter to*: 423; 42 n., 218.
Rogers, Henry, 342 and n.
— Samuel, *Letters to*: 152, 180, 189, 306, 319, 327, 341, 381, 505, 518, 543, 554, 603, 622; at Rydal and Keswick, 485 and n.; *Italy*, 153, 329, 544, 603; 119, 153, 155, 237, 260, 376, 439, 443, 450, 495, 504, 510, 637, 667.
— Miss Sarah, 190, 260, 342, 544.
Rolfe, Robert Monsey (later 1st Baron Cranworth), 516 and n.
Romans, the, 361.
Rome, 677.

719

Romilly, Sir Samuel, 452 and n.

Rooke, Revd. George, 399 and n., 409.

Rose, Revd. Hugh James, *Letter to*: 684; *Museum Criticum*, 558 and n.; *State of the Protestant Religion in Germany*, 558 and n., 684 and n.

— William Stewart, *Letter to*: 185; his translation of Ariosto, 185.

Rose Castle (nr. Carlisle), 391 and n.

Rotterdam, 621, 634.

Rough, William (later Sir William), 112 and n.

Rubens, 544.

Rushworth, Mr., 502.

Russell, Lord John, 594 and n.

— Revd. John, 81, 82.

— Thomas, his sonnet on Philoctetes, 125 and n.

Russia, 669.

Rydal, storm at, 286.

— Chapel, 169 and n., 233; opened, 301; 396, 416, 432, 607, 673; W. W.'s verses on, 180 and n., 183, 185–6, 187.

— Hall, 355, 551.

— Mount, repairs to, 129–30; the Wordsworths' satisfaction with, 242, 293; garden and terrace, 165, 241, 306, 354, 433; additions to, 329 and n., 432; in spring, 350–1, 353; threatened with move from, 370, 412 and n., 416–17, 432, 448, 472, 477; purchase of adjacent field, 412, 416, 433, 448, 472.

— Water, 214; in winter, 104, 240–1, 293, 521; 474.

Sackville-West, George John, 5th Earl de la Warr, 409 and n.

Saddleback, 586, 628.

St. Bees College, 413 and n.

St. Clare, Dr. William, 397 and n., 427.

St. James's Chronicle, 528 and n.

St. John, Gospel of, 351.

St. Paul, quoted, 301.

Sandford, Miss (governess), 318.

Satterthwaite, Dr. James (rector of Lowther), 6, 26, 133–4, 136, 139, 227, 231, 298–9, 348, 355, 453, 548; death of, 559.

— Col. J. C., 348 and n.

— Mrs., 355.

Scafell, 82, 274.

Scarlett, James (later Sir James), M.P., 461 and n.

Schaffhausen, Falls of, 237.

Schlegel, August Wilhelm von, 245 and n., 616 n.

Schwarts, Professor, 564.

Scotland, Church of, 534; its scenery in general, 303; *see also* D. W., Visits and journeys.

Scotland, Account of the Principal Pleasure Tours of, 163; *Select Remains of the Ancient Poetry of*, 216 n.

Scott, Charles, 627 and n., 628.

— John (editor of the *London Magazine*), death of, 43 and n., 44, 47, 70.

— Mrs. John, 44 and n.

— Sir Walter, *Letters to*: 71, 356, 366, 422, 627; 69; *Bride of Lammermoor*, 163; medallion by Lacey, 193; at Storrs, 381 n.; at Rydal, 387 and n.; bust sent to W. W., 400, 422, 432; his bankruptcy, 424 n., 432; revelation of authorship of Waverley Novels, 522 and n.; 402, 608, 612, 631.

— Walter (son), 366 and n., 628.

— William, 615 and n.

Sebergham Estate, 326 and n., 336.

Sedbergh School, 105, 150.

Sedgwick, Professor Adam, 682 and n.

Senhouse, Humphrey (of Netherhall), 78 and n., 84, 548.

— Miss Elizabeth, 548.

Seward, Anna, 357 and n., 366–8.

Seymour, Admiral Sir George Francis, 409 and n.

— Sir George Hamilton, 400 and n., 409.

Shakespeare, William, *Macbeth*, 237; 284, 402, 546; *Pericles*, 648.

Sharp, Richard, *Letters to*: 118, 155, 156, 159, 495; 152, 181, 308.

Sharpe, John, 584 and n.

— Revd. Joseph (of Kirkby Lonsdale), 116 and n.

Shaw, Mr. (printer), 526.

Shelley, Percy Bysshe, 124 and n.

Sherwen, Richard (attorney), 59.

Shuttleworth, Revd. Philip Nicholas, 353 and n.

Sidmouth, Lord, *see* Addington, Henry.

Skelton, John, 403 and n.

Skelwyth Bridge, 197.

Skinner, George, 558 and n.

Slee, Isaac (land agent), 501 and n., 502.

Smith, Elizabeth, 571 and n.

— Horatio, 476 and n.

— Thomas (of Gorton), 385 and n.

Smollett, Tobias, quoted, 118.

Snow, Benjamin (surgeon), 345 and n.

Snowdon, 276, 278, 279, 297, 303, 322, 387, 429, 431, 438, 477.

Sockburn, 619.

Sotheby, William, *Letter to*: 515; *Sonnet, A Fancy Sketch*, 515; *Georgica Hexaglotta*, 515, 691.

Soulby, John (sub-distributor), 220.

Southey, Bertha, 346, 351, 352; at Rydal Mount, 395, 398; 475 and n., 612.

— Cuthbert, 81, 126, 292.

— Edith, at Rydal Mount, 219, 517, 518, 521; 102, 240, 245, 288, 292, 331, 346, 351, 389, 394, 433, 570, 572-3, 590, 612.

— Herbert, 292 and n.

— Isabel, death of, 473, 475, 479, 484, 612.

— Kate, at Rydal Mount, 395, 398; 612.

— Robert, *Letters to*: 101, 225, 517, 542, 686; quarrel with Byron, 101 and n., 123, 212, 307-8; his bust at Rydal Mount, 400, 422; elected M.P., 469 and n.; visits Holland, 346, 351; his operation, 625, 628; *A Vision of Judgment*, 22 and n., 23 and n., W. W.'s comments, 24-5, D. W.'s comments, 53 and n.; *History of the Peninsular War*, 123 and n., 183, 225, 517; *Book of the Church*, 123 and n., 328, 660; *A Tale of Paraguay*, 123 and n.; *Oliver Newman*, 123 and n.; *The Roman Catholic Question—Ireland*, 687 and n.; contributions to the *Quarterly Review*, 123 and n.; 6, 24, 73, 78, 80, 84, 96, 107, 125, 137, 150, 230, 244-5, 274, 287, 292, 317, 324, 326, 355, 358, 368, 379, 389, 398, 411, 423, 429, 474, 475, 479, 484-5, 514-15, 549, 586, 594, 612, 616, 632, 635, 638, 653, 655, 659, 692.

— Mrs., 245, 292, 612, 619.

Southeys, the, at Harrogate, 530, 533.

Spain, French intervention in, 179 and n., 180, 499.

Spenser, Edmund, 284, 362 n., 402.

Spring Cottage (Loughrigg), 340, 540.

Stafford, Lord, *see* Leveson-Gower, George.

Stafford Gallery, 543, 544, 555.

Stamford, 267.

Standard, The, 528 and n.

Stanger, James, 83 and n.

— Joshua, 331 and n.

— Mrs., 352.

— Miss, 83.

Stangers, the, 351.

Stanley, Edward (of Ponsonby), 658 and n.

Steble, Revd. Allison, 39 and n., 41.

Stockton-on-Tees, collapse of Tees Bank, 428, 436, 450.

Stoddart, John (later Sir John), 10, 494.

Stowe (Brecon.), 263, 267, 318, 325, 339, 351, 353, 355, 436, 437, 479, 482, 483.

Strickland, Mr., 469.

Suffolk Chronicle, 64.

Sun, The, 482.

Switzerland, invasion of, 97; scenery of, 303; 120, 677.

Sykes, Godfrey (solicitor of the Stamp Office), 66 and n.

Tabley, Lord de, *see* Leicester, Sir George.

Tacitus, *Agricola*, 547.

Talfourd, Thomas Noon, 7 and n., 45 and n.

Tallentire Hall (nr. Cockermouth), 549 and n.

Taylor, George, 238 and n.

— Henry (later Sir Henry), *Letter to*: 488; 236 and n.

— Jeremy, Heber's edition of his works, 429; *Holy Living* and *Holy Dying*, 542 and n.

— John (of the *Sun*), *Letters to*: 382, 494, 577; 495; *Poems*, 577; W. W. praises sonnet, 578.

Taylor and Hessey, *Letter to*: 537.

Telford, Thomas, bridge at Conway, 274, 277; bridge at Menai, 275; aqueduct at Llangollen, 277 and n.

Test Act, 312; motion to repeal, 594 and n., 604–5.

Theobalds, Alice, 116.

— Edmund, 116.

— Emanuel (of Keartswick), 116.

Theocritus, 278.

Thistleton, Mrs. (friend of C. C.), 65 and n.

Thompson, Miss (of Lowther), 661 and n.

— Henry Teshmaker (of Bridekirk), 247 and n.

— Joseph (solicitor), 636.

— Revd. William, 59.

— Mr. and Mrs., 536 and n.

Thomson, James, 402 and n.

Tickell, Thomas, 403 and n.

Ticknor, George, 627 and n.

Tierney, George, 399 and n., 409.

Tillbrooke, Revd. Samuel, 8 and n., 53, 63, 65, 68, 76, 99, 150, 169, 194, 196, 218, 233, 243, 352, 353, 416, 540, 628, 730.

Times, The, 37, 424, 455.

Tindal, Sir Nicholas, 531 and n.

Todd, Capt. George, 202 and n.

Torquay, 291, 318, 325.

Toussaint l'Ouverture, Pierre-Dominique, 30 n., 48 and n.

Towers, Richard (of Duddon Grove), 39 and n., 41.

— Mr. (surgeon), 370.

Townshend, Chauncy Hare, 8 and n., 16.

Trent (river), 561.

Treuthel and Wurtz, 652, 655, 657.

Trossachs, the, 144.

Troutbeck, 231.

Tufton, Charles, 10th Earl of Thanet, 309 and n., 369 and n., 466.

— Hon. Henry (later 11th Earl of Thanet), 369 and n.

Turner, Ellen, 437 and n.

Tweed (river), 161, 356.

Tyndall, Revd. George, 400 and n., 409.

Ulverston, 208.

Unknown Correspondent, *Letters to*: 67, 144, 224, 380, 414, 484, 486, 578, 699.

Utrecht, 634.

Valpy, Abraham, 652 and n., 655, 657.

Vane, Lady Caroline (*née* Lowther), 153.

Vaughan, Dr. Peter, 399 and n., 409.

Venables, Dr. Richard, 590 and n.

Vice-Chancellor (office of), 28 and n.

Virgil, 125, 235, 250–2; his versification, 247; *Aeneid*, 244, 250–2, 445; *Georgics*, 250.

Wake, Charles, 637 and n.

Wakefield, Edward (Osman Ricardo's steward), 437 and n.

— Edward Gibbon, 437 and n., 481.

— John (banker), 458, 466.

— — (jnr.), 219 and n., 338, 458, 461, 466, 467.

Wakefield's Bank, 582.

Wales, 226, 242, 259, 263, 267, 269, 272, 273, 448, 477–8, 606, 608, 663, 688; its scenery in general, 302–3.

Walford, Mr. (C. C.'s neighbour), 88.

Walker, Hannah, 392.

— Revd. Robert, memoir of, 485 and n., 486.

Wallace, Mr. (dentist), 233, 234, 235, 238, 239, 434.

Walter, Revd. Henry, 300 and n.

Walton, Revd. Jonathan, 19 and n., 442; *Perilous Times*, 442 and n.

Ward, John William, 4th Viscount Dudley, 553 and n., 560.

Wardell, William (banker), 582 and n.

Wartons, the (Joseph and Thomas), 648–9.

Wastdale, 274, 486.

Waterloo (Belgium), W. W. at field of, 634.

Waterton, Charles, 415 and n., *Wanderings in South America*, 415 and n.

Watson, Joshua, 268 and n.

— Mrs. Richard (of Calgarth), 83 and n.

Watsons, the, 429.

Watts, Alaric, *Letters to*: 283, 376, 380, 383, 390, 418, 424, 425, 455, 487, 527; *Literary Souvenir*, 377, 391, 405, 487, 515, 525–6; 344, 377, 389, 397, 405, 428, 439, 443–4, 450, 583, 653, 680, 692–3.

— Mrs., 389 n., 418.

Webbers, the (tenants of Ivy Cottage), 352.

Webster, George (architect), 412 n.

Weir, Anna (schoolmistress at Appleby), 630 and n.

Wellesley, Lord (brother of Wellington), 518.

— Lady, 585 and n.

Wellington, Duke of, 517, 518.

West, Richard, 80 and n.

Westmorland Election (1820), 369 and n.

— — (1826), 446 and n., 448, 451–2, 455–69, 475, 480, 507; expenses, 470–1.

Westmorland Gazette, 144.

Wethercote Cove (Yorks.), 69.

Whewell, Revd. William, *Letter to*: 681; 682.

Whigs, the 97, 528.

Whish, Revd. Henry Francis, 400 and n., 408.

Whitaker, Eliza (*née* Horrocks), 292 n.

White, William (sub-distributor), 59–60, 117, 171, 210, 282, 283.

— Mrs. William, 59–60.

Whitehaven, 274, 282, 318, 340, 482, 553, 638, 655.

Whitwick (Leics.), 557 and n., 559, 575, 588, 590, 595, 599, 605, 607, 611, 618, 628, 634; parsonage and church, 639, 656, 666, 671, 672, 676, 683, 698. *See also* D. W., Visits and journeys.

Wilberforce, William, 462, 470.

— Mrs. William, 90.

Wilkie, David (later Sir David), *Letter to*: 264; 258.

Wilkin, John (tax official), 20 and n.

Wilkinson, Revd. Henry (of Sedbergh), 63 and n., 670.

— Revd. Thomas, 164 and n.

Willan, Jacob (horsedealer), 85 and n.

Willes, Miss Anne (Lady Beaumont's sister), 323 and n.

— Mrs. Francis (Lady Beaumont's cousin), 556, 560.

Wilson, Betty, 392.

— Christopher (banker at Kendal), *Letter to*: 449; 39, 464.

— Col. George (of Dallam Tower), 456 and n., 457, 467.

— Isaac (solicitor), 94 and n.

— James (Professor Wilson's brother), 654 and n.

— Capt. John (of The Howe), 451 and n.

— Professor John ('Christopher North'), 216, 382 n., 494.

— Mrs. Margaret, 154 and n., 494.

— Miss, 494.

— Revd. William, will of, 236.

Winchester College, John and Christopher (C. W.'s sons) commoners at, 7 n.; Christopher's prize from, 9; John and Christopher's return to, 13; 21, 190, 191, 407.

Windermere, 76, 529.

Winter's Wreath, 583 and n.

Wise, John, 670.

Wood, Anthony, *Athenae Oxoniensis*, 576 and n.

— Miss (Humphrey Senhouse's aunt), 548 and n.

— William (attorney), *Letter to*: 636.

Worcester, 435, 506, 531, 556, 557, 560, 561, 677.

Wordsworth, Catherine (W. W.'s daughter), grave of, 141.

Index

Wordsworth, Charles (C. W.'s son), at Harrow, 7 and n., 9, 46; 298; distinctions at Oxford, 529 and n.; 530, 531; at Bowness, 539; Student of Christ Church, 568; 581, 583, 587, 588, 589, 633, 639, 654, 694, 695.

— Dr. Christopher (W. W.'s brother), *Letters to*: 136, 296, 441, 453, 556, 633, 657; Vice-Chancellorship, 15 and n., 21, 53 and n., 504, 604; day in the life of, 15–17; fails to secure Divinity professorship, 558 and n., 560, 658; at Rydal with sons, 148; at Coleorton, 396; at Brinsop, 570, 572; in Paris, 639; on authorship of *Eikon Basilike*, 296–7 and n., 302; second pamphlet, 604, 635 and n., 658, 686; 21, 34, 76, 108, 112, 128, 246, 265–6, 268, 271, 299, 301, 329–30, 371, 421, 448, 575, 589, 599, 605, 698.

— Christopher (C. W.'s son), *Letters to*: 535, 556, 638, 668, 671; D. W.'s description of, 9; prize from Winchester, 9; distinctions at Cambridge, 529; 530, 531; at Bowness, 539; 587; wins Chancellor's Medal and prizes, 613, 620–1; in France, 633, 639; 657.

— Dorothy (W. W.'s sister), Family and friends: contrasts W. W.'s writing habits with Southey's, 50; on Charles and Mary Lamb, 93, 512; cares for Mrs. Quillinan, 132–5, 139–41; settles E. Q.'s affairs, 145–7, 169, 193–4, 196, 241, 243; new teeth, 233–5; on the last illness of Thomas Monkhouse, 325; on Mrs. Coleridge's troubles, 346; on George Beaumont's marriage, 354; on the character of Mrs. Luff, 393; on Miss Jewsbury, 405; on the threatened move from Rydal Mount, 416; on Sir Walter Scott's bankruptcy, 432; writes to De Quincey about his family, 492–4; on Sir George Beaumont's last illness, 520; seeks post for George Green, 562–3, 566–7; on W. W.'s

'freakish Muse', 618.

Interests: reads novels, 375; on affairs in Haiti, 30–1; comments on economic distress, 33, 51, 64, 432, 433; on negro emancipation, 230; on *The Recluse*, 292; on Scott's bust, 432.

Visits and journeys: at Playford, 1, 270; at Trinity Lodge, 7, 13, 15, 22, 267–9; visits John W. at Sedbergh, 19; on Fairfield, 62, 626; at Windermere, 76; in Borrowdale and Wastdale (with Dora W., 148), 274; second tour of Scotland, 154, 156, 157, 169, 173, her itinerary 159, 161, 177; at Haweswater and Longsleddale, 231; at Coleorton, 241–2, 485, 673; at Oxford, 254, 256; in London, 256–64; at Lee Priory, 265; at Clapton, 265; at Kendal, 315–19; suggests Italian tour, 373; at Hallsteads, 392; tour on the Continent (1820), itinerary 406; at Brinsop, 426, 431, 434–8, 472, 479, 481–2; at Manchester, 427; at Halifax, 536, 567; up Kirkstone, 548; at Keswick, 612; at Isle of Man, 613 n.; at Whitwick, 656, 659, 671, 676, 697–8.

Writings: *Journal of a Tour on the Continent* (1820), 2 and n., 25, 43, 53–4, 64, 77, 89, 100, 104, 115, 165, her own view of 271, 337, 406, 426, 516; *Journal of my Second Tour in Scotland* (1822), 628; *Recollections of a Tour Made in Scotland* (1803), 104, proposes to publish, 152–3, 155, 180–1.

Wordsworth, Dorothy ('Dora', W. W.'s daughter), *Letters to*: 547, 549, 589; D. W.'s descriptions of, 31, 76; leaves school, 100, 104; teaching at Miss Dowling's, 214, 217, 223; at Penrith Ball and Races, 230, 234; proposal of marriage, 423; has French hairstyle, 608; at Coniston with Joanna H., 148; at Stockton with S. H., 159, 167, 173, 177; at Harrogate, 200, 201, with W. W., 529–32, 533; in

724

London, 239, 249, 257–8, 259–62, 607, 612; at Hendon, 239, 240; at Lee Priory, 265; at Cambridge, 266, 599; in Wales, 273–4, 276, 278, 297; at Hindwell, 275; at Coleorton, 297; at Kent's Bank, 392; at Keswick, 433, 442, 539; at Brinsop, 544, 553, 557, 561, 572; at Bristol, 588, 617; Continental tour with S. T. C. and W. W., 614–22, itinerary, 623, 634, 637; health, 89, 148–9, 167, 204, 208, 214, 339, 491, 493, 498–9, 501, 504, 505–6, 509, 511, 516, 519, 520, 538, 552, 555, 699; 34, 37, 47, 63, 134, 135, 136, 166, 190, 195, 216, 219, 221, 222, 242, 267–9, 271, 272, 332, 346, 353, 356, 375, 386, 387, 390, 393, 395, 398, 416, 434, 472, 474, 536, 558, 569, 576, 581, 590, 608, 639, 656, 663, 665, 688.

— John (W. W.'s son), 37; at school, 76; disposition and love of study, 104–5; at Sedbergh, 150; admission to Oxford, 174–5, 187–8, 190–1; at New College, 199, 222, 227, 246, 256; ill, 214, 217; at Whitehaven, 274, 282, 318; at Rydal, 292, 298, 339; College Collections, 353; tries for Fellowship at Merton, 407–8, 412–13, 418, 449; takes degree, 499, 501; Christmas at Sedbergh, 504; stands for University Club, 512, 516; at Windermere, 529; at Bowness, 535–7; intends to take Orders, 539; prepares for curacy, 551, 575–6; offer of curacy at Whitwick, 557, 559–60; College expenses, 582, 589–90, 596; ordained deacon, 588, 595; reads prayers at Grasmere, 597; at Whitwick, 600, 603, 605, 607, 611, 618, 624, 631, 634, 638, 639; his professional character, 660, 676, 698; ordained priest, 671, 696, 698; offered living of Moresby, 683, 688, 691; accepts 696, 697, 698; 178, 203, 204, 205, 206, 207, 208, 213, 221, 346, 350, 355, 373,

374, 392, 395, 433, 509, 554, 573, 580, 599, 673.

— John (C. W.'s son), *Letters to*: 329, 529; at Winchester, 7 and n.; D. W.'s description of, 9; 15, 265, 267, 268, illness, 298; elected scholar of Trinity, 330; 442, 504; at Bowness, 539; 573; in France, 633, 639.

— John ('Keswick John', R. W.'s son), 33 and n.; at school, 74; mild and amiable, 231; at Rydal, 536, 635, 671; his education, 635, 670–1.

— Mary (W. W.'s wife), *Letter to*: 589; her Journal of Continental tour (1820), 53, 64, 77, 89, 115, 406, 516; at Keswick, 89, with the Southeys, 539; lameness, 92, 104, 110; at Lowther Rectory, 134, 135; at Matlock, 140; at Hallsteads, 141; at Coleorton, 186, 189, 190, 191, 392, 395, 396, 404, 572; visits London, 189, 609 n., 612, 618; at Lee Priory, 192, 198; tour in Holland with W. W., 198 and n.; at Harrogate, 202, 392; at Penrith Races and Ball, 234; Welsh tour, 273 and n., 279, 297, 663; at Kent's Bank, 392; at Brinsop, 544, 555, 557, 567, 572, 581; at Bristol, 588, 617; at Whitwick, 618, 624; 136, 170, 254, 255, 256, 263, 269, 339, 386, 389, 493, 599.

— Richard (W. W.'s brother), administration of Sockbridge estate, 501–2, 635.

— Mrs. Richard, *Letter to*: 501; 33 and n., her character, 74, 231.

— Thomas (W. W.'s son), grave of, 141.

— William, Family and friends: takes care of Julia Myers, 34; dances at Miss Dowling's ball, 101; seeks position for Thomas Hutchinson, 120–1; gets John W. into Oxford, 174, 187–8, 190–1; receives medallion of Scott, 193; at Penrith Races, 230, 234; tribute to Thomas Monkhouse, 329; on

Wordsworth, William, Family and friends: (*cont.*):

friendship, 350; tries to get Fellowship at Merton for John W., 398, 407, 410, 412, 414, 418; receives bust of Sir Walter Scott, 400, 422; his bust of Southey, 400, 422; threatened with leaving Rydal Mount, 370, 412, 416–17, 432, 448, 477; purchase of field adjacent to Rydal Mount, 412, 433, 444, 448; skates, 422, 423, 521; rejects suitor for Dora W., 423–4; suggests Welsh itinerary for H. C. R., 477–8; suggests Irish itinerary for H. C. R., 478; tribute to Sir George Beaumont, 519; advice to an heiress, 541–2; criticizes W. R. Hamilton's verses, 545–6; orders bust for Quillinan and Charles Wordsworth, 568, 569, 654, and for Barron Field, 694; descriptions of W. W. on tour, 616 n., in town, 625 n.; consults Huntly Gordon about Willy's future, 651; anxiety about Willy's future prospects, 657.

Health: eye trouble, 68, 74, 78, 82, 85, 89, 92, 112, 122, 123, 128, 138, 148, 162, 170, 208, 223, 232, 234, 236, 239, 339, 345, 368, 397, 404, 472, 481, 493, 500, 507, 512–13; origin of complaint, 123; tries Blue Stone, 489; accident at Bampton, 133, 135, 136–7, 139.

Finance: investments, 155–7, 159 and n., 160, 269, 293, 299, 309, 380, 500; receives legacy, 298, 301; Patterdale estate, 416.

Distributorship: 4, 14 and n., 23 and n., 25, 26, 29, 55, 59, 77, 116, 117, 131, 132, 151–2, 171–2, 208, 220, 236, 247, 295, 373, 430, 587, 621, 636; duties of, 56 and n., 57; income from, 58; proposed abolition of, 54 n., 66; extension of district, 182–3 and n.

Interests: proposes to qualify as a magistrate, 121; views on Scottish scenery, 143–4, 334; on chimney boys, 248; seeks London newspaper, 293, 294; on John Gauden, 296–7; on the aesthetics of landscape, 302–3; on the Grasmere enclosure, 304–5; on the picturesque, 321–2, 334; on the Dutch and Flemish schools of painting, 321–2; on the sublime, 335; on the 'Religion of gratitude', 351; on Swiss and French scenery, 523; on the education of the young, 565; on toothache, 688.

Visits and journeys: at Lowther, 26, 69, 70, 141, 152–3, 226, 380–2, 453–5, 465, 544, 547–50, 635; at Cambridge, 45, 266, 272, 604–6; plans tour in Ireland, 68, 293; at Keswick, 89, 292, 351; with E. Q. to Yorkshire, 92 and n., 93; at Dungeon Gill, 110; at Lowther Rectory, 134; at Hallsteads, 141, 489; at Coleorton, 186, 188, 189, 190, 191, 240, 241, 253–4, 297, 390, 395, 404, 552–60; in London, 189, 192 and n., 256–64, 609–15, 622–6; at Lee Priory, 192, 198, 265; tour in Holland, 198, 226; at Harrogate, 202, with Dora W., 529–31, 532–3; at Haweswater and Longsleddale, 231; at Oxford, 254, 256; at Clapton, 265 and n.; Welsh tour, 273–4, itinerary and descriptions, 275–9, 281, 289, 291, 297, 307, 321, 663; at Hindwell and the Stowe, 273, 275, 291, 297; at Kent's Bank, 376, 378, 392; at Manchester, 405; at Appleby, 455–65; at Buttermere, 485; at Sedbergh, 504; at Birmingham, 561; at Brinsop, 568, 569; at Liverpool, 575; at Hampton Court, 612; Continental tour (1828), 614–22, 624, 637, itinerary, 623, 634; at Enfield, 626; at Whitwick, 631.

Current affairs and politics: newspapers in public houses, 11; selection of schoolmasters, 11, 12; recipe for social improvement, 11, 26, 28; Yeomanry Corps, 27, 28, 40, 410; abuse of Press, 28 and n.; increase in freeholders, 39 and n.; Poor Rates, 39 and n., 40; Catholic Question, 42 and n., 55 and n.,

58, 97–8, 309–15, 347–8, 358–65, 527–8, 678–9, 687; Dissenters, 12, 55, 58, 98; defends his political opinions, 96–9; liberty of the Press, 97–8; Parliamentary reform, 97–8; extension of franchise, 98; Irish question, 98, 289, 309–15, 358–65, 527–8, 687; Church establishment, 98; state of press, 124; on French politics, 156, on religion in French politics, 668–9; on Cambridge University elections, 158; on Whigs, Tories, and Radicals, 245; on priests, 290, 363; on Romish system, 311, 314, 360–5; on local drunkenness and violence, 370; on the foundation of the proposed London University College, 371–2; on local politics, 410, 446–7; on Canning, 527–9; on the election of Chancellor at Oxford, 553–4; on the property of the Church of England, 679, 687; on the education of girls, 685–6; on the Madras system, 685; on international copyright, 690–1, 697.

Views on literature: *Mirandola*, 44; on contemporary poetry, 44; on use of Latin by modern poets, 79; on contemporary estimates of Pope, 106 and n.; on Hazlitt's misrepresentations, 106; on German critics, 118; on Gray, 118–19; on writing Latin verse, 125; on writing sonnets, 126; praises Cunningham's *Songs*, 138; on Rogers's *Italy*, 153, 329; on Ariosto, 185; on Dunbar, 209; on his own poetic powers, 224; on Byron's plagiarisms, 237, on plagiarism, 238; on religious myths, 244–5; on Dante, 245–6; on translating Virgil, 247, 250–2, 253–4; on Alaric Watts's poems, 284, 377; on Landor's *Imaginary Conversations*, 289–90; on C. W.'s *Who Wrote Eikon Basilike?*, 296–7, 302; on Medwin's *Conversations of Lord Byron*, 307–8; on Jacob Fletcher's tragedies, 333–4; on Longinus and the sublime, 335; on Maria Jewsbury's *Phantasmagoria*, 342–4; on Maria Jewsbury, 377; on Border poets, 402–3; on poems in *Friendship's Offering*, 476; on *The Amulet*, 524; on the logical faculty in poetry, 546; on the text of Collins's *Ode on the Popular Superstitions of the Highlands of Scotland*, 648–50.

Works, General: proposes to change his publisher, 306–7, 320, 327–9, 372, 376, 379, 381, 418; fresh negotiations with Longman, 383, 390–1; terms from Hurst and Robinson, 439, 443, 450, 487; reopens negotiations with Murray, 496, 515; returns to Longman, 500; course of negotiations, 510; rearranges his poems, 328; proposes new edition, 332, 337, 341, 384; preparing new edition, 372, 433, 473; asked to write an epitaph, 385; revising poems, 418, 433; his poetic intentions, 401; defends classification, 440, 444; prepares new (1827) edition for Longman, 502, 504, 505, 508, 510, 516, 521, 526, 543; declines to write for periodicals, 383, 391, 525, 552, 583, 592–3; on poetical paraphrases of Scripture, 534; two of his poems translated into German, 564; proposed selection of his poems for the Scottish peasantry, 568, 578, 609, 653–4, 694, 703–4; contributions to *Keepsake*, 580 and n., 590 and n., 592, 616; writing verses, 582; proposed selection for schools, 597–8; discusses textual variants with Barron Field, 600–3, 640–7; Galignani's pirated edition, 656, 658, 690, 691, 697; refuses to write for *Literary Gazette*, 625, 632.

POETRY:

Ecclesiastical Sketches, 4 n., 51 and n., 63 and n., 74, 92, 104, 110 and n., 112, 118; Wordsworth's own view of, 119, 181; 124, 178, 180; Rogers's opinion of, 180; 307, 320; hostile review, 127 and n.

Wordsworth, William, Works, General: POETRY: (*cont.*):

Excursion, The, second edition, 2 and n.; Sir George Beaumont's view of, 5 n.; 126, 292, 320; revision of, 354; 376, 381, 384, 390–1, 443, 450, 473, 495; third edition, 502 and n., 508; 526, 646.

Itinerary Poems of 1833, 4 n.

Memorials of a Tour on the Continent, 1820, 92 and n., 99 and n., 104, 108, 110 and n., 113, 118, 124, 127, 178, 271, 307, 320; hostile review, 127 and n.; W. W.'s favourite poems, 181.

Miscellaneous Poems (1820), 2 and n., 320, 384, 390–1, 495.

Poetical Works (1827), 502 and n., 508, 526.

Prelude, The, referred to, 50.

Recluse, The, 50, 74, 126, 292, 474, 500, 582.

Aeneid, translation of, 228, 235, 246, 294, 558, 559.

Anecdote for Fathers, 25 n.

Beggars, 601 and n., 640 and n., 641.

Blind Highland Boy, The, 641–2.

Composed in one of the Catholic Cantons, 181.

Country Girl, The, 590 and n.

Cuckoo and the Nightingale, The, 389.

Descriptive Sketches, 642 and n.

Desultory Stanzas, 113, 127.

Eclipse of the Sun, The, 119, 124, 174, 181.

Egyptian Maid, The, 663 and n., 665, 667, 671, 675, 689.

Elegiac Stanzas (*Addressed to Sir G. H. B. upon the Death of his Sister-in-law*), 323–4.

— (to Goddard), 94 and n., 113, 500 n.

Emigrant Mother, The, 643.

Evening Walk, An, 125.

Filial Piety, 602 and n., 699.

Flower Garden, A, 324.

Force of Prayer, The, 603.

French Revolution, As it Appeared to Enthusiasts at its Commencement, 601 and n.

Gipsies, 645.

Goody Blake and Harry Gill, 285.

Gravestone upon the floor in the Cloisters of Worcester Cathedral, A, 695 and n.

Green Linnet, The, 643.

Idiot Boy, The, 285, 643.

Inscription, The, 324.

I wandered lonely as a cloud, 285.

Laodamia, 244, 440.

Monument commonly called Long Meg and her Daughters near the River Eden, The, 4 n., 430.

Morning Exercise, A, 644.

Old Abbeys, 112.

Once I could hail (howe'er serene the sky), 474–5.

On the Power of Sound, 689.

Peele Castle in a Storm, 645.

Peter Bell, 646.

Rural Architecture, 642.

Ruth, 440, 590, 642.

Sailor's Mother, The, 642.

Simon Lee, 601 and n., 653–4.

Three Cottage Girls, The, 181.

Tintern Abbey, 237, 444.

To the Clouds, 474.

To the Cuckoo, 644.

To the Daisy, 644.

To Enterprise, 118, 444.

To the Lady E. B. and the Hon. Miss P., 277.

To the Lady Fleming, 180, 183, expanded, 184, 185–6, 187, 602 and n.

To Mary M., 287, 292, 294.

To Rotha Q., 286–7, 292, 294.

To Sir Geo. H. Beaumont, Bart., 324.

To a Skylark, 644.

To the Small Celandine, 285, 644.

To the Torrent at the Devil's Bridge, 279 and n., 297, 299.

Tradition of Oker Hill, A, 699 and n.

Triad, The, 590 and n., 591, 656, 689, 691, 692, 695.

Wishing-Gate, The, 590 and n., 691.

Yes, it was the Mountain Echo, 600–1, 645.

Sonnet composed at Cambridge, 45 and n.; parody of Ben Jonson,

88, 90, 103; epigrams on Byron's *Cain*, 102 and n.; Political sonnets, 178; sonnet on the Russians, 178; Guerrilla sonnets, 179; sonnet to Lady Beaumont, 414.

PROSE:

Guide to the Lakes, 4 n., 37; third, and first separate, edition, 120 and n.; fourth, and second separate, edition, 178 and n., 664; 223, 430, 689.

Convention of Cintra, The, 97.

Memoir of the Rev. Robert Walker, 485 and n., 486.

Wordsworth, William ('Willy', W. W.'s son), visits Cambridge, 7 and n., 8, 9, 13, 18; lying, 13, 36; at Playford, 18; possibility of being on foundation at Charterhouse, 67, 81–2, 85 and n.; removal from Charterhouse, 105, 115, 142, 147; dropsy, 142, 147, 158, 159, 161, 164–5, 173, 177, 178, 181; recovery, 145, 162, 170, 183, 190, 197; riding, 203; fishing and rowing, 214, 223; at school in Ambleside, 223, 232, 239, 256, 281; studying with John Carter, 345; 'preparing for Oxford', 368; at Kent's Bank, 392; skating, 521; thinks of career in army, 551; dislikes idea of University or Church, 556, 582; tries to arrange commission, 385–7; averse to Church,

608; unfitted for Law, 612; possibility of University, 629–30, 634–5; or situation in public office, 651–2; or study abroad, 655, 657, 660, 661–3; W. W.'s 'painful uncertainty' about him, 665, 669–71, 674; to be sent to tutor at Bremen, 687, 689–90; 'preparing for mercantile life', 699; 32, 35, 36, 43, 54, 74, 90, 95, 208, 215, 219, 274, 292, 298, 339, 345, 378, 386, 388, 390, 395, 398, 449, 521, 529, 532, 539, 554, 573, 574, 590, 626, 656.

Wrangham, Archdeacon Francis, 576 and n., his edition of Zouch, 576 and n.

Wybergh, Thomas, 456 and n., 458.

Wycliffe, John, 557 and n., 560.

Wye (river), 281, 307, 477, 539, 557.

Wyndham, Charles, 2nd Earl of Egremont, 408 and n.

— George O'Brien, 3rd Earl of Egremont, 247 and n.

Wythburn, 304; picnic under Raven Crag, 539; Nag's Head, 633.

Yates, Anthony (of Kendal), 550 and n.

Yeomanry Corps, 25 and n., 27, 40.

York, 202.

Yorkshire, election (1826), 453 and n.

Zouch, Dr. Thomas, 576 and n.

ADDENDUM

356a. W. W. to SAMUEL BUTLER[1]

Address: The Revd Archdeacon Butler, Shrewsbury.
Stamp: Kendal Penny Post.
MS. Alan G. Hill. Hitherto unpublished.

Rydal Mount near Ambleside.
29th August [1828]

Dear Sir,

The Enclosed is from an old Acquaintance of mine, whom I advised, when I saw him in Town a few weeks ago to place his Son[2] in your School, promising that I would write to you upon the occasion.

His Letter sufficiently, perhaps, explains particulars, but he seems not aware that you may not have room for his Son as early as Christmas. Will you have the kindness to write to him and let him know if you can receive the Boy.

Hoping that you are well
I remain dear Sir faithfully yours
Wm Wordsworth

Tillbrook is at Rydal, well I believe, but I have not seen him, having only just reached home.—

---

[1] Headmaster of Shrewsbury (see L. 180 above). W. W. had met him some time before this: probably when Butler was staying at the Ivy Cottage, Rydal, with his friend Samuel Tillbrooke in the summer of 1826. (See Samuel Butler, *The Life and Letters of Dr. Samuel Butler*, 2 vols., 1896, i. 310.)

[2] Probably Philip Warner Courtenay (b. 1814), son of W. W.'s financial adviser, who entered Shrewsbury later this year. He left in 1831, and went on to Jesus College, Cambridge, where he graduated four years later.